SDP

The Birth, Life and Death of the Social Democratic Party

• • • •

Ivor Crewe and Anthony King

OXFORD UNIVERSITY PRESS

Oxford University Press, Great Clarendon Street, Oxford OX2 6DP

Oxford New York
Athens Auckland Bangkok Bogota Bombay
Buenos Aires Calcutta Cape Town Dar es Salaam
Delhi Florence Hong Kong Istanbul Karachi
Kuala Lumpur Madras Madrid Melbourne
Mexico City Nairobi Paris Singapore
Taipei Tokyo Toronto Warsaw
and associated companies in
Berlin Ibadan

Oxford is a trade mark of Oxford University Press

Published in the United States by
Oxford University Press Inc., New York

© Ivor Crewe and Anthony King 1995

First published 1995
First issued in paperback 1997

British Library Cataloguing in Publication Data
Data available

Library of Congress Cataloging in Publication Data
Data available
ISBN 0-19-828050-5
ISBN 0-19-829313-5 (Pbk.)

1 3 5 7 9 10 8 6 4 2

Printed in Great Britain
on acid-free paper by
Bookcraft (Bath) Ltd
Midsomer Norton, Avon

To Jill and Jan,
who have waited so long

Preface

• • • •

This book bears a disconcerting resemblance to a biography of someone who showed early promise but died young. The SDP existed for only seven years. It has taken us rather longer to complete our book about it.

We decided to write the SDP's history on 26 November 1981, the day that Shirley Williams won the Crosby by-election. We were not sure that the new party would survive, but we thought that it might and that, if it did, someone ought to be on hand to chronicle its early years. We were conscious of the fact that at the beginning of this century no one had taken the formation of the Labour Representation Committee very seriously, with the result that historians of the Labour party (as the LRC soon became) have had considerable difficulty ever since in piecing together the early history of what soon became a major political force.

In the event, of course, our analogy with the Labour party proved wrong. The SDP did not survive. It went up like a rocket but came down like the stick. We believe, nevertheless, that its story is worth telling, partly for its own sake, partly for what the SDP's failure tells us about the British political system and partly because the episode can be read as a series of cautionary tales. There must be many former members and supporters of the SDP who, to this day, are wondering what befell their old party—a party in which so many of them had vested so much hope. Many others outside the party must be equally puzzled.

Both of us were initially attracted by the idea of the new party and knew many of those who set it up. Without ever formally joining the SDP, we sat on one or two of its committees in the early days. However, once the party's headquarters had been established, our involvement gradually ceased. For most of the party's short history, we viewed it from the outside as intrigued—and sometimes astonished—spectators. In the endless quarrels between the Jenkinsites and the Owenites, we usually found it easy to see both sides' points of view. We also found it easy to see why some people stayed in the Labour party in 1981–2 while others felt forced to leave. Our detachment probably unfits both of us to be politicians. We hope it does not unfit us to be sympathetic political observers.

Several of the early chapters of *SDP* were drafted soon after the events to which they relate, and we have largely resisted the temptation to revise them in the light of hindsight. The narrative chapters, in particular, are meant to catch the mood of the time, however false to reality that mood may now appear. The book is a genuinely collaborative effort. Although one or other of us prepared a first draft of each chapter, every chapter is the result of our joint efforts.

Two features of the book's structure should be pointed out. First, it is divided into five parts and they are not quite chronological. Parts I and II tell the story of the SDP's birth and infancy, from its origins in the divisions of the Labour party up to the general election of 1983. Part IV describes the SDP's development under David Owen up to the 1987 election and Part V recounts the subsequent split over the issue of merger and the demise of the party. These sections of the book are largely narrative and historical. Part III is more anatomical: it analyses the party's structure—its constitution, finances, media relations, membership and electoral support—for the whole of the 1981–7 period. Secondly, all the tables have been gathered together at the end of the book, to avoid interruption of the narrative. Readers interested in the statistical evidence for our arguments can look it up in Appendix 5.

We have relied throughout on four main sources. One of the last acts of the SDP, before it merged with the Liberals in 1988, was to donate the party's papers and archives to the Albert E. Sloman Library at the University of Essex. We have used these materials extensively, but they still contain a great deal that will be of interest to students and scholars of British party politics. We are enormously grateful to Robert Butler, the University's librarian, for the patience and professional skill he displayed in organizing and cataloguing this very extensive collection.

Secondly, we have made use of the considerable numbers of memoirs and diaries that have become available since we first started work. James Callaghan's *Time and Chance*, Susan Crosland's biography of Tony Crosland and, to an even greater extent, Denis Healey's *The Time of my Life* reveal much about the internal conflicts in the Labour party during the Wilson, Callaghan and Foot years. Tony Benn's diaries, in their full rich candour, are also useful. On the Liberal and SDP side we have drawn on David Steel's *Against Goliath*, Roy Jenkins' *European Diary 1977–1981* and *A Life at the Centre* and David Owen's two volumes of memoirs, *Personally Speaking* and *Time to Declare*. Since David Owen is so often accused of re-writing history, we should perhaps say that his version of the SDP's history largely coincides with what he was telling us at the time about his opinions and actions.

Thirdly, we have relied heavily on the contemporary press, whose reporting of the SDP, especially in *The Times*, the *Guardian*, the *Observer* and latterly the *Independent*, we found to be full, accurate and largely reliable. The *Guardian* frequently acted as, in effect, the SDP's parish magazine. The most perceptive newspaper commentators at the time were the late Peter Jenkins, Adam Raphael, Geoffrey Smith and Hugo Young. Two books by journalists on the SDP's early years were particularly helpful: Ian Bradley's *Breaking the Mould?* and Hugh Stephenson's *Claret and Chips*. Mr Bradley deserves credit for having, unfashionably for the time, included the question mark in his title.

Finally, many chapters are largely based on the interviews that we conducted throughout the 1981–8 period with members of the SDP and the Liberal and Labour parties. We interviewed many of the leading participants in the SDP's story on a number of occasions, and we are grateful to them for giving us so much of their time, especially since some of the interviews lasted for several hours. David Steel, when he saw us arriving in his office on one occasion, said jokingly, 'Oh no, not you two again!' But he spoke to us in the most friendly and helpful manner all the same—as did all our other interviewees.

The total list of those we interviewed comprises: Paddy Ashdown, Rosie Barnes, Alan Beith, Tom Bradley, Christopher Brocklebank-Fowler, Roger Carroll, John Cartwright, Tim Clement-Jones, Alex de Mont, Lord Diamond, Bernard Doyle, Andy Ellis, Tom Ellis, Roy Evans, Frank Field, (Sir) William Goodhart, John Grant, Tony Halmos, Lord Harris of Greenwich, Alan Haselhurst, Richard Holme (Lord Holme of Cheltenham), Sarah Horack, John Horam, Peter Jenkins, Roy Jenkins (Lord Jenkins of Hillhead), Charles Kennedy, Roger Liddle, Clive Lindley, Edward Lyons, John Lyttle, Bryan Magee, Alec McGivan, Robert Maclennan, David Marquand, Paul Medlicott, Sir Leslie Murphy, Julia Neuberger, Dick Newby, Matthew Oakeshott, David Owen (Lord Owen of the City of Plymouth), John Pardoe, Chris Phillips, Giles Radice, Bill Rodgers (Lord Rodgers of Quarry Bank), John Roper, David Sainsbury, Neville Sandelson, Christopher Smallwood, Anne Sofer, (Sir) David Steel, Dick Taverne, Mike Thomas, Polly Toynbee, Jim Wallace, William Wallace, Alan Watson, Ken Weetch, Phillip Whitehead, Shirley Williams (Baroness Williams of Crosby), Des Wilson, Eric Woolfson and (Sir) Ian Wrigglesworth. We received helpful correspondence from Bruce Douglas-Mann, Lord Gilmour of Craigmillar, Vincent McKee and Bob Mitchell.

Our gratitude to our interviewees extends to a large number of other people and organizations. The Nuffield Foundation provided us with generous financial support during the early stages of our research, and we were also supported financially by the Research Endowment Fund of the University of Essex. The staff of the picture libraries of the *Daily Telegraph* and the *Guardian* went out of their way to be helpful. First-class research and administrative assistance were provided by Alun Evans, John Bartle, John Brice, Deborah Crewe, Brian Fearnley, Graeme Hall, Stuart Hollinghurst, Peter Hollister, Graham Kinshott, Luke Morris, David Page, Melvyn Read, David Samways and Adam Searing. For painstaking and patient secretarial assistance we are grateful to a number of staff at the University of Essex Department of Government, including Sarah Bayes, Hazel Burke, Linda Day, Jane Horder, Chris Jennings, Caroline Morris and Jenny Mortimer. Finally, we are indebted to our experienced and sharp-eyed copy-editors, Heather Bliss and Hilary Walford, for pouncing on our typescript's slips and inconsistencies.

The manuscript has been read in its entirety by a deliberately variegated group of people, including Jeremy Beecham, Vernon Bogdanor, Seth Dubin, Jan King, David Marquand and Dick Newby. Graham C. Greene, Peter Pulzer and Hilary Rubinstein read the earlier chapters and made valuable comments. Individual chapters were read by Andrew Gilmour and Holli Semetko. We are grateful to all of them for their help, even though their comments forced us to change a considerable number of passages that we were reluctant to change. In return for their help, we grant them the usual absolution.

We referred earlier to our feelings of detachment. Perhaps we should add that, as we write, neither of us has any party affiliation. Between us we would probably vote for Roy Hattersley in Sparkbrook (if he were standing again), Sir David Steel in Tweedale, Ettrick, and Lauderdale (if he were), Richard Ryder in Mid-Norfolk, Charles Kennedy in Ross, Cromarty, and Skye, Giles Radice in North Durham, Nigel Forman in Carshalton and Wallington and Robert Maclennan in Caithness and Sutherland. Readers can make of that what they will.

I.C.
A.K.

Colchester, Essex
January 1995

Acknowledgements

• • • •

We wish to acknowledge the *New Statesman and Society* for permission to reproduce an extract from 'SDP Sunk in Private Gloom' by Peter Kellner (12 November 1982).

We wish to acknowledge the following for permission to reproduce photographs: *Daily Telegraph*, Srdja Djukanovic, *Guardian*, Tom Kidd, Press Association, Ian Southern Photography, *Sunday Telegraph*. Whilst every effort has been made to trace the copyright holders, this has not been possible in every instance. The Publishers would be glad to hear from any copyright holders who proved untraceable.

We wish to acknowledge the following for permission to reproduce cartoons: *Daily Telegraph*, Nick Garland, *Guardian*, *Independent*, Bryan McAllister, *Sunday Telegraph*.

Contents

• • • •

CONTENTS

Part IV: Maturity and Death

Part V: Obituary

List of Plates

••••

List of Figures

• • • •

List of Tables

• • • •

List of Cartoons

• • • •

Abbreviations

•••••

APEX	Association of Professional, Executive, Clerical and Computer Staff
ASDC	Association of Social Democratic Councillors
AUEW	Amalgamated Union of Engineering Workers
BBC	British Broadcasting Corporation
BCC	Broadcasting Complaints Commission
CBI	Confederation of British Industry
CLP	Constituency Labour Party
CLPD	Campaign for Labour Party Democracy
CLV	Campaign for Labour Victory
CND	Campaign for Nuclear Disarmament
CPPB	Committee on Party Political Broadcasting
CSD	Campaign for Social Democracy
DHSS	Department of Health and Social Security
EEPTU	Electrical, Electronic, Telecommunications and Plumbing Union
ETU	Electrical Trades Union
GMWU	General and Municipal Workers' Union
IBA	Independent Broadcasting Authority
ITN	Independent Television News
MEP	Member of the European Parliament
MP	Member of Parliament
NATO	North Atlantic Treaty Organization
NEC	National Executive Committee
NFPW	National Federation of Professional Workers
NUM	National Union of Mineworkers
PEB	party election broadcast
PLP	Parliamentary Labour Party
PPB	party political broadcast
PPS	parliamentary private secretary
PR	proportional representation
PWR	pressurized water reactor
SDA	Social Democratic Alliance
SDP	Social Democratic Party
STV	single transferable vote
SWP	Socialist Workers' Party

ABBREVIATIONS

TSSA   Transport and Salaried Staffs' Association
TUC   Trades Union Congress
USDAW   Union of Shop, Distributive and Allied Workers
VAT   value added tax

Part I

. . . .

BIRTH

1
· · · ·
Pre-History: 1964–1979

The British Social Democratic party or SDP was launched at the Connaught Rooms in London on 26 March 1981. It ceased to exist in its original form in the early months of 1988, when, as the result of a majority vote by its members, it merged with the long-established Liberal party. This book tells the story of the birth, life and death of the SDP. It also assesses the SDP's impact on British politics and the longer-term significance of the party's short but dramatic history.

The SDP, like any new political party, was a product of its time—specifically of an era of governmental failure in Britain which lasted from 1964 until at least 1979 (and, some would say, continues to this day). The political and economic failures of successive governments, both Labour and Conservative, conditioned the conduct of political debate throughout the 1960s and 1970s and had a profound impact on the ideological direction taken by both of the major political parties. There had long been talk of a major realignment in British politics. By the late 1970s the conditions for such a realignment—if one was ever to occur—seemed to have been firmly established.

The general election of October 1964 is a good place to begin our story, because we can see in retrospect that it marked the end of the post-war era of stability and relative optimism in Britain's political life. On 15 October 1964 the Labour party won a four-seat majority in the House of Commons, a majority it increased to a much more comfortable ninety-seven seats following a second election in March 1966.

Labour was probably the last party to come to power in Britain confident that it had the capacity to solve the nation's economic problems. Incoming administrations since then have been hopeful and determined; but none has been as optimistic as Labour was in 1964. After thirteen years in opposition, Harold Wilson and his colleagues believed that they had a better theoretical understanding of Britain's economic problems than the Conservatives. They also believed that, unlike the Conservatives, they could develop new institutions—such as the Ministry of Technology, the Department of Economic Affairs and the Industrial

3

Reorganization Corporation (IRC)—that would make it possible for the government, the trade unions and industry to work more closely together and at the same time harness the talents of a new generation of liberal-minded scientists, specialists and technocrats. Wilson presented his party and himself as moderate, sensible and pragmatic, but also as dynamic, thrusting and purposeful. 'Let's GO with LABOUR', proclaimed the party's 1964 election posters, 'and we'll get things done'.[1]

The reality, sadly, was different.[2] Labour accomplished a great deal in its own terms between 1964 and 1970. Comprehensive schools became the norm in secondary education; more than 350,000 houses were built each year; liberal legislation was passed in such fields as race relations, abortion and homosexuality; and the steel industry was nationalized. But, taken as a whole, the period was not a happy one. Labour's National Plan, published to a great fanfare of trumpets in November 1965, had collapsed by the following summer. The government's ambitious expenditure plans frequently had to be cut. The pound was devalued. The annual rate of inflation doubled between 1964 and 1970 from 3.2 to 6.4 per cent. Unemployment likewise rose sharply from 1.6 per cent in 1964 to 2.5 per cent in 1970. In some ways worst of all, Britain's rate of economic growth, which Labour had come to power pledged to increase, actually fell from a fairly impressive 5.4 per cent in 1964 to a mere 1.8 per cent in 1970. Labour had been elected in 1964 and re-elected in 1966 in order to get the British economy moving again. It had signally failed in its attempt.[3]

Harold Wilson's style also caused offence. The Wilson government not only failed: it failed without dignity. Wilson had presented himself to the nation and the party in 1964 as a planner, a technocrat, a man with a broad vision of Britain's economic future, who would lead the country into, then through, 'the white heat of the scientific revolution'. But what the nation and the party actually got was a succession of *ad hoc* responses to *ad hoc* crises, a substantial proportion of them created by the government itself. The country got, not 'planning', with that term's connotations of continuity and long-term thinking, but a prime minister who responded to new situations and problems with an endless procession of gimmicks, fixes, wheezes and ploys. Words became a substitute for deeds, ministerial reshuffles and the renaming of government departments a substitute for the making of difficult decisions. The phrase that Harold Wilson will best be remembered by, 'A week is a long time in politics,' epitomized his whole administration. It was not for nothing that he became known as 'The Artful Dodger'.

Nemesis duly arrived, in June 1970. Following the devaluation of sterling in 1967, the economy as a whole had begun to revive, and the country's balance of payments, in deficit throughout most of the 1960s, had begun to move into surplus. Labour's standing in the opinion polls likewise improved, and a better-than-expected set of local election results in May 1970 persuaded Wilson to go to the country nearly a year earlier than the law required. The decision proved unwise. Defying the opinion polls, the Conservatives under Edward Heath won an

4

easy victory, gaining sixty-six seats (a post-war record) and an overall majority of thirty in the House of Commons.

It was now Heath's turn to fail.[4] Edward Heath and his colleagues came to office determined to introduce 'a new style of government' and to replace the Wilson government's rampant interventionism in industry with policies designed to promote private enterprise and the free market. Lame-duck firms and industries were no longer to be bailed out; interventionist bodies like the IRC were to be abolished. The Labour party in office had relied heavily on both voluntary and statutory incomes policies in order to keep down the rate of inflation. The new Conservative administration was committed to rejecting utterly 'the philosophy of compulsory wage control'.

As in the case of the Wilson government, the reality was sadly different. The IRC was indeed abolished, and the Heath government succeeded, where the Wilson government had failed, in taking Britain into the European Economic Community (EEC). But in almost every other respect the Heath government's new economic policies soon collapsed. When firms like Upper Clyde Shipbuilders and Rolls-Royce got into difficulties, they were almost immediately bailed out; the Rolls-Royce aeroengines division, despite the government's earlier pledges, was actually nationalized. Rising unemployment led to increases in government spending and also to a massive increase in the money supply. Far from sticking to its commitment to eschew state intervention in industry, the Heath government put on the statute book the Industry Act of 1972 which gave the secretary of state for trade and industry comprehensive powers to assist ailing firms and even to take them over. The pledge to reject compulsory wage control was followed in November 1972 by the introduction of the most draconian price and wage controls in British peacetime history. Under Heath the phrase 'U-turn'—almost never used in connection with politics before—became part of the country's permanent political vocabulary.

The Heath administration's U-turns would probably have been acceptable if they had produced lasting and beneficial results. But they did not. Partly thanks to the 1972-3 oil crisis, Britain's balance of payments during the early and mid-1970s plunged deeper and deeper into the red. The annual growth rate over the 1970-3 period was a disappointing 2.3 per cent, scarcely more than under Labour and considerably less than in most of Britain's industrial competitors. Unemployment rose, from 2.5 per cent in 1970 to 2.7 per cent in 1973 (the Heath government's last full year in office). Inflation, which the Conservatives had pledged to cut 'at a stroke', rose from 6.4 per cent in 1970 to 9.2 per cent in 1973 and looked certain to go on rising for years to come. The Conservatives had found Britain's economy in an unsatisfactory condition in 1970. Despite their U-turns, they left it in an equally unsatisfactory condition three and a half years later.

Moreover, the Conservatives under Heath also managed, like Labour, to conduct their affairs in a way that caused offence. Whereas Harold Wilson's style had been tawdry and undignified, Heath's was pompous and brusque, the new prime minister's stubborn self-righteousness substituting for his predecessor's low cunning. Heath, unlike Wilson, was extremely dogmatic; but Heath's dogmatism was of a strange variety: it managed to survive endless changes of policy. Facing in one direction, Heath and his colleagues insisted they were right. Facing in the opposite direction, they went on insisting they were right, with, if anything, even greater conviction. Heath contrived to appear implacable and stubborn, even though, in practice, he was almost infinitely flexible. His style of government was new, certainly, but it impressed the British public no more than Wilson's had.

The end was not long in coming. Faced with an overtime ban in the coal industry, followed soon afterwards by an all-out strike, Heath decided in February 1974—over a year before a general election was due—to go to the country on the slogan 'Who governs Britain?' The answer was not the one that he either wanted or expected. Labour's vote in the February 1974 election fell sharply, but the Conservatives' fell even more; and, thanks to the vagaries of the electoral system, following the election Wilson was able to form a minority administration even though Labour's share of the vote had actually been smaller than the Conservatives'. Wilson himself then went to the country in October 1974; but, although he did secure an overall majority in the House of Commons, it was a tiny one of only three seats.

In the event, the ensuing five years of Labour government bore an uncanny resemblance to the party's previous period in office.[5] Like the 1964–70 government, the 1974–9 administration was endlessly buffeted by unexpected developments and crises, and, even after James Callaghan succeeded Harold Wilson as prime minister in April 1976, it seemed to lack coherent policies or a clear sense of direction. The 1974–9 government, like its predecessor, had repeatedly to cut its forward expenditure plans. It saw the value of the pound plummet to unprecedentedly low levels. In 1976 it was forced to call in the International Monetary Fund and to borrow large sums from the international banking community. Above all, the 1974–9 government was no more successful than its predecessors in bringing about a fundamental improvement in Britain's economic performance. Growth remained sluggish; unemployment more than doubled from 2.7 per cent in 1973 to 5.6 per cent in the first quarter of 1979 (with more than 1,300,000 men and women on the dole); and although by 1978 inflation had been brought down to under 10 per cent from a peak in mid-1975 of nearly 30 per cent, it was still at historically high levels and in the winter of 1978–9 threatened once again to run out of control.

For its own failings and the failings of the British economy under it, the Callaghan government, like its Labour and Conservative predecessors, paid a heavy price. In November 1976, as a result of defections from Labour's ranks and a series of by-election defeats, the government lost its overall parliamentary majority and from then on was forced to rely on the goodwill of the minor parties in the House of Commons. From the spring of 1977 until October 1978, it was able to count on the Liberals' support after Callaghan and the Liberal leader, David Steel, had negotiated a formal pact; but the Liberals' decision to end the Lib–Lab pact in 1978 meant that the government's existence became even more precarious. The so-called Winter of Discontent, with tens of thousands of both private- and public-sector workers simultaneously out on strike, together with the failure of the Callaghan government's referendum on Scottish devolution, combined to bring the administration down. It lost a no-confidence vote in the House of Commons on 28 March 1979 and was then defeated in the ensuing election on 3 May. The swing to the Conservatives under Margaret Thatcher in the 1979 general election, 5.2 per cent, was the largest to any party since the Second World War.

Three separate governments had thus attempted since 1964 to govern Britain successfully and to restore its economic fortunes. All three had failed, and all three had been rebuffed at the polls. It had been a depressing period.

One of the causes—and also one of the consequences—of the successive failures of the Wilson, Heath and Callaghan governments was a new militancy on the part of Britain's trade unions.[6] Beginning in the mid-1960s, the unions fought large numbers of demarcation disputes; they fought to defend their traditional restrictive practices; and they also fought to defend their members' real wages against the rising tide of inflation (thereby causing the inflationary tide to rise still further). The number of working days lost through industrial action soared. For example, the number of working days lost as a result of strikes in 1964 was 2,277,000. A decade later the equivalent figure was nearly seven times as large, 14,750,000.[7] Moreover, the official figures, however dramatic, tended to underestimate the total amount of working time lost through strikes since they omitted very short stoppages and often failed to take into account layoffs and short-time working in firms and industries that were only indirectly affected. The cumulative economic damage—not to mention the damage to Britain's reputation overseas—was incalculable.

Although formidable, the bald strike figures by themselves also failed to capture the full extent of the disruption caused to people's lives. Deliveries were late. Journeys had to be postponed. Familiar goods disappeared from supermarket shelves. A miners' strike in the winter of 1971–2 caused extensive power cuts; the further miners' overtime ban and strike in 1973–4 resulted in the imposition of a three-day working week in industry. Five years later, during the Winter of Discontent, hospital wards were closed, icy roads were left untreated, sacks of garbage were left to rot in city squares, and, on at least one occasion, the dead were left unburied. The unions' actions throughout the 1970s induced an atmosphere of pervasive uncertainty. They seemed at times to threaten not merely the country's economic well-being but the very fabric of society.

In the face of the trade unions' new militancy, successive governments in the 1960s and 1970s appeared utterly powerless. The first Wilson government had some success between 1966 and 1969 in persuading the unions to co-operate with a prices and incomes policy designed to prevent excessive wage claims; but that policy was abandoned in 1969, and in the same year trade-union pressure forced the government to withdraw its proposals, embodied in the white paper *In Place of Strife*, for reforming the laws on the unions and industrial relations.[8] The Heath government did succeed in 1971 in putting on the statute book a more ambitious Industrial Relations Act, but union resistance ensured that it, too, was soon a dead letter.[9] The unions accepted for a time the stringent wage and price controls introduced by Heath in November 1972; but the miners' overtime ban and their subsequent strike in 1973–4 were a direct threat to wage control and were resisted by the government for that reason. In the ensuing confrontation between the government and the miners, it was the government that lost; and the incoming Labour administration then conceded all of the miners' main demands. For a time between 1975 and 1978, the Wilson and Callaghan governments also succeeded, despite these precedents, in operating an informal, extra-legal wages policy in conjunction with the unions; but that policy, too, collapsed in the Winter of Discontent. It was beginning to be said, and to be widely believed, that Britain was becoming ungovernable.[10]

Confronted with these harsh facts of governmental and national failure, the two major parties began, not surprisingly, to diverge sharply in their outlooks and policies. Desperate ailments seemed to demand desperate remedies; and the so-called 'post-war settlement', with its emphasis on full employment, the mixed economy, expanding welfare provision and Keynesian economic management, began slowly—at first almost imperceptibly—to break down. The Conservatives, following a weekend conference at the Selsdon Park Hotel in Surrey early in 1970, proclaimed their new-found faith in private enterprise, the free market and selective welfare benefits (even if the Heath government subsequently proved less than single-minded in pursuing these objectives). Later, after 1975, the Conservatives, under Heath's successor, Margaret Thatcher, went much further, effectively abandoning Keynesian economic ideas in favour of monetarism and insisting on the inherent superiority of the capitalist system over any form of socialism. The Conservatives' abandonment of the post-war settlement's commitment to full employment followed soon afterwards. Meanwhile, the Labour party was moving hard in the opposite direction, adopting between 1970 and 1974 policies that were far to the left of anything known since the war. Throughout the 1970s the two major parties shouted imprecations at each other across an ever-deepening ideological chasm.[11]

There was one issue, however, that cut across these widening party differences. That issue was whether or not Britain should become and remain a member of the European Economic Community. On the Conservative side, EEC membership was opposed mainly by traditional Tories who feared for the future of British agriculture, who objected to any loss of British sovereignty and who were also keen that Britain should retain its traditionally close ties with the United States and the countries of the old Commonwealth. On the Labour side, membership of the EEC was opposed principally by left-wingers who dismissed it as nothing more than a capitalist club, who objected to the constraints that the EEC's rules would place on socialist planning in the United Kingdom and who, most profoundly, saw British involvement in the EEC as meaning the end of their dream of building a socialist Jerusalem in England's green and pleasant land.

In the 1970s the impact of the European issue was greatest on the Labour party.[12] Despite widespread initial reluctance within the party, the Wilson government decided in 1967 to apply for full EEC membership, and a majority at the Labour party conference that year adopted a resolution strongly supporting the government's initiative. But many of the most powerful trade-union leaders—and many, probably a majority, of Labour's rank-and-file members—were in fact not at all keen on the European idea, and when the party returned to opposition in 1970 their underlying hostility to Britain's EEC membership rapidly reasserted itself.

On 28 October 1971, when the Heath government laid before parliament the terms for British entry that it had succeeded in negotiating with the other member countries, the great majority of the parliamentary Labour party, including the former prime minister, Harold Wilson, voted to reject them despite their previous commitments; but no fewer than sixty-nine MPs on the Labour side, including Roy Jenkins, the party's deputy leader, and three other members of the shadow cabinet—Harold Lever, George Thomson and Shirley Williams—voted with the Conservatives in favour of the EEC, and a further twenty abstained. This rebellion, involving as it did so many leading frontbenchers, was on a scale and of a type unprecedented in Labour's history.

A few months later, in March 1972, Jenkins, Lever and Thomson (though not Williams) went a good deal further and resigned from Labour's shadow cabinet rather than accept its decision to commit a future Labour government to holding a second general election or referendum on the EEC issue. Jenkins and his allies disapproved of referendums in principle and also maintained that the shadow cabinet's decision in favour of a referendum amounted to a disgraceful reversal of the outgoing Labour government's firm pledges on the same issue. Later that year, in October 1972, a row over Europe in the Lincoln constituency Labour party precipitated the resignation from parliament of Lincoln's Labour MP, Dick Taverne. Taverne then fought and won the resulting by-election, fighting as a 'Democratic Labour' candidate.[13] Pro-Europeans like Jenkins and Taverne were convinced that Britain outside the EEC had no chance of reversing its long-term economic decline; they were adamant that Britain should be an outward-looking not an inward-looking country; and they rejoiced at the spectacle of the leaders of different European nations, many of them so recently at war, working amicably together in trying to solve the continent's problems.

When Labour returned to office in March 1974, the new Wilson government devoted its first twelve months to 'renegotiating' the original terms of entry negotiated by Heath. And, true to its word, the government then put these new terms to the British people in a national referendum—the country's first—on 5 June 1975. The referendum campaign saw a majority of Labour MPs and a minority of Conservatives fighting side by side against continued EEC membership and the great majority of Conservatives and a minority of Labour MPs fighting side by side in favour of the EEC. The Liberal party was overwhelmingly pro-European from the start. The organization that campaigned for a 'yes' vote in June 1975, Britain in Europe, brought together prominent figures from all three parties, notably Edward Heath, Roy Jenkins and David Steel, and they worked together in conspicuous harmony. On the day itself, the pro-European forces won by a convincing two-to-one majority.

As we shall see in Chapter 6, the European issue was not quite so crucial to the subsequent emergence of the SDP as is usually supposed. Nevertheless, the split in the Labour party on the issue, and the subsequent camaraderie of the Britain in Europe campaign, undoubtedly loosened some of the psychological bonds that tied leading pro-European Labour politicians to the Labour party; and at the same time it afforded them a glimpse of how attractive and effective co-operation across traditional party lines could be. It was no accident that, when the time came, Roy Jenkins, George Thomson, Shirley Williams and Dick Taverne were all among the SDP's original founders.

Europe was undoubtedly the most important issue that cut across party lines in the 1970s; but it was by no means the only one. During most of the post-war period from 1945 to 1970, the lines of political cleavage in Britain had mainly been party lines. To know someone's views on any one major issue of the day was to know his or her views on almost all of them. Politicians' opinions tended to come in neatly tied bundles, and the bundles were usually tied in either red or blue ribbon. By the early 1970s, however, this simple two-party pattern was becoming increasingly blurred. There were more and more issues—environmental and women's issues as well as Europe—on which the Labour and Conservative parties either had no policies at all or else were internally divided. Thus, the pattern of political debate in Britain and the pattern of party politics no longer corresponded as neatly as they once had. They were, so to speak, 'out of phase'. As a result, many politically aware men and women came to feel increasingly disoriented and alienated from both the Conservative and Labour parties.

As for the mass of ordinary non-political voters, their response to the events of the 1960s and 1970s was predictable. Both major parties had failed in office. Both were adopting more and more extreme policies. Both were talking a language that increasingly cut athwart voters' perceptions of what was politically sensible and allowable. A large proportion of voters naturally responded by ceasing to feel engaged with either of the major parties and by showing an increasing reluctance to vote for either of them at elections. Disenchantment with the two major parties and electoral volatility increased in tandem.[14]

Table 1.1 in Appendix 5 charts the decline of the two-party system among the electorate over the twenty years from the 1959 general election, when the system was still at its height, to the election of 1979, when it succeeded only partially— and temporarily—in reasserting itself. As can be seen, roughly 90 per cent of all voters supported either the Conservatives or Labour until the early 1970s. Then, in

1974, the total of major-party supporters fell sharply to 75 per cent; and even in 1979 it was still only a little over 80 per cent. The Conservatives failed to obtain as much as 40 per cent of the vote at either of the two 1974 general elections; and the Labour party failed to obtain as much as 40 per cent in either 1974 or 1979. Labour's two 1974 'victories' served only to conceal the true extent of Labour's long-term decline. Meanwhile, as the table also shows, the extent of 'very-strong' and 'fairly-strong' voter identification with the two major parties was also tending to diminish.

The main beneficiary of this growing disenchantment with both the Conservatives and Labour was, of course, the Liberal party. In 1964 a combination of Conservative unpopularity and continuing doubts about Labour's fitness to govern enabled the Liberals, then led by Jo Grimond, to win as much as 11.2 per cent of the popular vote even though the party fielded candidates in only 365 of the country's 630 constituencies. In the 365 seats that the Liberals did fight, their share of the vote was actually 18.5 per cent. In 1966 and 1970 the Liberal party's support fell, when first Labour and then the Conservatives recovered for a time their electoral appeal; but then, in the February 1974 election, held in the midst of the three-day working week and the miners' strike, the Liberals, now led by Jeremy Thorpe, fielded 517 candidates and won 19.3 per cent of the vote (fully 23.6 per cent in the seats they contested). The Liberals did not fare quite so well in October 1974 (when their candidates took 18.3 per cent of the vote) or 1979 (when they took 13.8 per cent); but they were now, all the same, an electoral force to be reckoned with. From 1974 onwards the Liberals contested over 500 seats at every general election; and their share of the vote never fell back again—or ever looked like falling back—to the single figures that had marked their electoral performance in the 1950s.[15]

The Liberals improved their position during the 1970s, not because large numbers of voters were positively attracted to them, but because an increasingly large proportion of them were repelled by both of the other parties. On the one hand, the Liberals were seen as amiable, moderate and relatively harmless—a 'cuddly' party, hard to dislike even if hard to take seriously. On the other hand, few voters knew much (or anything) about the Liberals' policy positions except that they were not the Conservatives' or Labour's. The only thing that the voters did know for sure about the Liberals was that they had no realistic chance of winning. The fact that the voters knew the Liberals could not win helped to ensure that they did not. The Liberals found it almost impossible to overcome the 'wasted-vote' argument. Fortunately for them, they happened to be led throughout the 1960s and 1970s by a succession of personable and popular leaders: Jo Grimond until 1967, Jeremy Thorpe until 1976 and David Steel until 1988. All three were capable of attracting a disproportionate amount of publicity; all three had considerable personal magnetism.

Jo Grimond in the 1960s had no illusions about the Liberals' chances of winning power on their own. He reckoned they were zero. But at the same time he wanted his party to be in a position, if possible, to exert influence on government and government policy; he repeatedly spoke of the Liberals 'getting on or getting out' and on one well-publicized occasion announced his determination to lead his Liberal troops 'towards the sound of gunfire'.[16] At worst, Grimond hoped that his party might one day hold the balance of power in the House of Commons and be able to exercise power by that means (though he knew the odds against that happening were extremely long). At best, he hoped that Labour would split and that the Liberals could then take part in a major realignment of the party system. Such a realignment would involve moderate Labour politicians and possibly some of the more progressive Conservatives as well as his own small band of Liberals. As we shall see, this was a vision that Grimond bequeathed to his fellow Scot and eventual successor as leader, David Steel.

All the parties were affected by the political turbulence of the 1960s and 1970s and by the pervasive atmosphere of crisis that hung over them; but none was more affected than the Labour party. Labour was not only divided on Europe: it was divided on almost every major question of philosophy and ideology; and it was these divisions inside the Labour party that, above all else, eventually led to the formation of the SDP.[17]

The two periods of Labour government in the 1960s and 1970s were reckoned almost universally—inside the party as well as outside it—to have been failures. Moreover, the failures did not appear to be accidents. On the contrary, they appeared to be all of a piece. Especially to those on the left of the party, the 1974–9 government resembled a remake of an old film: the details were different, but the title, the plot and even the cast of characters remained largely the same. Left-wingers and large numbers of ordinary rank-and-file activists felt terribly betrayed. If they had been Chinese rather than British, they might well have accused Wilson, Callaghan and their ministerial colleagues of 'the three great betrayals'.[18]

The first of the three was electoral. The Wilson and Callaghan governments, like all previous Labour governments, had been dominated by the right wing of the party; and it had always been the right's contention that it and it alone could deliver electoral success—a contention that had seemed to be borne out by the victories of 1964 and 1966. Only Labour's right wing, so the argument went, was in a position to appeal to Britain's floating voters, the great majority of whom were political moderates. These same floating voters were deeply alienated by the Labour left, intensely disliking both its policies and its leaders. It followed that a Labour party led by the left could never win.

This line of argument was plausible in the abstract; but in the specific circumstances of 1970 and then of 1979 it was Labour governments led not by the left but by the right that had been in power and had been defeated. The left could in no way be blamed. Worse, the Wilson and Callaghan governments had not merely been defeated; they had handed over power to governments—Heath's in 1970 and Thatcher's in 1979—that Labour activists universally regarded as being the most reactionary and aggressively anti-socialist of the twentieth century. 'Selsdon Man' was followed within less than a decade by 'That Bloody Woman'. The right wing of the party, by its ineptitude and lack of principle, had helped install both Heath and Thatcher in office.

The Wilson and Callaghan governments' second betrayal in the eyes of the Labour left was their betrayal of socialism. Despite the introduction of comprehensive schools, despite the various acts of nationalization, despite the building of council houses, despite the pension increases and despite the other social reforms, Britain was, in the eyes of most people in the Labour party, no more genuinely socialist in 1970 than it had been in 1964 and no more genuinely socialist in 1979 than it had been in 1974. British society was no more egalitarian; the citadels of establishment power had not been stormed; and Britain was still a member of NATO, still a supplicant ally of the United States and still a nuclear power. Not only that, but the Wilson and Callaghan governments had failed to create a command economy or even an economy marked by any substantial degree of central economic planning. To many in the Labour party, socialism *meant* planning; but there was precious little of it in evidence in the 1960s and 1970s. The National Plan of 1965 died within a few months, and the Labour governments' macroeconomic policies—those pursued by Labour's three chancellors, James Callaghan, Roy Jenkins and Denis Healey—were largely orthodox in character. Labour economic ministers perhaps offered enlightened welfare-statism; they certainly did not offer socialism.

Labour activists' experiences with the 1974–9 government were, if anything, even worse than with the 1964–70 government. The 1964–70 government had at least tried to fulfil its election promises. The 1974–9 government made no such attempt; or, rather, it operated on a 'pick-and-mix' basis, fulfilling those commitments that it thought were reasonable and jettisoning the rest. The left especially resented the second Wilson government's calculated refusal to introduce a radical Industry Act, one that would give the government sweeping powers to give grants to private-sector companies, to intervene in their internal affairs and even to nationalize them in the absence of legislation specifically designed for that purpose. Something called an Industry Act was, to be sure, introduced in 1975, but it was a pale shadow of what the Labour party in the country had wanted and thought it had been promised. A promised wealth tax similarly failed to materialize. By 1979 one did not have to be of an unusually conspiratorial cast of mind to conclude that the great majority of socialist ministers could not be relied upon to introduce socialism.

But it was the third of the great betrayals that was in many ways the worst. The Wilson and Callaghan governments totally failed in their declared aim of rejuvenating and revivifying the British economy.[19] In particular, unemployment rose sharply during both of Labour's two periods of office—to the point where in 1979 the Conservatives could, with cruel irony, campaign on the slogan 'Labour isn't working'. Labour governments were supposed to be full-employment governments. That was their *raison d'être* in the minds of Labour voters and activists. It was largely the two Labour governments' failure to solve the country's economic problems—and especially their failure to curb rising unemployment—that caused large numbers of Labour voters and supporters to begin to desert their former party.

Moreover, just as the party's right wing was held to blame for the party's electoral failures, so right-wing leaders and right-wing policies were held to blame for the Labour governments' economic failures. After all, right-wingers like Anthony Crosland and Roy Jenkins had pitched their claims high. *They* were the experts. *They* knew economics. *They* had mastered the fine arts of Keynesian demand management. *They* knew how to intervene selectively and forcefully in industry. *They* would be able to co-operate effectively not just with the trade unions but with leading industrialists in forums such as the National Economic Development Council. Yet all the right's economic expertise, its Keynesianism, its interventionism and its corporatism, had come to naught in the 1970s as it had in the 1960s. Not only was Britain not a notably more socialist country than it had been before; it was, if anything, even weaker economically. The left naturally blamed the right. Under the circumstances it was not at all clear whom else it could blame.

The Labour right's failures in office had a number of consequences. One of the most important was to ensure that the party's rank-and-file membership became much more left wing and militant than it had ever been before. To some extent, this shift to the left in the 1970s was a consequence of existing members of the party changing their minds; but to a much greater extent it was a result of old members leaving the party and new ones joining. Traditionalists and moderates left. Left-wingers stayed—and added significantly to their numbers.

The Labour party at the grassroots had always been kept alive by thousands of ordinary men and women for whom socialism meant above all improving the living conditions and life chances of Britain's working classes. Most members of the Labour party were practical idealists, not theoreticians. Some were very active in the party, but most merely contributed small sums to the party's funds, attended occasional meetings and helped out for a few afternoons or evenings during election campaigns. After 1964, faced with the Wilson government's failures— and especially its apparent lack of sympathy for ordinary workers (their wages restrained, their unions attacked, unemployment among them rising)—local Labour supporters of this type resigned from the party in droves—or, more commonly, simply failed to renew their subscriptions. According to Labour's official figures, the party's individual membership fell from 830,000 in 1964 to 680,000 in 1970.[20] These figures, however, were misleading and the actual decline was almost certainly much greater. It is doubtful whether Labour's individual member-ship in the early 1970s stood at much above 300,000.[21] It remained at a low level throughout the decade.

A decline on this scale deprived the Labour party of human and financial resources; but it also altered significantly the party's internal political balance. Those who left were disproportionately on the right of the party and relatively apolitical; those who stayed behind were disproportionately on the left of the party and far more highly politicized. Moreover, as like attracted like, new recruits to the party were also mainly left-wingers. The typical Labour party member gradually ceased to be a lorry driver, bricklayer or miner, concerned with the day-to-day well-being of working men and women, and became instead a much more ideologically minded teacher, local-government officer or social worker. The constituency Labour parties had always tended to be on the left of the party (voluntary party workers everywhere tend to be enthusiasts); but in the 1970s many of them moved even further to the left than they had been before.[22]

A large part of Labour's left wing in the 1970s also underwent a change of character. Men and women began to join the Labour party with opinions that lay far outside the liberal-democratic mainstream of the party, which had hitherto been dominant.

Tensions between right and left in Labour's ranks had, of course, existed as long as the party itself. To read the report of a debate at a Labour party conference in the 1920s or 1930s is to be transported immediately into a familiar world.[23] The right had always been reformist rather than revolutionary, gradualist rather than apocalyptic, concerned with the welfare of the nation as a whole, not just with the welfare of manual workers. Right-wingers believed in the mixed economy, not in the wholesale state ownership of the means of production, distribution and exchange (whatever Clause IV of the party's constitution might say). They also believed in a strong national defence; and, seeing themselves as 'more Methodist than Marxist', they acknowledged, however reluctantly, that a democratic political party like Labour might find itself forced to have enemies to its left. By contrast, Labour's left wing had always taken up positions that were more or less the opposite. It was radical, committed to the class struggle, determined to extend the economic power of the state, impatient, deeply hostile to the existing establishment. In short, the Labour left was genuinely revolutionary, in word if not always in deed. In some other country, with a different electoral system, the two wings of the Labour party would almost certainly have been in different parties.

But there was one point on which, until the 1970s, both the right and the left were largely united: they both believed in parliamentary democracy. They believed in free elections, a free press, competing political parties and the desirability of peaceful rather than violent political change. Both wings had doubts about the morality, as well as the efficacy, of extra-parliamentary political action, and both were opposed, for example, to the calling of strikes for political as distinct from industrial purposes. Parliament was where the country's political battles, including the battle for socialism, should be fought out. Moreover, this was not merely a matter of theory. Left-wingers like Aneurin Bevan and Michael Foot, devoted to parliament, were also distinguished parliamentarians, able to shine in and often to dominate the House of Commons chamber. The fact that the right and the left in the party shared these assumptions about political conduct meant that, although the disagreements between the party's disparate wings were often bitter, they were kept within bounds. Whatever their differences, right and left felt themselves to be members of the same political family—even if, more often than not, it was a warring family.

Beginning in the late 1960s, however, new kinds of left-wingers began to appear inside the party and to make their presence felt. And, as Labour's grass-roots membership declined, so the importance of this new element inexorably increased. Many of the newcomers were in no conceivable sense democratic socialists; instead they were revolutionary Marxists, Maoists and all manner of Trotskyites. Most had previously belonged—many still did belong—to obscure bodies with names like the Socialist Workers' party, the International Marxist Group and the Revolutionary Communist League (shortly to be rechristened the Militant Tendency). Many of them entered the Labour party because extreme-left organizations had decided that they should enter it: parts of the far left had deliberately adopted an 'entryist' tactic. Their infiltration was made easier, in addition, by the fact that in 1973 Labour's National Executive Committee, already left dominated, abolished Labour's list of proscribed organizations. The existence of the list had hitherto prevented members of bodies like those just mentioned from becoming members of the Labour party (or at least from doing so openly).[24]

The far-left newcomers frequently differed among themselves; their personal quarrels and ideological splits were notorious. But what they had in common was a contempt for liberal-democratic norms and institutions. They believed in extra-parliamentary action, and they also believed that the coming of socialism would require the total destruction of the existing capitalist order. Many of them regarded violence as a legitimate revolutionary weapon; and, as in the case of the British Communists between the wars, their repertoire of day-to-day tactics included harassment, verbal abuse and even physical intimidation. Gradually, as the 1970s went on, these newcomers—'infiltrators' or 'entryists', as their enemies called them—extended their influence in trade-union branches and constituency Labour parties in many different parts of the country (notably, but not only, in Liverpool, Manchester and inner London).[25] To right-wingers it was ominous that on many specific issues, and on the general question of their right to join the Labour party and organize within it, the newcomers increasingly had the support of leading figures on the party's traditional left, such as Ian Mikardo and the former and future Labour cabinet minister Tony Benn.

Tony Benn was a crucial figure—probably *the* crucial figure—in the Labour politics of the 1970s. For most of its history, the left wing of the Labour party had not had an effective leader. Aneurin Bevan in the 1950s had been too wayward and unpredictable—and too lazy—to put together a cohesive group of MPs that was capable of effective political action (and in 1957 he largely parted company from the left when he abandoned the cause, if he had ever taken it up, of unilateral nuclear disarmament). Benn was in a different class. He worked hard, he was a brilliant tactician, and he had both staying power and a clear sense of political direction. For more than a decade from 1970 he was the single most influential figure within the Labour party, using the party's extra-parliamentary organs to push the party further and further in the direction he wanted. Labour's evolution in the 1970s owed more to him than to any other individual, and attitudes towards him provided a litmus-paper test of people's ideological position in the party. Some in the party worshipped him; others merely followed him; many loathed him.[26]

One episode in the mid-1970s served notice of the left's intentions within the party and also of the tactics that some on the left were prepared to employ. The constituency of Newham North-East was represented in parliament by Reg Prentice, a former union official who had once been in the centre of the party (and had twice topped the poll in the annual elections to the shadow cabinet) but was now moving rapidly to the right. In 1975 Prentice was education secretary and a prominent cabinet minister, but his local party was increasingly dominated by the far left, and (probably partly for that reason) he began to speak out vehemently against the left and also against the trade unions for seeking to undermine the government's anti-inflation policy. When the Newham North-East party moved to deselect him as the local Labour candidate in 1975, more than half the parliamentary Labour party, 180 MPs, published a declaration in support of him, and Roy Jenkins and Shirley Williams spoke on his behalf at a rowdy meeting in the Mile End Road (where someone threw a flour bomb at Jenkins). Nevertheless, the local party insisted on proceeding against the beleaguered minister, and Labour's National Executive turned down his appeal. As Prentice had always supported Labour policy in the House of Commons and as there were no serious complaints about his record as a constituency MP, his deselection and the extreme left's infiltration of the Newham North-East party were seen by many on the right as scarcely veiled threats to their own position.[27]

Just as the local constituency parties were moving to the left, so were many of the largest trade unions, controlling among them the majority of votes at the annual Labour party conference and the majority of seats on the National Executive. The Labour party could not have moved to the left without the unions moving in the same direction; with the unions moving to the left, the party was bound to do the same.

One factor in the unions' leftward shift has already been referred to: their new assertiveness and militancy beginning in the late 1960s. As workers found their real incomes being squeezed by inflation, they became readier than in the past to join trade unions, to take industrial action and to elect union leaders who would fight aggressively on their behalf. And the union leaders who were the most militant in their approach to wage-bargaining also tended to be militant and left wing in their approach to politics. A new generation of leaders also appeared, somewhat fortuitously, at or near the top of a number of the largest unions. Historically, trade-union leaders had tended to be right-wingers, staunch supporters of the parliamentary leadership and the status quo; but the new men—notably Jack Jones of the Transport and General Workers' Union and Hugh Scanlon of the Amalgamated Engineering Union—were both committed left-wingers and self-declared radical socialists. Their causes included unilateral nuclear disarmament, wholesale nationalization and the creation in Britain of something approaching a Soviet-style command economy. In the National Union of Mineworkers, this process of generational change culminated in 1981 in the election of Arthur Scargill as the union's president.[28]

Developments like these in the unions would, on their own, have had serious repercussions inside the Labour party; but the unions' determination to play a larger role in the making of Labour policy was reinforced in the 1960s and 1970s by the repeated encroachments of Labour governments into what trade-union leaders had hitherto considered 'their' domain: that of industrial relations and wage-bargaining. The unions resented government-enforced incomes policies. They resented even more the first Wilson government's attempts to reform them and their activities with *In Place of Strife*.

The unions therefore decided even before Labour left office in 1970 that from now on they would play a more active part in the party's internal affairs. Until the late 1960s, the trade-union and political wings of the labour movement had operated on the basis of a tacit division of labour: the trade-union wing would look after collective bargaining and industrial matters; the political wing would look after politics. But the disputes of the 1960s undermined this agreement. The politicians were seen to be intervening in industrial matters: the unions must therefore intervene in politics. From the late 1960s onwards, trade-union leaders spoke more forcibly than in the past at Labour party conferences, they established closer links with union-sponsored Labour MPs, and they asserted themselves to a far greater extent on Labour's National Executive.

A concrete sign of the unions' enhanced role was the establishment in 1972 of the TUC–Labour Party Liaison Committee. For several years after 1972 this committee was the labour movement's authoritative voice on all matters concerning the trade unions and the party. It was the liaison committee that in the early 1970s drafted the so-called 'social contract', which was meant to govern union–government relations when Labour again came to power. Moreover, since the unions had already moved sharply to the left on most important matters of policy, it was inevitable that sooner or later they would use their influence to move the party as a whole in the same direction.

Like the unions, the constituency Labour parties from the late 1960s onwards became not only more left wing but also far more assertive than they had been in the past, far more inclined both to claim their rights in the party and also to try to extend those rights. In the past, left-wing trade unions and activists in the country had often rebelled *against* authority; now they sought to *become* authority. A large proportion of the party's new recruits were 'children of the Sixties', passionate young men and women who had been at college or university at the height of what Samuel H. Beer has called 'the romantic revolt'.[29] They believed in activism, participation and grass-roots decision-making. They rejected tradition—including the peculiarly British tradition of deference—and with it all forms of social and political hierarchy. One of the hierarchies that they rejected was the one, based in the House of Commons, that had hitherto dominated the Labour party.

The unions' and constituency parties' new assertiveness manifested itself in a number of ways. One had to do with the selection of parliamentary candidates. Until the late 1960s, most constituency Labour parties, although left wing in their general outlook, were not too concerned about whether the individual they selected as their local parliamentary candidate was himself a left-winger. All they wanted was 'a good Labour man' (or, occasionally, woman). Beginning in the late 1960s and early 1970s, however, many CLPs adopted a new set of criteria. They themselves had left-wing views: surely the man or woman they adopted as their candidate should also have left-wing views? As the 1970s wore on, right-wingers found it increasingly hard to win selection as parliamentary candidates; pro-Europeans, in particular, whatever their views on other issues, were virtually boycotted by most local parties. Not surprisingly, many right-wingers, wanting to become MPs, took to dissimulating their real views. Constituency Labour Parties (CLPs) wanted to hear left-wing noises: left-wing noises were what they got. Whereas in the past the choice at a typical Labour selection conference had usually lain between a right-winger and a left-winger (or even, occasionally, between two right-wingers), the choice in the 1970s lay increasingly often between two left-wingers, one of them on the 'soft left', one on the 'hard' (though this particular language did not come into use until later).

The results of this process naturally took some time to work themselves out: the amount of turnover among MPs at any one general election is limited. But by the late 1970s and the mid-1980s the cumulative effects on the political composition of the parliamentary Labour party of the changes taking place at the constituency level were there for all to see: each cohort of new Labour MPs was considerably more left wing than the one it replaced. The Labour party in the House of Commons—the last bastion of right-wing power in the party—was gradually, very gradually, falling into left-wing hands.[30]

The National Executive Committee (NEC), the party's governing body between annual conferences, also fell more and more into left-wing hands. In the period immediately after the war, the NEC typically consisted of a majority of trade-union members and other members elected by the unions, who were typically loyal to the parliamentary leadership, along with a minority, often a small minority, of left-wingers, mainly elected by the constituency parties. As late as 1964, the constituency section was more or less equally divided between right and left (James Callaghan, for example, was a constituency member), while the women's section boasted a solid right-wing majority. By 1974, however, only a single right-winger, Denis Healey, remained in the constituency section, and only one right-winger, Shirley Williams, remained in the women's section. By the end of the 1970s, Healey had gone, and at the end of a typical debate at the NEC the traditional right could seldom muster more than three or four votes, if that, out of the total of twenty-nine.[31]

This shift to the left on the NEC and at the annual conference—where the left had established an overwhelming majority even before Labour left office in 1970—had an inevitable effect on party policy. When Labour was in power, the right—still with a majority in the parliamentary party and among the party leadership—could mostly get its way; but in opposition the left, spurred on by Tony Benn as chairman of the NEC's home policy subcommittee, swept all before it.

The manifesto on which Labour fought and won the 1964 election under Wilson had been a self-consciously moderate document—practical, middle-of-the-road, aimed at the floating voter, devoid of the language of militant socialism (indeed largely devoid of the language of socialism altogether). The only industry to be taken into public ownership was steel. The manifesto adopted for the February 1974 election, by contrast, was an emanation from another political world. Despite the fact that Harold Wilson had earlier managed to veto a call for the national-ization of 'twenty-five leading companies', the February 1974 manifesto promised to take into public ownership all the building land in the country that was required for development; and it went on:

We shall also take shipbuilding, ship repairing and marine engineering, ports, the manufacture of airframes and aeroengines into public ownership and control. But we shall not confine the extension of the public sector to the loss-making and subsidized industries. We shall also take over profitable sections of individual firms in those industries where a public holding is essential to enable the government to control prices, stimulate investment, encourage exports, create employment, protect workers and companies, and to plan the national economy in the national interest. We shall therefore include in this operation sections of pharmaceuticals, road haulage, construction, machine tools, in addition to our proposals for North Sea Oil and Celtic Sea gas and oil.[32]

The 1974 manifesto's rhetoric also went further than anything known since the war. Labour pledged itself to bring about (the phrase was Benn's) 'a funda-mental and irreversible shift of power and wealth in favour of working people and their families'. 'The aims set out in this manifesto', the party proclaimed, 'are socialist aims, and we are proud of the word.' Attitudes and policies like these were deeply unpopular with the electorate, and it was no surprise that at the February 1974 election Labour's share of the vote fell to its lowest level since the 1930s. Indeed, it was one of the more bizarre features of the politics of the 1970s that, because Labour 'won' the two 1974 elections in the sense of winning more seats than the Conservatives, Tony Benn could claim, as he frequently did, that the two elections, which were in fact substantial setbacks for Labour, ought actually to be regarded as socialist triumphs.[33]

The unions' and constituency parties' new assertiveness led, in addition, to demands for major changes in the party's constitution. Increasing numbers of activists decided that the party's rank and file should be given a bigger formal and constitutional say in the making of party policy and in choosing the party's leaders. In the past, party conferences had often passed left-wing resolutions, and sometimes these resolutions had even found their way into Labour election manifestos. But then, more often than not, nothing much had happened. Members of the party were blandly told by Labour ministers that circumstances had changed, or that the proposal in question had proved on further investigation to be impracticable, or that not enough money was available, or that not enough parliamentary time was available . . . or whatever. Left-wingers, after more than a decade of this kind of thing, were fed up. They wanted action. They wanted power. Above all, they wanted socialism, and they suspected that many leading right-wingers in the party had no serious intention of carrying out Labour's more radical manifesto commitments—a suspicion that, from 1974 onwards, was undoubtedly well founded.

Grass-roots pressure began to build up in the mid-1970s for a series of amendments to the party's constitution that would enable the left not merely to determine the forms of words in Labour party policy documents but also, in future, to control the actions of Labour governments and Labour MPs. First, the left wanted to make it easier for a CLP to refuse to readopt a sitting MP if it did not like his or her political opinions. Secondly, it wanted the trade unions and CLPs to be given a substantial say in the election of the party's leader and deputy leader. Thirdly, it wanted to give the party in the country, represented by the NEC, exclusive control over the contents of the party's election manifesto. In 1974, following Harold Wilson's veto of the NEC's 'twenty-five leading companies' proposal, a group of local activists formed a grass-roots organization to campaign for all three of these constitutional reforms. The organization was called the Campaign for Labour Party Democracy (CLPD). At first, almost no one noticed CLPD: there were so many left-wing organizations with all kinds of different initials it was impossible to keep track of them. But CLPD was soon to have a decisive effect on Labour's future—and on the formation of the SDP.[34]

By the end of the 1970s, the Labour party had acquired not merely new policies, a newly constituted NEC and a new organization campaigning for constitutional change; it had also acquired a new ethos. The divisions in the party had once been between a dominant right and a rebellious left. Now the right was rapidly becoming marginalized, and the real question was no longer whether the party would move to the left, but how far and how fast. The balance of the argument inside the party had swung decisively in the left's favour. One small indicator of the scale of the change was the behaviour of the General and Municipal Workers' Union (GMWU) under the leadership of its new general secretary, David Basnett. The GMWU, the country's second largest union, had once been a bastion of the right—solid, sensible, reliable. Now in the late 1970s it remained a 'moderate' union in current Labour party terms, but its moderation increasingly consisted, not of fighting the right's battles against the left, but of seeking to play a balancing role between the two.[35] The GMWU remained in the party's mainstream, but the mainstream itself was flowing in new channels. After so many disappointments and dashed hopes, the day of the left appeared at last to be dawning.

21

The Labour party by the late 1970s was thus at all levels a very different party from the one it had been only a few years before. As party members considered the implications of Labour's defeat in May 1979, the left-wingers among them must have had ambivalent feelings. On the one hand, they were angry and, as they had in 1970, believed they had been betrayed. But, on the other hand, and looking ahead, they could feel that the party was at last moving in their direction. The size of the left's majorities at party conferences and on the National Executive was growing. The substance of the party's policies, at least on paper, was more and more to their liking. There seemed to be a reasonable prospect that the changes they desired would eventually be made to the party's constitution. And there also seemed to be a reasonable prospect that, given time, a majority of Labour's MPs could be brought round to their point of view. As Labour left office in the spring of 1979, the left was angry and frustrated but at the same time had solid grounds for optimism about the future.

The way in which the right, on the other hand, responded to these developments can easily be imagined. The right was bewildered, dismayed and disoriented. During the early 1970s, while Labour was still in opposition, leading right-wingers had been forced to retreat on issue after issue and to swallow forms of words and policies that they would have rejected with disdain only a few years before. It is doubtful whether as many as half of the members of the shadow cabinet who fought the February 1974 election believed in either the details or the rhetoric of their own manifesto. Some of the pledges in the manifesto, for example on nationalization, they would go on to fulfil, often against their own better judgement; but others they would ignore. During this period, an element of world-weariness and despair—the unkind would say cynicism and hypocrisy—began to enter the souls of many on the right of the party.

The question arises: why had the right not organized and fought back? Why had they put up with so much?

There are a number of reasons. One is that the right continued to provide the bulk of Labour's leadership in the House of Commons. Harold Wilson, although originally elected as a left-winger, had become solidly right wing by 1970; and Callaghan, Jenkins, Crosland and Healey were already on the right. These five men dominated the shadow cabinet in the early 1970s and would be certain to dominate any real cabinet that Labour might form in the future. So long as they were in this position, they could prevent occasional items that they disliked from being included in any election manifesto, and, more important, they knew—and knew that everyone else knew—that if Labour won an election and were returned to office they, rather than either the National Executive or the contents of the manifesto, would determine the Labour government's policies. This being so, why should they, while in opposition, fight to the death conference resolutions and manifesto pledges that amounted in practice to no more than forms of words? Most of them also believed, in the early 1970s, that the early return of a Labour government was most unlikely: why, therefore, fight over forms of words that were likely to remain just that, forms of words?

The right was also handicapped at this stage by personal differences and rivalries among those who should have been its natural leaders. Wilson, then as always, chose to play a balancing game. Callaghan and Healey were both loners, anxious to lead the party themselves one day and therefore anxious not to do or say anything in the meantime that would alienate potential supporters. Jenkins and Crosland were just as ambitious on their own behalf—and, having once been close friends, had by this time become serious rivals. Susan Crosland has provided a wry account of how the two men devoted a whole evening in 1973 to trying to re-cement their old friendship, only to subject it to even greater strains, 'like two dogs with a bone'.[36]

But the main reason the right did not fight back in the 1970–4 period was almost certainly that it knew that, if it did, it would lose. Things had changed since the great days of the Campaign for Democratic Socialism. In Hugh Gaitskell's time, it had seemed likely that the victory on unilateral nuclear disarmament won by the left at the 1960 party conference would prove merely an aberration. And so it did.[37] But now the left's position in the trade unions and in the party in the country was infinitely stronger. If the right fought and fought and fought again, as Gaitskell had in the 1960s, it would probably lose and lose and lose again.[38] Right-wingers asked themselves why they should run risks and wear themselves out only to go down to defeat. Like politicians everywhere, they hoped something would turn up. Perhaps the unions would come to their senses. Perhaps the post-1970 shift to the left would turn out to be yet another example of Labour's tendency to move to the left whenever the party was in opposition. In the event, the right fought really hard only on Europe. And in the end something did turn up: to everyone's great surprise, Labour won the February 1974 election.

But, as we have seen, the 1974–9 government did not go well, and following Labour's defeat in 1979 most right-wingers in the party were deeply depressed as well as disoriented. The right's version of democratic socialism had by now been tried twice within a generation. On both occasions, it had been at best a partial success, at worst an abject failure. Many members of the Wilson and Callaghan cabinets felt that they had, in personal terms, acquitted themselves well; they felt that, as individuals, they had nothing to be ashamed of. The outgoing government had, in difficult circumstances, performed considerably better than it was given credit for; in particular, the poor, the old and families with children had all been protected against the worst effects of the 1970s recession. Former ministers were irked by the left's seemingly wilful refusal to recognize that the Callaghan government during its last two and a half years had only had minority support in the House of Commons and had been in no position, even if it had wanted to, to implement all the pledges in the 1974 manifesto.

All the same, excuses apart, the outlook for the right following the 1979 defeat could hardly have been gloomier. Right-wingers knew they were now in a minority in all the Labour party's decision-making bodies except the shadow cabinet, and it was clear that the post-election debate was going to be conducted entirely on the left's terms.

In addition, Labour's right-wingers had a more fundamental problem, though it is doubtful whether more than a handful of them recognized it at the time for what it was. The fact was that, after dominating the Labour party intellectually for at least forty years, the right had run out of ideas. They still had ideals. They still had values. They still had preferences. But they no longer had a programme and a theory of how the world worked. They did not really understand, or even claim to understand, the functioning of late-twentieth-century capitalism, and they had no clear conception of how the capitalist system should be, or could be, transformed. The Labour right had been mining a rich seam of revisionist 'Croslandite' socialist ideas for more than a generation, and now that seam was exhausted. In the debates in the Labour party that were to come, right-wingers were seriously handicapped by the fact that, while they knew what they were against (Thatcherism, Thatcher herself and the Labour left), they were much less clear about what they were for. The left had both a theory and a programme, however misguided both might be. The right suffered more than it perhaps realized from the fact that it did not really have either.

Even before polling day in 1979, there was evidence of how hard the right was going to find it to organize for the coming struggle for power. Two right-wing organizations had been established between 1974 and 1979—the Manifesto Group in the House of Commons and the Campaign for Labour Victory in the country—and neither had been notably successful.

The Manifesto Group of Labour MPs was formed shortly after the October 1974 election in order to counter the influence of the Tribune Group and other similar left-wing groups in parliament. It did succeed in publishing a few pamphlets and in securing the election of some of its members to Parliamentary Labour Party (PLP) offices; but it did not—because it could not—succeed in preventing the PLP from gradually becoming a more left-wing body. Pressure from the constituencies saw to that. Pressure from the constituencies also led to the officers of the Manifesto Group deciding that it would be imprudent to publish the group's membership list (while the left-wing Tribune Group had no such inhibitions). It was a further sign of the times that the group chose to call itself the Manifesto Group—and to have as its declared object implementing the party's 1974 election manifesto—even though the majority of the group's members undoubtedly disapproved of a large proportion of that manifesto, not least its sweeping nationalization proposals and its revolutionary sounding promise of a 'fundamental and irreversible shift in the balance of power and wealth in favour of working people and their families'. It was clear right from the beginning that the Manifesto Group was, as the Americans say, 'running scared'.

The Campaign for Labour Victory (CLV), a considerably larger group, was meant to be the equivalent in the Labour party in the country of the Manifesto Group in parliament. The idea was that it should belatedly begin to perform in the 1970s the same functions that the Gaitskellite Campaign for Democratic Socialism had performed in the early 1960s—that is, rally the right's forces in the party in the country, encourage right-wingers who had left the party to rejoin it, influence opinion in the trade unions and, if possible, secure the selection of right-wing parliamentary candidates. CLV was formed in the aftermath of the 1976 Labour party conference, at which the left increased its already large majority on the NEC and, among other things, passed resolutions demanding the immediate national-ization of Britain's four largest clearing banks and seven largest insurance companies.

The man who took the chair at CLV's inaugural meeting—held at Central Hall, Westminster, in February 1977—was Bill Rodgers, the MP for Stockton-on-Tees. Rodgers had been secretary of the Campaign for Democratic Socialism in the 1960s and in 1971–2 had organized the pro-European forces within the parliamentary party. By 1977 he was a member of the cabinet as transport minister. His presence on the platform, however, was largely honorific. CLV's real founders were two relatively junior backbenchers, John Cartwright and Ian Wrigglesworth. The new body declared that 'the Labour party must be a broad national party open to all who believe in democratic socialism based on our parliamentary system'. It further proclaimed that 'socialism must be based on the need for practical politics to secure social justice and equality, and not on narrow ideological class warfare'.[39] In 1979 it was too early to say that CLV had failed—it had been in existence for only two years—but so far it had succeeded in picking up only limited support within the trade unions, and its network of rank-and-file supporters in the constituencies was thin and patchy. Even CLV's most optimistic supporters acknowledged that there was a long way to go.

At the time of the 1979 general election, and even for a considerable period of time after that, very few Labour MPs had any conscious thoughts of leaving the party. The future was gloomy, but it was still uncertain: something might, yet again, turn up. After all, the right had lost control of the party in the early 1970s but had regained it (or at least had seemed to regain it) when Labour won in 1974. Nevertheless, when we came much later in the course of writing this book to interview former Labour MPs who had defected to the SDP, we were struck by the fact that a large proportion of them dated the beginnings of their alienation from the Labour party, not to the tumultuous two years to be described in what follows but to considerably earlier events and developments.

Here is what some of them had to say:

It was like water on a stone, and it began almost as soon as I was elected [in 1966]. I had a running battle with the left in my constituency, and there was always a temptation not to do what I believed in because my people—the moderates—wanted to avoid trouble.

I soon realized when I was elected in '74 that, if you were an ambitious backbencher, it wasn't an asset any longer to be a right-winger. The new formula for success was 'trendy left views plus opportunism'.

Even before the referendum on Europe, the thought did cross my mind that the pro-European 'party within the party' might some day become a real party.

In my case, it goes back to the '76 conference. There were a lot of very unpleasant people there, who just didn't give a damn about trying to save this country's currency. Healey was on his way to an IMF meeting and was brought back to the conference from the airport. And he was booed all the way to the rostrum. I was horrified. I hated it: that bloody mob, those clenched fists, those pointing fingers.

Even when I disagreed with them, I used to think of the people at Labour party conferences as my people. Then a few years ago I looked around and realized they weren't my people any more.

It was out of feelings like these that the SDP was born.

2
• • • •
The Gang of Three

Members of the Labour party expected a period of acute controversy following the May 1979 election defeat. What they got was more like civil war. No one in the party who lived through the years 1979–81 remembers them with pleasure. The struggle between right and left, fought without mercy on either side, was passionate, relentless and sometimes degrading. To the right, the left wing of the party seemed a hate-filled lynch mob. To the left, the right wing, especially MPs and former ministers, were traitors, men and women who, out of a mixture of cowardice, dishonesty and incompetence, were undermining both the party and the socialist cause. In an atmosphere of unreason, words changed their meanings, former colleagues became sworn enemies, and every issue, however trivial, became a test of socialist virtue. The few who refused to throw in their lot with either side were viewed with contempt by both. The SDP broke away in March 1981 in the midst of this tumult, but Labour's civil war continued.

The central figure in the war, as he had been throughout the 1970s, was Tony Benn. Benn espoused every currently fashionable left-wing cause, whether it was Chile, South Africa, Irish unity, withdrawal from the Common Market, unilateral nuclear disarmament, public ownership, centralized economic planning, the abolition of the House of Lords, workers' control of industry or popular control of the mass media. He seemed to have no idea how much electoral damage his crusading on behalf of left-wing socialism was doing to the party. Equally important, he was adamant that the struggle for socialism should embrace in one broad coalition almost all those who chose to call themselves socialists. Accordingly, he led the way in welcoming into the Labour party supporters of Marxist fringe groups like the Militant Tendency.[1]

Benn's personality, not just his opinions, aroused strong feelings. Supporters and opponents alike could not make out whether his socialist convictions were genuine or whether he was a consummate hypocrite. He always seemed to mean what he said; yet at the same time what he said always seemed somehow to coincide with what the left wing of the Labour party currently wanted to hear (and year after year he came near the top of the poll in the elections to the constituency section of the NEC). On the public platform, his staring eyes and restless hands, carving the air as though it were meat, gave him the appearance of either a messiah or a fanatic, depending on one's point of view. Capable of being good-natured, good-humoured and even charming in private, Benn in public could be a hard and cold man. His jokes were designed to provoke derision rather than laughter. By the late 1970s, most right-wingers in the party positively loathed his self-serving sanctimoniousness and his insistence on always implying, without ever actually saying, that his opponents were acting from the worst of motives. They called him 'loony Benn' and wondered whether he might not, literally, be mad. On the left, some were devoted to him. Others were more suspicious; but even they, for the time being at least, acknowledged him as their leader. Tony Benn was not the sole cause of the right–left conflict that followed the 1979 election, but he did much to intensify it and his brooding presence ensured that it was far more rancorous than it would otherwise have been.

The right did not have any positive objectives in the months immediately following the election; they just wanted to hold their own. The left, by contrast, had a very specific—and carefully worked out—agenda. With the Campaign for Labour Party Democracy in the lead, the left after May 1979 set about putting in place the three changes to the party's constitution referred to in Chapter 1.[2]

First, the left sought the 'mandatory reselection' of Labour MPs. The Labour party had traditionally taken the view that Labour MPs owed their principal allegiance to the party at large and that they should therefore not be subject to undue pressure by activists in their local constituency party. A local party had the power to sack its MP—that is, refuse to reselect him as the party's candidate for the next election—but only if it passed a no-confidence vote in him personally; and even then the MP who was threatened with dismissal could appeal to the NEC. This procedure had already been eroded somewhat in the early 1970s when the NEC, without changing the rules formally, decided that MPs in difficulty could no longer appeal to it on substantive political grounds but only on the ground that their CLP had not followed the proper procedures.[3] This represented an advance from the left's point of view, since in the past the right-dominated NEC had often disallowed the sacking of right-wing MPs by left-wing constituency parties on ideological grounds; but the left still believed that sitting MPs were too difficult to dislodge and that the process of getting rid of them—or at least calling them to account—should be made easier. Specifically, CLPD and the left wanted the rules changed so that every MP would have to submit himself to a formal process of reselection at least once during the lifetime of each parliament. Such a procedure would make it easier for a local party to sack its MP, since, instead of having to pass a specific vote of no confidence in him as an individual, it would only have to put up a rival candidate against him—and then make sure the rival candidate got more votes.

The second change sought by CLPD related to the election of the party leader. Ever since the party was founded in 1900, the leader had been chosen by Labour's members of parliament; the person chosen became leader of the whole party by virtue of being leader of the parliamentary party. The left no longer accepted this arrangement. The PLP over the years had usually elected right-wing leaders, and, even when it had not, as in the case of Harold Wilson in 1963, the new leader had invariably moved to the right once in office. The left wanted to increase its chances of electing its own man or woman as leader. Even more important, it wanted to ensure that the leader, once elected, could be held to account by the party at large and even dismissed by it. The obvious way of reaching this objective would be to remove the election of the leader from the PLP and give it to the annual conference or to some kind of specially constituted electoral college of which MPs would form a part but not necessarily the largest part. As early as 1976, the annual conference passed a resolution calling on the NEC 'to consider appropriate means of widening the electorate involved in the choice of the Leader'.[4]

Thirdly, CLPD and the left wanted to give the NEC sole responsibility for drafting and promulgating the party's election manifesto. The NEC already had a good deal of say in drafting it, especially when the party was in opposition; but under the existing procedure the final document had to be approved by a joint meeting of the NEC and either the cabinet when Labour was in power or the shadow cabinet when it was not.[5] This procedure gave ministers and shadow ministers—and especially the party leader—an effective veto over the manifesto's contents, including a veto over the inclusion of policies that had been approved by the NEC and the conference. The nationalization of 'twenty-five major companies' had been vetoed in 1973–4; and in 1979 James Callaghan had likewise made it clear that he would not fight the coming election on a pledge to abolish the House of Lords. The left was infuriated by what it saw as this deliberate snubbing of the conference and the extra-parliamentary party by the House of Commons leadership. A resolution was therefore tabled for the 1979 conference demanding that the party's constitution be amended to give the National Executive 'the final decision as to the contents of the Labour Party general election manifesto'.[6] If the parliamentary leadership was not prepared to write the manifesto in the way that the NEC and conference wanted, then it would not be allowed to write it at all.

The left's objective in seeking these three constitutional changes was simple. In the eyes of the left, the party's most active and committed members *were* the party and should therefore control the party's leader and policies. Labour candidates likewise stood for election on the party's behalf; they should, therefore, be selected by the activists in the party. The leader was similarly the leader of the whole party; he should, therefore, be elected by its active members. The election manifesto, which was the embodiment of the party's policies and programme, should by the same token be drawn up by those who had worked out those policies and drawn up that programme. What could be more democratic? Who could possibly object?

The proposed reforms had the additional advantage from the left's point of view that they would enormously strengthen the left's position in the party. That, of course, was what they were all about. Once the reforms were in place, it was almost certain that there would be more left-wing MPs, that many right-wing MPs (since they would now be accountable to their constituency activists) would move to the left, that future leaders would be further to the left and also more responsive to the left, that future election manifestos would be even more left wing than those of 1974 and that, ultimately, genuinely socialist governments would implement genuinely socialist policies. Constitutional issues and issues of power in the party were thus inextricably linked. Left-wingers made no attempt to conceal the fact. Theirs was a Leninist vision of 'vanguard democracy'.[7]

Needless to say, the right was horrified by all this. At one level, right-wing MPs tried desperately to rebut the substance of the left's arguments. They pointed out that it was already possible for dissatisfied constituency parties to deselect their MP (several had already done so); and they insisted that a member of parliament owed a duty not just to his local Labour activists but to his whole constituency. Members of the PLP, they claimed, were far better equipped than union leaders and local activists to choose the party leader, partly because they had far greater opportunities to observe the leadership contenders at first hand, but partly also because, since they were MPs and were therefore sensitive to electoral considerations, they had a greater stake than the activists in ensuring that the party leader was someone who would be acceptable to the electorate as a whole. The right also pointed out that, since Labour MPs and parliamentary leaders would have to carry out the party's manifesto, it would be wrong to deprive them of a major say in drawing it up.

These arguments were conscientiously advanced; right-wingers believed what they said. But underlying all this rhetoric, for the right as well as for the left, was the different and far more important question of who was ultimately to be in control of the party. If the right had dominated the constituency parties, it would not have minded mandatory reselection; if it had controlled the annual conference (or been confident that it could control an electoral college), it would not have been too worried about a new method for electing the party leader; if it had still controlled the NEC, it could have lived with a procedure under which only the NEC drew up the manifesto. The right's problem was that it could no longer be confident of controlling any of these bodies. It therefore feared—just as the left hoped—that procedural changes would lead to substantive changes. The struggle over the constitution was a struggle for power. The right knew it—and was determined to resist the CLPD and its allies if it could. And its resistance was not confined to those who later defected to the SDP.

The trouble from the right's point of view was that, often wrong-footed ideologically in the past (if they were socialists as they claimed, why had they not introduced socialism when they were in office?), they were now wrong-footed tactically. Quite apart from the fact that the left was still gaining ground in the constituencies and unions, it was in practice very hard to resist a campaign that claimed to be in favour of democracy. Moreover, it was in fact true, as the left claimed, that the right in power, especially in 1974–9, had failed to honour many of Labour's manifesto commitments, in either the letter or the spirit. Equally awkward from the right's point of view was the fact that the party's existing constitutional arrangements were extremely hard to defend on grounds of principle. The provisions that the left was trying to change were sanctified by history rather than logic. As the left kept pointing out, Labour was almost the only democratic socialist party in the world that confined the election of its leader to its parliamentarians. As the left also pointed out with regard to mandatory reselection, it was actually easier for a local Conservative association than for a local Labour party to sack its sitting member.

The right's tactical difficulties were compounded by the fact that, to a quite remarkable extent, it had been taken unawares by the new developments. Right-wing ministers and MPs had been very busy people until May 1979. They knew, of course, that if Labour lost the election they would have a fight on their hands. But most of them had not noticed—had simply not had time to notice—that the fight would largely be over the party's constitution rather than policy, that on this issue the left was already well organized in both the constituencies and the unions and that the grass-roots organization that they should be taking notice of on the other side of the argument was CLPD. In 1979 most right-wingers had scarcely heard of CLPD, and most of them found it almost impossible to distinguish it from dozens of other, similar-sounding left-wing organizations.[8]

The right, largely for these reasons, had really not begun to regroup when the 1979 party conference was held in Brighton in early October. The 1979 conference in Brighton was a peculiarly unpleasant occasion, even by the standards of that peculiarly unpleasant time. The party's MPs attending the conference had been herded together—probably more by accident than design—into a kind of ghetto on the floor of the conference hall to the left of the speaker's rostrum. Delegate after delegate came to the rostrum not only to denounce Labour's record in office but to point an accusing finger, literally, at the MPs, who huddled together in ever-increasing physical and moral discomfort. A Liverpool delegate derided his own constituency's former MP, and went on: 'When I look at the seats just below me which are reserved for Members of Parliament I have a feeling that there are probably other constituencies who are badly represented at the present time'—a remark that was greeted with loud applause.[9] The party's general secretary, Ron Hayward, put the boot in repeatedly. He reminded conference that every Labour candidate signs a piece of paper to the effect that he will abide by the party's constitution:

That means the conference. I am very worried when they forget it once they get there. I still say that we did not—and you over there did not—select, raise the money, work to send an MP to the House of Commons to forget whence he came and whom he represents. (*Applause*) I read all the papers. One I read the other day . . . said that one MP said 'If I do not get my way at this conference I will resign.' I have got some advice for them. Do not worry about that. I have got a queue a mile long that wants to go to the House of Commons. (*Laughter and Applause*) It is a very short queue that wants to be Branch Secretary. (*Applause*)[10]

Callaghan had been prime minister of Britain only a few months before, but his speech was listened to in total silence, and Tom Litterick, a former Birmingham MP who had lost his seat, drew loud applause when he reminded delegates of the leader's role in the party's May defeat: ' "Jim will fix it," they said. Ay, he fixed it. He fixed all of us. He fixed me in particular.'[11] The atmosphere was poisonous. One observer likened it to an impeachment trial.[12]

The conference's decisions were of a piece with its rhetoric. A resolution calling for the party leader to be elected by an electoral college was narrowly defeated (some unions still did not want to appear to be playing too large a part in the party's affairs), but mandatory reselection was accepted; and, even though the subject was appearing on the conference agenda for the first time, the principle was also accepted that control over the election manifesto should in future be vested in the NEC. The left's strike rate on the central issues of the constitution was thus two out of three. In addition, the conference passed resolutions suggesting that Labour might have to 'reconsider' Britain's membership of the Common Market and calling on the party in parliament to declare that state assets sold off by the new Thatcher government would be restored to public ownership by the next Labour government 'without compensation'.[13] Predictably, the left also consolidated its hold on the National Executive, with Tony Benn easily topping the poll. CLPD's secretary described 1979 as 'a breakthrough year' for his organization.[14] He was right. Right-wingers, completely taken aback by the speed and scale of their defeat, were despondent.

Their response over the next few months—in so far as they made a concerted response—took two forms. One concerned the question of where the battle lines inside the party should be drawn. Historically, battlelines in the Labour party—whether in the parliamentary party, the unions or the CLPs—had always been drawn straightforwardly between left and right. For a brief period in 1979–80, however, they were also drawn between the parliamentary party (including the shadow cabinet) on the one hand and the National Executive on the other, with right-wingers, still in the majority in the parliamentary party, seeking to mobilize all their fellow parliamentarians against what they regarded as the NEC's (and the conference's) intolerable usurpations. For a year or so, it was to be 'MPs versus the rest'.

Impetus for this particular response was given by the setting-up in the autumn of 1979 of a commission of inquiry into the party's affairs. The PLP formally asked to be represented on this commission, but at its meeting on 24 October 1979 the NEC, despite an impassioned plea from Callaghan, turned down the MPs' request and voted instead to constitute the inquiry in such a way that it would be entirely dominated by the left. Meeting afterwards, the shadow cabinet expressed its 'deep displeasure', and the Manifesto Group maintained that the NEC's decision had been 'a real slap in the face for the whole PLP'.[15] This united front, presented by the shadow cabinet and the majority of the PLP to the National Executive, was to remain reasonably solid until the autumn of 1980.

The right's other response was of more long-term significance. It related to the line the right should take in replying to the left's insistence that it wanted the Labour party to be more internally democratic. The left's claims sounded plausible; but the right regarded them as dishonest. Here was the left talking about democracy. But what would the kind of democracy the left was advocating really mean in practice? Would it mean mass participation in party affairs, well-attended meetings, a concern to be responsive to Labour's supporters, an openness to all points of view within the party, fair debates and secret ballots? Not at all. Right-wingers believed that in practice it would mean tiny handfuls of union leaders meeting in smoke-filled rooms to decide how to cast their enormous bloc votes at party conferences and that, in the constituencies, it would mean tiny groups of extreme left-wingers meeting to pass—in the name of the whole labour movement—solemn resolutions on the class struggle, Cuba, Chile, Nicaragua, wholesale nationalization, the abolition of the House of Lords and anything else that anybody could think of. Labour's individual membership by 1979 was down to about 250,000, of whom at most 10 per cent, or 25,000, regularly attended party meetings. In the right wing's view, it was preposterous to talk as though this tiny group of people—scarcely enough to fill a medium-sized football ground on a Saturday afternoon—should be allowed to speak in the name of the whole membership of the party, let alone of millions of Labour voters. The right was further incensed by its knowledge that, in some constituencies, abuse and intimidation were used in order to silence the left's opponents and drive them out of the party.

The right had no alternative, however, but to find some means of responding to the left's challenge. Moreover, it had to do so in terms of the debate about democracy that the left had initiated. Gradually, the idea emerged that the right should abandon any notion of digging in to defend the party's existing arrangements but instead should try to outflank the left by advocating the extension to all the party's decision-making organs of the principle of 'one member, one vote'. The principle could be applied to the selection and reselection of parliamentary candidates; it could be applied to the election of party conference delegates; it could even be applied, as in the Liberal party, to the election of the party leader. A London Labour activist named Jim Daly advocated 'one member, one vote' as early as 1976 in an article in the right-wing discussion journal *Socialist Commentary*, and many right-wingers began to look on the idea favourably after their election defeat.[16]

From the right's point of view, 'one member, one vote' had three advantages. First, it was attractive in itself. Secondly, it provided a good argument of principle with which to beat the left. Thirdly, if the principle were to be adopted, the right's position in the party would be strengthened, since almost everyone on the right believed that most ordinary Labour party members were moderates and would, if given half a chance, vote at party meetings and in party elections in favour of middle-of-the-road resolutions and candidates. 'One member, one vote' appeared to have everything going for it. The extension of the principle might even have the effect of reversing the decline in the party's membership and of bringing back into the party some of the moderate working-class supporters who had recently deserted it.

The three advantages of 'one member, one vote' were matched, however, by three equally—and ultimately fatal—disadvantages. The first was that, precisely because the principle was likely to strengthen the right, it was totally unacceptable to the left—and the left now had the votes. Secondly, whereas the constitutional changes advocated by the left built on the party's existing institutions, 'one member, one vote' would probably undermine them. CLPD, to take an obvious example, wanted to extend participation in the election of the party leader to the trade unions. Some unions might object that they did not want to participate, but at least if they did it would be on the basis of their existing rules and procedures. By contrast, the principle of 'one member, one vote', if adopted, would be likely to undercut many trade-union leaders' power within their own organizations. 'One member, one vote' was an exceedingly radical idea in Labour party terms. That was precisely its weakness.

The third disadvantage of 'one member, one vote'—psychologically even more damaging than the others—was that, in adopting it, the right had yet again wrong-footed itself. If 'one member, one vote' was a good democratic principle in 1979, when the left was in the ascendant, why had it not been an equally good democratic principle for the previous eighty years, when the right had been on top? To this obvious question, there was no answer. The charge that right-wingers were introducing 'one member, one vote' into the discussion at this late stage simply in order to shore up their own position stuck for the simple reason that it was true. With regard to the constitution, the right had always operated on the comfortable principle 'If it ain't broke, don't fix it.' Now that it was broken, it was much too late to fix it. The next few months were to show that 'one member, one vote', so attractive to the right in principle, was for the time being all but useless in practice.[17]

No one on the right wing of the party was more dismayed by the steady increase in the left's power than Bill Rodgers, the man who had taken the chair at the Campaign for Labour Victory's inaugural meeting in 1977. Rodgers was one of those politicians who, though little known to the public at large, wielded considerable influence in the House of Commons. At the time he helped organize the 1971 Common Market rebellion in the House, he was only 43, but younger MPs already looked to him for leadership and advice. Firmly on the gradualist, reformist wing of the party, Rodgers saw himself as standing in the line of ideological descent running from R. H. Tawney through Evan Durbin and Hugh Gaitskell to Anthony Crosland. He had been general secretary of the Fabian Society.

He had also, as we noted in the Chapter 1, been secretary of the Campaign for Democratic Socialism in the early 1960s.

Rodgers owed his seat at Stockton—Harold Macmillan's old seat—partly to the patronage of Hugh Dalton, Attlee's first chancellor of the exchequer, who had spent his twilight years promoting the careers of able younger men. Between 1964 and 1979, whenever Labour was in office, Rodgers was in office too—at the Department of Economic Affairs, the Foreign Office, the Board of Trade, the Treasury, the Department of Defence and the Department of Transport—but he did not achieve cabinet rank until Callaghan became prime minister in 1976, probably because Harold Wilson had always regarded him as being too conspicuously committed to the right. In the autumn of 1979, Rodgers was—somewhat incongruously, given Labour's rapid slide towards unilateralism—the party's defence spokesman in the House of Commons.

Rodgers' reputation was as an organizer, a skilful behind-the-scenes operator; but he was in fact an emotional man, capable of passionate commitment to both people and causes. His socialism had a firm intellectual foundation (he had not been secretary of the Fabian Society for nothing); but, in addition, like many children of the Thirties, he had initially been influenced less by abstract ideas than by the sights and sounds of the place where he grew up, in his case Liverpool:

The smell on the docks and in the commercial centre of the city was of seed cake and molasses, fresh grain from the prairies and the strange, sweet, persistent odours of the East.

But that was not the whole of the story. Liverpool was also a city of much less romantic smells. It was a city of poverty and deprivation, despite the wealth of the great ship-owning families and the fine civic monuments to their generosity. It was a city of slums and sickness, where two accident hospitals dealt with the daily total of injuries on the docks. It was a city of imported fever and self-generated crime, of religious intolerance, of men without jobs and children without coats and shoes . . .

It was the visible wrongs of society, seen in one place and at a moment in time, that did much to establish . . . instincts, values and emotions that have endured.[18]

Rodgers had been a Labour supporter since he could remember. He did not invite Conservatives to his house.

But he was now becoming increasingly unhappy about the way the party was going. Like Durbin and Gaitskell before him, he hated tyranny—whether of right or left—even more than he hated the evils of capitalism, and in the 1970s he could see Labour being influenced more and more by the undemocratic left—the 'illegitimate left' as he came to call it. Rodgers was especially conscious of the honour and dignity attached to being an elected MP and was, therefore, even more outraged than most MPs by the activists' onslaughts on them at the Brighton conference. Like many, he felt increasingly alienated from the NEC's and the party conference's decisions on issues like Europe, defence and nationalization, and he had also become disillusioned with the role of the trade unions. As transport secretary during the Winter of Discontent, he had sometimes seen Labour ministers stand up to the unions, but more often he had seen them defer to them uncritically.

It is [he wrote later] a dangerous presumption that the views of NUPE on the health service or the NUM on energy or the NUR on transport are in the public interest. They are the views of a lobby, relevant and entitled to be expressed, but far from decisive.[19]

On 22 November 1979 Rodgers had lunch at his favourite London restaurant, Il Comolario near Sloane Square, with his former parliamentary secretary at the Transport Department, John Horam. Horam had come to the conclusion on his own that the Labour party was finished: it always avoided the tough economic decisions, especially under pressure from the unions, and, worse, it had no idea how to create wealth. But Horam felt the need to try out his ideas on his former boss, whom he had always taken to be an out-and-out party loyalist. Horam was pleasantly surprised to discover by the end of the meal that Rodgers was largely agreeing with him. Rodgers recalls that, until his lunch with Horam, the thought of possibly leaving the Labour party had never occurred to him. 'I liked and respected John,' he said later, 'and no one had ever talked to me before in those terms. It made a very big impact.' The conversation reinforced a decision Rodgers had already made: to develop his thoughts on the party's future in a speech he was due to make in Abertillery a few days' later. He took great trouble over the text of the speech, showed a draft of it to friends and made sure that the press knew that something important was in the offing.

Rodgers delivered his Abertillery speech on 30 November 1979, and it was widely reported in the next day's papers. A party of the far left, he said, would have little appeal to the millions of voters who rejected doctrinaire and extreme solutions. 'If such a party were to defy the lessons of experience and win a general election, it would impose a heavy burden on our parliamentary system and our mixed economy.' He doubted whether many in the parliamentary Labour party would want to be 'on such a gravy train to disaster'. Then Rodgers gave the first public hint that the activities of the National Executive and the conference could lead to a split in the party. After defending Labour's traditional principles, he continued:

If our party should abandon or betray these principles, it would be a tragedy. But they would not die. They would survive because there would be men and women prepared to carry on the fight. The enthusiasm and the vision would endure and the standard bearers would not be lacking.

'Our party', he added, 'has a year, not much longer, in which to save itself.'[20]

Rodgers' Abertillery speech did not produce immediate results; it was not meant to. But it was a clear indication that, in the view of at least some on the right, time was running out. Afterwards in the House of Commons Rodgers was amused to note that, while some MPs came up to him to congratulate him on his speech, others whom he knew agreed with it nevertheless went out of their way—even retreating into the lavatories—in order to avoid being seen with him. 'It wasn't hostility,' he said, 'it was fear.'

During the winter of 1979–80, as the left's assaults continued, the right continued to dig itself in. In January 1980 the left-wing majority on the National Executive refused to agree to the publication of a report by the party's former national agent, Reg Underhill, which described in detail, with supporting documentation, the pattern of Trotskyite infiltration of Labour parties in the constituencies. The press was full of exposés of the activities of various Trotskyite organizations, including the Militant Tendency, but Tony Benn declared that no good socialist should ever be expelled from the party and told the Trotskyite-dominated Young Socialists that they were 'an integral part of the Labour party and rooted within its finest traditions'. Another left-winger, Ron Brown, the MP for Leith, said that the arguments of the Militant Tendency were 'winning more and more respect from rank-and-file party members'. Eric Heffer, also on the left, claimed that the party was indeed suffering from entryism, but from the right not the left. He invited those who could no longer accept the party's socialist principles to take themselves off to another party more to their taste: in the words of the song, he said, 'We don't want to lose you, but we think you ought to go.'[21]

On the right, a fringe group called the Social Democratic Alliance (SDA) deliberately courted expulsion from the party by threatening to put up alternative candidates against eleven sitting Labour MPs who were alleged to have 'anti-democratic sympathies'. The list included Tony Benn and Eric Heffer and also the name of a young Welsh MP, Neil Kinnock.[22] In January 1980 a widely discussed opinion poll in *The Times* showed that 60 per cent of voters agreed with the proposition that 'the Labour party is moving too much to the left for my liking'; 54 per cent expressed at least some inclination to support a new centre party. In February the Campaign for Labour Victory issued a manifesto advocating the principle of 'one member, one vote', to be exercised by means of postal ballots and meetings open to all party members. 'The Labour party', said CLV, 'is at the crossroads.' In March thirty Labour backbenchers signed an appeal to the leader and shadow cabinet calling for changes in the party rules to preserve party unity and protect MPs' rights. The appeal argued that all party members, not just the minority of activists, should be involved in choosing or replacing parliamentary candidates. Among those who signed the appeal were nine former ministers, including Gerald Kaufman, Peter Archer, Dickson Mabon, John Horam, Robert Maclennan and John Grant, and three Manifesto Group officers, John Cartwright, Mike Thomas and Ian Wrigglesworth. The signatories were believed to have the support, from within the shadow cabinet, of Bill Rodgers, Roy Hattersley, Roy Mason, David Owen and Peter Shore.[23]

Owen, the former foreign secretary, was rapidly emerging as one of the right-wingers' most trenchant spokesmen. His speeches in the country attracted more attention than those of almost anyone else on the right, and they were couched in unusually aggressive language. 'The trouble in the past', he said in Wolverhampton, 'was that too often the centre-right of the party has disdained from fighting within the party, has not been prepared to muddy its feet on the doorsteps, not fought for a place on the National Executive, not taken the battle enough into the constituency parties.' But that, he said, had now changed.[24] In Newcastle-upon-Tyne, he reiterated CLV's call for an inclusive, broadly based party. 'We must not be afraid', he said, 'to challenge openly authoritarianism, dogma or the threat posed by the elitism of the activists . . . We have not challenged vigorously enough those who are contemptuous of consensus and scornful of compromise.' Apart from attacking the left, Owen urged the party to substitute the themes of fraternity and co-operation for those of statism and increased centralization. 'Centralized statism', he said, 'had undermined people's sense of identification with their surroundings . . . and reinforced the tendency to run away from cooperative community action.'[25]

In some ways David Owen was a strange person to find in the midst of an internal Labour faction fight. Unlike Bill Rodgers, who was born into the party and only later went into politics, Owen was brought up in a politically conscious family but did not become a member of the party until he was in his 20s. His background was middle class, his mother had Liberal leanings, and it was only while he was a medical student at St Thomas's Hospital in London that he found himself drawn towards socialist politics. Even then, his motives were more humanitarian than ideological. He was not what anyone thought of as 'a Labour man'. Nevertheless, his political apprenticeship was brief and his ascent of the political career ladder extraordinarily rapid. A parliamentary candidate at only 26, he was an MP at 28, parliamentary secretary at the Department of Defence at 30, minister of state at the Department of Health and Social Security at 36, minister of state at the Foreign Office at 38 and (following Anthony Crosland's sudden death in 1977) secretary of state for foreign and Commonwealth affairs, still at the age of only 38. Owen had been a member of a loose circle of MPs around Roy Jenkins in the early 1970s; he had resigned from the front bench when Jenkins resigned in 1972; and he had gone along with the preferences of the rest of the Jenkins group in the party-leadership election of 1976. But he was not by nature a team player. He was a loner, someone with a close family life, a man who kept his own counsel. His 1979–80 speeches constituted the first time he had taken an active part in the party's affairs outside the House of Commons.[26]

To his fellow politicians, Owen was an enigma. Not many people in politics knew him well; most of those who did disliked him. He invariably gave the impression of being well pleased with himself, and in personal encounters he was frequently brusque to the point of rudeness; one word widely used to describe him was 'arrogant'. Yet at the same time Owen had a rare streak of self-detachment. If he made a mistake, he admitted it. If he hurt someone's feelings (and realized he had, which was not always), he apologized. When he became foreign secretary at the age of 38, it was he who described himself as 'overpromoted'. He had a reputation for being cold and insensitive; but he was, if anything, even more emotional than Rodgers, with intense likes and dislikes in people, a capacity for forming almost unreasoning commitments to causes and also a very short temper. No one denied his physical and moral courage. Nor did anyone doubt his intellectual capacity; by the late 1970s he had written several books on subjects as diverse as defence, health policy and human rights. If he had a quality that even his friends found disconcerting, it was a tendency to begin by arguing passionately on one side of an issue and to wind up arguing equally passionately on the other— without seeming to realize that he had changed sides along the way.

Just such an abrupt change of front now occurred. Well into the spring of 1980 Owen was vehement, in both public and private, that the right–left battle must be fought out within the party. If it took several years for the battle to be fought and won, then so be it. In his Wolverhampton speech, he was categorical:

The most foolish course now for those who are determined to swing the Labour party back to sensible socialism would be to abandon the struggle within the Labour party, to talk of founding new parties, to break out from the Labour party just at the very moment when, at long last, we are beginning to fight back from within.[27]

He took the same view at what many described as a 'cathartic' Campaign for Labour Victory meeting in Birmingham in late May. About half of those present were for soldiering on within the party; the other half thought that there had to be a cut-off point. Owen was furious with the latter group. He rounded on CLV's secretary, a young man called Alec McGivan, saying: 'If CLV is about leaving the Labour party, then I'm having nothing to do with it.' In his speech at the meeting, he called for, if need be, 'ten years' hard slog'.

A few days later, however, something happened that caused him completely to change his mind. On 31 May 1980 the Labour party held a special one-day conference at Wembley. No one seemed to know quite why the conference had been called (organizing it had cost a vast amount of money), but its formal business was to approve an NEC policy statement entitled *Peace, Jobs, Freedom*. The atmosphere at Wembley was fractionally less poisonous than it had been at Brighton, partly because the general election was further in the past and partly because the conference was not very well attended. Even so, there was still a great deal of bitterness and rancour. Tony Benn's closing speech flatly contradicted the opening speech made by James Callaghan, who was, after all, a former prime minister and still the party's leader. One delegate asked of Callaghan: 'Could we not suggest that he might retire to his farm and make room for somebody who will do a better job?' Another delegate dismissed Callaghan's speech as 'mealy-mouthed' and 'shallow'. Denis Healey's progress to the rostrum was accompanied by shouts of 'Out, out'. Right-wingers in general were labelled 'weakhearted, traitors and cowards'. At a left-wing fringe meeting, Frances Morrell, one of Tony Benn's aides, referred to the members of CLV as 'our opponents', adding: 'Their conduct has been absolutely appalling.'[28]

Owen sat at the back of the hall throughout all this, his gorge rising. Apart from Callaghan, no one defended the PLP, no one defended the Labour government's record, no one defended, in particular, the Labour government's record in foreign affairs. Owen had not originally intended to speak, but finally he could stand it no longer. He strode to the rostrum and 'spoke from the gut' in defence—specifically—of the Labour government's decision to site American cruise missiles on British soil. The conference's official transcript records the reception that the former foreign secretary received:

DAVID OWEN: . . . I must say to the party that anyone who wants to play a role in international arms control negotiations—it is no use expecting us to have a place at SALT 3 if we are going to take decisions on cruise missiles before we have even entered into the negotiations. Oh no, it has to be faced in this country. It is no use expecting your friends and allies to expect you to have a place in those negotiations if you are pre-empting it. I am telling you as someone who has dealt with these negotiations. (*Cries of protest from floor*.) I will say it to you again. If you think you enter into arms control negotiations with your hands tied behind your back, with no form of leverage, you are deluding yourselves.

CHAIRMAN: Order. The speaker has a right to be heard, comrades. Please be quiet.

DAVID OWEN: . . . This party had this argument some years ago. We do not want that again. The emphasis in this document is on negotiations—and rightly so—on peace. But peace is not won by one nation pursuing its own policy in total isolation from others. It is in pooling, in making a bargain, in making a deal, in negotiating with the Soviet Union from a position of strength, not a position of weakness.

CHAIRMAN: Thank you, David. I am sorry to have to remind comrades that this is a serious conference and it is not a shouting match . . .[29]

Afterwards, Owen recalls, he felt very lonely, but a retired regional organizer came up to him and said that in fifteen years' time his speech would be one he would be proud to have made.[30]

The Wembley conference—notably the attacks on Callaghan and the entire PLP, the repudiation of the whole of the 1974–9 government's record and the angry abuse during his own speech—transformed Owen's attitude towards the Labour party's future. There was no longer to be any question of ten years' hard slog: what was needed was action—now. 'David burns,' a friend said later. 'You don't quite know how he burns, but he burns away. Wembley was an extraordinarily deep shock to him. The effect was a big one.' A few days later, he took the first of a series of steps that was to lead him out of the Labour party and, three years later, to the leadership of the SDP.

The Wembley conference was held on a Saturday. On the following Tuesday, 3 June 1980, Owen happened to run into a journalist acquaintance, Malcolm Rutherford of the *Financial Times*, in the tunnel that leads to the Palace of

Westminster from the neighbouring underground station. Rutherford informed him that John Silkin, a shadow cabinet member and a long-standing anti-Common Marketeer, was about to chair a meeting of the Safeguard Britain Campaign, the outcome of which was to be a statement calling on the next Labour government to withdraw from the Common Market unconditionally. Owen was beside himself with anger. Here was the left deliberately reopening the whole European controversy, which, on every political and moral criterion imaginable, should have been closed by the vote of the British people in the referendum five years before. 'Why now?' Owen asked himself: only because John Silkin wanted to improve his chances of obtaining the leadership for himself when Callaghan retired. Further along the tunnel towards the House of Commons, Owen, still angry, bumped into Bill Rodgers. He told him what was happening and said they must do something. Rodgers agreed. He was due to see Shirley Williams on Friday, three days later: why didn't David join them? Owen thought this was a good idea and said he would phone Shirley to warn her that he was coming (he had to ask Rodgers for her home phone number).

The three met in Shirley Williams' modest flat in Rochester Row on Friday, 6 June 1980. They had not talked seriously before, partly because Williams had lost her seat in the 1979 election. Since then she had been abroad a good deal, mainly lecturing at Harvard, and when in London she had been immersed in writing a book at the Policy Studies Institute. But she and Rodgers were old friends. They had been at Oxford together, and in the mid-1950s she had followed in his footsteps as general secretary of the Fabian Society. Like Rodgers, but unlike Owen, she had spent the whole of her political life in the labour movement. Her mother and father were both intellectual socialists; she had joined the Labour party in her teens; she had run a Labour candidate's election campaign when she was only 20; she herself had fought a constituency for the first time when she was only 23. In the 1964–70 government she had served in various ministerial posts, at the Ministry of Labour, the Department of Education and Science, and the Home Office. Between 1970 and 1974 she had been regularly elected to the shadow cabinet, frequently coming at or near the top of the poll. Partly for that reason, in 1974 she had been promoted into the cabinet, ahead of both Rodgers and Owen, serving first as secretary of state for prices and consumer protection, later as paymaster-general and education secretary.

Although Owen, Rodgers and Williams resembled each other in many ways— they were all university-educated, lovers of the arts and frequent visitors to the United States (Owen's wife was an American)—Williams' relationship with the labour movement was of a somewhat different character from theirs. Although always firmly on the party's moderate wing, she had never been labelled, in quite the way that Rodgers had, a hard-line right-winger. She had not taken part in the Campaign for Democratic Socialism in the 1960s, and she was interested in issues like race relations, immigration, education and the Third World that tended to bring Labour's right and left wings together instead of driving them apart. Unlike

Owen and Rodgers, she had never been involved as a minister in foreign affairs and defence. Equally important, her relations with the trade unions were—for one of Labour's so-called 'intellectuals'—unusually cordial. She liked many of the trade-union leaders, and they liked her. Largely for this reason, she was elected year after year, on the strength of trade-union votes, to the National Executive Committee. Owen and Rodgers were chiefly House of Commons figures; Shirley Williams was much better known, and held in much higher esteem, in the party in the country.

Williams owed her NEC membership and her standing in the party largely to her personal qualities. She was, by common consent, one of the nicest people in British politics—warm-hearted, outgoing and genuinely interested in other people. Non-politicians could easily identify with her. Although a politician, she seemed unlike politicians. As the French say, she was 'authentic': exactly the same person in private as in public. Moreover, her friendliness and warmth were matched by her candour; she appeared to be, because she was, more interested in advancing causes close to her heart than in advancing her own career. Others sensed this, and, unusually among politicians, she was almost universally acquitted of the charge of self-seeking.

Shirley Williams had, however, a widespread reputation for being indecisive. The truth was more complicated. In fact, she had little difficulty in making decisions on political and administrative matters. She had gained confidence and experience in ministerial office in the 1960s and was a forceful and successful member of the 1974–9 cabinet. She was certainly very outspoken on the NEC. But she did sometimes find it hard to make up her mind in matters concerning herself and her own future. Decisive on matters of policy and principle, she could be less decisive when it came to political tactics and personal manœuvering. Male politicians often overlooked the fact that, following the breakup of her marriage in the early 1970s, she was a single parent with a teenage daughter still at school. Having lost her seat in the House of Commons in 1979, she also had to earn her living; she was in great demand on both sides of the Atlantic as a writer, broadcaster and lecturer. Under the circumstances, it was hardly surprising that, disposed to be unpunctual anyway, she often contrived to be very late, even for important engagements with important people.

Everyone naturally focused on Shirley Williams' niceness; but the very fact that she was nice often caused people to overlook the fact that she was also, by instinct, a fighter, someone who enjoyed a good political punch-up. She had been involved in many over the years. She was about to be involved in many more.

Williams' growing alienation from the Labour party, like Rodgers', stemmed from the extreme left's political beliefs, but also, in her case even more, from its methods. The Trotskyites and their allies talked of democracy, but they did not look like a very democratic bunch to her. Williams' background was as much anti-fascist as pro-socialist, and she had no more liking for red fascism than black. She was one of the first senior Labour politicians to launch a sustained attack on Trotskyism's philosophical basis; she had even taken the trouble to read Trotsky's works.[31] Moreover, unlike Owen and Rodgers, she had a small but vocal Trotskyite contingent in her Hertfordshire constituency party. By now she knew what Trotskyites looked like and sounded like, and she detested them.

Williams was also worried that Labour was still too much of a class-based party and was tending, if anything, to become even more so. The party still relied heavily on working-class voters, and the fashionable talk on the left was of class war and the working-class struggle. Williams did not like the undertow of violence in that kind of language, and she also thought it was hopelessly out of touch with reality. She wanted to create a classless society, not a single-class one, whether dominated by the workers or anybody else; and she reckoned that in any case class-war rhetoric was not a very sensible way of trying to win votes in a society that was becoming less and less class conscious. Her political outlook was further coloured by her membership of the NEC. She had become an NEC member in 1970, just as the left was gaining its majority; and over the next decade she had seen the left gradually but inexorably tightening its grip. 'Look at the minutes,' she said later. 'Towards the end, there were just three of us, me, John Golding and Tom Bradley. On the rare occasions when we even got a close vote, we thought we'd done well.' She wanted to fight back inside the party; she wanted to win. But, more than Owen and Rodgers, she had for a long time, because of her NEC experience, been deeply pessimistic about the chances of success.

On 6 June 1980, in Shirley Williams' flat, the three former ministers agreed that they should issue a joint statement and that it should focus on Europe—in other words, that it should be a direct riposte to the Silkin-inspired *démarche*. Owen was instinctively pro-European; he had made a pro-Common Market speech as early as 1962. Williams' views on Europe were, if anything, even stronger; she had travelled extensively on the Continent as a teenager soon after the war, and she had seen for herself just what a divided Europe could lead to. She had written pro-European Fabian pamphlets in the 1950s. Rodgers, however, despite having helped organize the 1971 Common Market rebellion, was by no means a Euro-fanatic. He believed, of course, that the issue was important; but he now saw it primarily as a test of Labour's fitness to govern. In the circumstances of June 1980, Rodgers' view was that Europe was not the right issue on which to try to rally the party: it was too narrow, too old-hat ('Oh my God, not that again') and too likely to put off right-wingers who were either anti-Common Market or else not particularly interested in the issue. Accordingly, he agreed that, if Williams and Owen could draft a sensible statement on Europe, he would be prepared to sign it—but only on condition that the others accepted that this would be only the first thing that they did together. A much fuller statement, on a much broader range of issues, would have to follow. The others said 'OK', and the task of drafting began.

The passages on the Common Market itself were easy. The difficulty was over whether the statement should contain any reference, however veiled, to the possibility that the three of them might, at some stage, feel obliged to quit the Labour party. As one of them put it later: 'It was a long discussion. Everyone of us was a hawk at some stage, a dove at another. But at the end we were all hawks.' Their statement was issued the following day and received wide publicity in the Sunday newspapers of 8 June. It concluded:

For the Labour party to decide now on a manifesto commitment to leave the Community in 1983 or 1984 would be irresponsible, opportunistic and short-sighted. We could have no part in it. Five years ago it was a Labour government that uniquely gave the British people the opportunity to choose the future destiny of our country. Decisively the British people from all political parties chose continued membership of the Community. A clear majority of Labour voters freely chose to remain in the Community.

Is this decision endlessly to be reopened? Are the old divisions to be stirred up again and again . . .

There are some of us who will not accept a choice between socialism and Europe. We will choose them both.[32]

Most political correspondents recognized that these words brought measurably closer the possibility of Labour's splitting.

Rodgers, Williams and Owen were a good group for purposes of political action. Of the under-50s in the Callaghan cabinet, they had been, along with Roy Hattersley and John Smith, among the few really able ones.[33] Rodgers contributed his contacts in the parliamentary party and a sense of the politically possible; Owen contributed single-mindedness and determination; Williams, because she was trusted and widely loved in the party, ensured that the group was far more attractive to the rank and file than it would otherwise have been. But at the same time the three were all relatively new to political leadership—until now they had been majors and colonels rather than generals in the Labour army—and in mid-1980 they would have preferred it if leadership could have been provided by someone older and more senior, ideally by either Denis Healey or Jim Callaghan. Healey, however, although he continued to make all the right noises (his speech at the special Wembley conference contained a characteristic attack on 'the clapped-out dogmas [of] the toytown Trotskyists of the Militant group'), showed no signs of being prepared to fight any corner but his own; and Callaghan, now that he had ceased to be prime minister, was proving to be a bitter disappointment, not just to Owen, Rodgers and Williams, but to the whole of Labour's right wing.[34]

The majority of the PLP and the shadow cabinet believed that it was the duty of Callaghan as party leader to act as the PLP's spokesman on the internal commission of inquiry appointed the previous autumn. The commission by this time had been meeting in a desultory way for several months. MPs, including even some left-wingers, wanted Callaghan to take the lead in opposing mandatory reselection, NEC control of the manifesto and the setting-up of an electoral college to choose the leader. Some MPs also wanted him to be ready to impose a PLP veto: if the left on the commission used its majority to force through constitutional changes unacceptable to the PLP, then Callaghan should in effect say, 'You can publish your manifesto, and you can elect your leader, but we will issue *our* manifesto and elect *our* leader. If we do that, either you will back down or we will go to the country with our manifesto and our leader and you can get stuffed.'

Callaghan, however, was an old party operator, used to doing deals with the unions. He did not think a direct clash between the PLP and the NEC was either desirable or necessary. He hoped, as usual, that some kind of deal could be struck. He seems to have calculated that, if he and the other right-wingers on the commission made limited tactical concessions, they could limit the amount of damage inflicted on the party and at the same time preserve some show of party unity. In any case, there was a good chance that, whatever recommendations the commission made, some of them, at least, would be rejected by the unions at the coming annual conference. The inquiry commission was due to hold a long session at Bishops Stortford over the weekend of 14–15 June, and at the shadow cabinet beforehand angry words were exchanged. Bill Rodgers and Roy Hattersley, already suspicious of their leader's intentions, told him that at Bishops Stortford he should not give an inch. 'Do you mean to say I can't negotiate?' Callaghan asked. 'No,' the others replied, 'Don't negotiate. We might give too much away.' 'We', of course, was Callaghan.

The Bishops Stortford weekend produced a complicated package of recommendations that satisfied no one and ensured that there would be even more wrangling over the constitution. Callaghan and the party's deputy leader, Michael Foot (who, although a left-winger, disliked the inroads being made into MPs' constitutional position), tried to persuade the meeting to leave the election of the leader in the hands of the parliamentary party; but, having failed, the two reluctantly agreed to the setting-up of an electoral college. The college was to be made up in the proportions: 50 per cent MPs, 25 per cent trade unions, 20 per cent constituency parties and 5 per cent other affiliated organizations; and it was to have two duties: to elect the party leader and also to make the final determination of the contents of the election manifesto. In addition, the commission at Bishops Stortford confirmed the Brighton conference's decision in favour of mandatory reselection. The members of the commission presented the package to their colleagues as a compromise. On the one hand, the right had conceded mandatory reselection and the principle of an electoral college; on the other hand, the left had conceded half the vote in the electoral college to the PLP and had also agreed that the electoral college, rather than the NEC, should have the final word on the manifesto.

But the commission's findings failed to satisfy anybody. Left and right were equally indignant. With regard to the leadership, CLPD pointed out that the parliamentary party, if it put forward only one candidate, could effectively determine who won (since, with 50 per cent of the vote, it would only need the support of one trade union, CLP or other affiliated organization to put its nominee over the top). With regard to the manifesto, the left complained that the MPs' strong position in the electoral college would mean that the parliamentary party and its leader would still have as much effective control over it as in the past. Still, the left could console itself with the thought that the principle of the electoral college had been conceded and that, overall, the role of the parliamentary party had been reduced. Right-wingers had no such consolation. For them, the acceptance of an electoral college represented a complete betrayal. Certainly, MPs were to have 50 per cent of the votes in the college for the time being, but who was to say that this percentage would not in the future be reduced by some left-dominated annual conference? The PLP had been a largely autonomous body ever since its creation in 1906. Now, it seemed, it was to be autonomous no longer. Most MPs were extremely gloomy following Bishops Stortford, and at a PLP meeting at the end of June speaker after speaker rose to condemn everything that had been done there.[35]

The Bishops Stortford episode seriously weakened Callaghan's position as leader. It was already widely assumed that he would resign sometime in the autumn, and the newspapers were full of 'Will he? Won't he?' stories and speculation about possible successors. Bishops Stortford cost him support, not just on the back benches but in the shadow cabinet. Hitherto more or less united, the shadow cabinet was now split down the middle, with Callaghan ('When he is feeling unloved, he can be very unlovable') brutally attacking Rodgers, Owen and Hattersley for publicly disowning the Bishops Stortford compromise and they for their part accusing him of double-dealing and near-supine weakness. 'It was all', one of them recalled, 'very, very nasty.' Owen condemned the whole business—in a phrase that was later to become familiar—as yet another example of compromise and retreat, of 'fudging and mudging, mush and slush'. Whatever else it did, Bishops Stortford made it clear that there was no longer any point—if there ever had been any—in the right's looking to Callaghan for leadership. As prime minister, he had fought long and hard. Perhaps for that very reason, there was little fight left in him. In any case, he was obviously on the way out. The right-wing leaders of the next generation were on their own.

While the PLP and the shadow cabinet were agonizing over the inquiry commission's report, Rodgers, Williams and Owen were still working on the text of the broader statement that they had agreed to prepare at their meeting on 6 June. Rodgers wrote the first draft, and it went through at least eight versions before finally appearing on 1 August as an 'open letter' in both the Guardian and the Daily Mirror (a paper with a large working-class pro-Labour readership).

The letter's contents were not strikingly original, but its very existence and the tone in which it was written ('The Labour party', it began, 'is facing the gravest crisis in its history') indicated that the authors meant it to be understood as throwing down the gauntlet not just to the Trotskyite left but to everyone in the party who was seeking to undermine its traditional principles and commitments. The letter attacked the doctrine of class war, nationalization in the form of big public monopolies, the idea of an alternative economic strategy based on general import controls, the constitutional changes proposed by the inquiry commission and the National Executive, the notion that Labour had lost votes in the past by not being sufficiently left wing and, in general, left-wing 'dishonesty and escapism'. It defended parliamentary democracy, the mixed economy, profit-making, Britain's memberships of NATO and the European Community and the record of the last Labour government. It called for multilateral rather than unilateral disarmament, increased aid to the Third World, investment assistance for small businesses and, as an essential part of the attack on inflation, an incomes policy 'based on regular discussions among the trade unions, employers, professional organisations and the government'.

Almost all this remained within the limits of the traditional Labour consensus. The open letter's concluding paragraphs, however, stepped sharply outside them. The majority on the NEC was accused of disregarding 'all its own fine words about participation, consultation and democracy when it doesn't suit it'.

No wonder there is growing anxiety about the Labour party's commitment to parliamentary democracy, reinforced by the willingness of some leading NEC members to flirt with extremists who openly regard democracy as a sham ...

[If] the Labour party abandons its democratic and internationalist principles, the argument may grow for a new democratic socialist party to establish itself as a party of conscience and reform committed to those principles. We are not prepared to abandon Britain to divisive and often cruel Tory policies because electors do not have an opportunity to vote for an acceptable socialist alternative to a Conservative government.

There are those who say that the Labour party cannot survive its present battles, but must now tear itself to pieces. Others believe that soft words and a little skilful evasion of the issues can paper over the cracks again. We do not share either of these views. If there is one lesson, it is that there can be no compromise with those who share neither the values nor the philosophy of democratic socialism. A Labour party committed to these values and this philosophy can defeat Tory reaction. We shall fight for such a Labour party. We ask all those who share that conviction to fight for it too. It is Britain's best hope.[36]

Implicit in this last sentence was the thought that the Labour party, even if it remained Britain's best hope, was no longer its only hope.

Reactions to the open letter were predictable. Some MPs were unqualifiedly supportive. Others were favourably disposed but were reluctant to say so openly; Jim Callaghan let it be known that he agreed entirely with the letter's contents but regretted its timing and the manner of its publication. The left, for its part, damned its authors, its contents and its timing alike. Stuart Holland claimed that the three signatories were increasingly speaking for themselves and no one else in the party; he added, 'If they think they will have a damaging effect by leaving, they are wrong.'[37] The letter resulted in one bonus: Rodgers, Owen and Williams found that they had been given a collective name: the Gang of Three, on the model of China's then notorious Gang of Four. The name was originally given to them by their left-wing critics, but it was soon in general circulation. It had considerable advantages. It connoted 'togetherness', it gave the three a clear corporate identity, and it fitted comfortably into newspaper headlines.

The Gang of Three, although they attracted more publicity than anyone else, were by no means alone. Sympathetic Labour MPs expressed their support, if sometimes only in private; and like-minded MPs occasionally met under the umbrella of the Manifesto Group and CLV. But the Manifesto Group and CLV included many who were not prepared to contemplate breaking with the party, and prior to the 1980 annual conference Rodgers, Williams and Owen did not have anything that could remotely be described as an organization, whether in parliament or anywhere else. In September 1980, however, shortly before the conference, a group of twelve MPs—with some links to the Gang of Three but not many—published a detailed plan for the reform of the party's organization and structure. The plan embodied the principle of 'one member, one vote', which was to apply to the selection and deselection of Labour candidates, to the choice of constituency officers and to the separate election of a party leader in the country (as distinct from the leader in the House of Commons, who would continue to be chosen by MPs). The plan also called for the reform of the NEC so that ordinary party members, local councillors and the PLP would be directly represented.[38]

The group of twelve—inevitably known as the Dirty Dozen—was convened by Mike Thomas, the 36-year-old MP for Newcastle East. It comprised MPs of all ages, from all parts of the country and with widely varying amounts of parliamentary experience. The twelve were: John Cartwright (Woolwich East), Tom Ellis (Wrexham), Alan Fitch (Wigan), Willie Hamilton (Fife Central), John Horam (Gateshead West), Eric Ogden (Liverpool, West Derby), Arthur Palmer (Bristol North-East), George Robertson (Hamilton), John Roper (Farnworth), Mike Thomas (Newcastle East), Tom Urwin (Houghton-le-Spring) and Ian Wrigglesworth (Teeside, Thornaby). Seven of the twelve subsequently joined the SDP; five did not. Towards the end of September, sympathetic Labour supporters took a full-page advertisement in *Labour Weekly* which maintained that the Gang of Three was actually 'a gang of thousands'.[39]

As the 1980 party conference approached, the right-wingers who favoured root-and-branch reform of the party became more conscious of a dilemma, one that had been inherent in their position from the beginning. On the one hand, the Gang of Three and the Dirty Dozen advocated 'one member, one vote' and were increasingly unhappy with the role that the unions were playing in the party (and also in the country generally); but, on the other, they knew perfectly well that, if the leftwards march of the party were to be halted and the various constitutional reforms supported by the left either defeated or reversed, this could be achieved only by the trade unions, which among them controlled some 90 per cent of the votes at the conference. In other words, the reformers were completely dependent on the goodwill of the very people whom they were most anxious to reform (and of whom they were frequently most critical). The Dirty Dozen, conscious of this dilemma, warned Callaghan and the party leadership that it would not be enough merely to rely on trade-union bloc votes at the conference to restore the status quo: more fundamental changes were needed. But neither the Dirty Dozen nor anyone else explained how these fundamental changes were to come about. In the end, this dilemma was never resolved; it simply went away when the most committed reformers left the Labour party to join the SDP. The issue was not to resurface in the Labour party until nearly another decade had passed.[40]

Labour's 1980 annual conference opened in Blackpool on 29 September. If the previous year's conference had been unpleasant, the 1980 conference seemed to most right-wingers to be not only unpleasant but positively insane. On the very first day, Tony Benn announced from the platform that the next Labour government would require three major pieces of legislation within a month of coming to office. Within days, a new Industry Act would be needed to give the government powers to extend public ownership, to control capital movements and to provide for industrial democracy. Within weeks, a second bill would be needed to restore to Britain all the powers transferred to Brussels when Britain joined the Common Market in 1973. Moreover, since neither the new Industry Bill nor withdrawal from the Common Market could be expected to get through the existing House of Lords, that body would have to be abolished immediately, if necessary by means of the creation of a thousand additional peers. 'Comrades,' he said, 'this is the very least we must do.'[41] Rank-and-file delegates roared their approval, but the shadow cabinet was appalled by what they saw as Benn's demagoguery. Denis Healey, as ex-chancellor of the exchequer, hinted that even a single day would be too short a time in which to stop the flight of capital that would follow the announcement of such a programme. Other former ministers told the press—though not for attribution—that they thought Benn 'must have gone over the edge'.[42] Even some left-wingers stared in disbelief.

By chance, a CLV meeting had been scheduled for later that day. With Owen and Rodgers seated next to her on the platform, Williams, almost beside herself with frustration and anger, told the left exactly what she thought of them. The left, she said, lived in a dream world, out of touch with reality, making promise after promise that could not possibly be kept. She ticked off Benn's three promised pieces of legislation. 'And all this', she said with heavy irony, 'would be done in a couple of weeks! I wonder why Tony was so unambitious. After all, it took God only six days to make the world.' Amidst a good deal of heckling, she said that she had been to many Labour meetings where party members had been frightened because they had been abused and shouted at. She wanted to know why Communists like Mick McGahey were being allowed to play a part in changing Labour's constitution; she had seen him meeting with the mineworkers' delegation. She went on:

I was brought up as a youngster to learn about fascism. My parents fought against fascism, and they were both on the Gestapo blacklist, so I know something about it. But there can be fascism of the left as well as fascism of the right.

She recalled that a conference delegate, quoting Edmund Burke, had said that, for evil to triumph in the world, all that was needed was for enough good men to remain silent.

Too many good men and women in this party [she went on] have remained silent. Well, the time has come when you had better stick your heads up and come over the parapet, because if you do not start to fight now, you will not have a party that is worth having.[43]

Later in the week she caused considerable consternation by suggesting that the Gang of Three might give the Labour party till the coming January, but not any longer.

That evening, after both the Benn and the Williams speeches, a miscellaneous collection of right-wingers gathered round the television set in Shirley Williams' room at the Imperial Hotel, where she was staying as a member of the NEC. They shook their heads as the day's scenes were replayed before them on the news. David Owen, according to one MP who was there, got fiercer and fiercer. Ken Weetch, the Ipswich MP and Bill Rodgers' former parliamentary private secretary, lectured anyone who cared to listen about the dangers of their becoming like the post-war socialists in Czechoslovakia, selling out to the Communists. 'How long can we go on?' Weetch asked. 'We just don't have the troops on the ground.' Phillip Whitehead, the right-wing MP for Derby North, took one of the Dirty Dozen, John Cartwright, aside and asked, 'You're not going along with all this talk of quitting, are you?' Cartwright thought for a moment, then said, 'I'm not sure.' Many who were present recall the gathering in Williams' room as the first occasion on which they had heard open discussion of the possibility of a Labour split and the formation of a new party.

With one exception, all the decisions taken at the 1980 conference went in the left's favour. CLPD's proposal that the NEC should alone decide the contents of the party manifesto was narrowly defeated; but mandatory reselection was carried, and so was the proposal that the franchise for electing the party leader should be widened to include trade unions and CLPs. Somewhat quixotically, however, all the specific proposals relating to the composition of a possible electoral college were defeated, and it was accordingly agreed that a special conference to resolve the issue should be held in three months' time. Amid the hubbub, the compromise package so carefully worked out at Bishops Stortford was ignored. In addition, the conference adopted a string of new policies, including socialist planning, the immediate extension of public ownership and industrial democracy, a universal thirty-five-hour week without loss of earnings, immediate withdrawal from the Common Market (carried by five to two) and unilateral nuclear disarmament, including the closure of all nuclear bases in Britain (carried on a voice vote without anyone even bothering to call for a card vote). At the same time, although Williams held her own seat, the left made a net gain of three seats on the NEC.

The decisions of the 1980 conference were a triumph for the left. It had wanted radical change. It had argued for it and organized for it and campaigned for it. And now, at last, it had got it. But, of course, the left's triumph represented the right's undoing. One right-winger later recalled that on the Friday afternoon after the end of the conference he was driving in brilliant sunshine down the M6 motorway from Blackpool to London. As he drove along, he suddenly realized that he was thinking hard, not about whether there should be a new party, but about what its name should be.

3

● ● ● ●

Jenkins and the Jenkinsites

The events just described took place entirely within the Labour party; but during this period events were also taking place outside the party—and on the fringes of it—that were to have an important bearing on the SDP's formation and subsequent history. So far we have mentioned Roy Jenkins only occasionally and in passing. The time has come to give him a central place in the narrative.

In 1980 Jenkins had been out of British politics for four years as president of the European Commission in Brussels. He was no longer an MP, his name was seldom in the newspapers, and he almost never appeared on television. Nevertheless, he was still widely regarded as one of the more substantial figures in British public life. First elected to the House of Commons in 1948 at the age of only 27, he had waited out Labour's thirteen years in opposition between 1951 and 1964 and then had advanced rapidly in the 1964–70 Wilson government, serving first as aviation minister, then as home secretary and finally as chancellor of the exchequer. He served as deputy leader of the party from 1970 until his resignation over the Common Market issue two years later. He then returned to the Home Office when Labour unexpectedly found itself back in power in 1974.

Given his success at both the Home Office and the Treasury, and his intelligence and consummate parliamentary skills, Jenkins was widely presumed in the 1960s and early 1970s to be a future leader of the Labour party; but, when his chance finally came, on Wilson's resignation as prime minister in 1976, he was all but humiliated on the first ballot, receiving only 56 votes (compared with the 174 that James Callaghan and Michael Foot shared between them). When Callaghan then failed to offer him the foreign secretaryship, he decided to leave British politics, at least temporarily, for the presidency of the European Commission. He was not due to return from Brussels until his four-year term as president expired on 31 December 1980.[1]

Jenkins got so few votes in the leadership election partly because he and the Labour party had already fallen out of love with each other. Jenkins was a leading European at a time when Labour was turning against the Common Market; he was, in his own words, 'an unreconstructed Keynesian' at a time when the party, at least in the country, was more and more attracted to the ideas of socialist planning; he was a supporter of the Atlantic alliance at a time when the party was moving towards unilateralism, even neutralism.

The causes of the estrangement, however, went beyond disagreements on specific issues. Labour was a working-class party and also a socialist party, but Jenkins found himself increasingly uncomfortable with a political approach defined in such terms. Labour should, of course, appeal to working-class voters and, where appropriate, try to advance working-class interests; but its principal aim, he thought, should be to seek to build a radical coalition comprising men and women drawn from all classes. Within the working classes, the interests of the better-off, he believed, did not necessarily coincide with those of the really poor and disadvantaged; and in any case conducting politics on a class-war basis seemed a curious way of trying to eliminate class attitudes and cleavages. As for 'socialism', the word had long since been emptied of any meaning for Jenkins, and gradually, being an intellectually fastidious man, he stopped using it. People in the party noticed; and a certain coolness began to develop between him and even many of those who broadly shared his views. He was no longer 'one of us'.[2]

This sense that Jenkins had deserted the labour movement, in spirit if not yet in fact, was reinforced by the pattern of his political friendships. Politics in Britain has always been—in contrast to, say, American politics—highly partisan. The courtesies may be observed, but it is simply not done for Conservative politicians to be seen dining with their Labour opposite numbers or for Labour politicians to be known to enjoy country-house weekends with leading Conservatives. The major political parties are little subcultures, with their own habits and customs and a suspicion of outsiders. Jenkins simply did not think in these terms. He found it easy to identify congenial souls in all parties, numbering among his friends Liberals like David Steel and Mark Bonham-Carter and Conservatives like Sir Ian Gilmour and (later) Edward Heath. He even belonged to the Whiggish Brooks's Club in St James's. In particular, Jenkins had derived enormous pleasure and personal fulfilment from the all-party Britain in Europe campaign during the Common Market referendum. Even someone as pro-European, anti-left wing and generally ecumenical as Shirley Williams found his hobnobbing with Conservatives and Liberals at the Waldorf Hotel, their large limousines parked outside, somewhat hard to take.[3]

Mere political differences might have been borne; but Jenkins' personality and style also caused offence. He was a very grand person. Everyone said so. Without being in any way haughty or rude, he nevertheless contrived to give the impression that he thought of himself as a great world statesman and that he expected to be treated as such. A shy man, he often found it difficult to make contact with people who did not share his background and interests, and his nervousness sometimes manifested itself as brusqueness, even pomposity. He totally lacked the knack of putting people at their ease. In his utter refusal to do anything that was out of character, even in order to further his own interests (no one could ever imagine him standing in a picket line or telling funny stories), he was reminiscent of Shakespeare's Coriolanus.

But, if Jenkins himself did not tell funny stories, such stories were certainly told about him. They might or might not be true: the fact that they were repeated was what mattered. Visiting a prison as home secretary, he was said to have remarked absent-mindedly to one of the inmates, 'How nice to see you here.' During the leadership election in 1976, Jenkins' supporters urged him to be seen more around the House of Commons: he should chat to people, they said, buy them a pint of beer. Jenkins did buy one elderly Labour MP a pint, but then said 'I must be off now'—and left the MP to drink it alone. One working-class Yorkshire member, asked whether he would vote for Jenkins, replied firmly, 'No, lad. We're all Labour here.'[4]

The former chancellor was also known for his love of chauffeur-driven cars, well-cut suits (though he did not wear them especially well), good restaurants, good wine and long weekends at his Oxfordshire country home. The impression he gave was of a man who thought that he was just slightly superior to most of those around him—an impression reinforced by his odd accent, with its 'w's instead of 'r's (so that 'rural' became 'wuwal'). The satirical magazine *Private Eye* dubbed him 'Smoothychops'. Others thought of him as a 'Whig grandee'. It also did not help that, although naturally a kind man, Jenkins also had a very good turn of phrase; and, even when a phrase that occurred to him might be personally wounding, he could not always resist the temptation to use it. Jenkins' victims were apt to remember some of his more cutting remarks a good deal longer than he did.[5]

That was how his enemies—and even some of his friends—saw him. But there was another side to him, and everyone knew it. In a world of political pygmies, Jenkins was a giant. People might dislike him, but they never looked down on him. In addition to his intelligence and experience, he was a man of undoubted vision; he thought more deeply about politics than most politicians and saw further ahead than they did. He began to fight for British membership of the Common Market almost as soon as the EEC was formed in 1957—long before the cause became fashionable—and he was one of the first people in the Labour party to conclude that Britain's adversarial, class-based system of party politics was no longer working, if it had ever worked, in the national interest. Moreover, Jenkins as a politician was (to use the kind of old-fashioned word that he liked to use himself) steadfast. Once committed to a cause, he never wavered in his devotion to it. His resignation as Labour's deputy leader over the Common Market in 1972 is well remembered; less well remembered is the fact that, as early as 1960, he resigned from the Labour's front-bench economic team, to which he had only just been appointed, to be free to campaign on the European issue.[6]

Even his enemies conceded that Jenkins had vision and integrity. He had been a great reforming home secretary, one of the greatest of this century. They also conceded that he had courage. It was not easy for an ambitious politician year after year to make out the case for the Common Market to increasingly unsympathetic—and, latterly, downright hostile—Labour audiences; and his resignation in 1972 as deputy leader put his whole career at risk. Jenkins' courage, however, was not of the 'happy-warrior' type. Unlike Shirley Williams, he did not actually relish a good fight. On the contrary, he had to screw himself up to take risks and to confront opposition. In the words of one of his 1974–6 cabinet colleagues:

It happened again and again. Something would come before cabinet that Roy—and a lot of the rest of us—didn't like. You could see that Roy didn't really want to get involved, didn't want yet another fight; but then, wearily, he would wade in—and he was always very clear, very forceful, very effective.

Jenkins' courage was thus a reluctant courage—and one consequence was that he was liable to fight only when he was absolutely sure he was right and could also see clearly the way ahead (or could see equally clearly that there was no way back). Many on the Labour right were disappointed, following his 1972 resignation, when he neither challenged Wilson for the Labour leadership nor indeed did anything at all beyond making a series of worthy but mainly unprovocative speeches around the country.[7] He even denied that these speeches were meant to be critical of Wilson's leadership, though they patently were. Later, when Labour returned to power, Jenkins allowed himself to be sent back to the Home Office, where he could have no real impact on economic policy, rather than risk being excluded from the government altogether by insisting on returning to the Treasury. Jenkins' periods of courageous assertiveness thus seemed to alternate with periods of something approaching lethargy. One of his heroes was Herbert Henry Asquith, the last-but-one Liberal prime minister, on whose political epitaph were inscribed the words 'We had better wait and see.'[8]

Jenkins had another characteristic that set him apart and that was to have a considerable influence on the events of the next few years. Most British politicians are individualists, not just in temperament but in their operating styles. When in office, they have officials to serve them; when out of office, they typically have a loyal secretary and maybe a couple of other personal assistants. But, unlike politicians in, say, France or the United States, they do not normally have a political entourage, a group of people who are loyal to them both personally and politically and who expect to have a continuing relationship with them.

Jenkins in this respect was different. At least since the late 1960s, he had had such an entourage. It was a loose and disparate grouping, and its membership altered gradually over the years. Different people were associated with it to differing degrees. At any one time it might include John Harris (Lord Harris of Greenwich), Jenkins' former press adviser who had served under him as a minister at the Home Office; Dick Taverne, another of his former ministerial associates, the man who had been deselected by the constituency Labour party at Lincoln and had then fought the seat as an independent; David Marquand, a former (and future) academic who had resigned his Nottinghamshire seat in parliament in 1976 and followed Jenkins to Brussels; Tom Bradley, the MP for Leicester East, who had been Jenkins' parliamentary private secretary (PPS) for many years and was, along with Shirley Williams, a member of Labour's National Executive; Anthony Lester, one of Britain's leading civil-rights lawyers; and a number of younger Labour activists, such as Clive Lindley, Colin Phipps, Jim Daly, Michael Barnes and Matthew Oakeshott.[9]

Most of the Jenkinsites were able people, successful in their own spheres; but they were not—and knew they were not—politically important in themselves. None had ever been a cabinet minister; several had never been MPs; and, with the partial exception of Taverne, most people outside politics had never heard of them. They were a supporters' club rather than the nucleus of an army. Jenkins enjoyed their company, tried out his ideas on them and appreciated their loyalty. For their part, they were conscious of being associated with one of the most experienced, most intelligent, most serious-minded men in British public life—a truly great man in their view. They also, unlike many who saw him only from a distance, liked him and found him warm and personally sympathetic. They sensed, beneath the *hauteur*, a degree of personal vulnerability. They and he needed each other. The loyalty that they gave him he fully reciprocated. Patronage or the hope of patronage scarcely came into it. One young MP admitted that he stood 'somewhat in awe' of the former chancellor. Another—someone who was actually on the outer fringes of the group—volunteered: 'I admit it: I would have gone to the stake for him.'

The very existence of the group, however, caused problems. To insiders the Jenkinsites appeared serious, dedicated, even selfless; but many outsiders regarded the Jenkinsite group as being cliquish and stand-offish, almost too good to be true. Its high moral tone was widely regarded as a thin disguise for its leader's personal ambitions. The Jenkinsites were variously dismissed as his acolytes, idolaters, even sycophants. The group's existence also affected in an important way Jenkins' relations with the press. Jenkins' activities, ideas and plans received far more publicity than anyone else's. The reason was simple. To find out what Owen, for example, was thinking, you had to talk to Owen; to find out what Williams was thinking, you had to talk to Williams; to find out what Rodgers was thinking, you had to talk to Rodgers (or possibly his assistant, Roger Liddle). But to find out what Jenkins was thinking you could talk to any one of half a dozen people, each of whom had some reasonable claim to be his spokesman—and, if you did not talk to one of them, there was a very good chance that one of them would talk to you. The Jenkinsites in this way constituted a formidable propaganda machine (even if it was not always under Jenkins' personal control). Few other politicians could rival it.

Jenkins resigned as home secretary in September 1976 and took up his post in Brussels at the beginning of the following year. By all accounts, he was bored and unhappy in Brussels. His preferred way of working—well suited to the Treasury or the Home Office—was to identify important issues and then to take firm decisions on them, on the basis of thorough briefings from his officials. He liked an orderly flow of paper that would lead to a determinate outcome. He also wanted to be the boss and to be seen to be the boss. But the presidency of the European Commission was a post that required primarily negotiating and administrative skills, and it was also one whose status, as compared with that of Europe's heads of government, was not at all secure (it was not clear, for instance, what role the president should play at international summit meetings). Jenkins, accustomed to political leadership, found himself performing as a sort of quasi-diplomat, quasi-civil servant. The role gave him little pleasure. Being exiled in Brussels also deprived him of his power base, which was in Britain, and his familiar political surroundings, which were also in Britain. He responded by reading the British papers every day, by spending as many weekends as possible at home in London or Oxfordshire and by spending long evenings discussing British politics with the many British ministers and MPs (Conservative and Liberal as well as Labour) who visited Brussels in the course of their duties. The Labour figure he kept most closely in touch with was Bill Rodgers, a friend and confidant from Hugh Gaitskell's time.

Jenkins not surprisingly viewed with dismay Labour's growing hostility to the European Community in the late 1970s, its failure as a government to cope with Britain's economic problems and, not least, the confrontation between the Callaghan government and the unions that marked the Winter of Discontent. He did not want Labour to win the 1979 election, and he did not himself vote; his wife Jennifer (and also the one Jenkinsite who had worked with him in Brussels, David Marquand) voted Liberal. Without saying anything publicly, he had already decided that, if he returned to British politics at all, it would not be as a member of the Labour party. But was there any way forward outside Labour? If so, what was it? Jenkins was pondering these questions and not coming to any very satisfactory conclusions when, in the spring of 1979, he received an invitation from the BBC to deliver the annual televised Dimbleby Lecture. He presumed that the broadcasters expected him to talk about Europe, but the subject was left open and he decided to see whether he could use the occasion to explore new political ground. He showed a draft of the lecture to John Harris, David Marquand and a few others. Bill Rodgers glanced through it late one night but did not think much about it.

Entitled 'Home Thoughts from Abroad', the lecture was delivered on 22 November 1979, the same day that Rodgers was having lunch with John Horam. It did not sound on the face of it like a call to battle: it was full of learned historical allusions, and its language, probably deliberately, was somewhat opaque. But its general drift was clear enough. Jenkins condemned 'the constricting rigidity— almost the tyranny—of the present party system', which he believed was contributing to Britain's relative economic decline, to its over-rapid policy changes ('queasy rides on the ideological big-dipper') and to the public's growing political disenchantment. He called for a fairer electoral system, with the introduction of proportional representation. If that led to the formation of coalition governments, so much the better, provided that the members of the coalitions were sufficiently close in spirit to each other and to the national mood. Coalition governments had worked well on the Continent, and in any case how could men and women who practised an adversarial system of politics call in good conscience for an end to Britain's adversarial system of industrial relations? Scattered throughout the lecture were references to the need for a new political force:

This, some people will say with horror, is an unashamed plea for the strengthening of the political centre. Why not?

I believe that . . . if [the electorate] saw a new grouping with cohesion and relevant policies it might be more attracted by this new reality than by old labels which had become increasingly irrelevant.

The response to such a situation [of internecine warfare in the Labour party], in my view, should not be to slog through an unending war of attrition . . . but to break out and mount a battle of movement on new and higher ground.

Jenkins concluded with yet another reference to the need for 'a strengthening of the radical centre'.[10]

Remarks like these were not lost on many among his audience. 'It was like a Victorian lady showing her ankle,' Jenkins observed afterwards. 'The mere hint evoked a response.' Scores of letters of support were received by the BBC and in Jenkins' office in Brussels, and the writers' names and addresses were carefully card-indexed. John Horam wrote to say how much he agreed with the lecture. In the Labour party, however, the general response, even on the right of the party, was at best sceptical, at worst hostile. Shirley Williams thought it was a mildly interesting academic lecture, not much more. David Owen took it more seriously but was irritated by its unreality, and he and Tom Bradley had a row in Westminster underground station when Bradley tried to defend it (Bradley later saying that he had been tempted to push Owen under an oncoming train). Bill Rodgers was more enthusiastic (he admitted afterwards that during the lecture he suddenly had a vision of himself, with his sleeves rolled up, organizing a new party), but his enthusiasm was short lived. At this stage he was only just beginning to con-template leaving the Labour party, and most other worried right-wingers had not got nearly as far as he had. Almost all of them were angry at the time, because speeches like Jenkins' would make their battles inside the party that much harder to fight: they would be accused of treason before they had committed it or had even thought of committing it. Jenkins was widely accused of being no more than a rider on the European gravy train and of refusing to 'soil his hands' in the party's internal battles.[11]

Despite the hints in the Dimbleby Lecture, Jenkins was still by no means clear what he should do next: 'I felt like a climber on a ledge half way up a rock face. I couldn't see how I was going to get either up or down.' The various possibilities were discussed endlessly at fortnightly, sometimes weekly, Jenkinsite meetings in various London flats. Jenkins himself was occasionally present but usually not. The

Source: *Daily Telegraph*, 16 January 1981

'I came . . . I saw . . . I thought about it!'

hawks at the meetings consisted of Michael Barnes, Colin Phipps and, to begin
with, Dick Taverne. They took the view that the whole parliamentary Labour party
was gutless, that no Labour MPs would come over and that in any case they did not
'matter a row of beans'. The hawks' strategy was that a political office should be
established—rather in the style of an American presidential campaign—'for when
Roy landed at Dover' in January 1981. A skeleton political party would already
have been set up; its leadership would be vacant, and Jenkins would just walk into
it. The hawks were optimistic that such a Jenkins-only party, in alliance with the
Liberals (they took the need for such an alliance for granted), would sweep
everything before it.

The doves at the meetings—which one person who went to them found
'almost comically conspiratorial'—consisted of David Marquand, Clive Lindley, Jim
Daly, John Harris and, increasingly as the discussions progressed, Taverne. The
doves' view was that a purely Jenkinsite party might have to be formed in the end
but that such a party would stand little chance electorally on its own, and that it
would be far better if it were joined by at least a few Labour MPs, including, ideally,
Bill Rodgers and Shirley Williams. Rodgers because of his standing in the
parliamentary party, Williams because of her popularity in the country, were
thought to be crucial; David Owen, in their eyes something of a Johnny-come-
lately, was thought to have less to contribute. With regard to all of them, the doves
counselled patience, believing that Rodgers and Williams would probably come
over given time and that, if they came over, perhaps half a dozen other MPs would
too. Substantial Labour defections would give the new party credibility and further diminish that of Labour. Most of the Jenkinsites, even some of the hawks,

recognized, however, that the whole enterprise might still fail—that it might never get off the ground or that, even if it did, it might quickly crash.

During the whole of this period—in the months before and after the Dimbleby Lecture and before and after the Gang of Three's open letter to the *Guardian*—there were few people in the Labour party, even among those who were considering the possibility of leaving it, who quite knew what they were doing. Jenkins and the Jenkinsites could not see their way forward; and the Gang of Three and those who sympathized with them were torn between their desire to win their fight inside the Labour party and their knowledge that, if they did win it, it would be on the strength of trade-union bloc votes. They were also conscious that, whatever the outcome of any one vote at conference or on the National Executive, Labour would probably never again be the party that it had once been and that they had originally joined. Thus, on the unhappy right wing of the Labour party confusion reigned. There was in the midst of this confusion, however, one man who knew exactly what he wanted and had known for a considerable period of time. He was the Liberal party's leader, David Steel.

Steel, although only 42 in the summer of 1980, had already been leader of his party for four years. He was an assured, confident, straightforward politician, a man without any very firm grasp of policy, especially economic policy, but with clear ideas about the broad direction in which he wanted British politics to go. He had the additional advantage of being unusually skilful at communicating his ideas, whether on public platforms, in newspaper articles or on television.

Steel's vision of Britain's political future resembled Jenkins' in almost every particular. He was in favour of the welfare state but against detailed state control of the economy, in favour of private enterprise and the free market but against untrammelled capitalism and the ethics of selfishness and greed, in favour of free trade unionism but against the kind of war of all against all that the unions had conducted during the Winter of Discontent. He was, like Jenkins, an enthusiast for Europe, for an incomes policy based on consent and for an end to what he saw as sterile bickering over the boundaries between the public and private sectors (Jenkins' 'ideological big-dipper'). Also like Jenkins, Steel was a staunch liberal on social issues and matters of conscience. Just as Jenkins had helped in the 1950s to liberalize the law on obscene publications, so Steel in the 1960s had, with Jenkins' help, been largely responsible for liberalizing the abortion laws.

More fundamentally, Steel, again like Jenkins, thought that there was something wrong with a political system in which both of the two major parties were almost wholly dependent on a single vested interest, big business in the Conservatives' case, the trade unions in Labour's. Such a politics was bound to be unprincipled; it was also bound to heighten class and sectional differences instead of accommodating them. Steel sought a politics—and a society—of co-operation instead of confrontation, of working together instead of endlessly pulling apart. That was why he had joined the Liberal party, and that was the goal towards which he was now working as leader.

Steel had a vision; but he also had a vivid sense of the realities of his and his party's situation. The Liberals had made steady progress in recent years. Their share of the popular vote had gone up from 5.9 per cent at the 1959 general election to 13.8 per cent in 1979; their seats in the House of Commons had risen during the same period from six to eleven. At their best post-war election, that of February 1974, they had got 19.3 per cent of the popular vote—nearly one vote in five—and a total of fourteen seats. But Steel knew that, whatever some Liberal enthusiasts might say during an election campaign, there was no way in which, under the first-past-the-post electoral system, the Liberals on their own could break through and win a parliamentary majority. The Liberals' third-party status discouraged many people from voting Liberal; and, even when, as in February 1974, the Liberals obtained a substantial popular vote, they still won relatively few seats in the House of Commons.

While some Liberals continued to dream of the day when the party on its own would form a government, others were in fact quite comfortable envisaging it as a permanent minority, as a sort of guerrilla band that would harass the other parties and fire off occasional rounds of ammunition in their direction but would not seriously try either to join them or to replace them. Steel objected strenuously to this latter approach: he was an ambitious man who wanted to be a cabinet minister one day; and he thought it was wrong in principle to claim that one wanted to change the political system, but then to refuse to co-operate with other parties towards that end simply in order to preserve one's independence and *amour propre*.

Steel practised what he preached. He had worked with Jenkins in reforming the law on abortion; he had co-operated with both Labour and Conservative politicians, notably the Conservatives' Iain Macleod, in resisting the first Wilson government's efforts to restrict the entry into Britain of Asian holders of British passports from east Africa; he had been active in the 1975 all-party referendum campaign; most recently, he had masterminded the Lib–Lab pact, which had sustained the Callaghan government in power during 1977–8 (and the termination of which had helped to bring down that government in 1979). Steel concluded from the experience of the Lib–Lab pact, not that such pacts should not be entered into, but that they should be entered into by whole political parties, not just their parliamentary leaders.[12]

Against that background, Steel in the spring and summer of 1980 found himself performing a strange and elaborate quadrille, with Jenkins as one of his principal partners in the dance. Steel and Jenkins had often worked closely together in the past, and they liked and trusted one another as well as seeing eye to eye on almost everything. They also saw a good deal of each other socially, especially since Steel visited Brussels from time to time. It was of considerable importance to their relationship that they belonged to different generations. Steel, eighteen years younger than Jenkins, could defer to the older man without in any way demeaning himself. Jenkins, for his part, took an almost avuncular interest in Steel. They were in no sense rivals.

Steel, however, had a problem: he was the leader of a political party, but he did not want other people to join it. The choice in 1980, as he saw it, lay between, on the one hand, a small handful of Labour MPs and ex-MPs joining the Liberals as individuals and, on the other hand, a much more substantial breakout from the Labour party, leading to the creation of a new political organization independent of the Liberal party but operating in close collaboration with it. The Liberal leader had no doubt which alternative he preferred. He did not want Jenkins or any other solitary politician 'to do a Chris Mayhew'. Christopher Mayhew, a former Labour junior minister, had left the Labour party and joined the Liberals on his own in 1975, but he had then failed to secure re-election to parliament and, except as a minor Liberal peer, had scarcely been heard of since. The precedent was discouraging.[13]

Instead Steel was keen to encourage defections from Labour on as large a scale as he could, and he knew that far more Labour MPs would defect to a new party than would ever defect to the Liberals. He therefore did nothing to encourage Jenkins or anyone else to join the party of which he was leader, even though, if Jenkins had joined, he would have been the party's most formidable recruit of the twentieth century. Fortunately, Jenkins and Steel understood each other perfectly. Steel did not ask Jenkins to join the Liberals. Jenkins himself never raised the question as a practical possibility. It suited the convenience of both men to have a purely tacit understanding that Jenkins would form a new party if he could, with some kind of pact between the new party and Steel's Liberals to follow in due course.[14]

So far as the other Jenkinsites were concerned, they, like their leader, respected the Liberal party on the whole, recognizing its radical, non-socialist approach as being akin to their own. But at the same time they had no particular wish to join the Liberals. They did not think of themselves as Liberals; they rarely moved in Liberal circles; and, like Steel and Jenkins, they were aware that the defection of a few individuals like themselves would cause, at most, a momentary stir. Still, the Jenkinsites were not determinedly anti-Liberal and could see themselves joining the Liberals as a fallback position if a sufficiently large breakout from the Labour party failed to materialize. Some of them accordingly kept their lines to the Liberals open. Clive Lindley, for instance, organized a small private conference of Liberals and Jenkinsites at his country home in January 1980 and was in regular contact with Roger Pincham, that year's chairman of the Liberals' national executive. David Marquand similarly debated social-democratic principles at the 1980 Liberal assembly. But such contacts—unlike those between the two principals—were very sporadic.[15]

The other partners in Steel's quadrille were the Gang of Three—and the three of them he kept at a considerable distance. Owen, Rodgers and Williams belonged to another political party and for the time being were saying that they intended to go on fighting inside that party. Steel did not feel it was any of his business to get involved in the Labour party's internal wrangles. Moreover, whereas he knew

Jenkins well, he did not know David Owen at all, he scarcely knew Shirley Williams, and he knew Bill Rodgers only as a result of their having worked together during the referendum campaign. In view of what was to happen later, one of the strangest features of the year 1980 is that personal communication between Steel and the Gang of Three was at this point (in the words of one of them) 'non-existent'. They neither saw each other nor spoke to each other.

Instead, Steel addressed both the Gang of Three and his own party via a series of speeches and newspaper articles. At the 1979 Liberal assembly in Margate, well before serious talk of a Labour split had begun, he claimed that the challenge to the Liberals was to recreate the great coalition of idealists, progressives and radicals that had sustained the party of their grandfathers:

We have to bring together into one political movement those on whom the Labour party has turned its back—the poor, the unemployed, the libertarians driven by opposition to socialism into the Conservative camp. And from the other side the moderates whose ideas the Conservative leadership has now decisively rejected.[16]

In February 1980, writing in the *Sunday Times*, he called, still rather tentatively, for 'a central point from which to redraw the map of British politics' and put forward 'the outline of an agenda, which could unite liberals, progressives and radicals with those social democrats and even conservatives who share our analysis'. The agenda included electoral reform, worker participation and profit-sharing in industry, help for small businesses and a combining of the social security and tax systems.[17] Later, following the publication of the Gang of Three's open letter to the Labour party, Steel published his own open letter to the Gang of Three. He insisted that the events of recent months had proved that the right wing's fight inside the Labour party was 'lost, and lost beyond recall' and that the time had come to sort out the structure of a new radical coalition:

Given the limitations of our electoral system, there would be nothing worse than the emergence of two or three competing progressive parties, each with overlapping philosophies and policy proposals, all appealing to the same sections of the electorate. That would guarantee another Conservative victory, even on a reduced proportion of the vote. We are forced therefore to combine if we would succeed.

He concluded that it was time for the Gang of Three to end their dialogue of the deaf and to start talking to the Liberals with a view to offering a credible alternative government to the voters in 1983 or 1984. Puckishly, he signed his open letter 'Yours fraternally, David Steel'.[18]

Not surprisingly, Steel's public pronouncements—all of which envisaged a genuinely new political formation and not just an expansion of the Liberals—caused a certain amount of unease in his own party. To some extent, Steel's private office and those politicians closest to him—men like Richard Holme, William Wallace, Stuart Mole and Lord Tordoff—constituted a distinct element in the party. There was an air of separateness, even remoteness, about them. Steel himself was

63

the son of a Church of Scotland moderator, and his single-minded pursuit of a centre-left realignment appeared to have much of the manse's lofty rectitude and inner self-confidence. Steel occasionally seemed more concerned with pursuing his personal political vision than with the feelings of his flock. Some rank-and-file Liberals, however, were increasingly disturbed by the possibility that their party might be swamped by a more numerous, more aggressive social-democratic party, while others had genuine intellectual doubts about the compatibility between liberal and social-democratic ideas. But the Liberal leader for the time being ignored all such fears. His tactics might be flexible; but his long-term strategy was fixed.

While David Steel was sounding more and more confident in his calls for a new cross-party coalition of the centre left, the newspapers were increasingly sprinkled with stories about Jenkins, the Jenkinsites and their plans. The leakers in the Jenkinsite camp, whoever they were, clearly wanted to make sure that their man was not forgotten and that a feeling was created in the political world that something important was about to happen. A story appeared in the *Observer*, for example, reporting that talks between Steel and Jenkins had taken place and that former Labour MPs like Marquand and Taverne were holding regular meetings.[19] Later, the day after Rodgers, Williams and Owen had issued their initial statement on Europe, all the leading Sunday papers published reports that Jenkins intended when he returned from Brussels to form an independent centre party along the lines of the American Democrats. It was expected that an electoral pact with the Liberals would follow. Most of the Jenkinsites—Taverne, Marquand, Phipps, Barnes and Lindley—were named.[20]

These last stories also heralded a speech that Jenkins was due to make to the Parliamentary Press Gallery the next day. In this speech, Jenkins went considerably further than in his Dimbleby Lecture. He drew attention to Labour's 'major lurch to the left' at the special Wembley conference and to the huge tracts of political territory that the Labour right had been forced to surrender:

I therefore believe that the politics of the left and centre of this country are frozen in an out-of-date mould which is bad for the political and economic health of Britain and increasingly inhibiting for those who live within the mould. Can it [he asked] be broken?

Towards the end of the speech, answering his own question, he altered the metaphor:

The likelihood before the start of most adventures is that of failure. The experimental plane may well finish up a few fields from the end of the runway. If that is so, the voluntary occupants will have only inflicted the bruises or worse upon themselves.

But the reverse could occur and the experimental plane soar in the sky. If that is so, it could go further and more quickly than few now imagine, for it would carry with it great and now untapped reserves of political energy and commitment.[21]

Jenkins' phrase about breaking the mould was quoted endlessly during the coming months, but it was the 'experimental-plane' metaphor that better captured his feelings of hope—but also of uncertainty—at the time.

Throughout this period, Jenkins had very few personal contacts with members of the Labour party. The Jenkinsites and David Steel inhabited one political camp; the Gang of Three and other right-wingers in the parliamentary Labour party inhabited another. There was little communication between them.

Only a handful of Labour MPs kept in touch with Jenkins and his entourage. Tom Bradley, though still a member of Labour's NEC, made it clear that, if Jenkins left the party, he would too. John Horam went along to some early meetings of the Jenkinsite 'conspiracy' but then decided the whole thing was too dangerous. Robert Maclennan, a barrister and the MP for Caithness and Sutherland, saw Jenkins in Brussels from time to time during his time as a junior minister at the Department of Prices and Consumer Protection (initially under Shirley Williams); Maclennan believed that he and Jenkins tacitly agreed that the issue was, not whether they would leave the party, but when. Another young MP, Ian Wrigglesworth, who sat for Teeside Thornaby, next door to Bill Rodgers, talked to Jenkins on the phone occasionally and urged him on. It was also generally assumed that Tom Ellis, the MP for Wrexham, and Neville Sandelson, the MP for Hayes and Harlington (who had fallen out with his constituency Labour party), were Jenkinsite sympathizers. But they were virtually the only Labour MPs who were in touch with Jenkins and his supporters (or with Steel for that matter) during most of 1979–80—a total of about half a dozen.

Likewise, as we have seen, Jenkins' relations with the Gang of Three at this stage were almost as tenuous as theirs were with David Steel. Jenkins scarcely saw Owen before the autumn of 1980, and he saw Williams and Rodgers only very occasionally. Moreover, meetings between Jenkins on the one hand and Williams and Rodgers on the other tended to diminish in number—they certainly did not increase—as time went on. Given that all of them appeared on the face of it to be pursuing similar goals, why should this have been so? What kept the two groups apart?

Part of the answer is personal. Although Rodgers and Jenkins got on well, and had done so for years, Jenkins was not a close friend of either of the other two. Shirley Williams admired Jenkins in a rather distant sort of way and agreed with him on a wide range of issues. But he was not really her kind of person. He was grand; she was an instinctive egalitarian. He liked to be treated with proper respect; she liked to pull people's legs. They were perfectly civil to each other but did not seek out each other's company (she had been much closer to Jenkins' erstwhile rival, Tony Crosland). In the case of David Owen, the personality clash was more serious. Owen had worked with Jenkins on the European issue in the early 1970s and had resigned from the Labour front bench with him in 1972, but their relations had deteriorated while Jenkins was president of the European Commission and Owen British foreign secretary. Jenkins thought that Owen fought harder for narrowly

British interests than was appropriate in a body like the Community (one Jenkinsite dubbed him an 'infantile Gaullist'). Owen for his part thought that Jenkins did not appreciate how hard it was to fight on European issues inside a government like Callaghan's. Specific incidents also rankled, as when Jenkins' telegram congratulating Owen on being appointed foreign secretary appeared to have been drafted by a junior official in Jenkins' office. In general, they were just different sorts of people. Owen resembled a large dog, an Alsatian. Jenkins was more feline.[22]

Personality differences alone would not, however, have prevented Jenkins and the Gang of Three from working together during these months; after all, they were able to work together for a considerable period of time later on. There were also important political disagreements between them. Their nature emerged shortly after Rodgers delivered his 'one year, not much longer' speech at Abertillery. A few days before Rodgers made the speech, Jenkins, who did not know he was going to make it, phoned him and suggested that the two of them ought to have a talk. Rodgers said he was going to be in south Wales on the coming Friday: perhaps he could come back by train the next morning and they could have lunch at Jenkins' Oxfordshire home at East Hendred. Jenkins said fine: he would see if he could also get hold of Williams. As it worked out, Jenkins met both Rodgers and Williams at Didcot station on the next Saturday, 1 December 1979, and drove them to his home four miles away, where they had a long talk over lunch.[23] Afterwards Rodgers took the trouble to write Jenkins a long letter arising from their conversation. The letter reveals much, not only about Rodgers' (and, by implication, Williams') thinking in the winter of 1979–80, but also about a range of issues that were to have an important bearing on the SDP's eventual formation and history.

Rodgers, as his letter makes clear, was worried about the course that Jenkins, Taverne and the others seemed bent on pursuing. He wanted to distance himself from the Jenkinsites—not very far, but far enough that there should be no misunderstanding. He was particularly concerned that Jenkins should bear in mind the strength of the ties binding people to the Labour party:

I know that you don't underestimate the personal factors—sentiment, habit, hardship, ambition—that will affect the judgment of members of Parliament. A number of our older colleagues—Alan Fitch, Ernest Armstrong, Ivor Davies—are as strong as ever, but they are approaching retirement and not looking for too much upset in their remaining time. A number of our young ones—Giles Radice, Phillip Whitehead, Ian [Wrigglesworth]— probably feel that they have not yet had a chance to prove themselves and perhaps save the party.

As for myself, if Denis [Healey] were elected leader and asked me to become shadow chancellor (not likely but not quite impossible) mightn't I be tempted to believe that I was now in a better position than ever before to be an influence for good from the inside? I mention this because I don't want to mislead you about the immense personal pressures on all of us still on the inside if faced with the choice of helping to launch a [new] party.

Rodgers was polite enough to say that he knew Jenkins was not underestimating such personal factors; but of course he was worried that Jenkins was doing precisely that.

Rodgers also wanted Jenkins to be clear that in his, Rodgers', mind the fight in the Labour party had to go on for the time being. It might, after all, be won. Even if it were not, only by fighting could one persuade other Labour MPs that one had done one's very best, that the cause was now hopeless and that therefore they had no choice but to consider breaking away. If there had to be a break, it should come further down the road, when more people would be prepared to join:

I have no doubt that during this period [up to the October 1980 party conference] I should do all I can towards a satisfactory outcome. I realise that this will increase the likelihood of fudge and compromise and no clear breaking point. But I still think that it would be better to save the Labour party than venture out into the unknown with a new Fourth party (as I suppose we should call it). This may prove impossible and my own optimism continues to diminish. But unless some of us can say—and show—that we have tried and failed, we shall not carry with us the troops that we shall need if the break should come.

As he made clear, Rodgers' doubts were partly tactical; but they were by no means wholly so. Jenkins had talked in his Dimbleby Lecture about 'strengthening the centre', but Rodgers did not think of himself as a man of the centre and he did not want to participate in founding a centre party:

In the simplest terms, I would want a Fourth party eventually to take over 90 per cent of the existing Labour vote. It would be a party of the left, winning towards the centre as it discarded the outside left.

I'm not sure whether we agreed about this. But I have no confidence in (and no great warmth towards) a party of the centre. It would not work. The Conservative party will always be with us . . . A Fourth party will only succeed if it sets out to usurp the traditional Labour vote.

Rodgers emphasized in his letter the element of electoral calculation, but it is clear from his tone—'no great warmth towards'—that it was not only, or even mainly, electoral considerations that he had in mind. He had not spent his entire life in the Labour party and the labour movement suddenly to emerge as a wishy-washy centrist, expected to operate somewhere on the left fringes of the Conservatives.

Predictably under the circumstances, Rodgers was especially worried about the Jenkinsites' evident enthusiasm for flirting, including publicly flirting, with the Liberals. He suspected that many Liberals would not welcome a new party; he knew that any talk of a deal with the Liberals at this stage would be lethal to his efforts to save the Labour party; and he did not want any fourth party simply to be the Liberals' junior partner. His language was probably more restrained than his feelings:

I am most concerned here about dealings with the Liberals. When the time comes—if the time comes—there will be a need for an electoral pact . . . But I think it is a great mistake to assume that the Liberals will fall over backwards to welcome and facilitate a Fourth party. I have great respect for David Steel, who has vision and might be more concerned with a major realignment of politics than his own party's precise position in it. But this is far from true of all his colleagues and the Liberal party has its own sentimental and institutional ties.

In these circumstances, and particularly if serious negotiations lie ahead, an arm's-length relationship with the Liberals seems to me essential. They should certainly not be privy to any discussions that we—all of us still in the Labour party—may have. Here again, any whisper at this stage of a getting-together with the Liberals would be damaging to the cause. If a Fourth party is launched and succeeds, it will absorb much of the Liberal party—but on its own terms, and not without a struggle.

In short, Rodgers was rejecting every element of the Jenkinsite strategy, especially that of its hawkish wing. Rodgers wanted, ideally, to stay in the Labour party; he did not want a centre party; he did not want to do a deal with the Liberals except a deal that was strictly in the interests of any new party that might be formed. Rodgers later attended an 'Easter seminar' at East Hendred with Tom Bradley and others; but, given Rodgers' views, it is little wonder that he and Jenkins did less and less political business together and that, by the summer of 1980, Jenkins was feeling that he had been deserted by many of those who should have been his friends. Isolated in Brussels without his closest supporters around him, 'he was', according to one Jenkinsite, 'very miserable and depressed'. The Dimbleby Lecture was now largely forgotten; it had anyway been ill-received by the Labour right; the Jenkinsites' activities were scarcely visible in the press or on television; Hugo Young in the *Sunday Times* referred dismissively to 'the phantom divisions of the Centre'.[24] No one realistically expected a new party to be formed.

Owen and Williams did not read Rodgers' letter to Jenkins; they probably did not know of its existence. But his views were undoubtedly theirs—and they might have expressed them less politely. They, too, wanted to save the Labour party, did not want to join a centre party and did not want to become over-matey with the Liberals. In addition, with Jenkins far away in Brussels, their energies were absorbed, day after day, speech after speech, in fighting the battle inside the Labour party. Jenkins and his talk of a centre party seemed at best a distraction, at worst a confounded nuisance. In consequence, they not only did not go out of their way to seek out Jenkins and Steel and elicit their views: they denounced the idea of a centre party and distanced themselves from the Liberals in all their public pronouncements. In doing so, they had the whole-hearted support of all but a tiny handful of the most hawkish Jenkinsites.

Most outspoken was Shirley Williams. When early talk of a Jenkinsite centre party coincided with the Gang of Three's statement on Europe, she said on radio that she was not interested in a centre party because it would have 'no roots, no principles, no philosophy and no values'.[25] She clearly liked this phrase and used it repeatedly over the coming months. Similarly, when Steel wrote his open letter to the Gang of Three in August, Williams told the press: 'We are none of us looking for a party to join—we have got one already.'[26] Rodgers was even more dismissive:

It is predictable and routine that Mr. Steel should have made such a statement, but there is no point whatsoever in having talks. We do not support a centre party, and that includes the Liberals.

We are democratic socialists, seeking to save the Labour party and to ensure that it is a convincing alternative government to Mrs. Thatcher's.[27]

Indeed, so sustained and adamant were the Gang of Three's public denunciations of a centre party and of any deal with the Liberals that by the end of the summer of 1980 Steel, like Jenkins, was becoming increasingly depressed and somewhat irritated. 'We need your help,' he said, appealing to moderates in other parties at the September 1980 Liberal assembly, but he then went on:

Many of the Labour party are waiting to see what will happen at their conference. If the left further entrench their takeover, some will find it no longer possible to stay. But I predict that that is not what will happen. Rather, I believe there will be a fudged compromise, allowing the left to continue its attempts to control the Labour party, while those of publicly proclaimed tender conscience will be enabled to remain within it in the hope of picking up places in the next Labour cabinet.[28]

Everyone knew that the jibe about 'those of publicly proclaimed tender conscience' was aimed at the Gang of Three.

This was broadly the position on the eve of the Labour party's 1980 conference at Blackpool. Roy Jenkins, still in Brussels, was calling increasingly explicitly for the formation of a new centre party. A few Jenkinsites in London were discussing how such a party might be launched. David Steel of the Liberals was talking to Jenkins and some of his people and hoping that a new party would be launched and would form an alliance with the Liberals to strengthen British politics' radical centre.

On a completely different piece of political ground, David Owen, Bill Rodgers and Shirley Williams were talking of breaking with Labour but were still determined to fight and to try to win within the Labour party. The Gang of Three thought of themselves as being further to the left than Jenkins and Steel; they found the talk of a new centre party unhelpful and unattractive; and they had no direct dealings—and did not want to have any direct dealings—with either Jenkins or the Liberals. Moreover, on the eve of the Blackpool conference, it still seemed possible that the Labour right might win or at least might mount a successful holding operation. As Steel's speech implied, there was some reason to believe that Callaghan would be able to shift enough union bloc votes to defeat the three constitutional changes being proposed by the left.

But then, as we saw at the end of Chapter 2, the hopes of the right were dashed. The left won overwhelmingly at Blackpool. The whole situation in the party was transformed.

Chapters 4 and 5 will tell the story of the formation of the SDP; but it is important to note now that, by the late summer of 1980, the seeds of many future controversies and misunderstandings within the SDP had already been sown. The Gang of Three were fighting and gaining support within the Labour party. Two of them, Rodgers and Owen, were Labour MPs and members of the shadow cabinet; and the third, Williams, was a member of Labour's NEC. Their perception, indeed their assumption, was that, if a split in the Labour party occurred and a new party was formed, it would be because they had left the party and because a number of Labour MPs, local councillors and activists had followed them. Rodgers, Owen and Williams did not see either Jenkins or Steel as central to their enterprise. It is doubtful whether, in the first nine months of 1980, the three of them—with the possible exception of Rodgers—spent altogether more than a few hours thinking about Jenkins and Steel. Not unnaturally under the circumstances, when the SDP was eventually formed, the members of the Gang of Three thought it was their party. They had formed it; they had made sacrifices for it; they had borne the heat of the day; the new party could not have come into being without their efforts.

But the Jenkinsites' perception was completely different. Jenkins was by far the most senior political figure contemplating a break with Labour. He was a former home secretary and chancellor; and he was currently president of the European Commission, a far more exalted position than any of the Gang of Three could reasonably aspire to. The Jenkinsites believed, probably rightly, that their man was held in higher esteem by the British public than any of the other three. Moreover, it was Jenkins who had first had the vision and the courage to say publicly that Labour's day was done and that it was time to fight 'on new and higher ground'.

Jenkins could, after all, have left the European Commission quietly, retired to the country with his substantial pension and devoted the rest of his days to chairing royal commissions, writing biographies and acting as a highly paid consultant for a merchant bank—an elder statesman, comfortably off, able to travel the world, respected. Instead, at considerable risk to his reputation, he was proposing to re-engage himself in British politics, to become a figure of controversy again, to risk his political life in his dangerous 'experimental plane'. It was Jenkins who, inviting ribaldry from sceptical politicians and journalists, and with no initial backing from the Gang of Three, had held out the hope of creating a new party if the right's position inside the Labour party became intolerable. Only Jenkins had kept the faith. Not unnaturally, when the SDP was eventually formed, Jenkins and his supporters saw it as his party, one that the Gang of Three had somewhat belatedly agreed to join.

These two views were incompatible; they were bound to cause trouble. But that was for the future. For the moment, the war inside the Labour party went on.

4

••••

Anguish: 'Severe Mental Pain'

The right-winger who drove down the M6 from Blackpool following the 1980 Labour conference and who found himself thinking about what a new party might be called had, without having previously realized it, 'resigned psychologically' from the Labour party. He had taken no positive action, but an emotional tie had been broken. How many Labour MPs at the beginning of October 1980 were in a similar position, assuming already that sooner or later they would leave Labour and join some new political grouping? The short answer is: almost none. Probably the only ones who had already made the break in their own minds were the Jenkinsite MPs mentioned in Chapter 3, together with Richard Crawshaw, the moderate MP for Liverpool Toxteth. Few others, if any, had travelled that far—certainly not any of the Gang of Three. One reason was that the total rout of the right at Blackpool had come as a complete surprise as well as a shock, and it was going to take some time for its full implications to sink in. But a far more important reason was that most Labour MPs, however right wing, could hardly bring themselves to contemplate leaving the party they loved.

A religious person who has ever been afflicted by doubt will know how they felt, since Labour has always historically been much more than a mere political party. It is a cause, a way of life, a church—self-contained, comfortable and secure. The Labour party has its heroes and martyrs: the farm labourers of Tolpuddle, Keir Hardie, Arthur Henderson, Clem Attlee, Ernie Bevin and Nye Bevan. It has villains and traitors, led by Ramsay MacDonald and Philip Snowden. It has its single moment of supreme triumph, 1945, to remember and its more numerous moments of defeat and despair, such as 1931 and 1959. To be a Labour activist is almost to be defined by party conferences remembered, by Fabian summer schools, by fish and chips in the shop behind Blackpool's Imperial Hotel, by fond memories of that Welsh regional organizer—what *was* his name?—who, amazingly, knew every verse of 'The Red Flag'.

Labour has been in power frequently since the Second World War, but the sense that the labour movement is a movement of struggle—beleaguered, constantly having to fight just to hold on to the ground it has already won—remains. At the party conference, speakers refer to one another as 'comrade'. This does not mean that they like each other—in fact they often hate each other—but it does mean that they share a sense of fighting shoulder-to-shoulder together, of being soldiers in the same army. Thus, the Labour MP, especially if he has been in politics for long, is enmeshed in a tight network of friendships, loyalties and associations. The MP's diary, the books on his shelf, the address book in his pocket, the photos in his album, combine to tell him who he is, what he has been, what he may yet become. One does not give up all that lightly. One tries, if one can, to avoid even thinking about giving it up.[1]

With the end of the Blackpool conference, the battle inside the party moved back to London and the House of Commons. The Gang of Three, though conscious by now that they might some day be driven out of the party, were still determined to win the battle inside it if they could. In a speech at Blaenau Festiniog over the post-conference weekend, David Owen reminded his listeners that the parliamentary party had repeatedly rejected the principle of an electoral college for the election of the leader. The PLP, he said, must be totally convinced that any decision to widen the franchise for choosing a prime minister or opposition leader would produce a genuinely democratic decision:

Widening of the franchise can only be considered on the basis of genuinely greater democracy. The parliamentary Labour party must, as a matter of principle, insist that any scheme for widening of the franchise is seen by the country as a whole to be open, fair and democratic.[2]

Bill Rodgers in Cambridge a few days later said that the time had come 'to assert the rights, duties and role of the parliamentary Labour party without equivocation'.[3] Rodgers also called for Callaghan's resignation. He wanted a new party leader to be in place before the special conference called for January had agreed on the composition of the electoral college. He also wanted to see someone elected who, unlike Callaghan, would bring some 'purpose and passion to the leadership of the party in the very difficult period ahead'.[4]

On 15 October 1980, less than a fortnight after the conference, Callaghan did finally stand down. He was tired; his efforts to work with the trade unions behind the scenes to stem the left-wing tide had failed; and, like Rodgers, he wanted his successor to be elected by the parliamentary party on the old basis. Although he did not say so publicly, Callaghan almost certainly wanted his successor to be Denis Healey, who was widely presumed to be the favourite among Labour MPs and whose chances of election were likely to be far greater in the PLP than they would be in any electoral college, however it was composed. Healey announced immediately that he would be a candidate, as did John Silkin, the man whose anti-European manœuvres had first caused the Gang of Three to come together in June. Peter Shore, another anti-European who had been regarded, not entirely accurately, in previous years as a staunch left-winger, also threw his hat in the ring. Shore hoped to be the left's only candidate; but, after several days' hesitation, Michael Foot, someone who was more popular on the left than Shore and who would almost certainly go on to win in the electoral college if he won in the PLP, announced that he, too, was putting his name forward. Tony Benn declined to stand, righteously declaring that, after Blackpool, it would be presumptuous of the PLP to monopolize the election. Although Benn and others on the left insisted that the contest should be deferred till after the January conference, the PLP majority accepted the shadow cabinet's recommendation that it should be held at once.

The majority of right-wingers in the PLP very much wanted Healey to win. They were determined, or at any rate anxious, to remain in the party and believed that Healey constituted their only hope of restoring it to some semblance of sanity. If Healey won, his victory would constitute a significant defeat for the left and would revive the right's morale. It might even force Healey into a position where he had no choice but to become, like Gaitskell, the right's publicly avowed leader—if only to head off the challenge to his position that the left would certainly mount once the new electoral college had been established. Even some right-wingers who thought that, no matter who won the election, the game was up nevertheless voted for Healey, believing that they owed it to themselves and to the party to go on fighting so long as the faintest glimmer of hope remained. They 'felt bound', as one of them said, 'to exhaust the existing procedures'.

It quickly emerged, however, that Healey was going to be a far from ideal candidate from the right's point of view. Once Foot had come into the race, Healey declared that, if elected, he would serve as leader for as long as the majority of the PLP wanted him to, and he also said that he would lead the PLP's fight 'both on the issue of how reselection works and, of course, on the question of having an electoral college which is at least as democratic in its way of operating as the present system'.[5] But that was as far as he was prepared to go. He did not repudiate mandatory reselection. He did not repudiate the principle of an electoral college. He did not make stirring speeches on policy matters like unilateralism, nationalization, the trade unions and the Common Market. In fact, he did not do or say much of anything, except to indicate that he was available 'at any time of day or night' to answer MPs' questions.[6] Healey's calculation, on which this low-profile strategy was based, was that right-wing MPs were bound to vote for him anyway (they had no real alternative) and that, if he insisted on making stirring right-wing speeches, he would antagonize the small but significant group of MPs in the centre of the parliamentary party on whom the outcome of the election was likely to depend. Foot was presenting himself as the candidate of unity; Healey did not want to be presented by others as the candidate of disunity.

Healey's calculation seemed sensible, but it had the effect of further disheartening many right-wingers who were already losing heart. They were on the look-out for strong leadership, and Healey was clearly not going to provide it. A member of the Gang of Three described a meeting with him:

We spent two hours with him about the time of the party conference. What we were really saying was, 'Come on, Denis, tell us where you stand.' And after it we were profoundly depressed because he did not give the right answers on anything. The Labour party wasn't in much of a mess; the trade unions could sort it out in any case; and it didn't matter about policy, because you could say what you liked in opposition and then put it right in government. The main thing was to be in power. It was a typical Healey performance. I got very angry with him.

During the leadership contest the officers of the Manifesto Group arranged a meeting with him to ask a series of questions that they were putting to all the candidates. Foot was friendly and polite. Healey was nonchalant to the point of rudeness. At the end of the meeting, somebody said to him, 'Your answers have been very unsatisfactory. There are an awful lot of us. Why should we vote for you?' 'That's easy,' Healey is said to have replied. 'You have nowhere else to go.' Mike Thomas recalled that, when the SDP was launched a few months later, he was tempted to send Healey a telegram: 'Have Found Somewhere Else to Go.'

The results of the first ballot were announced on 4 November. Healey led with 112 votes; Foot was second with 83; Silkin had 38; Shore had 32. Silkin and Shore were thus eliminated on the first ballot and advised their supporters to transfer their support to Foot on the second. Most of them did so and, when the result was announced on 11 November, Foot was the new leader. He had beaten Healey by 139 votes to 129, a margin of ten; five votes the other way and there would have been a tie, six and Healey would have won. It is evident from the result, given the known left–right balance in the parliamentary party, that in order to win Foot must have picked up the votes of a considerable number of centrist and right-wing MPs. Why did they vote for him?

Some of them undoubtedly did so because they disliked Healey, because they liked and respected Foot (who was personally popular well outside the ranks of the left) or because they wanted a quiet life and reckoned that Healey, simply by being Healey, was bound to stir things up inside the party (some right-wingers honestly believed that Foot, because he was seen as a man of the left, would be capable of restoring party unity). But there is another possibility: that some right-wing MPs, possibly a critical number, voted for Foot, not because they wanted to heal the wounds in the party but because, on the contrary, they wanted to open them up still further. Already determined to defect, they wanted to inflict the maximum possible damage on the party and also to increase the chances that a large number of other MPs would follow them. Some Labour loyalists believed at the time that a number of defectors had deliberately cast wrecking votes for Foot, and some further believed that such wrecking votes had been sufficiently numerous to defeat Healey and elect Foot. Healey refers to this possibility in his memoirs:

Though I believe most of the MPs who ultimately joined the SDP voted for me in the Leadership election, I am certain that several voted for Michael Foot in order to be able to justify their later defection; their few votes alone were sufficient to explain my defeat.[7]

What is the truth? Certainly many of those who later defected to the SDP were aware during the 1980 election that they might subsequently be accused of employing wrecking tactics; and so, in order to avoid any hint of suspicion or mis-understanding, many of them actually showed each other their ballot papers, with their 'X' firmly marked beside Healey's name. Bill Rodgers voted for Healey in both ballots. So did David Owen, the latter announcing that he, at least, was 'not about to play silly buggers'. Shirley Williams would certainly have voted for Healey if she had still been in the House. But some MPs who subsequently went over to the SDP did vote for Foot, knowing what they were doing and why they were doing it. One of them said frankly afterwards:

It was dirty politics. I admit it. I—and I reckon quite a few others—thought that Foot had to be elected in order to convince the waverers that the game was up and that we had no choice but to move. I was particularly concerned about Shirley: if Healey had won, I still think she wouldn't have come over.

This MP was not alone. But were there enough like him to have made the crucial difference? To find out, we approached all the living Labour MPs who defected to the SDP (Richard Crawshaw had died in the interim) and asked them, either orally or in writing, to tell us in confidence whom they had voted for in each of the two ballots in the 1980 election. Most of them replied. Most said they had voted for Healey in both ballots, and many were obviously surprised that we should even have asked the question. But five, whose names we cannot reveal, including the MP just quoted, acknowledged that they had voted for Foot, in the second ballot if not the first. One of them added: 'I voted for Foot because I thought he would make the worst leader for Labour, not only in a personal capacity, but also because he was nearest to the left.'

In other words, we know that enough of those who subsequently deserted Labour for the SDP voted for Foot to have produced a tie in the election. We suspect that at least one other did so. If he did, he would have provided the margin by which Foot won. If our findings are correct, Foot was indeed the left's candidate in the leadership election, but he was also the candidate of a crucial minority of the future SDP. He was the product—and Labour the victim—of what the French call *la politique du pire*, the politics of the worst.

Be that as it may, most Labour right-wingers—including the great majority of those who subsequently left the party—were appalled by Foot's victory. Foot favoured almost everything they opposed: unilateral nuclear disarmament, with-drawal from the Common Market, sweeping nationalization, import controls, the making of maximum concessions to the trade unions, the planning of every aspect of the economy except wages. Foot's election, moreover, meant that almost every bastion of power in the party had now fallen. The left had won on policy; it had won on the constitution; now it had won the leadership. The right had been totally routed—on top of which it now looked as though the whole party would be routed at the next general election. The full range of Foot's disabilities as a political leader had not yet emerged and were not to emerge for some months; but already it seemed certain that the new combination of left-wing policies and left-wing leadership would prove lethal in 1983 or 1984. Even if it did not and even if Labour somehow won, the resulting government would be a shambles. No single event did more to persuade right-wing MPs to quit the party than Foot's election, coming as it did on top of the multiple disasters of the Blackpool conference. It was, as one of them said, 'a thundering blow'.

Moreover, the consequences of Foot's election were compounded by the behaviour of Healey, who, following the election, meekly pledged his loyalty to Foot, accepted the deputy leadership of the party and showed no signs of believing that anything especially important had happened. Had Healey roared his defiance, had he pledged himself even at this late stage to put himself at the head of a right-wing counterattack, or even if he had shown a modicum of personal sympathy towards some of his right-wing colleagues, he would have made it all but impossible for them to desert the party—which, under those circumstances, would have been tantamount to deserting Healey personally. But as it was, Healey's actions—or, rather, his inactions—made the Gang of Three and the Jenkinsites feel that they had been still further betrayed and that there was now nothing to hope for from Healey's generation of Labour leaders. In the words of one MP:

So far as I was concerned, Healey didn't have to win, he just had to fight. Healey, as you know, likes to bluster and shout and bully people, but he's really just Ferdinand the Bull. He gets up and bellows once in a while, but most of the time he just sits there, sniffs flowers, drinks gin and tonic and listens to his records. He'll fight for himself if attacked—but fight for a cause or a principle? Never.

'Of course,' the same MP added, 'it might be different if Denis believed in something—anything. But he doesn't.' In this negative sense, Denis Healey should be regarded as one of the SDP's principal founding fathers.

Although the election of Foot came as a shock to most right-wing MPs, it did not immediately precipitate a split. Even now, most right-wingers were by no means ready to defect: they were not mentally prepared; they had not thought the problem through in either personal or political terms; they did not have an organization. Most were looking for almost any excuse to delay taking a final decision: perhaps Foot, whom most of them liked as a human being, would not turn out to be such a bad leader after all; perhaps the right would sweep the board in the coming shadow-cabinet elections; perhaps—and this was the straw at which they increasingly clutched—a majority of the unions could be got to support the principle of 'one member, one vote' at the forthcoming special conference. At the very least, the conference, scheduled for 24 January 1981 at the Wembley Conference Centre, would provide the clearest signal yet of the way in which the party was moving. If it accepted 'one member, one vote', fine. If, as was more probable, it established an electoral college and gave a majority of votes in the college to the unions and the constituency parties, then at least the unhappy right-wingers could console themselves with the thought that they had done their best.

Anguish—according to the dictionary, 'severe bodily or mental pain'—is not a word to be used lightly; but many on the right of the Labour party were undoubtedly in a state of genuine anguish during the eleven weeks between mid-November 1980 and late January 1981. They had no idea what was happening or what they should do. Many of them slept badly; many drank too much; many quarrelled with their wives; many suffered from strange psychosomatic illnesses; many became increasingly, and exasperatingly, irritable. Some of them cannot remember, do not want to remember, the details of what occurred during that period. Asked to retrace the sequence of events from Blackpool to Wembley as they affected him, one MP replied:

I find that the most difficult thing to do, because it was the most intense period. It was the most personally painful period. I was very confused about what I wanted and about what I thought was possible . . . There is a huge confusion in my mind except over one or two incidents . . . I had a great uncertainty over what to do.

The precise details of the post-election, pre-Wembley period are, therefore, hard to reconstruct: there are almost as many accounts as there are people—and in every account there are gaps.

In one sense, everyone now had no choice as an individual except to make up his or her own mind. 'Do I stay in the party and fight, or do I leave?' They had to answer to that question; no one else could answer it for them. But, in another sense, that was not the question. These were not so many Martin Luthers, isolated in monastic cells; they were politicians. What they did would inevitably depend on what others were going to do—or, more precisely, on what they thought others were going to do. For weeks, Shirley Williams wondered whether Bill Rodgers could bring himself to make the break, David Owen wondered about Shirley Williams' next move, Rodgers was anxious lest Owen should do something too precipitous, and so on. Other potential defectors, unsure themselves what to do, could only guess about the Gang of Three's intentions. Partly, all of this was a matter of calculation: a new party could succeed only if enough people, the right people, joined it. But it was also partly a matter of reassurance and moral support: one could only be sure oneself that one was doing the right thing if others were doing it too. The most private decisions were thus not taken privately; the uncertainties of each compounded—and were compounded by—the uncertainties of others. Misunderstandings were frequent, tempers were frayed, hard words were spoken. The fact that nevertheless the Gang of Three steadily gathered support during these eleven weeks is a measure of how completely many right-wing MPs had come to despair of their party.

Of the Gang of Three, David Owen was the one with the clearest notion of what he wanted. He wanted if possible to reassert the right's dominance in the Labour party. But he no longer believed that that was possible, so as a second best he half wanted and half expected to abandon Labour and form a new party. He was well aware, however, that the chances of the new party's succeeding depended largely on how many other Labour politicians, including the rest of the Gang of Three, could be persuaded to defect. And that, in the weeks immediately following the Blackpool conference, was not at all clear. Owen chose therefore to play a waiting game, combining greater strategic boldness than his colleagues with, if anything, even greater tactical caution. Rodgers and Williams feared that, because Owen was so angry and frustrated, he would do something rash; but he never did— at least not then.

In the midst of the leadership election, on 5 November 1980, the shadow cabinet met to discuss the line that the parliamentary party should take at the special conference on the proposed electoral college. Hitherto, the shadow cabinet and the PLP, while not declaring flatly that they would refuse to accept a leader elected by the electoral college, had nevertheless resisted the whole idea of the college. Hence the dismay in June when Callaghan had accepted the Bishops Stortford compromise.[8] The shadow cabinet and the PLP's resistance appeared to be backed by almost the entire right wing on the shadow cabinet, not just by Rodgers and Owen, but also by Roy Hattersley, Eric Varley, Gerald Kaufman and Roy Mason. Peter Shore took the same line. Now, however, Hattersley astonished his colleagues by submitting a paper proposing his own version of a constitutional compromise: an electoral college in which the PLP would have 55 per cent of the vote, with the rest going to affiliated organizations such as CLPs and trade unions on the basis of a postal ballot of their members. Six days later, on 11 November, at its first meeting under Foot's chairmanship, the shadow cabinet accepted the Hattersley compromise after a three-hour wrangle by 8 votes to 7. The next day a thinly attended meeting of the PLP also accepted the new proposal, by 68 votes to 59 (out of a total PLP membership of 268). Rodgers' and Owen's counter-proposal, for the leader to be elected by a ballot of all party members ('one member, one vote'), got nowhere.[9]

For Owen, the shadow cabinet's acceptance of the Hattersley compromise was the last straw. Not only did it, in his view, demonstrate Roy Hattersley's personal perfidy (the dissident right-wingers needed a hate-figure and Hattersley was well cast in the role), but it showed beyond any doubt that, when push came to shove, the right-wing majorities on the shadow cabinet and in the PLP were simply not prepared to stand up to the left-wing majorities on the NEC and in the party conference.[10] Rodgers, Owen and many right-wing backbenchers had hoped that the shadow cabinet and the PLP would be powerful collective weapons in their struggle against the left; now these weapons had broken in their hands. Owen's response was to decide not to stand for re-election to the shadow cabinet, and he so informed Foot on 21 November. At the same time he told his constituency Labour party in Plymouth Devonport that there were three points on which he believed there could be no further equivocation: commitment to the success of the mixed economy, commitment to a genuinely international socialism and commitment to representative democracy. 'I believe', he added, 'that there can be no further movement in the party away from these commitments and that, in fact, substantial ground has to be won back.'[11] He wanted the freedom of the back benches in order to be able to carry on his anti-left campaign.

Convinced that future success lay, if anywhere, in numbers, Owen had meanwhile begun to gather around him a group of sympathizers in the House of Commons. The 'ticket of admission' was not a desire to leave the Labour party, let alone a commitment to leaving it, but merely a willingness to contemplate the possibility of leaving it at some indefinite time in the future—a willingness 'to think the unthinkable'. Before anyone new was admitted to the group, all the existing members had to give their consent. Security was tight, and even some potential sympathizers had only a vague idea that 'something was going on'. Early recruits included most of the Jenkinsite MPs—Horam, Maclennan, Bradley, Ellis and Wrigglesworth—and also Mike Thomas, the outspoken Newcastle member who was carrying on an increasingly personal campaign for 'one member, one vote' in the party in the country.[12] John Cartwright, formerly a member of the National Executive, joined later, as did John Roper, the strongly pro-European MP for Farnworth in Lancashire. Roper remembers that the decisive day for him was 18 December. The Owen group was due to meet that day. So was another little group that Roy Hattersley was putting together. Roper had invitations to go to both. He went to Owen's. He then tried, but failed, to recruit Phillip Whitehead, the MP for Derby North (Whitehead subsequently realizing that he had been 'softened up' by Roper). Edward Lyons, the MP for Bradford West, later a founder SDP member, never joined the group; he became aware later that he had been sounded out, but his responses must not have been enthusiastic enough. Some known sympathizers, notably Neville Sandelson, were deliberately omitted because they were thought to be too leaky. There was, in addition, another absentee of whom everyone was acutely conscious: Bill Rodgers.

Because his Labour roots were so much deeper than Owen's and because his closest friends in the party included many who were determined to stay on and fight whatever happened, Rodgers was far more torn than Owen. He had fired the first shot in the war against the left with his Abertillery speech, but he was far less clear than Owen what he wanted the outcome to be. More than either Owen or Williams, Rodgers clung to the hope that Foot would prove a tolerable leader and that in the future, as so often in the past, he would stick up for the rights of Labour members of parliament. Rodgers was also reluctant to do anything that would damage either the party or the right-wingers' cause within it. He therefore reluctantly decided to stand for re-election to the shadow cabinet, though Owen had taken it for granted that he would not and was dismayed when he did. It was a measure of the right's continuing numerical strength in the parliamentary party that, despite the election of Foot and his own increasing outspokenness, Rodgers easily held his place in the shadow cabinet, finishing joint eighth out of twelve places with 116 votes (compared with Tony Benn's 88).[13]

But what happened next further alienated Rodgers from both the Labour party and Foot. Rodgers realized that, given his hostility to unilateral disarmament, the new leader was unlikely to keep him as the party's defence spokesman; but, given his ministerial experience and his status as one of the principal right-wingers in the House of Commons, he presumed that Foot would offer him a senior post, one in keeping with his well-known fields of interest and expertise—if not quite the shadow chancellorship, which was too much to hope for, then perhaps trade, industry or energy. Instead Foot, apparently not recognizing either the need to secure his own power base in the party or the imminent danger to Labour's unity, offered him a series of posts—health detached from social security, social security detached from health or Northern Ireland—that the younger man thought were either beneath his dignity or else too far removed from his own fields of interest. After a series of increasingly embarrassing meetings, non-meetings and phone calls, Rodgers concluded that Foot did not take him seriously, that he did not take the forces that he represented in the party seriously and that he would, therefore, be best advised not to accept any shadow portfolio but, instead, while remaining a member of the shadow cabinet, to reserve to himself the right to speak on any topic he deemed important. Rodgers thus found himself accepting collective responsibility and also not accepting it at the same time, while Foot found himself with a totally disaffected colleague. His own position apart, Rodgers concluded that Foot as a politician and party leader was hopelessly inept and unprofessional (a conclusion that many others were soon to reach on their own).[14]

While Owen was deciding that he would not stand for the shadow cabinet, and Rodgers was simultaneously deciding that he would, Shirley Williams, no longer an MP and preoccupied with completing a book she had been working on for some time, was contemplating her future. Like Rodgers, her roots in the party went deep; like Owen, she increasingly believed that the right's cause in the party was hopeless and that there would soon be no alternative but to get out. But, unlike both Rodgers and Owen, Williams was not only not an MP; she was not totally committed to the idea of standing for parliament again: she did not altogether like the House of Commons, especially if it meant making futile speeches in opposition instead of actually accomplishing something as a minister. For her, therefore, the choice was more complicated than for Rodgers or Owen. For them, it was stay in the Labour party or found a new party; for her, it was stay in the Labour party, help found a new party or leave politics altogether.

One decision forced itself on her very quickly after Blackpool. By October–November 1980 the 1979 election had been fought well over a year before and the Hertford and Stevenage CLP was keen to get on with the business of readopting her as its parliamentary candidate. The local party was also under some pressure from Walworth Road to decide by the end of the year who its candidate was going to be. Williams decided, reluctantly and to the dismay of her local supporters, that, whoever the candidate might be, it was not going to be her. 'I have not changed,' she told a meeting in Stevenage on 28 November, 'but the party has.' She went on, in the words of *The Times*' report:

[The party] now wants withdrawal from the EEC, without consulting the people through a referendum . . . Conference's defence resolutions were absurd . . . [On] incomes policy the conference faced both ways; on social policy it did not come to grips with priorities; on the Third World the conference had little to say.

Added to [which] is the threat to representative democracy implicit in the mandatory reselection of Labour MPs, in the proposal to impose control by local parties over elected Labour groups . . . and in the attempt to create an electoral college to elect the Labour leader, and potential prime minister, of which the trade union block vote would be a part— a block vote cast on behalf of some who are neither members nor supporters of our party, but may be Conservatives, Liberals or Communists.

She said she could not be a Labour candidate at present because she could not 'honestly expound and defend' the policies agreed at the October conference; she did not want to mislead people into thinking that she endorsed or acquiesced in those policies. She added, in a carefully worded phrase, 'There is no other party in Britain today I could contemplate joining.'[15] At a Fabian meeting the next day she repeated that she was not interested in joining some centrist grouping made up of 'rag, tag and bobtails from the Liberals and the Tories alongside ex-Labour people'.[16] For the time being, however, she was ready to remain a member of Labour's NEC. Although no longer prepared to fight under Labour's new banner, she would go on fighting to change the banner.

Thus, at the beginning of December 1980 the Gang of Three were in considerable disarray. Rodgers had stood for the shadow cabinet; Owen had not; Williams had declined to stand as a Labour parliamentary candidate but remained, somewhat incongruously, a member of the National Executive (she had promised Tom Bradley that she would not leave him to fight on alone). Similar tactical disagreements and uncertainties likewise manifested themselves when Foot came to choose the other members of his front-bench team. John Horam and Ian Wrigglesworth said they did not want to be considered for appointment, but Robert Maclennan, one of the earliest of the potential defectors from the party, accepted an offer to serve as one of Healey's foreign-affairs team. The tactical disagreements among the Gang of Three and their supporters were seized on by hostile commentators. Bernard Levin in *The Times*, under the heading 'The gang is breaking up early for Christmas', enjoyed himself hugely at their expense:

A week to two ago I was drawing attention to the fact that the Gang of Three had become two Gangs, of Two (Mr Rodgers and Dr Owen) and One (Mrs Williams) respectively. Since then there has come news to make it clear that further amoebic fission has taken place, so that the two Gangs have now become three, each consisting of a membership of one. Perhaps, indeed, the process of reproduction by division has not yet run its course; in time, it may be, an arm will fall off Dr Owen, one of Mrs Williams's legs will become detached, and Mr Rodgers will lose his head, thus doubling the total number of Gangs, and, in the end, as the fragmentation continues by geometric progression, the count will be so large that the very streets will become impassable for the clutter.

Levin predicted that, if the time for a split ever came, precious few would be found to desert the Labour party.[17]

In fact, however, Williams and Rodgers were both coming round to Owen's view: that they had no alternative but to break with Labour and set up in business on their own. Events in the outside world played some part; a motion by Mike Thomas that the parliamentary party should decline to accept as legitimate any version of the electoral college that did not provide for postal ballots was again defeated, and David Steel again renewed his invitation to Labour dissidents to form their own grouping and seek an alliance with the Liberals.[18] But the hardening of Williams' and Rodgers' positions that took place from early December onwards was largely the result of developments in their own thinking, developments that were also taking place in the minds of other right-wing MPs.

In Williams' case, she was depressed by a long series of conversations that she had had with Healey and Foot, some before the leadership election and some afterwards, when it was already clear that she might leave the party. They had both urged her not to go, pointing out the damage that this would do to the party and to the anti-Conservative forces in the country generally, and making the obvious point that, if she remained loyal to the Labour party, she could look forward to holding high office whenever it returned to power. But they had failed completely, in her view, to address themselves to the real issues of internal party democracy and Labour's credibility as an alternative government. It seemed to her that Foot and Healey simply did not want to address these issues; and the same seemed to be true not just on the NEC, where she was by now in a permanent minority, but across much of the party's moderate wing. She was not surprised, but she was very depressed, by the failure of men like Hattersley and Varley to stand up and fight.

She was also positively frightened by the power that Marxist extremists were amassing in the party. She was, she said, constantly reminded of a book she had read, *The Nazi Seizure of Power*, which described how the Nazi minority in a small German town had been able to gain total control of the town largely as the result of its opponents' feebleness and short-sightedness.[19] She increasingly felt that a class-based Labour party could no longer accurately reflect the interests of a more and more classless society and that it would be unforgivable to leave the electorate without any alternative except that between dogmatic right-wing Thatcherism and dogmatic left-wing Marxism. More than anything, Williams felt that, after Blackpool and the election of Foot, the right's cause in the Labour party had become hopeless. If the Gang of Three and their supporters stayed, they would accomplish nothing and merely provide the far left with what amounted to an electoral fig-leaf. If, on the contrary, they left and started a new party, such a party might succeed; even if it did not, the breakout might have the effect of bringing

Labour back to its senses. Over the 1980 Christmas holiday Williams had still not finally made up her mind, and she refused adamantly to be rushed. But she was increasingly inclined to abandon the Labour party—though it felt much more as though Labour were abandoning her—and to embark on something new. Thoughts of leaving politics altogether gradually subsided.

The way Williams' mind was moving mattered to more people than just herself. She was the right's conscience. If she left, others would feel they could leave too. If, on the other hand, they left while she stayed, they would feel guilty and wonder whether they had done something wrong. Some in the party felt that they almost needed Williams' benediction. Equally important, politicians in all parts of the party were conscious that Williams was widely loved and respected in the country and that her defection—far more than Owen's or Rodgers'—would damage Labour and promote a new party's prospects. Hence Healey's and Foot's efforts to persuade her to stay. Hence, too, the reluctance of many people to make their move until she had made hers. She was, in the minds of many, 'the key personality': 'she made the SDP possible.'

No one was monitoring the way that Williams' mind was moving more closely than her old friend Bill Rodgers. He was even more torn than she was. Indeed, afflicted with back trouble for several weeks in January 1981, Rodgers appeared to his friends to be stretched, almost literally, on a rack. His whole life had been in the Labour party. Now he was being urged—was urging himself—to turn his back on it. Over Christmas he had lunch with Roy Jenkins and told him that he was not proposing at the moment to leave. He was not saying that he would never do so, only that he had not reached the point at which he could.

However [he said later] I'd got this very bad back, and I went to bed and lay in bed and couldn't move. I lay on my back and read Bernard Crick's *George Orwell*, and in the course of lying on my back and reading *Orwell* and reflecting on my lifetime I decided to leave the Labour party. There were two influences. One was Orwell, not because he was an awkward, angular, difficult character, but because he believed in a lot of the things I believed in: the importance of freedom, the nature of totalitarianism, whether left or right. The other was my father. He's been dead for quite a long time, but he was always true to himself, and when I went into the House I remember him saying something about preferring to see me stay on the back benches rather than abandon the things that matter to me.

Those two things, and I simply thought, 'I've had twenty years in the House of Commons. I've done a lot of things I've enjoyed doing. Am I just going to live in the House of Commons and politics for the next ten to fifteen years having to support what I believe to be wrong—corrupt—and being increasingly unhappy?' And I said, 'No, I'm not.'

That was when I crossed the river. Before that, I hadn't made up my mind not to cross it. I simply found I couldn't. I think what happened was that I walked up to the river and paced up and down the muddy bank and just couldn't quite see my way to crossing. Then I just lay on my back and suddenly said, 'What's the point?—I'm going to do it.' And I rang up Roy and Shirley and said, 'Shirley, I've made up my mind. I'm coming.' And then everything was settled.

Other defectors who reached their moment of decision at about the same time give strikingly similar accounts. Two themes predominate. One is the sense in late 1980 and early 1981 that, for them, the game in the Labour party was up, that there was simply no point in soldiering on. One of the founders of CLV said that he had once had a 'five-year battle plan'. The first year would be spent recapturing conference, the NEC and so on; the next two years would be spent reversing the various constitutional and policy changes; the final year or two would be spent relaunching the party. 'But then', he said, 'I realized that it was no good, that the first phase alone was going to take years. We just didn't have the time.' Another leading figure in CLV reached the same conclusion:

Roy Hattersley, I remember, invited me to Gayfere Street to discuss 'Whither the party?', and he claimed to be surprised when I told him there was probably going to be a breakaway. 'Talk me out of it,' I said. All Roy could say was, 'We will win.' I replied, 'Where have you been all this time?' All this time I could feel myself sliding out of the party. I was sleeping badly. Shirley kept saying, 'Do you really think the party can be saved?' That was the one that always sunk me.

The second theme, common to almost all of them, was the sense that they could no longer live with themselves, that if they stayed in the party they were going to become increasingly unhappy. 'I was tired of living a lie,' a working-class MP said; 'I couldn't go on week after week defending the indefensible.' 'I was at the end of my tether,' another remembered; 'I just didn't want to go on seeming to stand for policies that I didn't believe in—and that I actually didn't think were going to be implemented.' The account given by an older northern MP shortly after he defected was strikingly similar:

I enjoy being an MP. I like being in parliament and I like serving my constituents, so if you ask me, 'Am I afraid of losing my seat?', the answer is, 'Yes.' But the choice in the end was between ten years in which I kept my head down and crept into the division lobbies but didn't really respect myself and three glorious years—short, maybe, but glorious. The fact is that latterly I was having the greatest difficulty making any kind of pro-Labour speech.

Probably more than any other single factor, it was the sense of living a lie—and of knowing that, if one remained in the Labour party, one would have to go on living the same lie for many years to come—that in the end drove Shirley Williams and twenty-seven Labour members of parliament out of the Labour party and into the SDP.

5
. . . .
Born in Despair

The Gang of Three and their supporters felt they were being driven out of the party; but, as we saw in the last chapter, they were anxious, before making their final move, to make sure that they could take as many Labour MPs as possible with them. For obvious reasons, they were also anxious to find out what a new party's electoral prospects might be like. Would a breakaway group of the kind they were envisaging be committing electoral suicide? Or would it have some chance, however slight, of getting off the ground and winning at least a degree of electoral support?

Early in December 1980, Shirley Williams invited two University of Essex professors, Ivor Crewe and Anthony King, to come to her London flat one evening to discuss a new party's electoral prospects with an unidentified group of Labour MPs. Both professors were friends of hers and both were thought to be know-ledgeable about electoral matters. Those present turned out to comprise Shirley Williams herself, Bill Rodgers, David Owen, John Horam, Mike Thomas, John Roper, Ian Wrigglesworth and one of the Jenkinsites who was not an MP, Matthew Oakeshott. The occasion was oddly academic in tone. Crewe and King arrived carrying a large flip-chart, and they subsequently circulated a detailed memor-andum. Their message was that a new centre-left party would indeed have a chance. On the one hand, the Conservative and Labour parties still had—and would continue to have—large blocks of committed supporters, and the electoral system would of course make it difficult for any new party to break through; but, on the other hand, more voters were up for grabs than ever before, support for much of Labour's ideology and many of its policies was declining fast, and declared support in the opinion polls for a new centre party was rising. The Conservatives were likely to be deeply unpopular by 1983 or 1984, and a new party with Roy Jenkins and Shirley Williams among its leaders would have considerable electoral appeal.

Crewe and King took it for granted that any new party would have to form some kind of alliance with the Liberals: there was simply not enough electoral room to accommodate both the Liberals and a new party. While the two were holding forth, Shirley Williams' daughter, Rebecca, asked whether she could come into the room: she said she wanted to see history in the making. But, as they left, one of the MPs said mock-caustically, 'It's all very well for you academics to pontificate: I've got my seat to think about.' It was clear that most of the MPs present were still hesitating and were far from being committed to the new venture.

As in the twelve months following the general election of 1979, so in the summer, autumn and early winter of 1980, relations between the Gang of Three and Roy Jenkins remained virtually non-existent. The occasional lunch, the occasional phone call, were all they amounted to. Owen, Williams and Rodgers were too preoccupied with developments in the Labour party to have the time—even if they had had the inclination—to plot high strategy with Jenkins, who was still physically remote in his Brussels office. But towards the end of 1980, as the special Labour party conference and Jenkins' return from Brussels approached, it was clear to both sides that lines of communication had to be established. Jenkins needed the Gang of Three and as many other defectors from the Labour party as he could get. The Gang of Three for their part thought Jenkins would probably be an asset to the new party, and anyway he was available and had long since made his intentions known: it was obvious that, if there were going to be a new party, Jenkins would be a part of it. Beginning in late November 1980, the two hitherto-separate political streams represented by the Gang of Three and the Jenkinsites began to flow together to form a considerably larger river.

It was Owen who, although not personally close to Jenkins, knew that Jenkins could not be ignored. He took the initiative, inviting himself to lunch at the Jenkinses at East Hendred on 29 November. Jenkins recorded the occasion in his diary:

David Owens with their children came to a long lunch . . . He told me firmly, for the first time, that he was prepared to join a new party, and that he thought that Shirley would come too, though he was curiously less sure about Bill. He was also, although agreeable in other ways, very firmly geared up to tell me that he thought that Shirley should be leader; they very much wanted me to play a full part in it, but that it was his view that Shirley should be leader because of her great popularity, etc. And it was made clear that it was his view to be not a centre party but a 'Socialist International' party, and I was joining them rather than vice versa.

We will see how that works out, but at any rate it is a great advance which no one would have thought possible some time ago. There will now be a real break in the parliamentary party, and I may well get, at the end of the day, much more the sort of party I want than the sort of ex-Labour Party that for the moment he wants. But we will see . . .[1]

Owen in his memoirs, published eight years later, describes the same lunch; and, although the two men's accounts are broadly in agreement, there is one important difference of emphasis between them. Jenkins in the diary extract just quoted makes no mention of the principle of 'one member, one vote' as one of the key principles on which the new party would need to be founded; but, in his account of the lunch, Owen writes of little else:

Before I went I discussed the visit with other MPs. In our debates over how we should try to launch the party, we had agreed that there would have to be a form of collective leadership for the period during which the party would be built up and its democratic origins established. We were all very concerned about how the leader of a party should be elected, because this was the question at issue dominating the running battle currently going on in the Parliamentary Party. We were all committed to one-member one-vote. . . . We were suspicious that Roy . . . would prefer to keep the old system of choice by members of parliament only. So I, and some other MPs, were very interested in finding out what was Roy's view on one-member one-vote. At that meeting with him at lunch—with Debbie present—I asked him. His answer was clear. In the past he had always favoured selection by the Parliamentary Party, but he now thought that time had moved, and that the wider franchise should be accepted, and that it would be here to stay. So he would accept that what we were campaigning for inside the Labour Party—one-member one-vote—should apply to a new party. This was, I thought, agreed, therefore, and was very, very important, because I—and others—had been suspicious of his views and to be frank we wanted to be sure that Shirley and nobody else was likely to be leader of a new party . . . She had the charisma and she had the public appeal. I didn't think Roy would be the ideal leader of the party. I wanted therefore to have a leadership election system whereby he would not become leader automatically, as given the make-up of the MPs who were likely to create the new party, he otherwise would.

From that moment on the lunch went very well, our old friendliness revived in a relaxed atmosphere . . . Effectively the Gang of Four came into existence at that moment. From then on, when Roy was in Britain, he came to our meetings.[2]

No one who was not present can be sure what was said on 29 November 1980, but it is highly unlikely that Owen did not raise the issue of 'one member, one vote', and he certainly came away with the impression both that he had indeed raised it and that Jenkins had acceded to it. Jenkins for his part did not attach the same importance to the principle as Owen and his little group of MPs did, and it may be that he appeared to assent to what Owen was saying while keeping his mental reservations—which he undoubtedly had—largely to himself. Such misunderstandings, if there was a misunderstanding on that occasion, were to be a recurrent feature of the SDP's history.[3]

Whatever was said at East Hendred that day, Owen was now confident that Jenkins and the Gang of Three could reach an accommodation, and he was also confident that Jenkins acknowledged that, if there were to be a new party, it would be founded on the principle of 'one member, one vote'. Jenkins meanwhile still saw himself as the one person, apart possibly from Owen, who had definitely made up his mind what he was going to do and as a man therefore who was forced to bide his time while others like Rodgers and Williams came round to his point of view. One Jenkinsite at the time likened him to a French fisherman, sitting on the bank of a river, his line in the water, waiting patiently to catch his fish. This sense, that Jenkins was the active participant while the others were merely waiting passively to be fitted into his master plan, was natural, but it was later to cause great irritation. Owen was already referring to Jenkins attending '*our* meetings'.

In his public statements during these weeks Jenkins was concerned to make the coming-together of him and the Gang of Three as easy as possible. Williams' phrase about a centre party having no roots, principles or philosophy was being quoted endlessly, so when Jenkins was interviewed on television in mid-December, while still in Brussels, he went out of his way to deny that he had ever advocated forming a centre party: 'What I want to see is a strengthening of the moderate left forces, a radical centre.' He added that he had the greatest respect for Williams, shared her political outlook and would be glad to work with her again.[4] In a radio interview in mid-January, after returning from his Community post, he was at pains to criticize Margaret Thatcher's economic policies as well as Labour's slide to the left.[5] He was careful in everything he said not to appear to be claiming the leadership of any new party. He spoke only of 'working with those I respect and admire in politics'.[6] There was no hint of a Jenkinsite takeover.

It is worth noting that until late November 1980 press comment on the possibility of a Labour split was extremely muted. The Gang of Three's speeches and statements were duly reported, and Sunday columnists with nothing better to write about speculated in a leisurely way about the Gang's ultimate intentions. But almost no one believed that anything would really happen: Williams and Rodgers were well-known Labour loyalists, and over the years there had been endless talk of splits in the Labour party, but none of them had ever come to anything. But towards the end of November, following Williams' announcement that she would not be standing again as a Labour candidate, lobby correspondents and columnists suddenly realized that something important was happening and that a breakaway party might indeed be established. Hugo Young wrote in the *Sunday Times*: 'A new party is in the making before our very eyes.'[7] And Peter Jenkins a few weeks later wrote a column in the *Guardian* that was to prove remarkably prescient. Jenkins maintained that a breakaway from Labour had moved from being a mere possibility to being a probability and predicted that Roy Jenkins and the Gang of Three would have no difficulty in coming together. Their problems, he believed, would lie in other directions: in the discrediting of social-democratic ideas by the experience of the Wilson and Callaghan governments and also in the extraordinary difficulty of mobilizing enough disaffected voters for long enough to dislodge one or other of the established parties. Describing the setting-up of any new party as 'a desperate venture', he concluded that those about to embark on it 'had better reckon with reality':

The Labour party *is* probably in decline and in the course of time there will probably be some kind of realignment in the centre-left. But it could take a long while, perhaps extend over two or three elections; meanwhile promising careers will be wasted in the wilderness, the Conservatives will probably be kept in power . . . and many failures may precede eventual success. Those who set out had better be prepared for a long haul into the unknown.[8]

Peter Jenkins was right, but in the euphoria that followed the SDP's launch his words of caution tended to be forgotten.

The increased press interest in Roy Jenkins and the Gang of Three was in itself important because it suddenly forced the pace of events. The potential defectors were no longer afforded the luxury of procrastination. As each new moment of crisis arrived, the press wanted to know precisely what the Gang of Three and their supporters in the Labour party were going to do. If they acted, well and good. If they did not, that in itself would be interpreted as action of a sort. Either way, the eyes of the political world were now on the Labour dissidents in a way they had not been before. Expectations built up rapidly, and some of them, at least, had to be fulfilled: otherwise the Gang of Three would lose credibility and their followers would lose heart. Specifically, everyone now took it for granted that the Gang would have to take some action—even if it meant deciding to take no action— immediately following the special Labour party conference in January, especially if, as seemed probable, the conference voted to confirm the creation of an electoral college and also voted not to introduce either 'one member, one vote' throughout the party or postal ballots within the unions and CLPs. Sometime over the 1980 Christmas break, 24 January 1981 ceased to be any date and became the critical date. An opinion poll at about this time also suggested that, if Jenkins and the Gang of Three were going to act at all, they should be getting on with it: it showed a social-democratic–Liberal alliance leading both of the other parties.[9]

Although Roy Jenkins as president of the European Commission still had a few engagements to fulfil, including attendance at Ronald Reagan's inauguration in Washington, the first fortnight of January 1981 saw the final transformation of the Gang of Three into the Gang of Four. Jenkins was committed to a new party. Owen was equally committed (unless the Wembley conference astounded everybody by going for 'one member, one vote' or something like it). Williams had made her final decision, though she was still refusing to be pressured into declaring herself in public till she was absolutely ready. Rodgers had told her he was coming. The four were now in touch with each other continually, either face-to-face or through emissaries; and at a meeting on 14 January, ten days before the conference, they agreed on a detailed plan of action. A joint statement of principles would be issued the day after Wembley, and a Council for Social Democracy would be set up which Labour MPs would be invited to join. The council would function within the Labour party for the time being, but it was clear that it was meant to form the nucleus of a new party when the time came.

When would the time come? David Steel from outside was pressing the Gang of Four to make the break by Easter—otherwise he would find it hard to prevent local Liberal associations from adopting parliamentary candidates in seats that the

Source: Owen, *Personally Speaking*, 172

Sawing off the branch on which they sat

new party might want to fight—but David Owen, cautious as ever, insisted that a new party organization would take months to establish and that perhaps they should not finally commit themselves to quitting the party till the autumn. Shirley Williams, too, was inclined to favour delay, hoping (vainly as it turned out) that a few moderate unions like the electricians and her own union, APEX, might be persuaded to support the new party.

Also on 14 January a valedictory meeting of the Manifesto Group was held at the House of Commons. Some of those present knew they were leaving; others knew they would be staying. All knew that the group had failed in its original purposes. Ian Wrigglesworth and Mike Thomas were reproached for their unwillingness to fight on; Roy Hattersley and Giles Radice were reproached for not having fought hard enough in the first place. But the atmosphere was more sad than rancorous. David Owen appealed for tolerance. 'We may need each other again', he said, 'in a few years' time.'[10] It was a phrase he was to use years later in a different context.

The Gang of Four were due to meet again on Sunday, 18 January, at East Hendred, Roy Jenkins' house in Oxfordshire. The meeting was supposed to be private, but that morning Shirley Williams, attending an Anglo-American conference at Ditchley Park a few miles away, opened the *Observer* to find on the front page a picture of Jenkins standing in front of his house looking rather like the lord of a large manor; and underneath the picture was a story that began, 'Mr Roy Jenkins has asked Mrs Shirley Williams, Dr David Owen and Mr William Rodgers to a summit meeting at his Oxfordshire home today to discuss the prospects for a new Social Democratic party.'[11] Williams was furious: the meeting was supposed to be private, yet here it was all over the front page—and Jenkins must either have been responsible for the leak or, at the very least, have knowingly connived at it. The *Observer* story, moreover, left the reader with the distinct impression that Jenkins had graciously invited the Gang of Three to *his* house to assist him in forming *his* party. Williams was damned if she was going to be bounced in this fashion into declaring publicly that she was leaving the Labour party. She was also damned if, after all the Gang of Three had been through, Jenkins was going to be allowed to create the impression that the new party was his personal property and that the three were merely his associates—or possibly subordinates.

Beside herself with anger, Williams phoned Jenkins at East Hendred to say that, so far as she was concerned, the meeting was off. Several phone calls later, Jenkins succeeded in persuading her to join him and the others, but not at East Hendred, instead at Bill Rodgers' house in north London. Only partially mollified, Williams accepted the arrangement—only to have her anger redoubled when, arriving at the Rodgers' house in Patshull Road, she found the street outside thronging with journalists, photographers and TV camera crews. As she walked from her car to the house, she tried, unsuccessfully, to shield her face from the intruding lenses. Inside, her anger took a long time to subside, and she only allowed the business part of the meeting to begin after she had extracted a half-apology from Jenkins for the day's excitements. 'I am sorry', Jenkins is said to have muttered, 'that this great enterprise of ours is starting up in the same spirit as the worst of the Wilson cabinets.'[12] Fortunately for the enterprise, once the four got down to business—working on two drafts of their proposed joint statement, one by Jenkins, one by Williams—they found that agreement came easily. They decided to meet again at David Owen's house on the following Sunday, after the outcome of the Wembley conference was known. There was nevertheless a permanent casualty of the row: Williams never entirely trusted Jenkins or the members of his entourage again.

The day before the Wembley conference there was yet another row, again at Bill Rodgers' house but this time with a different cast. Three of Rodgers' younger friends in the parliamentary party, Giles Radice, Ken Weetch and George Robertson, had asked to see him to find out whether, even at this late stage, they could find some way of preventing the party from splitting. But Rodgers was, if anything, even angrier with them than Shirley Williams had been with Jenkins. His visitors begged him not to desert the party, not to desert his friends, above all not to take a step that might allow the Tories to remain in power for a generation. But Rodgers, showing the effects of weeks of mental and physical strain, completely lost his temper, accusing Radice, in particular, of being one of those tedious middle-class socialists who always feel guilty about the working classes. 'It's all very well for you,' said Rodgers, pointing a finger at Radice: 'you're a rich man and a public school boy.' Weetch, who had been Rodgers' PPS at the Department of Transport, put his face in his hands and said sadly, 'I can't believe this is happening.'

On 24 January, Jenkins watched the special party conference on television; Williams, still a member of the National Executive, sat on the platform; Owen and Rodgers, as Labour MPs and therefore *ex officio* members of the conference, roamed the body of the hall. By that morning it was clear that the device of an electoral college for the election of the party's leader and deputy leader would be confirmed, and the only doubts concerned the detailed composition of the college. The Wembley atmosphere was not quite as sour as that at Blackpool or Brighton. Owen's plea for 'one member, one vote' was listened to in relative silence, punctuated only by a few jeers; but a rank-and-file delegate was yelled at and booed when he declared from the rostrum: 'This is a deeply corrupt assembly. It's not only deeply corrupt, but also deeply intolerant.'[13] Foot as leader of the party pleaded with the conference to give members of parliament half the vote in the electoral college, while the NEC recommended a straight three-way split, with the PLP, the unions and the constituencies having one-third of the vote each.

It was generally assumed that the NEC's proposed solution would be adopted; but instead, when the crucial votes were taken, a motion was carried by 3,375,000 votes to 2,865,000, giving the trade unions 40 per cent of the vote in the electoral college and MPs and the constituency parties only 30 per cent each. There were gasps of astonishment when the result was read out. Several of the biggest unions had clearly used their bloc votes, not merely to defy Foot and the NEC, but to secure for themselves a larger say than anyone had ever imagined possible in the election of future Labour leaders. The unions were displaying their power and, at the same time, increasing it substantially. Rodgers, Owen and Williams—watched by the television cameras—showed no outward signs of emotion as the result was declared. But inwardly they were delighted. Their claims about the left's growing power in the party were now seen to be fully vindicated; the cause of the right appeared even more hopeless than before; and a number of big unions had shown that they were ready to use their power blatantly in the left's interests.[14] The events at Wembley were bound to do Labour the maximum amount of damage. More important, the breakaway would now be widely seen as inevitable and justified— and would attract additional support. Williams slipped off the platform shortly before the ritual singing of 'The Red Flag', commenting that 'Four trade union barons in a smoke-filled room [was] no way to elect a prime minister'. Owen called the vote 'a disaster'. To Tony Benn, however, the Wembley decisions were 'marvellous', and he called for further constitutional changes to bring the parliamentary party under even stricter rank-and-file control.[15]

That evening at Bill Rodgers' house, and the next morning at David Owen's in Limehouse, the Gang of Four and their advisers—John Lyttle for Williams, Alec McGivan for Owen, Matthew Oakeshott for Jenkins and Roger Liddle for

Rodgers—put the finishing touches to the joint statement that they had agreed on earlier. Afterwards they handed it out to newsmen and posed for photographers in the bleak East End street outside Owen's front door. Williams insisted on changing her blouse; Rodgers insisted on *not* changing his battered old pullover and trousers. The photographs and news of the group's imminent defection from the Labour party were on the front page of every newspaper on 26 January, and that day nine Labour MPs, in addition to Owen and Rodgers, declared their support for the Council for Social Democracy. Eight of the nine were expected: Bradley, Ellis, Horam, Maclennan, Roper, Sandelson, Thomas and Wrigglesworth. The ninth, Richard Crawshaw, had not so far been publicly identified with Jenkins or the Gang of Three, and the presence of his name came as something of a surprise to journalists.

The joint statement setting up the Council for Social Democracy—dubbed by John Lyttle 'the Limehouse Declaration'—consisted largely of a restatement of the Gang of Four's well-known political positions. Large parts of it were concerned with policy. The declaration spoke of reversing Britain's economic decline, of creating 'an open, classless and more equal society' and of the need for Britain 'to recover its self-confidence and be outward-looking rather than isolationist, xenophobic or neutralist'. Its section on the economy amounted to a call for a more humane capitalism, with the market economy's benefits to be diffused more widely:

We want more, not less, radical change in our society, but with a greater stability of direction.

Our economy needs a healthy public sector and a healthy private sector without frequent frontier changes.

We want to eliminate poverty and promote greater equality without stifling enterprise or imposing bureaucracy from the centre. We need the innovating strength of a competitive economy with a fair distribution of rewards.

We favour competitive public enterprise, cooperative ventures and profit-sharing.

There must be more decentralization of decision-making in industry and government, together with an effective and practical system of democracy at work.

The document's approach, broadly, was that of the Social Democrats in West Germany, part of Owen's 'Socialist International'.

But it was the more narrowly political passages in the document that attracted the greatest attention. Shirley Williams' objections to a centre party were laid to rest in a carefully phrased sentence: 'We do not believe in the politics of an inert centre purely representing the lowest common denominator between two extremes.' She and the other signatories declared that, in establishing the Council of Social Democracy, their intention was 'to rally all those who are committed to the values, principles and policies of social democracy'. Some would previously have been active in the Labour party; some would not:

We do not believe the fight for the ideals we share and for the recovery of our country should be limited only to politicians. It will need the support of men and women in all parts of our society. The council will represent a coming together of several streams: politicians who recognize that the drift towards extremism in the Labour party is not compatible with the democratic traditions of the party they joined, and those from outside politics who believe that the country cannot be saved without changing the sterile and rigid framework into which the British political system has increasingly fallen in the last two decades.

The document concluded with its only rhetorical flourish:

We recognize that for those people who have given much of their lives to the Labour party the choice that lies ahead will be deeply painful. But we believe that the need for a realignment of British politics must now be faced.[16]

The word 'realignment'—a word that the Liberals had long been using—had been inserted in an early version of the document, then taken out, then inserted again. Its presence meant that the four were now irrevocably committed to forming a new party. Wembley had finally resolved any lingering doubts in Williams' mind.

The next few weeks, between the Limehouse Declaration in January and the launching of the SDP in late March, seemed to those involved to be both tumultuous and glorious. They provided the Gang of Four and most of their supporters, hitherto so fearful and hesitant, with the time of their lives. The sense of release was tremendous, the pace of events exhilarating. Indeed the rush of events was such that the new party's founders felt more like surfboarders borne along by events than sea captains calmly charting a long voyage. Those in at the beginning of the SDP remember the time leading up to the new party's launch with unaffected nostalgia.

For one thing, the initial response of the general public far exceeded anything that the Gang of Four had anticipated. A full-page advertisement in the *Guardian* on 5 February, a fortnight after the special conference, elicited 25,000 letters of support and more than £70,000 in cash. At the time of the actual launch in March, letters were still arriving at the rate of about 300 a day and each post brought another £1,000 in donations.[17] Shirley Williams opened the door of her flat one morning to find that the postman had left, not just the usual handful of letters and bills, but several whole mail bags.

The *Guardian* advertisement, which reprinted the Limehouse Declaration in full, was also important in giving an indication of the breadth of support that the new party might attract. The advertisement's 100 signatories included three former Labour cabinet ministers in addition to the Gang of Four—Edmund Dell, Lord Diamond and Lord George-Brown—and six other former ministers—Kenneth Robinson, Dick Taverne, Evan Luard, Austin Albu, Lord Kennet (Wayland Young) and Lord Donaldson of Kingsbridge. The business world was represented by David Sainsbury and Sir Leslie Murphy (a former chairman of the National Enterprise Board), science by Lord Flowers (rector of Imperial College London) and Sir Frederick Dainton (a distinguished chemist and former chairman of the University Grants Committee), economics by James Meade (a joint winner of the

Source: *Guardian*, 2 February 1981

*'What do you mean, can't we slow down a bit? We haven't even started the
motor yet!'*

Nobel Prize) and Frank Hahn (another Cambridge professor), the wider academic
world by Lord Bullock (Alan Bullock, the biographer of Hitler and Bevin), Lord
Young (Michael Young, who had been a close friend of Tony Crosland), Michael
Zander (professor of law at the London School of Economics) and Jean Floud
(principal of Newnham College Cambridge). The only prominent trade unionist to
sign the advertisement, Frank Chapple, was one of the very few signatories who did
not in the end become a member of the SDP.[18]

At the same time, even before the new party had been launched, eight opinion
polls in a row suggested that a social-democratic party in alliance with the Liberals
might conceivably sweep all before it. The polls were, of course, greeted with a good
deal of scepticism, including by the social democrats; but their virtual unanimity
made it hard to disregard them altogether. For example, an NOP survey published
in the *Observer* shortly before the launch found fully 46 per cent of voters saying
that they would vote for a Liberal–social-democratic alliance if there were a general
election tomorrow, compared with 27 per cent who said they would vote Labour
and only 25 per cent who said they would vote Conservative. The new party's
potential impact was suggested by the fact that, when NOP asked respondents to
choose only from among the existing parties, with the social democrats left out, the
findings were: Labour 45 per cent; Conservatives 36 per cent; Liberals 13 per
cent.[19] The social democrats thus appeared to be the crucial ingredient.

The only warning notes were sounded by other surveys which suggested that in fact the new party would take more votes from the Conservatives than from Labour, that Labour was actually still in the lead in the constituencies of the eleven declared social-democrat MPs and that support for the new party, although extensive, was by no means deeply rooted. The evidence suggested in other words that support for the social democrats was currently exploding but that some day it might, equally rapidly, implode.[20]

But for the time being the Gang of Four and those around them were preoccupied with creating the beginnings of a semblance of a party organization. The Gang of Four met for lunch every Monday, usually in a private room at L'Amico, an Italian restaurant not far from the House of Commons. It was agreed that David Owen would chair the parliamentary group, Roy Jenkins would co-ordinate policy, Bill Rodgers would build up the grass-roots organization and Shirley Williams would be responsible for communications and publicity. So great was the rush to be involved in the new party, and so anxious were the Gang of Four not to offend those eager to help, that all four, especially Jenkins and Williams, soon found themselves at the centre of a vast, amorphous network of committees, sub-committees, task forces and advisory groups, the meetings of which often merged into one another.

Alec McGivan and Ian Wrigglesworth meanwhile looked for premises. McGivan seriously considered a small suite of rooms in Strutton Ground off Victoria Street, but there was a street market just outside and McGivan decided that the fastidious Jenkins could not be expected to clamber to the party's headquarters over empty fruit crates and piles of old vegetables. Wrigglesworth instead found larger, more suitable accommodation in nearby Queen Anne's Gate. To handle the party's funds, trustees were appointed: Clive Lindley, a businessman friend of Jenkins; David Sainsbury, whose uncle, Lord Sainsbury, was one of the first SDP peers; Sir Leslie Murphy, late of the National Enterprise Board; Lord Diamond, chief secretary to the Treasury under Harold Wilson; and Ian Wrigglesworth. The trustees were there to see that the money pouring into the party was handled honestly as well as efficiently. In addition, because the Council for Social Demo-cracy at this stage had no formal constitution, it needed, for legal reasons, to be given some kind of formal corporate existence. Robert Maclennan drafted a legally sound but somewhat bizarre document that made Jenkins, Owen, Rodgers and Williams, in effect, the party's owners.

But the most pressing organizational need was the launch of the party itself, which Mike Thomas and Ian Wrigglesworth were determined should not only attract favourable publicity but should also establish the party's separate political identity and be the basis on which it could attract members and funds. The two had been appalled that the Gang of Four had almost forgotten to include a reply coupon in the *Guardian* advertisement of 5 February. Wrigglesworth drew up and super-vised the budget for the launch, and he and Thomas ensured that members of the public could join the party, or give money to it, using credit cards. Because they were among the few social-democrat MPs with business experience, Thomas and

Wrigglesworth, and to a lesser extent John Horam, were largely left alone to sort out the details. Since the new party was meant to be a national party, not just a London-based party, it was decided, at Shirley Williams' suggestion, to hold the launch more or less simultaneously in nine different cities. From the use of credit cards to the design of a distinctive 'red, white and blue' logo, the party was intended by Thomas and those working with him to be—and to be seen to be—a genuine party of the 1980s, not, like the others, a party born into some earlier historical epoch. They wanted television and the press to portray, and to comment favourably on, the new party's professionalism. Whatever else it was, the launch was going to be an American-style 'media event'.

Meanwhile, all the SDP's founding members (except Roy Jenkins who had quietly allowed his party membership to lapse) were going through the extremely painful process of disengaging from the Labour party. They did not resign immediately, partly because some of them could still not bring themselves to, partly because some felt that they owed it to their constituency supporters to make any formal announcement directly to them and partly because, in late January and February 1980, there remained a good deal of confusion about when the new party was going to make its début. Michael Foot renewed his pleas to Owen, Rodgers and, especially, Williams to stay in the party and to continue their fight there; and on 2 February the three spent an hour with Foot and Healey in Foot's room at the House of Commons. But no one's mind was changed.

At the same time, loyalists in the Labour party were becoming increasingly irritated by the fact that the social democrats were staying on in the party, and even sitting on its committees, while simultaneously plotting its destruction. Tony Benn commented, referring to Shirley Williams: 'I do not think it is moral for someone to sit in the highest echelons of one party in order to get enough time to prepare another party.'[21] Neil Kinnock, newly elected to the shadow cabinet, was even more pungent. The supporters of the Council for Social Democracy could go, he said, or they could stay; but:

They cannot retain any credibility or claim to integrity if they prolong their public agonizing, taunts and threats in such a way as to deliberately inflict harm on the party which has given them office, opportunity, importance and not a little affluence. Renouncing a political allegiance is a defensible act. Making a meal of the hand that fed them is indefensible . . .[22]

The remark about affluence was a dig at Roy Jenkins, who had not only brought back from Brussels a substantial pension but had just accepted a part-time vice-chairmanship of the merchant bankers Morgan Grenfell.

In fact, on the very day that Kinnock was speaking, 30 January, David Owen was telling his constituency party in Plymouth Devonport that he would not be standing as a Labour candidate at the next election. Bill Rodgers had resigned from the shadow cabinet three days earlier. On 9 February Shirley Williams resigned her place on the NEC. And during the rest of February and early March all the other defectors informed their constituency parties that they were no longer to be regarded as Labour MPs or candidates. On 2 March all of the Council for Social Democracy's supporters in the House of Commons followed Tom Ellis and Richard Crawshaw in resigning the Labour whip. They were joined by nine members of the House of Lords. The Labour defectors in both houses announced that they wished henceforth to be known as 'Social Democratic' members. By mid-March the disengagement process was complete. It had seemed to take forever, though it had actually—from the Limehouse Declaration—taken less than seven weeks.

Although each SDP MP made a statement giving his own reasons for leaving the party, Shirley Williams probably spoke for all of them in her letter to Ron Hayward, the party's general secretary, in which she resigned from the NEC:

Dear Ron,

It is with great regret that I must tender my resignation from the NEC . . .

Many party members will criticize me for resigning, even though they will agree that the 1980 Blackpool annual conference and the January 1981 Wembley conference were disastrous. They will say that I should continue to fight for sensible democratic policies on the NEC and in the party generally. I can only say that with a handful of others on the NEC and outside it I have done my share of fighting over the last decade. Because so many comrades have only now realized how serious is the plight of the party and how far it has drifted away from its own supporters, there have been too few of us to be able to change or even stop its course.

We have almost always been defeated and we have been defeated by larger and larger majorities as the years have gone by. I see no prospect that that will change.

Some leading members of the parliamentary party are now seeking a compromise on the leadership election issue . . . Politics is the art of compromise, and compromise must be based on give and take. I have found, however, that compromise in the NEC is just another name for endless retreat. The party that is now emerging is not the democratic socialist party that I joined but a party intent on controlling those of its members who are elected to public office by the people of Britain. I believe that to be incompatible with the accountability of MPs to their electors which lies at the heart of parliamentary democracy. Despite fierce and sustained ideological differences with many of my colleagues on the NEC, I have been treated on the whole with comradeship and courtesy which I appreciate.

To those who have been friends and allies on the NEC I can only say how sorry I am to part company with them. I do so only because I believe the party I loved and worked for over so many years no longer exists . . .

Yours ever,

Shirley [23]

Initially, eleven members of Parliament, all Labour, declared their support for the Council for Social Democracy; but between 26 January and the new party's launch two months later another three MPs signed on, taking the membership of the parliamentary group to a total of fourteen. John Cartwright, the MP for

Woolwich East, had long been expected to defect, but his announcement on 27 February still came as a considerable shock to Labour loyalists because—working class in origin, long active in the co-operative movement, a former party agent—he was universally thought of as being Labour through and through. Edward Lyons, the MP for Bradford West, a human-rights barrister hostile to the Soviet Union and suspicious of the state, followed a few weeks later. But the big surprise had come three days earlier on 16 March, shortly before the launch, when, during the parliamentary debate on the deflationary 1981 budget, Christopher Brocklebank-Fowler, the Conservative MP for Norfolk North-West and a long-standing critic of the Thatcher administration, dramatically crossed the floor of the House of Commons to join the little Social Democratic group on the opposition benches. There were rumours during the rest of the year that other anti-Thatcher Tory backbenchers might be about to follow; but, for reasons to be explained in the next chapter, none ever did.

All of those who defected, including Cartwright, Lyons and Brocklebank-Fowler, made it clear that, although they had changed parties, they nevertheless had no intention of resigning from parliament and fighting by-elections under their new colours. Privately, some were uneasy; but publicly, they took the line that, although they had changed parties, they had not changed their views and that therefore they had no need to face their electors a second time. As Owen put it to his constituency supporters in Plymouth, 'I have not changed my support for the manifesto on which you and I fought the 1979 election, and I will conduct myself in parliament over the years ahead, until the next election, within the spirit of that manifesto.'[24]

This line of argument was somewhat disingenuous, since not all the Labour defectors were supporters of the 1979 manifesto (with its pledges to extend public ownership and to introduce compulsory planning agreements in industry) and since in any case they all knew perfectly well that they had been elected, not as supporters of this or that pledge in the party manifesto, but as the person who happened to be the Labour candidate in their constituency. There was thus moral force in the claim of Labour loyalists that the defectors who were MPs should resign their seats and fight by-elections as 'the honest thing to do'. But the SDP defectors never seriously considered adopting that course. They genuinely believed their views had not changed. More important, they knew perfectly well that to resign and fight by-elections before the new party had established itself properly would be to risk committing political suicide, especially since the Labour chief whip (abetted by his Conservative counterpart) would, of course, not dream of allowing the SDP by-elections to be held all on one great dramatic day but instead would see to it that they were held in dribs and drabs over a number of weeks, even months—and in the most damaging possible order from the SDP's point of view. The defectors felt that they were having a hard enough time already. They did not fancy being martyrs—and they certainly did not fancy being martyred ignominiously one by one. Until the next general election, they would stay put.[25]

As can be imagined, David Steel and other leading Liberals watched all these developments with considerable satisfaction, though with some puzzlement as to why the whole business was taking so long. Steel continued to apply what pressure he could from the outside, partly to signal to potential defectors that he personally would welcome them into an alliance with the Liberals, but partly also to warn them that they should not take him and his fellow Liberals for granted: any alliance between them would have to be made quickly, and it would have to include agreement on policy as well as a share-out of seats. The social democrats, Steel realized, did not wholly appreciate that some Liberals were not wildly enthusiastic about merging the Liberals' fortunes with those of renegades from another party, some of whom, moreover, persisted in calling themselves socialists.

Prior to the Wembley conference, in an effort to establish common ground with the social democrats, the Liberal leader issued a ten-point plan for economic recovery, including industrial co-operation, a long-term incomes policy, the expansion of youth training and government aid to growth points in industry.[26] On the eve of the conference, he bluntly told the Gang of Three to stop 'dithering', and Alan Beith, the Liberal chief whip, said that, before he personally did any deal with the Labour dissidents, he would want to know whether they could in fact win more seats than the Liberals could on their own.[27] Following Wembley and the Limehouse Declaration, Steel took advantage of a Liberal party political broadcast to tell the country that there was now a golden opportunity 'to do what so many of us have dreamt for years': 'to break the mould of a failed political system and to produce a realignment of the progressive and hopeful forces in Britain.' He continued: 'If the social democrats' valuable experience of government is added to our nationwide community campaigning experience, I believe we could prove an unstoppable combination.'[28] Many Liberals, however, continued to urge the social democrats to move faster. Richard Holme, the party president, said that, if the Labour defectors really wanted to help the Liberals, they should 'get their skates on'; and Steel pointed out that the two sides would have to move very quickly if an agreed Liberal–social-democratic policy statement were to be put to the Liberal assembly in September.[29] Prospects for co-operation between the two sides were substantially improved when, on 27 February 1981, David Owen for the first time declared himself to be in favour of electoral reform.[30]

Meanwhile, the question of what the new party should be called was in a curious way answering itself. At first the Gang of Three and the Jenkinsites, in their idle moments, had toyed with all kinds of names: Social Democratic, to be sure, but also New Labour, Democratic Labour, Progressive Labour, Radical, just plain Democratic, just plain Progressive. A few Jenkinsites even preferred Centre. Names containing the word Labour were dropped because they failed to distinguish sharply enough between the new party and the old one (and also because they made the new party sound too much like what it was, a straightforward breakaway from Labour). Names containing words like Progressive and Radical were dropped because such words were thought to be too vague and, in the case of Radical, possibly to have the wrong connotations. The only objections to Social Democratic were that it was a trifle long and that it might be thought too continental-sounding, as though the new party belonged somewhere in Germany or Scandinavia. But when the newspapers and television began to label the Labour dissidents 'social democrats' and when no one seemed to mind—and when everyone seemed to understand what was being referred to—the name stuck. No formal decision was come to. A consensus simply emerged.

Determining the date of the launch proved considerably more difficult. Owen, as we have seen, was inclined to aim for the autumn. He felt that, before the party was launched, time would be needed to raise money, to mobilize potential sup-porters, to work out at least an outline constitution, to consider the new party's general political direction and, not least, to establish that the SDP was indeed going to be a new party and not just some kind of splinter group. 'Anyone', someone told the *Observer*, 'who thinks that you can set up a new party in a matter of days is living in cloud cuckoo land.'[31] But such a timetable, whatever its theoretical advantages, turned out to be unrealistic. The Liberals needed a new party in exis-tence so that they would have someone to negotiate with; the media would have a field day if Jenkins and the Gang of Three, having dithered during most of 1980, proceeded to dither during most of 1981; and a protracted delay would risk dis-appointing, perhaps even alienating, many of the well-wishers who were writ-ing in and sending money to the Council for Social Democracy's headquarters. But, above all, what were Shirley Williams and the defecting MPs supposed to do pending the new party's formal inception? Stay in the Labour party, where their position would quickly become completely intolerable? Or pass out of the Labour party into some kind of non-partisan limbo, in which case they would look ridiculous?

For these reasons, delay made little sense and the date of the launch was gradually brought forward, from the autumn to some time after the May local elections, then to Easter, then from Easter to a few weeks before Easter. The date finally settled on was Thursday, 26 March, less than nine weeks after the issuing of the Limehouse Declaration. The May elections provided a good example of the decision's political logic. The original idea had been that Labour councillors who were thinking of joining the social democrats should not be embarrassed into having to declare themselves while they and their colleagues were in the midst of standing for re-election; but then it became clear that postponing the launch would make the position of such councillors worse, since, if they really did mean to defect, they would be sailing politically under false colours and would constantly be pressed during the election campaign to say what their true intentions were. In the end, the May elections turned out to provide yet another argument for launching the new party earlier rather than later.

The launch on 26 March was, as intended, a media spectacular. It was the first item on every television news bulletin, a main headline on the front page of almost every newspaper. The new party's red, white and blue logo was everywhere. So were the Gang of Four: on the platform for a televised news conference in London's Connaught Rooms; climbing in and out of cars, trains and aeroplanes in London, Glasgow, Cardiff, Southampton, Leeds, Norwich, Birmingham, Manchester and Plymouth; in television studios and at public meetings and press conferences all over the country. More than 500 of the world's press were present in the Connaught Rooms at 9 a.m. ITN's *News at One* devoted all but two of its 25 minutes to the new party, and by the end of a long day Mike Thomas estimated that the SDP had attracted more than £15 millions' worth of free publicity. This was, after all, the launch of the first new national political party since 1900—a party, moreover, that included four ex-cabinet ministers and two or three of the country's most admired politicians.[32] It was bound on its own to attract a great deal of media attention. Even so, Thomas could be well satisfied with the results of his personal efforts. In mid-afternoon, he slipped away to the House of Commons to intervene in prime minister's question time and establish his claim to be the first SDP member to speak in the House of Commons.[33]

Roy Jenkins told the news conference in the Connaught Rooms that the SDP offered not only a new party but an entirely new political approach: 'we want to get away from the politics of out-dated dogmatism and class confrontation . . . to release the energies of the people who are fed up with the old slanging match.' David Owen said the new party would be 'the most democratic party in the country', with all decisions to be made on the basis of 'one member, one vote' and with its funds coming from individual members, not from big business or the unions. Shirley Williams echoed Owen in saying that the SDP would be a 'left-of-centre party' and called for policies that would heal the growing divisions between classes and regions and give real equality of opportunity to women and ethnic minorities. Bill Rodgers went out of his way to assert the new party's separate identity. Asked whether the SDP was a new kind of socialist party or part of a centre alliance with the Liberals, Rodgers replied:

No, we are not a new centre party, we are very plainly a left-of-centre party. David Owen and my other colleagues have demonstrated that we recognize fully that the Liberals have played an important part in British public life and we want a cooperative relationship with them.

We need it for electoral purposes. We do not want to be fighting each other when the general election comes. We need to cooperate in the House of Commons. But we are a distinct and new party with new ideas and a new momentum.

Rodgers then, without prompting, volunteered that he hoped the SDP would fight half the constituencies in the country at the next election.[34]

The new party on its first day went out of its way to emphasize the collective nature of its leadership. At the morning news conference, the Gang of Four sat side by side in strict alphabetical order from left to right: Jenkins, Owen, Rodgers and Williams. And they spoke in that order. All four fielded questions. None was 'the leader'. In an article that day in *The Times*, Shirley Williams commended the SDP's collective leadership as challenging 'the conventional pyramid structure of the old parties':

It also offers great dividends: complementary experience and complementary knowledge of a wider range of government departments and subjects than any single leader could ever have. The collective leadership reflects in ourselves the participation and mutual respect we stand for, in industry, the social services, and in the family itself. The days of the paterfamilias are as dead as those of the autocratic employer. So why should such concepts survive unchallenged in politics?[35]

The SDP's subsequent experience was to suggest, however, that the days of the dominant leader were not quite as *passé* as Williams supposed.

The mood on 26 March 1981 was euphoric. Indeed it is hard a decade and a half later, when the SDP has ceased to exist as a separate political force, to recall just how euphoric the mood was. And it remained that way for many months to come. For that reason it is worth remembering that the SDP was initially born in March 1981 far more out of feelings of despair than out of feelings of hope. Those who founded it had given up on the Labour party, the party they had loved; and they knew that the electoral odds were heavily stacked against a new party, just as they had been stacked against the Liberals for half a century. The fourteen MPs who took part in the launch were very well aware, as Peter Jenkins had said, that they were setting out on 'a long haul into the unknown'. All fourteen of them subsequently stood as SDP–Alliance candidates in the general election of 1983. Only four of them held their seats. Of the remaining ten, eight finished third, a ninth finished fourth, and only one managed to finish second. If the ten MPs who were to be defeated in 1983 had been told on the day of the launch that they would undoubtedly lose their seats in two years' time, they would have been disappointed—but they would not have been surprised. They were all taking a chance, and they all knew it.

6

•••

Defectors and Loyalists

Thirteen ex-Labour MPs and one ex-Conservative were among the founders of the SDP in March 1981. Thirteen more ex-Labour members joined during the remainder of 1981, and two more came over in 1982, making a grand total of twenty-nine SDP MPs. As we shall see in Chapter 8, the spectacle of a steady progression of members of parliament out of the Labour party's ranks and into those of the SDP was one of the major factors giving the new party its early momentum.

James Wellbeloved joined the party in July 1981, Michael O'Halloran in early September. In October, after the Labour party conference, the SDP attracted another seven recruits: Dickson Mabon, Bob Mitchell, David Ginsburg, James Dunn, Tom McNally, Eric Ogden and Ron Brown, the brother of the former Labour foreign secretary George Brown (who also joined the SDP). In November another Labour member, John Grant, came over, and in December so did another three, Jeffrey Thomas, Ednyfed Hudson Davies and Bruce Douglas-Mann. In March 1982 Bryan Magee joined the new party, to be followed a few weeks later, in June, by George Cunningham. By the summer of 1982 the SDP parliamentary group had grown from fourteen at the time of the launch to double that number, and there were now nearly three times as many SDP MPs as there were Liberals.

But the reader may already be aware of a puzzle. A large number of Labour MPs, and one Conservative MP, defected. But an even larger number in both parties did not defect, and many of those who remained loyal to their existing party held political views that were similar or even identical to the minority who switched. For every Bill Rodgers, there was a Roy Hattersley; for every David Owen, a Denis Healey or Eric Varley. There is, therefore, a considerable defector–loyalist puzzle; and if the SDP, and indeed the other parties, are to be understood, an attempt must be made to solve it. Two members of parliament hold similar or identical views. One defects to the SDP. The other does not. Why?

It is important to notice the scale of the puzzle. Not only was the SDP the first substantial new political party to be launched in Britain since 1900: the resignation of twenty-eight Labour MPs to form the SDP was the largest breakaway from any party for nearly a century. Not since 1886, when seventy-eight MPs led by Joseph Chamberlain broke with the Liberals over Irish Home Rule, had any party suffered desertions in such numbers.[1] Moreover, the split appears even larger if account is taken of the eighteen Labour peers and thirty-one former Labour MPs— eight of them former cabinet ministers—who likewise joined the new party. (They are listed in Appendices 1 and 2 at the end of the book.)[2] Yet at the same time, although the breakaway was very large in absolute numbers, the number who resigned from the Labour party did not constitute a very large percentage of the parliamentary Labour party. On the contrary, there were 269 Labour members of parliament in 1981: the twenty-eight defectors amounted to about one in ten of them. More to the point, the defectors constituted only a small proportion even of Labour's right wing.

The term 'right wing' is used loosely in most of this book to refer to all those Labour members and activists who did not think of themselves as left-wingers and did not belong to left-wing organizations such as the Tribune Group or the Campaign for Labour Party Democracy. On this broad definition there were probably about 150 MPs on the Labour right in the House of Commons in 1981, comprising most of those who did not vote for Michael Foot on the first ballot in the 1980 party-leadership contest. The twenty-eight Labour defectors to the SDP amounted to less than 20 per cent of this group. A somewhat narrower definition of 'right wing' might reduce the size of the right in parliament to about 120, somewhere between the number who voted for Denis Healey on the first ballot in 1980 (112) and the number who voted for him on the second (129).[3] Even on this narrower definition, the proportion of Labour right-wingers who defected to the SDP still comes to well under a quarter. Either way, those who followed the Gang of Four in quitting Labour's ranks were heavily outnumbered by those who might have done so but did not.[4]

Moreover, the twenty-eight who did defect never constituted even a loose grouping, let alone an organized faction, when they were in the PLP. Far from being a 'tightly knit group of politically motivated men' (to adopt Harold Wilson's description of the seamen's leaders in 1966), the twenty-eight formed no more than a cluster of mini-groups, which only partly overlapped. The Jenkinsites, as we saw in Chapter 3, formed such a mini-group; and some defectors, including several of the Jenkinsites, had been officers in the Manifesto Group.[5] Similarly, some of them had been associated with Britain in Europe in 1975 (Tom Bradley, Dickson Mabon, Bill Rodgers, John Roper and Ian Wrigglesworth), and several more had been members of Labour's delegation to the European Parliament later in the same decade (Ron Brown, George Cunningham, Tom Ellis and Bob Mitchell). At least nine had personal ties to one or more of the Gang of Four, having been junior ministers under them or else their parliamentary private secretaries.[6] But there remained a number of defectors—Bruce Douglas-Mann, Ednyfed Hudson Davies, Edward Lyons, Bryan Magee, Tom McNally, Jeffrey Thomas—who stood outside even these mini-networks and whose switch cannot have been prompted by feelings of loyalty to any group or clique. What the Labour party lost was not a group or even a splinter group but a number of tiny fragments.

The defectors were not even united in their views. Obviously, none of them had been out-and-out left-wingers, but before defecting a considerable number would have described themselves as centrists. They certainly did not constitute an ideologically distinct group within the Labour right. On the issues that had divided the Labour right during the 1970s—notably Scottish and Welsh devolution and trade-union reform—the twenty-eight were as divided as everyone else. Most of them were in favour of or indifferent to the Callaghan government's devolution proposals; but Crawshaw, Ogden and Mitchell voted against them from time to time, and Cunningham and Douglas-Mann were leading figures (together with many left-wingers) in the main rebellions against the legislation. Cunningham indeed was largely responsible for the '40 per cent rule', which in the end killed the proposal for a Scottish Assembly (and also, indirectly, the Callaghan government).[7] The divisions on the issue of trade-union reform were just as great, as events inside the SDP were to show.

But the issue that most tellingly reveals the SDP's ideological disparateness is Europe. It is tempting now—and was tempting in 1981—to regard commitment to the European Community as being at the very heart of the Social Democrats' beliefs. 'The 1971 split over Europe', Peter Jenkins wrote in *Mrs Thatcher's Revolution*, 'prefigured the schism of 1981.'[8] This assumption was also shared within the Labour party, as Tony Benn's postscript commentary on his diary entries for 1971–2 reveals:

During the long and protracted argument about Europe which followed . . . it became clear that a group of pro-European Labour MPs would never accept an adverse Conference decision on this question, and had therefore decided that if their dream of an enlarged Common Market conflicted with their membership of the Labour party, then the Party would have to be sacrificed. It was this commitment that ultimately led to the formation of the SDP in 1981.[9]

But was it? It is true that the Gang of Four were united by their unswerving support for the Community. All four had voted to join Europe in the October 1971 debate, and it was on Europe that the Gang of Three had issued their first joint statement. It is also true that constituency Labour parties had increasingly come to regard opposition to the Common Market as a touchstone of doctrinal purity, with the result that several MPs who later joined the SDP were involved in rows on Europe with their local activists.[10]

But passionate commitment to Europe was not in fact what bound the SDP defectors together. Of the twenty-eight Labour MPs who defected, twenty-two had served in the 1970 parliament and had therefore been in a position to vote in the House of Commons on 28 October 1971, when sixty-nine Labour MPs, organized by Rodgers, had supported the Heath government on the outcome of its negotiations with the EEC. If it were true that enthusiasm for Europe was an essential condition of subsequent SDP support, then the great majority of those twenty-two should have voted in 1971 in the pro-European lobby. In fact, however, only half of them, eleven, did so, with two others abstaining. The other nine voted with the Labour majority against joining the EEC on the Heath government's terms. Of these nine, some, like John Horam and John Grant, were indifferent rather than hostile to British EEC membership and were not positively anti-European; but at least two of them—George Cunningham and Michael O'Halloran —regularly defied the Labour whip in 1977 and 1978 and voted against direct elections to the European Parliament, as did one of the 1971 abstainers, Jim Wellbeloved.

Moreover, not only was devotion to the European cause not the ideological cement that bound the twenty-eight SDP defectors together: views on the issue hardly distinguished the Labour right-wingers who did defect to the SDP from those who did not. In 1981, thirty of the sixty-nine rebels in 1971 were still in the House of Commons. Eleven of the thirty, as we have just seen, defected to the SDP, but the other nineteen did not. A majority of the 1971 'Euro-fanatics', in other words, remained loyal to the Labour party.[11] There was thus no neat one-to-one relationship between being pro-European and defecting. On the contrary, most of Labour's Europeans did not join the SDP and some of the Labour MPs who did join were not notably pro-European.[12]

Policy differences within the Labour party did, of course, play a part in the split: those who defected were united in their dislike of Labour's shift to the left. But even broad policy differences were certainly not a sufficient condition of a Labour MP's making the switch: only a small minority of those who disliked what was happening inside the party in fact defected. Indeed some SDP MPs (especially the later defectors such as Grant, McNally and Cunningham) were probably closer in their views to many of those they left behind than to their new SDP colleagues. Therefore, we still need to ask: when two Labour MPs agreed on all major issues, what other factors persuaded one to stay but the other to leave? More precisely, when five were agreed on all the issues, what persuaded four to stay but the fifth to leave?

For some loyalists, their emotional attachments to the Labour party were simply too strong for them to contemplate leaving. The loyalty of men like Roy Hattersley, Roy Mason, Merlyn Rees and Eric Varley can probably be explained in this way.[13] They might or might not share the Social Democrats' diagnosis of the state of the party. But they had been born in the party, they had spent their whole life in it, and they wanted to die in it. Moreover, such an absolute commitment had the attraction of irrevocability: there was no need to agonize, no need to calculate or dissemble, no need to lose sleep. One simply made up one's mind to stay in the party and then carried on as normal.

A second, more cerebral factor was the differing assessments that MPs made of the Labour right's prospects. Labour MPs could share identical views on policy yet genuinely disagree about the right's chances of recovery. Optimism came more easily to some than to others, but everyone could, if they tried hard enough, find reasons for continuing to hope; the trade unions, for example, might switch their votes at the next party conference. Giles Radice, a leading Manifesto Group activist who remained loyal, instinctively took the long view: 'In politics patience is a virtue. Labour party politics is a matter of time and tides.'[14] Another loyalist whom the SDP had hoped to recruit, Ken Weetch, made the same point: 'When I was his PPS, Bill Rodgers used to tell me to play Labour politics long; I followed his advice even if he didn't.' Many of the loyalists believed—or persuaded themselves to believe (it was sometimes hard to tell which)—that, despite everything, the party could yet be saved.

A third factor in helping to make up people's minds was more strategic. Breakaways from a party always help the other side—whether outside one's old party or inside it. The departure of leading lights on the right would only serve further to strengthen the Labour left. Worse, as Peter Jenkins pointed out in his *Guardian* article, to split the party might mean splitting the anti-Conservative vote and handing office to the Thatcherites, possibly for a generation.[15] The historically aware referred back to the almost twenty-year Conservative hegemony that had followed the Liberal Unionist breakaway in 1886. The European-minded, like Denis Healey, remembered the role played by a divided socialist movement in the rise of German and Italian fascism. Loyalists like Giles Radice and Phillip Whitehead concluded on these kinds of grounds that it was better to quit politics altogether than to set up in opposition to Labour. This was, in fact, a course taken quietly during this period by many disillusioned Labour activists and local councillors.

But, although assessments of the Labour party's long-term prospects and a genuine fear of splitting the opposition were undoubtedly crucial factors in many cases, they are not entirely satisfactory as an explanation of the overall pattern of loyalty and defection. On the one hand, many who remained loyal to Labour were not confident that the party could be saved.[16] On the other hand, most of the defectors were as well aware as the loyalists of the disadvantages of splitting Labour and setting up a rival party: the new party might fail, and under Britain's electoral system the Conservatives under Thatcher might indeed remain in power for an indefinite period on a minority vote. What distinguished defectors from loyalists cannot, therefore, have been only their differing judgements about Labour's future.

What role did deselection or the fear of it play? Labour loyalists and some Liberals claimed that many of the SDP MPs defected only because they were about to be deselected as parliamentary candidates by their local party: they jumped before they were pushed. There can never be certain answers to hypothetical questions; but the balance of evidence strongly suggests that deselection or the fear of it played only a marginal role in MPs' decisions to quit the party.

Altogether eleven SDP MPs had been seriously at odds with a substantial section of their local party, but of these no more than four would have remained in the Labour party had they been reselected or expected to be reselected: James

Dunn possibly, Eric Ogden and David Ginsburg probably, Michael O'Halloran certainly.[17] James Dunn's political views made him an unlikely Social Democrat and his prospects of reselection by his Militant-dominated Labour party in Liverpool Kirkdale were slim. But poor health was in any case forcing him towards retirement and his constituency was due to disappear under the boundary revisions. Dunn could have remained in the Labour party and retired with dignity. Instead he joined the SDP. The other three cases are clearer cut. After being narrowly deselected by his Liverpool West Derby CLP in June 1981, Ogden resisted the blandishments of SDP MPs to join them until he had learned that the local Liberals would allow him to stand as the Alliance's candidate for his seat.[18] Ginsburg had little chance of reselection in Dewsbury, having concentrated on his business affairs in recent years and chosen to live in Hampstead rather than the constituency. He joined the SDP a month before his local party was due to draw up its reselection short list, by which time he had received only one nomination from among the Dewsbury party's five branches. O'Halloran's defection appeared to be wholly opportunist. His ambivalence towards the EEC and his taste for Islington-style machine politics hardly made him a natural Social Democrat. At odds with the hard left in his Islington North constituency since his original selection in 1969, he was equally isolated from the right and would not necessarily have won their support in a reselection contest. After joining the SDP, he made little contact with its largely middle-class local membership and played no active part in the party nationally. In March 1983, after boundary changes had eliminated his prospects of securing the Alliance nomination for an Islington constituency, he resigned to become an Independent Labour candidate at the general election that shortly followed.

Thus, at most only a handful of the SDP MPs joined because of deselection. And, in addition, fewer than half of those Labour MPs who actually were deselected as candidates seriously considered joining the SDP. Seven of the eight deselected Labour MPs were right-wingers, but only one, Eric Ogden, defected.[19] A similar story can be told of those right-wing Labour MPs such as Clinton Davis (Hackney Central), Reg Freeson (Brent East) and William Hamilton (Fife Central) who only just fended off left-wing challenges to their selection or who, like Joel Barnett (Heywood and Royton) and Charles Morris (Manchester Openshaw) were squeezed out by left-wing MPs where boundary revisions obliged sitting members to compete for the same seat. Only one, Freeson, gave so much as a hint of wishing to join the SDP.[20]

The deselected, the almost deselected, those who had been squeezed out for ideological reasons after the boundary revisions—all would seem to have had good reasons for joining the SDP. They had been rejected or nearly rejected on account of their political views, which were closer to the SDP's than to those of Foot's Labour party. Their struggle for political survival had often been unpleasant and exhausting and some had been very shabbily treated. Most would have been welcomed into the SDP and would then have had the support of a much more congenial and compliant local party membership. What stopped them from joining?

Some lacked the spirit and energy: switching to the SDP would have meant building up a local membership, attending countless fund-raising functions and cultivating the local press, all the while knowing that the battle was going to be uphill. Potential aggravation from local Liberal activists was an added complication for some inner-city MPs such as Arthur Lewis (Newham North-West) or Stanley Cohen (Leeds South-East). There seemed little point in wriggling free from the Labour left only to become entangled with an equally prickly collection of Liberals. Retirement, or a nominal campaign as an Independent, seemed easier options.

Some simply left it too late. Usually the possibility of deselection did not stare MPs in the face until sometime in 1982, and after the spring of 1982 joining the SDP was a less attractive option than it had been: SDP or Liberal candidates were largely in place, and by that time the SDP's ratings in the opinion polls had begun to slide.[21]

The SDP was not, therefore, whatever people might say, a refugee camp for casualties in Labour's civil war. But of course the ferocity of the fighting in someone's constituency often did have a bearing on whether that person switched or stayed. The SDP's three most unexpected recruits—Cunningham, Grant and McNally—were escaping from especially bitter faction fights.[22] And some of the switchers who survived reselection—or expected to—emphasized that they were not so much afraid of death as unhappy at the idea of a guerrilla way of life:

We always out-voted them [i.e. the local left] by out-organizing them, but there were increasing costs: endless phone calls, membership recruitment on Sunday mornings, and so on. I felt my independence was being gradually compromised. The temptation was not to do what I believed in because the moderates did not want trouble—and also had to have everything explained to them.

Cunningham told the press how much he resented having to devote time to counter-intriguing: 'If they get two votes here, can I get three votes there? If they control the Young Socialists, can I win the Women's Section? I cannot do my job properly and spend time on that kind of shenanigans as well.'[23]

If some MPs defected because they were tired of in-fighting in their local party, the reverse is also true: some who might otherwise have defected remained loyal because their local party was moderate and supportive. Most CLPs had moved some distance to the left in the 1970s, but the advance of the hard left was extremely patchy, and many of Labour's traditional heartlands lay outside the party's main left–right battlezones and saw only sporadic fighting. One Labour member who almost defected told us: 'But for the good relationship I had with my party I would have gone. But I had educated them about Militant.' Another waverer with a moderate CLP said: 'I simply couldn't go along to these people, with whom I'd been out in all weathers, and say I was leaving them. I simply couldn't.' Political ties were reinforced by ties of friendship. As one of the Gang of Four put it:

In some places MPs had an uncharacteristically nice party and therefore either didn't see, or didn't feel in their guts, the pain of what it was like to be up against the other side of the party . . . They didn't really understand what we were going on about.

Less impressionistic evidence confirms that MPs with moderate constituency parties were substantially less likely than those without to be tempted into defecting. A CLP's vote in the 1981 deputy-leadership contest provides a good indicator of whether or not it was moderate: a CLP that voted for Healey had obviously not been captured by the left. Table 6.1 (in Appendix 5) divides CLPs according to whether they voted for Benn or for Healey in both rounds. In order to judge whether those Labour MPs who might have been expected to defect but did not were also among those who happened to have moderate CLPs, the table examines the CLPs not only of the twenty-eight actual defectors but of forty 'potential defectors'. These potential defectors comprise the October 1971 EEC rebels who were still MPs in 1981 and who stayed in the Labour party—nineteen in all—plus twenty-one others who were mentioned in the press or in our interviews as potential SDP recruits. Not all of them, it must be emphasized, ever talked or even thought of defecting; it is simply that others, such as journalists and SDP MPs, thought of them in these terms. They are listed in Appendix 3 at the end of the book.

Among the sixty-eight defectors and potential defectors the contrast between the decisions of those with Bennite CLPs and those with Healeyite CLPs could hardly be more striking. Of those with Bennite local parties, a majority, twenty-two out of forty, actually did switch. Of those with Healeyite parties, only four out of twenty did so. Turning the same figures around emphasizes the contrast (see Table 6.2). Of the 551 CLPs that recorded a double-vote for either Benn or Healey, no fewer than 80 per cent backed Benn. Among the actual defectors' CLPs, the proportion was even more overwhelming: 85 per cent.[24] By contrast, almost half of the loyalists' CLPs, 47 per cent, voted for Healey in both rounds. These constituency parties were thus not only more moderate than the defectors' CLPs: they were substantially more moderate than the total of constituency parties.[25]

The character of a potential defector's constituency party was thus an important factor affecting whether or not he went over. Age also played a part—or rather old age did. As Table 6.3 shows, about half of the potential defectors in their 30s, 40s and 50s did defect; the other half did not. But, of the sixteen in the group as a whole who were in their 60s in 1981, only three—Brown, Crawshaw and Ginsburg—made the move. Most of the other thirteen, the loyalists, were working-class stalwarts, men like Tom Urwin, Harry Gourlay and Alan Fitch, who were dubbed by one SDP MP 'the gold-watch brigade'. Saddened and disillusioned by what was happening in their party, they nevertheless could not bring themselves to make the break. There was anyway no need for them to do so: they would soon be retiring.

In 1981–2 the SDP's recruiting sergeants were convinced that one major determinant of a Labour MP's willingness to come over was his financial prospects. An MP who reckoned that, if he lost his seat, he could easily get another job without significant loss of income was much more likely to defect than one who risked a big drop in his income or even finding himself on the dole. One early defector reported a working-class Labour MP as confiding in him ruefully: 'Its all very well for you: if you lose your seat, you can easily get another job.'[26] This financial theory of defection is certainly plausible. It cannot, however, account for the loyalty of the thirteen potential defectors who were already in their 60s (several of whom had in any case planned to retire before the next election); nor is there any real reason for thinking that money considerations weighed heavily among more than a handful of the younger MPs.

One relevant bit of evidence lies in the occupational profiles of the actual defectors and the potential defectors or loyalists (see Table 6.4). The MPs with most to lose if they lost their seats were those who had had manual, technical or clerical jobs before entering parliament and who, if defeated, might find it difficult to obtain a job straightaway—and might find it impossible to match their current salary. At a time of high unemployment, this was especially true of those in their late 40s and 50s. But in fact the defection rate among the small number of former manual, technical and clerical workers in the total group, 36 per cent, was only a little lower than among those who had held better-paid jobs, 45 per cent. The class profiles of the loyalists and defectors were actually remarkably similar: in both groups, as for Labour MPs in general, the majority had a background in the professions, research or business.

Of course not all MPs who had had professional jobs before entering parliament could count on picking up the threads immediately if they lost their seats (although David Owen declared that he would go straight back to medicine). But a tentative assessment based on the potential defectors' pre-parliamentary occupations and extra-parliamentary sources of income suggests that prospective financial loss was seldom a significant factor in a Labour MP's decision to stay or leave. We estimate that defection was almost as frequent among those who had good reasons to anticipate a drop in income (48 per cent) as among those who did not (53 per cent).[27]

Financial calculations thus counted for little. Far more important was the depth of an MP's roots in the labour movement. This was especially true of older members. The labour movement was the air they breathed. Their relationship with it was not unlike Ernest Bevin's explanation of Winston Churchill's loyalty to Lord Beaverbrook: ' 'E's like the man who's married a whore: 'e knows she's a whore but 'e luvs 'er just the same.'[28] Most older members represented solidly working-class areas in which they had lived for most of their lives. They were unwilling to end their public life under a cloud and to retire to a community where they would be vilified as traitors by former friends and colleagues.

The member for the Durham mining seat of Houghton, Tom Urwin, was typical. The son of a miner, married into a mining family, he had lived in Houghton all his life. A branch official of the Amalgamated Union of Building Trade Workers since 1933, its full-time organizer since 1954, a member of the Labour party since 1940, the chairman of the local council's Planning Committee for fifteen years, he was elected as Houghton's MP in 1964. In one capacity or another—union organizer, local councillor, member of parliament—he had served the labour movement for almost fifty years. To divorce the Labour party would be to divorce family and community, not just party. It was too much to expect.

Irrespective of age, the length and depth of an MP's involvement in the labour movement had a direct bearing on his or her decision about whether or not to defect. A person's connections with a trade union is a case in point. Members of unions were much less likely to leave (34 per cent) than were non-members (57 per cent). Union sponsorship was even more important: exactly half of the forty non-sponsored Labour MPs among the potential and actual defectors joined the SDP, whereas only 29 per cent of the twenty-eight who were union sponsored did so. Active involvement in a union's internal affairs was even more important. Ten of the sixty-eight actual and potential defectors had held union office.[29] Of these, only one, Tom Bradley, the treasurer and then president of the Transport Salaried Staffs' Association, switched to the SDP. The SDP recruits were almost entirely without union experience, certainly during their careers in parliament.[30]

Local-government experience reveals a similar contrast between switchers and stayers. People who have served as local councillors, especially for a considerable length of time, are likely to be more firmly anchored in their local party. Their network of local contacts is more extensive; their obligation to local party workers is stronger; their acceptance of party discipline is of longer standing. The defection rate in 1981–2 of those with local-government experience was just over one in four, 28 per cent, whereas the defection rate of those without such experience was nearly twice as high, 51 per cent (see Table 6.5). This contrast was similarly reflected in where the MPs in the two groups lived. Barely a third of defectors, 36 per cent, lived in or near their constituency, whereas two-thirds, 66 per cent, of the loyalists did. The defection rate of 'local' MPs, 28 per cent, was likewise only half that of 'absentees', 56 per cent. In fact only five of the defectors —Tom Bradley, John Cartwright, Richard Crawshaw, Bob Mitchell and Jim Wellbeloved—can be said to have been heavily involved in the local politics of their area.[31]

If we combine all our indicators of Labour 'roots'—trade-union and local-government experience together with place of residence—the full contrast between defectors and loyalists is further underlined. Of the twenty-eight defectors, twenty had neither trade-union nor local-government experience; and of these twenty at least twelve (but probably more) were absentee MPs in the sense of living well outside their constituencies (see Table 6.6). Of the forty loyalists, only sixteen, 40 per cent, had neither trade-union nor local-government experience; and of these sixteen, only four were absentees. There is, therefore, something in the accusation made by Labour loyalists at the time of the split that most of those who broke from Labour had not been all that tightly bound to it in the first place. Most of the defectors were MPs who happened to be Labour, rather than pillars of the labour movement who happened also to be MPs.

What of the Conservatives? The question needs to be asked because in 1980–1 there seemed almost as many reasons to expect a Conservative breakaway as one from Labour. The wets on the back benches and in the cabinet were dispirited by the government's economic strategy and alarmed at its consequences for both unemployment and their party's support in the polls. Yet they felt helpless to change the government's direction, especially after the dismissal from the cabinet of Sir Ian Gilmour, Lord Soames and Mark Carlisle in September 1981. The Conservative party, in their view, had been hijacked by a bunch of doctrinaire crackpots and rescue was nowhere in sight. They were utterly depressed.

Yet only one Conservative MP, Christopher Brocklebank-Fowler, the courageous if somewhat impulsive member for Norfolk North-West, defected to the SDP; and this solidarity in the Conservatives' ranks was not confined to members of parliament. None of the original group of peers who declared for the Social Democrats was a former Conservative (though later the Duke of Devonshire, a junior minister in the Macmillan and Douglas-Home governments, did join). Likewise, not one of the 'Guardian 100' was an active Conservative; and, again, by contrast with Labour, only a handful of former Conservative MPs or candidates deserted their party.[32]

Brocklebank-Fowler was a broad-minded 'One Nation' Conservative with unusually progressive and therefore unpopular views on matters such as race relations and overseas aid. He had grown increasingly unhappy with his party's tone and policies under Margaret Thatcher and was particularly critical of the prime minister's economic strategy. The deflationary 1981 budget confirmed his worst fears, and, as we noted in the last chapter, he dramatically crossed the floor of the House after making a critical speech in the debate on the budget.[33] However, Brocklebank-Fowler was far from being alone in his views. Wets on the back benches were appalled by the 1981 budget, and those in the cabinet, led by Jim Prior, were furious at the lack of warning and consultation that preceded it: the Thatcherites had simply bypassed them. Yet no one followed Brocklebank-Fowler's lead.

The SDP's leaders were disappointed—and genuinely surprised—that no other Conservatives came over. As early as January 1981, Robert Hicks (Bodmin), a back-bench wet, told a television interviewer that up to twenty Conservative backbenchers might join a new centre party—a remark intended to give vent to the wets' frustration rather than signal an imminent breakaway, but a hint none the less that was picked up by social democrats.[34] Hicks was one of a small group of Conservative MPs who, in the autumn of 1981, actually discussed with the SDP leadership the possibility of joining the new party. Others, according to leading members of the SDP, included Stephen Dorrell (Loughborough), Hugh Dykes (Harrow East) and David Knox (Leek), as well as two somewhat less liberal backbenchers who had fallen out with the Conservative party managers, Keith Stainton (Sudbury and Woodbridge) and John Wells (Maidstone). Some SDP leaders were also encouraged, mistakenly, by the flurries of press speculation about Edward Heath.[35]

The Conservative–SDP discussions were at their height in late 1981 when, as one SDP leader put it, referring to the Croydon and Crosby by-elections, 'We really had the Tories on the run.' Why in the end did they prove fruitless?

One reason was that the SDP never launched a concerted campaign to recruit potential Conservative defectors. Social Democrat leaders talked to those individual Conservative members who approached them but rarely sought potential defectors out. A number of Conservative wets whose possible defection formed the subject of press speculation were not once propositioned and neither, as far as they knew, were their fellow wets. There was no parallel to Owen's and Rodgers' systematic recruiting efforts among disaffected Labour backbenchers in the late autumn of 1980.

A second reason was the absence of a lead from any senior Conservative. Brocklebank-Fowler was only a backbencher and an uninfluential one at that, who had made no attempt to bring others over with him. One potential defector explained, 'Had Prior or Gilmour said, in effect, "This is a turning point in history; we must consider joining the SDP", I would have thought very carefully about it.' But there was no Gang of Four—not even a Gang of One—to lead people like him out of the party. None of the senior wets seriously contemplated joining the SDP; indeed they discouraged any backbenchers they came across who were musing about defection, arguing that it was better to oppose from within than to abandon the party to the Thatcherites. 'It is not Margaret Thatcher's party,' Sir Ian Gilmour told Julian Critchley, 'it is as much ours as hers.' And anyway, 'the Social Democrats can't last—they are not interest-based'.[36]

Financial pressures were important. The potential defectors were, in the main, middle-aged men with families and mortgages but without substantial private means. They reckoned that their chances of being elected in their safe Conservative constituencies as a Social Democrat were slim. Most of them loved the parliamentary life, even if they were thoroughly fed up with the way their party was governing the country. They were not prepared to risk their career and financial security for such an uncertain prospect as the SDP. Some may also have worried that they would lose consultancies and directorships, as Brocklebank-Fowler claimed had happened to him, virtually overnight. 'Call it cowardice, if you like,' one backbencher said, 'but I had been out of parliament once, had a very difficult time sorting myself out and did not want to go through that again.'[37]

In one or two cases there were social and family pressures. In some rural and small-town constituencies the local Conservative MP is more than a mere politician: he and his family are figures in local society. In their case to renounce the party is to renounce an important social position, to exclude oneself from the traditional round. Moreover, this social ostracism affects not just the member but his whole family, and a few MPs—and their wives—were naturally unwilling to make the sacrifice. One Conservative backbencher who was very close to defecting but pulled back explained ruefully to a colleague that 'he could not deliver his wife—it was almost a divorce issue'.

Another reason for the lack of Conservative defections was that the discussions simply took place too late. A few potential Conservative defectors told members of the SDP in late 1981 that, so far as they were concerned, coming over was a matter not of if but when. They were in the same position as many Labour right-wingers had been a year earlier: depressed by the steady retreat of their brand of Conservatism and fearful that the position could not be reversed for many years, but still hoping against hope that somehow the party would change course. Some of them also hoped (in vain as it turned out) that Sir Ian Gilmour, now on the back benches, would organize and lead a revolt of the anti-Thatcher dissenters. The dissenters decided on these grounds to wait at least until the 1982 budget. And then, during the winter of 1981–2, the political tide turned. First, the results of the annual 1922 Committee elections, held in November 1981, turned out not to be the Thatcherite walk-over that many of the wets had feared. Then, early in the New Year, the Alliance's support began to slip in the polls. More important, the previously downward economic trends began slowly to level off, the public was increasingly optimistic about the economy, and the 1982 budget, when it came, was less deflationary than had been expected. Finally, in April 1982 the Falklands War broke out, after which any thought of defection evaporated: defection at that stage would have been tantamount to treason at a time of national crisis. Thus, potential defectors among Conservative MPs were saved by the last-minute miracle for which Labour MPs only a year earlier had been waiting in vain. Unlike their Labour counterparts, the Conservatives were never completely convinced that their party could not be saved.

The SDP's inability to recruit Conservative MPs, especially senior politicians like Gilmour, Heath and Prior, was a serious failure. An influx of liberal Conservatives would have provided additional parliamentary numbers and talent and would have encouraged other Conservative activists and voters to switch their allegiance. Even more important, it would have given increased validity to the Social Democrats' claim that they were in the business of realigning the entire British party system. Without Conservative recruits in significant numbers, the SDP appeared merely as a breakaway party from Labour, reshaping one side of the party system only. At least half of the political mould remained visibly intact.

In the absence of Conservative recruits, many in the SDP began their new political lives by having to come to terms with their party's relationship with the traditions and ideas of their old party, the Labour party. They were founding a new party, but in many cases they were not quite sure how new they really wanted it to be.

7

· · · ·

What Kind of Party, and Whose?

The events that led twenty-eight Labour MPs to break with their party in 1981–2 were as dramatic as any that British domestic politics is likely to provide; they inflicted heavy damage on the Labour party and in the end destroyed the careers of some of Britain's most promising politicians. That being so, a number of important questions need to be asked and answered—more explicitly than they have been so far. Why did the Gang of Four leave the Labour party? Why did they found a new party? What kind of party did they think their new party was going to be? There are also a number of intriguing 'what-if?' questions which it is at least worth attempting to answer.

To begin with, why did the Gang of Four and the other defectors leave the Labour party? We can dismiss one possible answer straightaway: their departure had little to do with the party's adoption of an electoral-college method of electing its leader—and even less to do with its failure to adopt the principle of 'one member, one vote'. In the first place, the change in the method of electing the leader was only one instance, and not in itself a very important instance, of the party's general shift to the left; if this particular change had not brought about the break, some other would have. Secondly, it is simply impossible to believe that the original Gang of Three would have opposed—passionately and in public—the idea of an electoral college if they had believed that it would result in the election of leaders whom they could trust; they did object to the electoral college in principle, to be sure, but they objected far more to its probable consequences. Thirdly, 'one member, one vote', as was pointed out in Chapter 2, was not at all a good issue from the Gang of Three's point of view: they were bound to lose on it; it was not an issue that ordinary voters were likely to get exercised about; it had the effect of making the Gang of Three and their followers appear hypocritical, since they had never shown any public interest in the subject when their faction of the party controlled it; and, on top of all that, the Gang of Three was far from being united on the issue. Owen felt very strongly about it (at least after he had taken it up) and Williams felt reasonably strongly about it (especially when it became clear that outright Communists could help to elect the leader of the Labour party); but Rodgers did not feel at all strongly about it—and indeed made no secret of the fact that on balance he thought the leader should continue to be elected by members of parliament. As for Jenkins, he shared Rodgers' view about the role of MPs and had anyway distanced himself from Labour long before the issue of 'one member, one vote' ever arose.

The electoral college and the principle of 'one member, one vote' became the sticking-point in the autumn of 1980 largely by accident, partly because it provided the beleaguered right-wingers with a relatively simple issue on which to stand and fight (either the party adopted the principle or it did not), but chiefly because the question of the electoral college happened to be the one question that was left over from the Blackpool conference to be decided at Wembley. The Gang of Three did not choose 'one member, one vote' as the issue on which to leave the Labour party: it chose them. The electoral college and 'one member, one vote' provided the occasion of the split; but they were not the 'causes' of the split any more than the cutting-off of Jenkins' ear 'caused' the minor war of that name in the eighteenth century.[1]

Another possible cause of the split, referred to frequently at the time and ever since, was Europe. It was indeed more important than 'one member, one vote', but not quite in the way that is often supposed. Jenkins, the Gang of Three and those who founded the SDP all favoured British membership of the European Community. Moreover, a few of them—Jenkins and Williams certainly—would have left the Labour party if it had ever become irrevocably committed to leaving the Community, regardless of other circumstances. For them, Europe was indeed a make-or-break issue. But, as we saw in Chapter 6, such 'Euro-fanatics' (as their Labour enemies liked to call them) or 'Euromaniacs' (as Thatcher liked to call them) were not in fact all that numerous among the defectors. Indeed, a substantial minority were decidedly lukewarm towards Europe. For most of those who were not Euro-fanatics, the Common Market was undoubtedly important in itself—they believed in it and wanted Britain to remain a member of it—but to them it was much more important for what it symbolized. To be in favour of the Common Market, in their eyes, was to be in favour of a Labour party and a Britain that were internationalist and forward-looking, that had succeeded in coming to terms with the real world; to be against the Common Market was to be parochial and backward-looking, hopelessly wedded to a vision of things that had never been and never could be. If the Labour party during the 1970s and 1980s had been becoming more anti-European on purely pragmatic grounds—say, because of opposition directed specifically at the Common Agricultural Policy—then those who were not extreme Euro-fanatics might not have minded so much. At least they could have been taking part in a rational argument. But that was not at all what was happening. Instead, the European issue was caught up in a much larger—and less rational—argument about the future of socialism and the future of the Labour party. What really mattered was not Europe in itself but that larger argument.

To make the point, suppose that by 1980–1 the European issue had actually been settled, that the Labour party, for whatever reason, had become reconciled to British Common Market membership. But suppose at the same time that everything else in the party had remained the same: that it was leaning ever further to the left on the leadership, on mandatory reselection, on incomes policy, on central economic planning, on nationalization, on the trade unions, on unilateral nuclear disarmament, on Britain's relations with America and the Soviet Union, on the whole rhetoric of revolutionary socialism and the class war. Would Jenkins, Owen, Rodgers and Williams, under those circumstances, Europe apart, have been content to stay in the party? The answer is surely 'no'. Europe, in short, was a sufficient condition to leave the Labour party for a few of the defectors, including some of the leading ones; but it was almost certainly not a necessary condition for any of them. The simple view that the formation of the SDP was nothing more than a mass migration of pro-Europeans out of the Labour party into the new party suffers from the additional defect that, as we saw in Chapter 6, many if not most of Labour's pro-Europeans did not migrate at all but stayed behind.

The role that the far left—the Trotskyites and their allies—played in bringing about the defections is more complicated. The far left's presence in the Labour party, and the fact that the traditional left was prepared to co-operate with it, undoubtedly made it very hard for some right-wingers to remain. Williams and Rodgers, in particular, were passionate anti-totalitarians; they loathed the Trotskyites and their thuggish allies, and in time they came to loathe almost as much the more old-fashioned left-wingers—like Ian Mikardo and Tony Benn—who took advantage of the far left's votes and support, who refused to have bodies like Militant Tendency expelled from the party, who refused to permit the Trotskyites' activities to be exposed publicly and who even denounced those who had the temerity to criticize the far left's tactics. Williams, Rodgers and others felt almost defiled by having to share their party with such a mob. The far left—and the welcome it received in some quarters—undoubtedly weakened the party's hold on their affections.

But such right-wingers would have been the first to acknowledge that what mattered was not the far left's presence in the party as such (unpleasant though that was) but rather the extent of its influence. One therefore has to ask: were the extremists in fact playing a crucial role in shifting Labour's constitution and policies to the left or were they really just an unpleasant nuisance? To put the same question another way, suppose that all the extreme left-wingers had been expelled from the party, as many on the right wanted: would their expulsion have made any significant difference to the ideological balance of power in the party, or would the move to the left have continued much as before, even in their absence?

The truth seems to be that many on the right, appalled and disgusted by the extreme left, considerably exaggerated its significance. The Labour party did indeed move to the left on the constitution, on a wide range of policy matters and in terms of the parliamentary leadership (witness the election of Foot). But there is no substantial evidence to suggest that these changes were brought about by

Trotskyites and other Marxist revolutionaries bent on destroying the parliamentary system. On the contrary, the available evidence strongly suggests that they were brought about by trade-union leaders and constituency activists who held more or less traditional Labour-left opinions and who naturally wanted to see those opinions become party policy.

These trade unionists and activists had come to the not unreasonable conclusion that the party's customary right-wing leaders could not be relied on to implement left-wing party policy and that, therefore, they must either be replaced or else made more strictly accountable to the party's rank and file. To explain the growth of the left's power in the party, it is not necessary to hypothesize the existence of vast numbers of insidiously influential Marxist revolutionaries burrowing away in the party: it is only necessary to take into account the factors outlined in Chapter 1: the post-1968 shift to the left in the trade unions; the widespread disillusionment in the party with the failures of the Wilson and Callaghan governments; the decline in the party's mass membership, especially its working-class membership; the organization and activities (perfectly above board) of the Campaign for Labour Party Democracy; and the feeling, very widespread in the party, that left-wing socialism was the only adequate response to the right-wing Conservatism of Edward Heath and Margaret Thatcher. The best evidence suggests, to repeat, that the party's shift to the left came about through means that were perfectly democratic and perfectly in accordance with the party's procedures. It occurred because the shift to the left was what the majority of Labour party members wanted; and it would undoubtedly have occurred even if the Trotskyites and their allies had never existed.[2]

But, of course, if the aim is to explain why those who defected from Labour did so, the extreme left's actual role matters less than what the defectors believed it to be—and there can be no question but that some of the defectors, including Williams and Rodgers, believed it to be very important indeed. (Others were less concerned, either because, like Horam, Thomas and Roy Jenkins himself, their alienation from Labour predated the rise of the extreme left or because in some cases, like that of David Owen, they had had little personal contact with it.) The question therefore needs to be asked: if some of the defectors had a tendency to exaggerate the extremists' influence, why did they do so? There are a number of answers, and they are easier to disentangle in retrospect than they were at the time. One answer undoubtedly has to do with the differing degrees of individuals' personal contact with the hard left: the more one saw of the Trots and their friends—and the more one saw them on the winning side—the more serious and significant they seemed to be. Williams, in particular, was much influenced by her experiences in her constituency and by her membership of the NEC. And, as Chapter 6 showed, right-wing Labour MPs with left-wing constituency parties were much more likely to defect than those with moderate parties. There was also almost certainly a 'noise factor' operating: the extremists, with their loud voices and clenched fists, were so vociferous that it was easy to mistake a vocal minority for an invading army. Moreover, the extremists were not only vocal, they were extremely menacing. Even allowing for the possible exaggeration of their influence, the consequences of being wrong, as in the case of 1930s Germany, were too horrible to contemplate.

An additional factor was that, in the political climate of the Labour party of the 1970s and early 1980s, it became more and more difficult to distinguish between the Militant Tendency and the Tribune Group, between the real hard-line revolutionaries on the one hand and the more traditional left-wingers on the other. After all, the two groups almost invariably supported each other; they attended meetings together; they voted for both the same constitutional changes and the same policies. One could be forgiven for finding it increasingly difficult to tell them apart—especially since the acknowledged leader of the parliamentary left, Tony Benn, by now both looked and sounded like a cross between Saint-Just and Lenin.

But there may have been another, more subconscious, reason why many on the right of the party—including some who did not defect—tended to exaggerate the importance of the hard left: they may have been reluctant to face the truth. If one could somehow convince oneself that the extreme left had 'taken over' the party, had succeeded in usurping power in some illegitimate way, then one could go on believing that all was actually still well, that the party's heart was still in the right place, that there were still thousands of ordinary, sensible men and women in the party, just waiting to be rallied. If, however, the extreme left was no more than a nuisance, and if it was actually the case that the party membership had, more or less of its own accord, moved significantly to the left, then the outlook was altogether gloomier. It is hard to escape the impression that many right-wingers exaggerated the extreme left's importance because the alternative possibility—that they were now in a permanent minority within their own party and had been put there democratically—was too distressing even to contemplate. It may be no accident that some of those who laid most stress on the influence of the hard left, including Williams and Rodgers, were among the last to reach their decision to leave. They were the ones most closely tied to the party; they, not surprisingly, found it hardest to accept the new reality.[3]

Be that as it may, it is probably true that neither the extreme left nor Europe (and certainly not the issue of 'one member, one vote') was crucial in causing the March 1981 breakaway. As so often on these occasions, the best explanation is probably the simplest. Those who defected did so, in the main, for two reasons. The first was that on issue after issue the party was adopting policies that they did not believe in and could not defend; the MP summed it up best who said that he was having the greatest difficulty in making a pro-Labour speech. The second reason was that the defectors had concluded, rightly or wrongly, that their cause was hopeless, that the changes that had taken place in the party were irreversible. Had they not come to the latter conclusion as well as the former, they probably would have stayed. As we saw in Chapter 4, leaving the Labour party caused most of them genuine anguish, genuine 'mental pain'.

Having decided to leave the party, why did the defectors decide at the same time to set up a new party? The short answer is, of course, that in the case of most of the defectors the two decisions were the same decision. Most of the defectors were members of parliament: short of simply resigning their seats, they had no choice but to go somewhere. All the same, several of the SDP's founders did seriously contemplate leaving politics altogether. David Marquand, a Jenkinsite, had actually left in the mid-1970s. John Horam and Ian Wrigglesworth, likewise, would probably have resigned their seats and gone into business if there had not been enough defectors to make a new party viable. Shirley Williams, too, seriously contemplated finding some alternative employment; she was no longer an MP and could easily have established—as she has since—a second career as a writer, lecturer and part-time (possibly even full-time) academic. In her case, the balance was probably tipped by her sense of duty and her love of politics, by the feeling that, if others were prepared to fight, she should be too, and also by her hatred of—and fear of—the hard-left extremists. For her, the SDP was intended to be more than just a means of expressing left-centre political opinions: it was meant to be a means of defending liberal democracy against anti-democrats of both ideological extremes.

Still, neither the defections nor the formation of the SDP were inevitable, and there are several 'what-if?' questions that are worth speculating about. What if, to begin with, Healey rather than Foot had won the Labour leadership election in November 1980? (The margin, after all, was exceedingly close.) The best guess is that, if Healey had won, defections on the scale that took place in March 1981 would probably not have occurred—or, if they had occurred, would have occurred much later. Jenkins might well have set up his new party, and it might well have been joined by a few of the Jenkinsite MPs, including, say, Neville Sandelson and Tom Ellis. But the Gang of Three would certainly not have left, nor would the great majority of those who followed them. Everything then would have turned on what kind of leader Healey turned out to be and how successful he was at stemming the left-wing tide. Had he turned out to be an aggressive Gaitskell-style leader, and had he shown that, given time, he could defeat the left, then most of the defectors would undoubtedly have stayed. Had he, alternatively, turned out to be a Gaitskell-style leader but had then lost, then the break, when it came, might well have been on an even bigger scale, with Healey himself possibly leading a breakout of dozens of right-wingers. If, however, Healey had turned out to be not a Gaitskell but a Callaghan, doing deals with trade-union leaders, prepared endlessly to compromise with the left in the interests of party unity, then the break, though postponed, would not have been prevented and, again, might have been on an even larger scale. One's judgement in the end depends on what one thinks of Denis Healey and on one's assessment of the balance of political forces inside the Labour party. Our judgement is that he would not have fought and that, if he had, he would have lost. The Labour party in the early and mid-1980s could only be led successfully from somewhere on the left.[4]

What if Healey, having lost to Foot, had nevertheless gone on to put himself at the head of the right wing in its battles within the party and, at the same time, had been joined in so doing by other like-minded right-wingers, Hattersley, Varley, Shore, perhaps Merlyn Rees, possibly Gerald Kaufman? The answer to this question is as certain as answers to such hypothetical questions can ever be: Jenkins might still have set up his personal party, but almost no one in the parliamentary Labour party would have joined him. Rodgers and Williams would have remained in the Labour party and, if they had remained in these circumstances, Owen almost certainly would have remained too. They would have stayed, partly because such a broadly based right-wing alliance would have held out some hope of success, but partly also because they would have found it impossible to desert—would not have wanted to desert—such a large number of their closest political friends and allies. And, of course, it goes without saying that, if the Gang of Three had stayed, so would most of the others who defected. Nothing did more to cause the break in March 1981 than the Gang of Three's sense that they were completely isolated within the party and that none of the other right-wingers in the shadow cabinet had the guts or the determination to join them in trying to fight back. In this sense, to Healey's name as one of the founding fathers of the SDP must be added the names of most of the other people just mentioned, certainly that of Roy Hattersley, whose failure to co-operate with the Gang of Three—worse, whose willingness to undercut them—caused them the greatest pain and outrage and also, fairly or unfairly, induced in them the greatest cynicism.[5] What would have happened if the right had fought back in a more or less united fashion and had nevertheless still lost—as seems probable—is anybody's guess. There might have been a larger breakaway than in March 1981. There might, alternatively, have been a mass exodus from active politics.

What if the Wembley conference had gone differently? There was no chance that it would accept the principle of 'one member, one vote'—and the Gang of Three and their allies must have known that when they decided to make it an issue—but there was always the possibility that it would indeed create an electoral college, but one in which the parliamentary party was given, not 30 per cent of the vote, as eventually happened, but, say, 50 per cent, as Michael Foot was advocating. If that had happened, the Gang of Four would almost certainly have gone ahead and issued their Limehouse Declaration (they would still have objected to the principle of trade-union bloc votes playing any part in the election of the party leader), but it is doubtful whether they would have attracted nearly so many other defectors, and they would certainly have been deprived of the immense pro-paganda victory that the actual Wembley result gave them (with even many of those who remained in the party describing it as a disaster and a disgrace). Indeed, rereading the record of the period, one is struck by the almost pathetic desire of many of those who finally defected to be afforded any reason, any excuse, any glimmer of hope, to enable them to reconsider their decision. At Wembley late on 26 January 1981 they must have begun to wonder whether there was not some sort of divine conspiracy to drive them out of the party. One of them actually said:

'I began to think that someone up there was trying to tell me something.' If the Wembley result had been significantly different, even with the electoral college, the formation of the SDP might have been delayed, it might have attracted less support, it might even not have occurred at that stage.

Two other 'what-if?' questions are closely related and concern the matter of who was chiefly responsible (apart from the left wing of the Labour party and, in his way, Denis Healey) for the launching of the SDP. Who deserves the credit or blame? Whose party was it?

The first of these two questions can be phrased in the form: suppose that Jenkins and the Jenkinsites had gone ahead on their own to form a new party but that, for whatever reason, they had not been joined by the Gang of Three: what would have happened then? The answer to that question seems incontrovertible: a new party would have been formed, but it would have been very small, it would have attracted the support of very few MPs, and at least in the short term it would have amounted to little more than a satellite party of the Liberals. The fact is that Jenkins as an individual had very little pulling power among right-wing Labour MPs. Even those who were thinking seriously about defecting regarded him as a remote figure. He was too conservative, he was no longer a politician, he was not really one of them. Almost all the people we talked to at the time, asked to distinguish between the role of Jenkins and the role of the Gang of Three in forming the SDP, downplayed Jenkins' role and emphasized that of the Gang of Three.[6] Moreover, Jenkins' standing in the country, although still considerable, was no longer what it once had been. A purely Jenkinsite party would not have been likely to attract popular support on anything like the scale that the SDP in fact secured in its first few months. And, of course, doubts about the new party's electoral prospects would have made Labour MPs, other than the few Jenkinsites, even more reluctant to defect than they already were.

The second question is simply the first turned the other way round: suppose the Gang of Three had gone ahead and formed a new party but that, for whatever reason, they had not been joined by Jenkins and his allies: what would have happened then? Again, the answer seems incontrovertible: a new party would have been formed, it would have been nearly as large as the SDP actually was, it would have attracted the support of nearly as many Labour MPs as the SDP actually did, and it would have had considerable popular appeal—though probably not quite as much as the SDP had in the event, with Jenkins among its collective leadership. It was, in short, the Gang of Three who led the breakaway, it was they who had the capacity to carry a significant mass of back-bench Labour MPs with them, and it was they who had the capacity actually to split the Labour party and not just to establish a new grouping in opposition to it. Jenkins contributed a great deal to the SDP—courage, vision, experience, a degree of popular appeal, widespread contacts in the outside world and in the City and industry—but the central fact is that the SDP could have been, and would have been, created without him. He was, as they say in the computer trade, an 'add on'. In that sense, the Gang of Three were not his lieutenants; he was theirs. That, however, was not the way he saw it—as has already emerged and will again.

The question still needs to be asked: what did Jenkins and the Gang of Three think they were doing when they set up the SDP? What kind of party was it to be? What sort of electoral appeal was it supposed to have, and to whom?

And here there is a problem, because it is hardly too strong to say that they did not know what they were doing. More precisely, each of the party's founders did have more or less clear ideas about what he or she wanted, but there was no very high level of agreement among the four or even any very serious attempt to reach such agreement. The SDP, at its very heart, was a muddle—and by and large was allowed to remain so.

This state of affairs may seem strange, but the reasons for it are obvious. Jenkins and the Gang of Three had long been comrades in the Labour party, they got on reasonably well together, they broadly shared the same goals, they knew that none of them was either a Thatcherite or a left-wing socialist. Above all, they were in a tremendous hurry: decisions about what to do or say next had to be taken every day, every hour, almost every minute. Under the circumstances, there was no incentive for them to have long discussions about what the nature of their new party ought to be. On the contrary, there was every incentive for them not to have such discussions, because, quite apart from taking up time, they would probably reveal differences that it was in no one's interests to reveal at this stage. They said to each other, in effect: 'Let's not talk in too much detail now. Any differences there are amongst us may not turn out to be all that important, and anyway, given time, they may sort themselves out on their own. Why interrupt what we're doing?'

In the midst of putting the finishing touches to the design of an 'experimental plane' one does not stop to argue about whether, if the plane flies, one is going to fly it to Washington or New York: one gets on with the job. Jenkins and the Gang of Three simply got on with the job.

Nevertheless, although there was no very precise agreement about the nature of the new party, it is possible to discern in the various statements that were issued and the speeches that were made in 1980–1 several different conceptions, all somewhat hazy, of the kind of party the SDP ought to be. The haziness derived largely from the fact that few people held only one of these conceptions; most of the SDP's founders drew on more than one; and people constantly changed their minds.

The simplest conception, and the one that was most attractive to many backbench MPs who joined the new party, might be called—and was called at the time—the 'Mark II Labour party' conception. On this analysis, the SDP's task was quite straightforward. There had once been a sensible, moderate, democratic Labour party. That party no longer existed. It should, therefore, be restored to life again as quickly as possible in the form of the SDP. In the words of one MP defector, 'I wanted us simply to announce that we *were* the Labour party.' Such a party— Labour resurrected—would be shorn of the hard left and the Bennite left; but it would still stand, like Labour in the past, for Keynesian economic management,

large-scale public ownership, government aid to industry and co-operation between government and unions. This conception had, in electoral terms, a simple
corollary. Just as the Labour party in the past had appealed mainly to working-class
voters, so now the SDP should do likewise. Bill Rodgers did not believe in any simple sense in a Mark II Labour party; but it was this conception he was alluding to
when, in his letter to Roy Jenkins quoted in Chapter 3, he spoke of any new party
'eventually taking over 90 per cent of the Labour vote'.[7] The holders of the Mark II
conception did not think of the SDP as competing with Labour in a new multiparty
system; they saw it as replacing the Labour party and eventually driving it out of
business altogether.

Another conception might be called—though it was not so called at the
time—the 'radical-idealist' conception. On this analysis, there were two things
wrong with the Labour party, not just one. One was that it had moved much too
far to the left on issues like nationalization, nuclear disarmament and Europe;
but the other, paradoxically, was that the party had in many ways become too
conservative. Instead of having become a classless party, it was still too closely tied
to the working classes; instead of having become a party concerned equally with
all sections of the community, it was still too closely tied to the trade unions.
Moreover, a new party should, as befitted a new party, be concerned with new
issues: Third World issues, internationalist issues, women's issues, environmental
issues, issues of racial equality. The radical idealists were much more critical of the
trade unions than were the proponents of the Mark II Labour party, and in general
they were more sceptical of the idea that big government could solve the world's
problems. They did not at this stage repudiate nationalization, economic planning,
government–union co-operation and such like, but they were more inclined to
favour devolution, decentralization, worker participation, co-operatives and profit-
sharing—the dispersal of power rather than its concentration.

Although they did not say so, the proponents of the Mark II Labour party
conception were in fact harking back to the 1950s and 1960s in their notion of
what the new party's electoral appeal should be: they simply wanted a new Labour
party substituted for the old one. The radical idealists were more agnostic. The new
party might, in an ideal world, simply replace Labour, but the danger was that, if
that happened, the SDP might just inherit the Labour party's old ideas and likewise
become too closely attached to old Labour party interest groups like the unions. On
balance, therefore, it would perhaps be better if the new party struck out on its own
and, instead of merely replicating Labour's old appeal, tried to reach out to new
kinds of voters and to win the kinds of educated middle-class parliamentary
constituencies in which Labour in the past had never done well.

Just to confuse the issue, the proponents of the Mark II Labour party
conception and the radical idealists, although they had different interests and
(incipiently) different ideas about where the new party's electoral appeal should
lie, both maintained that they were on the 'centre left', or even just 'the left', of
politics—and said that that was where they wanted the SDP to be too.

These two 'left-of-centre' conceptions may be contrasted with what could be called—and was called at the time—the 'centrist' conception. On this view, the SDP ought to be concerned, not so much to pursue specific lines of policy as to promote a new approach to politics. Britain was a deeply divided society, between class and class, between unions and management, between holders of extreme views on both left and right—and the SDP's first aim accordingly should be, together with the Liberals, to bring the country together again. Policies should be based as far as possible on consensus, and there should be as much continuity in the content of policy as possible, without the 'queasy rides on the ideological big-dipper' of recent years. In particular, bouts of nationalization should not be followed by bouts of denationalization; the existing frontiers between the public and private sectors might not be ideal, but it was better to leave them as they were rather than be continually trying to redraw them. The centrists, like the proponents of the Mark II Labour party, harked back to the 1950s and early 1960s; but, when they did so, they had in mind not so much Labour's then electoral appeal as the broad political consensus—'Butskellism'—that was the hallmark of the post-war period. The centrists did not see the SDP as supplanting either the Conservatives or Labour but rather as introducing into British politics a moderating third force, capable of working with like-minded people of all parties and of none.

Implicit in the centrist conception was a whiff of the old idea of 'a ministry of all the talents' or 'a government of national unity'. Overall, the centrist approach was mildly statist, mildly conservative, certainly not radical. The new party's electoral appeal, on this view, should not be to specific social classes but to men and women of good will in all sections of the community. The party should go out of its way to recruit people who had not previously been active in politics, possibly because they had been politically alienated by both the Labour party's and the Conservative party's extremism.

These conceptions were, as has been said, hazy, and it would be a mistake to distinguish too sharply among them. They overlapped; their lines crossed at many points. Even so, it can be seen that they did not all amount to the same conception and that there were many potential points of conflict between them—over the substance of policy, over political style, over whom the new party should be appealing to, over relations with the Liberal party. Intellectually as well as personally, the SDP was thus a somewhat disparate coalition even before it was born.

At least to begin with, it is probably fair to say that Bill Rodgers straddled the Mark II Labour party and the radical-idealist conceptions, David Owen was, more or less without qualification, a radical idealist, while Shirley Williams was a radical idealist on policy but had a Mark II Labour conception of whom the SDP should appeal to, while Roy Jenkins was a centrist, though with radical-idealist leanings. As time went on, all four changed their views to varying degrees, David Owen most of all, and new lines of cleavage began to emerge. Nevertheless, a large part of the history of the SDP remains the history of how these initial conceptions were—and were not—resolved.

Part II
. . . .
INFANCY

8
•••••

The Golden Age:
March–December 1981

The SDP was launched in late March 1981, and during most of its first year the party had quite astonishing momentum. Everything seemed to go right for it and wrong for its rivals. Success inspired favourable publicity; favourable publicity in turn inspired continuing success. The experience reminded one observer of a giant Saturn rocket lifting off from Cape Canaveral, another of the massive explosion of Mount St Helen's in the American state of Washington that had taken place in the previous year. The whole British party system seemed to be tearing itself apart. Such momentum could not, of course, be sustained, and the let-down, when it came, was severe; but in the meantime all those involved with the SDP hugely enjoyed themselves.

It was a stroke of good luck for the SDP that 1981 turned out, by coincidence, to be a ghastly year for both the Labour and the Conservative parties.[1] On the Labour side, the Gang of Three's departure was followed by a damaging struggle for the party's deputy leadership between Denis Healey and Tony Benn and by the rapid exposure of Michael Foot's supreme political incompetence. Foot not only failed to unite his party, though he had been elected to do just that: his speeches and his rambling answers to television interviewers' questions were positively embarrassing in their incoherence. The satirical magazine *Private Eye* dubbed him 'Worzel Gummidge' after a character in children's fiction who resembled an amiable but demented scarecrow. His dishevelled clothes, his puppet-like walk and his cane reminded others of Charlie Chaplin. By the end of 1981 the opinion polls were reporting that the British people had less regard for Michael Foot than they had had for any other opposition leader since opinion polls began (and he was to sink lower, much lower, in the months to come).[2]

Meanwhile, Healey and Benn were touring the country publicly abusing each other (though never by name) and offering totally discordant visions of Labour's and the country's future. Benn appeared frequently on television, and, since he was one of the most unpopular politicians in the country, his television appearances probably did the party almost as much damage as Foot's. The party's annual conference in October 1981 made matters, if anything, worse. Healey succeeded in defeating Benn for the deputy leadership but only by the narrowest of margins and after a series of bizarre revelations of how various unions had gone about deciding how to cast their ballots; the conference then went on to call, in all solemnity, for unilateral nuclear disarmament, unconditional and immediate withdrawal from the Common Market, the introduction of a thirty-five-hour week without loss of earnings, the total rejection of incomes policy in any form and the introduction of a 'fully socialized economy', with a massive extension of nationalization.[3] The 1981 conference, like those of 1979 and 1980, might almost have been designed to alienate ordinary voters. It certainly had that effect.[4]

On the Conservative side, things were every bit as bad. The Thatcher government's standing was damaged by inflation, which stood at over 10 per cent, and by high and rapidly rising unemployment, which doubled from 6 per cent when the Conservatives came to power in 1979 to 12 per cent at the end of 1981.[5] Worse in some ways, the government appeared incompetent even in its own terms. It could not meet its own public-spending targets, it could not meet its own tax-cutting targets, it could not meet its own interest-rate targets; it could not even meet, despite its emphasis on monetary policy, its own money-supply targets. Not surprisingly, given the government's failures on the economic front, both the cabinet and the Conservative party were divided and demoralized. Anti-Thatcher wets and pro-Thatcher dries fought running battles in public; accounts of flaming cabinet rows appeared regularly on the front pages of the newspapers; and there were even disagreements in public between the government and its allies in the business community, notably the Confederation of British Industry (CBI). The prime minister, however, insisted that there would be no changes in policy, and, as she did so, her personal standing with the public plummeted. In October 1981— resembling Michael Foot in this if in nothing else—Thatcher set a new record, becoming the least well-regarded British prime minister of the opinion-polling era.[6] It was during this period that she acquired such nicknames as 'Queen Margaret', 'Attila the Hen' and 'The Immaculate Misconception'.

This combination of Labour and Conservative unpopularity, occurring simultaneously, gave a tremendous boost to the Social Democrats and their soon-to-be Liberal allies. Figure 1 sets out the main parties' standings in the Gallup Poll during the eighteen months between October 1980 and March 1982. The statistics tell the story of one of the most remarkable transformations in the history of British politics. As the data in the figure show, the Liberals on their own at the beginning of the period were in the doldrums. At about 14–15 per cent, their standing had not declined since the 1979 election, but it had not improved either. In January– February 1981, in the midst of all the talk of the formation of a new party, the Liberals gradually edged upwards; and then, beginning in March 1981, with the SDP's launch, the SDP and the Liberals together made substantial gains, moving into second place behind Labour and staying there—either ahead of the Conservatives or neck-and-neck with them—during most of the summer and early

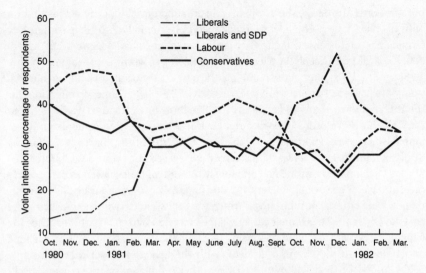

Fig. 1 The standing of the parties in the Gallup Poll, October 1980–March 1982

autumn. But it was after the Labour and Conservative conferences in early October that the real breakthrough came. To everyone's astonishment, the Liberals and the SDP moved into first place in the polls, staying there either on their own or tied with Labour (once) for the whole of the next six months. Early in 1982 the Liberals and SDP fell back somewhat, but, as the figure shows, they were still strongly in contention. A third-party surge on this scale and of this duration had never been seen before.[7] Some in the SDP, tempting fate, even began to talk about the share-out of offices in an SDP–Liberal government. (The Liberals, sufferers of so many disappointments in the past, tended to be more cautious.)

The new party's success owed much to the older parties' perceived failures; but it undoubtedly owed something, too, to the SDP's youthful ebullience and to its image of brightness, modernity and efficiency. Here was something different, a party that represented a break with the past and held out high hopes for the future. The party's founders seemed to be genuinely nice people and to have put behind them the meanness, the pettiness and the endless self-serving that disfigured the older parties in the eyes of voters. Instead of conflict, the SDP offered co-operation; instead of dogma, reason; instead of doctrinal rigidity, an apparent desire to meet opponents half-way. For large numbers of ordinary people, weary of decades of stale controversy that were leading the country nowhere, the new party had enormous appeal.

That was not, of course, how everybody saw it. There was a good deal of cynicism about the SDP among politicians and even among otherwise sympathetic journalists. Many outsiders viewed the new party with moral and even aesthetic disdain. The SDP's public image struck its opponents as a sickly over-sweet mixture of Little Lord Fauntleroy, Mary Poppins and the sanctimonious George Washington with his cherry tree. The new party claimed to be a break with the past, but Roy Jenkins had first been elected to parliament as long ago as 1948 and the Gang of Four had all been deeply implicated in the Labour governments' failures of the 1960s and 1970s. They could repudiate the past if they wanted to, but, if they did, they were going to have to repudiate themselves. The SDP claimed to offer hope for the future, but to many older hands the Limehouse Declaration was little more than a rehash of dozens of earlier right-wing Labour pronouncements (and one journalist, reading it, instantly dubbed the SDP 'the Boring party'[8]). As for the SDP's being especially nice, almost everyone agreed that that description fitted Shirley Williams, but no one had previously thought of David Owen as particularly nice, and views about Bill Rodgers and Roy Jenkins varied. Labour loyalists, in particular, were bitter about the way in which the SDP's leaders were now vilifying the party to which they owed their careers. They had refused to go on fighting inside the Labour party, yet they were now being fêted for their courage. They had declined in a holier-than-thou way to do deals with the Labour left, yet they were now being lauded for their willingness to meet other people half-way. 'Arrogant', 'self-centred' and 'opportunist' were words heard frequently on Labour loyalists' lips.

If the defectors themselves were bad enough in Labour loyalists' eyes, even worse were many of their supporters. Any MP can tell you that politics is a rough business, a matter of making difficult choices and being prepared to live with the consequences. Yet here were a bunch of people—the political equivalent of a well-heeled suburban church congregation—who seemed to think that all one had to do to solve the world's problems was to think the right thoughts and occasionally write out a modest cheque on one's substantial bank balance. A cartoon in *Private Eye*'s Great Bores series depicts an eager young housewife holding forth about the SDP to her neighbours over coffee:

I don't know but I'll probably vote for the SDP next time I mean the other two parties have completely failed and I really think that these people do offer something different I have enormous respect and admiration for Shirley Williams who I think has shown tremendous courage and they're very good you know on housing and welfare and so forth it really is very exciting what they're doing making a real change in the whole political thing breaking up you know this old way they have of doing things and offering a genuine alternative you know that hasn't been tried before because everything the other parties have tried has just failed that's why I think we should all vote SDP . . .[9]

Her neighbours grin well-meaningly. Likewise, a badge on sale at the 1981 Labour conference read simply: 'Take the politics out of politics: join the SDP'. Moreover, as the SDP's standing in the polls rocketed, the party's founders became a little hard to take as saints and martyrs: saints and martyrs are not supposed to enjoy worldly success on quite such a large scale.

In the weeks after the launch, the Gang of Four's time was largely taken up with speeches around the country (their meetings, though little reported, often attracting crowds numbering in the thousands) and also with the establishment of the new party's structures. As we shall see in Part III, permanent premises were found at 4 Cowley Street, a few minutes from the House of Commons; a business-man was appointed the party's chief executive; the SDP's membership records were put on a computer at the Midland Bank; and a marketing manager was put in charge of producing a colourful range of SDP T-shirts, tea towels, bumper-stickers and mugs. The drafting of a constitution was likewise put in train, and a network of 'area parties' was established throughout the country. Various policy commit-tees similarly began their work, with an interim steering committee in charge. Someone had the bright idea that the SDP's first conference, to be held in the autumn, should not take place in a single venue but should be a 'rolling con-ference', with journalists and the party's leaders transported from one town to another in a specially chartered train. In every way, the new party was to be as unlike the existing ones as possible.

Working relations with the Liberals also began to be established. At the Anglo-German Königswinter conference in early April, Bill Rodgers and Shirley Williams had a long talk, their first, with David Steel; they found to their surprise that they agreed with him about almost everything. With Steel determined that the two parties should reach broad agreement on policy and not merely on the terms of an electoral pact, representatives from the two sides met in May and early June to draft a short 'statement of principles'. The statement, published on 16 June 1981, was entitled *A Fresh Start for Britain*. It acknowledged that the Liberals and the SDP stemmed from different traditions and had separate identities but went on to say that they shared a common concern about the country's political and economic future. Therefore, it said, they intended to establish joint commissions on a number of major areas of policy and to consider 'how to avoid fighting each other in elections'. When the joint statement was launched, Shirley Williams and David Steel were photographed together sitting side by side on the lawn of Dean's Yard, Westminster, looking for all the world like two young lovers.[10]

The SDP at this stage made much of its collective leadership, and the Gang of Four as a concept was by now firmly established in the public's mind. Outsiders could be forgiven for supposing that the Gang collectively took all the major decisions affecting the SDP's future. But most politicians are individualists, not team players; they have as their first priority the furthering of their own political careers; and the Gang of Four were no exception. Even during the period of collective leadership, from the March 1981 launch until the election of the first leader of the party in July 1982, the Gang of Four took collectively all those decisions that had to be taken collectively; but they did not take collectively those decisions that directly affected them as individuals, even if those decisions were almost certain to have an important bearing on the future of the party as a whole. From the outside, the Gang of Four probably looked like the board of directors of a large public company. And to some extent they acted like that. But, at the same time, they remained very much four separate individuals, each in political business on his (or her) own account. The extent to which this was true began to emerge only a few weeks after the party's launch, in May 1981.

Late that month, Sir Tom Williams, the right-wing Labour MP for Warrington near Manchester, resigned his seat to become a judge. A by-election would have to be held during the summer or autumn, and there was immediate speculation about whether the SDP would fight it. On the face of it, it seemed a no-win proposition from the new party's point of view. The SDP had no organization in Warrington and no candidate. More to the point, although the Liberals and Social Democrats were doing extremely well in the national polls, the Labour party was still ahead and Warrington was a very safe Labour seat. Labour had got 62 per cent of the vote there in 1979, the Liberals a mere 9 per cent. Moreover, the constituency, was solidly working-class, in a region that, as a whole, was staunchly pro-Labour. The SDP's dilemma was obvious. If the party did not fight Warrington, its claims to be taken seriously as a national party would immediately be called in question; if however, it did fight and lost, as seemed certain, much damage would have been done. The most the party could hope for was to come a respectable second; the worst it had to fear was that it would be totally, perhaps fatally, humiliated.

Under the circumstances it might have been supposed that the Gang of Four would decide together what line the party should take. Indeed the Gang, together with the steering committee, did decide that the new party should fight the seat; but no collective thought was given as to who the candidate should be. In particular, the Gang did not consider whether the candidate should be one of the two of them, Roy Jenkins and Shirley Williams, who were not already MPs. The two were left entirely on their own to decide for themselves. Failing either of them, it seemed that the candidate would probably be some lesser figure, possibly someone in the constituency. David Marquand's name was mentioned; so was that of Sir Tom Williams' son, David, who, unlike his father, had defected from the Labour party and who desperately wanted to fight the seat. Whoever in the SDP finally took the plunge, the Liberals in the constituency, of whom there were not many, said that they would be happy to stand aside.

Most people in the SDP hoped and believed that Shirley Williams would be the candidate. She was believed to have far more appeal to manual workers and their families than the other possible contenders, and the fact that she was a Catholic seemed likely to help in a constituency with a substantial Catholic minority. A private poll commissioned by the party showed Labour well in the lead whoever the SDP candidate was; but it also suggested that Shirley Williams would attract more votes from Labour—and also from the Conservatives—than either Roy Jenkins or an unnamed 'Social Democrat with Liberal support'.[11]

However, after thinking the matter over for a few days, Williams decided that Warrington was not for her. Her reasons were partly political, partly personal. Politically, she thought it would simply be too risky for the new party to field one of the Gang of Four in Warrington: the chances of success were minimal; the risks of humiliation were too great to be worth running. Personally, she was deterred by the fact that no one knew when the Labour chief whip would move the by-election writ. It might not be until the autumn; but Warrington was a long way from London and, if the by-election were long delayed, Williams would find herself having, in effect, to commute between the two cities for several months. She did not wish to be away from her daughter so frequently and for such long periods, and a prolonged by-election campaign would also cut substantially into her freelance income. (Unlike Owen and Rodgers, she did not have an MP's salary; unlike Jenkins, she did not have an EEC pension.)

But others put a different construction on her decision. They thought she had simply funked it. She had been upset at losing her seat in the 1979 election; she could not, it was said, face the thought of losing an election a second time. Owen, in particular, was appalled. He wanted Williams to be the leader of the new party, and now she might not even have a seat in the House of Commons when the time came.[12] Worse, her decision raised serious doubts about her courage. Owen's feelings were shared by other MPs and members of the SDP's steering committee and were also reflected in the press. If the SDP was supposed to be a crusade, why had one of the crusaders-in-chief not unsheathed her sword? Williams was said to have 'declined to take up the challenge', to have 'flinched' in the face of the odds.[13] There were many phrases like these. They stung.

Meanwhile, Jenkins, ever the fisherman, was sitting on the river bank waiting to see what Williams decided to do. He was no more keen to fight Warrington than she was. Indeed, he was probably less keen, since he had more to lose than she did: if he lost badly at Warrington, that would probably be the end of his political career. But Williams' decision not to stand, and the negative response that greeted it, immediately forced his hand. He badly wanted the party leadership, and he knew that, if Williams did not fight Warrington, he had to: otherwise he, too, would be accused of being gutless. The by-election would also provide Jenkins with a wonderful opportunity to demonstrate that he was not in fact a remote grandee but was capable of fighting an effective election campaign in an industrial constituency. Williams' decision did indeed force Jenkins' hand—but at the same time it made things easier for him. He would now not lose too much in personal terms if he did badly; if he did well, his claims to the SDP leadership would be considerably strengthened.

In the event, the Warrington by-election was a triumph for the former chancellor. On 11 June 1981 Jenkins travelled by train to the constituency, to be acclaimed as the SDP's candidate at an enthusiastic and crowded meeting.

The idea [he said] that I have served my political life in rolling pastures or leafy suburban avenues, which some newspapers seem to suggest, is ludicrous. I have represented one of the most industrial seats in Birmingham for 27 years. I believe I had happy relations with them. I certainly won nine elections there.[14]

The Conservatives chose as their candidate a London bus driver, Labour a man called Doug Hoyle, a left-wing member of the National Executive who had lost his seat at Nelson and Colne two years earlier. Labour's chief whip, seeking to deprive the new party of time in which to build up a local organization, called the election for 16 July, far sooner than anyone had expected.

It was anybody's guess how Jenkins, with his reputation for grandness and remoteness, would be received in the town; and his campaign began rather slowly, with the opinion polls suggesting that Labour would romp home, with the SDP being lucky to take as much as a quarter of the vote. But in fact the citizens of Warrington seemed to enjoy having a celebrity in their midst—and Jenkins increasingly looked as though he enjoyed being there. Shy at first, he became more and more relaxed—and his grin became broader and broader—as the campaign wore on. The presence of the whole Gang of Four—plus the Liberals' David Steel at the final eve-of-poll rally—turned what would otherwise have been a routine by-election campaign into something like a midsummer carnival. Shirley Williams was especially well received, with smiles and kisses blown at her everywhere. Even so, only a few moments before the result was declared, Bill Rodgers, not normally a pessimist, confided to someone standing next to him that he thought Jenkins would be doing well if he got as much as 30 per cent of the total vote.

When the returning officer read out the actual result there was uproar in the hall. Hoyle had won as expected; but Labour's 1979 majority of 10,274 had fallen to a mere 1,759, and Labour's share of the vote had shrunk from 62 to 48 per cent. Jenkins, a rank outsider, the candidate of a party that had not even existed only four months before, had captured 12,521 votes, 42 per cent of the total. Even Jenkins' most sanguine supporters were amazed, and Robert McKenzie, on BBC television in the small hours next morning, called Warrington 'the most sensational by-election result of the century'. Jenkins, in his speech of thanks to the returning officer, cast aside his prepared notes and proudly declared that, while this was his first election defeat in thirty years in politics, in reality it was the greatest victory he had ever participated in.

The result of the Warrington by-election gave the SDP credibility in a way that no number of opinion polls could possibly have done. Far from being humiliated, the SDP had come a close second in a seat it had never dreamt of winning. It was the Labour party that had been humiliated. 'There have', the *Guardian* wrote, 'been false dawns before; but there has been no time when a fundamental change in the pattern of British politics looked more likely to come than it does this morning.'[15] Journalists and politicians began to talk about the possibility of the SDP and the Liberals holding the balance of power after the next election; they even contemplated the possibility that the two parties might win outright. Warrington also transformed Roy Jenkins' personal position. No longer merely one of the Gang of Four, he was now its dominating figure. The SDP MPs were especially impressed. Most of them had tended to think of Jenkins as a has-been and something of a poseur. No longer.

Warrington also made clear what should have been apparent already: that for the foreseeable future the new party was going to live or die by by-election results.

Everything would, therefore, depend on whether the seats that happened to fall vacant were, or were not, winnable by the SDP or their Liberal allies. The two parties had already agreed in principle on a national electoral pact, but they had not yet had time to work out in detail which party would fight which individual seats. Instead David Steel persuaded the Gang of Four that, so far as by-elections were concerned, they should simply, for the time being, take turns. Since the Liberals had given Jenkins a free run in Warrington, it followed that the next seat to come up would automatically be fought by the Liberals.

The next seat to fall vacant in fact did so unexpectedly quickly, following Jenkins' adoption in Warrington but before the result there was known. It was Croydon North-West, a marginal seat in outer London whose sitting Conservative MP, Robert Taylor, had died. With the Conservative party doing badly in the polls, Croydon appeared to be a far better bet for the alliance than Warrington had been—and, for that reason, the question of whether the Liberals or the SDP should contest it became fraught. It was undoubtedly the Liberals' turn; and, moreover, the Liberals already had a candidate in place, a combative bearded local-government officer named Bill Pitt. The only trouble with Pitt was that he had already fought the seat three times and on all three occasions had finished a bad third; in 1979 he had actually lost his deposit. If the SDP and the Liberals were to maintain their momentum, a seat like Croydon North-West had to be won, and Pitt did not begin to look like the person to win it. Steel—not too bothered by the inter-party agreement to take turns or by the fact that he was the Liberals' leader rather than the SDP's—wanted the seat to be won and reckoned that the person who could win it was Shirley Williams. She, therefore, should be the candidate. She for her part, still stung by the suggestions that lack of courage had led her not to fight in Warrington, was more than willing. Croydon also had the advantage of being near her London home.

But it was not to be. Before the Warrington result was declared, Pitt appeared to be willing to stand down in favour of a more prominent candidate from either the Liberals or the SDP; but Jenkins' near-miss in Warrington not unnaturally caused him to change his mind: 'Bill Pitt *MP*' suddenly seemed a real possibility. Considerable publicity was being given to the possibility that Williams might be the Croydon candidate, but Pitt now refused to budge. A private lunch with Steel made no difference; neither did an orchestrated campaign of phone calls from other leading Liberals. 'Why', Pitt's wife wanted to know, 'should the Social Democrats think only the top nobs can stand? If the alliance with the Liberals is to succeed, there should be ordinary candidates too.'[16] It was a fair point.

In the end Williams withdrew, gracefully, freely acknowledging the Liberals' prior claim to the seat. But David Owen, already showing signs of being less keen on the alliance with the Liberals than many of his colleagues, was irked. In his view, Williams should have announced that she was going to fight the seat no matter what the Liberals did; if Pitt insisted on standing, too bad: Williams would beat him. But Owen knew he was in a minority on the issue and kept his thoughts largely to himself. The Conservatives meanwhile still regarded the seat as an old-fashioned Labour–Conservative marginal, despite the Warrington result, and accordingly determined on a leisurely timetable for the by-election. It would not be held until the autumn. The Conservative chief whip apparently hoped that the Conservative party conference in October would restore the Conservatives' flagging fortunes while the Labour party's conference would further damage Labour's. Pitt and the Liberals seem scarcely to have figured in his calculations.

The difficulties over Croydon were a disturbing reminder that forging an alliance between the fiercely independent Liberals and the SDP, dominated as it was by defectors from the Labour party, was not going to be easy. As a result, there was a degree of nervousness in the two parties' leaderships about what might happen at the Liberals' own annual assembly, due to be held in September 1981 at Llandudno in north Wales.

Any serious doubts that existed before the assembly, however, were almost immediately dispelled. The editors of the Liberal magazine *New Outlook* had organized a joint Liberal–SDP meeting to take place at the beginning of the conference week. On the platform at the *New Outlook* meeting David Steel was joined by Roy Jenkins and Shirley Williams and also by Jo Grimond, the former Liberal leader. Grimond's presence was important, because he was thought to be somewhat tepid about the idea of the Liberals and the SDP getting together; he was a small-'l' liberal and appeared to suspect that the Social Democrats, for his taste, were too centralist and government oriented. In the event, the atmosphere in the large Llandudno hall where the meeting was held was electric. People cheered, stamped their feet and applauded till their hands hurt. A few cried. Williams was given a spontaneous standing ovation, and Jenkins was interrupted by loud and prolonged applause when he called for Bill Pitt's election in Croydon. Some found the meeting almost too emotionally charged.

At the Liberal assembly proper, a motion calling for an electoral pact between the two parties was carried by 1,600 votes to 112. A motion designed to delay ratification of the pact was defeated by a similar margin. On the final Friday, in his leader's speech, Steel, looking more confident and commanding than ever before, insisted that the future of the country would depend on the Liberals' foresight, conviction and courage in the coming years. He looked forward, he said, to the formation of 'a great reforming government' by his own party and its Social Democratic allies:

Now at last we have the reality in our grasp. We must have the nerve and courage not to let it slip. I have the good fortune to be the first Liberal leader for over half a century who is able to say to you at the end of our annual assembly: go back to your constituencies and prepare for government.[17]

The SDP's own rolling conference—coming only a week after Labour's acrimonious conference in Brighton—was an even greater success. The new party still lacked a proper constitution, and the conference therefore had only consultative status, but the debates were friendly and earnest, the speeches by the Gang of Four and the SDP's MPs were listened to attentively, and all those present evidently believed they were in at the beginning of a great undertaking. The decision to have the conference make a circular tour of the country by chartered train—from London to Perth in the Highlands of Scotland, then to Bradford in the industrial north of England and finally back to Central Hall, Westminster, symbolically close to the Palace of Westminster—turned out to be inspired. The train's arrivals and departures made good television, far better than the usual pictures of bored-looking delegates in seaside conference halls; and most of the journalists covering the conference, whatever their own views, were amused and intrigued by the occasion's sheer novelty. On the train itself songs were sung, drinks drunk, stories told. And the atmosphere was one of tremendous good will and camaraderie. The symbolism of the whole occasion worked: the chartered train and the new party were both on the move.[18]

The train was fun; but more important in sustaining the new party's momentum was the spectacle during 1981 and 1982 of a steady progression of MPs out of the Labour party's ranks into the SDP's. Admittedly, some of the newcomers were not quite as welcome as others. Michael O'Halloran, as we saw in Chapter 6, was the product of an old-fashioned Irish political machine in north London. He played scarcely any role in the House of Commons and was clearly one of those Alan Beith had in mind when he referred to 'machine men' whose machines have broken down. Eric Ogden had been denied re-selection by his CLP. But, taken as a whole, the new defectors were an impressive group. Dickson Mabon had been a junior Scottish Office minister and then minister of state at the Energy Department. Tom McNally was a former head of Labour's International Department and had been a political adviser to Callaghan as both foreign secretary and prime minister. John Grant had been a junior minister in three departments: Civil Service, Employment and Overseas Development. George Cunningham was one of the ablest and most respected backbenchers in the House of Commons. The SDP was particularly gratified to have attracted McNally and Grant. Like John Cartwright, they were both genuine Labour men. It cost both a great deal to come over.

The favourable impression created by the continuing defection of Labour MPs was reinforced by the defection of Labour councillors in many parts of the country and also by a long run of Liberal and SDP successes in local by-elections. Until 1981 no one had paid much attention to the results of local by-elections, which were held rather sporadically, often in obscure towns and villages, frequently with minuscule turn-outs. But the rise of the SDP caused political correspondents and the parties themselves to begin to monitor them closely—and they increasingly told a story of Liberal–SDP gains. In late July, for example, the Liberals and the SDP each captured a very safe seat from Labour in the London borough of Lambeth. The SDP then went on to capture a safe Labour ward in Hemel Hempstead in Hertfordshire, and the two alliance parties together captured a total of three council seats in Guisborough in Cleveland. The Liberals with SDP support gained a seat in Buckinghamshire, and the Liberals also held a Merseyside seat with a 50 per cent increase in their share of the poll. Similar results were reported month after month, and the Liberals, in particular, became adept at ensuring that they received maximum coverage in the media.[19]

The Croydon North-West by-election meanwhile was held on 22 October 1981. It was already clear that postponing it until the autumn had been a serious blunder from the Conservatives' point of view. By October 1981 the Labour party had, as expected, slumped still further in the polls, but so had the Conservatives, with unemployment still rising and the government in disarray. Bill Pitt, who described himself as a Liberal–SDP Alliance candidate (with a capital 'A') on his ballot paper, won the seat easily, turning a Conservative majority of 3,769 into a Liberal majority of 3,254. He nearly quadrupled his previous share of the vote, from under 11 per cent in 1979 to 40 per cent. It was the Conservatives' first by-election loss since the general election, and Labour found itself driven for the first time into third place (in a seat that, until recently, it had hoped to win). The Liberals contributed an efficient organization, largely brought in from outside, and thousands of enthusiastic workers. The SDP contributed workers and also the presence of the Gang of Four. By polling day, Shirley Williams was looming almost as large in Bill Pitt's campaign as Pitt was. Afterwards it was universally agreed that, if the Alliance could win with Bill Pitt, it could win with anybody. Warrington, it seemed, had by no means been a flash in the pan. Roy Jenkins declared, following the announcement of the Croydon result, that British politics would 'never be the same again'.[20]

The SDP's momentum during its first year was, as we said earlier, driven by by-elections. The succession of by-election campaigns overlapped, with the enthusiasm and organization of each spilling over into the next. Well before the campaign in Croydon North-West was over, another was already well under way—and this time the Alliance's candidate was, at last, Shirley Williams.

The third Alliance by-election, also caused by the death of a sitting Conservative, Graham Page, came in Crosby in Lancashire. Crosby, like Warrington, was far from being ideal from the Alliance's point of view—but for opposite reasons. Despite being situated on Merseyside to the north-west of Liverpool, Crosby was a Conservative bastion, a prosperous middle-class suburb with few working-class enclaves. Its leafy streets were lined with golf courses, private schools and stockbrokers' Tudor mansions. The late Conservative MP's 1979 majority had been 19,272, more than five times the Conservatives' majority in Croydon North-West. Politics apart, this was not the kind of seat that Shirley Williams wanted to fight. Crosby was, for her, an altogether too comfortable sort of place; she would have preferred to fight a Labour-held inner-city constituency. Also, Crosby was even further than Warrington from her London home. But this time she had no choice. Not to fight Crosby, after having let Warrington and Croydon go by, would be to risk being dismissed out of hand as a political lightweight and coward. She had to demonstrate, quickly, that she was capable of acting decisively in her own interest.

All the same, she arrived in Crosby by a somewhat circuitous route. As soon as the seat fell vacant, she made it clear to the rest of the Gang of Four that she was interested in fighting it; and she and they discussed the situation with David Steel in Perth at the start of the SDP's rolling conference. But there were two complications. One was the fact that the Crosby Liberals already had a candidate: Anthony Hill, a law lecturer who had stood for the party in 1979, winning 15 per cent of the vote. The other was that, following the ratification of the SDP–Liberal electoral pact at Llandudno, each party was now committed to fighting only the seats allocated to it as the result of inter-party negotiations—which, however, had not yet taken place. The principle of taking turns in by-elections was supposed to have lapsed. Steel was nevertheless clear in his own mind that Williams ought to be the agreed candidate in Crosby. He wanted to sustain the Alliance's momentum, and he reckoned that in a place like Crosby, with its huge Tory majority, only Williams could do it. He, therefore, as he had in Croydon, set about trying to persuade the prospective Liberal candidate and the local Liberals that, even though Williams was a Social Democrat, she should be offered the nomination.

Steel, however, had scarcely begun the private process of persuasion in Crosby when Williams, determined after Warrington to restore her reputation for boldness and decisiveness, declared in public her readiness to be the candidate. She made her announcement, without having warned either Steel or the rest of the Gang of Four, at the Bradford session of the SDP's rolling conference. Crosby, she declared, was a high mountain, but even the highest of mountains had to be scaled.[21] Fortunately, the Crosby Liberals did not seem to resent her public pronouncement—they may even have been flattered by it—and a month later, on 19 October 1981, three days before the announcement of Pitt's victory in Croydon, they adopted her as their candidate. With Anthony Hill beside her on the platform, Williams told a cheering crowd that Crosby would, of course, be a challenge but that after Warrington no seat in the country was unwinnable.[22]

Shirley Williams' campaign in Crosby reproduced the carnival atmosphere of Warrington but on an even more exuberant scale. The rest of the Gang of Four and David Steel were in the constituency during much of the campaign, and thousands of Liberal and SDP supporters flocked into Crosby from elsewhere on Merseyside and from all over the country. Even in the midst of the carnival atmosphere at Warrington, Jenkins still tended to play the world statesman. He had preserved a certain detachment. That was not at all Williams' style. She threw herself into a fourteen-hour-a-day schedule of meetings, walkabouts, debates and canvassing; she was preceded everywhere she went by a sound truck blaring out the theme music from *Chariots of Fire*. Someone dubbed her 'the tiny tornado'. The only slightly worrying element, early on, was the Conservatives' determination to remind voters, in a constituency in which an above-average number of parents sent their children to fee-paying schools, of her well-known opposition to such schools. Fortunately for her, she seemed to manage to deflect the issue, pointing out, among other things, that the SDP could not abolish independent schools even if it wanted to, since the European Declaration of Human Rights contained a guarantee of freedom of parental choice.

Polling day was 26 November 1981. As it approached, the opinion polls were unanimous in forecasting an SDP victory. Even so, the scale of the new party's victory was breathtaking, dwarfing the results in both Warrington and Croydon. On a 69 per cent poll—only 6 per cent down on the general election—Shirley Williams converted a Conservative majority of 19,272 into an Alliance majority of 5,289. The Conservative share of the vote fell from nearly two-thirds to less than half. The Labour candidate, as in Croydon, finished third. Williams only just failed to achieve an absolute majority, and her share of the vote was more than three times that of the Liberals in 1979. In her victory speech she declared that she now had no doubt that the SDP and the Liberals would sweep on to victory together at the next general election:

This is not for us a party but a crusade, an attempt to find a democratic alternative to what we believe to be the growing extremism of politics in Britain, the move in the Labour party towards the rejection of parliamentary democracy and the move of the Conservative party to a level of unemployment that threatens the very social fabric of our society.

She quoted Dryden: 'It is well old age is out and time to begin anew.'[23] Williams was the first person to be elected to parliament under the SDP's own red, white and blue banner.

The result in Crosby reflected the Liberals' and the SDP's standing in the opinion polls and also gave it an additional impetus. As can be seen from Figure 1, the Alliance in the Gallup Poll took the lead over both the other parties in October 1981, increased that lead slightly in November and then increased it substantially in December. The figures in December 1981 were scarcely believable: 51 per cent of Gallup's respondents said they would vote Liberal, SDP or Alliance at an early general election, the highest level of support recorded for any party during the 1979 parliament. A mere 23 per cent said they would vote Conservative, the lowest figure recorded by Gallup for either major political party since the 1930s when opinion polling in Britain began. Gallup's findings may have been the result of a sampling fluke—no one will ever know—but it was findings like these that led to loose talk, as in Williams' victory speech, of an imminent Alliance government.

For all those active in the SDP, the months from the launch on 26 March until the end of 1981 were immensely exhilarating. There was no time to think, scarcely even time to take breath; but relations among the Gang of Four were good, relations at party headquarters were good, and relations with the Liberals were also good. The SDP and the Liberals were sweeping all before them. It was a time, rare in politics, of genuine comradeship, when differences of opinion and personal rivalries were almost completely submerged by people's sense that they were engaging in a common enterprise—an enterprise that, moreover, looked as though it might succeed beyond anyone's wildest expectations. The SDP, born in despair, was now full of hope. There seemed every reason to be optimistic about the future, no real reason not to be. But, in truth, events and circumstances, which had conspired in the SDP's favour throughout 1981, were about to conspire against it. The party was never again to be so lucky. Although no one knew it, as they celebrated the coming of the 1982 New Year, the SDP's golden age was already over.

9
• • • •
Jenkins as Leader: 1982–1983

The period from the autumn of 1981 to the early spring of 1982 marked the high point of the SDP's fortunes. During that period the new party won parliamentary and local by-elections, did well in the polls and was seldom out of the news; talk of an SDP–Liberal government, though far-fetched, was not absurd. But in the early months of 1982 the Alliance began to lose momentum. First, it failed to win new support and then, gradually, it started to lose its existing support. By-election victories became less frequent, press and television coverage less lavish. The Liberals and the SDP continued to claim in public that they hoped, indeed expected, to form the next government; but in private such optimistic talk gradually petered out.

Figure 2 sets out the three major parties' standings in the Gallup Poll from October 1981 until the eve of the general election in June 1983. The two Alliance parties, as can be seen, suffered a small loss of support between late 1981 and early 1982, but they nevertheless continued to do well and to lead both Labour and the Conservatives until April 1982 (except in March when they tied with Labour). But then there began a steep decline, which saw the SDP and the Liberals fall below 30 per cent in May 1982 and stay there for the rest of the parliament. In May 1983, an especially bad month, the proportion backing the Alliance, according to the Gallup Poll, was scarcely greater than the number who had said they would vote for the Liberals on their own in late 1980, before serious talk of forming of a new party had even begun. Labour probably benefited to some slight degree from the Alliance's decline; but the major beneficiaries were the Conservatives. Between November 1980 and April 1982 the Conservatives' standing in the Gallup Poll never rose above 40 per cent; between May 1982 and June 1983 it never fell below that figure. The initial explosion of Alliance support was thus followed by an almost equally massive explosion of Conservative support. What, from the Alliance's point of view, had gone wrong?

It is clear that the principal causes of the Alliance's downturn in early 1982 had very little to do with the Alliance. The SDP and the Liberals did not do anything

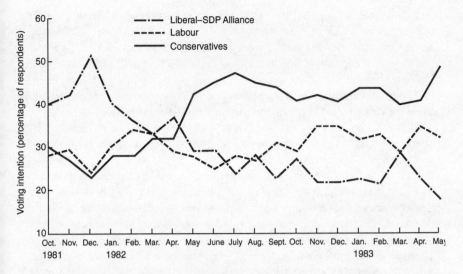

Fig. 2 The standing of the parties in the Gallup Poll, October 1981–May 1983

spectacularly wrong; their problem was that, at long last, the fortunes of the Thatcher government began to improve. The rate of inflation began to fall in the spring of 1982, from 11 per cent at the beginning of the year to 9 per cent in the early summer; and unemployment, while it continued to rise, did so less rapidly than before, the overall figure stabilizing at around 12 per cent.[1] The real incomes of those who were in work increased at the same time, and there was a sharp improvement in most people's economic expectations. As David Sanders and his University of Essex colleagues have shown, it was this improvement in the economy, more than any other single factor, that accounted for the government's and the Conservative party's recovery.[2] It was already clear from the opinion polls and the Croydon and Crosby by-elections that a significant proportion of the voters who were attracted to the Alliance were dissident Conservatives—people who had voted Tory in 1979 and, other things being equal, would probably vote Tory again. If they were sufficiently alienated from a Conservative government, they would not switch to Labour, but they might support a centre party. In 1982–3, however, the economic recovery was making them feel better about both Margaret Thatcher and her policies. The Conservatives' standing was given an additional boost in the spring of 1982 by Britain's victory in the Falklands War. In the four months before Argentina invaded the Falklands, the Conservatives' average standing in the Gallup Poll was 30 per cent; in the following four months, it was 45 per cent. Thatcher had had the stench of failure about her. Now she wore the crown of success.

That said, the Alliance's decline probably did owe something, if not a great deal, to the Alliance itself. Otherwise, it is hard to explain the whole of its continuing downward drift, even allowing for the improvement in the economic situation.

One problem was that the media lost interest in the Social Democrats. This was largely inevitable. A new party is news; a party that has been in existence for nine months is no longer news. By early 1982 television and the newspapers had had enough of pictures of Roy Jenkins looking statesmanlike and Shirley Williams looking winsome. Moreover, as Chapter 14 will show, the SDP had never been all that popular with the national press, most of which was strongly pro-Conservative or (in the case of the Mirror Group) strongly pro-Labour. As soon as the SDP and the Liberals ran into trouble, journalists and their editors were eager to draw attention to the fact. A few of them probably felt guilty about having given the SDP so much media-hype in the first place.

Another factor—a consequence as well as a cause of the Alliance's decline— was the emergence of some degree of internal stability in the Labour party. Healey's victory over Benn was quickly accepted as final by both sides, and for the time being the left seemed content to consolidate its advances without trying to make new ones. A tacit truce was thus declared in Labour's civil war. It prevented a further erosion of Labour's electoral support during 1982. More important, it reduced Labour MPs' incentives to defect to the SDP. By the spring of 1982, most of those who were ever likely to defect had probably done so already; but another half-dozen or so might have gone over if life in the Labour party had become even more intolerable. The fact that it did not meant that the once-steady migration of Labour MPs out of the party into the SDP at first slowed, then stopped altogether. The fewer who defected, the fewer who were likely to defect—and the SDP lost another source of publicity.[3]

Meanwhile, the new party and the Liberals were beginning to lose their reputation for niceness. On Sunday, 3 January 1982 the *Observer* carried a front-page story in which Bill Rodgers announced that he had, on the SDP's behalf, broken off negotiations with the Liberals over the share-out of parliamentary seats. As we shall see later, the immediate difficulties following Rodgers' declaration were soon smoothed over and the negotiations were quickly resumed; but the episode left a bad taste in many people's mouths and was widely blamed for the Alliance's loss of support in the polls. An SDP MP remarked: 'It made us look no different from other people.'[4]

The tensions between the SDP and the Liberals were matched by tensions within the SDP. In early February 1982 the parliamentary party split three ways over a trade-union reform bill introduced by the employment secretary, Norman Tebbit. The bill placed restrictions on the closed shop and also widened considerably the range of actions taken by trade unions and their members for which the unions could be held financially responsible. The majority of the SDP MPs thought the parliamentary party should vote in favour of the second reading of the Tebbit bill and then table amendments embodying the SDP's own union proposals. Led by David Owen, the majority were personally sympathetic to the purposes of the Tebbit bill and were also keen that the SDP should be seen to distance itself from the Labour party and the Trades Union Congress (TUC); they wanted the SDP to shed

Source: Published with kind permission from the *Daily Star*, 10 February 1982

*'Classic SDP symptoms—votes for something, votes against it and abstains,
all at the same time'*

its Mark II Labour party image. They were also aware that the bill was very popular with the electorate and with a majority of the SDP's rank and file in the country (who were turning out to be quite hawkish on trade-union matters).

But a minority of the MPs, most of them relatively new recruits, disagreed. Led by John Grant, a former employment minister, they objected to the substance of the bill, which they believed would damage industrial relations, and they were also worried that the new party, which badly needed trade unionists' support, would come to be labelled as anti-union. In the end, seventeen of the party's twenty-seven MPs voted with the government on the bill's second reading, five voted against it, and five others were paired or absent. The incident was not terribly important in itself and did not have serious long-term repercussions; but it made the SDP's parliamentary group look foolish, and, following the previous month's dispute with the Liberals, it further dented the Social Democrats' image of amiability and 'togetherness'.[5]

The gradual decline in the SDP's fortunes coincided with the beginnings of the Gang of Four's disintegration. The process did not have an identifiable beginning or end, but it proceeded inexorably. The party's spectacular successes in

1981, paradoxically, contributed to the disintegration. Widely attributed to the SDP's collective leadership, the party's successes might have been expected to contribute to the Gang of Four's cohesion; but, against that, it had always been agreed that the SDP would sooner or later have to have a single leader, and events like Warrington and Crosby had the effect of making the leadership appear a far greater prize than it had seemed at the time of the launch. By the end of 1981 it was not inconceivable that whoever was elected SDP leader might be the next prime minister or at least a major figure in a coalition government. The downturn that followed made this seem less likely but did not entirely eliminate the possibility: after all, the downturn might turn out to be only temporary, with some new reversal of the Conservatives' fortunes. The Gang of Four's persistent individualism was thus increasingly compounded, in the winter of 1981–2, by rivalry. Moreover, the Gang of Four had no formal organization, not even any informal set of 'rules of the game'. It was easy, therefore, for all four to get into the habit of making more and more decisions on their own and for the group's weekly private lunches at L'Amico to become at first fortnightly, then monthly.

There were at this stage no real 'ideological' differences within the party. The differences that did exist were over tactics and specific points of emphasis. The split over the Tebbit bill, for example, did not coincide with splits over anything else; and a man like John Horam, increasingly known for his free-market, even Friedmanite, economic views, was also known for being doubtful about the wisdom of deploying American cruise and Pershing II missiles in Europe. Few in the party were consistently 'right wing' or 'left wing' and almost no one was firmly identified with any of the conceptions—Mark II Labour, radical idealist or centrist—outlined in Chapter 7. The lines of division in the SDP on policy matters thus resembled those in the traditional Conservative party much more than those familiar on the Labour side. SDP policy disagreements tended not to reinforce each other.[6]

That said, it was clear to everyone by this time that, while rigid ideological divisions in the SDP might not exist, there did exist personal differences, which were increasingly showing themselves in the form of competing factions. It was almost impossible to put one's finger on what exactly the personal differences were or to say what they amounted to in strategic or policy terms; but they were real all the same. Not everyone took sides, of course; but those who did seemed to know, almost by instinct, which side they were on. Indeed in many ways the fact that the differences were so subtle and so hard to pin down made the impending struggle for control of the party all the more passionate and intense. While outsiders (including many bemused rank-and-file party members) wondered what all the fuss was about, insiders allowed themselves to get very worked up.

Predictably, the factions comprised the Jenkinsites on the one side and the anti-Jenkinsites on the other. Jenkins himself and Bill Rodgers were in one camp, Shirley Williams and David Owen in the other camp. At one level, the distinctions between them were undoubtedly political and philosophical. Jenkins, in the language of Chapter 7, was a 'centrist', who wanted to replace the politics of confrontation with the politics of accommodation and to build bridges between Britain's warring parties and classes. He also wanted the closest possible links with the Liberals, partly because he broadly shared David Steel's political vision and partly because he was in a hurry (he was already in his 60s and his active political career would soon be over) and believed that in the short term only a close Liberal–SDP Alliance stood any real chance of doing well enough in an election to form a government or become a major partner in a coalition. Rodgers supported Jenkins largely out of personal loyalty. By contrast, Williams and Owen were radical idealists. They too wanted to replace confrontation with accommodation; but they also wanted to change the world. By nature, they were movers and shakers rather than compromisers. They were prepared to do business with the Liberals (Williams had been given a standing ovation at the Liberals' Llandudno assembly), but, having sacrificed so much to found the SDP, they were adamant about maintaining its separate identity. After all, if they had wanted to join the Liberal party, they could have done so; but they had never even thought of joining it.

These limited political differences existed. They were compounded, however, by temperamental differences and differences of style that, fundamentally, were much more important. The Jenkinsites were comfortable, emollient, sometimes complacent-seeming; the anti-Jenkinsites were pushier, more aggressive, more disputatious. While the Jenkinsites chatted in front of a blazing fire or sat round a table laden with good food and wine, the anti-Jenkinsites were—or felt themselves to be—essentially outsiders, with their noses pressed against the glass. The Jenkinsites' snootiness and air of ineffable superiority, their pleasure in making cutting remarks about their rivals and opponents, infuriated those who were not of their company. The Jenkinsites tended to be secretive, members of a mysterious private club; one heard about their doings indirectly, usually at second or third hand. The anti-Jenkinsites saw themselves as being altogether more open and above board: 'What you see is what you get.' The Jenkinsites were typified by Jenkins himself, the anti-Jenkinsites by Mike Thomas, the MP for Newcastle East, who was as combative, cocky and argumentative as the average Jenkinsite was— or appeared to be—smooth and debonair. Jenkins dubbed the outspoken Thomas 'Pavarotti', and the implied put-down was typical. What most annoyed the anti-Jenkinsites was the Jenkinsites' sense that they *owned* the SDP, that it could not possibly be led by anyone other than the Great Man himself. The anti-Jenkinsites were not about to let that particular claim go unchallenged.

To begin with, the struggle for control of the party took the somewhat arcane form of a debate over the principle of 'one member, one vote'. Commitment to this as a principle, as we saw in Chapter 5, varied considerably within the party. Williams and Owen passionately believed in it; but Rodgers merely went along with it, making clear that he did so only because of his two colleagues' strong feelings on the matter. Rodgers persisted in believing that a party's leader should be chosen by its MPs. Rodgers apart, it is probably fair to say that most of those who joined the SDP, whether MPs or not, simply assumed that the principle of 'one member, one vote' would be written into its constitution. Most of the well-known SDP MPs had campaigned on the issue. Not to adopt 'one member, one vote' would be to imply that the defectors from Labour had been less than honest when they had advocated the principle—and laid so much stress on it—inside their old party.

Jenkins, however, had different ideas—ideas that, at first, he kept largely to himself. Not having participated in Labour's internal quarrels after the 1979 election, he had never become personally identified with the principle of 'one member, one vote'. Like Rodgers, he did not actually believe in it, at least for the election of a party leader. Moreover, following his personal triumph in Warrington, he had also come to the conclusion, on a tactical level, that his chances of becoming SDP leader would be greater if the choice remained with the party's MPs at Westminster instead of being handed over to the rank-and-file membership in the country. His calculations were perfectly straightforward. No one knew for whom the rank and file, given a chance, would vote in a leadership contest; Shirley Williams was widely assumed to be the favourite among ordinary party members; the parliamentary group, on the other hand, was becoming increasingly Jenkinsite. Initially, most of the party's MPs had been somewhat suspicious of Jenkins, but his campaign in Warrington had greatly impressed them, and many of the defectors who came over after the launch also happened to be Jenkins supporters. By the late summer of 1981 Jenkins undoubtedly had a majority in the House of Commons. It was obviously in his interest that the election of the leader should remain the prerogative of MPs.

Accordingly, when the SDP Steering Committee came in the autumn of 1981 to consider how the new party's leader should be chosen, Rodgers, with Jenkins' backing, formally proposed that the party's MPs alone should choose him or her, though their choice should be subject to ratification by the Council of Social Democracy and, if need be, by the entire party membership. Owen was stunned. When he had had lunch with Jenkins in November of the previous year, he had come away believing that Jenkins was committed—explicitly, in so many words—to the idea that the principle of 'one member, one vote' should be embodied in the new party's constitution. Now Jenkins appeared to be reneging in the most blatant and unscrupulous way. Moreover, Jenkins and Rodgers had not warned him of the line they were going to take at the Steering Committee, even though both of them had spoken to him only a day or two before. Furious as only he could be, Owen decided then and there that he would do everything he could to beat the Jenkinsites on the issue of 'one member, one vote' and that, whatever the outcome on that issue, either he or Williams would challenge Jenkins for the party leadership. He was damned if Jenkins and his crowd were going to have the top prize simply handed to them on a plate.

Despite Owen's protests, the Steering Committee decided to recommend to the constitutional conference, due to take place in London in February 1982, a formula very similar to the one that Rodgers had proposed; but it also agreed that the ultimate decision would have to be made by the entire party membership and that the February conference, rather than the Steering Committee, should determine the precise range of alternatives to be put to the members. In the event, the conference decided to put forward three options: election by the MPs alone; 'one member, one vote'; and a compromise formula under which the 1982 election would take place on the principle of 'one member, one vote' but with the choice of leader subsequently reverting to the MPs after the next general election, when it was hoped that there would be many more SDP MPs, all of whom would have been elected under the SDP banner. The debate at the February conference was abstract in content and mainly decorous in tone. Only Mike Thomas significantly raised the temperature, saying that he reckoned that the vast majority of those who had joined the SDP had done so believing that its constitution would embody the principle of 'one member, one vote' and that if he, Mike Thomas, were not a member of the Steering Committee he would seriously consider suing it under the Trade Descriptions Act for daring to bring forward its MPs-only proposal.[7]

The party's members backed Thomas. In a postal ballot, only 23 per cent voted for election by MPs only; the other 77 per cent split their first preferences between permanent 'one member, one vote' and the compromise formula of 'one member, one vote' now and MPs later. When the members' second preferences were taken into account, permanent 'one member, one vote' edged out, though only narrowly, the compromise proposal. The membership also voted to bring forward the date of the leadership election, originally scheduled to take place in November 1982, to July. Most of the 37,382 rank-and-file members who took part in the postal ballot must have done so on the basis of abstract principle, neither knowing (nor caring) what was at stake in personal terms; but the same can have been true of very few on the Steering Committee or in the parliamentary party. For the great majority of them, the struggle was between the Jenkinsites and the anti-Jenkinsites. And the antis, led by Owen and Williams, had won the first round.[8]

In the course of all these arguments, it seems to have been taken for granted that the new leader, however he was elected, should at the time of his election be a sitting MP. It was strange that this assumption should have been made, because, at the time the constitutional debates were at their height, during the winter of 1981–2, Roy Jenkins was the only one of the Gang of Four who did not have a seat in parliament, and it might have been supposed that one of his supporters would advance the idea that it ought to be possible for a non-MP to be a leadership candidate (though of course, if elected, he would have to find a seat eventually). No one did so, however. Nevertheless, as time went on, and especially after Shirley Williams took her seat after the Crosby by-election, the Jenkinsite camp became increasingly anxious. Would Jenkins in fact be eligible to compete for the leadership that he so much coveted? Would there be a by-election in a winnable constituency in time? Over the 1981 Christmas holiday this anxiety began to resemble panic.

Fortunately for Jenkins (and for the great majority of the SDP, who badly wanted him back in the House of Commons), on 2 January 1982 the Hillhead division of Glasgow fell vacant on the death of Sir Thomas Galbraith, a former

Conservative junior minister who had been the local MP for thirty-three years. Glasgow Hillhead had long been on the Alliance's list of target seats. It was a socially mixed constituency, containing some of the richest parts of Glasgow but also desperately poor working-class neighbourhoods along the River Clyde. Hillhead was also, according to an analysis in *The Times*, the best-educated constituency in the whole of Britain, with a large professional middle class and many students and teachers at Glasgow University.[9] Following the 1979 general election, it was the only Conservative-held seat left in the city.

Despite the pressures on him to return to parliament, Jenkins hesitated. The risks from his point of view were formidable. A good second place in Warrington, before the rise in the Liberals' and the SDP's fortunes, had been a personal triumph; a good second place in Hillhead, after the spectacular Alliance victories in Croydon North-West and Crosby, would be a disaster. It would probably put paid to his hopes of becoming party leader; and it might well put an end to his whole career, since he could hardly tout himself around the country month after month fighting by-elections indefinitely. In addition, Jenkins was aware that, as an Anglicized Welshman, he might be handicapped as a candidate in a Scottish constituency. Nevertheless, his advisers—Robert Maclennan (one of the only two Scottish SDP MPs), Lord Harris and Matthew Oakeshott—urged him to fight. And anyway he really had no choice. Hillhead could be won by a good Alliance candidate, and the whole world knew it. Even more important, if he failed to fight and win, he would almost certainly be unable to contest the SDP leadership, since another winnable seat was most unlikely to come up in the limited time available. Jenkins was a courageous man, but in this case his undoubted courage was reinforced by something approaching desperation.

The only problem was the local Liberals. The Hillhead Liberal association had already selected a candidate, a computer executive named Charles Brodie, and there was every reason to think that Brodie would 'do a Bill Pitt'—that is, dig in his heels and refuse to stand down on Jenkins' behalf. It would certainly have been understandable if he had; and on 9 January 1982 Jenkins spent a tense and uncomfortable two hours at his home in Kensington Park Gardens, with Brodie and the Hillhead chairman, Ken Wardrop. The two Glasgow Liberals tried to impose what the Social Democrats regarded as 'impossible conditions' on the fighting of a joint campaign in the constituency. While the three men were closeted together, Jenkins' wife, Jennifer, one of his aides, John Lyttle, and an adviser to David Steel, Paul Medlicott, sat waiting outside. After an hour and a half, Jenkins came out furious, saying he needed a drink. 'That's the last time', he said, 'I'll take advice from Matthew [Oakeshott].' In the end, it was Medlicott who, with David Steel's backing, laid down the law to the Liberals, informing them bluntly that either Roy Jenkins fought Hillhead or that was the end of the SDP–Liberal Alliance. Brodie and Wardrop backed off, and when the actual campaign started the two parties co-operated quite amicably.

Croydon and Crosby had been relatively easy; in both cases, especially Crosby, it was clear from the outset that the Alliance was very likely to win. Hillhead was harder. The campaign went on for nearly two and a half months; the weather was terrible; and at least two opinion polls showed Jenkins trailing badly in third place. Nerves on the campaign staff became seriously frayed, and the candidate himself became more and more irritable. The worst day— 'black Sunday'—was 14 March 1982, only eleven days before polling day, when three opinion polls were published, none of them showing Jenkins in the lead. A poll in the *Observer* placed him third, with only 23 per cent of the vote; and the paper that morning led with a story by Adam Raphael headed 'Jenkins faces defeat in fight for Hillhead'. The mood in the party's Pond Hotel headquarters was one of near despair. But that turned out to be the low point, and between then and polling day on 25 March the intense Alliance campaign began to produce results. Jenkins worked harder than ever before in his life; and, as in Warrington, the people of Hillhead appeared flattered rather than alienated by his international fame and grand manner. If the Warrington, Croydon and Crosby campaigns had been like carnivals, Hillhead resembled a noisy lecture series or one of Gladstone's earnest campaigns in the nineteenth century. The meetings of all the main candidates were filled to overflowing, and by polling day journalists reckoned that something like 10,000 people—nearly a fifth of the entire eligible electorate—must have attended at least one election meeting. The omens on polling day itself were good: three opinion polls that morning all showed Jenkins in the lead.

The result itself, coming in the midst of the serious decline in the Alliance's national fortunes, was good if not marvellous. Jenkins won, with 33 per cent of the vote, more than double the 14 per cent that the Liberal candidate had polled in 1979. The Conservative came second with 27 per cent. The Labour candidate (a nineteen-stone Bennite supporter) finished third with 26 per cent and the Scottish National Party's candidate fourth with 11 per cent. Jenkins' share of the vote was considerably lower than that of the SDP and Liberal candidates in Warrington, Croydon and Crosby, but the swing to the Alliance in Hillhead, from both the Conservatives and Labour, was substantial by historic standards. The general view was that the Alliance bandwagon had continued to roll, if somewhat more slowly.[11] But what really mattered was the essential fact of Jenkins' triumph: at the age of 61 he was an MP again. In the words of *The Times*, he had established 'an irresistible claim' to the SDP's leadership.[12]

The claim may have appeared irresistible but, as we know, it was about to be resisted: David Owen would see to that. The question in his mind was not whether Jenkins would be challenged for the party leadership but by whom. In fact, although Owen did not know it, Shirley Williams had already informed Jenkins, even before the Hillhead by-election, that she had decided that she would not be a candidate herself. Williams believed that she was quite capable of leading the new party; indeed she thought that on balance she would probably make a better leader than Jenkins. But the truth was that, in her heart of hearts, she did not want the job. By instinct she was more of a team player than her colleagues. She hated political infighting (and had left the Labour party partly for that reason). Above all, she was a very private person and had always found the attentions of the prurient press deeply repugnant. She feared the effect that being a major party leader would have on her private life and her family and friends. It was probably this love of privacy and this lack of ultimate ambition that gave Williams her reputation for being indecisive. The reputation was largely undeserved; but people probably rightly sensed—even if they misinterpreted—a deep-seated reluctance on her part to advance herself and her interests regardless of the personal price.

Although Williams had told Jenkins in so many words that she would not be a candidate, the Jenkinsite camp nevertheless continued to view her with considerable alarm. They saw her, probably rightly, as the one member of the original Gang of Three who might conceivably prove more popular with the rank and file than Jenkins. Either because they feared that she might change her mind or because they had not been told about the conversation between Williams and Jenkins before Hillhead, several of the Jenkinsites spent a good deal of time in the weeks after the by-election trying to destroy the credibility of a possible Williams candidacy. Since she had not publicly announced her intentions, it was put about that she was, as usual, dithering. It was patronizingly suggested that, while she was not suited to be leader of the party, she would make a 'natural party president'. At a later stage it was likewise put about that, even if she did want to stand for the leadership, she would not in any case be able to do so because she would not be able to obtain the requisite five nominations from SDP members of parliament.[13]

These tactics backfired badly, from both Jenkins' point of view and the SDP's. They angered Williams and her friends and at the same time reinforced Owen's determination that, come what may, the leadership of the party was not going to go uncontested. On 26 March, the day after Hillhead, Williams described Jenkins as 'the Alliance's natural leader, on the basis of seniority, experience and acceptability to both the member parties'; but at the same time she and some of Jenkins' other critics floated the idea that, while Jenkins should probably be leader of the Alliance, he should not necessarily also be the leader of the SDP. Perhaps there should be a troika, with Jenkins as Alliance leader, Steel as Liberal leader and some other member of the Gang of Three as SDP leader. In that way the SDP's tradition of collective leadership could be maintained.[14] Over the following weekend, Williams, clearly irritated by the Jenkinsites' bland assumption that the SDP was now their personal property, insisted in a speech in London that the new party's style of collective leadership had been 'a remarkably successful one' which 'had captured the public imagination'. She warned that 'the SDP must not now slip towards a hierarchy dominated by a single person, however wise or brilliant'. Mike Thomas spoke in a similar vein on the same day.[15] David Steel, however, immediately vetoed the troika proposal—'I don't think that's a practical proposition,' he said on television—and few in the SDP seemed keen on pursuing the idea.[16] The sense was widespread, not just among the Jenkinsites, that too much had already been said too publicly. But Jenkins and those close to him were now alerted to the fact that

Jenkins could not become party leader by simply laying claim to what he seemed to think was his natural inheritance.

During the next few weeks, between early April and mid-May 1982, the result of the first of the postal ballots was declared, indicating that the membership favoured the election of the leader by 'one member, one vote' and that the date of the leadership election should be brought forward to July. In view of the tensions following Hillhead, it was agreed that, if there were a leadership contest, it should be conducted without any overt campaigning by either side and without the candidates' debating against one another on television. No one wanted to see the party damaged even more.

Partly for that reason, and partly because they were still not absolutely confident that their man would win, some Jenkinsites continued to try to prevent an election contest from taking place at all. The press was briefed to the effect that the overwhelming majority of SDP MPs wanted Jenkins as their leader, that not to elect Jenkins would be to humiliate him (thereby gravely weakening the Alliance's collective leadership) and that no SDP leader other than Jenkins would be acceptable to the Liberals—this last despite the fact that David Steel repeatedly insisted that he would be happy to work with whomever the SDP decided to choose. In addition, it was suggested by the Jenkinsite camp that it would somehow be 'disloyal' if a leadership contest were forced—as though it was perfectly proper for Jenkins to stand for the leadership, but not for anyone else; Jenkins was, or should be, the party's acknowledged leader; anyone else was a mere 'challenger'. Immense pressure was brought to bear first on Williams, then on Owen, to let the victor of Hillhead have a clear run. 'You wouldn't believe', one of them said later, 'the kinds of things that were done to try to persuade me not to stand.'

The Jenkinsites' anxiety was increased by the effect on domestic politics of the Falklands War. The Hillhead by-election was held on Thursday, 25 March; Jenkins took his seat in the House of Commons on Tuesday, 30 March; on Friday, 2 April Argentina invaded the Falklands. The war that then took place lasted until 14 June, just three days after the close of nominations for the party's leadership. During the ten weeks of the Falklands War, David Owen ceased to be merely one of four leaders of a small, albeit growing, political party: he became a national figure. As the SDP's spokesman on foreign affairs, he spoke for the party on countless occasions in the House of Commons and on television and radio. Moreover, he spoke with great authority, having been Britain's foreign secretary during the last Falklands crisis in 1977, when the dispatch of British warships to the South Atlantic had apparently averted an imminent Argentinian attack.

And he had another advantage. Most of the opposition party leaders during the Falklands War were somewhat ambivalent in their attitude towards it. On the one hand, they wanted Britain to win (or at least publicly said they did); but, on the other, they could not work up any enormous enthusiasm for the dispatch of a huge and expensive naval task force to rescue 1,800 Falkland Islanders and their sheep, and they were conscious that, if the task force were to fail in its mission, as at first seemed possible, then the Thatcher government, which they loathed, would be badly, perhaps fatally, wounded. In other words, men like Foot, Jenkins and Steel, although they could never say so in public, and although they probably did not admit the fact even to themselves, had a vested interest in a British defeat—as well as conscientious doubts about the wisdom of British policy. In subtle ways, this fact undoubtedly communicated itself to the British public.

David Owen had no such ambivalence. A thoroughgoing patriot, the MP for a Plymouth dockyard constituency, a former Royal Navy minister, a somewhat belligerent man in any case, Owen wanted Britain to win; he said so repeatedly, and it was perfectly clear that he meant what he said. He carried far greater conviction than anyone else on the opposition side. Yet at the same time he had no difficulty in distancing himself from the Thatcher government's policies. He deplored the incompetence that had allowed Argentina to invade the Falklands in the first place, and he insisted that simple British sovereignty over the islands could not provide a long-term solution to the island's problems and that some kind of deal would eventually have to be struck with the Argentinians, ideally through the United Nations. The sincerity of Owen's patriotism, the distinctiveness of his personal position and the force with which he argued his case enormously increased his political standing.[17]

Both Jenkins and Williams were meanwhile somewhat eclipsed by the war. Neither had a particular claim to speak on the SDP's behalf, and both harboured doubts about the wisdom of Britain's actions. They had very little to say on the subject; what they did say was in no way memorable. In Williams' case, the fact that it was gradually becoming clear that she would not be a leadership candidate also made her a less important figure than she had been hitherto. One of the SDP's original stars, she never entirely fell out of its firmament; but, from the spring of 1982 onwards, it was clear that she was going to play a more subordinate role in the party than many SDP supporters had originally envisaged for her. The large numbers who had hoped that she would one day be the SDP's leader were deeply disappointed.

Nevertheless, Owen for a considerable period of time remained keen that Williams, rather than himself, should be the anti-Jenkinsite candidate. Quite simply, he thought she had a better chance of winning than he did, largely because she was so much better known among the SDP rank and file. But during a series of conversations between the two in mid-May 1982 Owen did not succeed in shaking her determination, which had already been conveyed to Jenkins; and on 18 May she issued a simple one-sentence statement: 'I will not be standing for the leadership.' Owen quickly let it be known that he, on the contrary, would be. Jenkins had long since made his own intentions clear. When nominations closed on 11 June, Jenkins and Owen were the only two candidates—and the lie was immediately given to the notion that Jenkins had the 'overwhelming support' (the words the Jenkinsites always used) of the SDP MPs. Of the party's twenty-seven members of parliament apart from Jenkins and Owen, fourteen declared themselves for Jenkins, twelve, including Williams, for Owen, and one, Michael O'Halloran, remained uncommitted.[18] Most of the twelve who declared for Owen would have been just as happy, or even happier, with Williams.

The ensuing leadership contest was almost exclusively an exercise in personal and political rivalry: the two contenders had almost no policy disagreements. The arguments in favour of Jenkins were that he was vastly experienced, that he was highly respected in the country, that he had good personal relations with the Liberals, especially David Steel, and that, unlike Owen, he would be a plausible contender for the prime ministership in the coming general election. Jenkins had been a highly successful chancellor and home secretary. The arguments in favour of Owen were that he was more genuinely radical than Jenkins, that he would work harder on behalf of the party than the lethargic-seeming Jenkins and that a new party such as the SDP needed a more dynamic and aggressive leadership style than Jenkins was likely to provide. Ironically, in view of later developments, Owen in 1982 was undoubtedly seen as the candidate of the 'left' of the party, that is, of those who still thought of themselves as being essentially socialists even though they had left the Labour party. Indeed during the election contest it was frequently alleged—and as frequently denied—that Owen wished to do no more than create a Mark II Labour party.[19]

On one point, however, there was a sharp disagreement between Jenkins and Owen, although it was not a point that, in the circumstances of 1982, had immediate practical consequences. It arose out of their attitudes towards the Liberal party. Jenkins, the biographer of two Liberal politicians, Sir Charles Dilke and Asquith, was not in any way antagonistic towards the Liberals. Indeed he was sympathetic towards them. He had helped to form the SDP because he judged, wholly pragmatically, that a new party in alliance with the Liberals would probably turn out to be a more powerful political force than the Liberal party on its own, even if the latter party were augmented by a few Labour defectors. He judged, equally pragmatically, that many more Labour MPs would be likely to defect to a new social-democratic party than to the Liberal party. Jenkins also wanted to create a close alliance with the Liberals because he saw such an alliance as the only means, not just of breaking Britain's political mould but of breaking it quickly. He very much wanted to be prime minister, and it was a reasonable assumption that the coming general election would provide him with his last real chance of attaining the highest office. As one journalist put it, he was, in truth, 'an old man in a hurry'.[20]

Owen was younger, and, although there was a greater air of urgency about him than about Jenkins, he was in fact personally in less of a hurry. He could afford to bide his time: he had a great deal of it. More important, Owen had a view of the future of the SDP and of its relations with the Liberals that differed fundamentally from that of Jenkins. During the course of the leadership contest, Owen gave an interview to a short-lived magazine called *Alliance*. He was asked at the very beginning of the interview: 'What do you stand for that is different from Roy?' His answer consisted exclusively of his thoughts about the relationship between the

SDP and the Liberals. Because of its bearing on later events, his answer is worth quoting at length:

The area of possible difference is the emphasis we might give to the nature of the relationship with the Liberal party. In some senses I think I know the Liberal party better than most members of the Social Democratic party—after all I was brought up in the West Country. My political life has been in the West Country where the Liberals are a strong political force.

I respect them deeply; of all the Social Democratic leaders I think I am the strongest decentralist . . . Many Liberals are surprised when they hear my views [and] discover how much we have in common, and yet I'm often portrayed as the person who is less committed to a close relationship.

They are wrong; I believe that our relationship is strengthened by retaining our separate identities. We are in danger of losing the tremendous strength that comes from the diversity that the two parties represent.

The Liberal party has roots in history; it has forged an identity which is unique. It has a capacity to attract a very wide spectrum of interest groups. The strength of the Social Democratic party is its newness. It is able to say, 'Look we are a new party.' That is one of the most powerful electoral assets that we have and we must not lose that element of newness.

What I'm proudest about in the Social Democratic party is that 60 per cent of our members are people who have not belonged to any political party before. That is our most precious asset. We must use their experience outside politics . . . to refashion our political system and build up our own political identity. I am not a believer in trying to establish a political party that is identified with the Labour party, the Conservative party or, with respect, the Liberal party. I'm in business to fashion a new Social Democratic party, a totally new force in British politics.

If we blur our identities too much, and the Liberals and the Social Democrats look as if they are 'an Alliance party', nothing would please the Conservatives and Labour party more; they would narrow us to what they would brand as a centralist band of opinion.[21]

The themes of Owen's 1982 *Alliance* interview—the SDP's newness, its need to forge a separate identity and its need to keep its distance from the Liberals—were, and were to remain to the end, the defining elements of his personal political strategy.

The leadership contest was for the most part, as intended, decorous and restrained. The two candidates prepared short election statements which were issued to the SDP's 78,000 members with their ballot papers. The two statements were impersonal and unrevealing; the few messages they contained were in a code so obscure that it could probably be cracked only by someone who already knew what the messages were. Jenkins' statement was full of autobiographical allusions. Owen's reiterated the point that the SDP and the Liberals should not merge into a single 'Alliance party'.[22] Otherwise each candidate's statement could easily have been written by the other. Apart from the statements, the campaign consisted largely of the two men appearing occasionally on television and contributing somewhat stilted articles to up-market newspapers. Both sides also took the trouble to brief lobby journalists, who wrote stories hinting darkly at the bitterness of the SDP's internecine feuding. 'Knives out for SDP leadership' said the *Daily Telegraph*. The *Guardian* went further: 'SDP leadership election turns into traditional Labour-style infighting'.[23] Headlines like these reflected accurately the degree of mutual irritation that existed between Jenkins' and Owen's more fervent supporters—and the Owenites, as the underdogs, had to be restrained from playing it rougher as the campaign went on. But the infighting probably made little impact on rank-and-file party members in the country, and most members of the general public were probably only vaguely aware that a leadership contest was taking place at all.

Apart from the Falklands War, the only event that might have given the Jenkins camp pause was the publication, on the Sunday before the party members' ballots were due to be received in Cowley Street, of an NOP poll in the *Observer* showing that Owen was preferred over Jenkins by a very wide margin among ordinary voters. Of the 75 per cent of NOP's sample with views on the issue, 63 per cent said they wanted to see Owen as the SDP's first leader; only 27 per cent favoured Jenkins. Far more Alliance voters than supporters of the other parties, fully 90 per cent, did have views on the issue; and, even among a group that inevitably included Liberals as well as SDP supporters, Owen's margin was the same: 63 per cent to 27 per cent. Owen was thought by NOP's respondents to be more intelligent than Jenkins, more businesslike, more patriotic, fairer and more honest; Jenkins was thought to be more experienced but also smugger, more arrogant and less in touch. It surprised observers at the time that, whereas Jenkins was on balance preferred by Labour voters, Owen was the favourite by quite a wide margin among Conservatives. The difference, not surprisingly, was put down to the effects of the Falklands War.[24]

The *Observer* poll may possibly have had a slight effect on late voters; but Jenkins won comfortably nevertheless. On a turn-out of 75.6 per cent, he secured 26,256 votes, 55.7 per cent of the total; Owen secured 20,864, 44.3 per cent.[25] If anything, Owen's tally was the more impressive of the two, since Jenkins' claims to the leadership were, on the face of it, much more compelling than his and since only a year or so previously few people would have thought of the ex-foreign secretary as a serious candidate. His substantial share of the vote probably reflected a widespread sense among the rank and file that the SDP under Jenkins would indeed be too centrist in orientation and too statesmanlike and lethargic in style. They wanted more excitement and dynamism.

Jenkins was hugely relieved at the outcome. 'It's a better result than I expected,' he said, 'but I am a bit used to winning from behind.'[26] Owen, by contrast, was annoyed at being defeated: until the result was actually read out, it looked as though he might conceivably win; and, apart from the no-hope contest that he fought at Torrington in the 1964 general election, it was the first time in his political career that he had been beaten. Publicly at least, however, he was philosophical. He told one newspaper, 'Roy has won and his view must be dominant,' and another, 'Some people thought we would repeat the horrors of the Labour party, but there was no bitterness or enmity. Roy Jenkins is a friend of mine, and we will work very much together.'[27] Despite rumblings from the Jenkinsite camp suggesting that the 'disloyal' Owen needed to be put in his place, Jenkins appointed him deputy leader of the parliamentary party when the MPs re-assembled in the autumn, and the arrangement worked well for the rest of the parliament.

There were two sequels to the leadership contest, neither of which did the party much harm but which did not do it much good either. One was a further election contest, this time for the presidency of the party—the post that, under the new party's constitution was to provide, in effect, the SDP's leadership in the country as distinct from the House of Commons. The general assumption had been that the post would go more or less automatically to Shirley Williams; she was the darling of the SDP's own members and was also very popular among ordinary voters. But Bill Rodgers doubted whether Williams had the necessary organ-izational ability and, a Jenkins supporter, he may have been irked by Williams' backing for Owen in the leadership contest. Since much of his own work for the party had thus far been backroom organizational work, he probably also felt the need to re-establish himself publicly. At any rate, he announced in late June that he would be standing. The election was held in September and, as expected, Williams won easily in a lowish poll. She got 65.9 per cent of the vote, Rodgers 19.4 per cent and a little-known outsider, a self-styled 'rank-and-file' candidate, Stephen Haseler, 14.8 per cent.[28]

The other sequel was a reminder of how great the tensions between the Jenkinsites and the Owenites remained underneath the surface. The rolling conference in 1981 had been a great success, and it was decided to organize another in 1982. Unfortunately, the media were by now somewhat bored with the whole exercise (and, by a stroke of malign fate, the SDP's chartered train in 1982 contrived to break down one dark night in the wilds of rural Cambridgeshire). Worse, a session of the conference at Great Yarmouth resulted in both the party leadership's first defeat on a major policy question and a highly public display of Jenkins–Owen acrimony. The SDP's National Committee had tabled a motion calling on the conference to endorse unequivocally the principle of a statutory, albeit temporary, incomes policy if the Alliance were to come to power. Although the motion was strongly supported by the party's newly elected leader, Jenkins, it was opposed by a delegate from Westminster named Ruth Levitt; and, on a show of hands, it was defeated by a large majority. What almost everyone knew was that Ruth Levitt was David Owen's unpaid research assistant; and Owen could be seen on the platform vigorously applauding her anti-leadership speech. Jenkins was furious, interpreting both Levitt's speech and Owen's applause as calculated acts of disloyalty; and Shirley Williams, even though she had supported Owen in the leadership contest, was every bit as angry. She told Owen that if he did not apologize publicly she would make a speech denouncing him. Owen realized, quite apart from Williams' threat, that he had gone too far and he made what was intended to be—and was interpreted as—a gracious apology. But far more had been revealed about the nature of the two men's relationship than either would have wished.[29]

The Hillhead by-election victory that made possible Jenkins' election to the leadership was, as it turned out, the last by-election victory that the SDP (though not the Alliance) was to enjoy in the 1979 parliament. During the remainder of 1982, the SDP and the Liberals fought by-elections on seven other occasions—at Beaconsfield, Mitcham and Morden, Coatbridge and Airdrie, Gower, Peckham, Birmingham Northfield and Glasgow Queen's Park—but, although the Alliance's candidate in four of the seven seats moved up from third place to second, increasing substantially the Liberals' 1979 share of the vote, the two parties' overall performance was disappointing.[30] Not only were no victories forthcoming, but the loss of publicity and morale that accompanied the successive defeats meant that the by-election results were even more discouraging.

The only one of the seven that attracted significant television and press coverage was the one in Mitcham and Morden in south London in early June. The sitting Labour MP for the constituency, Bruce Douglas-Mann, wanted to join the SDP group in parliament but felt that, in good conscience, he could do so only if he first fought and won a by-election. His decision caused a good deal of resentment in the SDP's ranks: a good seat in the House of Commons was being put at risk, and other SDP MPs did not greatly appreciate the contrast that Douglas-Mann was implicitly drawing between the quality of his conscience and the quality of theirs. However, after a certain amount of grumbling at both national and local levels, Douglas-Mann was eventually endorsed as the official SDP candidate. Unfortunately for him, the Falklands War and the Conservatives' recovery intervened between his decision to resign and the actual by-election, and, although he finished a creditable second and more than trebled the 1979 Liberal candidate's share of the vote, Mitcham and Morden was lost to the Conservatives' Angela Rumbold.

The continuing by-election failures and the defeat at Great Yarmouth were not the only set-backs that Roy Jenkins suffered during this period. Eleven months almost to the day transpired between his election as SDP leader on 2 July 1982 and the general election that was held on 3 June 1983; and during those eleven months it emerged that Jenkins was not at all well suited by either aptitude or temperament to be the leader of a struggling new party (or even, probably, the leader of a struggling old one). As the Labour peer Harold Lever is said to have remarked: 'Roy would make an admirable prime minister if only he could somehow be dropped into Downing Street by helicopter.' Unfortunately, that means of transport was not available. Jenkins was not as inept as Foot, but the contrast between him and both Thatcher and Steel (and also his own hero Hugh Gaitskell) was marked.

Within the party, both at Cowley Street and in the House of Commons, Jenkins largely failed to establish his authority. The working methods that had served him well in Whitehall, and rather less well in Brussels, did not serve him well at all as leader of the SDP. Staff support and office accommodation adequate to his purposes were both lacking; and, in his new role, issues simply did not present themselves in the orderly, methodical, Whitehall-like manner he preferred. Rather, they came at him from all directions, at all times of the day and night, and in no discernible order. He found it exceedingly hard to cope. More important, the challenge for the new leader of a fledgling political party was not one of taking decisions presented to him in a pre-packaged form but of reaching out for decisions, of making an effort at all times and under all circumstances to try to seize and hold the political initiative. Jenkins seldom did so. But neither did he immerse himself in detail, with the result that MPs and members of the Cowley Street staff lacked direction in small matters as well as large. Finding himself uncomfortable in his new role, Jenkins retreated, even more than in the past, into his close circle of friends and advisers. Those MPs and members of the party staff who were not members of his circle often found him hard to reach; and, when they did succeed in reaching him, he could be irritable and brusque. Few of these internal problems surfaced in public, but they tended to reinforce the sense of *malaise* inside the party that was anyway being created by the SDP's poor showing in by-elections and the polls.

More visible were the problems that Jenkins faced in the House of Commons. The House was an altogether rowdier place in 1982 than it had been when Jenkins had left for Brussels five years earlier. Hard-left Labour MPs like Dennis Skinner and Bob Cryer were hard in both senses of the term. They endlessly barracked and interrupted their political opponents, and they were usually allowed to get away with it by the then Speaker, George Thomas. Jenkins in 1982 found himself forced to sit on the opposition benches below the gangway in the midst of men like Skinner and Cryer, and the 'new barbarians', as one of Jenkins' staff called them, deliberately set out to make life difficult for him. They largely succeeded. 'Roy,' one of them would say in a loud stage whisper, 'your flies are undone.' Jenkins was also discommoded by having to speak for the first time in many years from the back benches, with nowhere to put his hands or notes. He looked and felt awkward. His old authority slipped from him, and the more trouble he had in commanding the House of Commons' attention, the more hesitant and nervous he became.

The parliamentary sketch writers found the spectacle irresistible:

Still no sign of the eventual outcome in the South Atlantic: but there was some movement yesterday on the home front. It took the form of Mr Roy Jenkins.

The movement was initially confined to those rather distinguished jowls of his. They began to roll [as] Mrs Thatcher arrived for prime minister's question time. While she answered other members, the rest of Mr Jenkins began to move importantly in his seat below the gangway facing her.

He consulted some notes. He advanced to the edge of his seat with some deliberation. It was clear that he was going to put a question. This was in itself an event of a certain significance. Nothing had so far been heard from him in this crisis. Since it arose, he had all but disappeared from the public gaze . . .

Dr Owen is at home with such matters. Mr Jenkins is not. Like Switzerland, he is prosperous, comfortable, civilized and almost entirely landlocked. His only previous contact with the high seas has been in various good fish restaurants.[31]

There was more, much more of the same.

Jenkins' nervousness and ponderousness were just as evident—and evident to far more people—on the television screen. His straight-to-camera pieces were dull and wooden, and his answers to interviewers' questions, although far more coherent than Foot's, were always lengthy and orotund when they should have been short and to the point; his long experience of government and his grasp of detail, which ought to have given him added confidence and authority, seemed instead to weigh him down. He looked on television more like a diffident don or civil servant than like someone who was about to shatter the mould of British politics. Jenkins' print journalism—he frequently contributed articles and book reviews to serious newspapers—continued to be elegant and thoughtful; but his television manner, with millions of potential Alliance voters looking on, remained to the end leaden and dreary.[32]

Predictably, his standing with the general public declined steadily during the eleven months that he led the party. He was elected in early July 1982, and in that month 50 per cent of the Gallup Poll's monthly sample thought he would do a good job as the SDP's leader. At the end of the year, in December 1982, only 34 per cent thought that he was actually doing a good job; and by the eve of the general election, in May 1983, that figure had fallen to only 30 per cent. Symptomatic of Jenkins' difficulties in communicating his views and his personality was the fact that, even after he had been SDP leader for nearly a year (and after he had been prominent in public life for fully thirty-five years), no fewer than a quarter of the electorate, sometimes more, still replied 'don't know' to the Gallup Poll's standard question about him.[33]

Feelings of disappointment with Jenkins were by no means universal in the party; some in the SDP still praised him for his strategic vision and his remarkable ability to pace himself. But the great majority felt let down. Interviewing SDP MPs and members of staff in the winter of 1982–3, we were surprised at how many of those who had voted for Jenkins for the leadership were now disappointed, some even wishing they had voted the other way. Typical of the comments made at that time were these:

I used to be a Jenkins idolater . . . But, alas, he's a soft man in tough times.

I voted for Roy. I thought he would make the best prime minister. But he's certainly not the best person for getting himself there. I now think that maybe David or Shirley would have been better.

Most of the staff at Cowley Street voted for Jenkins, but many of them wouldn't now. He's not a party leader. He sometimes shows up not properly briefed. Committee meetings that ought to be taking practical decisions get turned into seminars.

It's hard to say it, but to me he looks like an old man—old and ill.

Owen's stock was meanwhile rising rapidly:

He's an arrogant bugger, but he has a first-class brain.

He's stroppy and difficult, but he does have a cutting edge.

If you want to scale sheer rock faces, David's the man to do it.

It was also clear that the SDP under Jenkins' leadership continued to have a serious problem of self-definition. What kind of party, exactly, was it to be? At the end of 1982 the SDP's leaders had still failed to come up with an answer that was both generally acceptable within the party and also had some minimal degree of precision. Meanwhile, however, the electorate—by what it said and, more important, by what it did—was providing its own definition of the SDP. The party offered itself to the voters in its terms; the voters responded to it in theirs. As we shall see in more detail in Chapter 16, the great majority of voters viewed the new party—whether those inside the SDP liked it or not—as a centre party. Bill Rodgers had written in 1979 of a new party's being 'a party of the left' and of its eventually taking over '90 per cent of the existing Labour vote'; and many in the SDP continued long after the launch to envisage their party's electoral appeal in those terms. But that was not how the voters saw it. They thought of the SDP as being a centre party, with policies that fell midway between those of the Conservatives and the Labour party. At the same time, the new party's experience on the ground was showing that it was just as likely to attract ex-Conservative voters as ex-Labour voters. A party of the kind that Rodgers had had in mind would not have been doing nearly so well in places like Crosby and Hillhead—and would have been doing much better on council estates.

Partly because most voters saw the SDP as a centre party, they increasingly saw little need to distinguish clearly between it and the Liberal party. More and more voters, asked how they would vote if there were a general election tomorrow, replied simply 'Alliance' rather than either 'Liberal' or 'SDP'. The two centre parties, never very distinct in most voters' minds, gradually began to be fused together completely. An additional reason for this fusion, of course, was the fact that the Liberal and Social Democratic parties were now working so very closely together. So far our focus in this book has been on the SDP in isolation. It is time to consider in more detail the evolution of the Liberal–Social Democratic Alliance, the political arrangement that the two partners were pleased to call their 'partnership of principle'.

10

••••

A 'Partnership of Principle'

The average Labour MP, if asked during the 1960s or 1970s what he thought of the Liberal party, would probably have replied that he barely thought of it at all. One might or might not like the Liberals; one might or might not agree with them. But they were not serious. Of the twenty-eight Labour MPs who eventually defected to the SDP, twenty-six had had Liberal opponents at the 1979 general election; in twenty-five of the twenty-six cases, the Liberal candidate had finished third or worse. It is doubtful whether in more than a handful the Liberal's intervention had made any difference to the outcome.

In so far as Labour politicians did think about the Liberal party, their image of it was blurred and, in the main, faintly derisory. Of the Liberals' recent leaders, Jo Grimond was generally regarded as a likeable but ineffectual eccentric, and Jeremy Thorpe, Grimond's successor, was thought of as something of a clown who had anyway come to a bad end. Only David Steel stood out. He was different; he alone had the aura of a real politician. No one in the SDP doubted that he was a man with whom one could do business. As for the other Liberal MPs and activists in the country, almost no one in the SDP or the Labour party knew the first thing about them.

What the Liberals stood for was also not terribly clear. Their general ideological tilt was evidently towards Labour rather than the Conservatives. They supported the welfare state and were increasingly opposed to nuclear weapons; they had refused to keep the Conservatives under Edward Heath in power in 1974 and had been ready, even eager, to sustain the Callaghan government in office in 1977 and 1978. But they parted company from Labour in being much more critical of the trade unions than most Labour politicians and in not believing in centralized government control of the economy. The distinctive feature of their policy was probably their dislike of concentrations of power—any concentrations of power, including inside their own party. Pluralists as much as liberals, they advocated wider share ownership in companies, greater employee participation in industry, proportional representation and the devolution of power to Scotland, Wales

167

and the English regions. In effect, their slogan was 'small is beautiful' (though they were in favour of British membership of the Common Market). The Liberals also practised something called community politics, which seemed to mean trying to win votes by mobilizing local discontents about such matters as dangerous road crossings and overdue council-house repairs. How this particular tactic related to actually running the country, at either national or local level, was not clear.

That was as much as—perhaps more than—most people in the Labour party knew about the Liberals, except, of course, that the Liberals never won elections and therefore had no leader who had ever held national office. The average Labour politician knew little of Liberal policy, nothing about the Liberal party's con-stitution, nothing about the Liberals' internal culture and nothing about the debates and resolutions at the annual Liberal assembly. It was thus on a basis of near-total ignorance of the Liberals on the part of the SDP's leaders and MPs that the Liberal–SDP relationship began.

The Liberals certainly played no part in the Gang of Three's decision to leave the Labour party. As we saw in Chapter 3, Owen, Rodgers and Williams ignored Steel's persistent overtures throughout 1980, in private as well as in public. Of the twelve original defectors from the parliamentary Labour party, only John Horam and Tom Ellis seriously contemplated joining the Liberals.[1] It did not occur to most of them even to consult individual Liberal supporters, let alone join them. The Gang of Four certainly did not trouble to find out what Liberal party policy was before drawing up the Limehouse Declaration. The Liberal party was not so much rejected as ignored—a minor blip on the experimental plane's radar screen.

Moreover, in early 1981 most SDP defectors were wholly preoccupied with the tribulations of disengaging from Labour. Not all felt they were making an irrevocable break; most initially conceived of the SDP as a reconstituted Labour party, appealing to traditional Labour voters on the basis of moderate, up-dated Labour policies. They still subscribed to Williams' 'no roots, no principles' dismissal of any new centre party.[2] Association with the failed, centrist, largely middle-class Liberal party would distance them too far from the local Labour voters on whose continued support their chances of re-election would depend. No doubt an accommodation of some kind with the Liberals would be needed; but it could wait. The immediate task was to build a new party.

Most defectors' thoughts about the Liberals remained unformed and tentative for much of 1981. In so far as they had an overall view, it was usually one of amiable neutrality. But, from the beginning, David Owen's view was both much better formed and much less amiable. The SDP, in his view, had to have as its first—almost its only—priority the development of its own distinctive identity. Any alliance with the Liberals, Owen believed, should be entered into from a position of strength, with a large and loyal membership, with a constitution and an organization in place and with an already worked-out programme of policies; it should be the final stage, not the first, in the new party's development. In the meantime, Owen believed, the SDP should co-operate with the Liberals only to the degree necessary for the furtherance of the SDP's electoral interests—and only for a single election. This would require an electoral pact, although not necessarily on a fifty–fifty basis, and would also require agreement on a minimum programme for government, including early elections on the basis of proportional representation. Such co-operation did not, however, in Owen's view, require joint policy-making, joint candidate selection, joint broadcasts, dual party membership (a particular *bête noire* of his), the pooling of resources or any other form of Liberal–SDP assimilation. On Granada's *World in Action* programme, shortly before the launch, Owen demurred at Steel's reference to an 'alliance', preferring to talk of a 'coalition'.[3]

Why Owen wanted the SDP to take such a hard line with the Liberals remains something of a mystery. Neither his personal history nor his political career contained any traumas that might explain it.[4] A large part of the explanation was probably temperamental. Owen's whole approach to life was aggressive, almost military. He liked discipline and decisiveness; he was, like Margaret Thatcher, one of nature's warriors, not, despite his former profession, one of its healers. By contrast, the Liberals, as he saw them, were nothing but a miscellaneous collection of limp-wristed wets, frequently feeble as individuals, collectively incapable of action. Owen saw himself as essentially a man of government—tough, hard-headed, matter of fact. He saw the Liberals as unreliable and wholly inexperienced—a species of dangerous children.

Owen thus regarded himself from the outset as the principal guardian of the SDP's independence and integrity. He had not left the Labour party to join some other party, the Liberals; he had left it to form a new one, the SDP. 'We have not defected,' he insisted. 'We have created an entirely new party. We are founders, not defectors.'[5] He had, moreover, a clear conception of what the Social Democrats should be: united, radical and a party of the left, a member of the Socialist International, not a party of the 'soft centre'.[6] He did not want the Social Democrats' enterprise to become bogged down in an endless series of deals and compromises with the woolly Liberals. From the beginning, he was very suspicious of all those—both Liberals and Social Democrats—whom he imagined to be plotting an ultimate merger between the two parties or even of being prepared to contemplate such a merger.

Owen's line was consistent, and no one who cared to read his mind, or his speeches, should have been in any doubt about it. Publicly, Owen was polite about the Liberals, sometimes even cordial; but in private he made no effort to conceal his contempt for them. But many Social Democrats were apt to dismiss his views as either a personal eccentricity or a minor matter of political tactics. The differences between Owen and the other SDP leaders on the future of Liberal–SDP relations were never resolved. Worse, they were never really confronted, with the result that over the next half-dozen years genuine differences of opinion were consistently compounded by misunderstandings and mutual suspicions, which ultimately proved fatal to the whole SDP enterprise.

Even Owen, however, accepted in 1981 that the immediate issue between the Liberals and the SDP was one of practical co-operation. Foremost was the need for some form of electoral pact. The Liberals found the task of winning seats formidable enough; most people in the SDP thought the party would find it totally insurmountable if it competed against the Liberals for the same non-Labour, non-Conservative vote. Yet initially very little thought was given to what an electoral pact with the Liberals would mean in practice. In the weeks leading up to the party's launch the issue was never discussed among the Gang of Four, let alone with Steel or other Liberals. Everybody was too busy.

The most modest expectations were held by some of the Jenkinsites. From their early contacts with Liberals they assumed that Jenkins and Williams would be allowed a clear run in a promising by-election or at a general election but that, if the SDP set itself up in nation-wide competition as a fourth party, the Liberals would resist fiercely and co-operation would quickly become impossible.[7] They hoped for—and would have been content with—a clear run for existing SDP MPs and up to a hundred other SDP candidates.[8] Others, such as Rodgers, appeared to assume that the new party would confine itself to Labour seats, leaving the Liberals to fight Conservative seats.[9] But, as the polls showed the Social Democrats forging ahead of the Liberals, many in the Social Democratic camp began, probably unconsciously at first, to up the ante. David Owen and Mike Thomas, in particular, envisaged the SDP establishing a sufficient electoral dominance over the Liberals to dictate the terms of an eventual electoral arrangement. They were, therefore, astonished to hear Rodgers, at the party's launch in the Connaught Rooms, effectively committing the SDP to a fifty–fifty share-out of seats with the Liberals, when no precise figure had even been discussed, let alone agreed, by the Gang of Four or the Steering Committee. Rodgers regarded the fifty–fifty figure as a pre-emptive move *against* the Liberals; Owen and Thomas, by contrast, regarded it as a wholly premature concession *to* the Liberals. At the time, Owen and Thomas said nothing in public, but in later years they cited it as an early milestone on the SDP's mistaken road to merger with the Liberals.[10]

The Liberals' own reaction to the emerging SDP was at first divided. Some senior Liberal MPs, disillusioned by the empty returns of the Lib–Lab pact, were irritated by Steel's manœuvring. Cyril Smith, in particular, said he had no wish to jump on board Jenkins' experimental plane: 'It could be that when his plane arrived on the runway, he would find another plane waiting to take off . . . It would be so much easier therefore to transfer the passengers from the second plane to the first.'[11] His reasoning was blunt: 'I do not see the logic of creating two political parties to go for the same vote.' The SDP, he insisted, shortly before the launch, 'should have been strangled at birth'.[12]

Infanticide, however, was not in the Liberals' power. Most Liberals' reaction to the new party was therefore somewhat ambivalent, alternating between fear of a potential rival and welcome for a potential ally. The first opinion polls underlined the Liberals' dilemma. They revealed the benefits the two parties would reap if they co-operated but also the price they would pay if they fought. A Gallup poll in April initially gave Labour 30.5 per cent, the Conservatives 30 per cent, the SDP 19 per cent and the Liberals 18 per cent. But the same poll then asked respondents how they would vote 'if the new Social Democratic Party made an Alliance with the Liberals so that a candidate from only one of those parties would stand in each constituency'. The result was spectacular: Alliance 48.5 per cent, Conservatives 25.5 per cent, Labour 24.5 per cent.[13] The message was clear. Fighting separately, neither party would be anywhere close to a breakthrough. Fighting together, they could beat the major parties, they might obtain proportional representation, and they might even win outright. Moreover, the sum of an alliance would be greater than its parts. It would not only combine the Liberal and SDP votes but would apparently attract the support of perhaps as much as 10 per cent of the electorate who were unprepared to vote for either of the two parties on its own.[14]

Under the circumstances, most Liberals recognized that some form of collaboration was essential. Yet there continued to be murmurs of unease. The SDP—its members, its policies, its eventual size—were still unknown quantities. If it competed with the SDP, the Liberal party might be sidelined; but in any alliance with the SDP it might be swallowed up. Either way, its identity was under threat.

Different Liberals, however, defined the Liberals' identity differently and therefore had different fears. Most Liberal MPs owed their election to a personal vote built on assiduous constituency work. They were political personalities in their own right, acting as quasi-independents at Westminster and accustomed to more media attention than most backbenchers receive. Some were piqued by the amount of attention being paid to the SDP defectors, and they also feared being swamped in parliament by the Labour refugees.

Dark mutterings also came from the Liberal party's well-organized and increasingly influential anti-establishment, the Association of Liberal Councillors. The ALC represented a younger generation of urban radicals. Committed to community politics, often proudly provincial (the ALC's headquarters were in the small Yorkshire town of Hebden Bridge), the ALC bore many of the hallmarks of the 1960s New Left. Its new liberalism was thoroughly antithetical to the high-growth, consensus corporatism of most of Labour's social democrats, and its community politics was often directed against big-city Labour councils. The leading ALC people—people like Tony Greaves and Michael Meadowcroft—saw themselves as being just as distant from social democracy as from conservatism. They believed in the dispersal of power, a weak state and the primacy of the individual. Ex-Labour social democrats were not their obvious allies.[15]

A less coherent uneasiness was felt among some more traditional Liberals, whose identity resided not in ideology but in the very survival and independence of their local Liberal associations. Being a Liberal meant being an outsider, pursuing lost causes, staying on principle in the political wilderness. Suddenly making common cause with refugees from the Labour party smacked of opportunism.

There was also a widespread suspicion in Liberal ranks of tacit deals and

Source: Guardian, 17 September 1981

All aboard the Alliance stagecoach

secret compromises and much of this unease came to focus on the issue of the complexion of the Liberals' putative partners. Whom would the SDP admit to their ranks? Labour's moderate wing had a wide span. The libertarians and internationalists, represented by the Gang of Four, were welcome; but the conservative, authoritarian Labour right from the big trade-union and town-hall machines was far less congenial. Equally uncongenial were some of the right-wingers threatened by deselection and contemplating taking refuge in the SDP. Liberals grew suspicious whenever the SDP, with its eye on the Labour vote, claimed to be the true descendants of the Labour tradition.

Underlying all these anxieties were reservations about the Liberal party's own leadership—reservations that were easily aroused at the best of times. The SDP was a Westminster contrivance, not a spontaneous country-wide movement. Liberal encouragement for it had come almost entirely from one person, Steel. In one sense, Liberal suspicions of Steel himself were well founded. He and his close associates did indeed have an unequivocal commitment to an alliance with the SDP, and they were almost the only Liberals who had. Steel's objective, as we saw in Chapter 3, was to restructure the entire party system—the Liberal party included—by pursuing a strategy of close collaboration with other parties. It was an objective unique to him and to those immediately around him. Always moving towards his ultimate goal, Steel rarely took his eye off the ball, and he was adept at deriving maximum advantage from minor political opportunities. But he could not always count on carrying the rest of his team with him.

The Liberal party was a difficult one to lead. It lacked organizational or ideological cohesion or even an ethic of cohesion. The MPs were their own men; the party structure was devolved and federal; the constituency associations were almost wholly autonomous. The pervading spirit was one of participation and parochial rights, not one of compliance and collective solidarity. Without patronage or electoral success to bestow, Steel's only resources were persuasion and his legitimacy as the party's elected leader.

Given the character of his party, Steel not unnaturally adopted a hands-off, detached, somewhat secretive leadership style, avoiding direct dealings with his party workers whenever possible and relying instead on a small group of advisers to act as fire-fighters and intelligence agents. He kept out of internal party disputes, did not cultivate any faction and handled dissent by means of manoeuvring and fixing. He chose to communicate his views through the national media or *Liberal News*—or via his lieutenants—rather than face to face. It was a style that protected him from the snares of faction but could also cut him off from his party's thinking. Usually it worked—but not always.

Since the Dimbleby Lecture, Steel had envisaged a four-step path to his goal of realignment. Step 1 was the formation of a Social Democratic party out of a splintered Labour party. Step 2 was an SDP–Liberal agreement on policy. Step 3 was an electoral pact. Step 4 was an integrated election campaign under a single leader.

Step 1 was effectively completed, even before the launch, with the issuing of the Limehouse Declaration. A week later, Steel published a letter to Liberal candidates calling for a Liberal and Social Democratic Alliance 'in which we would each retain our separate identities, structure and detailed policies while having in common a programme of national priorities and, if possible, agreement not to have opposing candidates in any one constituency'.[16] Shortly before the launch Steel's close lieutenant, Richard Holme, went further, calling for a partnership of equals with a joint policy and pooled resources.[17] Steel had good reasons for wanting to press ahead rapidly. He wanted to dangle the prospect of an electoral pact before Labour MPs who were still contemplating defection; he wanted to climb on board the SDP's plane to avoid the Liberals being left on the runway; and he was anxious to forestall Liberal dissidents from organizing any effective opposition. He was also conscious of the political timetable. The principle of an alliance would have to be decided at the annual Liberal assembly in September; but an agreement would actually be needed before then—to slow up the adoption of Liberal parliamentary candidates (there were already 200 in the field) and also to allow time for Liberal sceptics and agnostics to grow accustomed to the idea of co-operating with the Social Democrats.

The first formal moves towards co-operation took place in parliament. In February 1981, even before the launch, the two parliamentary groups formed a joint consultative committee consisting of Owen, Steel and also John Roper and Alan Beith, the two whips. The purpose was to co-ordinate parliamentary tactics. The committee met every Thursday to discuss the choice of speakers in forthcoming debates, membership of committees and voting in parliamentary divisions. There soon followed fortnightly joint meetings of the two parliamentary parties as a whole, chaired by Owen and Steel alternately. Liberals occasionally bridled at Owen's high-handedness, but the meetings were businesslike and generally cordial, and agreement usually came easily. The split over the Tebbit bill was the only occasion in the 1979–83 parliament when SDP and Liberal MPs went into different division lobbies.[18]

At the same time both parliamentary parties retained their autonomy. They had their own whips; they met separately before convening jointly; and they sat close by but apart in the chamber, the SDP on the front bench below the gangway, the Liberals on the bench behind. Despite their small numbers, each party maintained its own parliamentary spokesmen (partly because, as a result, the Speaker felt obliged to call speakers from both parties early on in big debates). All these arrangements reinforced Owen's views on SDP–Liberal relations. They demonstrated that the two parties could co-operate perfectly well without sacrificing their individual identities. Indeed, weight of numbers, the priority given to leading Social Democrats over Liberals in the chamber and Owen's personal dominance of the joint meetings effectively made the SDP the senior partner.[19] The relationship was precisely the model Owen personally had in mind for the two parties at large.

Steel meanwhile was concerned that the steady increase in the number of Liberal associations adopting parliamentary candidates would store up trouble for Liberal–SDP co-operation. He, therefore, continued to press for a policy agreement—the precondition, as he saw it, of any viable electoral pact. While he was considering how to proceed, he and Richard Holme found themselves in early April 1981 attending the Anglo-German Society's annual Königswinter conference. Shirley Williams, Bill Rodgers, John Roper and David Marquand were also there, having been invited completely separately. Despite the incessant media talk of alliances and pacts, this was the first occasion on which leading Liberals and members of the Gang of Three had been together in the same place for any length of time since the previous autumn. Until Königswinter, Steel, Rodgers and Williams had frequently addressed each other via the press; but, so preoccupied were the Gang of Three with launching their own party, that they had not actually had a chance to talk to their Liberal opposite numbers.

On the final day of Königswinter, Steel, Holme, Williams, Rodgers and Roper lunched together—in full view of everyone else at the conference—and their conversation quickly turned to future Liberal–SDP relations.[20] Steel knew precisely what he wanted, but Williams and Rodgers had given little thought to the matter. Somewhat to their surprise, they found that they accepted almost all of Steel's game plan.[21] The next steps, they agreed, should be a joint statement on policy principles and an electoral pact; and they also agreed that the two parties should move fast. Holme drafted what became known as the 'Königswinter Compact' on a paper napkin. Cautiously worded, with a reference to 'autonomous parties from different traditions and backgrounds', it proposed the establishment of a joint negotiating committee to draw up a common statement of principles by June, the subsequent setting-up of two or more joint policy commissions, probably on industry and on constitutional reform, and also 'the informal exchange of vital electoral priorities for each party'—a coy phrase for negotiations over parliamentary seats. After lunch, Steel and Williams went for a long walk in the mountain forest behind Königswinter, with journalists following discreetly at a distance, like chaperones.

The Königswinter meeting marked the moment when leaders of the Liberals and the SDP first agreed to form a pre-election alliance. The Königswinter Compact effectively set the agenda for Liberal–SDP relations until the 1983 general election, and all steps proposed in it were eventually accomplished. The encounter at Königswinter also allowed the two sides to discover for the first time how much they had in common and how well they could get on. Each was pleasantly surprised. Owen was later to refer to the meeting as the moment at which 'relations with the Liberals went critically wrong', and it was certainly the moment when Rodgers' and Williams' attitude towards the Liberals began to diverge from his.[22] Before Königswinter, the only SDP leader who knew and respected Steel was Jenkins. After Königswinter, the only SDP leader who did not know and respect him was Owen.

On their return, Rodgers and Williams recounted their discussions with Steel to the newly formed SDP Steering Committee. There were a few, but only a few, sceptical murmurs. The next day, however, when they reported to a joint meeting of the Steering Committee and the Parliamentary Committee, they ran into a storm of opposition. The resistance, led by Ian Wrigglesworth, Edward Lyons, Robert Maclennan and Mike Thomas, was partly fuelled by the MPs' feeling that they had been bounced (the Königswinter proposals had already appeared in the press) and that Rodgers and Williams had overreached their authority; but it mainly reflected the objectors' scant regard for the Liberal party. Why should the SDP rush out its policies for the sake of the Liberals before the SDP's own constitution and policy-making machinery were in place? A premature agreement on policy would alienate party members, dissolve the party's image before it had time to gel and discourage further recruitment as a result. It would also place the SDP in a weak bargaining position *vis-à-vis* the Liberals when the opinion polls showed that the SDP, not the Liberals, was the stronger of the two. An agreement over policy and candidates would no doubt be needed before the next general election, but it was not all that urgent: the Liberals, after all, needed a pact just as much as the SDP did, if not more.

It was eventually decided at the meeting to postpone further discussion of joint policy-making (although the joint commissions could go ahead) and also to propose a moratorium on the selection of Liberal candidates as a quid pro quo for starting to discuss negotiations over seats. Owen later recalled that he 'had never seen so much anger and fury in the Steering Committee' and claimed that Williams had made 'a profound mistake'; but at the time he kept his counsel.[23]

Steel meanwhile was anxious to ease the growing worries inside his own party. Undaunted by the row at the SDP's post-Königswinter meeting, Steel seized on the opportunity offered by the forthcoming Warrington by-election. The Liberals, he said, could hardly be expected to withdraw their candidate in Warrington without knowing what the SDP stood for and without having a common programme to campaign on. The two parties therefore agreed to draft a brief 'joint statement of principles'.

Despite ritual public references to the two parties' different ideological roots, agreement on principles proved to be easy.[24] The Limehouse Declaration contained nothing for Liberals to object to, and Owen's recently published book, *Face the Future*, with its critique of centralized planning and its advocacy of the 'enabling state', had come as a pleasant surprise to Liberals.[25] In reality the political outlook of leading Liberals and Social Democrats was virtually indistinguishable. On constitutional reform, the mixed economy, the welfare state, Europe, NATO and civil liberties, the two parties were agreed. The SDP was less committed than the Liberals to a 1970s-style incomes policy, while the Liberal party contained substantial unilateralist and green minorities, who had few counterparts in the SDP. But in early 1981 it was almost meaningless to talk of SDP 'policies', as distinct from broad principles; shades of difference between the two parties, in matters of substance as distinct from style, were only dimly discernible.

Hurriedly produced without wide consultation, *A Fresh Start for Britain* was published on 16 June.[26] It stuck to a short and general reformulation of the two parties' existing agreed principles and papered over the potential cracks. It called for 'an agreed strategy for incomes', 'the conservation of resources and the protection of the environment' and 'the proper defence of Britain through membership of NATO'. Detailed proposals on employment, industrial recovery and constitutional reform would come later, from the two joint policy commissions. Finally, it announced that 'the two parties wished to avoid fighting each other in elections' and would therefore explore ways of making an electoral alliance effective. *Fresh Start* added little to previous statements by the two parties but was of critical importance symbolically. It pleased Liberals by omitting the word 'socialism' and by embracing electoral reform, environmental protection, co-partnership in industry and 'a more equitable distribution of the world's resources'. The SDP's sceptics were relieved by Williams' press-conference assurance that it did not preclude the issuing of separate manifestos. *Fresh Start* underlined what the parties had in common and cleared the way to Warrington and Llandudno. It was the moment at which the two parties formally announced that they were to do business together.

The momentum towards a close alliance was boosted by the Warrington by-election, but the months between *Fresh Start* and the Llandudno assembly nevertheless brought intimations of the protracted problems that an electoral pact might produce. Those in the SDP who had doubts about the Liberals took the Warrington result as evidence that the SDP could win or come close in seats where the Liberals had no chance. Where the Liberals had historically been weak, the SDP could well be strong. For men like Thomas and Wrigglesworth, Warrington did indeed underline the advantages of an electoral pact—but one in which the SDP took the lion's share of the seats.[27] The opinion polls likewise suggested that Social Democrat supporters comfortably outnumbered Liberals.[28] The Croydon Liberals' successful resistance to Shirley Williams' replacing Bill Pitt as candidate suggested that the Liberals wanted nothing so much as a free ride on the SDP plane. Mike Thomas called on half the Liberal prospective candidates to step down: they had been selected in the Liberals' strongest seats, and the Liberals had to understand that the SDP 'had not come into existence merely to water the ground so that Liberal seedlings might grow'.[29]

Liberals drew matching, but opposite, conclusions. According to them, Croydon in particular showed that Steel was prepared to sacrifice local Liberal interests to national SDP interests and that he might even agree to a centrally imposed distribution of seats despite the warnings he was already receiving from senior Liberal party officers.[30] To Steel's critics, Croydon also showed that local obstinacy paid. Some adopted Liberal candidates after Croydon promptly announced their refusal even to contemplate withdrawing.[31]

Steel got his way at Llandudno. The assembly's overwhelming approval of an alliance with the SDP in September 1981 was the triumphant culmination of

Steel's skilful matchmaking over the previous eighteen months. Yet he had still had to assuage last-minute doubts, assuring a critical meeting of the Liberal Candidates' Association that no candidates who had 'energetically been building up their local organization and support over several years' would have to stand down. Responding to fears about the next wave of Labour defectors—described by Alan Beith as 'machine men whose machines have broken down'[32]—William Wallace, one of Steel's close advisers, had to pledge, when he moved the motion ratifying the alliance, that Labour party defectors would not automatically become alliance candidates.[33] Even after Jenkins' and Williams' rapturous reception at the *New Outlook* meeting, David Penhaligon, the Truro MP, brandished an alleged SDP computer list of the Alliance's best seat prospects, read out the names of the top four seats, all of them held by Liberal MPs, and warned Social Democrats on the platform: 'You believe that you must have access to at least half of the best fifty on the list. Wish the pact well, as I do, I would tell you that it is not on.'[34]

The day after the great alliance debate, Liberal delegates again asserted their independence of the Social Democrats, voting by a large majority against the siting of cruise missiles in Britain, against the purchase of the Trident II missile system and in favour of a nuclear-free Europe. Since opposition to an independent nuclear deterrent—i.e. Polaris—was already official party policy, the Liberals were thus in all but name embracing unilateral nuclear disarmament and endorsing the breaking of many of Britain's commitments to NATO—the very positions that all the defectors to the SDP had fought so hard against inside the Labour party. Small wonder that many in the SDP—especially those, like Owen, who had not been present to breathe the heady air of Llandudno—continued to harbour doubts about the Liberal connection.

In August 1981 the two parties had begun an informal exchange of ideas about the best procedures for determining the share-out of constituencies under an electoral pact, and after the Liberal assembly these discussions turned into protracted behind-the-scenes negotiations. Disputes immediately arose over the composition of the negotiating bodies, the size of the regional 'negotiating units' and the rights of potential SDP defectors. The haggling foreshadowed the trouble that the actual seats negotiations were to run into during the following year.

Rodgers led for the SDP. Although a Jenkinsite, he was as adamant as Owen would have been that the new party should get the best possible deal. He approached the discussions with three considerations in mind.[35] The weightiest was his fear that the Liberals, having already adopted 230 candidates, mainly in their strongest areas, would end up with most of the elected MPs, riding the crest of an electoral wave that had actually been powered by the SDP.[36] A way therefore had to be found of allocating at least half the winnable seats, preferably more, to the Social Democrats. His second concern was to ensure the automatic selection as candidates of all the SDP MPs, both as a reward for existing defectors and as an inducement for potential ones—of whom there was still a considerable number. The third was his lack of confidence in the skill of ordinary SDP members at negotiating with local Liberals, who, at least in the most promising territory, were more numerous and more partisan. All three considerations pointed to the need for national or at least centrally controlled negotiations.

Steel himself would probably have welcomed a national allocation, but he could not deliver one. Constituency autonomy over candidate selection was an article of Liberal faith—and of the Liberal party's constitution. Steel had neither the constitutional nor the political authority to impose a centrally negotiated agreement.

The negotiating guidelines, when they were finally published in October 1981, instead attempted a compromise between the two parties' conflicting views. (They are reproduced in Appendix 4.) The Liberals secured the principle of constituency autonomy and locally based negotiations, while the SDP obtained an agreement that the total number of seats fought by each party would be in 'rough parity' and would be a social and political 'mix'. The guidelines also guaranteed that all MPs sitting for their party on 1 January 1982 would be adopted for their existing constituency. The obvious possibility of joint local selection by the combined members of both parties was brushed aside.[37]

Like most compromises, the October 1981 guidelines ducked several hard realities. Two weaknesses were to prove particularly troublesome. The first was the combination of the 'local-strength' criterion and the 'political-mix' criterion. The former allowed the Liberals to claim seats where they had done well in 1979 or in subsequent local elections or where they already had a candidate in place—thus covering almost all their good prospects. The SDP could almost nowhere claim comparable local strength, but it could claim winnable seats on the basis of the 'political-mix' guideline.

The crux of the problem was the identification of winnable seats. Had the two parties appealed to largely distinct groups of voters, allocating seats between them would have been relatively straightforward. But the limited evidence available by late 1981 suggested that the two parties appealed to sections of the electorate that heavily overlapped. The SDP's strength apparently lay not in any specific appeal but in its capacity to mobilize a substantial centre vote that had existed for many years but had eluded the Liberals on their own. The SDP's negotiators therefore assumed that what was winnable for the Liberals was winnable for them—and should be equally shared.

The Liberals, however, regarded the SDP's claims to many of their most promising seats as both inequitable and foolish. They claimed that there was no such thing as a 'natural' Liberal or Alliance seat. Winnable Liberal seats became so only as a result of long, hard toil by Liberal associations and candidates. Such locally generated support would not necessarily transfer to SDP candidates. The SDP's job was not to take advantage of the Liberals' strength but to build up its own, concentrating on seats where the Liberals, for whatever reason, happened to be weak. The whole purpose of any alliance, many Liberals insisted, was to create new winnable seats, not to eject existing Liberal candidates from old ones.

The guidelines' second main weakness was that constituency autonomy was potentially incompatible with the concessions on the ground that an electoral pact was bound to require and was certainly contradicted by the protection clause for defectors to the SDP. Few Liberals outside Steel's office faced up to this conundrum, and Steel kept his own thoughts to himself. The problem was, however, immediately highlighted by the defection in October 1981 of Dickson Mabon, a former Labour junior minister and MP for the Clydeside seat of Greenock and Port Glasgow. The guidelines clearly entitled him to the seat; but Greenock Liberals insisted that they could win the seat for the Alliance while Mabon could not.[38] They would refuse to work for him and had already adopted an experienced local councillor and solicitor as their candidate. Backed by the Scottish Liberal party, they announced that they would not stand down.

The seats negotiations, when they finally got under way, quickly ran into the sand. After a few meetings in December 1981, SDP negotiators were reporting back dismaying news about the behaviour of the other side. The Liberals, they complained, were being impossible, declaring all the best seats to be non-negotiable under the 'local-strength' guideline, ignoring other guidelines when it suited them and refusing to be bound by agreements that they had already entered into.

By Christmas, Bill Rodgers was convinced that the Liberals were systematically breaking the national inter-party agreement and that the negotiations would soon grind to a complete halt. He was particularly frustrated by Steel's unwillingness to instil a sense of realism into local Liberals, whom he was allowing to act as if negotiating an electoral pact could be a game without losers. On New Years' Eve, Rodgers informed the *Observer*'s political correspondent, Anthony Howard, that he was suspending all further negotiations, and three days later the story of a major rift in the Alliance broke.

What triggered the row was a triviality magnified by a misunderstanding.[39] However, Rodgers' display of temper was conscious and tactical.[40] It was calculated to jolt Steel out of his complacency while stiffening the resolve of local SDP negotiators. The least glamorous of the Gang of Four, Rodgers may also have been tempted to show his mettle. Tactically his *démarche* worked, but politically it misfired. Rodgers fully intended to go public but expected the media to treat the suspension as a tough bargaining ploy, not as a major split between the Alliance parties. The resulting publicity was immensely damaging, with both sides rushing into print and accusing each other of bad faith while at the same time appealing for unity.[41] Steel, trying to make light of the shambles, quipped that Rodgers had evidently 'eaten too many mince pies', but in a pre-echo of disputes to come he also observed: 'The Liberal party is not an authoritarian party, and the SDP perhaps is.'[42] Journalists made fun of the hitherto sanctimonious Alliance partners: 'Suddenly,' as one wrote, 'the choir boys appeared with bruised knuckles and swollen ears.'[43] The dip in the Alliance's support in the opinion polls that took place in early 1982 was widely, if inaccurately, attributed to the row.[44]

A few days later, with the forthcoming Glasgow Hillhead by-election in mind,

Steel and Rodgers made peace over a well-publicized lunch. The Liberal leader yielded considerable ground, conceding the crucial point that 'parity of seats' meant 'parity of representation'. The press reported a tacit understanding, never denied by the Liberals, that to achieve parity at 200 parliamentary seats the SDP would forgo its claims to the Liberals' first fifty preferences (the so-called 'gold' seats) in return for two-thirds of the next 150 (the so-called 'silver' seats). A 'ring-fence' was placed around Greenock, and negotiations were resumed.[45] A precedent had now been set for leader-to-leader agreements and for settlements imposed from above.

Whether wise or not, Rodgers' tactic broke the log-jam. Liberal resistance to SDP claims softened while the SDP became more assertive.[46] Agreement was reached on over 500 seats by the original 1 April 1982 deadline—no mean achievement, either politically or logistically. Nevertheless, negotiations over the remainder dragged on through the spring and summer of that year. Frustrated by the delay and by the time that they were having to spend on the issue, Steel and Jenkins, by now the SDP leader, decided they must put a stop to the seemingly endless bickering. Neither was particularly exercised by the allocation of largely unwinnable seats, but both were increasingly impatient with the chauvinism of local Liberal associations—of which fifty in August 1982 were still refusing to ratify agreements they considered unfavourable. In early September 1982 they did a deal—including some reversals of allocation—over the outstanding problem seats, a deal that Steel pushed through a reluctant Liberal executive on the eve of his party's annual assembly. In the end, only three rebel Liberal associations held out until the 1983 election, fielding Liberal candidates against the official SDP–Alliance standard-bearer.[47]

The 1981–2 seats negotiations provide a case study of the difficulty of organizing an electoral pact between two separate political parties, even parties as friendly as the Liberals and the SDP. The core problem was that the negotiations were inevitably a zero-sum game: the seats that one party gained the other lost—even if the hope was that both would gain in the end in terms of seats in the House of Commons. Since they were playing a zero-sum game, the negotiators inevitably became adversaries rather than partners. In addition, the inevitable conflicts of interest were reinforced by differences in the two parties' styles and structure. The SDP's approach was managerial and professional. It adopted a national plan and Rodgers treated the negotiations as virtually a full-time job for six months. Negotiating teams were briefed from Cowley Street with vast quantities of infor-mation and computer calculations about constituencies, including recommended trade-offs, bottom-line positions and rank orderings disguised in code (in case Liberal negotiators could read the figures upside down). The local SDP teams generally kept to an agreed line and operated on the assumption that settlements made at the joint meetings were binding.

By contrast, the Liberals' approach was *laissez-faire*, amateur and democratic to a degree. Liberal negotiators often did not know each other and would arrive at

Source: *Daily Express*, 19 September 1981

'When the music stops, we each try to grab
as many seats as we can'

meetings without a leader or an agreed line; the national negotiator present would largely keep himself in the background. The Liberals ignored psephological expertise in favour of their personal interests and their knowledge of individual constituencies, in which they had an almost primitive faith.[48] The Liberals also attached far more importance than the SDP to local organization, the strength and impact of which they often exaggerated. They had little sense of—and even less concern for—the national implications of their local negotiations. Agreements were treated as provisional recommendations subject to acceptance by local associations, meaning that any one association could effectively veto a whole set of them.

These differences of style served to confirm the stereotypes each party held of the other. To Social Democrats, the Liberals were undisciplined, parochial and small-minded. Their obsession with local rights and their indifference to overriding national considerations revealed a massive failure of political imagination. A historic opportunity had suddenly opened up before them, but they were incapable of seizing it. To the Liberals, the SDP appeared opportunistic, overweening and unappreciative of the Liberals' long years of as yet unrewarded toil. The SDP, in their view, was doing all the taking; they were doing all the giving. If SDP negotiators came away asking 'Do the Liberals seriously want power?', Liberals came away asking 'Do the SDP want anything but power?'

Most leading figures in the SDP were well satisfied with the eventual outcome. What mattered was that the deal should be comprehensive, should be adhered to and should be settled with as much speed and as little fuss as possible so that the two parties could present a united front to the electorate. The allocation of particular constituencies to one party or the other did not, in the final analysis, matter nearly so much. By these standards, the deal was a considerable success. Agreement had been reached on 630 out of 633 constituencies well before the 1983 election; 40 per cent of adopted Liberal candidates had been bullied or wheedled into standing down; and, although inter-party relations had soured in a few areas, there had been no widespread breakdown.

Longstanding critics of the over-close relations between the two parties, however, saw their worst fears confirmed. Many Liberals felt Steel had betrayed them: he had broken his Llandudno pledge to protect energetic local candidates, he had imposed a final settlement without proper consultation, and he had allowed himself to be turned, in effect, into a mediator between the local Liberals and the national SDP. The SDP's doubters felt equally bitter about what they claimed was their party's failure to obtain a fair share of the winnable seats. They pinned much of the blame on Jenkins. Instead of placating Steel, in order to secure a deal before the 1982 Liberal assembly, Jenkins should, in their view, have insisted on further Liberal concessions in order to obtain parity of representation. The day after the Jenkins–Steel seats deal was concluded, Thomas wrote to the new leader:

We have obtained nothing like the 2 : 1 advantage in the 'silver' seats that the [SDP] Steering Committee set as the terms for conceding to the Liberals their fifty 'gold' seats . . . On the basic mathematics the seats deal is very bad for us. We could easily end up with only 15–25 of the first 100 seats and 5–10 of the first 50 . . . We are now in danger of getting the worst of all worlds: a seats deal that is very bad for the SDP, and a blurring of the SDP's image within the Alliance that minimises the total number of seats won and reduces to humiliating levels (at which our Party might not even survive) the seats within that total won by the SDP . . . I shall not publicly oppose [the deal], but I should not like my self-enforced silence to be interpreted as assent.[49]

In one sense Thomas was right. The Liberals must have retained the majority of seats on their mysterious 'silver' list (a list that was never published or even admitted to exist). They kept 72 per cent of the seats with an above-average Liberal vote in 1979 and sixty-seven of the ninety-six seats where they had made the most progress since February 1974.[50] But, in a much more important sense, Thomas was wrong. As Table 10.1 (in Appendix 5) shows, on the basis of the actual constituency results in 1983, the seats deal would in fact have given the SDP parity of representation with the Liberals if the Alliance in 1983 had succeeded in winning more than 100 seats. In an Alliance group of between 40 and 100 MPs, the SDP would have been outnumbered by the Liberals' by about three to two; but beyond that the number of SDP MPs would have virtually matched the number of Liberals if the Conservatives had been losing votes to the Alliance, and would have been larger if the Labour party had been.[51] A full account of how the SDP came to obtain parity of representation despite its failure to secure two-thirds of the silver seats is told in the Appendix to this chapter.

The inter-party deal was thus a fair one, and there is no convincing evidence that, if the allocation between the parties had been any different, the Alliance would have won more seats in 1983. That said, however, the Alliance as a whole almost certainly did lose votes through the protracted public quarrelling over the seats negotiations. The relentless drip of news stories about local squabbles took its toll, largely destroying the SDP's unrealistic but important appeal as a party that was 'above party'. But whether the seats negotiations could actually have been handled in a way that caused any less damage is doubtful. Leaving negotiations entirely in local hands, as many Liberals advocated, might have led to less squabbling, but would have left the SDP with an even smaller proportion of the best parliamentary prospects.[52] If the SDP was to survive, national monitoring and intervention in the seats negotiations were essential, and the disputes they gave rise to were probably a price that had to be paid. Nevertheless, the succession of local rows caused some leading Social Democrats to draw the opposite conclusion from that of anti-Liberals like Mike Thomas and to conclude that some form of local joint selection had to be adopted next time round.[53]

The final deal on the allocation of seats in the autumn of 1982 completed the agenda of co-operation between the parties that had first been broached at Königswinter eighteen months before. Throughout this period, David Owen managed to swallow his misgivings, at least in public. He was infuriated by Steel's failure to dislodge Bill Pitt in Croydon North-West, dismayed at the Liberal assembly's quasi-unilateralism at Llandudno and contemptuous of the Liberals' negotiating tactics on—and the eventual outcome of—the seats allocation.[54] But he did not speak out. Instead, in a series of speeches he developed his own views on what the proper relationship should be between the two parties.[55] His line was entirely consistent: there should be no fusion of the two parties, no blurring of identities, no 'Alliance party', but rather co-operation between two independent and distinct parties along the lines of West Germany's then coalition partners, the Free Democrats and the Social Democrats. Owen restated his position regularly, yet most other Social Democrats only half registered how deep Owen's antipathy to the Liberals was.

One reason was that Owen did not make a major issue of his anti-Liberalism (except to some extent during the 1982 leadership contest); he seems to have felt constrained to adhere in public to the more accommodating views of the rest of the Gang of Four. Moreover, Owen's warnings were always somewhat ambiguous. On the one hand, he carefully set out a version of collaboration that fell far short of merger or assimilation. On the other, he often flattered the Liberal party; he claimed to recognize the need for electoral co-operation; he referred, like Jenkins, to 'our principled partnership' between the parties; and he extolled the virtues of coalition government.[56] His public tone towards the Liberals was diplomatic and respectful, not at all overtly hostile. He left it to his feisty supporter, Mike Thomas, to express in public the impatience and belligerence that he privately felt.

The only outward sign—but an important one—of Owen's coolness towards the Liberals was his disengagement from most SDP–Liberal activities. This was sometimes accidental, as in the case of the Königswinter conference, but it was usually deliberate. He kept his distance partly to make a political point and partly out of personal distaste for Liberal company. His visits to by-election campaigns were usually short 'duty attendances', when he would make a speech but not, unlike Rodgers or Williams, join the party workers on the streets. He took no part in the seats negotiations and he deliberately absented himself from the annual Liberal assembly. With a seat in parliament already, he had less reason than either Jenkins or Williams to court Liberal popularity or to feel any debt of gratitude when the Liberals in by-elections made way for the SDP. He was rarely exposed to instances of warm and genuine co-operation between ordinary members of the two parties—that is, to the informal alliance on the ground that was emerging in many parts of the country. He thus experienced none of the Alliance's more exhilarating moments—not the activists' enthusiasm at Warrington, not the *esprit de corps* at Croydon and Crosby, not the Alliance's Llandudno apotheosis. The Alliance's more positive achievements passed him by. Largely unnoticed, David Owen brooded—and waited.

There was one other problem that the Liberals and the SDP had to solve before the coming general election: whether the Alliance should fight the election with two leaders or only one and, if with only one, with whom. The arguments appeared evenly balanced. On the one hand, the Liberals and the SDP were two separate parties, and the SDP in particular emphasized the virtues of collective leadership; there was, therefore, clearly a case for having two leaders. Against that were the obvious problems that a dual leadership would give rise to. The two leaders would be bound to differ publicly on something during the election campaign. The difference might be slight, merely a matter of nuance and detail; but it would be ruthlessly exploited by the media and the Alliance's opponents. Moreover, many voters might be alienated by a dual leadership. It was widely believed that voters at elections in Britain demand to know not only which party they are being asked to vote for but which potential prime minister. Leaving that question unanswered, it was alleged, would confuse many voters and make the Alliance look at least faintly ridiculous.

In fact, although the arguments were finely balanced, the issue was initially resolved without any difficulty—in marked contrast to the seats allocation. At a private meeting at Kiddington Hall in Oxfordshire in February 1982, the leaders of the two sides agreed that there should be a single Alliance leader who would become prime minister in the event of victory.[57] Who the single leader should be would be decided in private discussions between the leaders of the two parties; there would be no ballot of the parties' MPs, let alone of their members. Agreement on a single leader was reached so easily largely because there was little doubt in anyone's mind at that stage about who the single leader would be: Roy Jenkins. He alone in the Alliance looked and sounded like a potential prime minister and had the necessary governmental experience. Everyone at Kiddington Hall knew that Jenkins was the one leader under whom Steel would be happy to serve without any controversy, bickering or heart-searching.

Over the remainder of 1982 it was taken for granted, without being announced, that Jenkins would become leader of the Alliance in due course. But as the year went on the crucial phrase 'leader of the Alliance' underwent a little-noticed but important shift of meaning. At the Kiddington Hall conference, it was assumed to refer not only to the putative prime minister of an Alliance government but to the Alliance's leader in the coming election campaign. Within a few months, however, Steel had very slightly—and unilaterally—shifted his ground. Fearing a hostile reaction from his own party in the wake of the struggle over seats, he let it be known that the Liberal and SDP leaders would have co-equal roles in the election campaign and would present themselves as joint Alliance leaders. The term 'leader of the Alliance', according to Steel, simply signified who would represent the Alliance in the process of forming a government. In the late summer Steel came under pressure from his party not to 'give up the crown' to his SDP opposite number. Many Liberals felt that too much had already been conceded to the SDP in the seats negotiations; but the chief reason was the growing evidence from opinion polls that, of the two leaders, Steel was by far the more popular with the voters.[58] Rightly or wrongly, voters appeared to give less weight to ministerial experience than to television images when judging potential prime ministers. Liberals feared that as soon as Jenkins was formally designated Alliance leader the media would concentrate on him at the expense of the more telegenic Steel, thus damaging both the Liberals and the Alliance as a whole.

These worries were further reinforced by the Alliance's slide in the polls following the Falklands War. With support at barely 20 per cent, reference to an Alliance prime minister seemed merely pretentious. What the Alliance now needed was a leader who might reverse its slump in the polls, and the obvious man for the job was Steel. He was not only more popular with the public than Jenkins—in fact, he was the best liked of all the four party leaders—but he had had practical experience of the tough business of leading a small party in an election campaign.

Steel resisted Liberal pressure throughout the autumn, merely reiterating the view that the two leaders should work 'in harness' in the coming campaign. He, too, was coming to believe that Jenkins might prove an electoral liability, but he was reluctant to jeopardize their close partnership or the fragile relationship between the two parties by taking the initiative in claiming the leadership for himself. He hoped that Jenkins might make the move himself, possibly in response to pressure from within the SDP (which, after all, had even more to lose than the Liberals did from having a vote-loser at the head of the campaign).

However, Jenkins' SDP critics remained silent. They saw the electoral dangers of a Jenkins-led campaign, but they were reluctant to give up the prospect of an

SDP prime ministership, remote though it was, especially as they expected to return fewer MPs than the Liberals. Moreover, they knew the media would rightly interpret a decision to make Steel Alliance leader as a humiliation for Jenkins and therefore the SDP. Accordingly, Steel continued to play for time. But by March, after the Liberals' spectacular win in the Bermondsey by-election, the opinion polls were recording even larger majorities in favour of Steel as both Alliance leader and Alliance prime minister, and Steel was again called upon by Liberal MPs, led by David Penhaligon and David Alton, to bid for the joint leadership.[59]

In late April 1983, with a general election confidently expected to be called within weeks, it was finally confirmed that Jenkins was indeed to be the Alliance's 'prime minister-designate'.[60] But at the same time Steel persuaded Jenkins that in return he, Steel, should be chairman of the Alliance's campaign committee and, in that sense, leader of the Alliance campaign. The distinction, when it was announced, was lost on most of the electorate—and indeed on almost everybody except Jenkins, Steel and a few Liberals close to Steel who had been privy to the various discussions. So far as the outside world was concerned, Jenkins was the Alliance leader just as Michael Foot was Labour leader and Margaret Thatcher the Conservatives' leader. But, in Steel's eyes, the gradual decoupling of leader-as-prime minister from leader-as-campaigner-in-chief was now complete—and neatly met the problem of Jenkins' electoral drawbacks. It was a misunderstanding that, as we shall see in the next chapter, was to have considerable repercussions.

Inevitably it was the differences and conflicts between the two parties that made the news in 1981–3. But it would be misleading to characterize relations between the SDP and the Liberals solely in terms of the rows and bickering that intermittently broke the surface. On the contrary, what was remarkable was the high degree of co-operation and unity that was achieved. On the ground, there was optimism and good will, fuelled only to some extent by overheated expectations of an electoral breakthrough. Among most of the politicians, the attitude was also one of good will, of constructive, if occasionally wary, pragmatism. Even among the small minority in the SDP who were suspicious of the Liberals, few were wholly irreconciled to the idea of some form of tactical arrangement.

Co-operation and unity were achieved across a wide range of the two parties' activities. At Westminster the two parties' MPs went through the division lobbies together night after night, week after week, almost as though they were taking the same whip. The casuistic formula for the Alliance leadership was the product of a neat compromise that satisfied honour on both sides; and the 1983 election manifesto made the most of the many views that the two parties shared (successfully masking underlying differences on defence, nuclear power and incomes policy). The great majority of local parties likewise worked in harmony, campaigning jointly in local elections and occasional by-elections.[61] The discipline and scale of the electoral pact was without precedent in British political history.[62] The forming of the Alliance was a notable achievement, not least in a country with a political culture as adversarial and partisan as Britain's.

The forging of this 'partnership of principle' was, however, largely an internal matter—a case of the two parties working together to try to build a successful marriage. But the Alliance in early 1983 was on the eve of having to face a much more severe test—the external and ultimately more important test of its credibility with the electorate as a whole.

Appendix

• • • •

How the SDP Obtained Parity of Representation from the 1982 Seats Deal

The SDP obtained parity of representation despite its failure to secure two-thirds of the silver seats because it was much more sophisticated than Liberals in its use of psephological evidence. It adopted three definitions, not one, of winnable seats. The first was based mainly on Liberal strength at the 1979 election. The second derived from a research paper by Ivor Crewe which, on the basis of opinion-poll data, examined variations in Alliance support across different sociological categories of constituency.[63] This confirmed that relatively strong Liberal areas in 1979 showed up as promising Alliance territory in 1981; but it also revealed three categories of seat with only an average or below-average Liberal performance in 1979 but above-average Alliance support in 1981: 'affluent-worker' seats, especially the New Towns, university towns and 'single-member service centres'.[64] Whatever the cause of this Alliance surge, the SDP negotiators thought they should try to secure as many as they could of such seats in the allocation. The third definition was based on a computer calculation by the SDP whip, John Roper. This picked out 'low-threshold' seats, i.e. those that the Alliance could win with a relatively small proportion of the national vote. Many of these were classical two-party marginals in which the third-placed Liberals had not been too heavily squeezed and where an Alliance candidate might therefore 'sneak through' to victory.

Most of these second and third categories of 'winnable' seat appear not to have been on the Liberals' silver list and were thus quite easily secured by the SDP in the negotiations. The SDP took 64 of the 94 low-threshold seats, 49 of the 81 affluent-worker seats, 9 of the 10 distinctive New Town seats and 32 of the 41 university seats. Local Liberals, by contrast, were often dazzled by the 'second-place illusion' and successfully bid for large numbers of utterly unwinnable, ultra-safe Conservative seats simply on the basis of a poor Liberal second place in 1979.

There are ironies in this unappreciated outcome of the negotiations. The SDP got a better bargain than it had imagined because it flouted Guideline 3, incorporated for its benefit, by which the parties were meant to fight a similar social mix of seats. The Liberals, however, exploited the 'local-strength' guideline, inserted at their insistence, and thereby, as the result of the much-vaunted 'superiority' of their own local knowledge, dealt themselves a bad hand.

The seats negotiations not only would have achieved a reasonable parity of representation between the two parties; retrospective analysis of the 1983 election results shows that it passed other tests as well. In hindsight, fewer than a dozen seats were misallocated in the sense that the Alliance would probably have polled better if it had been represented by the other party—and even then the difference was only a few percentage points.[65] Moreover, there is no convincing evidence that misallocation cost the Alliance a single seat.[66] The 1983 election was to prove that the SDP negotiators were right to assume that, on the day, the electorate would vote for the Alliance and not for the Liberals or the SDP specifically. By June 1983, in the eyes of most voters, Liberal and SDP candidates were interchangeable.[67]

11

....

Disappointment: June 1983

Despite the forging of the Alliance, it was a chastened SDP that Roy Jenkins led into 1983. The seats negotiations with the Liberals had reached a largely satisfactory conclusion, but electorally the Alliance was in the doldrums. The by-elections in the latter half of 1982 had not gone well, and the first Gallup poll of 1983 showed that only 22.5 per cent of the electorate thought they would vote Liberal or SDP at an early general election, leaving the Alliance well behind Labour and even further behind the Conservatives. The Conservatives' commanding lead in all the polls made it look increasingly as though the next general election would come within a few months and not in 1984 as had previously been supposed. Conscious of the need to try to attract new publicity and raise morale, the Alliance organized a big rally in Central Hall, Westminster, towards the end of January. The fact that the press insisted on dubbing the rally an Alliance 'relaunch' was a measure of how far the two parties' fortunes had fallen. Predictably, the rally attracted little attention.

Yet at the same time there did not seem any reason to be too downhearted. Despite the Falklands, many of the factors that had caused people to turn against the Conservatives in the first place—high interest rates, high unemployment and swingeing cuts in some of the social services—were still operating; and the Labour party, although it had got over the worst, was still led by the risible Michael Foot and was still committed to such unpopular policies as massive state intervention in industry and unilateral nuclear disarmament. Alliance support had expanded suddenly in 1981. It had contracted suddenly in 1982. It might suddenly expand again.

A reminder of how unpredictable the British electorate had by now become was soon forthcoming. Towards the end of 1982, Robert Mellish, a former Labour housing minister and chief whip, resigned his docklands seat of Bermondsey near the heart of London south of the river. Mellish had held the seat since 1950. His majority in 1979, in a very small electorate, had been 11,756. Bermondsey was one of the safest Labour seats in the country. But the local Labour party had recently been taken over by the far left, and Mellish's successor as Labour candidate was an Australian named Peter Tatchell, who made little effort to conceal the fact that he was a homosexual and who festooned the lapels of his black leather jackets with badges advertising every imaginable left-wing cause. He was against racism, in favour of unilateral nuclear disarmament, in favour of a woman's right to choose and, apparently, also in favour of Labour's resorting to 'extra-parliamentary action' to dislodge the Thatcher government. A sort of one-man walking street demo, he stood for everything that millions of working-class voters found unattractive about the 1980s-style Labour party. Even Foot at first wanted to disown him because of his alleged support for extra- (and implicitly anti-) parliamentary action.

Tatchell managed to conduct himself with dignity during an increasingly vicious by-election campaign (an anonymous leaflet asked, 'Which queen would you vote for?'); and he won the sympathy of his political opponents and some of the more fastidious journalists. But it was to no avail. On 24 February 1982 Labour's massive majority of nearly 12,000 was turned into a majority for the Liberal Simon Hughes of over 9,000—a swing of almost 48 per cent. The transfer of votes was on an even bigger scale than at Crosby. The Conservatives, who had finished second only four years before, fell into fourth place behind a rebel anti-Tatchell former Labour councillor. The Alliance bandwagon was, it seemed, rolling again. *The Times* headlined its story the next day, 'Alliance goes into electoral orbit'. Bermondsey, moreover, was the first Labour-held seat to fall to the Alliance; Croydon, Crosby and Hillhead had all been Conservative seats.[1]

The repercussions of Bermondsey were felt immediately. There were renewed calls inside the Labour party for Foot's resignation as leader; the Alliance surged in the polls; and talk of a June election abruptly ceased. But it was not clear whether Simon Hughes' victory in Bermondsey had been a fluke, the result of Labour's extreme unpopularity and the nomination of someone like Tatchell, or whether it represented the beginnings of a genuine reversion to the three-party politics of 1981, before the Alliance's decline and the Falklands War. As luck would have it, that issue was about to be settled in yet another by-election, this time in Darlington, in County Durham, where the sitting Labour MP, Ted Fletcher, had just died.

Darlington was as unlike Bermondsey as could be imagined. A medium-sized town with only one MP, it was socially mixed and quietly prosperous, with a long history and considerable civic pride. Although the town's lone parliamentary constituency had been Labour for the previous nineteen years, it was in fact highly marginal, and Ted Fletcher's majority in 1979 had been only just over 1,000. In addition, the Labour party in the north-east was more recognizably its old self politically than in almost any other part of the country. There were some left-wingers in Darlington, but few of them were on the far left, and the Darlington Labour party would not have dreamt of nominating anyone as exotic as Peter Tatchell. Its candidate, Ossie O'Brien, was a well-respected teacher and former local councillor, a man in Labour's traditional mainstream. Even so, the first poll to be taken in the constituency—only two days after Bermondsey—showed the Alliance ahead of the Conservatives, with Labour a poor third.[2] In addition, the Alliance's candidate, Tony Cook of the SDP, appeared to be near ideal. A personable young family man, he was already well known to Darlington voters as a popular presenter on Tyne–Tees Television.

In the event, Darlington proved an utter humiliation for the SDP, one felt all the more keenly for coming so soon after the Liberals' triumph in Bermondsey. Labour's Ossie O'Brien and the Conservatives' Michael Fallon turned out to be just as personable as Tony Cook—and much better informed. The three men took part in two televised debates, and in both of them Cook appeared totally out of his depth. He was humourless and ignorant and seemed to have nothing in his head but banalities. Darlington was a self-contained community, and the canvassers for the three parties agreed that voters were unusually quick to form impressions of the three candidates. Their impressions of Cook were unflattering. Moreover, the SDP's overall campaign in Darlington lacked any of the flair and excitement that the Alliance's previous by-election campaigns had generated. Partly because the Social Democrats initially thought they were ahead, the campaign seemed designed to soothe rather than arouse. Worse, as it went on, and as the opinion polls made it seem increasingly unlikely that Cook would win, his London-based advisers became more and more agitated and began to argue among themselves and also with the candidate. Bill Rodgers was supposedly in charge of the Alliance campaign, but in practice it seemed that no one was. Cook, instead of being encouraged to say as little as possible, was briefed for his public appearances in more and more detail. But, wholly inexperienced, he was unable to assimilate the detail and, having previously been bland, became increasingly flustered. 'It was', one frustrated SDP man said afterwards, 'like trying to force-feed a goose with a throat obstruction.' On the day, Ossie O'Brien doubled Labour's majority, with the Conservative coming second. Cook, although he put the 1979 Liberal share of the vote up from 10.2 per cent to 24.5 per cent, finished third. In other circumstances, Darlington might not have been any worse than most of the other post-Falklands by-elections; but, after Bermondsey, it was a disaster. The Liberals' Bermondsey success, had indeed, it seemed, been a fluke—or did the Darlington defeat possibly owe something to the fact that the SDP and not the Liberals had been the party fighting the seat?

Darlington proceeded to revive many of the tensions within the Alliance described in Chapter 10. In Liberal circles, Tony Cook's defeat was widely put down to the SDP's inferiority in matters of by-election technique. The Social Democrats, it was said, were too inexperienced, too ready to give credence to favourable-seeming canvass returns and too fastidious in not attacking the Labour party's national policies and leadership.[3] The failure to win Darlington was also put down to Roy Jenkins' limitations as one of the Alliance's leaders; and a joint meeting of Liberal and SDP MPs a week after Darlington, although it rejected a proposal that the whole idea of a joint Alliance leadership should be scrapped, could agree only that a final decision on the leadership should be postponed yet again.[4] The two parties would probably have gone on postponing the decision indefinitely, with the result that press coverage of the Alliance would have concentrated increasingly on the leadership question; but by the end of April, partly as a result of Darlington, a June 1983 election had come to seem more rather than less probable. The Conservatives remained well ahead in the polls; the Alliance and Labour were both floundering; the prime minister seemed to be waiting only for the results of the May local elections. It was against this background that Jenkins and Steel finally agreed on their novel division of labour between Jenkins as Alliance prime minister-designate and Steel as leader of the Alliance campaign.[5]

The leadership decision was announced only just in time. The Conservatives did well enough in the 5 May local elections to put to rest any residual doubts Thatcher may have had, and four days later, on Monday, 9 May, she announced that parliament would be dissolved at the end of that week, with polling to take place exactly a month later, on Thursday, 9 June. The SDP and the Alliance were thus about to face their first major electoral test. It was a measure of how far their fortunes had fallen that no one any longer thought that they had any realistic prospect of winning power on their own. The most they could hope for now was to hold the balance of power in the new parliament and possibly to relegate Labour to third place in the popular vote. The SDP had been launched two years before as the party that was going to transform British politics. Now it was a party that *might* transform British politics but in all probability would not. The party went into the election hopeful and determined rather than—as would have been the case in 1981—positively optimistic.

No fewer than five strategic decisions confronted the SDP and its Liberal allies as the campaign began. All five had been mulled over—and decisions, in varying degrees, taken on them—over the previous year and a half.

The first concerned whether the Alliance, despite its recent decline in the polls, should nevertheless declare that its aim in fighting the election was to win power outright, i.e. to obtain an absolute majority in the House of Commons. The Liberals were well aware of the arguments on both sides of the question: they had faced them at every general election in the recent past. On the one hand, for any third party like the Liberals, or now the Alliance, to declare that it was 'going for government' was to risk appearing absurd, since it would be asserting a claim that had no basis in reality. 'You must be joking' would be a natural, and justifiable, voter response. Such a claim would also risk causing voters to think of the election in question as being wholly concerned with the formation of a government; and, if voters began to think in those terms, they would be likely to vote for a party that could reasonably claim that it could actually form a government on its own: in practice, either the Conservatives or Labour. Any claim to be a potential party of government also required the party making the claim to spell out detailed policies during the campaign and not merely to advance broad themes. In that respect, too, the 'going-for-government' strategy was a high-risk strategy: detailed policies are always open to detailed attack.

That was one side of the argument; it suggested that the Alliance should approach the voters in a spirit of due humility. But the other side of the argument seemed to almost all those involved in the discussions to be even more telling. If a third party declared that it was merely setting out 'to establish a bridgehead in British politics' or to 'create a new third force', it would in effect be conceding defeat right at the outset; it would be opting out of the one issue that British general elections have always been supposed to be about: the choice of who is to run the country. It would, in effect, be inviting voters to opt out: knowingly to cast their votes in favour of a party that had no chance—and did not even claim to have a chance—of winning. Such an approach would almost certainly deter voters. It would also demoralize parliamentary candidates and their supporters. How could anyone justify putting up an Alliance candidate in every constituency in the country, and justify urging Liberal and SDP activists to come out and work on their behalf, if the sole aim of the exercise was to pile up votes across the country as distinct from electing actual MPs and possibly securing a majority? Candidates, activists and leaders alike had to believe that, even if the goal of electing an Alliance government was remote, it was nevertheless achievable. Otherwise most of them would find it almost impossible, within themselves, to function effectively. Moreover, in the specific circumstances of 1983, Jenkins, Steel and most of those around them did believe that an Alliance government, though extremely unlikely, was not impossible; and they saw no advantages whatsoever in not being seen to be working towards that end. They were conscious of the arguments in favour of a more cautious approach, but they dismissed them. Jenkins, in particular, insisted in speech after speech that the Alliance's aim was to form a government and nothing less; and when it appeared the joint Alliance manifesto bore the subtitle *Programme for Government*.

The second decision that had to be taken concerned whether the Alliance should present itself during the campaign as primarily an anti-Conservative or an anti-Labour force. Attacking Labour would have the advantage of appealing to Conservative-inclined voters and possibly also of attracting some Labour waverers; but at the same time attacks on Labour that were too vehement might make the Alliance appear more right wing than it wanted to, thereby alienating another group of potential supporters. The alternative strategy, of attacking mainly the Conservatives, had the same disadvantages but in the opposite direction. Such a strategy would run the risk of making the Alliance look more left wing and pro-Labour than it wanted to, thereby alienating yet another group of potential supporters. This anti-Conservative strategy had the added disadvantage that Conservative propaganda was still anxious to portray many of the SDP leaders, especially Shirley Williams and David Owen, as crypto-socialists, people who had not really changed their views even though they had left the Labour party; to be too anti-Conservative might seem to confirm this image. In fact, there did not seem to be any obvious electoral advantage in pursuing either strategy in the circum- stances of 1983, and, since Jenkins, Steel and most of the other Alliance leaders were genuine in their distaste for the policies and leaders of both major parties, the decision was taken, without a great deal of discussion, that the Alliance should not lean either way. It should distance itself equally from both the other parties.

The Alliance's third strategic problem was related to the second: what to say to voters during the campaign about how the Alliance would comport itself if, as a result of the election, it found itself holding the balance of power in a hung parliament. Would the Alliance put a Conservative government in power or a Labour government?

This question was easy to answer, at least in principle, because the same reasoning that applied to tactics during the campaign clearly also applied to any post-election situation: the Alliance would not, unless given good reason to, lean in either direction. Jenkins and Steel made it clear from the start that, in the event of a hung parliament, they would be prepared to negotiate with the leaders of either major party—but only on the Alliance's terms. From Labour they would demand a scaling-down of its public-expenditure proposals, an incomes policy, continued British membership of the European Community and the dropping of unilateralism. From the Conservatives they would demand an expansionary economic programme with the aim of bringing down unemployment. From both they would demand a commitment to introducing some form of proportional representation (though whether with or without a popular referendum on the issue was never made clear). The Alliance, its leaders said, would be prepared, depending on the circumstances, to join a coalition government or, alternatively, to give parliamentary support to a minority government formed by one of the other parties; but either way a clear agreement on policy would have to be worked out in advance, and the agreement would have to be ratified by the Liberal and SDP MPs. Steel had spent many months ruminating on the Liberals' weak position under the 1976–8 Lib–Lab pact. He had even written a book on the subject. He was not going to repeat the mistakes the Liberals had made at that time.[6]

The fourth problem concerned policy: what should the Alliance say to the electorate during the campaign in substantive terms? The answers to this question were provided in (and by) an enormous pile of policy documents that the Liberals and the SDP, and the joint commissions of the two parties, had been accumulating ever since the new party's formation. The documents—there were dozens of them—had titles like 'Towards Full Employment: A Common-Sense Approach to Economic Policy', 'Partnership for Prosperity: Strategy for Industrial Success', 'Decentralising Government' and 'Electoral Reform: Fairer Voting in Natural Communities'. The problem was to cull from those of the documents that had been approved formally by one or other of the two parties the proposals that the Alliance leaders most wanted to emphasize during the coming four weeks. Rather than risk protracted arguments when it was clear that an election was imminent, Jenkins and Steel, having up to this point postponed the drafting of a joint manifesto, now announced that there would have to be one and that it would need to be drafted in days rather than weeks. They handed over the job of preparing a draft to a single individual, the SDP's policy co-ordinator, a former civil servant named Christopher Smallwood; and they then got the Joint Policy Committee of the two parties to agree to delegate final approval of Smallwood's draft, when it was finished, to the two chief whips, Alan Beith and John Roper. Some Liberals predictably objected to the lack of consultation; but there was not a lot that they could do about it at this late stage.[7]

In fact, the final version of the manifesto, agreed by Beith, Roper and the two leaders, was not a cause of serious dissension in either party. Entitled *Working Together for Britain*, it was launched at a press conference a mere four days after Thatcher called the election, well before the manifestos of the other two parties. The document's central commitment was to a reduction in the number of Britain's unemployed to a million over the coming two years, but without any increase in the rate of inflation. The programme to bring down unemployment was to be paid for by increased government borrowing of £3 billion and by the cancellation of the Trident nuclear weapons system. The programme would be buttressed by a 'fair and effective pay and prices policy'. The manifesto proposed a radical restructuring of the welfare state, including the eventual integration of the tax and benefit systems, a wide range of measures aimed at reducing the incidence of poverty, greater democracy in the trade unions, industrial democracy including profit-sharing and employee share-ownership, a massive expansion of education and training, especially in the 16–19 age group, and an immediate halt to both nationalization and privatization (that of British Telecom, in particular, would not be proceeded with).

This programme of economic and social reforms was to be underpinned by a wide range of constitutional changes. Under an Alliance government, the terms of the European Convention on Human Rights would be written into British law in the form of a bill of rights, and legislation would be introduced providing for wide access to official information. More radically still, a quasi-autonomous parliament would be established in Scotland, with a full range of devolved powers, including the power to tax (though not the power to run a deficit). Devolution to Wales and the English regions would follow if there appeared to be a widespread demand for it. Most radically of all, *Working Together* proposed the introduction of a system of proportional representation based on multi-member constituencies and the single transferable vote. The manifesto described PR as 'the linchpin of our entire programme of radical reform':

Alone of the political parties, the Liberal party and the SDP recognise that our economic crisis is rooted in our political system. As class-based parties, Labour and Conservative represent and intensify our divisions . . . Electoral reform is thus a precondition of healing Britain's divisions and creating a sense of community . . . A switch to proportional representation will transform the character of our politics . . .

These constitutional proposals, more than any others in the manifesto, distinguished the Alliance's policies from those of the other parties.

The fifth and final strategic problem arose out of the division of labour that had been agreed upon between the two Alliance leaders: what exactly were Roy Jenkins, as 'prime minister-designate', and David Steel, as 'leader of the Alliance campaign', going to do during the coming days and weeks? The short answer was that they were going to do almost exactly the same things. Both would appear at the joint Alliance press conferences. Both would appear frequently on television. Both would tour the country. Both would appear at several of the 'Ask the Alliance' rallies to be held in a number of big cities.[8] In other words, the division of labour was not to be a division of labour at all; the two men were to differ only in title. The only concession made to Jenkins' somewhat more exalted status was that he, rather than Steel, would appear as the Alliance's spokesman in the two big set-piece television interviews of the campaign—with Brian Walden on *Weekend World* and Sir Robin Day on *Panorama*. It was also expected that Jenkins would spend more time than Steel in his constituency, since Glasgow Hillhead was so much more marginal than the Liberal leader's seat in the Scottish borders. These largely informal arrangements were not the result of hard bargaining between the two sides; they merely reflected each of the two parties' determination that its leader should play a prominent part in the campaign and Jenkins' and Steel's personal willingness to offer a genuinely dual leadership.

We have labelled all five of the decisions just described as 'strategic', and in a sense they were: they involved big issues, ones that could only be taken at the top. But, in another sense, little or no strategic thinking actually took place in the run-up to the 1983 campaign. Both Jenkins and Steel were, in their way, political visionaries, and Steel at least was a consummate political tactician—'brilliant', as an SDP admirer had said, 'over six yards'; but neither was really a political strategist in the sense of being a leader who, conscious of his long-term goals, nevertheless pauses occasionally to examine the changing terrain in which he finds himself in order to assess the best means of achieving those goals. In this sense, Jenkins and Steel were both instinctive politicians, people who preferred 'to fly by the seat of their pants' (a phrase that was often used of Steel). Being such people, they did not confer regularly between 1981 and 1983 on broad strategic issues as distinct from day-to-day matters, and they were not conscious of any need to assess, and then to reassess, the Alliance's political situation as it developed.

As a result, the Alliance's broad strategy for the 1983 campaign was, in effect, taken off the shelf. The themes that the British electorate were offered in 1983 were, for better or worse, the same themes that Jenkins and Steel, especially Jenkins, had been developing over the previous four years: the themes of national unity, of the need for all sections of the community to work together and of the profound dangers inherent in 'confrontation politics' and 'extremism'. These themes had been spelt out in the 1979 Dimbleby Lecture; they were now repeated in the phrases and sentences of *Working Together for Britain*:

a new road of partnership

an alternative government pledged to bring the country together again

a halt to confrontation politics

our whole approach is based on cooperation

our greatest need is to build a sense of belonging to one community

It remained to be seen whether large numbers of voters would respond to these themes in mid-1983 as they had apparently done in the SDP's and the Alliance's halcyon days two years earlier.

If Jenkins and Steel were not, in the sense just outlined, strategists, they were not in any conceivable sense planners, and the coming of the 1983 election took both men largely unawares. The Liberal–SDP Alliance in early 1983 was a reality in terms of both the seats allocation at the bottom and the dual leadership at the top; but it was not at all a reality anywhere in between. In particular, the two party's headquarters staffs—the SDP's at Cowley Street and the Liberals' a mile or so away at the National Liberal Club—had not in any way been integrated and were not under any form of joint management; many members of the two staffs, even senior members, scarcely knew each other. Until the calling of the election, the SDP and the Liberals had in organizational terms been 'working together but in parallel'.[9] There was not even a joint Liberal–SDP campaign committee.

Such a committee was hurriedly established on the eve of the dissolution; but, since it consisted of Jenkins, the entire Gang of Three, Lord Diamond (a former Labour cabinet minister who was to co-ordinate the campaign from London), Bernard Doyle (the SDP's chief executive), John Lyttle (Jenkins' chief assistant), Steel himself, Stuart Mole (one of Steel's advisers), Paul Medlicott (the Liberals' press officer) and John Pardoe (a former Liberal MP whom Steel had drafted into the campaign at the last moment), and since it was clear that many of its members would be away during most of the campaign touring the country or working in their constituencies, it was agreed that the committee as a whole would only meet in London at weekends. It was hardly an executive body. In so far as anyone was supposed to be in overall charge of the campaign, Jenkins and Steel themselves were expected to play this role (even though for days at a time they might not be together in the same town) along with their immediate advisers, Lord Harris of Greenwich and John Lyttle for Jenkins and Lord Chitnis, Paul Tyler and Richard Holme for Steel (though Holme would mainly be absent in the seat that he was fighting, Cheltenham).[10]

The rest of the joint organization similarly resembled one of Heath Robinson's more complicated contrivances. With Lord Diamond trying to maintain some semblance of order, both physical and emotional, more than 100 members of the Liberal and SDP headquarters staff were crowded into the SDP's Cowley Street headquarters and spent the ensuing four weeks sharing offices, attending innumerable meetings, making and answering innumerable telephone calls (though a newly installed telephone system at first refused to work) and desperately seeking to liaise with each other, with their superiors, with the two leaders' campaign organizations and with other prominent Liberal and SDP figures, including the Gang of Four, who were scattered the length and breadth of Britain. Fortunately, it had been agreed that the Alliance's daily press conferences during the campaign would be held in the relative calm of the National Liberal Club, away from this pandemonium. In the event, although almost everyone in the two parties agreed afterwards that the organization of any future Alliance campaign should be better integrated and planned, nothing went too badly wrong, and it is doubtful whether the best campaign organization in the world would have made more than a fractional difference to the outcome. Lord Diamond's blend of firmness and emollience probably helped avert any major disaster. He had not been chief secretary to the Treasury for nothing.

The first three weeks of the campaign itself were almost unbearably frustrating.[11] The Conservatives, as everyone had expected, remained comfortably ahead in the opinion polls; neither Francis Pym's suggestion that it would be undesirable for the Conservatives to have too large a majority ('Landslides on the whole don't produce successful governments') nor the discovery that Ian Wrigglesworth's Conservative opponent in Stockton South had twice stood as a National Front candidate seemed to make much difference. The Labour party, as everyone had also expected, remained far behind and fell still further behind as the campaign progressed. A member of the shadow cabinet dismissed Labour's manifesto as 'the longest suicide note in history', Michael Foot proved hopelessly inept on television and the hustings (a Tory journalist, asked at a Labour press conference whether Foot filled him with confidence, replied 'Absolutely'), and Labour's unilateralist defence policy was publicly condemned, first implicitly by Denis Healey, the party's foreign-affairs spokesman, and then explicitly—and categorically—by James Callaghan, the former prime minister. The Alliance's campaign began quietly but it also began reasonably well; the Alliance manifesto was published first, the two leaders stuck to their agreed line of attacking Labour and the Conservatives equally while keeping their distance from both, and the first Alliance television broadcast, with its theme of 'working together' and featuring Jenkins and Steel heaping praise on one another and emphasizing their willingness to co-operate, was widely judged a success.[12]

But none of this seemed to have even the slightest effect on the Alliance's standing in the polls; the Alliance's needle on the charts was stuck—and remained stuck for fully three weeks. The polls published in the first full week after Thatcher's announcement of the election date showed the Alliance on just under 18 per cent—rather worse, if anything, than during the preceding few months. The polls published in the second full week showed it still on just under 19 per cent. And the polls published in the third full week showed it, yet again, on just under 19 per cent.[13] Not only were the averages bad, but few individual polls showed the Alliance on significantly more than 20 per cent; three suggested that it might have slumped to as little as 14 or 15 per cent. On this basis, neither the Liberals nor the SDP could expect to gain a single extra seat, and almost all the SDP MPs and several Liberals could expect to lose their seats. Questions to the two parties' spokesmen at the daily press conferences became increasingly concentrated on the Alliance's poor opinion-poll showing, and David Steel, in particular, felt compelled to claim that, in the 1983 campaign as in past campaigns, the polls would start to move his way as soon as voters came to appreciate the unattractiveness of the major-party alternatives. 'There is still', he insisted a fortnight into the campaign, 'everything to play for'; but even he admitted that the Alliance had 'got to do much better'.[14] He and his aides repeatedly insisted that an upturn in the polls could be expected at any time.

Jenkins, Steel and those travelling with them were genuinely puzzled by the polls' failure to move in the Alliance's direction. Both men, and other prominent Liberal and SDP figures, including Owen and Williams, were attracting large and sympathetic audiences to all their meetings; they were being received warmly in the streets and on the doorstep; they still sensed among ordinary voters the same underlying hostility to Margaret Thatcher and the same suspicions of the new-style Labour party that they had encountered so often in by-elections. Why, then, did the polls seem to be stuck? They had no easy answer. But, as day followed day and week followed week, puzzlement slowly gave way to frustration and frustration in turn gave way to something like desperation. Some explanation *must* be found, something *must* be done—*soon*, before it was too late. The growing mood of desperation was felt most strongly among activists on the ground, especially in seats that the Liberals and the SDP hoped to gain or hold. The leaders and their entourages were at least busy; they could vent their frustrations in action—and at the same time bask in the warmth of the response they were receiving. But many of their followers around the country felt increasingly let down, out in the cold, helpless—and bitterly angry. They could see the whole election and the Alliance's once-great prospects slipping away, the results of years of patient work in their constituencies squandered.

Almost everyone in both parties admitted to being puzzled—up to a point; but a growing number believed that they did know what the problem was, that it lay in the two parties' dual leadership and that it lay, in particular, in the prominent role that Jenkins was playing in the campaign with his fancy title of prime minister-designate. Canvassers who had been out on the doorstep reported that very large numbers of voters either did not grasp the concept of a dual leadership or, worse, did grasp it and did not like it; 'why can't you people make up your minds?' voters wanted to know. But Jenkins himself was seen as the greater problem. Steel was fluent and relaxed as a campaigner; Jenkins, by contrast, was almost always ponderous and ill at ease. His two performances on *Weekend World* and *Panorama* were generally thought to have been unhelpful at best, ghastly at worst; instead of presenting the Alliance's case with confidence and vigour, he had seemed hesitant and defensive in replying to Walden's and Day's questions. Millions of voters had watched the two programmes, especially *Panorama*—and so had thousands of Liberal and SDP party workers.

Moreover—and far worse—this was not just a matter of individual party activists' impressions: the opinion polls were telling the same story. A survey published in the *Daily Express* on the day parliament was dissolved showed that, whereas only 7 per cent of voters thought Jenkins would make the best prime minister for Britain, 19 per cent—nearly three times as many—thought the same of Steel.[15] A few days later, a Harris poll for the *TV-Eye* programme concentrated on the two Alliance leaders and asked which of them voters thought would make the better prime minister. The results did further damage to Jenkins' reputation, especially since, as a former minister, he was supposed to be more 'prime ministerial' than his Liberal counterpart. Among Alliance voters, the figures were Steel 76 per cent and Jenkins 21 per cent. Among all voters, the figures were Steel 65 per cent and Jenkins 22 per cent.[16]

And worse was to come. On 24 May, more than a fortnight into the campaign, the results of an Audience Selection survey were broadcast on TV-am. The voting figures were fairly typical of the polls being taken at that time: Conservatives, 45 per cent; Labour, 32 per cent; Alliance, 20 per cent. But when Audience Selection's respondents were asked how they would vote if David Steel rather than Roy Jenkins were the Alliance's prime minister-designate, the results were sensationally different: Conservative, 42 per cent; Alliance, 29 per cent; Labour, 28 per cent.[17] In other words, a Steel leadership rather than a Jenkins leadership looked as though it would be sufficient, in and of itself, to add nine percentage points to the Alliance's share of the vote and to propel the Alliance past Labour into second place. The differences between the two sets of figures could be translated, literally, into dozens of seats in the House of Commons.

Not surprisingly, Liberals around the country were even more upset by such poll findings than were supporters of the SDP. Jenkins was not *their* leader; he was the leader of another party, who had been foisted on them by Steel. Senior Liberals recalled, with mounting irritation, that during the February 1974 election campaign—the last time they had fought a vulnerable-seeming Conservative government—they had been doing much better in the opinion polls on their own at this stage of the campaign without the benefit of the SDP, or the Alliance, or the dreary Jenkins. The whole arrangement manifestly was not working: why should they put up with it any longer? How far sentiment of this kind was based on cold reasoning, and how far it was based on an understandable if unattractive desire to find a scapegoat for the Alliance's poor performance, is impossible to say. But there was no denying the strength of it.

At quite an early stage, expressions of this Liberal frustration began to find their way into the press. Leading Liberals were clearly making use of their access to prominent journalists to put pressure on the Alliance leadership in general and their own party leader in particular. Richard Holme, well known to be one of Steel's closest confidants, told Laurence Marks of the *Observer* that, because Jenkins would inevitably be preoccupied with fighting to hold Hillhead during the campaign, Steel would be more available and would therefore be, in American terms, 'the

Source: *Daily Telegraph*, 24 May 1983

The scapegoat designate

Candidate'. 'If anyone asks', Holme went on, ' "Who is Prince Rupert of the Rhine, leading the cavalry?", it's David.'[18] Following Jenkins' appearance on *Weekend World*, the *Daily Telegraph* reported that he was under pressure 'to take a less prominent part in the campaign after giving what senior and normally friendly Liberals saw as a needlessly defensive performance'.[19] Such stories became even more frequent following the TV-am poll which apparently showed that, with Steel as leader, the Alliance would overtake Labour. During a campaign stop at Brighouse in West Yorkshire, Steel was asked why, in the light of the TV-am poll, he did not 'push Jenkins aside' and replace him as Alliance prime minister-designate. Steel replied: 'It is not my nature to push people aside.' But then he added: 'Obviously, we will have to look at our campaign over the next week to see how best we can project the idea that this is not a presidential campaign.'[20]

An obvious opportunity to reassess the Alliance campaign at once presented itself, in the form of the weekly meeting of the Alliance's joint campaign committee. Normally the committee would have met in London, but on Friday, 27 May, Steel informed the journalists travelling with him that, instead, he had invited the committee's members to meet him at the Steel family home at Ettrickbridge, an isolated village in the Scottish border country near Selkirk. The meeting would be held two days later, on Sunday, 29 May, and arrangements had been made to fly in the members of the committee and some of their aides by helicopter and private plane. The purpose of the hastily convened Alliance summit, the Liberal leader told journalists, was 'quite simply to reassess strategy in view of the collapse of the Labour party'.[21]

That may possibly have been one of the purposes of the meeting. It was not, however, the main purpose. The full story of the Ettrickbridge summit has never been told. It deserves to be. It constitutes one of the more bizarre episodes in recent British political history, with more than faint echoes of the second act of Macbeth.[22]

To understand what happened at Ettrickbridge one needs to understand that from the beginning the Alliance's dual leadership was based on a profound mis-understanding, but a misunderstanding that would probably never have surfaced if the election campaign had gone well.

For most people in the SDP, and certainly for Roy Jenkins, the dual leadership was exactly what it seemed. Jenkins was the prime minister-designate. What that meant was that, like the leaders of the Conservative and Labour parties, he would inevitably receive a disproportionate amount of media attention and that his pronouncements on behalf of the Alliance would likewise be regarded as especially authoritative. The great majority of Social Democrats recognized that, of course, David Steel was the more effective public speaker and television performer of the two. In consequence they were happy—more than happy—to see Steel as leader of the Alliance campaign sharing the spotlight with Jenkins. In the SDP's ranks the idea of a collective leadership still had a considerable appeal.

Many Liberals' conception of the dual leadership, however, was completely different. Pardoe, Holme and others saw Steel and only Steel as the leader of the Alliance army. Hence Holme's remark about Steel being 'Prince Rupert of the Rhine, leading the cavalry'. Jenkins' role in their view was to be hoisted aloft and carried into battle rather in the manner of a religious icon or the relics of a saint —visible to the troops and venerated by them but in no conceivable sense in operational command of them. On this conception, Jenkins would spend most of the campaign fighting his strictly local battle in Glasgow and would sally forth only very occasionally to make suitably weighty pronouncements for the benefit of the more earnest class of elector. Steel meanwhile would barnstorm around the country arousing voter interest and demonstrating his prowess as a campaigner, as he had done in so many by-elections and in the 1979 general election.

The Liberals' conception made perfectly good sense in its own terms; but in its practical execution it had two flaws. In the first place, nobody told Jenkins. Either David Steel himself did not fully understand or share his aides' conception, or else he did understand it but could not bring himself to tell the older man that his role was to be restricted in this way. Totally unaware that influential Liberals, including possibly Steel, conceived of the dual leadership along these lines, Jenkins and almost everyone else in the SDP simply assumed that the phrase 'prime minister-designate' meant what it said—and implied what it implied: Jenkins was to be leader of the Alliance just as the real prime minister, Margaret Thatcher, was leader of the Conservative party.

In the second place, the Liberals' conception was flawed because nobody told the television companies. The BBC, ITN, Granada and the others made exactly the same assumption about the dual leadership that the SDP did: that, of the two leaders, Jenkins was the more senior and was therefore to be treated on a par with Thatcher and Foot. The television companies in any case could not afford to have one senior reporter and one camera crew following each of Thatcher and Foot, but two of them following both of the two Alliance leaders. Forced to choose, they were at least as likely to choose Jenkins as Steel, and it was Jenkins who appeared on *Weekend World* and *Panorama*. Moreover, it was by no means clear how the television companies could have been informed of the Liberals' conception. Invited to treat the prime minister-designate as though he were little more than the SDP candidate for Glasgow Hillhead—and the leader of the Alliance campaign as though he were . . . what?—the television producers would probably have retreated into incomprehension—and then leaked the whole bizarre story to the press.

Nevertheless, almost all of those close to Steel thought their strategy was the right one; and they became more and more convinced of this as the Alliance failed to made headway in the campaign and Jenkins floundered. Not surprisingly, Steel came under increasing pressure to revert to the original strategy—or to adopt it if he had not been convinced originally. In the eyes of Steel's advisers, Jenkins was the problem; he, Steel, was the solution. By the third week of May, Steel himself had come round, however reluctantly, to this view. He did not do so out of personal ambition; his overriding objective was still to see an Alliance government installed in power with Jenkins as prime minister. But he could not escape the implications of the growing volume of evidence which showed that Jenkins was proving an electoral liability. It seemed that Jenkins' own career would benefit if Steel, even at this late stage, were visibly to take charge.

By now, however, the Liberal strategy in its original form no longer made practical sense. The effort to hint to the television companies and the press that they should treat Steel as Prince Rupert and Jenkins as a semi-retired elder statesman had patently failed, and a more dramatic gesture was now required: formally and in public Jenkins would have to renounce his grand-sounding but empty prime minister-designate title; he would have to stand down. Only in this way could television and the press be got to switch their attention away from him and on to Steel. But, of course, Jenkins would have to be persuaded: he would have to make the announcement himself, and he would have to appear to be making it voluntarily. There could be no question of a public execution of Jenkins. It was obvious to everyone, including Steel and his advisers, that any open split between the two parties and the two leaders at this stage would be electorally disastrous— the very opposite of what was intended.

Steel accordingly agreed to sound out Jenkins in private. He spoke to him several times in the week beginning Monday, 23 May, and he also raised the issue with David Owen in the course of an Alliance rally in Plymouth. Owen, no admirer of Jenkins, had no objection in principle to the SDP leader's ceasing to be the prime minister-designate; but he was firmly of the view that, just as it was Jenkins and Steel who had privately stitched the dual-leadership arrangement together, so it was for them, and only for them, to unstitch it if they wanted to. Anything the two leaders agreed between them was fine by Owen; but he had no intention of getting personally involved. Jenkins for his part was initially taken aback by the idea that he should, in effect, stand down; but he agreed to go away and think about it. He concluded, however, that the idea was genuinely not a good one: it would give the impression that the two Alliance parties were in disarray and had lost heart. He was probably also worried about the impact that his standing down might have on his chances of holding on to Hillhead. After consulting his wife Jennifer, Jenkins informed Steel that, although he had given the idea careful consideration, he intended to continue to play his current role. The discussions between the two men, although somewhat awkward, were perfectly polite and amicable.

And there the matter rested. Or, rather, there it seemed to rest. On 29 May Jenkins flew to the Ettrickbridge summit believing that the issue had been closed. Rodgers, Williams and most of the others in the SDP knew little, if anything, of what had been going on during the previous few days and, so far as they were concerned, the Ettrickbridge meeting was to be taken up, as advertised, with a review of Alliance strategy. But Owen, who happened to sit next to Pardoe on the plane on the way up to Scotland, suspected that something was afoot and asked him directly: 'What are you buggers up to?' And John Lyttle, Jenkins' assistant, became somewhat suspicious when a series of unexpected delays prevented him from reaching Ettrickbridge as early on the Sunday morning as had been planned. He realized later that in all probability the Liberals had wanted him kept out of the way while they plotted.

The summit was held in the intimacy of the Steels' combined kitchen/dining-room. Steel sat with one or two of the others in the window seat, and the Gang of Four, Steel's principal advisers and Lord Diamond arrayed themselves more or less randomly around the dining-room table. Only later did someone who was present think it significant that Owen had seated himself at the far end of the table from Steel. Perhaps, having some inkling of what was coming, Owen wanted to be seen to be distancing himself from the proceedings. Before the meeting started Shirley Williams pointed out that the dining-room window was open and that, with dozens of journalists hanging over the garden gate only a few yards away, what they said might well be overheard. The window was thereupon closed; but the atmosphere, for a time, remained casual. Judy Steel hovered in the wings. The Steels' dog wandered in and out.

The formal meeting began with a discussion of how the campaign had been going. It was universally agreed that there was still a mystery about the opinion polls. The polls persisted in showing the Alliance on 20 per cent or less; but all of the Alliance's private polls showed them doing much better, and they simply could not reconcile the published poll findings with the fact that everywhere they went they were drawing much larger and friendlier crowds than either the Labour party or the Conservatives. In fact, the *only* sign that the campaign was going badly was the polls; but the polls had of course to be taken seriously, since they had a bad effect on party workers' morale and since the Alliance desperately needed credibility if large numbers of people were to vote for them.

At this point, after about half an hour, John Pardoe spoke in response to a prearranged signal from Steel. The fact was, he said, that the dual leadership was not working. People did not understand the concept of a prime minister-designate, and Roy was not doing well on television. A lot of people were saying that they would vote for the Alliance if it were not for Roy. It was his, Pardoe's, view that the Alliance should have only one leader and that it should be Steel—or, failing that, that the media should be got to project Steel rather than Jenkins, who was not popular and was going down badly with the general public.

Before anyone in the SDP had a chance to respond to this totally unexpected onslaught on their elected leader, Steel, sitting at the head of the table, produced from his pocket a piece of paper. It contained a draft statement, which Steel suggested might usefully be issued to the press after the meeting. Steel read the statement out. Its gist was that Jenkins wished it to be known that he no longer wanted to be referred to as prime minister-designate and that for the rest of the campaign he would be spending most of his time in his constituency. Steel would take personal charge of the campaign, and from now on he and he alone would be the Alliance's undisputed leader. Jenkins, the draft statement said, recognized that the campaign was not going well and was taking this step in the interests of the Alliance as a whole.

As Pardoe and Steel spoke, Jenkins, who was clearly astonished, flushed with embarrassment and anger. Several on the SDP side were 'aghast'. Bill Rodgers, who spoke first, said he was *very* annoyed. He wanted to know why he and the others had not been told in advance that this issue was going to be raised, and he also wanted to know why it had not been raised on some earlier occasion, when half the country's press was not waiting outside. In any case, Rodgers insisted, the idea was simply impracticable. The proposal was to dump Roy, and everyone would see that that was precisely what it was. The Alliance would be seen to be divided. It would be seen to have a leadership crisis on its hands. The Tories would have a field-day. Rodgers, according to one witness, was 'pretty acid' and asked John Pardoe, who was not a parliamentary candidate, 'Just what seat do you think you're fighting?' Shirley Williams intervened to support Rodgers, making it clear that, so far as she was concerned, there could be no question of changing the leadership. But she accepted that television was not one of Roy's greatest strengths and suggested that for the rest of the campaign as much of the television as possible should be shifted to, as she put it, 'David, David and me'. She had thought all along that the Alliance campaign had focused too much on Jenkins and Steel and had not made enough of the SDP's old virtue of collective leadership.

And at this point the question of the leadership was dropped. Everyone seemed to agree with Williams that the Alliance leaders could find better ways of putting themselves over on television, and the discussion turned in a desultory way towards practicalities, with everyone agreeing that the two parties had so far succeeded in working together remarkably well. There seemed to be a general air of relief that a difficult corner had been turned.

But it had not. While the discussion proceeded, someone sitting opposite him noticed that Pardoe was 'boiling'. Finally, it seemed, he could stand it no longer. He demanded that they return to the leadership issue: they had talked around it, but they had not dealt with it. The trouble with this outfit, Pardoe said, was that it was constantly running away from the really difficult issues, but this one *had* to be faced. Backed by Stuart Mole, Steel's principal assistant, Pardoe repeated that Jenkins was a disaster on television, that the Alliance would be better off without him and that he ought to go. He was, said one of the Gang of Four, 'brutal'. But he was not speaking only for himself. Steel, though looking extremely uncomfortable, himself returned to the attack. 'I ought to make it clear', he said, 'that I've had many representations from the Liberal party and from the constituencies saying that they have very little faith in the current leadership and that there's a lot of unhappiness about.' By now there was no doubt in anyone's mind that several Liberals had come into the room with a carefully preconcerted plan for rendering the SDP leader's position impossible. 'We came not to bury Jenkins,' one of the Liberals admitted afterwards, 'but to embalm him.'

If so, they underestimated both Rodgers and Williams. Owen contented himself with indicating, as before, that, so far as he was concerned, the matter should be left up to the two leaders; but Rodgers and Williams were by this time livid. They thought the whole business was utterly dishonourable, and they also thought that the Liberals, as one of them put it, 'must be out of their minds'. Rodgers said it was 'disgraceful'. Why were they coming back to the leadership? They had settled the issue half an hour ago. The whole Alliance enterprise was founded on trust, and trust would disappear completely if this kind of thing were permitted to go on. Williams agreed. She said she had had her doubts about the leadership arrangements, but they had been settled a long time ago and it would be 'absolutely fatal' to change them now. She was appalled by what was being proposed, and she was not prepared to go along with it. If there was any suggestion of Jenkins standing down as prime minister-designate, she herself would withdraw publicly from the campaign—and would tell the press why. Lord Diamond also spoke, more quietly, on Jenkins' behalf.

As the argument swirled about him, Roy Jenkins, the former home secretary and chancellor of the exchequer, the former president of the European Commission, one of the founders of the SDP, whose political future was being debated almost as though he were not there, sat silent. Someone in the room said later that he was 'shaking', another that he was 'absolutely shattered'. He had befriended Steel. He had trusted and relied on him. Now, in full view of the leaders of both parties, he was being betrayed by him. There had been no real warning.

Williams was sitting opposite him and was terribly afraid he was going to throw in the towel. She was in no position to say anything to him directly, but she desperately tried to catch his eye and again and again mouthed the words, 'No, no, no.' Finally he seemed to understand and, almost imperceptibly, inclined his head. She was enormously relieved, and her relief was soon intensified when she realized that the Liberals were giving up. Pardoe appeared disposed to pursue the issue, but Steel said they had better drop it. Jenkins at this point broke his silence and said in a dignified way that, if he believed that changing his mind and standing down would do any good, he would be prepared to do it, but he was convinced that any such change at this late stage of the campaign would be 'counterproductive'. And that was the end; the meeting was over.

The party then broke for lunch, at which the leaders were joined by a considerable number of Liberal and SDP aides, who had not actually been able to hear what was going on in the Steels' dining-room but who in most cases must have had a pretty good idea. Although the atmosphere was strained, everyone did their best to keep up appearances. Jennifer Jenkins was, if anything, even angrier than her husband, and John Lyttle took her off into a corner to give her a chance to calm down.

The plot seems to have failed for a number of reasons. At least one of the plotters thought, before the Ettrickbridge meeting, that Steel had already cleared the draft statement with Jenkins and had, in addition, squared either or both of Rodgers and Williams. This Liberal was amazed when it became clear that none of the SDP leaders in the room, with the possible exception of Owen, can have had any prior knowledge of what was about to be suggested. Those on the SDP side could only assume that the Liberals imagined that, under pressure, one or other of the Gang of Four would crack. Perhaps Jenkins would give in and agree to go. Perhaps Owen, whose low opinion of Jenkins was well known, would come out against him. Perhaps Rodgers or Williams, both of whom were defending difficult constituencies, would agree with the Liberals' analysis of the situation. Perhaps . . . Whatever they thought, they were wrong: none of the Gang of Four cracked. As John Pardoe said ruefully afterwards, 'It was not the most glorious moment in my political career. But then I'm bad at co-operative assassination.'

The immediate impact of the meeting was, to say the least of it, paradoxical: in public Ettrickbridge did the Alliance nothing but good. Not a word of what transpired in the Steels' dining-room was leaked to the press, and the truth of what happened only began to emerge months later.[23] Instead Paul Medlicott, the Liberals' press officer, spent hours standing in the rain during and after the meeting giving journalists an account of it which, while it contained no material inaccuracies, gave a completely misleading impression of what had been going on.

'It was', said an admirer, 'a marvellous piece of press manipulation.' The next day's newspapers told precisely the story the Alliance wanted: that there would be no formal shake-up in the Alliance leadership but that from now on Steel would play a more prominent role. 'Alliance to move Jenkins out of the limelight', *The Times'* headline read. 'Steel', said the *Guardian*, 'replaces Jenkins as the front runner'. The *Daily Mail's* headline said simply: 'Roy takes back seat'. But best of all was the television coverage. The evening news bulletins that day portrayed the Liberal and SDP leaders as a band of happy warriors, full of confidence and rejoicing in one another's company; and this wholly misleading spectacle upstaged to a considerable extent Margaret Thatcher's appearances with President Reagan at the Williamsburg summit in the United States. Watching television and reading the newspapers the next day, those who had been present in David Steel's dining-room could hardly believe their luck.

And their luck had by no means run out. It was probably largely a coincidence, but at about the time of the Ettrickbridge summit the long-expected—and even longer awaited—improvement in the Alliance's standing in the opinion polls began to show itself. The Conservatives' support held up well, but Labour's slid badly as the party's divisions continued to be apparent and as Foot, stumbling up ladders, licking his lips nervously and ranting like a nineteenth-century non-conformist preacher, demonstrated how hopelessly miscast as Labour leader he was. Others in the Labour party meanwhile insisted on reminding voters of Thatcher's triumph in the Falklands campaign. Healey accused the prime minister of 'glorying in slaughter' and of exploiting the sacrifices of the servicemen in the Falklands for party advantage; and Neil Kinnock, when a heckler shouted at him that at least Thatcher had guts, retorted: 'And it's a pity that others have to leave theirs on Goose Green to prove it.' Such outbursts backfired badly. Before the end of May, only a scattering of polls had reported the Alliance to be on as much as 20 per cent; from 1 June onwards, none showed the Alliance to be on less than 20 per cent. An increasing number showed the Alliance level with, or even ahead of, the Labour party.[24]

The apparent surge in Alliance support transformed the morale of both the Liberals and the SDP and caused the media to pay far more attention to them than they had done before. So far as both television and the press were concerned, the story of the last ten days of the campaign was whether Labour or the Alliance would finish second in terms of the popular vote. Even the Conservatives, confident though they were, began to show signs of being slightly rattled. On 31 May Thatcher referred to the Liberals and the SDP for the first time in one of her election speeches (though she disdained to use the term Alliance), warning voters that deserting the Conservatives for either the Liberals or the SDP could let Labour in. On 3 June she startled television viewers—and many of her own supporters—by appearing to want to protect the position of Labour. 'The Labour party', she said, 'won't die; the Labour party will never die.' The Alliance's own rallies drew increasingly large and enthusiastic crowds. On 6 June, only three days before polling day, Jenkins and Steel drew more than 1,000 cheering supporters to an 'Ask the Alliance' meeting in Porchester Hall, Paddington; another 800 well-wishers waited in vain outside. In their final television appeal to the nation, the two leaders returned to their familiar themes of national unity and the need to bring the people of Britain together again.

Today [Roy Jenkins said] Britain is being divided, both by geography and class, more sharply than at any time since the Thirties. That problem will not be solved by voters aligning themselves in two intolerant armies, based on their rival strongholds in the North and South, hurling insults at each other across the divide.

David Steel invited the electorate to dump the menace of Marxism into the dustbin of history 'by voting for the Alliance and so relegating the Labour party to harmless impotence'.

The two leaders succeeded to the end in maintaining their distance from both the main parties and also in sustaining the fiction, at least in public, that the Alliance had a real chance of winning the election outright. The same general line was taken by almost all the Alliance's chief spokesmen. Only David Owen stood out. 'It is not the main thrust of my belief', he said in his constituency at the very beginning of the campaign, 'that we are likely to form the next government.'[25] Owen's view, implicit in all his speeches, was that the Alliance should be seen principally as an anti-Labour party, but one which at the same time was the country's best hope of curbing the excesses of Thatcherism. He was much readier than the other Alliance leaders to concede that the best the Alliance could realistically hope for was to hold the balance of power. He suggested on television that the role of the Alliance's MPs in the new parliament would be to 'curb and moderate and influence the future government'.[26] It was very easy to detect in Owen's public statements a certain disenchantment with the way the Alliance campaign was being conducted by the duumvirate that was supposed to be in charge. Interviewed by a *Times* reporter in his constituency a week before polling day, he observed: 'I have conducted a campaign which has at least had some intellectual consistency. The first phase was to get Labour out of the way, and the second is now to harness the desire to check Mrs Thatcher.'[27] Such remarks, although they were noticed by his colleagues, were not prominently reported at the time; the *Times* interview only appeared on an inside page. But they were clear indicators of the line that Owen was going to take, and stick to, in the future.

On polling day itself, 9 June, most leading figures in the Alliance, apart from being exhausted, were torn between hope and apprehension. On the one hand, the campaign had gone reasonably well, at least since Ettrickbridge, and the opinion polls that were published that morning held out the possibility that the Liberals and the SDP between them would poll more votes than Labour. But, on the other hand, it was patently obvious that even 25–30 per cent of the popular vote would not be translated into an equivalent number of seats and that most of the defectors to the SDP, including two or three of the Gang of Four, would in all probability lose their seats. No one could any longer realistically talk of an Alliance government or of Jenkins as prime minister, and the size of the Conservatives' lead in the final polls made the chances of a hung parliament also seem remote. The SDP's golden age, with its stunning by-election victories, now seemed not only over but very long ago and far away.

Even so, the results when they finally started to appear in the early hours of 10 June 1983 were deeply depressing for the Liberals and, even more, for the SDP. In one sense, the Alliance did not do at all badly. It won 25.4 per cent of the popular vote; one voter in four throughout the United Kingdom had supported it. This was the best performance by any party other than Labour or the Conservatives since 1923. The Alliance, moreover, very nearly beat Labour into third place: Labour won only 27.6 per cent of the vote, a mere 2.2 per cent ahead of the Alliance. This was the worst performance by Labour since 1918, when the party had been in its infancy. The Liberals held on to all but one of their thirteen seats (Bill Pitt's moment of fame in Croydon was over), and they gained another five. Michael Meadow-croft took Leeds West from Labour. Alex Carlisle took Montgomery from the Conservatives. Paddy Ashdown took Yeovil, also from the Conservatives. And in Scotland the Liberals gained another two seats, also from the Conservatives: Roxburgh and Berwickshire, where Archy Kirkwood, David Steel's friend and ally, was the victor, and Gordon, won by Malcolm Bruce.

But, in another and more important sense, the election was a disaster. The SDP in parliament was virtually obliterated. All but one of the twenty-nine sitting SDP MPs fought the election, all but four of them seeking to retain their previous constituency. Only five of the twenty-eight survived. David Owen held on in Plymouth Devonport, as did Roy Jenkins in Hillhead (which he had won only a little over a year before). The other three survivors were John Cartwright in Woolwich, Ian Wrigglesworth in Stockton South (where he probably survived because of his Conservative opponent's National Front past) and Robert Maclennan in Caithness and Sutherland. In addition, the SDP made one gain: Charles Kennedy, aged only 23, unexpectedly captured Ross, Cromarty and Skye from the Conservatives.

But everywhere else was desolation. Shirley Williams lost Crosby (though her personal vote would probably have re-elected her but for adverse changes in the constituency's boundaries), and Bill Rodgers also lost his seat in Stockton North, finishing third behind both his Labour and Conservative opponents.[28] Of the twenty-three SDP MPs who went down to defeat, only six managed to finish second in the seat they were contesting. Christopher Brocklebank-Fowler, the lone Conservative defector, was a creditable runner-up in Norfolk North-West; George Cunningham was defeated by only 363 votes in Islington South and Finsbury; Dickson Mabon likewise lost by only a narrow margin in Renfrew West and Inverclyde; and Jim Wellbeloved and Bob Mitchell did well in Erith and Crayford and Southampton Itchen. But the long list of those who trailed badly in third or fourth place included many of those who had been most prominent in founding the new party only two years before: Mike Thomas, Tom Bradley, John Horam, John Grant, Edward Lyons, Tom McNally, John Roper and Neville Sandelson. Twenty-four parliamentary careers were ended, all but one of them permanently.[29] Brocklebank-Fowler would certainly have retained his seat as a Conservative. Likewise almost all the Labour defectors would have held their seats if they had remained in the Labour fold. They had taken a calculated risk. They had lost. They had always known they might.

Could the Alliance have done better in the 1983 general election? No one will ever know. It is easy to comment on an election campaign in the style of a drama critic, much harder to show that some alternative style or strategy would in fact have worked better.

That said, four possibilities suggest themselves. One is that the Alliance might have won more seats if it had had one acknowledged leader and that one leader had been David Steel. This possibility is discussed in more detail in Chapter 16, but the evidence in favour of it is not strong. Undoubtedly a few voters were mystified by the idea of a dual leadership and were deterred from voting for the Alliance by it and it alone. Undoubtedly, too, some voters were put off by Jenkins and would have voted for the Alliance if Steel had been seen from the outset to be the Alliance leader. But there is no evidence to suggest that the number of such voters was very large, and it can be argued equally plausibly that many electors were positively attracted by the idea of two parties with two leaders working amicably together. It certainly did not help the Alliance that Jenkins was somewhat flaccid towards the beginning of the campaign and that, in particular, he did not perform well in the *Weekend World* and *Panorama* interviews. Steel probably would have done better. So, probably, would Owen. But Jenkins grew considerably more forceful as the campaign went on, and it is doubtful whether any alternative arrangement would have added more than a percentage point or two to the Alliance's final share of the vote (though, admittedly, that might have been enough to result in the Alliance's overtaking Labour).

A second possibility is that the Alliance leadership during the campaign should have been not less collegial but more so: that the other members of the Gang of Four should have been given equal prominence with Roy Jenkins so far as the SDP side of the campaign was concerned. Certainly Jenkins and his assistants, Lord Harris and John Lyttle, were criticized during the course of the campaign for giving Jenkins so much prominence and for relegating David Owen and Shirley Williams, in particular, to relatively minor roles. Jenkins appeared far more often at the Alliance press conferences than either Owen or Williams, and he played a much more prominent part in the Alliance's election broadcasts. Owen and Williams between them were quoted less than half as often as Jenkins in the main television news bulletins.[30] There is probably something in this line of argument: Jenkins had certainly not made a favourable impression on the public in the months leading up to the election. Nevertheless, Owen and Williams were, even as things stood, highly visible throughout the campaign; and it seems doubtful, again, whether any presentational change by itself would have made more than a marginal difference to the outcome.

A third possibility has already been alluded to. When the 1983 election was called, Jenkins and Steel did not stop to consider afresh what the Alliance's themes in the campaign should be; they simply took their existing themes—national unity, the need for all sections of the community to work together, the dangers of confrontation politics and extremism—off the shelf. The only disadvantage of this approach was that 1983 was not 1979 or even 1981. By 1983 the country was still divided in the sense that there were still extremes of wealth and poverty and wide variations in prosperity between different parts of the country; but it was no longer divided in the sense that different sections of the community were at each other's throats. The Winter of Discontent was four years in the past, there had been no major strikes for a considerable period of time, and the country was no longer riven by urban riots. On the contrary, a considerable sense of national solidarity had been created by the Falklands War and its aftermath. In giving such prominence to these old Liberal themes and the themes of the Dimbleby Lecture in the changed circumstances of 1983, Jenkins and Steel ran the risk of appearing dated and faded, of seeming to be ever so slightly out of touch. There is no hard evidence bearing on this point, but it is hard to escape the impression that the Alliance suffered to some extent from this failure to think through afresh its position in the new situation.[31]

The fourth possibility is related. The Alliance in 1983 did not fight a negative campaign in the sense that it spent its time attacking its opponents; but it was negative in the sense that the Alliance defined itself almost entirely in terms of what it was not. It was not a socialist party, tied to the trade unions and increasingly under the influence of left-wing extremists; and it was not a hard-line monetarist party, tied to big business and increasingly under the influence of right-wing Thatcherism. In effect, the Alliance's slogan was 'Neither Foot nor Thatcher'. But it was never made entirely clear what the Alliance was, as distinct from what it was not. As Chapter 16 will show, most voters, even those favourably disposed towards the Alliance, had only a hazy idea of what it stood for, even in the most general terms. It is hard to believe that this was not something of a disadvantage for the Alliance, probably in the short term, certainly in the long. The Alliance's vagueness meant that it could attract voters who were repelled by the other parties but that it had relatively little capacity to attract them on its own. John Cartwright got into the habit of saying of voters: 'They don't know what tune we're whistling.' He was right. They didn't.

Part III

····

ANATOMY

12

• • • •

New Institutions for a New Party

Those most active in setting up the SDP in 1981 included a number of MPs and supporters who were determined to create not merely a new party, but a new type of party. The SDP would be a party for the 1980s. It would offer a modern programme to a modern-minded electorate which had been alienated by the old politics of class. And it would be the very model of a modern party organization—democratic, efficient and, above all, professional. The individual donations and offers of help that poured into the Council for Social Democracy gave the party's founders the support and resources to start from scratch. The founders had no obligations to any existing grass-roots movement or local associations that might wish to press their own ideas and demands. They were not saddled with the traditions and rituals that weighed down the other parties. They could be experimental and innovative, creating a new party in their own image. It was a rare opportunity.

To these leading Social Democrats, creating a 'modern' party meant achieving three things. It meant writing a constitution that safeguarded the independence of MPs and limited the power of activists while vesting ultimate sovereignty with the mass membership. In this they broadly succeeded. It meant creating a party that would be administered by a professional central office staffed by high-quality officials, like a modern business. In this, too, they had considerable success. Finally, it meant, out of necessity, achieving financial independence from the trade unions, business or, indeed, any kind of organized interest; the SDP would have to be a party of ordinary members, funding itself from subscriptions and small donations and exploiting both state-of-the-art communications technology and the media to build up a mass membership. In this they largely failed. This part of the book describes the attempt of the SDP's founders to create a modern political party. We start with the party's constitution.

The making of the SDP constitution was a sluggish affair. For almost eighteen months after the Limehouse Declaration the party existed without any established rules or structure. Apart from financial responsibilities, which were vested with trustees, formal powers within the SDP lay wholly with the self-appointed Steering Committee, operating with skeletal interim rules. Minor rulings were often made *ad hoc* by Cowley Street staff, and in the country the provisional area parties tended to invent rules as they went along. But all the major strategic decisions were made exclusively by the Steering Committee. It created the party's committees and determined who among its members would chair them. With barely any wider consultation, the Steering Committee handled relations with the Liberals, keeping a close eye on the joint policy commissions, the seats negotiations and the fighting of by-elections. And it also attended in minute detail to the draft constitution which was to be presented in the fullness of time to local party representatives. Curiously, given the party's origins, SDP MPs made no attempt to exert their collective authority, even on matters directly affecting them. They did not demur, for example, when, at the Gang of Four's instigation, David Owen overnight became their provisional leader and John Roper their whip in a manner reminiscent of the old-style 'emergence' of Conservative leaders. The Steering Committee was in charge. Since its members consisted entirely of the Gang of Four's nominees, this effectively meant that the Gang of Four were in charge except when they were divided. 'Who owns the party?' Shirley Williams asked one of the party's legal advisers soon after the launch. 'You do,' came the reply.

The constitution was slow to take shape because there was no pressure for speed and some advantages in delay. The Gang of Four's collective leadership worked tolerably well throughout 1981. Jenkins occasionally irritated the Gang of Three by treating them as if he were prime minister and they his senior cabinet colleagues, but most decisions were genuinely collective. In fact the quadrumvirate brought considerable benefits. It meant that the hydra-headed 'leader' could do four things at once. The heavy initial burden of public meetings, party committees, interviews and articles was only tolerable because it was shared among the four of them. The arrangement also allowed the party to 'stretch' its policy appeal. When one leader's policy views were idiosyncratic or out of line, such as Shirley Williams on private schools, they could be deflected by the views of the others. Moreover, Jenkins and Williams appealed to different but complementary segments of the population—Jenkins to men and the middle-aged and elderly, Williams to women and the young; Jenkins to progressive Conservatives, Williams to Labour right-wingers.[1] Having both of them as co-leaders swelled the party's recruitment of members and its ratings in the opinion polls.

The Gang of Four also had personal reasons for favouring delay. Once the constitution was formally in place, the party leader would have to be chosen. Whatever method was adopted, the constitution was expected to stipulate that the leader be a member of parliament. When the first draft was approved by the Steering Committee and presented at the rolling conference in October 1981, neither of the two most likely contenders, Jenkins and Williams, was in the House of Commons and there was no telling how long it would be before two winnable by-elections turned up. Occasionally the idea of a leader drawn at least initially from outside parliamentary ranks was floated. But the problems were formidable: such an arrangement would inevitably create a rivalry with the caretaker leader in the Commons; too much would be at stake at any by-election contested by the leader; and the party's claim to be a contender for government would be undermined. Therefore, the best solution was to delay the formal incorporation of the constitution until both Williams and Jenkins were returned to Westminster. In the event, the constitutional convention, at which area party representatives were to decide upon the Steering Committee's final proposals, was delayed until as late as February 1982; and at the convention the date set for the election of the leader was pushed further back to the beginning of the next parliamentary session, i.e. November 1982. The Gang of Four were not in a hurry.

The protracted pace of constitution-making also reflected a central fact about the Gang of Four. None of them was interested in constitutional matters. As Labour MPs they only developed a serious concern about the party's constitution when their own positions were threatened.[2] Rodgers was a life-long student of Labour's procedures and structures, but his expertise was devoted to exploiting them, not changing them. Williams owed her secure position on Labour's NEC to the block votes of the engineers and the clerical workers, a debt that seemed to weigh lightly on her conscience until 1979 when she began to try to reform the block-voting system.[3] To the Gang of Four the Labour constitution was a piece of oddly designed but comfortable furniture to which one became accustomed, even attached—until somebody else took possession of it. As regards the SDP's constitution, each was a fervent advocate of a particular idea: Rodgers was committed to the multi-constituency area party, Jenkins to the election of the leader by SDP MPs alone, Williams to positive discrimination for women, Owen to the election of the leader by 'one member, one vote'. None of them, however, had a worked-out view of the overall shape of the constitution or even its underlying principles. Owen, Rodgers and Williams had each written an entire book about social democracy without once referring to party structure. It was simply not a subject that engaged their imagination or energy. It was a technical matter, best left to lawyers.

Origins

The two lawyers to whom they left it, both barristers, were Robert Maclennan, the MP for Caithness and Sutherland and one of the original twelve MPs to defect, and William Goodhart, a founder member of the party. Both were trusted as neutral by the two warring camps on the Steering Committee. Maclennan, for example, had supported Jenkins in Labour's 1976 leadership contest, but he was not part of Jenkins' immediate entourage and was also close to Shirley Williams, under whom he had served from 1974 to 1976 as a junior minister in the Department of Prices and Consumer Protection. He was anyway very much his own man.

Maclennan was the architect, Goodhart the draftsman; but they were handed no brief, offered no model to follow and were left on a loose rein. They did consult leading SDP figures intermittently but not widely or systematically; they did institute an informal group of academic specialists on European parties, but again this was not a major influence. Drafts and redrafts were presented to a succession of steering group meetings throughout 1981.[4] Significantly, none of the Gang of Four kept a supervisory eye on progress and, even after its subsequent revisions, the constitution was very much Maclennan and Goodhart's own work. They were the SDP's James Madison and Gouverneur Morris.[5]

The paper on the draftsman's board was not, however, entirely blank. The sheer course of events had left its mark. For example, after the launch volunteer organizers of local parties were just informed by Cowley Street that they and their neighbouring organizers belonged not to a traditional constituency party but to an 'area party' that might cover as many as eight or nine constituencies. Maclennan and Goodhart had little option but to incorporate this *fait accompli* into their preliminary proposals. Nor could Maclennan, in particular, ignore the ever-shifting personal politics of the Gang of Four. When the first draft of the constitution was being prepared in the summer of 1981, it was widely assumed that Jenkins was the preferred leader among SDP MPs but that Williams was the favourite of the mass membership. The method for electing the leader might therefore determine the result. Whether the election should be by MPs alone, by a ballot of the entire membership or by some combination of the two became a highly charged issue. Personal rivalry was also behind the proposal that the party should have two leaders: a parliamentary leader, who would be prime minister in an SDP government, and a national president, who would represent the party in the country. The German Social Democrats' leader/president system was cited in justification (somewhat misleadingly).[6] The system's real attraction was that the presidency would serve as a consolation prize for the loser in the leadership contest and as an insurance against either Jenkins or Williams failing to win a parliamentary by-election in time.

Many aspects of the constitution, however, were unaffected by such petty considerations and could be derived from first principles. The early drafts reflected two sets of influence.[7] First, there was some attempt to give the constitution a distinctively 'social-democratic' character. Maclennan saw the constitution as an electorally useful flagship for the party's distinctive values and style. The principle of decentralization, which had been mentioned specifically in the Limehouse Declaration, was to be implemented in the form of a strong regional tier, with powers to initiate policy proposals, to elect representatives to a policy-making council, to supervise finances and to oversee the selection of candidates. The party's commitment to a 'more equal society, one which rejects ugly prejudices based upon sex, race or religion', was to be reflected in elaborate provisions for the proportionate representation of women, ethnic minorities and the young on the party's regional and national bodies.[8] And Owen's and Williams' latter-day conversion to 'one member, one vote' in the Labour party, and to proportional representation for the country, lay behind the regular recourse to secret postal ballots of the membership by means of the single transferable vote.

These 'social-democratic' principles, however, were of only limited value. For one thing, they were too vague and undeveloped to act as a guide in most respects. (It did not occur to Maclennan or to anyone else to look to the Liberals for inspiration.) For another, they were not always wholly compatible, since they embraced both the democratic instinct for participation and the managerial instinct for control. On the one hand, the party claimed to be a party that 'belonged to its members'; on the other hand, it was deeply committed to the supremacy of parliament and therefore to the independence of MPs from those same members. From the beginning, Maclennan attempted, in his words, 'to balance the need for careful deliberation in the formulation of policy with the need to secure the widest involvement of members'.[9] It was to be a constitution allowing for member democracy as well as protecting MPs, one that both dispersed and shared power, a constitution of checks and balances.

The second of the two influences on everyone's early thinking about the constitution was more important, however, and it was wholly negative. It was their experience of Labour's bizarre and divisive constitution. Everyone wanted to avoid its drawbacks, but opinions differed on precisely what these were. David Marquand and John Horam, with the tacit support of Jenkins, were traditionalists. For them the pre-reform Labour constitution, stripped of its worst features, remained an adequate model. Their quarrel with the Labour party was essentially about policy, not procedure (both Marquand and Jenkins were in Brussels by the time constitutional reform was put on the Labour party's agenda and they had not been involved in the arguments). Moreover, this group regarded constitution-making as an electorally dangerous distraction from the serious task of building up the party organization, developing policy and working out a political strategy. Constructing a new constitution *ab initio* was bound to be protracted and probably divisive; and, as Labour's experience had demonstrated, the electorate punished parties that contemplated their navel. What was required was an off-the-peg constitution, not a bespoke-tailored one, with a minimum of consultation. For that purpose the pre-1981 Labour constitution, minus affiliated membership and the bloc vote, was more than adequate.

Another group was more radical. It was led by Mike Thomas, with explicit backing from Owen and Williams. This group regarded the constitution not as an electoral distraction but as an electoral opportunity—a means of demonstrating that the SDP was both more radical and more modern than Labour. The public judged parties at least partly by how they ran their own affairs, and on this view the SDP's claim to be in the business of changing the face of British politics would look more credible if its internal arrangements likewise broke new ground. Maclennan and Goodhart, as it happened, sided with the radicals.

The SDP's constitution was thus inspired as much by an anti-model as by a model. As early as February 1981, when interim rules were being drawn up for the Steering Committee, Goodhart's first sketch of a possible constitution included the following principles:

Party to be *unitary* org. with *no* affiliated bodies—one party in parliament and country.

SD MPs shd. *not* be mandated by party. Const. shd. reflect that. MPs shd. *not* be reqd. to fight election on manifesto they don't believe they can sustain as govt.

Downgrade National Conference as decision-making body.

There *must* be a filter. Applications to be vetted.

Power for some body to declare that membership is incompatible with membership of SDP. No person to be eligible if member of org. whose aims inconsistent.

Categories of membership. No special categories—no rts. for membership of affiliated bodies.[10]

The instinct to treat the Labour party as a negative reference point applied to quite minor parts of the constitution. One example was the placing of the party's finances wholly in the hands of eminent but 'non-political' trustees, an early decision of the Gang of Four's which was incorporated in the first—and the final—draft of the constitution. This was largely a reaction against the politicization of the office of treasurer in the Labour party, where candidates for the post (and for an automatic place on Labour's National Executive) were increasingly judged on their ideological rather than their financial credentials. Another example was the elaborate provision made for a quasi-judicial appeals tribunal, independent of the party's elected national bodies, to handle internal disputes about membership, expulsions, party elections and candidate selection. The idea, again, was to avoid the problems that arose in the Labour party, where such disputes were handled by the NEC and were inevitably caught up in its permanent factional warfare. The very assumption that such disputes would be commonplace was, of course, an inheritance from the Labour party. In the event, the elaborately constructed tribunals seldom met.[11]

Evolution

As the very existence of the tribunals suggested, the SDP's constitution, from its first to final draft, was a lawyer's document, not a politician's. Any constitution attempts to second-guess the future. The politician's instinct is to keep his options open and leave few hostages to fortune: his ideal constitution is short, vague and flexible. The lawyer's instinct, by contrast, is to try to insure against all foreseeable contingencies: his ideal constitution is comprehensive, elaborate, precise and rigid. The first published draft of the SDP's constitution comprised seventeen chapters and two annexes, which were organized into thirty-seven sections and 370 clauses—in all, 18,000 words, three times the length of the American Constitution.

The constitution evolved through a long series of drafts between the March 1981 launch and June 1982. An outline plan was discussed by the Steering Committee in June 1981. A more formal and detailed draft was submitted to the Steering Committee in September. This in turn was presented in amended form to the rolling conference in October and November. A new draft, with further revisions based on submissions from area parties, was circulated to area parties in December 1981 and formed the basis for the deliberations of the constitutional convention at Kensington Town Hall in February 1982. The convention adopted a number of amendments, and two issues—the method of electing the leader and positive discrimination for women in elections to the National Committee—were subsequently decided by a ballot of the membership. The final version of the constitution came into operation on 1 June 1982. Further but mainly minor amendments were passed at a second constitutional convention in May 1985.

The June 1981 outline already contained the bare bones of the constitution established a year later. A modestly sized Council for Social Democracy, meeting three times a year, would be the main national deliberative body—the 'parliament of the party'. Its members would be elected representatives, not mandated delegates, with provision for the proportionate representation of women, ethnic minorities and the young. The day-to-day management of the party would be supervised by a Steering Committee (later called the National Committee), consisting of representatives of the council, MPs and MEPs, and local councillors. A separate Policy Co-ordinating Committee, consisting of representatives of the Council, the Steering Committee and the Parliamentary Committee (i.e. the SDP MPs and peers), would 'supervise the preparation of the presentation to the electorate of the Party's policies'. It would be assisted by a party think-tank, the Consultative Committee on Policy, which would 'scrutinize policy proposals with a view to considering their cost, practicality and their relationship with other policy commitments'. There would be a regional tier of organization, acting as a buffer between the activists and the centre. The chairmanship of the council (subsequently the 'presidency') and the chairmanship of the Parliamentary Committee (subsequently the 'leadership') would be separate offices, but both would be filled by means of a postal ballot of party members.

In the long-drawn-out process of drafting the constitution, most of the initial proposals that were radical and innovative came under pressure, and many were whittled away. The story of the Jenkinsites' attempt to have the leader elected by MPs rather than the membership is told in Chapter 9.[12] But from the beginning less dramatic changes were also made. The June 1981 Steering Committee diluted the provisions for ensuring that the National Committee and council represented ethnic minorities and women, scrapped the idea of a Consultative Committee on Policy and initiated the first of a series of changes that weakened the proposed powers of the regional tier. At the same time, it restored some traditional practices: in response to the urgings of the publicity-minded, it agreed that the party should have an annual conference, although this was to take the form of a 'consultative assembly' without decision-making powers.

Another proposed innovation came under pressure at the rolling conference in October 1981. The rolling conference was meant to be advisory only, but it revealed the thinking of ordinary grass-roots activists. The Rodgers formula for the election of the leader generated much less excitement than it had on the Steering Committee in September: delegates appeared to be evenly but not very intensely divided. What exercised delegates was the creation of area parties. There were vociferous objections to their unwieldy size, especially in the shire counties, and to Cowley Street's retention of the entire subscription. What was the incentive to recruit more members, came the cry from the floor, if local parties got no kickback from their subscriptions? The proposals for positive discrimination in favour of women also encountered criticism. Here were early hints of the issues that would dominate the forthcoming constitutional convention.

The convention on the constitution was held on 13–14 February 1982 at Kensington Town Hall, attended by 300 elected representatives of the provisional area parties. They proved to be more assertive than the excessively polite sessions of the rolling conferences had led the Steering Committee to expect. By the end of proceedings, the platform had been defeated no fewer than eight times.

The Steering Committee's first set-back was a curious episode. The very first published draft of the constitution had opened with the ringing statement, lifted from the Limehouse Declaration, that the party 'exists to create an open, classless and more equal society which rejects prejudices based upon sex, race or religion', but the version offered to the convention for debate had been expanded by the Steering Committee to include mention of 'concern for the individual regardless of *gender*, race, colour, *sexual orientation* or religion' (emphasis added). 'Sexual orientation' had been slipped in, partly in response to expressions of interest in the party from gay rights groups, but mainly as a badge of modernity and radicalism. It was perhaps the last of the party's trendy gestures. Opponents moved an amendment to delete the phrase. They objected to the sociologese. What did 'sexual orientation' actually mean? A defender from the floor was blunt: 'Our prejudices are beginning to show. Let's not mince words. This amendment is designed to weed out queers.' Shuddering at what the tabloids would make of the added phrase ('the poofta's party'), delegates carried the amendment to delete it by 147 votes to 116. And for good measure they de-jargonized 'gender', turning it back to 'sex'.

Delegates were less radical than the platform about minorities' rights but more radical about their own. The draft constitution limited the initiative to propose policy to the party's policy committee alone (called the policy sub-committee until 1985), but the Steering Committee was pressured into accepting an amendment that gave ordinary council members the right to submit policy motions at council meetings for debate. Another amendment passed against the platform enabled the council to change the constitution by a simple rather than a two-thirds majority, subject to ratification by a ballot of the members. These were the first tentative steps in what proved to be a steady advance in the council's policy-making role.

The Steering Committee was given the expected drubbings on the size of the area parties and the share-out of subscriptions. Rodgers defended the idea of multi-constituency parties on various grounds: they enabled the stronger constituencies to help the weaker ones within the same area; they discouraged personal fiefdoms and takeovers by minority cliques; the administrative headaches promised by the imminent parliamentary boundary changes could be avoided; and area parties symbolized the party's commitment to proportional representation in multi-member constituencies. As regards the subscription, every penny was needed to support the party headquarters, which had no trade-union or big-business milch cow on which to suckle. A clawback by the area parties would inevitably lead to staff redundancies.

But delegates were not to be placated. Multi-constituency parties were the monstrous invention of a remote bureaucracy. Particularly in the rural areas, they encouraged the small unrepresentative power groups of 'the ambitious, the wealthy and the mobile' that the SDP aimed to eliminate. By decisive majorities, delegates passed amendments that allowed the formation of single-constituency area parties and the retention by area parties of 'not less than 20 per cent of the subscriptions' paid by their members. From the platform's point of view, the outcome might have been worse: the Steering Committee feared that a much tougher, mandatory clause establishing single-constituency parties would be passed, leading to organizational chaos.[13]

The subject that aroused most passion, however, was positive discrimination for women. Two fairly mild sops were passed comfortably: the reservation of four places for women, to be elected by the whole membership, on the thirty-nine-strong National Committee; and the stipulation that the short list for every parliamentary candidature must contain at least two women. But opinion was evenly and fiercely divided over the much bolder proposal that each area party should elect an equal number of women and men to the Council for Social Democracy. Opponents from the floor objected on the conventional grounds that merit should take precedence ('Shirley succeeded without special help'). The foremost advocates of the idea were David Owen and Shirley Williams. Part of their case rested on the usual arguments for positive discrimination; but the more important motive, summed up by Williams, was ideological and electoral: 'This party is about altering old customs and old approaches if it is about anything.' Large-scale positive discrimination would clinch the party's claim to be radical, would appeal to women voters, especially the doers and joiners, and would outflank Labour, whose record in this respect lagged far behind its rhetoric. The vote on the amendment seeking to eliminate equal representation on the council produced a 150 to 150 tie, at which point Jenkins as chairman ruled that the issue should be settled by a membership ballot. Only 16 per cent of the convention delegates were women. Had there been more, the proposal would almost certainly have passed.

On the issue of how to elect the party leader, the delegates were given the task, not of actually choosing the election method, but of deciding the range of alternatives that would subsequently be put to the membership in a ballot, this being the compromise agreed by the Steering Committee after its row in September.[14] The Steering Committee recommended a formula very similar to the one proposed by Rodgers, but it laid another seven, selected from area-party submissions, before the delegates for debate. In the event, as Chapter 9 relates, the convention decided to place three options on the ballot: election by MPs alone, 'one member, one vote' and an alternative formula under which the 1982 election would take place on the principle of 'one member, one vote' but with the choice of the leader reverting to the MPs after the next election. The debate on the floor revealed that many delegates regarded 'one member, one vote' as a founding principle which, if ignored, would leave ordinary party members feeling cheated.[15] When the various proposals were put to the vote, a majority of delegates backed the principle of 'one member, one vote' (55 per cent), and fewer than a quarter the MPs-only principle (21 per cent). Of the eight proposals, the Rodgers formula received the least support of all.[16]

In the postal ballot of members, declared in early May 1982, the Steering Committee was rebuffed on both the outstanding issues. Its proposal for positive discrimination was decisively beaten, by 21,377 votes (57 per cent) to 16,071 (43 per cent). And the principle of 'one member, one vote' carried the day, although not as comfortably as at Kensington Town Hall (see Table 12.1 in Appendix 5). On the first round of counting, 'one member, one vote' led the OMOV-now-MPs-later formula by 44 to 34 per cent (a slenderer margin than the 55 to 24 per cent majority at the constitutional convention), and election by MPs only trailed at 23 per cent. Because none of the options obtained an absolute majority, the single-transferable-vote (STV) rules required the second preferences of MPs-only voters to be redistributed. In this second round, 'one member, one vote' won by the barest of majorities (51.5 to 48.5 per cent).[17]

The Party's Structure and Constitution

The constitution that was finally put in place in June 1982 established five important institutions in the party: the area party, the Council for Social Democracy (CSD), the National Committee, the Policy Committee and the dual leadership of leader and president. Each of these institutions was unusual by the standards of British political parties. This section of the chapter describes their functions and interrelationships.

THE AREA PARTY AND ITS MEMBERS

There are, broadly, two conflicting views about the proper role of local parties and their members. Both views accept that ordinary members 'own' the party and that power ultimately rests with them. But the 'democratic' view regards the party as a confederation of autonomous local parties whose members are active participants in the determination of party policy and to whom the party leadership should be closely accountable. The 'managerial' view regards local parties as branches of the national party, their function being to campaign, to recruit members and to raise money on the party's behalf while the leadership is left to get on with the specialized job of policy-making. The Labour party gives its local organizations a democratic role, as befits a party created by a popular movement outside parliament. Having, like the Conservatives, been created by politicians, the SDP took a more managerialist line. This was reflected in the three principles that governed the party's rules about membership. First, only individuals were allowed to join. No provision was made for indirect membership through the affiliation of independent groups like trade unions—a deliberate reaction against Labour.[18] Secondly, individuals *belonged* to their area party but *joined* the national party. They might be recruited locally, but their application and subscription were submitted to national headquarters (which remitted 20 per cent to the area party). Thirdly, eligibility and expulsion were matters not for the area party but for the National Committee and the national Appeals Tribunal. The definition of eligibility was deliberately vague: members could not be members of any other United Kingdom party or 'members or supporters of any organisation whose purposes are incompatible with those of the SDP'.[19]

The basic unit of organization was the area party, which, in contrast to the old parties' structure, consisted 'of one or more parliamentary constituencies up to a maximum of seven'. In September 1986 there were 223 recognized area parties covering the whole country, and they typically comprised three or four parliamentary constituencies. Only forty-two single-constituency organizations had persuaded the National Committee that they were strong enough to warrant separate area-party status.

In the leadership's eyes, multi-constituency area parties had numerous advantages. They were less vulnerable to takeover by small cliques and thus to the fate that befell many moribund inner-city Labour parties—and their MPs—in the 1970s. At the same time, they solved (and hid) the problem of tiny membership and unviable organizations in some constituencies, especially in working-class areas. Area parties, in addition, would be an advantage when negotiating with the Liberals over the allocation of seats and would offset feelings of disenfranchisement among SDP members living in constituencies designated as 'Liberal-led'. The purely managerial case for area parties was also influential. A small number of large parties would be easier for headquarters to service and monitor than a large number of small parties: they would involve fewer agents, less correspondence and a lower incidence of rebel or dissident local organizations—in a word, less trouble for the centre.

THE COUNCIL FOR SOCIAL DEMOCRACY (CSD)

The Council for Social Democracy, the 'parliament of the party', was 'responsible for the adoption of the policy of the SDP'. It resembled an eighteenth-century American state convention more than a twentieth-century party conference. Designed to be a cautious, deliberative body, its voting membership was intentionally small, consisting of about 400 elected representatives from the area parties.[20] The small size was meant to instil a sense of cohesion (the original plan was for a body of only 200) and to discourage the development of factions. To foster a sense of continuity, the constitution also stipulated that the Council should meet not annually but at least three times a year, that its members be elected for two-year terms, that they be eligible for re-election and that any attempt to mandate them by their area-party members be prohibited. The principle of 'one member, one vote' by postal ballot was applied to the election of area council members, and there remained a modest provision to encourage more women members: area parties electing two or more council members had to ensure that at least one was a woman.

THE NATIONAL COMMITTEE

Formally, the most powerful body in the party was the National Committee, the party's board of management 'responsible for the management and conduct of the activities of the SDP outside Parliament'. Chaired by the president, it met monthly. (Its composition is set out in Table 12.2.)

With its complex mixture of separate elections by distinct constituencies, the National Committee superficially resembled Labour's equally hybrid NEC; but it was contrived so as to produce a body less in thrall to the constituency activists and more representative of the party's policy-making and 'responsible' elements. A significant feature was the reservation of up to ten places for MPs, who, in contrast to the Labour party, were to be elected by their fellow MPs, not by constituency activists or conference delegates. Local councillors and peers also had their reserved places, whereas local party activists were, at most, only indirectly represented through the regionally elected CSD members of the committee. The constitutional status of ordinary party members, however, was recognized via their right to elect eight committee members, although less democratic motives also lay behind this provision: it was seen as a reserve means of putting the so-called *prominenti*—national but non-parliamentary figures—on the committee.[21] The detailed provisions about sex, region, age and co-option (the latter was meant to ensure the presence of black members) were designed to produce a social balance on the committee. In the eyes of its members the National Committee never lived up to its formal powers. Its lack of policy-making functions left it with an administrative rather than a political agenda. Its large size and the disparate origins of its provincial members made it an unwieldy instrument for managing the party, although it remained a useful means of regular communication between the party in the country and the leadership. But power and status resided in the Policy Committee.

THE POLICY COMMITTEE

The Policy Committee's job was to initiate policy proposals, and its powers were considerable. It drafted provisional statements of policy ('green papers'), circulated them for comment among area parties and regional councils and presented final drafts ('white papers') to the CSD for debate and resolution. It could establish working parties on policy and also commission research and discussion papers. It had monitoring as well as initiating powers: policy proposals coming from area parties or regional councils were submitted not to the council but to the Policy Committee 'which shall state the action . . . [it] . . . considers appropriate whether by formulation of a draft statement of policy or otherwise'. Its control over the manifesto was almost absolute. The manifesto was to be 'based upon statements of policy adopted by the Council', but it was left to the committee to choose which statements; unlike in the Labour party, there was no obligation to include policy proposals passed by a certain majority. On issues the CSD had not debated, moreover, the committee could make policy as it thought best.

Membership of this powerful committee was deliberately stacked in favour of the MPs. This reflected one of the drafters' core constitutional convictions: since members of parliament are responsible, and electorally accountable, for putting policies into law they must have a major say in the formulation of policy. Significantly, the committee was chaired by the party leader, not the president, and was composed of:

- the leader
- the president
- all MPs belonging to the National Committee (up to a maximum of ten)
- nine other members of the National Committee, elected by the full committee.

After the 1983 general election, when only six SDP MPs were returned, MPs were in a minority on the Policy Committee; but, had SDP representation in the Commons exceeded ten, MPs would have commanded a majority and, moreover, could have influenced the selection of the nine Natonal Committee members.

THE LEADER AND PRESIDENT

The dual leadership was yet another 'check and balance' in the party. But the division of labour between leader and president was not marked out in the constitution, a reflection perhaps of the presidency's origins as a kind of con-solation prize. The leader was the SDP's parliamentary leader, chief election campaigner and potential prime minister. The president's functions, by contrast, were undefined, except that he or she chaired the CSD and the National Committee. Thus the job was what the holder chose to make of it, and relations with the leader were a function of personalities more than formal roles. This was to prove a source of strain under Owen's leadership, especially during the 1987 merger crisis. Yet the post, which was elective and held for a minimum of two and a maximum of six years, was more significant than the Labour party chairmanship, which rotated annually on the principle of Buggins' turn. In a larger and wealthier SDP, the president might have become a major election strategist, like the chairman of the Conservative party; but in the small SDP the president's role was confined to offering a second face to the voters, boosting activists' morale, acting as ambassador to the Liberals and attending to the nuts and bolts of the party machine. Judging from the turnout in the national ballots, party members regarded the presidency as a relatively unimportant post.[22]

Two other components of the party structure require only brief mention, because they wielded little power. The party's annual Consultative Assembly was a 'forum for discussion' of SDP policy and affairs by ordinary SDP members. Tacked on to the September meeting of the council at the beginning of the party conference season, it had no formal decision-making powers but, much like the Conservative conference, was regarded as a publicity-making rally. Regional councils were permitted but not mandatory as an intermediate layer between area parties and the CSD. Originally envisaged as powerful units in a decentralized party structure, their functions were restricted to the consideration of policy green papers circulated by the Policy Committee, the submission to the Policy Committee of policy proposals relating to their region and the holding of regional consultative assemblies. Regional councils were not established for all parts of the country, and only the Scottish and Welsh Councils displayed any vigour, mainly on the issue of devolution and the need for closer co-operation with the Liberals.[23]

The Distribution of Power in the SDP

Party constitutions distribute power as well as functions. They shape the relationship between members, activists, MPs and the leadership. Defenders of the SDP constitution described it as one of checks and balances, which vested ultimate power in the party membership while protecting the independence of MPs and the leadership's managerial prerogatives. Critics saw it as a façade behind which a 'barons' party' monopolized initiatives, controlled policy making and snuffed out dissent and faction.[24]

The distribution of power between members, activists, MPs and the leadership is illuminated by answers to four questions. Who elects the leader? Who selects candidates? Who determines policy? And what latitude is given to faction and dissent? The answer to the first question has already been given earlier. It remains to answer the other three.

CANDIDATE SELECTION

The rules about candidate selection, like so much else in the constitution, were deliberately designed to avoid the alleged abuses and weaknesses of the Labour party's procedures: 'rigged' short lists, disputes over selectors' credentials and selection (and deselection) by small and unrepresentative groups of activists. The prerogative of selection was therefore to rest with the ordinary members, not the activists, of the area party. 'One member, one vote' was the core principle. The result was a studiously democratic but extraordinarily elaborate—and expensive—system.

The role of the national party was limited to maintaining a panel of suitable candidates containing 'a reasonable balance between both sexes and different age groups and [including] representatives of different social and economic groups and of ethnic minorities'. The area party committee was then to short-list the applicants, who had to be on the national panel of eligible candidates unless a special exemption was obtained from the National Committee. In order to minimize rigging, the short list needed to be approved by a simple majority of members attending the selection meeting, contain at least five (but no more than nine) names and include at least two applicants from outside the area. To boost the selection of women, the short list had to contain at least two of each sex.

Short-listed candidates had the opportunity to address members at a selection meeting, but the final decision was taken by all members of the area party (including those living outside the constituency in question) in an STV postal ballot. Most members did not attend the selection meeting and, presumably, voted on the basis of the 250-word biography and 750-word political statement of each candidate that was sent out by the area party to its members. Since canvassing was 'strongly discouraged', selection was for many members a peculiarly impersonal process, like ordering gifts from a mail-order catalogue. Finally, the rules on reselection and deselection placed power firmly in the hands of members, not activists, and gave MPs a measure of protection. To be renominated as the parliamentary candidate, a sitting SDP MP needed only to secure the endorsement of a simple majority (by secret ballot) at a meeting open to all area party members. If the MP was rejected at the meeting, the issue was resolved by a postal ballot of all area party members.

In the SDP's short life as a national party, the leadership nibbled twice at the powers of the membership. The May 1985 constitutional revisions stipulated that when a by-election arose the existing parliamentary candidate was automatically deselected and the National Committee 'in consultation with the local party' would choose someone. This change was intended to avoid another Darlington, where the national party had been embarrassed by a candidate who was locally selected but unsuitable.[25] Later in 1985 the National Committee, at David Owen's prompting, excluded an active SDP member, Neville Pressman, from the candidates' list on the grounds that he was a member of the Campaign for Nuclear Disarmament (CND) and spokesman for the ginger group Social Democrats for Peace.[26] Compared with the two main parties, however, candidate selection proceeded with very little friction (perhaps because so few of the candidates had a serious chance of winning).

POLICY-MAKING

No party activity was more subject to checks and balances in the constitution than policy-making. As described earlier, the crucial powers of initiative, formulation and temporary veto were vested in the indirectly elected Policy Committee. The CSD's role was carefully worded. It did not 'initiate' or 'formulate' or even 'decide' party policy: it 'adopted' it. Until September 1985 the council could only consider policy documents laid before it by the Policy Committee or by regional councils. Motions from council members could be considered only if they were signed by twenty-five or more council members. After September 1985 policy motions could be put to the council by an area party but subject to various restrictions which reflected a fear of activist power.[27]

The CSD, therefore, did not normally initiate policy. Nor did it have the decisive or ultimate say in the matter: 'no motion or amendment shall become the policy of the SDP unless it is adopted both by the Council and by the Policy Committee' (chapter V, section E, clause 10). In other words, when the CSD approved of proposals made by the Policy Committee, they become official party policy; but if such proposals were amended, referred back or rejected they were reconsidered by the Policy Committee, which prepared revised proposals for the next CSD. Proposals initiated by a regional council, an area party or individual council members had to be approved by the Policy Committee as well as the council in order to become party policy. Only if council and the Policy Committee could not agree 'on an issue of policy of major importance' were ordinary members given a role. Such disputes were to be settled by a postal ballot of all SDP members. Thus, ultimate sovereignty lay with neither the council, the Policy Committee nor the party leader, but with the national party membership.[28]

As well as according rank-and-file members this power of arbitration, the constitution obliged the party to go to elaborate lengths to consult them over policy. Green and white papers were circulated in advance of council meetings to all area parties, which could submit amendments or (after September 1985) a motion. The annual consultative assembly and the party's Fabian-style policy think-tank, the Tawney Society, were open to all party members. Any member with a keen interest in policy had ample opportunity to get involved. Nevertheless, the actual involvement of ordinary members was modest. A survey of area party activities showed that members were hardly chafing at the policy bit: barely a fifth of area parties discussed the party's green papers 'extensively'; most of their agendas were dominated by social events and organizational matters.[29]

While the policy-making role played by members and activists was modest, it did grow as they gained experience and confidence and secured helpful procedural amendments. One indicator is the number of policy resolutions that activists, as opposed to the Policy Committee, submitted to the CSD either as individual members or through regional councils or area parties. As Table 12.3 shows, the Policy Committee's role in initiating policy motions was much more dominant in the seven councils that preceded the 1985 constitutional revisions (66 per cent of all policy motions) than in the four that followed them (47 per cent).

Evidence that activists grew in confidence as the years passed can also be found in the increasing proportion of amendments tabled by area parties and the increasing number carried by the council (see Table 12.4). Altogether 127 area parties (out of about 220) submitted policy motions or amendments; but that left about a hundred which in four years of council meetings took no policy initiatives at all.[30]

The contribution of area parties to the policy agenda was thus limited. Their contribution to the substance of policy was more limited still. It is, in fact, impossible to point to any example of rank-and-file members significantly reshaping SDP policy as it proceeded through the various consultative stages. (Their impact on the party constitution was another matter.) Most green papers 'turned white' with only marginal changes, the few important revisions usually being at the behest of the Policy Committee. And most white papers progressed through council meetings unscathed, with only the occasional minor amendment being passed.[31] SDP Councils were mostly bloodless affairs.

Nevertheless, there were occasional rebellions, notably over incomes policy at the first council meeting in Great Yarmouth and over plastic bullets in Northern Ireland at the Buxton council.[32] At the special conference on revisions to the constitution in May 1985, council members not only won area parties the right to submit policy motions but only just failed (by 111 to 102 votes) to gain for themselves, as distinct from the national membership and the Policy Committee, the ultimate say on policy questions. But the overall tone of councils was well mannered and low key, the atmosphere almost suffocatingly reasonable and respectful. There was no counterpart to the fierce prejudices of Conservative activists, the sectarian passions of Labour delegates or the whimsical enthusiasms of Liberals.

This does not mean that party activists were ignored. There were no policy issues, plastic bullets excepted, on which the party leadership deliberately defied or by-passed the council. But this was because there was no need: the ethos of the party precluded it. The relationship between members and leadership in the SDP differed from that in the other parties. Labour and Liberal activists instinctively distrust authority and are naturally rebels; Conservative activists make a cult of leadership and loyalty. SDP members, by contrast, were almost compulsively 'reasonable'; they were natural compromisers. Part of the explanation lay in the party's origins. Few joined the SDP because they felt passionately about any policy issue, except perhaps for Europe. Most joined out of a general distaste for the 'extremism' and 'dogmatism' of the two major parties, especially Labour. Often they objected to the style of the other parties' policy debate even more than to the substance of the outcome. The SDP's very newness was also a factor. Policy proposals had little symbolic or historic importance, and past battles had not made them points of honour. They could be treated pragmatically rather than ideologically. What counted about a policy proposal was not its conformity to a principle but whether it was likely to achieve its objectives.

SDP policy was therefore shaped by its Policy Committee, which in turn relied on the working groups it established to deal with policy in different fields. In principle the working groups were open to ordinary members with the requisite interest and expertise; in practice their memberships and modes of operation were, with one or two exceptions, divorced from the world of the rank and file. From the start, the Gang of Four and a small circle of trusted friends exercised control, and they loosened the reins only gradually. The first eleven working groups were established in September 1981, before the party's constitution was in place, by a self-appointed Policy Committee dominated by the Gang of Four. The chairman of a group was usually a trustworthy MP or former MP close to the party leadership, such as David Marquand or Dick Taverne. The chairman submitted a list of names to the Policy Committee, which added its own nominees. Chairmen also chose from a list prepared by Cowley Street containing the names of ordinary subscribers who had written in expressing their interest. But most policy groups were packed with the great and the good, looking more like Royal Commissions than working parties of the rank and file. Thus the SDP in its formative stages relied on a trusted circle of the prestigious and the expert for its policy-making. It was almost immediately plugged into what someone dubbed the 'dinner-party network' of academic policy thinkers, specialist journalists and reformist lawyers. Julia Neuberger, a member of the citizens' rights policy group, described her shock at the first meeting:

I found I knew twelve of the fourteen people there. Tony Lester, who had got me to join the SDP, was a member of my congregation. Michael Zander worked for my father-in-law; Paul Sieghart was a nephew of a family friend; I knew Celia Goodhart because I taught her daughter and Bob Maclennan's brother was the boyfriend of my sister-in-law.

Not all policy groups were as incestuous, but they did draw on a narrow, heavily overlapping London circle formed by the social-science establishment, specialist staff on the *Guardian* and *The Economist* and Fabian Society refugees. The SDP was particularly well connected with research institutes such as the Policy Studies Institute and the Royal Institute of International Affairs.[33]

Especially in its first two years, the party was thus served by a formidable array of intellectual talent. Its working groups were top-heavy with academics who were well equipped to make theoretical and research contributions but had little experience of the sharp end of government. Their vantage-point was usually the captain's bridge, rarely the decks below. The policy group on education and training, for example, included the chairman of the University Grants Committee, three university and college heads, but only one comprehensive school teacher. The economic policy group was, if anything, even more distinguished, boasting a Nobel prize winner in economics, Sir James Meade, and a clutch of leading academic economists.[34] Not since the arrival of the 1964 Labour government had a party provoked such a rush of academic blood to the head. The result was a portfolio of policy green papers that in coherence and expertise generally out-classed anything produced by the Conservative or Labour parties when in opposition.

This small network had a real sense of participation in a new party. Their actual influence is more difficult to gauge. The more prestigious members of the policy groups soon drifted away, out of pressure of time, leaving it to handfuls of people to draft and revise the first set of policy proposals. The important green paper on trade-union reform was drafted by Roger Liddle, Roger Rosewall (a former Socialist Workers' Party (SWP) organizer who worked for the Electrical, Electronic, Telecommunications and Plumbing Union (EETPU)) and Tony Halmos, a TUC official who subsequently joined the SDP staff. The radical green paper on poverty and taxation was largely written by Dick Taverne. Most others were the joint work of Christopher Smallwood (the party's policy co-ordinator until 1983) and the policy group's chairman. And, as we have seen, most green papers turned into white papers, and subsequently official policy, with little alteration from the Policy Committee or the CSD. After David Owen became leader, the working group structure was by-passed more frequently, policy-making being concentrated far more in Owen's personal office. He was more prone than Jenkins or the Gang of Four to make (or unmake) policy on the hoof, notably on defence and on conditions for participation in a coalition government, and to rely mainly on *ad hoc* contacts with a small number of advisers before making statements to the media.[35]

The elaborate structure of consultation hid from view a policy-making process that was, in fact, concentrated in remarkably few hands. 'In practice', one policy group chairman argued,

policy-making is bound to be élitist. It was far too democratic and took far too long. Members should be organizing, not discussing policy. It should have been left to the policy group chairmen and a few bright young recruits from the City and universities. Then the whole exercise could have been completed in two or three weeks.

Had policy been made in such a way, ordinary members would have felt excluded, but otherwise it is hard to believe that the end result would have been very different.

FACTION AND DISSENT

With the Labour party, as ever, in mind, the SDP's constitution was designed to discourage caucuses and factions and to minimize the institutionalization of dissent. Power was formally divided between national bodies and the rank-and-file membership, at the expense of activists. The institutional bases for faction in the Labour party—the mandating of delegates to higher bodies and the affiliation of independently organized groups with voting powers—were explicitly prohibited. The Social Democratic Alliance, which preceded the SDP and might have turned into a party faction, was deliberately sidelined by the party leadership: those prominent in it were excluded from the Steering Committee, and its candidates in the 1981 local elections were not endorsed.[36]

The constitution permitted 'Associated Organizations', but only under the thumb of the National Committee, which determined whether they received funding, accommodation at Cowley Street and representation on policy subcommittees, and which could revoke their status.[37] By 1985 there were seven associated organizations—for students, young Social Democrats, local councillors, women and trade unionists as well as the Association for a Social Democratic Europe and the Tawney Society. With the exception of the Young Social Democrats and SDP Students, they all had small memberships and lacked active local branches. All seven regarded themselves as support organizations for the national party rather than as ginger groups or organs of dissent.[38] The party also recognized single-cause groups, such as the SDP Friends of Ireland and the Social Democrats for Peace, but these had no official status or rights. The more active of them published pamphlets, placed articles in the party press, held fringe meetings at the Consultative Assembly and tried to orchestrate policy motions and amendments. But none had more than a couple of hundred members and none had more than a marginal influence on policy.[39]

The only group of organized dissent to make any impact was the so-called Limehouse Group. It was established in 1984 in response to Owen's advocacy of a social-market economy and aimed to keep the party left of centre and close to the European Social Democratic (as opposed to Liberal) parties. It stood for the redistribution of wealth, strong trade unions and an extension of collective and co-operative ownership in their various forms; it also championed the rights of the CSD against the Policy Committee and an 'authoritarian' leadership. It recruited a stable membership of 150 and achieved a public profile within the party, but it failed to secure majority votes at the CSD for its constitutional and policy objectives, most notably legislative supremacy for the CSD and the gradual transfer of both the public sector and major private companies to a 'citizen's trust'.

Thus the SDP appeared to the outside world as a homogeneous and passionless party, largely devoid of division or faction. The squabbles at the top were usually too muffled to produce more than a faint echo below. The constitution discouraged organized dissent, and the party's culture of deference and reasonableness did not nurture it. 'Our members are far too obedient,' Shirley Williams complained. Yet there were unacknowledged rifts in the party, notably over co-operation with the Liberals. These rifts were largely hidden from the public and from ordinary members because they ran deepest within the party leadership itself, and the leadership operated largely through small and informal networks, beyond the reach of the constitution. When these divisions erupted into the open after the 1987 election, the constitution was effective in resolving them, but it could not contain them.

In modern times a party constitution needs to combine three principles which are not readily compatible. The first is internal party democracy: sovereignty must be vested in the party membership. The second is organizational effectiveness: only leaders and a small executive can take initiatives, respond quickly to events, represent the party to the public and run it from day to day. The third is a measure of independence for the party's MPs, who owe their position both to the party that nominated them and to the ordinary voters who elected them.

The SDP's existence was too short for definitive judgements about the success of its constitution, but it probably brought these principles into better balance than the old parties had done. The time and consultation devoted to its drafting was worthwhile. In its brief operation, the constitution worked as its architects, Maclennan and Goodhart, intended. Leaders could exercise considerable powers of initiative but were accountable to the membership on major issues (as Owen's resignation in 1987 after the ballot on merger was to demonstrate). Policy-making was handled more realistically than in the Labour and Liberal parties, less autocratically than in the Conservative party. Policy initiatives and formulation were left to small groups of leading politicians and specialists but were subject to protracted deliberation within the wider party. Contrary to left-wing critics, there was ample opportunity for ordinary members who wished to get involved in policy-making to do so, even though most did not.[40] Activists were denied the mischief-making power they had in both the Labour and the old Liberal parties, without any detrimental effect on the recruitment of members for constituency work. Candidate selection proceeded without the rows and shenanigans associated with the Labour party, although this may have been because few seats were seen as winnable. Factions were discouraged without being proscribed. The SDP showed that there were ways of creating a national party organization that was both democratic and manageable.

The measure of the constitution's success was the fact that it was adopted, in most respects, by the Liberal Democrats—the party formed out of the Liberals and pro-merger Social Democrats. The more anarchic institutional features of the old Liberal party which had proved so electorally embarrassing for the leadership, such as the Liberal Council and the open-access annual conference, were replaced by the SDP's more regulated policy-making framework. The Labour party, too, has moved towards some of the principles incorporated in the SDP constitution.[41]

One consequence of the SDP's elaborate provisions for consulting the ordinary membership and its frequent council meetings was, however, unanticipated: it put a heavy strain on the party's finances, its organization and its members' time. The constitution was designed for a major national party, with a large headquarters, a mass membership and ample funds. As Chapter 13 shows, this was a position that the party nearly achieved, but not quite.

13

• • • •

Machinery, Members and Money

In creating the party's constitution the SDP's leaders were constrained to some extent by personal differences and also by what the members would accept. In building the party organization they enjoyed a much freer hand. Overnight the launch produced nearly 50,000 members, an abundance of volunteers and £500,000 in the bank. There were no major financial backers to humour or established organizations to incorporate. The only existing organization on the ground was the Social Democratic Alliance, from which the SDP leadership warily kept its distance. With only a few active branches, the SDA was too weak to claim a reserved place in the SDP's structure.[1]

The party's leaders were determined to begin with a clean slate, beholden to none. Yet the conditions for building a party organization were far from ideal. The structures that sustain the normal functions of a political party had to be established from scratch and all at the same time; there was a flood of applications and subscriptions to be processed; the new members, most of them fresh to party politics, needed help in setting up and maintaining area parties; the media's appetite had to be sated in the early months and whetted thereafter; a policy-making structure had to be erected. Moreover, within a few months of the launch, routine administration had to take a back seat to a succession of more urgent tasks, many of which pulled officials away from their London offices: by-elections in Warrington, Crosby and Hillhead, the first of the rolling conferences and the seats negotiations with local Liberals. For the first eighteen months the development of the party organization was, at best, chaotic.

Although some confusion and error was probably inevitable, it was aggravated by a lack of firm and co-ordinated direction from the top. The Steering Committee was too unwieldy and met too infrequently to do the job, and responsibility was spread instead among the Gang of Four. Roy Jenkins chaired the Policy Committee and was also the main ambassador to the Liberals. Bill Rodgers chaired the Finance and General Purposes Committee—an unusual retention of Labour nomenclature—because he had been the most familiar with Labour's

238

organization. David Owen chaired the Parliamentary Committee and was thus regarded as the SDP's leader in the Commons. Shirley Williams chaired the Communications Committee which handled publicity and the media 'because she had a background in journalism'. Specific one-off tasks were taken on by whoever among the other MPs was available.[2] It was an amicable but haphazard division of labour, and it emerged without any serious discussion about the party's long-term interests or the priorities to be given to different organizational tasks.

The spreading of responsibilities among the Gang of Four was politically understandable but mistaken administratively. It demonstrated the formally equal status of the four and forestalled too obvious an emergence of a presumptive leader, but it meant that nobody took ultimate responsibility for building up the party machine, raising money, establishing lines of authority and setting organizational priorities. As chairman of the Steering Committee, Jenkins was in the best position to do this, but he found the nuts and bolts of party machinery tedious. Rodgers came closest to taking on these responsibilities as chairman of the Finance and General Purposes Committee, but he lacked the time, and perhaps the status, to act on the whole leadership's behalf; and from the autumn of 1981 he was increasingly absorbed in the seats negotiations with the Liberals.

In the absence of a single leader, Cowley Street staff wasted time and delayed decisions trying to square each of the Gang of Four. Not the least of their problems was actually making contact with them. The Gang of Four's London offices were widely scattered: Jenkins' at Morgan Grenfell in the City, Williams' at the Policy Studies Institute in Victoria, Owen's and Rodgers' at Westminster. Moreover, the four were frequently on the road addressing and chairing countless meetings. Usually, they had no time to do more than attend committee meetings and hurriedly consult the relevant committee secretary. 'It's ridiculous for Shirley to be chairing the Communications Committee,' one committee member complained. 'She's not a natural executive. She doesn't follow through on decisions. She should be out in the country empathizing with voters.'

In fact, none of the Gang of Four, with the partial exception of Rodgers, was by either instinct or experience a natural executive. They were politicians. As cabinet ministers they had headed ready-made administrative machines which they were expected to steer in a general direction but neither to design nor to maintain. Like the great majority of politicians, the Gang of Four did not think organizationally, they had had little experience of running an organization, and they had had even less experience with building one up. They had ideas, of course, but they seldom had plans. Nor did any of them give organizational matters a high priority. In order to attract votes and members, what initially mattered, in their view, was publicity and political positioning in relation to the other parties; building a party machine would either take care of itself or could be put off till later. One result was that matters of organization were handled with far less clarity of purpose and much less long-term thinking than was going into shaping the SDP's constitution. A peculiar feature of the constitution, when it appeared, was that the architects' plans were not drawn up until after the foundations were laid; a peculiar feature of the party's organization was that there was no architect's plan at all.

Although no detailed blueprint was available (or sought), the party leadership operated on the basis of three broad principles. The first was to concentrate power and resources at the centre. The second was as far as possible to insulate the administration of the party from its internal politics. The third was to adopt up-to-date business techniques.

The first principle, centralization, was an administrative necessity as well as a political convenience. The 50,000 sympathizers who responded to the launch had no local branches to contact, and their only means of becoming a party member was to have their name added to a centrally compiled list. The new party's immediate objectives—maintaining the media's interest, making policy, preparing for the general-election campaign—could only be organized from the centre, and other tasks, such as by-elections and seats negotiations with the Liberals, were too important to risk leaving to inexperienced rank-and-file members. It was thought not only unwise but unrealistic to rely on grass-roots spontaneity. The new members and volunteers clearly expected an organization to be created for them.

These practical considerations coincided with the Gang of Four's personal stakes in controlling the new party's formative stages. They had risked their careers by leaving a Labour party whose parliamentary leadership had been eclipsed by the constituency parties and trade unions, and they had no intention of jeopardizing their futures again by exposing themselves to the uncertain and perhaps naïve notions of the new party's members. Moreover, they had the centralizing instincts of former ministers (only Williams had been a committed devolutionist in the Callaghan government) and they were all natural metropolitans, with homes in, and long-standing attachments to, London. None possessed the provincial loyalties commonly found among members of the Liberal party.[3]

The second principle—the attempt to keep politics out of the party's central organization—was yet another reaction against Labour practices.[4] The party's leaders took an early decision to vest its finances in appointed trustees who would not be entitled, while holding office, 'to seek selection as candidates for any parliamentary or European election or to seek elective office within the SDP'.[5] Later the party appointed an executive director and other senior staff on their administrative and professional merits rather than on their (often non-existent) political experience. The Gang of Four wanted neutral civil servants around them, not partisan intriguers.

A cult of modern business practice was the third dimension to SDP organization. It had a public-relations aspect. Most of those involved in the SDP believed that how a party ran its own affairs told the electorate a great deal about how it would run the country's. There was an aversion among the SDP leaders to the bootstrap amateurism of the Liberal party and to the archaic inefficiencies of Labour's 'penny farthing machine'. Serious parties, in their view, took organization seriously.

Source: Guardian, 17 March 1981

'There's nothing in the phone book under Social Democrats—perhaps if you want to join them you have to be an MP first'

The professionalism of the Connaught Rooms launch immediately gave the SDP the reputation for professionalism that it was seeking. It did not, in fact, deserve it. From the beginning the party organization was totally overwhelmed. Reluctant to turn down volunteers, the party was soon clogged by innumerable consultative committees and endless advisory subcommittees. A massive backlog of unanswered mail accumulated. When the party appointed a chief executive in September 1981, the new man found sacks of unopened post left over from before the Warrington by-election.

Ironically, the most administratively disruptive mistake was embodied in the SDP's principal symbol of high-tech modernity: its computerized register of members. The immediate intention was to give area organizers a print-out of local members as a first step to forming an area party. The long-term advantages would be considerable too. By ensuring the availability of a more accurate and up-to-date

Source: Guardian, 27 March 1981

*'It's very convenient, you can join by credit card and at the same time write
everything they stand for on the back of it'*

register than could be compiled locally, the computerized list would avoid the
Labour party's perpetual disputes over credentials. It would also form the basis of a
sophisticated communications system within the party, enabling the leadership to
ballot and survey the membership—and to appeal for funds.

That, at any rate, was the idea; the SDP would be a kind of political Hyatt
Regency. The reality was more like Fawlty Towers. The computerized register
quickly became a nightmare.[6] The party bought the computing services of the
registrar's department of the Midland Bank, but without enquiring sufficiently
closely into its capabilities. The bank's system, in fact, could print out only the
entire list of members' names and addresses: it lacked the facility to select members
according to a particular attribute such as residence—which was essential if lists
of local members were to be forwarded to area organizers. Numerous errors also
crept into the transcription of membership forms into computer records. Some

forms were difficult to decipher; in other cases the would-be member had submitted an incomplete address or given an initial rather than a full forename or the wrong local constituency.

The SDP staff were too busy, the Midland Bank staff too inexperienced, to spot and correct the mistakes. As a result, the local lists, expensively and time-consumingly extracted from the full list, were incomplete and inaccurate. Some early aspiring members heard nothing for an entire year; others were contacted two or three times by different people. In January 1982 some members who had joined only a month or two earlier received renewal notices, but others who had joined at the start received no notice at all. Attempts at correction led to further errors. Some names were duplicated, others deleted. These lapses generated the predictable correspondence and phone calls from the SDP's disappointed but often highly articulate members—adding still further to the load of an already over-burdened staff. Some early recruits undoubtedly departed, never to return.

Order was not in fact restored—or, rather, achieved—until late 1982, after the leadership election in June of that year and the ballot on the constitution three months earlier. At both ballots even more anomalies in the register became apparent. In Cowley Street there was considerable relief that the party was not embarrassed by leaks to the press about the disarray in the membership records of a party that prided itself on its efficiency and constitutional purity. Computerized efficiency? Old-fashioned filing cards would have served the party better.

The tradition in British political parties is to recruit their chief of staff internally, typically choosing someone with many years' experience in the party organization. The SDP decided, in this as in so many other things, to be different. To lick the organization into shape, it advertised for a chief executive ('general secretary' was thought too redolent of the Labour party). The idea was to recruit a high-flier from business or administration, and an appropriate salary (£25,000 p.a.) was accordingly offered. The person appointed from a field of 320, Bernard Doyle, applied out of the blue and was unknown to anybody in the party. He was an identikit SDP member, an almost perfect representative of the post-war generation of non-partisan meritocrats who were so strongly attracted to the SDP. Born into a lower middle-class family and educated at a northern grammar school and Manchester University, he had paid his way through Harvard Business School, joining Booker McConnell, the sugar-based conglomerate in 1973. He reached Booker McConnell's main board, as chairman of its engineering division, in 1979. Before joining the SDP he had never been involved or very interested in party politics. He described his sympathies as 'broadly with the Liberals'.[7]

Doyle's appointment was no more than a partial success. His relations with the SDP leadership were always strained. What the leadership needed was a civil servant familiar with the ways of ministers. What it got was a managing director used to a non-interventionist board. Accustomed to a clear structure of author-ity and corporate planning, Doyle found it almost intolerable to work for four bosses who frequently took unilateral initiatives, gave contradictory instructions and dealt directly with his subordinates. Someone with previous experience of politicians would have read the Gang of Four better, tolerated ambiguity and inconsistency, anticipated political traps and, finally, imposed his own agenda. Lacking political antennae, Doyle deferred to the Gang of Four, 'of whom he was in awe', but he grew increasingly resentful of their sporadic interventions and increasingly frustrated by their inability to give clear directives, their unwillingness to 'think long' and their apparent boredom with organizational matters, especially with regard to finance. The SDP leadership in turn complained of his 'massive sense of insecurity', subordinates of his 'indecisiveness'. After the 1983 election, Doyle left for the quieter world of the Welsh Water Authority. The SDP abandoned its experiment of having a chief executive and promoted its national secretary, the more relaxed and political Richard Newby, to head the party organization, without changing his title.[8]

All that said, Doyle's managerial abilities and workaholic commitment did succeed in creating administrative order out of what had been chaos. By early 1983 the SDP was in a steady state. Proper financial discipline had been imposed in the nick of time; policy had been formulated across a wide area; the constitutional structure of committees and councils had been put into operation; nearly 200 area parties had been established, covering the whole of Great Britain; regional offices had been set up in Cardiff, Glasgow, Bristol, Manchester and Birmingham; and the membership list had been transferred from the Midland Bank to a computer bureau and then straightened out. A newspaper for party members, the fortnightly *Social Democrat*, was launched in May 1982. The number of staff grew from eleven at the launch to fifty-five at the 1983 general election. In the space of two years a central party organization had been established which surpassed not only the Liberals' but the Labour party's in professional competence. It was a considerable accomplishment, and Doyle deserved much of the credit. Achieving it, however, left too little time to prepare for the coming election. It also left the party still weak in crucial areas, such as membership and finance.

'A Party in Nobody's Pocket'

British political parties largely have to pay for themselves. Their spending is restricted; they cannot buy time on radio or television, and strict limits are imposed on what candidates may spend on their constituency campaigns. Parties receive some state subsidies-in-kind in the form of free radio and television time for their broadcasts and free postage for their candidates' election addresses. But beyond that the parties have to find the money to pay for their own headquarters and staff, fund-raising and research activities, press and poster advertising and—if they choose to do any—opinion polling.[9] For these purposes the Conservative party has relied heavily on business and large individual donations and the Labour party on trade-union contributions.[10]

For a very brief period the SDP spurned the idea of institutional donations and made a virtue of its dependence on subscriptions and small donations. It had come into being to challenge the system symbolized by the unaccountability and potential corruption of business and trade-union political funding. The Conservative and Labour parties, the SDP proclaimed, had become mercenaries in the class war; the new party would be in no one's pocket. The Steering Committee was to be informed of any donation in excess of £5,000 and in the period up to the launch there were only three such donations: £25,000 from David Sainsbury, the finance director of the supermarket chain; £25,000 from Eric Woolfson, a successful musician and song-writer; and £10,000 from an anonymous donor. George Apter, a businessman supplying props to the television and advertising industries, paid for the 'Guardian 100' advertisement. The rest of the £170,000 raised by the launch, including £35,000 from the *Guardian* advertisement, came in small amounts. There were no shadowy paymasters behind the party, at least to begin with.

In building its financial base the SDP had no model to follow. The Liberals were a wholly negative point of reference. Since the war their central finances had been hopelessly inadequate; they were spread between too many conflicting bodies and were overdependent on the erratic donations of a few wealthy individuals. The Liberal Party Organization was not only underfunded; it was in chronic conflict with the parliamentary Liberal party, which looked to its own, independent sources of support. The nub of the problem was the combination of a decentralized party structure and an inadequate membership base. Too little revenue was raised from subscriptions, and too little of what was raised found its way to the centre. The SDP's Finance and General Purposes Committee had two early dilemmas to resolve. One concerned the size of the membership subscription. Should the party aim to maximize membership with a low fee or maximize revenue with a high fee? The committee could only guess at what economists call the 'price elasticity of demand' for party membership; and there was a political as well as a financial dimension. Opponents of a high fee feared it would leave the area parties with too few members, especially in working-class areas, and would reinforce the SDP's comfortable, middle-class image. Advocates of a high fee believed such a fee would not only increase income but encourage a more committed membership. The outcome was a compromise. There was to be a 'recommended' subscription of £9, making SDP membership considerably more expensive than membership of the other parties. But those unable to afford £9 could pay less, the minimum being £3. The party would also accept non-members as 'supporters', who in return for a donation were entitled to participate in SDP activities but not to vote. Provision was made for payment by credit card over the telephone, an arrangement that immediately became the media's symbol of the SDP's commitment to marketing, modernity and the middle classes.

With hindsight the £9 subscription turns out to have erred on the side of caution. More members subscribed more than £9 (35 per cent) than less (25 per cent), the average subscription being about £11.[11] This suggests that a slightly higher fee would have increased income and would probably not have depressed recruitment. Be that as it may, the high-fee strategy set the pattern for the following years. The subscription was steadily increased by more than the rate of inflation and by 1987 stood at £16 (with a minimum of £4), still well above those of the other parties.

Those most closely associated with membership and party finance hoped to recruit 100,000 members initially and hence have an annual operating budget of about £1 million. They were disappointed. The launch produced 54,000 members within two months, and the membership rose to an estimated 65,000 by the end of 1981.[12] This number was well below the estimated (but probably exaggerated) memberships of the Conservative party (about 1,150,000), Labour (275,000) and even the Liberals (150,000). It was less, too, than the membership of CND, which in 1981 grew much more rapidly than the SDP. After 1982, the party's membership declined (see Table 13.1 in Appendix 5). The Steering Committee's reluctant decision to remit part of the subscription to local parties (£3 out of £11 in 1982) did not produce more members or local self-sufficiency.[13] The renewal rate of those who joined in the first half of 1981 was 80 per cent—a very high figure for voluntary associations—but the rate among those who joined in the second half of the year dropped to well below 70 per cent. To maintain its membership, the SDP needed to recruit about 15,000 new members a year. For the first few months of 1982 it was on target. Once the Falklands War began, however, recruitment plummeted. 'Over a period of two or three weeks, the rate of recruitment halved. It was quite extraordinary.'[14] And it never again reached its former rate. By the summer of 1982 about 64,000 members were still on the register for the leadership ballot. Thereafter, renewal rates and new recruitment fluctuated broadly in line with the party's electoral popularity. In 1984, following the Alliance's 1983 election defeat, membership dropped to 45,000 (the party claimed 'around 50,000') but by 1986, following the Alliance's success in the 1985 county council elections and its by-election wins in Brecon and Radnor and in Ryedale, it had recovered to 58,000, where it stayed in 1987. The party claimed in addition to have over 30,000 'supporters' and donors.

With a mere 50,000–60,000 paid-up members, the SDP was spread very thinly across the country. A typical area party contained fewer than 300 members or about eighty to eighty-five in each constituency. These averages hid considerable variations from place to place. A regional analysis shortly after the launch (see Table 13.2) revealed a concentration of members in the south, especially in Greater London, where the typical constituency contained about 116 members. In Scotland and Wales, however, membership was sparse, averaging fewer than forty per constituency. There were also marked differences within regions and indeed within area parties. Most members lived in the shires, in prosperous medium-sized and small towns and in outer suburbs; very few lived in inner cities (outside London), the coalfields or on council estates.[15] The ten strongest area parties comprised cathedral and university towns (Cambridge, Oxford, Winchester), high-tech industrial towns (Bracknell, Eastleigh, Wokingham), well-heeled suburbs (Barnet, Hampstead, Putney, Richmond, Twickenham) and inner-city yuppiedoms (Battersea, Kensington) (see Table 13.3). By contrast, there was no SDP to speak of in the heavily industrial and solidly working-class belts of south Wales, central Scotland and the Black Country.

A total membership of little more than 50,000 was not sufficient to meet a national party's needs for electioneering, fund-raising and membership recruitment. The party accordingly looked for ways of topping up the revenue from members. It began by experimenting with a genuinely new form of party finance: discount merchandising. At the launch the SDP's bold logo had been emblazoned on badges, ties and even specially made tea mugs. Members snapped them up as mementoes. What began as a publicity gimmick quickly turned into a business. The SDP created the post of 'marketing and membership services manager', to which it appointed Anthony Martin in August 1981. A former marketing manager for both the *Sunday Times* and the *Financial Times*, he was unabashed at his political inexperience: 'We have something that is new and different, so we need to market it . . . the skills needed in promoting a newspaper are not that different from promoting a political party.'[16] The members' newsletter came to resemble a mail-order catalogue, the items on offer ranging from SDP pens, T-shirts, balloons, shopping bags and letter holders to an 'italic script reproduction on parchment paper of the Limehouse Declaration, individually handsigned by the Gang of Four' (for £12). There were even ambitious plans to extend 'membership services' to insurance and travel. Enthusiasts saw merchandising as a novel means of making money, recruiting members and publicizing the party all at the same time. Sceptics feared the creation of SDP Ltd.[17] But the experiment failed. Martin left after seven months, disappointed at the lack of funds for an advertising campaign and looked down upon by the political staff. The first year's profits from sales of merchandise amounted to a mere £14,509.

The party also looked to a more traditional source of income. By the end of 1981 it had abandoned its initial fastidiousness about institutional donations. While it was soon clear that nothing would be forthcoming from the trade unions, there was some optimism that companies could be persuaded to give. The SDP had recruited a number of prominent business leaders, including Sir John Harvey-Jones, deputy-chairman (and later chairman) of ICI, and Sir James Spooner, chairman of Vantona Viyella, as well as David Sainsbury.[18] It also had business and City connections through some of its leaders. Jenkins, for example, was a director of Morgan Grenfell, and Dick Taverne was on the board of BOC.

The party had, in effect, two sales pitches. One was that the SDP provided insurance against a Labour victory. In 1981 unemployment was soaring while inflation and interest rates remained high. Margaret Thatcher and her government were deeply unpopular. Business leaders feared that a Labour government, committed to a Bennite siege economy, would be returned *faute de mieux* on a wave of anti-government sentiment. The SDP invited business to hedge its bets. A strong centre party offered disillusioned Conservatives an alternative refuge to Labour and could also siphon off some Labour support. The SDP could stand between a defeated Conservative party and the return of full-blooded socialism.

The other sales pitch was the SDP's claim that it could provide business with the long-term economic and political stability it needed for investment, risk-taking and planning. The old two-party system, it was argued, produced a 'yah-boo' politics of confrontation, polarization and over-frequent changes of policy, which damaged business. A strong centre party would act as a brake on both the major parties' ideological enthusiasms. With enough seats, it would also push through proportional representation so that voters would be forced to choose in effect between moderate coalitions of the centre right and centre left. A three-party system, entrenched by proportional representation, would not only mean the end of socialism in our time: it would also mean the end of hyper-partisanship.

There was considerable sympathy with these arguments in Britain's board-rooms, especially in 1981 and 1982 when high interest rates, an over-valued pound and a sharp fall in demand were squeezing profits and producing a rash of bankruptcies. Proportional representation had been backed in some City quarters for many years. But the lunches and receptions for businessmen that were held at Cowley Street and elsewhere failed to produce any substantial company donations; and the direct mail appeals to smaller, private, companies yielded almost nothing.[19] The attitude of business was one of all support short of actual help.

Business contributions were discouraged by a combination of factors. None of the SDP leaders was accustomed to holding out the begging bowl, and some felt uncomfortable doing it ('Jenkins was hopeless, didn't speak their language at all').[20] More important, the overwhelming majority of directors were, of course, Conservatives, and on every board there were enough Conservative loyalists to block proposals to contribute to the SDP. The SDP's supporters were often compromised, in addition, by the fact that in the past they had opposed donations to the Conservative party on the grounds that the company should stay out of party politics. The larger companies thought their interests lay in political neutrality. They needed to be on good terms with the government of the day, whatever its partisan composition, and they were particularly reluctant to jeopardize relations with as unforgiving a government as Margaret Thatcher's: as one SDP person put it, 'They just wouldn't put their heads above the parapet.' Even after rising to be chairman of ICI, Harvey-Jones had to accept his board's strong preference for political neutrality. It was in any case too early to expect contributions in 1981 and 1982. The party was still very new and its electoral prospects, whatever the polls suggested, were uncertain. Most companies are naturally cautious and require a detailed prospectus before investing in a new venture. By 1983, however, when the SDP was more of a known quantity, the Conservatives were set fair to win the next election and most companies saw little benefit in propping up the SDP.

For all these reasons, the Social Democrats soon found that they would have to manage without the kinds of institutional life-support machines that the Conservative and Labour parties rely on. The lack of assets that could be used as security severely reduced the scope for borrowing and meant that subscriptions and private donations formed the party's entire financial base. It would have to live strictly within its means. In 1981–2 the party's central income for routine expenditure (i.e. excluding funds earmarked for the general election) amounted to a healthy £855,000 (see Table 13.4), raised almost entirely from subscriptions. As membership declined, however, so did the party's central revenue, despite a considerable increase in *ad hoc* donations. By 1984–5 subscription income was only half that of 1981–2 (and even less in real terms), and total revenue dropped to a low point of £663,000, a real fall of nearly 40 per cent. From 1985 onwards, the party's revenue increased in tandem with the increase in subscription income from its growth in membership, but also through a sharp jump in donations, which accounted for half its revenue by 1986–7.

Despite the party's success in attracting more donations, its income in 1986–7 was still 16 per cent below the level of its first-year income in real terms. The party's annual central income comfortably exceeded that of the Liberals, which ranged from roughly £400,000 to £500,000 during this period despite the Liberal party's larger membership, a difference that reflected the very different balance of power in the two parties between headquarters and constituencies. But the SDP's central income was only one-sixth of that of the Labour and Conservative parties.[21] One SDP MP used the phrase 'just enough, but not enough': the SDP's income was just enough to sustain a viable central organization, but not enough to finance a general-election campaign without reliance on large donations.

After the 1983 general election, the party belatedly gave a much higher priority to building up its membership and financial base, mainly at the prompting of its trustee and benefactor, David Sainsbury. The one department at Cowley Street to be spared drastic cuts was fund-raising and recruitment, which employed a staff of five; the press department, by contrast, was cut to three and the policy department to one office and a secretary.[22] The party then embarked on a variety of relatively minor fund-raising and recruitment ventures. A campaign to identify potential members and donors from the 1983 election canvass cards had a modest success, contributing to the small recovery in membership in 1984 and 1985. The Industrial Policy Association, which had been founded by Sainsbury and five other sympathizers in July 1982 as an SDP equivalent of Aims of Industry (its objective was 'to engage in research into and the promotion of business enterprise in a mixed economy'), recruited about sixty sympathizers from business and the City. After an abortive attempt to raise money through a parliamentary newsletter for the City, it turned into a discussion group, research trust and financial 'front organization'.[23] Another policy research group informally allied to the SDP was the Public Policy Centre, in which Taverne and Roger Liddle were active. Established in early 1983 as

249

a charity, it received support from, among others, the Bank of England, Shell and the BOC Group.

A more important initiative was a programme of direct-mail and direct-telephone fund-raising. The idea had a number of prima-facie advantages, not the least being that it fitted the SDP's structure and image. The party had already compiled a computerized list of members and sympathizers (unlike the other parties); and, in addition, many of its supporters were the type of busy, professional people who were happier writing out cheques than spending time raising money for the local party. As an added bonus, direct fund-raising, if successful, might reinforce the party's reputation for high-tech efficiency. In any case, since the earlier initiatives of selling merchandise and soliciting company donations had largely failed, there was nothing else that could be tried, and direct-approach techniques were enjoying great success in the United States.

Yet it was not certain that American-inspired methods could be transplanted into British soil. The tradition of political donations was weaker in Britain, and suitable mailing lists were not as easily available. Direct fund-raising was also a heavy and long-term investment requiring a substantial initial input of funds and the ploughing-back of early returns to develop the programme further.

As early as the autumn of 1982, Cowley Street tested a variety of direct-mail techniques, but the 1983 general election was called before anything very elaborate could be attempted. In 1984, following the election, the SDP consulted an American company, Craver Mathew Smith, the leading fund-raisers for the Democrats, and, with the help of a £40,000 donation from David Sainsbury, set up a direct-mail fund-raising unit, equipped with high-quality laser printers to produce smart, professional-looking letters. It started experimenting with computer-generated personalized election leaflets at the Tyne Bridge by-election in December 1985, and by the time of the Greenwich by-election in February 1987 had mastered the techniques of 'segmenting the market' and 'targeted personalized mail'—i.e. slanting leaflets according to the known social and political characteristics of the recipients.[24] In the 1987 general-election campaign, these techniques were extended to fund-raising. Three direct-mail appeals to members and supporters produced £700,000—four times as much, in real terms, as its appeal to members had raised in 1983 and more than the Conservative party had managed to raise by the same methods.[25]

As we shall see, these sums provided the bulk of the party's £1 million campaign fund in 1987 and saved it from having to depend as heavily as it had four years earlier on a few wealthy individuals. By the standards of a small British party largely reliant on small personal donations, the direct-mail initiative proved to be a considerable—and unexpected—success. By 1987 the SDP had, perhaps, begun to crack the problem of party finance.

Financing the 1983 and 1987 General Elections

In 1983, according to the leading authority on British political finance, the Alliance 'proved far more successful in collecting both small and large individual contributions than any third party since the First World War'.[26] This was almost entirely due to the SDP. About £150,000 came in small donations from 10,000 members in response to a campaign appeal. The remaining £850,000 was raised by the Financial Advisory Committee, a group of a dozen sympathetic business-men. David Sainsbury, the chairman, spent the first few days of the campaign telephoning his contacts: 'I was more successful than I expected. Many of those who had vaguely promised that they would do something but had then been quiet did cough up once the election was announced.' Some of the contributions came from the individual proprietors of firms, others from the pockets of those directors who had been unable to persuade their boards to contribute. In 1987 the Sainsbury committee raised £300,000 and would probably have drummed up more if it had been convinced of the need.

By far the most generous donor was David Sainsbury himself. A major shareholder in his family chain of supermarkets, as well as its finance director, he was one of the wealthiest men in Britain. Quiet and unassuming in manner, he was without immediate political ambitions of his own and served the party as a trustee from 1983 and as a member of its Finance Committee. He saw the party as a vehicle for his 'social-market' ideas about economic and industrial policy (he wrote a Fabian pamphlet on the subject in 1980) and was a strong supporter of Owen, whose policy views on the subject he came to influence. He earmarked most of his donations for specific purposes, including by-elections, the 1983 advertising campaign, public opinion research, a survey of members and the development of direct-mail fund-raising. The total amount he gave between 1981 and 1987 was probably in the region of £750,000. The SDP did not depend on Sainsbury for its day-to-day operations, but it was to him that it inevitably turned for new projects.

Corporate funding continued to be negligible. In the financial year covering the 1983 election, the SDP received six company donations totalling £12,300 and the Alliance four amounting to £15,500 (see Table 13.5)—compared with the £3.4 million donated either to the Conservative party or to one of its front organizations such as the Economic League and British United Industries. After Owen became leader in 1983, the party hoped to attract more company support. Owen was held in more respect in business circles than Jenkins, Williams or Rodgers and he cultivated his City contacts. He gathered around him a group of young entrepreneurs who supported his 'social-market' economics, applauded his tough stance on trade unions and admired his personal dynamism. From 1984 to 1986 the total of company donations did increase, but it was still modest. In the financial year covering the 1987 election, eleven companies contributed £57,000 to the SDP, and fourteen companies gave a similar amount to the Alliance— compared with the £4.5 million donated to the Conservatives and their allies. Most donations took the form of modest side bets: only three donations reached five figures, and in all but three cases the same company contributed an equal amount or more to the Conservatives.[27] Business had still not been won over to the SDP in any serious way.

The amount of revenue raised by the area parties was also meagre. In 1983 their 311 candidates spent £864,000 altogether, but almost half of this sum, £380,000, was provided by central grants (see Table 13.6). By comparison, 97 per cent of the constituency spending of Conservative candidates, 73 per cent of that of Labour candidates and 81 per cent of that of Liberal candidates was met by locally raised funds. This pattern was even more marked in 1987, when locally raised funds accounted for almost all the spending by Conservative, Labour and Liberal candidates but only 41 per cent of that of SDP candidates. In 1983 the average sum raised locally for each SDP candidate was only £1,556, well below the amounts found by local Conservative, Labour and Liberal parties.[28] In 1987 the average sum raised per SDP candidate by area fell in absolute terms (to £1,405) and was less than half that generated by Liberal associations for their candidates (£3,472). The reason did not lie in a lack of generosity or commitment on the part of SDP members; in fact the sum raised locally per SDP member was more than in the other parties in 1983 and equal to that in the Labour and Liberal parties in 1987. The reason lay simply in the sheer lack of members.

Despite the paucity of company donations, and contrary to the leadership's fears, the SDP did raise enough money centrally to mount adequately financed, if less than lavish, election campaigns (see Table 13.7). In 1983 it spent £467,000 in the run-up to the campaign (including about £250,000 on a billboard poster campaign in early 1983) and £1.07 million during the campaign itself, a total of £1.54 million. This accounted for the lion's share of the Alliance's central expenditure. The Liberals spent only £365,000, and a small joint Alliance fund disbursed a mere £47,000, making an Alliance total of £1.95 million. In 1987 SDP spending was one-third less in real terms—a total of £1.3 million—almost all of it spent during the campaign. The Liberals again spent much less (£280,000), but the Alliance fund spent more than in 1983 (about £250,000), making an Alliance total of £1.82 million—a drop of 25 per cent compared with 1983. Expenditure at both elections was an enormous advance on the mere £200,000 spent centrally by the Liberals in 1979—a sixfold increase in real terms—and indeed on Liberal spending at any post-war election.

Thus, for the first time since the 1920s a third party's campaign finance was such that it could compete with the two main parties on comparable, if still unequal terms. Michael Pinto-Duschinsky estimates that the disparities in central spending between the parties narrowed from a Conservative : Labour : Liberal ratio of 12 : 7 : 1 in 1979 to a Conservative : Labour : Alliance ratio of 12 : 7 : 6 in 1983. In 1987 it widened again to 12 : 6 : 3 (as much because of real increases in Conservative and Labour spending as of the real decline in Alliance spending).[29] Nevertheless, it was enough in both elections to make possible the professional production of party election broadcasts and the undertaking of some private opinion-polling, items that the Liberals had never been able to afford in the past. It also enabled SDP candidates, by means of a central grant, more or less to match their rivals' constituency spending (as Table 13.8 shows).[30] Every SDP candidate got some help, and no candidate in a realistically winnable constituency was genuinely short of money; Liberal candidates, on the other hand, received negligible sums in 1983 and none at all in 1987.[31] Compared with Liberal candidates in 1979, local campaign expenditure by SDP candidates increased in real terms by 76 per cent in 1983 and by 80 per cent in 1987. Funds were inadequate only for such luxuries as press advertising, which, being enormously expensive and of dubious electoral advantage, is almost certainly poor value for money.[32] In Cowley Street it was generally thought that finance was adequate and that no constituency result turned on lack of funds, as later research was at least partly to confirm.[33] The paucity of company donations and the relative poverty of area parties were more of a symptom of the party's electoral weakness than a cause.

Any judgement on the SDP's organization-forming efforts has to recognize that creating a new and durable national party is extraordinarily difficult. Most attempts soon fail, as the Greens' collapse after their success in the 1989 Euro-election illustrates. By historical standards the building of the SDP was a considerable success. Within fifteen months of its launch it possessed a skillfully constructed constitution, an elected leader, a comprehensive programme of policies and a professionally staffed headquarters. The SDP leaders achieved their objectives of establishing a centralized and professional national organization largely free from faction fighting. Its election funds were sufficient in 1983 for the best-financed third-party campaign for sixty years. At the centre, its organization and funding far outstripped that of the Liberal party, which claimed three times its membership. But, like the Liberals, the SDP was dependent for most of its short existence on the continued good will of a few wealthy supporters, in particular David Sainsbury, and it only began to develop a viable financial base and successful fund-raising methods in 1987. Its most serious weakness—and the main failure of the 1981–7 period—was the party's small membership base, which left it without a local organization to speak of in many areas and with an inadequate flow of cash to the centre.

The inadequate size of the membership probably reflected modern social trends more than mistakes on the part of the SDP's leadership. All the main parties have seen their membership decline since the 1950s.[34] Building up a membership is inherently slow and difficult in an era when the mass media have taken over many of the campaigning (and social) functions of local party organizations. In any case, recruiting members has probably become less important to a party than cultivating the good will of the press and television. Chapter 14 describes the SDP's attempt—and its failure—to secure that support.

14

• • • •

A Media Party?

From the moment of its birth the SDP was widely dubbed 'a media party'. Sometimes the phrase was used admiringly. More often it was used pejoratively. Those who used it pejoratively in some cases believed that the SDP was, literally, a media creation: that some combination of press barons and television higher-ups had first badgered the Gang of Four into leaving the Labour party and then ensured that the SDP, when it was launched, received a warm welcome. For example, in the view of the conspiracy theorists, the BBC had offered Roy Jenkins the platform of the Dimbleby Lecture knowing that he would use it to attack Labour and launch a new party. On this view, the SDP was not a genuine mass party with roots in local communities and organizations: it was an artificial concoction of public-relations executives and the metropolitan media—in James Callaghan's dismissive phrase, a 'piece of fluff'. According to *Tribune*, the BBC was 'stuffed with SDP men' and had 'its own political party now'; according to Tony Benn, the BBC was actually an 'agency of the SDP'.[1]

The belief that the media plotted to bring the SDP into existence was confined to Labour left-wingers and has no substance. The less partisan and conspiratorially minded nevertheless believed that they could detect a natural affinity between the SDP and the media, especially between it and the quality press. Much was made of the well-known journalists who lent their names to the 'Guardian 100' advertisement or subsequently revealed themselves to be SDP supporters: John Morgan, the political broadcaster; Marjorie Proops, the *Daily Mirror*'s veteran agony aunt; Anthony Sampson, the *Observer* columnist and author of *Anatomy of Britain* and Polly Toynbee, the *Guardian*'s columnist. Serious journalism, it was implied, tended to share with the SDP not only the same political outlook but similar values and life-styles. The SDP's emphasis on moderation had a natural appeal for broadcasters ingrained with the principle of partisan balance, and the party's revolt against the two major parties raised a cheer among people instinctively sceptical of the existing establishment.[2] Likewise its rejection of 'slogan politics' was attractive to people aware of the complexities of government, and its self-conscious modernity appealed to the professional trend-spotters in broadcasting studios and newspaper offices. The SDP, on this view, was not the artificial creation of media institutions: it was the natural party of media people.

The SDP itself was more than content to live with the 'media-party' tag. In the first weeks of its existence it was little more than a coterie of Westminster politicians looking for followers in the country. Without members, money or machinery, it was wholly dependent on the media to convey its purposes, mobilize potential support and sustain an identity. As one of the leaders told us, 'We had no choice: it was either media-creation or no creation at all.'

Two events in particular symbolized the party's apparently special relationship with the media: the official launch in March 1981 and the rolling conference in September. The Steering Committee's decision to treat the launch as a media event resulted in lavish publicity—£15 million worth of free advertising according to one calculation.[3] In all but one of the national dailies (the *Sun*) the launch made the main front-page story, and was the subject of the first leader and also the focus of a full spread of coverage in the inside pages. The reporting was done in a spirit of bemused good will, and leader comment ranged from benevolent neutrality in the partisan press—'This must be good for Britain' (*Daily Mail*)—to an unambiguous welcome in the less committed papers. The launch also achieved its practical political objectives. Within a fortnight, the SDP recruited over 40,000 members and saw its support in the polls jump by five percentage points.[4]

The style and scale of the Connaught Rooms launch had a significance beyond its immediate organizational objectives. It was intended to impress upon the other parties and the media that the Social Democrats were not just another minority party of naïve amateurs. The SDP was not going to allow itself to be bracketed with parties like Plaid Cymru and the Ecologists (as the Greens were then called), or for that matter with many Liberals, who took positive pride in their other-worldly rejection of the media's slick and superficial ways. The SDP saw itself as a party of shrewd and experienced politicians entitled to play in the big league. A professionally organized media event was a way of telling the world—and convincing themselves—that they were a force to be reckoned with.

The SDP's decision to 'roll' its first national conference from Perth to Bradford to London was likewise an attempt to revive media coverage, at the regional as well as the national level. Closeted on the northbound and then the southbound trains with leading SDP figures, journalists undoubtedly produced more copy—and friendlier copy—as a result. There was plenty to drink, the conversation flowed and the jokes were funny. The SDP press office circulated 'The Travelling Hacks' SDP Song-Sheet' so that a sing-song could be held on the 'moderates' express'. Everybody had a rollicking good time. It was the high point of media–SDP rapport.[5]

These early successes left the SDP with a reputation for obsessive publicity-mindedness and an uncanny ability to manipulate the media. It was alleged that in return the party received overgenerous media coverage and comment. The reality of the SDP's relations with the media throughout its history was, however, very different. It was a story of an almost complete failure with the press and only a partial success, after a sustained legal campaign, with television. The launch and the rolling conference turned out to be the only instances of the SDP creating a major media event, despite a number of attempts to repeat the trick in later years. Far from being the beginning of the party's special relationship with the press and television, they were the end of it. After 1981 the party faced the same central problem as other minor parties: it depended on the media far more than the media depended on it. Despite courting the press and television more aggressively than the Liberals or the other small parties had ever done, the SDP largely failed to attract media interest, let alone media support.

The SDP and the Press

It was not editorial plotting or journalists' personal preferences that gave the initial SDP breakaway and the launch their high press profiles; nor was it the supposed public-relations skills of leading Social Democrats. Rather, it was the fact that, by the conventional news criteria, the emergence of the SDP was an irresistible story.[6]

All the essential ingredients were present. There was novelty: the creation of the first major national party in Britain since 1900. There was conflict: the party emerged from—and further deepened—the turmoil in the Labour party. And there were real stars: the Gang of Four were all senior politicians and two of them, Roy Jenkins and Shirley Williams, were well known to the general public. Personal drama could be conjured out of their 'agonizing' over whether to leave the Labour party and their 'heartbreak' at doing so. The SDP and Liberal Davids could be portrayed as taking on the Labour and Conservative Goliaths. Opportunities for speculation were similarly endless: how many MPs would defect and who would be next? In addition, a serious issue arose: the future of the British party system and of the SDP's place in it. The breakaway was undoubtedly newsworthy. An equivalent breakaway from the Conservative party would have received attention on an equally grand scale.

But after the launch the SDP ceased to be news in anything like the same sense. Not only did the novelty and the drama fade, but the SDP was at a disadvantage in parliament, which is the media's primary source of political material. The SDP had no supply days on which to initiate debates and only a small number of MPs who could make a splash in debate or at Question Time. Because the Speaker strictly alternated between the government and the opposition benches in choosing whom to call, David Owen (as the party's unelected parliamentary leader from 1981 to July 1982) was normally the sixth in line, by which time journalists had long since left the press gallery to file their copy.

The SDP's and the Liberal party's low media profile is summarized in Figure 3, which plots the number of references of any kind made to the SDP or the Alliance between January 1981 and June 1983 on the front pages of three very different

---

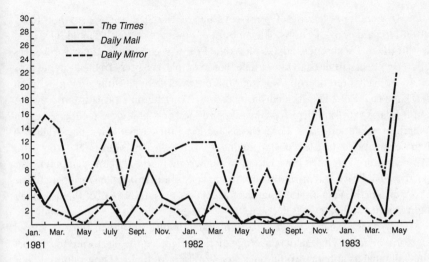

Fig. 3 Front-page mentions of the SDP, or the Liberal–SDP Alliance, in *The Times*, *Daily Mail* and *Daily Mirror*, January 1981–May 1983

newspapers: *The Times*, the *Daily Mail* and the *Daily Mirror*. The figure illustrates how quickly the press lost interest in the SDP. After its launch, the party virtually disappeared from the tabloids' front pages. For example, references to it of any kind appeared only twice a month on the *Mirror*'s front page during the Alliance's run of by-election successes and the SDP's recruitment of defecting Labour MPs in the autumn and winter of 1981–2. In the popular press the SDP was relegated to minor-party status almost as soon as it had been formed. Even in the quality press, coverage was largely confined to three areas: by-elections and opinion polls, party conferences and internal quarrels. There were bursts of publicity in June–July 1981 (Warrington), September 1981–March 1982 (defecting MPs, the rolling conference, Croydon North-West, Crosby, Hillhead and the seats row) and in May–June 1982 (Owen on the Falklands, local elections), but generally the SDP was mentioned no more than twice a week on *The Times*' front page.

In other words, there was no sustained press campaign on behalf of the SDP. Quality coverage was not only intermittent, it was generated by events over which the SDP had little control. Whenever, following the 1981 rolling conference, the SDP sought publicity by taking an initiative of its own—whether serious or gimmicky—it almost inevitably failed. In the autumn of 1982, for example, the SDP began to hold regular parliamentary lobby briefings much as the government and the Labour opposition did, but few correspondents turned up. Policy proposals and major speeches went unreported in the tabloids and earned only a few inches in the serious press. In January 1983, the relaunch of the Alliance to the accompaniment of the Aberystwyth Male Voice Choir in Central Hall, Westminster, was a flop.[7]

An additional feature of press coverage of the SDP was the extraordinary attention paid to by-elections. The amount of coverage certainly would have been less in the SDP's absence, but, so far as the SDP was concerned, the coverage was often sceptical rather than favourable. For example, the press treated Roy Jenkins as an unlikely pretender in Warrington. Contrasts were gleefully drawn between his *haut bourgeois*, EEC-funded life-style and Warrington's proletarian ways. A *Daily Express* cartoon depicted him stepping out of a first-class compartment at Warrington station, with Lord Harris behind him carrying his bags (labelled Brussels), and a puzzled porter saying to him: 'Wowwington? No, this isn't Wowwington. You must have got off at the wrong place.' Jenkins' campaign was portrayed as brave and intriguing but not as something to be taken seriously. In the Croydon North-West and Darlington by-elections, press treatment of the Alliance's lightweight candidates was derisive.[8]

Nor does publicity for the SDP and the Alliance appear to have produced electoral benefits. Had media coverage alone persuaded the electorate to support the Alliance, its support would have steadily risen in the local and national polls during the by-election campaigns; but there was no such trend. In Warrington the Alliance's support in the local polls did rise, but only in the final few days (for reasons that almost certainly owed more to late campaigning by the Gang of Four than to the media). In Croydon North-West and Crosby, Alliance support barely moved in the course of the campaign. In Hillhead it dipped midway before recovering at the end. Nationally (as Table 14.1 in Appendix 5 shows), support for the SDP and the Alliance generally remained steady in the month preceding a by-election and only jumped if they won or came near to winning. The SDP did not owe its early by-election successes to a good press. It owed its extensive press coverage to its by-election successes.

The truth that coverage depends ultimately on credibility was revealed in the 1983 and 1987 general elections. On both occasions the Alliance entered the campaign without any realistic prospect of forming a government or even, given the Conservatives' overwhelming lead in the opinion polls, of holding the balance. On both occasions its support slipped in the first week of the campaign, so that it looked as though the Alliance would barely improve on the Liberals' 19–20 per cent of the vote in 1974. And the Alliance was treated accordingly. On Martin Harrop's calculations, it received 16 per cent of the total party coverage among the eight national dailies in 1983 and 21 per cent among the nine in 1987, with slightly higher proportions in the quality press.[9] In the light of the polls, this level of coverage was not unreasonable.

The nature of the coverage, too, reflected the Alliance's minor-party status. Apart from brief inside-page summaries of the Alliance's manifesto early in the 1983 campaign, almost nothing about its policies appeared in the popular press. Why waste readers' time with proposals that would never be implemented? Interest in the Alliance was largely confined to the re-election prospects of the SDP leaders and to the Alliance's potential impact on Conservative and Labour fortunes. At its morning press conferences the Alliance's spokesmen were asked about little except the polls. Only in the final few days of the campaign, when the Alliance appeared to have overtaken Labour and had a glimmer of a chance of narrowing the Conservatives' lead, did the quality press (but not the tabloids) begin to take an interest in Alliance policies, notably on defence.[10]

One aspect of the party's treatment in the press particularly disappointed the SDP's leaders. Not a single national newspaper, daily or Sunday, ever unequivocally urged its readers to vote for it. In 1983 the newspapers that came closest were the *Guardian*, the *Observer* and the *Sunday People*, but their position amounted to 'not Labour, but not a Conservative landslide either'. All three regarded the Alliance as a means of preventing a runaway Conservative victory and therefore recommended tactical voting; but, in the absence of precise guidance about how or where to vote tactically, the advice was less than helpful to their readers—or the Alliance.[11] In 1987 the *Independent* supported David Owen's ideas about a social market but did not endorse the SDP, while the *Mail on Sunday* switched to the Conservatives after an earlier period of sympathy for the Alliance and *Today* urged its readers to vote tactically in favour of a coalition government.

It was, of course, no surprise that the overwhelming majority of newspapers continued to give unqualified support to the Conservatives; but on their past record one or two papers might have been persuaded to side more openly with the Alliance. *The Times*, for example, had campaigned in the early 1970s for a re-alignment of the left, specifically for a moderate centre grouping led by pro-EEC Labour politicians like Roy Jenkins, George Thomson and Shirley Williams; it had vociferously supported Dick Taverne in his 1973 by-election and Reg Prentice in his battle for reselection at Newham North-East; and in each of the four elections from 1966 to October 1974 it had urged its readers to return more Liberal MPs. Similarly, the day after the SDP was launched, *The Times* leader made sympathetic noises: 'Most of the policies which they put forward in their twelve-point programme yesterday are ones which we as a newspaper have long supported.' But little more than two years later the paper's election leader was dismissive: the Alliance was proposing an unworkable inflation tax, a pie-in-the-sky benefits reform and muddle over defence; it was 'not yet capable of achieving power or of knowing quite what to do with it'.[12]

There were two reasons for this shift in tone. The first was the change of ownership that took place in 1980. The new owner, Rupert Murdoch, was a staunch admirer of Margaret Thatcher, and a lunch with the Gang of Four left him less than impressed.[13] He chafed at the amount of coverage extended to the SDP in early 1981, and he bridled even more at the prominence given to anti-government news and comment. After the dismissal of Harold Evans in March 1982, *The Times* took an unswervingly pro-government line.

The second reason was that, in company with other Conservative newspapers, *The Times'* initial welcome for the SDP was premised on a particular right-wing view about what its place in the British party system should be. As a means of realigning the left, it was applauded. Its role was seen as being to offer the electorate a safe left-of-centre alternative to Labour, thereby isolating the extreme left in a weakened Labour party. This was what the SDP appeared to promise when it was founded. But the party's function was certainly not to challenge the Conservative party directly. Hence the Conservative press's increasingly sharp antagonism to the Alliance in the final few days of the 1983 campaign. *The Times* and other Conservative newspapers wanted an Alliance opposition rather than a Labour opposition, but that emphatically did not mean that they preferred an Alliance government to a Conservative government.

The *Guardian*'s lukewarm attitude towards the new party is harder to explain. In all but three elections since the war, the *Guardian* had recommended the return of more Liberal MPs, and since the mid-1970s it had repeatedly rejected the two major parties' more fundamentalist positions. When the SDP was formed, the *Guardian* described its principles as 'a mix of commitments close to that which this paper has advocated over the years'. Four of its leading journalists were SDP candidates at the 1983 general election—Malcolm Dean, Christopher Huhne, John Torode and Polly Toynbee—and another, Mary Stott, was elected to the party's National Committee. Peter Jenkins, its senior political columnist, and Derek Brown, its media correspondent, were known to be supporters. No newspaper had as high a proportion of Alliance supporters among its readers, and many SDP activists regarded it as akin to a house journal.[14] Labour's inept campaign in 1983 had turned the probability of defeat into a certainty. Thus all the circumstances seemed to point to an unequivocal *Guardian* endorsement of the Alliance.

The paper's internal politics probably best account for the ambivalent stance it eventually took. *Guardian* reporters belonged in almost equal numbers to the Alliance, mainstream Labour and an assortment of other socialist groupings. *Guardian* readers were also evenly divided between Labour and the Alliance; in the absence of anything more ideologically palatable, Labour activists, like Alliance activists, regarded the *Guardian* as their journal. Confronted with these conflicting loyalties and pressures, the *Guardian* chose to steer a safe course between the two main opposition groupings, best summarized as 'not a Conservative landslide'.

The Alliance's failure to win press backing meant that, among those who read a daily newspaper and who voted for it, the overwhelming majority—four out of five, or three million people—had ignored strident implorings to vote Conservative or, less frequently, Labour.[15] Such an outcome underlines the limits to newspaper influence, but it does not, of course, tell us how many potential Alliance supporters the partisan press succeeded in dissuading from actually voting for the Alliance. The press's electoral impact is difficult to estimate with any degree of precision because it cannot be entirely disentangled from other influences on the vote. Recent research suggests that the press tends to reinforce its readers' existing loyalties rather than converting them to new ones. Nevertheless, the partisan press can influence the uncommitted and younger voters, at least temporarily.[16] Table

14.2 shows the Alliance's share of the three-party vote at the 1983 and 1987 elections among the readerships of the national newspapers.

These figures offer a number of clues to the electoral damage done to the Alliance at the two elections by the partisan press. One is the much higher Alliance vote among *Daily Star* readers in 1983 (31 per cent) than in 1987 (16 per cent); this decline was probably partly due to the fact that the *Daily Star*, unlike its fellow tabloids, took a neutral line in the 1983 campaign (before eventually plumping for the Conservatives) but a combatively Conservative one in 1987. Another is the higher level of Alliance support among readers of the non-partisan or mixed-partisan press (such as the *Guardian* and the *Independent*) than among readers of the partisan press. Yet another is the very substantial Alliance vote of 43 per cent (ahead of both the Conservatives, 30 per cent, and Labour, 27 per cent) among the one in six minority who read no daily newspaper in 1983 and therefore relied primarily on television for their political news. These voters were not exposed to one-sided Conservative or Labour propaganda and probably for that reason found it easier to support the Liberals and the SDP.

Could the SDP have manoeuvred the press into giving it more favourable coverage? Many on the party's Communications Committee thought it could. If the Gang of Four paid personal attention to the senior editors of the Mirror Group, one early brief advised, they 'would be handsomely repaid'. A three-stage plan—involving a formal lunch, regular weekly briefings of the *Daily Mirror*'s senior political correspondents, Terry Lancaster and Joe Haines, and intermittent separate meetings with the three Mirror Group newspapers—was proposed. Nor, according to the brief, should other newspapers be entirely written off. Rupert Murdoch was 'usually open to persuasion, if not to be converted, at least to give us a fair crack'. At the Express Group 'Lord Mathews . . . is heavily Thatcherite. But if he is impressed with individuals . . . he tries to see that they are not too badly bashed.' In the early months, a few lunches in the editorial board rooms were arranged for the SDP leaders, but like the other elaborate plans for a media strategy they soon petered out. By the summer of 1981 the Communication Committee's agenda was filled with public-relations ideas for rekindling the press's attention, most of them wildly impractical. Few were attempted and almost none worked.[17]

By early 1982 the committee's public-relations specialists were urging the party to follow an 'events-based' strategy, which meant the devising of genuinely newsworthy events. But this advice, too, proved over-optimistic. The truth was that the party's ability to make news, as distinct from merely responding to it, was limited. The SDP was neither the government nor the main opposition party, and after May 1982 its chances of becoming either looked slim. The press accordingly became more interested in monitoring the party's prospects than its proposals.

An illustration of the SDP's weakness *vis-à-vis* the press was its decision to schedule its daily press conferences during the 1983 campaign to take place before those of the Conservatives and Labour. The idea was to shape the campaign agenda. But the attempt was in vain. The terms of the election debate were set by the Conservatives, who were the party in office and likely to remain there. John Lyttle, the SDP's experienced chief press officer, understood realities when he commented on the memorandum calling for an events-based strategy: 'This may be something of a snare and delusion . . . to make events the centrepiece of strategy may be to exaggerate our power to influence the news.'[18] This sober truth began to be reflected in the growing attention the SDP paid to television, where the prospects for wider coverage looked more promising.

SDP and Television

The SDP had good reason to expect television to be more rewarding than the press. The audiences for the early evening television news programmes on BBC 1 and ITV alone matched the total circulations of all the national dailies,[19] and the parties' election broadcasts similarly reached enormous numbers of voters.[20] Moreover, the public had always regarded television as more accurate and trustworthy than the press; it was by far the most persuasive of the media.[21] In BBC TV's 1983 election-day survey, 22 per cent of voters said their final decision on how to vote was influenced by a party election broadcast whereas only 7 per cent mentioned the influence of family and friends and a mere 4 per cent cited posters or advertisements in the press.[22] Party-election broadcasts were even more influential among those sections of the electorate who were crucial to the Alliance's prospects. The proportion claiming to have been influenced by party election broadcasts was 30 per cent among new electors, 37 per cent among vote switchers, 44 per cent among those who did not decide how they were going to vote until the campaign and 53 per cent among those who delayed their decision until the final few days. The number saying they were influenced in other ways was tiny in comparison.[23] Elections are won and lost in television studios far more than in editorial offices, let alone on doorsteps.

From the SDP's point of view, television had another advantage over the press. Newspapers consider it their right, even their duty, to be partisan; television is obliged to be impartial. Political advertising and editorializing are prohibited, and there is no equivalent of the newspaper leader. Although the definition of 'impartiality' and its enforceability in the courts is a matter of controversy (as the SDP was to discover), all the parties know that the BBC and IBA are acutely sensitive to charges of bias. This is partly because the broadcasting authorities, unlike the press, are ultimately beholden to politicians for their future, but also because the public-service norms of 'fairness' and 'impartiality' are ingrained.

Television's definition of fairness and balance has traditionally varied according to the type of programme involved. Outside election campaign periods, news bulletins reflect 'news values' and are under no injunction to afford the parties an equal or fixed portion of coverage. Current-affairs programmes, however, are subject to rough-and-ready quotas throughout the year. After the 1979 election, for example, the BBC set the tally for MPs' appearances outside election campaigns at 50 per cent Conservative, 40 per cent Labour, 8 per cent Liberal, 2 per cent others. In 1981, after some agonizing, it lopped 2 per cent off the major parties to give the SDP 4 per cent. Each party's allocation consisted of the mid-point between its share of the vote and its share of parliamentary seats, a compromise designed to deal with the unrepresentativeness of the electoral system.

An even more precise formula was formally applied to party political broadcasts (PPBs) and their election-campaign equivalents (PEBs). Since 1974 the formula for PPBs had been one ten-minute broadcast per year for every two million votes cast at the previous election, with a further ten-minute broadcast for 'remainders' exceeding one million votes.[24] The formula for PEBs was slightly more favourable to the Liberals and other small parties because it was primarily based on the number of parliamentary candidates that each party fielded. There was an additional and overriding assumption that, except for the news, broadly equal exposure should be given to the government and the official opposition.

This mixture of criteria defied consistency, reflecting the inherent vagueness of such principles as 'fairness' and 'balance'. But they had rarely been challenged because the broadcasters strove for and usually secured an agreement between the Conservative and Labour parties. The forum for negotiations on party broadcasts was a shadowy body, the Committee on Party Political Broadcasting (CPPB), chaired by the Leader of the House of Commons and attended by the party whips and senior officials from the BBC and IBA. The CPPB was a cameo of the cosy, two-party club of 'usual channels' and tacit understandings that the Alliance, excluded, wished to subvert. The committee's existence was not so much secret—it was set up as long ago as 1947—as carefully unpublicized. Votes were not taken, the aim being consensus, and its proceedings and its guidelines for allocations were confidential until prised open by the SDP. It certainly had no legal standing: the final decisions on PPBs rested with the BBC and IBA, who were under no obligation to broadcast PPBs at all.

Before the 1983 general election, the Social Democrats concentrated their campaign for more air time on the CPPB. Although the CPPB's remit was narrow, the SDP regarded its decisions as symbolically important. Moreover, direct representations to the broadcasting authorities by the SDP were invariably diverted to the CPPB. The SDP looked upon the Committee's deliberations as a useful dress rehearsal for any tougher action it might choose to take at a later stage.

The CPPB, however, proved incapable of agreeing on the entitlement to PPBs of a party that was new, initially very popular and in an electoral alliance with an established party. There was no 1979 track record to go on, of course, and given the parties' conflicting interests none of the obvious indicators of current strength was mutually agreeable. A meeting in December 1981 invited the SDP to present its case, agreed to include an SDP representative at future meetings and also to disclose its guidelines (although not its internal memoranda); but it refused to allocate the SDP any PPBs for 1982, whereupon Owen held a press conference and called for an emergency debate in the House of Commons, emphasizing the lack of disclosure and playing the open-government card.

It was the first shot in a long campaign which was to end up, three years later, in the courts. The next salvo was fired by Shirley Williams, after the broadcasting authorities had sidestepped the SDP's formal request for two five-minute PPBs prior to the local elections in May:

The broadcasting authorities are enjoined by the Broadcasting Act and the BBC Licence and Agreement to be impartial. Yet if the broadcasting authorities propose, the parties dispose. They control party political broadcasting through a committee which meets in closed session, holds no public hearings and is traditionally chaired by a government minister . . . The traditional quiet carve-up of broadcasting time between the Whips of the two old parties is as alien to open government as a conclave of the Mafia . . . we do not seek simply to join the club. Nor do we wish to interfere with the freedom of the two broadcasting authorities. On the contrary. They ought to be exercising that freedom right now—instead of letting Tory and Labour party managers trample over the rights of other parties. What we want is an open, impartial and defensible system for allocating broadcasting time, fair to all the parties and controlled by none of them.[25]

These remarks were made in the knowledge of a joint review paper circulated to the parties by the BBC and IBA which went some way towards meeting the SDP's demands. Stretching a provision in the committee's founding *aide-mémoire*, it proposed one five-minute PPB per year for the SDP until the next election.[26] More important, it accepted that the allocation of PEBs should be 'forward looking', reflecting changes of party popularity since the previous general election, and on that basis it proposed a 5 : 5 : 4 ratio between the Conservatives, Labour and the two Alliance parties.

At its first CPPB meeting as a bona fide member, in July 1982, the SDP demanded parity between the Alliance and the major parties on the basis of the previous eighteen months' by-elections, the local elections and the opinion polls. Reluctant to grant legitimacy to the young pretender, the Conservative and Labour parties proceeded to reject the joint review paper proposals, arguing that a new party consisting almost entirely of MPs elected under different colours was not entitled to any PPBs at all. The most they were prepared to agree to was a five-minute PPB for the *Alliance*, which could be devoted to the SDP if the Alliance parties wished. With Steel's agreement, Jenkins rejected the offer. Despite his warmth towards the Alliance, Jenkins was unwilling to accept an arrangement that questioned the legitimacy of the SDP—not only out of pride but because of the proposal's practical implications for the SDP's speaking rights in the House of Commons and its access to resources at Westminster. The rejection turned out to be a lost opportunity, because no more was on offer from the CPPB; in April 1983 the

SDP accepted an identical offer and presented its first (five-minute) party political broadcast—more than two years after the party was founded.[27]

The day after the 1983 general election was called the CPPB convened to decide on the allocation of party election broadcasts. The Alliance insisted on 5 : 5 : 5, the major parties on the 1979 ratio of 5 : 5 : 3. The BBC and IBA proposed 5 : 5 : 4. Far more than ten minutes of air time was at stake. By another of the unadmitted conventions that had evolved, the PEB ratio determined the parties' coverage in all political programmes, including the mass-audience news bulletins, for the duration of the campaign. A protracted and acrimonious meeting broke up without agreement. The BBC and IBA proceeded to impose 5 : 5 : 4.

As soon as the campaign began, normal news values were suspended in favour of the stopwatch. The formula entitled the Alliance to 28.5 per cent (i.e. four-fourteenths) of the news coverage of the parties; its actual coverage ranged between 25.6 per cent on Radio 4 to 30.9 per cent on Channel Four.[28] The same formula was applied to current-affairs programmes and interviews with the party leaders. Almost as many watched the extended interviews with David Steel and Roy Jenkins (14.0 million) as with Michael Foot (14.4 million) and Margaret Thatcher (14.9 million). The proportions who recalled watching at least one of the PEBs by the Conservatives (90 per cent), Labour (86 per cent) and the Alliance (72 per cent) also reflected the 5 : 5 : 4 ratio.[29] Thus the Alliance's disadvantage compared with the two major parties on television was very much narrower than in the press, including the quality press.

Despite the Alliance's protest at being denied 5 : 5 : 5 ('a monstrous injustice'), the broadcasters' decision was a generous one. The ratio had been 5 : 5 : 3 throughout the 1970s. When the BBC and IBA made their decision, the Alliance's electoral prospects looked no brighter than those of the Liberal party by itself in the two elections of 1974. Moreover, the allocation gave the Alliance far more exposure than it would have obtained on its 'news value' alone. Jay Blumler, the experienced academic observer of election news-making on television, found that journalists regarded coverage of the Alliance as a mildly tedious duty.[30] Although the Alliance did not present news, the news had to present the Alliance. It was soon dubbed 'the four-fifths party'. In the press, where no fairness doctrine applied, the party coverage ratio was 5 : 5 : 2.[31]

Television journalists' scepticism about the Alliance's news value, however, meant that, despite the stopwatch criteria, the Alliance was still side-lined. A detailed analysis of the 1983 campaign found that the Alliance featured in only 6 per cent of the lead stories on the television news, 16 per cent of the news headlines and 22 per cent of the first one-third of the extended news bulletins. Alliance-initiated stories fared even worse.[32] The Alliance thus got 5 : 5 : 4 in terms of quantity, not quality.

The journalists' view that the Alliance was less newsworthy than the two major parties owed something to prejudice and preconception; for most of them it was natural to 'think binary', to think of politics as conflict and of conflict as two sided: covering the Alliance was as awkward as having three boxers in a ring. Yet the journalists' assessment of the Alliance's intrinsic news value was on the whole realistic. At no point in the 1983 campaign, even when the Alliance looked set to overtake Labour in the opinion polls, did Liberals and Social Democrats have the remotest chance of winning or even holding the balance of power. They remained parties of protest rather than government, even if they were stronger and more credible than the Liberals alone had been.

Nevertheless, television did occasionally respond to Alliance overtures. When David Steel 'talked up' the opinion polls early in the campaign, the fact was duly reported on television. Another piece of media hype, the Ettrickbridge summit, was copiously covered at considerable inconvenience to the broadcasters.[33] Television was equally responsive to protests about real or imagined 'unfair' coverage. Early in the campaign, Cowley Street complained that the news broadcasts treated the Alliance as an also-ran, relegating it to the second half of the evening two-part campaign report when audience numbers were beginning to drop off. After a week, the BBC changed the format.

The Alliance undoubtedly benefited from its television exposure during the 1983 campaign; and (as Table 14.3 shows) it benefited more than its rivals. Among the one-fifth of voters who claimed to have been influenced by any of the PEBs, more voted Liberal–SDP (45 per cent) than Conservative (35 per cent) or Labour (20 per cent). Among the majority who denied being influenced, the Alliance vote was less than half as much (19 per cent). The apparent impact of the PEBs owed something to the relatively strong support for the Alliance among those voters— the switchers, the late deciders and the new electors—who had most reason to make use of the PEBs. But this is only part of the explanation. If these groups are further subdivided between the 'influenced' and 'uninfluenced', the Alliance's vote was consistently and substantially higher among the former.

Nor is there much doubt that it was the Alliance's PEBs that attracted recruits rather than Conservative or Labour PEBs that led to defections. The relevant measure is the *net* gain or loss to each party among all voters who cited that party's PEBs as an influence on their vote. In the BBC TV–Gallup election-day survey, 128 out of 3,429 respondents (3.7 per cent) said they were influenced in one direction or the other by a Conservative PEB. Among these there was a tiny surplus of 24 recruits over 18 defectors (the rest were loyalists)—a net gain of a mere 0.2 per cent. Among the 102 respondents who claimed to be affected by a Labour PEB, defectors outnumbered recruits by 21 to 14, a net loss of 0.2 per cent. The impact of the Alliance's PEBs was far greater. They were mentioned by 184 respondents (5.4 per cent), among whom recruits outnumbered defectors by 128 to 5, a net gain of 3.6 per cent.[34] Taking these figures at face value, each PEB was worth close to an additional 1 per cent of the vote to the Alliance. In the absence of PEBs, the Alliance would have been left with 22 rather than 26 per cent of the vote—at the probable cost of three SDP and four Liberal seats.

The persuasive power of the Alliance's PEBs was not a result of their being especially good; television professionals judged them as competent but not outstanding.[35] It arose, rather, from the simple fact that the amount of exposure given to the Alliance relative to the two main parties was so much higher during the campaign than before it. The same increase in exposure had helped the Liberals in previous elections. In 1979, for example, when the Liberals' support during the campaign doubled from 7 to 14 per cent, its three PEBs appear to have added at least 2 per cent to its vote. In fact Liberal support had risen in every campaign, bar one, since 1964.[36] The Alliance, like any other minor party, benefited from the replacement of newsworthiness by fairness as the criterion for coverage on television. The lesson was by no means lost on the SDP.

The SDP Goes to Court

Once the dust had settled on the 1983 election, the SDP again found itself almost entirely off the screen and the airwaves. The 5 : 5 : 4 election ratio was retained for PPBs—a considerable improvement on the pre-election allocation of 6 : 6 : 2.5[37] —and a broad balance was also applied to panel programmes like *Any Questions* and *Question Time*. But television and radio's main political output is news and in the news programmes the Liberals and the SDP rarely appeared. An SDP-commissioned content analysis of BBC TV's *Nine O'Clock News* and ITN's *News at Ten* conducted shortly after the election showed that the parties were covered in a ratio of Conservative 20 : Labour 16 : Liberal 1 : SDP 1 on the BBC and 51 : 36 : 1 : 1 on ITN.[38] A follow-up study a year later (13 February–20 April 1984) revealed little change: the ratios were now 12 : 4 : 1 on the BBC and 16 : 7 : 1 on ITN.[39] An independent study of the evening news bulletins' coverage of the miners' strike in 1984 reported a ratio of party coverage that was even more skewed—39 : 31 : 1— despite the SDP's claim to have a distinctive position on the issue.[40] Television coverage of the House of Lords debates was similarly restricted.[41] These figures were reflected in the public's unawareness of the Alliance parties and their leaders (as Table 14.4 illustrates). A September 1984 poll reported that a large majority claimed to have seen nothing on television about either Steel (62 per cent) or Owen (68 per cent) at any time in the previous month, whereas the proportion who could recall seeing something of them during the previous week was a mere 9 per cent for each.[42] Figures for press mentions are similar. To the ordinary public, the Alliance was almost invisible except at election time.

The varying amounts of coverage given to the different parties were, of course, largely driven by conventional news values. Downing Street acts; the opposition parties react. Not surprisingly, the Conservatives and Margaret Thatcher during the 1980s got the lion's share of coverage. The SDP found it almost impossible to create news despite David Owen's energetic campaign for media attention. On becoming leader, Owen turned his private office into a veritable assembly line for press releases. Barely a luncheon speech, conference address or evening meeting went undocumented or undistributed. The impact was marginal. The twice-yearly meetings of the Council for Social Democracy were too sedate and lacklustre for television; only the *Guardian* and *Independent* dutifully reported them in any detail. Publicity was effectively limited to the political calendar of the May local elections, the autumn annual conferences and the occasional by-election.[43]

Newsworthiness, however, did not entirely dictate the television coverage of the parties. The broadcasters felt obliged by the norm of balance to allow the opposition to respond to government actions and statements. But who, after the 1983 general election, was the opposition? In July 1983 the Alliance, led by the SDP, launched a campaign directed at the broadcasting authorities in which the two Alliance parties claimed equality of status with Labour on the ground that only two percentage points had divided their vote from Labour's in the election. That the Conservative party, as the government, received the most exposure was acceptable; that Labour should receive so much more than the Alliance, and that its spokesmen should be called 'shadow ministers', was not.

The BBC and IBA maintained that the election had changed nothing. In reply to Owen's and Steel's joint letter of complaint, the chairman of the BBC, Lord Howard, was blunt:

Parliamentary convention nominates the opposition party with most seats as Her Majesty's Opposition. As far as I know that continues to be the convention. It is one that we shall continue to observe in our coverage when seeking official comment on announcements of public policy. Your Alliance may disagree with the electoral system that awards you only 23 seats. But that is the reality . . . and the one that must be uppermost in our minds. So there can be no question of the BBC's granting to the Alliance near-parity of coverage with the Labour party.[44]

This pronouncement from on high left the SDP with no choice but to acquiesce or take legal action. Recourse to the courts might be dangerous. It would be construed as a threat to editorial freedom. It would cost money. Most important, the SDP's legal advisers were far from confident that the Alliance would win. Nothing in the BBC's charter or licence affected election broadcasting and, although in 1981 the Board of Governors had stated its objective to be 'to treat controversial subjects with due impartiality [in] programmes dealing with matters of public policy', such resolutions were not thought to be enforceable in the courts.[45] What little case law existed was likewise not wholly favourable. In 1979 a Scottish Session judge had ruled that it was 'not for the courts to lay down to the IBA how it should carry out its duties' (*Wolfe* v. *IBA*). In a more recent case brought by Provisional Sinn Fein against the BBC (*Lynch* v. *BBC*), the judge had ruled that the BBC had discretion in achieving balance and impartiality and was under no legal requirement to treat all parties equally, irrespective of their electoral support or number of candidates.[46]

The party therefore opted for a flanking attack. In June 1984 David Owen formally complained to the Broadcasting Complaints Commission (BCC)—a body set up by statute in 1980 and independent of both the BBC and IBA—that the Alliance was discriminated against in news and current-affairs programmes. Like the Press Council, the BCC did not possess the power to redress grievances or impose policy, but its judgements were published. Owen argued that the BBC's coverage was quite out of line with the Alliance's 1983 vote and its recent by-election support. Labour's status as the official opposition did not begin to justify the huge imbalance of coverage between it and the Alliance. In particular, the Alliance was entitled to the same opportunities as Labour to comment on government actions. The Alliance objected to references to Labour frontbenchers as 'shadow ministers'. The commission was requested to undertake a full investigation and, as a part of it, to call upon the BBC and the IBA to produce a record of party participation in all current-affairs programmes since the last election.

The BCC, however, quickly deflected this assault. The commission, its chairman replied, could only investigate complaints about a specific injustice in a *particular* programme, not about general coverage or editorial policy. The chairman later added for good measure that, even if Owen's complaint did fall within its terms of reference, the BCC would exercise its discretion and refuse to investigate: the commission was not in the business of reaching what would inevitably be a political judgement.

The issue now shifted to one of procedure: what recourse was open to an aggrieved political party if its case would not even be investigated, let alone decided, by the broadcasting body established to hear the public's grievances? It could not successfully petition the Ombudsman, who had no jurisdiction over the BBC and who denied having it over the Home Office in its role as the BBC's and the IBA's licensing authority. Owen, with Steel's support, thereupon applied to the Divisional Court to declare his original complaint to be within the BCC's jurisdiction and to order the commission to investigate it. The court's ruling, in January 1985, was mixed. Under the wording, if not the spirit, of the Broadcasting Act, the court said, the commission was wrong to claim that it had no jurisdiction. However, the nature of the SDP's complaint was essentially political, turning on the correct criterion for judging political balance. There were several rational and defensible approaches that the commission could take, but no clear guidance about which of them the commission should actually choose. Moreover, Owen's objective was a change of editorial policy, which the commission was neither intended nor empowered to recommend. The court held that the commission had not acted unreasonably in refusing to hear what the SDP had to say.

The SDP treated the case as a draw because it had to pay only its own costs; but, in effect, it had lost. Once again, a court had effectively declared that political broadcasting was a political, not a judicial, matter. Broadcasters could, if they wanted to, continue to play safe, taking a traditional line on the constitution, and depict British politics in parliamentary terms, divided two ways, rather than in electoral terms, divided three ways.

It was now open to the Alliance to sue either the BBC or the IBA. In May 1986 Owen and Steel decided to sue the BBC, because it was the 'more important and the public broadcasting corporation'.[47] The stated purpose of resorting to the High Court was to challenge the BBC on grounds of fairness and to force it to disclose its criteria and monitoring data; but a deeper purpose was to establish that the BBC was liable to judicial review and on that basis to exert further pressure for better coverage. In the event, the two settled out of court. The BBC agreed to provide the SDP with details of its monitoring data and also its criteria for assessing the fairness of news coverage in return for an SDP undertaking not to disclose the information. The questions of judicial review and fairness were not, however, pursued because the SDP was advised that, while it might win on the first, it would probably lose on the second and incur costs of £100,000 or more. The party had made some progress therefore, but very little, and coverage of the Alliance parties in news and current-affairs programmes did not increase noticeably. A content analysis of the evening news bulletins in 1986 reported that the Alliance parties accounted for only 6 per cent of all mentions and the SDP a mere 2 per cent.[48]

Yet politically the legal campaign was something of a success. It generated some much-needed publicity for the SDP in the quality press. More important, it was probably instrumental, together with the Alliance's successes in the Greenwich and Truro by-elections, in persuading the broadcasting authorities to grant the Alliance formal parity with the major parties for the 1987 campaign. It was allocated, as the Conservative and Labour parties were, five ten-minute PEBs, an improvement on the 5 : 5 : 4 ratio that had operated since 1983. By convention the Alliance, therefore, received an equal amount of coverage in news and current-affairs programmes during the campaign. This was a minor breakthrough in political television, the first time that the broadcasting authorities had effectively acknowledged the existence of a three-party system.

In contrast to 1983, moreover, television broadcasters also appear to have got used to the idea of three-party politics. A content analysis of the BBC's and ITN's main evening news bulletins in 1987 found that the Alliance was as successful as the two major parties in initiating stories and that it received equal coverage in copy initiated by the media. Stories about more than one party were usually about all three and not, as in 1983, confined to the Conservatives and Labour. And, although the Alliance parties appeared less frequently than the major parties in the early part of the news bulletins, especially in the lead stories, the discrepancy was less than four years earlier.[49]

Parity in the number of PEBs helped the Alliance parties, but by less than they had expected. Once again the Alliance's PEBs were particularly influential among the new electors, campaign waverers and late deciders. But in 1983 the Alliance's four ten-minute PEBs boosted its vote by an extra 3.6 percentage points; in 1987 its five ten-minute PEBs added only 2.7 percentage points, the equivalent of four seats (all won by Liberals).[50] The extra PEB—and thus the additional coverage in news and political programmes—for which the Alliance fought so hard turned out to be worth about an extra 0.5 per cent of the vote. It illustrated that formal 'fairness' of media exposure was a very limited asset when the party's own message lacked appeal.

For, despite television's policy of three-party equality, the Alliance totally failed to impose its own agenda on television's coverage in 1987. It was quite unable to focus media attention on its distinctive issue of constitutional reform or to mount any kind of sustained attack on the major parties. Tactical voting as a television topic was banned, because programme editors were told it might breach the law. Instead the Alliance found itself again on the sidelines, responding to attacks by the other parties and explaining away its own lack of lift-off in the polls and its internal divisions. Some of this failure stemmed from public-relations errors and the Alliance's political weaknesses, in particular the Liberals' splits over defence and the disagreements between Owen and Steel about their preferred coalition partners.[51] But, even if the Alliance parties had avoided these mistakes, so long as they remained in third place it was certain that the media would cast them in, at best, a supporting role. The media want to be where the action is. In 1987 that was not where the Alliance was.

The Alliance's procedural parity but substantive inferiority on television in 1987 symbolized the upper limit of its encroachment on the two-party dominance of the mass media. The Social Democrats' energetic campaign against the BBC and the IBA did compel the broadcasters to re-examine their policy on political broadcasting, disclose their criteria for balance and fairness and release their monitoring data; but it wholly failed to weaken the overwhelming importance of news values in political broadcasting between election campaigns or to eliminate their influence during them.

After its flamboyant launch, the SDP was unable either to create news about itself or, when it did, to influence the way in which it was portrayed. It never persuaded professionally sceptical journalists that, separately or together with the Liberals, it was a serious contender for office. Apart from occasional mid-term successes, what inevitably attracted most attention were rows and splits or unexpected set-backs in elections. The notion of a media inherently predisposed in favour of the SDP was a complete fallacy. The SDP's friends in the television studios and editorial boardrooms—whose numbers were anyway exaggerated—always put professional news values first. The media's inherent bias was in favour of the big parties, not the small ones, the winners, not the losers. The SDP, whatever anyone said, was always a minor party, never a media party.

15

• • • •

The Party of a New Class?

We have discussed whether the SDP was a new class of party. It is now time to consider a different question: whether it was the party of a new class. The formation of the SDP, one social historian wrote, was a 'delighted act of self-recognition by a new class coming out and discovering its common identity'.[1] But what new class? Answers at the time were not couched in terms of enduring economic or political interests but in terms of life-style and culture ('their homes are imitation farmhouses rather than miniature stately homes, with stripped pine rather than period furniture', and so on). Social Democrats, it was alleged, usually without a shred of evidence, were trendy and 'progressive' professional people, the advance guard of the claret-drinking, chattering classes, whose native habitat, as is well known, was NW3. Frank Johnson of *The Times* listed the SDP's factions as:

The Owenites; the Jenkinsites; the Elizabeth Davidites; those who want a successor to Polaris; those who want a successor to their Volvo; militant Saabs; supporters of Tuscany for August as opposed to the Dordogne; members of those car pools by which middle class families share the burden of driving the children to the local prep school; owners of exercise machines; people who have already gone over to compact discs . . . readers of *Guardian* leaders; and (a much larger group) writers of *Guardian* leaders.[2]

And similar yuppie characteristics were observed at an SDP conference by the Conservative politician and wag, Julian Critchley:

One has only to list the towns to which Social Democrats are prepared to travel—Bath, Buxton, Harrogate—to be told all one wants to know. Tories travel north in the company of a Jeffrey Archer [novel], Social Democrats take with them a copy of the Good Food Guide. And no wonder: Bath, Buxton and Harrogate between them number 18 entries in the good book; Blackpool has none.[3]

Party members saw themselves differently.[4] What distinguished them in their own eyes from members of the Conservative and Labour parties was not their style, but their ordinariness, not the class from which they came but their classlessness.

By this they did not mean that SDP members were drawn evenly from all social classes. Rather they meant that they did not define either themselves or the world in conventional class terms; and, to the extent that they thought along class lines at all, they did not associate themselves with the established classes to whom the Labour and Conservative parties pitched their appeal. As we shall see, the SDP members' notion of classlessness was not in fact inconsistent with their belonging to a new class.

Who joined the SDP? What and whom did they represent? An identikit picture can be constructed from no fewer than six sample surveys of SDP members, all conducted between 1981 and 1984.[5] The surveys revealed that the typical Social Democrat was a middle-class family man (man, not woman) in his late 30s or early 40s. He had a mortgage and lived in a suburb, a commuter village or one of the market or cathedral towns of southern England. He had moved into the area from another town to get a better job and would probably move again for promotion. His own parents were not poor but were of modest means, on the border between the 'respectable' working class and the lower middle class. He had passed the 11-plus, had gone to grammar school and had done well enough at school to enter university. He had just escaped national service. After school or university he had launched himself fairly successfully on a professional or management career. If he worked in the private sector, it was probably in the service rather than the manufacturing sector and on the 'staff' rather than the 'line' side of the organization. But he was more likely to work in the public sector, whether in a nationalized industry, the civil service, a local authority, a university or a hospital. He belonged to a professional association or a white-collar union, but without much enthusiasm, and he was certainly not a union activist.

In fact, until he joined the SDP he was not much of a joiner at all, being too busy furthering his career. Local politics tended to bore him because his roots in the local community were shallow, but he followed the national political scene closely in the quality media, especially the *Guardian*. He usually voted, sometimes Labour and sometimes Liberal, but again with little enthusiasm, and he did not get involved in party work until the SDP emerged. And even as an SDP member he was not particularly active, preferring to write out cheques for the party than to pound the pavements.

This caricature inevitably ignores minorities in the party. Many of the Labour refugees come from an older, working-class, community-minded generation with long experience of local politics. By contrast, the *prominenti*, who belonged to or advised the national policy groups, had had distinguished careers and belonged to one or more of the metropolitan policy-making networks. But most of the rank and file were remarkably similar to this caricature socially—and were remarkably unlike the electorate as a whole (see Table 15.1 in Appendix 5). Men outnumbered women by two to one. Almost half of all members (compared with about a third of the electorate) were aged between 25 and 44, despite the toll in time taken by family and career commitments at this age. Most significant of all, the members were indeed overwhelmingly middle class: three-quarters (77 per cent) of those with jobs were in the professions or management, compared with 16 per cent of the electorate, and only 10 per cent had manual jobs, compared with 54 per cent of the electorate. In the Newcastle-upon-Tyne party fully 85 per cent were owner-occupiers and only 5 per cent were council tenants, in a city where council tenants comfortably outnumbered home owners.

As well as being middle class, members were unusually well educated. In Newcastle 71 per cent had gone through some form of post-school education and 31 per cent possessed degrees—compared with 5 per cent of the local electorate. And among the most active members—those who attended the rolling conferences or the Councils for Social Democracy—these characteristics were still more pronounced. Activists were even more likely than ordinary members to be male, middle-class graduates in early middle age.

As soon as this bias became known, the media latched on to it. The SDP was said to be 'a residents' association' writ large, a 'middle-class club' run by 'Socially Distinguished People'. The only trouble with these labels, however, is that they do not distinguish between the SDP and the other parties, because (as Table 15.1 shows), the other parties' activists were equally male, equally middle class and equally middle-aged. Even at Labour party conferences, where there are numerous blue-collar trade-union delegates, a majority of the delegates (60 per cent) come from the professional and managerial classes. SDP activists were undoubtedly unrepresentative of the British electorate, but they were typical of British party activists as a whole.

Almost all active party workers are 'middle class' in the broad sense of that umbrella term. What distinguished SDP (and Liberal) activists from the Conservative and Labour counterparts was that they were concentrated in a particular segment of the middle class—the growing 'service class' consisting of highly qualified managers and professional people employed by large companies and public bureaucracies.[6]

This class has three distinctive characteristics which were shared by SDP activists and which are capable of shaping political values. First, SDP activists were upwardly mobile in class terms. The higher professional and managerial dominance of the SDP was only fractionally greater (82 per cent) than in the Conservative (79 per cent) and Liberal (80 per cent) parties; but the proportion who had risen from working-class or lower-middle-class beginnings was much greater (65 per cent compared with 43 per cent and 44 per cent). Labour activists, it is true, were even more likely to have come from the working and lower middle classes, but they were also more likely to have stayed there. The SDP's activists thus resembled Labour's in their social origins and the Conservatives' and Liberals' in their current status. They were, moreover, by far the most conscious of their modest origins, being the readiest to describe their childhood circumstances as relatively poor (66 per cent) rather than relatively good (34 per cent). They were acutely aware of having risen in the world.

Secondly, SDP activists had succeeded—and were conscious of the fact—
by virtue of their education and training. Their passport into the upper middle
class was their degree certificate or their professional qualification rather than
their capital, personal contacts or social polish. They were archetypal meritocrats.
Over half (53 per cent) had been to a grammar school, compared with much
lower proportions among Conservative and Labour activists (37 and 27 per cent
respectively); and over twice as many as in the Conservative and Labour parties (65
per cent compared with 27 per cent and 25 per cent respectively) had continued
their education beyond the age of 18. The SDP was *par excellence* the party of the
scholarship boy, the honours graduate and the self-made intellectual.

Thirdly, SDP activists tended to have jobs imbued with a public-service rather
than a profit-making ethic. They were not in the business of making money but of
communicating, caring and creating—as lecturers, teachers, researchers, consultants, journalists, editors, market specialists, social workers, nurses, community
workers, charity organizers, personnel officers and public servants. And they were
much more likely than Conservative or Liberal activists to work in the publicly
owned sector of the economy—the proportions were 54 per cent compared with
23 and 35 per cent—where the object was to provide services rather than make
profits and to maintain professional standards rather than achieve financial
solvency. (Labour activists worked in the public sector in ever larger numbers, of
course, but fewer in a professional or administrative capacity.) Few SDP activists (or
ordinary members) were self-employed: they were managers, not owners. In the
Newcastle-upon-Tyne party only 10 per cent were self-employed, no more than the
national average. The shopkeeper, small businessman and company director
continued to find his natural home in the Conservative party.

SDP members were not only drawn from a particular social sector: they came
from a particular generation. Half of all SDP members were born between 1937
and 1956. They therefore belonged to the fortunate generation that was too young
to remember the Great Depression or to have fought in the Second World War but
instead had come of age during the 'golden' Fifties and Sixties, the decades of
economic growth, full employment, educational opportunity and the securely
established welfare state. They were the beneficiaries of Butler's 1944 Education
Act, Beveridge's social security system and Bevan's National Health Service. They
had also escaped unscathed from the early 1980s depression (only 2 per cent of
SDP members were unemployed), although many of them were worried that their
children might not be so fortunate. By their own lights, the lives of SDP members
had been a success, and compared with both their parents and their children
success had come with relative ease. This they owed not only to their own efforts
but also to both an expanding educational system, which recognized their ability
and qualified them for their careers, and a growing public sector and corporate
private sector which were able to employ their skills. They had every reason to
hanker after the Butskellism of an earlier age that had served them so well.

The SDP, as we saw in Chapter 7, was born with blurred vision, the product of different views among its founders about the direction it should take. Seeking to establish a third force of the 'radical centre', Roy Jenkins envisaged the SDP appealing across a broad political spectrum to disillusioned moderates in both the Conservative and the Labour camp, to former Liberals who had given up in despair and to the non-partisan whom he believed were in search of a cause. The Gang of Three, on the other hand, regarded the SDP as a means of re-creating a modern party 'of conscience and reform'—what Labour had once been and might still have been if Gaitskell had prevailed over Clause IV. Their aim was to replace the existing Labour party on the left, not compete with it from the centre. The SDP, they assumed, would appeal mainly to disaffected Labour party members and supporters, that is, to people like themselves.

Jenkins, it is clear, had made the shrewder assessment of where the new party's actual members would be likely to come from. A *Weekend World* survey in November 1981 found that most SDP members (72 per cent) were joining a political party for the very first time. Only 15 per cent had ever belonged to the Labour party, and more than a third of them had let their membership lapse at least five years before.[7] An SDP survey in late 1984 found a similar pattern.[8] Not surprisingly, ex-Labour members and officers were more in evidence in the local leadership of the SDP, but even at this level they were in a decided minority.[9] While some area parties consisted of political innocents organized by ex-Labour 'pros', most were composed of novices led by other novices—the SDP's 'political virgins', as David Owen liked to call them.

As Jenkins envisaged, SDP members were drawn from across the entire political spectrum, not just from the left. Nevertheless, their ideological fulcrum was somewhat to the left of centre. Former Conservatives were in a small minority. At the 1979 election only 27 per cent of SDP members had voted Conservative compared with 44 per cent of the country as a whole. The remainder had split their vote equally between Labour (36 per cent) and the Liberals (35 per cent).[10] When an opinion poll asked them to choose a coalition partner, SDP members split 56 to 44 in favour of Labour despite the raw enmity that then existed between the parties. This bias to the left was even more pronounced among the activists: the 1979 vote of those who attended the 1982 rolling conference was 45 per cent Labour, 28 per cent Liberal, 23 per cent Conservative.[11] Asked what kind of party the SDP should become, many more said 'a party of radical change' (69 per cent) than said 'a party of moderate reform' (29 per cent). Ordinary members were much more cautious, however, and the figures were reversed: only half as many opted for 'radical change' (34 per cent) as opted for 'moderate reform' (65 per cent). The ordinary member, in other words, was cast broadly in Jenkins' mould, the activists in the Gang of Three's.

SDP members described both themselves and their party as being politically in the 'centre' or on the 'centre left'. Asked to place themselves on a nine-point scale running from 1 (far left) to 9 (far right), over three-quarters (77 per cent) of the Newcastle-upon-Tyne party members chose one of the central three points (4 to 6);

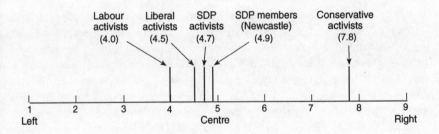

Fig. 4 The ideological self-placement of party activists

but more positioned themselves at point 4, just to the left of centre (34 per cent) than positioned themselves at point 6, just to the right of centre (15 per cent), and the average position of all members was a whisker to the left of centre, at point 4.9. Activists put themselves slightly further to the left (see Figure 4), a large majority calling themselves 'centre left' (62 per cent); a mere 13 per cent saw themselves as centre right or right.[12] As Figure 4 graphically shows, SDP (and Liberal) activists were positioned very close to their Labour counterparts but a long distance from Conservative activists. It was as if Labour, Liberal and SDP activists still considered themselves members of the same clan, despite family feuds, to whom the Conservatives remained the common enemy.

What did SDP members mean by 'centre left'? How did the phrase translate into views on policies? The *New Statesman's* then political editor, Peter Kellner, doubted whether the phrase had any ideological substance at all: SDP members were not 'united in anything more than their dislike of the other parties . . . the party appears to be more a marriage of convenience between disaffected ex-supporters of the other parties than a true meeting of minds on the centre ground'.[13] Did most SDP members possess a coherent ideology in the sense of having similar centre-left views on most major issues, or was their centre-left position, as Kellner suggested, merely the arithmetical average of a jumble of views that were otherwise unconnected?

Kellner's scepticism was in fact somewhat overdone. Although the policy views of early Conservative and Labour converts to the SDP usually differed in the expected direction, the distance between the two groups was generally narrow and narrowed still further as the SDP matured.[14] The only significant gaps were over a small number of issues that had traditionally divided the major parties: private schools, a wealth tax and the closed shop; and even on these issues differences between the two wings of the SDP rarely amounted to polarization: the majority of both wings almost always took the same side, even if by dissimilar margins.[15] Moreover, the gaps were bridged by the substantial proportion of members—fully 40 per cent—who were formerly Liberal or non-partisan. The party was not so much a marriage of convenience between strangers as a second—and largely harmonious—marriage between divorcees.

On most major issues, in fact, the SDP's membership was remarkably united, if unity is defined roughly as an agreement of at least three-to-one (see Table 15.2); on only a handful of issues was it divided, if this is defined roughly as agreement among 60 per cent or less. The party's unity was particularly conspicuous on the litmus-test issues that had led to the breakaway from Labour. Support for Europe, the 'good old cause', was almost unanimous (only 5 per cent favoured Britain's withdrawal), as it was for the sister cause of membership of NATO (93 per cent approved). On the economy there was a consensus for a statutory incomes policy (91 per cent) and a near-consensus for the status quo on nationalization (74 per cent). As regards industrial relations, members were at one on the need for compulsory secret ballots in trade-union elections and decisively in favour of the election of employees to the board of companies (76 per cent). Unilateral disarmament was heavily rejected by 78 to 22 per cent. And, on the sacred issue of proportional representation, there was, again, almost no heresy. On the main issues of principle, therefore, members of the SDP overwhelmingly endorsed the party leadership. They held a common set of views—views which might reasonably be described as 'centre left'.

Some of the specific policies subsequently adopted by the party, however, commanded less widespread agreement. Members were overwhelmingly in favour of an incomes policy in principle but were more divided on whether it should take the party's preferred form of an incentive tax (60 per cent) or voluntary restraint by trade unions (36 per cent).[16] The proposal to strip private schools of their charitable tax status had majority support (54 per cent), but significant minorities preferred either their full integration into the public sector (18 per cent) or no changes at all (28 per cent). The response to Scottish and Welsh devolution was lukewarm (58 per cent in favour, 42 per cent against) and the party's flirtation with parliaments for the English regions was decisively rejected (by 68 per cent to 32). Unlike the party leadership, in fact, the membership was cautious about constitutional change. The abolition of the House of Lords was massively rejected (by 86 to 14 per cent), a reaction in part to the idea's association with Tony Benn. The withdrawal of British troops from Northern Ireland, a popular proposal among the general public, was rejected by 62 to 38 per cent.

On most issues, however, SDP members shared a similar position which, while not unique to the SDP, nevertheless divided it sharply from one or other of the main parties. On macro-economic policy, for example, they adhered to traditional Keynesianism in opposition to the government's monetarism; the SDP's 1984 survey of its own members found widespread and strong agreement with the proposition that the 'government should spend more to create jobs, even if taxes go up for those in work'. Overwhelming majorities wanted the economy to be reflated by means of higher public spending (88 to 12 per cent) and preferred government investment to the free market by 81 to 19 per cent as a means of creating employment. There was less consensus on the priority to be given to tackling unemployment (63 per cent) as opposed to tackling inflation (37 per cent) and on the trade-off between higher public spending (57 per cent) and lower taxes (43 per cent); but the balance of opinion still clearly fell on the left.

SDP members were also on the left, but this time on the unpopular left, on a separate set of issues that might loosely be labelled 'minority rights'. There was strong majority support for 'positive action to give women equal opportunities' (79 to 21 per cent) and a clear, if less decisive, rejection (by 60 to 40 per cent) of the mildly worded proposition that 'voluntary repatriation of immigrants under some circumstances' might solve racial tensions. Finally, SDP members were evenly split over the death penalty (48 per cent in favour, 52 per cent against), but they none the less contained many more abolitionists than were to be found among the electorate at large.

Yet on other issues concerning individual rights SDP members adopted positions associated with the political right. In addition to supporting compulsory secret ballots in trade unions, a substantial majority wanted to proscribe the closed shop. The right of tenants to buy their council houses—which the Labour party opposed in the early 1980s—was also supported strongly (by 76 to 24 per cent). In the conflict between individual rights and collective solidarity, and between private choice and public provision, SDP members tended to side with the individual.

The party's members, therefore, did hold a distinctive set of views: their view on any one issue usually coincided with that of the members of one or other of the major parties, but the combination of views that they held was substantially different from that of either the Conservative or Labour parties.

But were these views in a meaningful sense coherent, shaped by consistent underlying principles, or were they merely a jumble of left, centre and even right-wing ideas—notes without a tune? One possible connecting thread was the common interests of the emerging 'service class' to which so many of the SDP's members belonged. The connection between class interest and policy beliefs should not be exaggerated. For one thing, the membership's most firmly held views—on Europe, NATO, nuclear defence and proportional representation—were on issues that do not lend themselves to analysis in class-interest terms. For another, it is not always obvious what the distinctive interests of a 'service class' are. Certainly many of the SDP members' economic views, notably the priority they gave to cutting unemployment rather than inflation, their support for higher income tax and their readiness to eliminate the private schools' tax advantages, were not obviously in the interests of the service class or themselves.

Nevertheless, most of the members' positions were those that one might expect from a well-educated, public-service salariat. Their Keynesian belief in reflation through state investment and state spending reflected the faith of the 'organization man' in economic planning as well as the happy experience of those who had grown up and begun to prosper during the Macmillan and Wilson years. The members' commitment to an incomes policy likewise made sense for salaried people in the public sector. Their support for employee representation on company boards and for a wealth tax sounds radical but was similarly consistent with their position as managers and experts rather than owners. Their marked hostility to the closed shop and trade unions' legal immunities, and their support for secret postal ballots, did not contradict their largely passive membership of unmilitant white-collar unions or their distaste for organizations that seemed to threaten their managerial and professional workplace authority. And their sympathy for progressive but unpopular causes such as women's rights, immigrants' rights and the abolition of the death penalty reflected the liberalism that higher education in Britain undoubtedly tends to foster. The values and outlook of this new section of the middle class—a concerned but not frightened or alienated middle class—thus did find a reflection in SDP policy.

They found a still more vivid reflection in the type of parliamentary candidates that they selected. 'He who can make nominations', an American political scientist once wrote, 'is the owner of the party.'[17] The SDP's studiously democratic procedures for candidate selection ensured that the party's members were indeed its 'owners'.[18] Not surprisingly, they chose candidates for parliament in their own image—and accentuated the image in the process. The party's ordinary members, as we have seen, were mostly male, middle class, middle-aged and well educated; the activists were more so; the candidates were almost uniformly so (see Table 15.3). SDP candidates in consequence were even more unrepresentative of the British electorate than the party members were: a mere 4 per cent were manual workers but 75 per cent were graduates. At the same time they resembled the types of candidates traditionally fielded by the other parties. In this respect, the SDP brought new faces, but not a different face, to British politics.

The SDP's selection procedure entitled all area party members to vote by secret postal ballot, whether or not they had attended the public meeting at which the short-listed nominees spoke. The possibility that glittering potted biographies would carry more weight than demonstrated political ability, to the advantage of 'celebrities', was raised after the embarrassing performance of Tony Cook in the Darlington by-election.[19] And there does appear to have been some preference for publicly known figures. All but one of the twenty-nine MPs seeking reselection were successful—and in their own constituency unless boundary revisions or the allocation of their seat to the Liberals had squeezed them out.[20] In addition, nine former Labour MPs were selected.[21] Moreover, a well-known name could compensate for inexperience: four *Guardian* journalists were selected, all but one of them new to electioneering.[22]

The SDP's mild discrimination in favour of women—every short list had to contain at least two women—produced only modest results. Women made up a mere 17 per cent of SDP candidates (forty-three in 1983, sixty in 1987), only slightly more than in the Liberal and Labour parties, which made no special provision for women. The root cause was the small number of women who presented themselves as candidates (only 11 per cent were on the national panel of accredited candidates), which in turn reflected the substantial time, travel and money that seeking a candidature, let alone being a candidate, involved—a case of household pressure rather than area party prejudice. Ethnic minorities fared even worse. Only 1.6 per cent of the SDP's candidates were black or Asian (four out of 311 in 1983, six out of 306 in 1987), about the same proportion as in the other parties.

More significantly, a mere 5 per cent of candidates (ten in 1983, fifteen in 1987) were manual workers, fractionally more than in the Conservative and Liberal parties but many fewer, of course, than in the Labour party (20 per cent). Thus the older, ex-Labour working-class element in the SDP was not picked to represent the party on the hustings. The main reason, yet again, appears to have been the very small number who put themselves forward, but the social atmosphere of the local parties probably played some part in dissuading them. The absence of any institutionalized trade-union presence in the SDP also effectively guaranteed that its parliamentary aspirants would be overwhelmingly middle class; as one commentator wryly observed, 'positive discrimination in favour of women appears to be acceptable . . . but no party appears concerned to rectify the under-representation of manual workers'.[23] As befitted a new party, the SDP's candidates were marginally younger than the major parties', but this was entirely due to the much larger number of incumbent MPs in the Conservative and Labour parties.[24]

There is nothing special about the SDP's candidates having been middle class. What did mark them out was their background in the intelligentsia rather than in the commercial and business sectors (see Table 15.4). Compared with Conservative candidates, far fewer were in business (22 as against 36 per cent) and considerably more were in the professions (54 as against 45 per cent). Even in the professions, many more were in education (30 compared with 10 per cent) and fewer in the law, finance or construction (16 compared with 26 per cent). Journalists and university teachers were particularly in evidence. The SDP fielded almost three times as many dons as the Conservatives did, despite contesting only half the number of seats.

SDP candidates were indeed formidably intellectual. Three-quarters (74 per cent) had a degree, and about one-quarter (24 per cent) a second degree, often from an American or a European university. An astonishing number wrote books: a preliminary analysis of the first 150 candidates selected in 1983 recorded fifty-two published volumes ranging from *Socialism without the State* (Evan Luard, Oxford West and Abingdon) to *The Geology of the Malvern Hills* (Colin Phipps, Worcester).[25] Like the ordinary members who chose them, moreover, they were meritocrats. Half of them (49 per cent) reached university via state schools (mainly grammar schools), the highest proportion for any of the parties. The privileged path from private school to university was taken by only half as many (26 per cent). In contrast, Conservatives with a university background were almost twice as likely to have gone to private as to state schools. The SDP's candidates were generally talented and articulate representatives of their class and generation.

The idea of classlessness was central to the SDP's public ideology and private self-image. In fact the SDP was as much the party of a class as the Conservative and

Labour parties were. Its members, activists and candidates were disproportionately drawn from an emerging 'service class' of young, well-educated, meritocrats occupying the middle and higher rungs of the public-service bureaucracies and multinational corporations. Their mildly progressive political views reflected the experience and interests of people who owed their success to higher education, professional qualifications and managerial skills. But could the members of such a class form the basis of a successful new party? We shall see in Chapter 16 that their interests were not sufficiently distinct or cohesive, and their numbers were simply not large enough, to break through the formidable barriers of the electoral system.

16

. . . .

The SDP, the Alliance and the Electorate

The SDP's founders chose an ideal time to mount their challenge against the post-war hegemony of the Conservative and Labour parties. In early 1981 the two main parties were more unpopular with the British electorate than at any time since the war.[1] The Conservatives were taking a heavy toll for the economic recession. Only a quarter of the electorate 'approved of the government's record to date' or expressed 'confidence in the government's policies for tackling the economic situation', and Margaret Thatcher's satisfaction rating as prime minister was the lowest recorded since opinion polls began.[2]

Public dissatisfaction with the government in mid-term is normal. Concurrent dissatisfaction with the opposition is much more unusual. Public disillusionment with the Labour party set in early in 1981, soon after Michael Foot's election as leader, and it deepened when Tony Benn's challenge for the deputy leadership further exposed Labour's bitter internal feuds. The number seeing Labour as divided and expressing little or no confidence in Michael Foot as leader grew to overwhelming proportions in the polls.[3] By the final quarter of 1981 Conservative support in the Gallup Poll stood at only 26 per cent, Labour support at only 27 per cent. Never before had the standing of either party or its leader sunk so low. Never before was a third party presented with such ideal circumstances for a breakthrough.

This immediate opportunity was, moreover, reinforced by deeper, longer-term trends in the British electorate. Crumbling class barriers, the spreading influence of television's non-partisan political coverage and disillusion with successive governments of both parties had already gradually eroded the popular foundations of the party system.[4] This 'partisan dealignment' took a variety of forms. The most telling was the growing reluctance of the electorate both to turn out and to vote either Conservative or Labour: the proportion doing both declined from over 80 per cent in 1951 to 56 per cent in October 1974. This decline was accompanied by a corresponding contraction in the proportion who felt a degree of psychological attachment to the Conservative or Labour parties and also by a quite rapid weakening of such attachments as did exist. As recently as 1964 two-fifths of the electorate considered themselves 'very-strong' Conservative or Labour supporters; by 1979 only one-fifth did so. The foundations of the two-party system were rotting in other ways too: party memberships plummeted, the smaller parties won by-elections and, as partisan bonds loosened, the electorate became more volatile. More and more voters seemed to be searching for a new political home.

Yet the SDP's founders knew they were taking a colossal gamble. The year 1981 may have offered the best chance for a third-party breakthrough in half a century; but there had been disappointments before. Partisan dealignment and short-term disillusionment with one or other major party had appeared to present openings to the Liberals (and the Nationalists in Scotland too) in the past; but these openings had never been consolidated into a permanent electoral, let alone parliamentary, breakthrough. Instead, what occurred were impressive but short-lived waves of third-party support in the mid-term of an unpopular government, waves that largely receded at the next general election.

These waves were known as 'Liberal revivals'. There had been three of them since the late 1950s, all when the Conservatives were in power. The first began with the Liberals' Torrington by-election gain in March 1958 and lasted about seven months; the Liberals rose temporarily to 19 per cent in the Gallup Poll, but in the 1959 general election they lost Torrington and saw their national vote reduced to a mere 5.9 per cent. The second began with the Orpington by-election in March 1962 and lasted about eighteen months. Liberal support for a time reached 25 per cent in the polls, but at the 1964 election the Liberals' vote was down to 11.2 per cent and they only just held on to Orpington. The third was heralded by yet another by-election victory, that in Rochdale in October 1972, and lasted for about two years. The Liberals gained four more seats at by-elections (Sutton and Cheam, Isle of Ely, Ripon and Berwick-upon-Tweed) and rose to as much as 28 per cent in the polls. But in the February 1974 general election they lost Sutton and Cheam, and also Ripon, and their vote fell to 19.3 per cent, slipping further to 18.3 per cent in the October election later that year.[5] Thus there was neither a sudden, tidal wave of Liberal support nor a continuously rising water level but rather the ebb and flow of a slowly advancing tide. Each incoming Liberal wave lasted longer, left a higher watermark and receded less; but recede it did.

The Alliance's Electoral Performance

The SDP's founders gambled that their party, in alliance with the Liberals, would break through the two major parties' sea defences on the next spring tide.[6] Although their gamble ultimately failed, their short-term successes were remarkable. The Alliance's 25.4 per cent of the vote in 1983 was the strongest showing by a third party for sixty years, and its 22.5 per cent in 1987 was the best, apart from 1983, since 1929. On the European continent no liberal or centre party has captured a quarter of the vote in any post-war election; the closest equivalent to the Alliance, the German Free Democrats, seldom takes more than 10 per cent. In large parts of suburban, small-town and rural Britain the Alliance replaced Labour as the main opposition to the dominant Conservatives: it took second place in 262 out of 397 Conservative seats in 1983, in 228 out of 375 in 1987.[7] Under a system of proportional representation the Alliance would have won 161 seats in 1983 and 143 seats in 1987 and almost certainly formed part of a coalition government. Under the British electoral system it won only 23 seats in 1983 and 22 in 1987; but even these modest numbers were the largest third-party totals since 1935.

In other types of election the Alliance did even better.[8] In local elections, where the disproportional impact of the first-past-the-post electoral system was less severe, the two Alliance parties advanced steadily, with net gains in every year from 1982 to 1987. In 1980 there were only about 900 local Liberal councillors; by 1987 there were some 3,600 Alliance councillors.[9] The Alliance did particularly well in the 1985 county-council elections, gaining large numbers of Conservative seats in the more rural areas to take control of six counties and hold the balance of power in sixteen others.[10] In its best local election years (1982, 1985, 1986 and 1987) the Alliance obtained the equivalent of 27 per cent of the national vote.

In by-elections the Alliance's performance was even more impressive. In the whole of the 1981–7 period the Liberals and the SDP between them won the equivalent of 37–8 per cent of the national vote in by-elections.[11] In the course of the 1983 parliament the Alliance won more votes in the aggregate than either of the two major parties. Altogether the Liberals and the SDP made eight gains in by-elections between July 1981 and March 1987, and in the 1983 parliament they took first or second place in fifteen of the sixteen by-elections that were contested. At by-elections, and in most parts of the country in local elections, the SDP brought about what the Liberal party alone had always failed to achieve: genuine three-party politics.

Moreover, the opinion polls during most of this period told an equally exhilarating story. Between October 1981 and January 1982, during the SDP's brief golden age, support for the Alliance in the polls rose above 40 per cent, and during the 1983 parliament it rose above 30 per cent on no fewer than fifteen occasions in the monthly Gallup poll.[12] During much of 1985 and 1986 the Liberals and the SDP were more or less level-pegging with the other parties. Support at those levels, had it been sustained at a general election, would have been enough to give the Alliance a substantial block of seats in the House of Commons.

But, of course, it was not sustained. At the 1983 and 1987 general elections, the Alliance did astonishingly well by historical and international standards, but it did not do nearly well enough. It lost four of its total of eight by-election gains (Crosby and Croydon North-West in 1983, Portsmouth South and Ryedale in 1987), and its share of the total vote subsided to the mid-20 per cent level. The Alliance's mid-term surges were stronger and more enduring than the Liberals' had been before the formation of the SDP, but their character was essentially the same. Like the pre-1981 Liberals, the Alliance performed better in by-elections than in mid-term opinion polls and better in both than in general elections.[13] The arrival on the scene of the SDP failed to make a crucial difference. Why should this have been so?

The Centre Vote Before 1981

To explain the SDP's failure one needs to look at the Liberal vote in the 1960s and 1970s. The Liberal party's failure to consolidate its innumerable advances reflected two facts.[14] First, the Liberals consistently underpolled their potential support. Reality never lived up to promise. This point was well illustrated by the two elections of 1974, when one in three electors (32 per cent) supported the Liberals in either February or October or both, but fewer than one in five voted Liberal in each of the two elections taken separately. Later, in 1979, 30 per cent of Liberal identifiers voted for some other party, whereas among Conservative and Labour identifiers the proportions were only 5 and 13 per cent. Similarly, opinion polls typically estimated the potential Liberal vote as lying between 30 and 35 per cent, sometimes more, yet at no post-war general election did the actual Liberal vote reach 20 per cent.[15] At every election far more people seriously considered voting Liberal than finally did so.

Secondly, the Liberal vote was subject to extraordinarily high turnover. It resembled a modest hotel, with large numbers of short-stay guests coming and going through its ever-revolving doors. By comparison the Conservative and Labour hotels were not only larger but also had far more long-stay residents. While the two main parties could normally count on keeping three-quarters of their voters from one general election to the next, the Liberals typically kept fewer than half of theirs. Most Conservative and Labour defectors returned from the Liberals to their original party, while new and equally temporary Conservative and Labour recruits to the Liberals replaced them. It thus made good sense to refer to the Liberal vote as the 'soft centre'—except that to imagine that a Liberal vote existed at all was misleading, since it actually consisted of a tiny core of Liberal regulars (a mere 2 per cent of all voters) surrounded by a much larger but highly volatile penumbra of occasional supporters. The Liberals thus not only failed to convert most of their potential sympathizers into voters; they failed to convert most of their voters into solid supporters.[16] In the climate of partisan dealignment in the 1970's the Conservative and Labour icebergs were slowly melting, but no Liberal iceberg was forming.

The Liberals attributed their failure to the electoral system, and they were largely right to do so. The first-past-the-post system heavily penalizes small parties whose electoral support, like that of the Liberals, is spread evenly across the country rather than being concentrated in specific geographical areas. Such a party may win a significant share of the popular vote yet win very few seats in parliament. Moreover, the system not only penalizes such parties in terms of seats: precisely for that reason, it also has the effect of discouraging people from voting for them in the first place. Thousands of Liberal sympathizers—knowing their Liberal candidate was unlikely to win and knowing, too, that the Liberals nationally were unlikely to be in a position to form a government—were unwilling to 'waste' their vote. The two-party system was thus self-sustaining. The fact that the party was small also meant that it failed to get a substantial share of press and television coverage. The Liberal party in the 1960s and 1970s was small because it got few votes—and it got so few votes because it was small.

It still needs to be asked, however, why the Liberal vote was so evenly spread and why Liberal supporters were so easily discouraged by the electoral system. Other small parties, like the Welsh nationalists, Plaid Cymru, or the Catholic parties in Northern Ireland, did not lack both local concentrations of support and strong partisans. Partisanship is based on the electoral system; but it is also based on the social and ideological divisions in the electorate. The Liberal vote was so soft and ephemeral because the Liberal party neither spoke for major interests in British society nor represented an ideological constituency that was in any way distinctive.

Election surveys in the 1960s and 1970s repeatedly found that the socio-demographic profile of Liberal voters was featureless. Although marginally younger, more middle class and better educated than the electorate as a whole, Liberal voters in general were a microcosm of the nation. Unlike the two major parties, the Liberal party did not receive the support of any organized group or social category. Most such groups—small businessmen, farmers, church-goers, trade unionists, Afro-Caribbeans—regarded either the Conservatives or Labour as 'their' party, the party that fellow members supported and that could normally be relied upon to take their side. No group thought of the Liberals in that way. The basis of the Liberal vote was political, not social.

It was not, however, political in any enduring, ideological sense. What moved people to support or reject the Liberal party was not its political principles, broad policy positions or stands on specific issues. Rather, when voters were asked to say in their own words what they liked or disliked about each of the parties, the Liberals' appeal, or lack of it, emerged as being altogether more diffuse. It lay partly in the party's image as 'moderate' and 'good for all classes', partly in the personality of whoever was its current leader, but mainly in its location as a small party separate from, but somewhere in between, the two major parties. The Liberal party's main claim on voters' attention was that it was not either of the other two.

This was true of those who actually voted Liberal as well as of the electorate as a whole. Compared with their Conservative or Labour counterparts, Liberal voters were particularly unlikely to cite issues or policies as their motive. In fact, most of them voted Liberal despite preferring the Conservatives or the Labour party on almost all substantive issues, and they tended to be unaware of, or even be misinformed about, Liberal policy, frequently projecting their own policy preferences on to the party. So far as most voters were concerned, the Liberal party was, in Bernard Levin's famous phrase, an 'aimless, all-purpose, wish-fulfilment machine'.[17]

Thus Liberal voters did not occupy what political scientists call a distinct 'issue space', sharing a cluster of policy views that set them apart from both Conservative and Labour supporters. Admittedly, Liberal voters occupied the 'middle ground', but they cohabited it with large numbers of Conservative or Labour supporters. To occupy the middle ground of politics was consistent with voting for either the Liberals or a major party and for switching easily from one to the other. People thought it a wasted vote to back the Liberals, not only because the Liberals had no chance of winning but also because the party was not sufficiently different from the major parties to be worth wasting a vote on.

It followed that, if the SDP were to break out of the Liberal party's cycle of surge followed by decline, it had either to exorcise the 'wasted-vote' curse, by persuading large numbers of voters that it really did have a chance, or else establish for the new Alliance a distinct social or ideological base in the electorate. If it could do both of these things simultaneously, that, of course, would be ideal.

Jenkins and the Jenkinsites initially emphasized the new party's credibility. Unlike the Liberals under such attractive but lightweight figures as Jo Grimond and Jeremy Thorpe, the SDP would present to the country well-known and experienced leaders, a strong national organization and a professional campaigning style. Jenkins as leader saw the Alliance's appeal as essentially that of the Liberals' writ large. The aim was to mobilize—as the Liberals on their own had never succeeded in doing—the full extent of the latent support for the centre that was known to exist in the electorate. It was assumed that voters would judge the Alliance on its overall image and positioning, not on its specific policies. It was also assumed that the SDP neither could nor should target specific groups of voters, not even working-class voters. Rather, it should be the party for everyone in the country, irrespective of their class or previous party affiliation, who wanted a moderate alternative to the polarized class politics of Thatcher and Benn.

Under Owen after 1983 the party's approach shifted. In Owen's view, the 1983 result had starkly revealed the limited number of votes that the Alliance could win over simply by radiating moderation and niceness. A bland image of caution and compromise would not do. In order to build up long-term loyalties among the electorate, the SDP, Owen believed, had to stake out a distinctive location on the ideological map by taking up distinctive positions on policy. The SDP needed, in other words, to sharpen its profile. This would give it, and by extension the Alliance, a new feeling of realism, competence and toughness—of its being fit to govern on those grounds. Seeking to substitute policy credibility for electoral credibility—or, rather, to turn the one into the other—Owen was readier than Jenkins to highlight rather than to play down the SDP's differences with the Liberals.

Those were the assumptions underlying the SDP's thinking about the electorate. What was the reality?

Partisanship and Volatility

The SDP's aim was to produce an enduring realignment of the party system. Any such realignment would need to be underpinned by higher and stronger levels of partisan identification with the SDP and the Liberals—or the Alliance together—among the voters. As Table 16.1 (in Appendix 5) shows, the SDP's achievement in this regard was limited. In February 1974, when the Liberal party on its own won nearly a fifth of the vote, 14 per cent of the electorate identified themselves with the Liberal party. In 1983, even though the centre vote almost doubled, Liberal and SDP identifiers between them amounted to exactly the same proportion: 14 per cent. Barely half, 51 per cent, of those who voted for the Alliance in 1983 identified with it; the remainder thought of themselves as Conservative or Labour supporters or as being non-partisan. The centre vote in 1983, like the Liberal vote in 1974, was a protest vote; it did not represent a fundamental shift in voters' loyalties.

By 1987 there were signs that the Alliance was beginning to sink roots. Although the Alliance's vote fell slightly in 1987, the proportion of Alliance identifiers rose to 19 per cent—the highest level recorded for a centre party since measurements began in 1964.[18] But these roots were very shallow. The increase consisted almost entirely of those with a 'not-very-strong' identification with the Alliance, and two out of five Alliance voters (42 per cent) still remained non-identifiers. Indeed the typical Alliance identifier in 1987 was not only less partisan than his Conservative and Labour counterparts but had a weaker commitment than his Liberal predecessor had had in the 1970s. And the number of Alliance true believers remained tiny: a mere 2 per cent of the electorate described themselves as being 'very-strong' Liberal, SDP or Alliance supporters. Like the Liberals before the arrival of the SDP, the centre consisted of a few dedicated loyalists together with a large penumbra of largely uncommitted hangers-on.

The SDP's failure to inject a firmer partisan commitment into the centre vote was reflected in the volatility of Alliance support. In the opinion polls, the Alliance, but especially the SDP, bobbed up and down on every wave of political fortune. After a good by-election or party conference, support for the Alliance would swell, but then would dip almost immediately; after a poor by-election or a row, Alliance support would plunge. When the Alliance was on the crest of a wave, SDP supporters outnumbered Liberal supporters by over two to one; but, when the Alliance was sandbanked, support for the two parties was roughly equal.[19] After 1981 the voters who floated to the centre mainly thought of themselves as SDP voters, not as Liberals. Within the Alliance, the Liberal party was the anchor, the SDP the sail.[20]

Who Voted SDP?

Who were these floating voters? Who voted SDP? The answer is complicated by the SDP's close relationship with the Liberals. The fact is that most voters thought of the Alliance as a single party or else made no distinction between it and the SDP, especially in 1987.[21] In any case, the minority who did think of themselves specifically as Social Democrats or Liberals frequently found that their preferred party had stood down for the other in their own constituency. But that did not seem to make any difference: psephologists could detect no systematic variation in the performance of Liberal and SDP candidates at either the 1983 or the 1987 general election. In similar types of seat the two parties performed similarly.[22] The question, therefore, is not where the SDP got its vote from, but where the Alliance, as a whole, got its.

On the face of it, the establishment of the SDP inflicted heavy damage on the Labour party and left the Conservatives intact. Between the elections of 1979 and 1983, the Conservative share of the vote slipped by a mere 1.5 percentage points, but the Labour vote slumped by 9.3 points and the centre-party vote increased by fully 11.6 points.[23] The obvious interpretation is that the SDP, in alliance with the Liberals, split the anti-Conservative vote, enabling the Thatcher government to be re-elected with a bigger parliamentary majority despite the small fall in its vote in the country.

The truth is more complex. As Table 16.2 suggests, the centre parties in 1983 did indeed advance at the expense of Labour more than the Conservatives. Twice as many Alliance voters identified with the Labour party (25 per cent) as with the Conservative party (14 per cent). Vote-switching revealed a similar pattern. Fewer than two in five of the Alliance's 1983 votes came from 1979 Liberals; among the remainder, Labour defections to the Alliance outnumbered Conservative by 32 to 20 per cent. This damage to Labour was reinforced by a somewhat higher rate of defection among 1979 Liberals to the Conservatives (14 per cent) than to Labour (9 per cent). But, although the Alliance made deeper inroads into Labour than into Conservative ranks, it recruited from across the partisan spectrum, as the Jenkinsites had assumed and wanted. Erstwhile Conservatives as well as erstwhile Labour voters defected.

Moreover, to infer in some simple way that the SDP split the anti-Conservative vote, thereby delivering victory to Thatcher, is to assume that, in the absence of the SDP, the Labour defectors would all have stayed loyal to Labour. But the evidence in Table 16.3 suggests otherwise. In 1983, when Alliance voters were asked to say which party 'had the best policies' and which party 'had the best leaders', the minority who did not answer 'the Alliance' preferred the Conservatives by an 11 to 5 per cent margin on policies and a 25 to 2 per cent margin on leaders. Not surprisingly, these margins were wider among 'not-very-strong' Liberal and SDP identifiers and among Conservative switchers to the Alliance; but even Labour-to-Alliance switchers put the Conservatives a fraction ahead of Labour on policies and comfortably ahead on leaders. Without the Alliance as a safe haven, many of these Labour deserters would undoubtedly have gone straight across to the Conservatives, producing an even larger Thatcher majority.

In 1987 Labour recovered some of the ground it had lost to the Alliance in

1983. Between the 1983 and 1987 general elections the Conservative share of the vote remained the same, Labour's rose by 3.2 points, and the Alliance's dropped by 2.9 points. These net changes were the product of a complicated two-way traffic of voters to and from the Alliance. The Alliance lost a slightly larger proportion of its 1983 supporters to the Labour party than to the Conservatives (12 per cent to 8), while it won over a slightly larger proportion of former Conservative than former Labour voters (18 per cent to 12). As in 1983, the Alliance made converts from— and lost defectors to—both sides of the main party divide, much as the Liberal party had done in the 1970s.[24]

The Social Base of the SDP and the Alliance

Such were the party antecedents of the SDP's voters. But what kind of people were they? In the party's early years journalists and other politicians were quick to label them. But the labels were usually inspired by what was known about the SDP's more prominent activists—a notoriously deceptive basis of judgement that, not surprisingly, produced a wide variety of not always consistent notions. Some imagined that, because the SDP was a new party, it must cater for a 'new class'.[25] Others assumed that, because the SDP was in the ideological centre, it must also be in the sociological centre, attracting support from the 'middle mass' straddling the manual/non-manual borderline. Yet others supposed the SDP to be the party of 'class misfits', such as foremen or routine non-manual workers or the upwardly mobile or white-collar trade unionists. As Chapter 15 showed, almost all saw it as the Socially Desirable Party, the party of the chattering and wine-drinking classes, the party of the affluent, the young, the well educated and the metropolitan, the party that stood to mop up the yuppie vote. Nobody suggested that the SDP had no distinctive social profile at all.

That, however, was broadly the case. The essential socio-demographic facts about the Alliance electorate are set out in Tables 16.4 to 16.6. They show that the voters for the Alliance in 1983 and 1987, like the Liberals' voters before 1981, were virtually a microcosm of the electorate as a whole—certainly in terms of sex, age and social class. Admittedly, Alliance voters were fractionally younger, more female and, in 1987, more middle class than the national average, but it is the narrowness of the differences, not the existence of them, that stands out.[26]

The Alliance's lack of a distinctive social base is brought out from a different point of view in Table 16.5, which sets out the 1983 and 1987 Alliance vote in each social category and its deviation from the national average. The figures are notable in two ways. First, they show that no social group preferred the Alliance to both of the main parties: not one gave the plurality of its vote, let alone an absolute majority, to the Alliance. Secondly, the level of support for the Alliance was remarkably similar across the social spectrum. In 1983, for example, when the Alliance took a quarter of the national vote, its support did not dip below a fifth or rise above a third in any of the main social groups. It did as well among the unemployed, the poor and welfare dependents as among managers and professional people. (So much for the SDP as the yuppies' party.) The Alliance's vote came from everywhere in general and nowhere in particular.

The Public Sector Salariat and the Alliance

In fact, the Alliance's reputation as being an essentially middle-class party, while misleading, cannot be dismissed altogether. A finer-grained social analysis of the Alliance vote (set out in Table 16.6) suggests that the Alliance did have a special— and growing—appeal to one specific segment of the middle classes: managers and professionals in the public sector.

The 1983 British Election Study found that the 'salariat'—managers, administrators and professionals with secure employment and above-average incomes— divided between the Conservative party and the Alliance (Labour was always in third place) quite sharply according to education and type of job. One source of division was higher education. Among those without any formal qualifications— most of whom had come up through the ranks—60 per cent voted Conservative in 1983 and only 22 per cent (less than the national average) for the Alliance. By contrast, among those with degrees, almost as many voted Alliance as Conservative (41 to 42 per cent). A second source of division was the economic sector in which a voter worked. The Alliance vote was higher among the public-sector salariat, especially those working in the civil service, local government and the National Health Service, than among the private-sector salariat (34 per cent to 28).[27] A third was that between 'line' and 'staff' jobs. Managers with supervisory 'line' responsibilities over employees gave an overwhelming 68 per cent of their vote to the Conservatives and only 20 per cent to the Alliance. By contrast, professional and semi-professional 'staff', such as teachers, computer programmers, nurses and technicians, gave only 44 per cent of their vote to the Conservatives and as much as 35 per cent to the Alliance. A final source of political division within the salariat was trade-union membership: among the unionized salariat the Alliance vote was 36 per cent; among the non-unionized it was only 24 per cent. The Alliance was, thus, far from being the party of the middle classes as a whole, but it was close to being the party of a middle-class minority. The Conservatives were the party of the commercial and profit-making middle classes; the Alliance represented a significant portion of the 'caring' and public-service middle classes.

One can only speculate about why this segment of the salariat had an affinity for the Alliance. Self-interest cannot be ruled out. Civil servants, academics and health-service administrators—to cite just three example—have a personal stake as well as a principled belief in the continued growth and status of the public sector. Thatcher's government, unlike previous Conservative administrations, made plain its intention to cut the public sector down to size, while Labour became identified with the increasingly militant public-sector unions. The Alliance offered itself as a champion of the public services but one that did not threaten the economic and occupational privileges of those who helped run them.

Yet social background and values were probably more important factors than crude self-interest. The liberalizing influence of university education was probably one such factor. Graduates tend to take a tender rather than a tough line on issues such as crime and punishment, civil liberties and the legislation of personal morality, and were probably alienated by Thatcher's populist authoritarianism. A second factor was probably this stratum's ambivalent position in the hierarchy of work. Professional employees without managerial responsibilities do not necessarily identify with 'management'; but they do not readily identify with 'the workers' either. The 'them-and-us' division at work, on which the Conservative–Labour conflict feeds, largely passes them by: to the public-sector salariat, management and workers alike are both part of 'them'. The fact that so many Alliance supporters worked in the welfare services was also important. Those who came into contact with social problems were often offended by the social consequences of the government's economic policies—and even more by the Thatcherites' apparent indifference to them. The caring professions like doctors and teachers swung particularly sharply from the Conservatives to the Alliance between 1983 and 1987.[28]

It would be an exaggeration, however, to claim that the Alliance established a social base in the public-sector salariat. Even among the university-educated salariat—a tiny 4 per cent of the electorate—the Alliance was the second party behind the Conservatives. Surveys record only two occupational groups—teachers and vicars—who preferred the Alliance to both of the major parties.[29] Had the Alliance survived beyond 1987, firmer loyalties might have been fostered among this sector of the salariat: it had a common sectional interest, was organized into interlocking networks and shared a similar life-style;[30] and schools, universities, hospitals, government ministries and town halls offered an organizational milieu for a social-democratic culture. But that stage had certainly not been reached by 1987. The Alliance remained most people's—including most professionals'—second preference, almost nobody's first.

The Ideological Basis of SDP and Alliance Support

A major obstacle to a realignment in favour of the centre before 1981 was the Liberal vote's lack of an ideological base. The advent of the SDP made little difference. Part of the explanation for its electoral failure was its inability to establish a new—or indeed any—ideological constituency in the electorate.

The point is made in Figure 5, which depicts the electorate's mental picture of the SDP's place, and also that of the other parties, on the contemporary ideological map.[31] It shows, first, that the SDP completely failed to differentiate itself from the

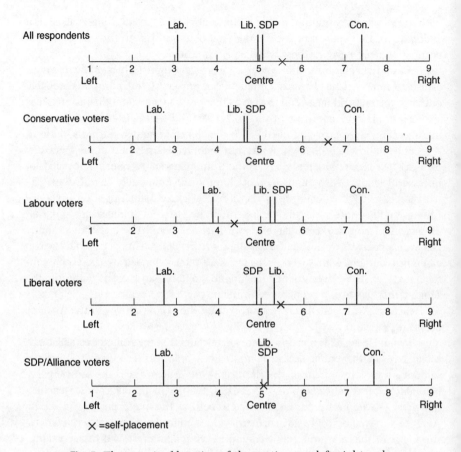

Fig. 5 The perceived location of the parties on a left–right scale,
July 1986–June 1987

old Liberal party: in most people's eyes the two Alliance parties occupied virtually identical ground. Leading Social Democrats, especially David Owen, regularly insisted that the SDP's traditions and values were quite distinct from those of the Liberals, but it is obvious that the distinction, although valid up to a point, was completely lost on most voters: they did not regard the SDP as a substitute, reconditioned Labour party; they regarded it as a substitute, reconditioned Liberal party.

Secondly, the SDP was seen by both its own supporters and the electorate as a whole as a centre party, not as a left-of-centre party. Neither the energetic early attempts of the Gang of Three to depict social democracy as a left-of-centre philosophy nor David Owen's subsequent redefinition of social democracy as economically 'tough' but socially 'tender' persuaded the electorate that the SDP was anything other than centrist.[32] Voters placed it almost equidistant between the two main parties (if a shade closer to the Labour party) and almost plum in the centre of the left–right spectrum (if a hair's breadth to its right). Moreover, SDP supporters placed not only their party but also themselves in the middle. Typical SDP voters by no means regarded themselves as moderate but somewhat left-of-centre voters who had been abandoned by a leftwards-lurching Labour party. Rather, they saw themselves as out-and-out middle-of-the-roaders. For many of them the Labour party had probably always been too left wing.

Of course, Alliance supporters may not have held genuinely middling opinions on most issues, leaning to neither left nor right. The picture in Figure 5 could be misleading: it could represent merely an arithmetic mean of a wide distribution of different views. Perhaps Alliance voters were left wing on some issues, right wing on others; or perhaps Alliance supporters held a wide variety of views ranging right across the political spectrum on each individual issue and thus really did not have a collective opinion at all. Which of these possibilities is closest to the truth emerges from Table 16.7, which sets out the balance of right-wing to left-wing views among Alliance voters on no fewer than thirty-three issues that engaged British politicians during the period the SDP existed.

The pattern across the full array of issues contains three important features. The first is the absence of any issue that clearly divided Alliance voters from both Conservative and Labour voters.[33] The Alliance had nothing to compare, for example, with the distinctive place of the Welsh-language issue in the Plaid Cymru vote or of an independent Scotland in the Scottish National vote. Not a single overriding Liberal or Social Democratic principle united Alliance voters against supporters of all the other parties. Either Alliance voters did not give clear majority backing to Alliance policies like the inflation tax or, if they did, as in the case of devolution to the regions, they were joined by majorities of Conservative and Labour voters. The only policy on which the Alliance took a special line that was endorsed by a large majority of its voters was proportional representation, but this was a policy supported by most Labour voters too. The Alliance, like the Liberal party of the 1970s, failed totally to establish its own policy constituency among the electorate.

The fact that no single policy position was embraced exclusively by Alliance voters does not preclude the possibility that the cluster of policies that they supported marked them off from Conservative and Labour voters. An elaborate argument of this kind was presented by Anthony Heath and his 1983 British Election Study team.[34] Abandoning the traditional one-dimensional left–right mapping of policy opinions in favour of a two-dimensional map based on an axis of 'class values' which is cross-cut by an axis of 'liberal values', the British Election Study concluded that the Alliance vote in 1983 was not 'an amorphous one without any distinctive character' but one that occupied a 'heartland every bit as distinctive as those of the other two parties'. The Alliance was 'not purely a party of the centre' but displayed 'a distinctive contour' comprising centre and right-wing positions on class issues and tender rather than tough positions on liberal issues. What differentiated Alliance voters from others, on this analysis, was that, unlike Labour voters, they tended to take a hard line on economic issues but, unlike Conservative voters, tended to take a soft line on matters of defence, foreign policy, minority rights and individual freedom. It appeared that the SDP had, after all, helped the centre to carve out its own ideological niche.

The Heath argument was sufficiently plausible at the time to persuade Alliance leaders to step up their 'tough-and-tender' campaign.[35] Closer inspection, however, reveals it to be flawed and to be unsupported by the data in Table 16.7.[36] The picture that emerges from the data is much less tidy. On class issues having to do with distribution, such as public spending, welfare and taxation, Alliance voters leaned to the left and resembled Labour voters more than Conservatives; in this sense they were traditional social democrats. But on class issues having to do with production, such as trade-union rights and renationalizaton, Alliance voters were well to the right and were closer to Conservative voters than to Labour voters; in this sense they abandoned traditional social democracy. On issues of public ownership, they took a position some distance from both Conservative and Labour supporters. Wary of frequent frontier changes between the private and public sectors (and relatively indifferent to the whole matter), they were unenthusiastic about both privatization and renationalization. In short, Alliance voters believed in the mixed economy and welfare capitalism. They wanted the nation's wealth to be generated by the market but to be redistributed by the state.

Moreover, not only did Alliance voters not take a consistently left-wing, centre or right-wing position on class issues; contrary to the tough-and-tender thesis, they did not take a consistently liberal line on non-class issues either. On nuclear defence, unlike Labour voters, they opposed unilateralism, believing in retaining the Polaris missile (but on balance rejecting the siting of cruise and other United States missiles on British soil).[37] On the repatriation of immigrants and aid to the Third World, they took a liberal view, if only just; but on capital punishment and censorship of sex and nudity in the media, they were hard-liners. They were less consistently liberal than Labour voters on such issues (except on abortion) and were sometimes closer to Conservatives.[38]

Alliance voters did not even take a consistent or distinctive line on constitutional questions, the policy area in which the Alliance parties had for longest been distinctive and radical. The Liberal party was the historic party of devolution and Europe, and attitudes to Europe in some ways symbolized the difference between the Gang of Four and the Labour party they left. Most Alliance voters did support the 'shifting of power to regions and local authorities', but by a smaller majority than among Labour voters.[39] Similarly, most Alliance voters in 1983 did oppose the official Labour policy of British withdrawal from the European Community (on no single issue were they so far removed from Labour voters), but not as overwhelmingly as Conservative voters. Later, however, when the Labour party had become reconciled to Britain's remaining in Europe and the issue had dropped off the political agenda, the majority of Alliance voters actually supported Britain's pulling out! Alliance voters were far less progressive than commentators —and leading Liberals and Social Democrats—assumed.

Another characteristic of Alliance voters, predictable by now, was their lack of agreement among themselves. Conservative voters agreed by a majority of at least two-to-one on twenty-one of the thirty-three issues in the table; Labour voters did so on nineteen; but Alliance voters did so on only thirteen. Alliance voters were spread across the policy spectrum, and their views were as widely divergent on the progressive agenda and on constitutional issues as on the old-fashioned left–right issues. Alliance voters were certainly not centrists in the sense of clustering tightly around the middle and vacating the far sides in favour of supporters of the major parties. On the contrary, they were no more likely than Conservative or Labour voters to take moderate views on specific policy questions.[40] The notion that Alliance voters were a collection of like-minded *Guardian* readers is completely false. Some indeed shared the *Guardian*'s views, but far more reflected the views of newspapers ranging all the way from the *Daily Mirror* to the *Sun*.

The Alliance's failure to mobilize support behind distinct principles or policies was also reflected in the reasons people gave for voting for it. When the idea of a social-democratic party was first mooted, its appeal came from its newness, its 'moderation' and its leadership, not its principles or policies.[41] In response to an open-ended question about their reasons for voting SDP, Jenkins' supporters in the Warrington by-election mostly cited 'the extremism of other parties' (35 per cent) and 'fed up/want a change' (26 per cent); references to the SDP's policies came only fifth (9 per cent).[42] In Croydon North-West respondents were asked to match a series of statements against their 'impressions of the parties'. The two most frequently attributed to the SDP (and more so than to the Conservative and Labour parties) were 'represents all classes' (26 per cent) and 'has good leaders' (24 per cent); a bare 9 per cent associated it with policy statements.[43] The picture barely changed after the Alliance had developed its detailed programme. As Table 16.8 shows, voters for the Alliance displayed much less confidence in their party's ability to achieve desirable policy goals than Conservative and Labour voters displayed in theirs. In 1983 only 50 per cent of Alliance voters chose the Alliance as the party best able to deal with a range of problems; by 1987 the proportion had fallen back to 42 per cent, not much more than the proportion of Liberals backing their party on the same issues in 1979 (35 per cent).[44] In this respect David Owen's efforts to give the SDP programme a cutting edge did not succeed in providing a firmer policy base. The majority of Alliance voters were in no doubt that between them the two Alliance parties could provide the best person to be prime minister;[45] but they regarded another party—or perhaps no party at all—as best able to deal with the main problems facing the country.

People were not attracted to the Alliance by Liberal or SDP policy partly because they (or many of them) had only a hazy notion of what it was. In 1983 a Gallup poll on the parties' images found that 50 per cent described the Alliance as having 'vague policies' whereas only 30 per cent described it as having 'clear policies' (see Table 16.9). By 1987 the Alliance had somewhat raised its policy profile, but on balance more people continued to regard its policies as vague (44 per cent) rather than clear (39 per cent). Not surprisingly, only one out of five Alliance voters gave a positive and specific reason for their vote; almost twice as many gave a negative and general reason such as 'time for a change'—the hallmark of the protest voter.[46]

What did distinguish the Alliance from the two main parties in voters' eyes was that it was a party of good, if somewhat vague, intentions. Large majorities described the Alliance as being good for all classes rather than just one class (64 to 8 per cent) and as being 'moderate' rather than 'extreme' (74 to 6 per cent). By contrast, the Conservative and Labour parties were seen as class based and extreme. The perceived 'extremism' of the two major parties, especially Labour, was an important impetus behind the Alliance vote, an impetus that strengthened over time.[47] In 1979 16 per cent of Liberal voters said the way they voted was influenced by 'Conservative extremism', 20 per cent by 'Labour extremism'. In 1983 the figures for Alliance voters were 24 and 34 per cent respectively, and in 1987 29 and 46 per cent.[48] Thus the most powerful appeal of the Alliance was almost wholly devoid of policy substance: the Alliance was seen as a safe and decent alternative to the two established parties, the Labour party in particular. It was seen as a moderate force in an increasingly immoderate age. But this amiable appeal was not strong enough to produce an electoral breakthrough or a partisan realignment. It is difficult to be partisan, let alone passionate, about niceness, moderation and common sense.

Could the Alliance Have Done Better?

In short, the Alliance failed to establish itself as a major parliamentary force principally because it was unable to mobilize all or even most of its potential support and because it failed to establish any kind of solid social or ideological base. It was a grouping that aroused warmth but little heat, a considerable amount of generalized sympathy but little passionate enthusiasm.

The Alliance's failure to establish a distinct ideological identity was serious. People complained that the Alliance 'lacked clear policies'. When they said that, however, they did not mean that the Alliance failed to publish clear and specific policy proposals on most matters of public importance; in most cases they did not know whether the Alliance had produced such policies or not. What they meant, rather, was that the Alliance's innumerable policy proposals were beads without a string. They lacked an underlying theme or big idea. Voters felt unable to predict which way the Alliance would jump when difficult decisions had to be made. Nor did they know what big changes, if any, an Alliance government would bring about (other than electoral reform, which did not interest them). As they contemplated the Alliance, voters knew approximately *where* the new grouping stood—between the two main parties, sometimes above them. But they did not know for *what* it stood for, or for *whom*.

The Alliance's failure to mobilize its own potential support was equally serious. In 1983 no fewer than 14 per cent of all voters said that they had seriously considered supporting the Alliance or had actually voted for it in either local elections or a by-election, but had decided against doing so at the general election. If all of them had backed the Alliance, it would have obtained 40 per cent of the vote and, in all probability, taken office. Similarly, in 1987 the number of potential but unrealized Alliance supporters amounted to fully 27 per cent. If this 27 per cent is added to the 23 per cent who did vote Liberal or SDP, the Alliance would have had the backing in that election of up to 50 per cent of the voters. Of course, people's claims to have 'seriously considered' voting for the Alliance must be taken with a pinch of salt. But these kinds of figures are in line with the Alliance's ratings in the opinion polls in 1981–2 and with its share of the vote in many by-elections.

The main reason why the Alliance failed to mobilize its full electoral support was, of course, the same structural factor that had formerly crippled the Liberals: the reluctance of electors to 'waste' their vote. Their belief that the Alliance could not win and their fear that voting for it would advantage the real enemy (whether the Conservatives or Labour) were mentioned as reasons for not backing the Alliance by no fewer than 57 per cent of the Alliance's potential supporters in 1983 and by as many as 67 per cent in 1987.[49] This factor was reflected in the pattern of constituency results: where the Alliance came third in 1983 it was squeezed in 1987. Nationally its vote fell by 2.9 percentage points, but in seats where the Conservative and Labour candidates had taken first and second places in 1983 it fell by 4.7 points. In marginal seats where the Conservative majority over Labour was less than 15 per cent, it fell by even more—5.4 points.[50] The SDP proved no more able than the Liberals to shake off the wasted-vote curse.

In many parts of the country, however, the Alliance should have been able in 1987 to turn the wasted-vote argument against its enemies: in the 311 seats where the Alliance came second in 1983 it appeared to be in a position to squeeze the other parties rather than be squeezed. This was particularly true of those seats in which there remained a substantial Labour vote and in which ex-Labour voters might have been expected to switch to the Alliance. Both Alliance parties targeted such seats and they should have been helped by 'TV 87', the national campaign to encourage anti-Conservative tactical voting, which received a degree of support in some newspapers.[51] In the event, tactical voting in favour of the Alliance was both modest and patchy.[52] So limited was its scale that, even where it occurred, the Alliance's share of the vote fell compared with 1983.[53] Most of the Alliance's target seats with a sizeable Labour vote proved quite resistant to tactical blandishments.[54] Even when the structural situation seemed to be in its favour, the Alliance was unable to take full advantage of it.

It can be argued that, despite the disappointing election result in 1987, the

Alliance by then had made some headway in its long-term aim of breaking the two-party hegemony. By 1987 there were signs that the Alliance had begun to establish a larger and more enduring base in the electorate. The proportion of voters identifying with the Alliance parties was slowly increasing, the public-sector middle classes were coming to regard the Alliance as 'their' party, tactical voting for the centre was slowly starting to catch on, and the number of Liberal and SDP local councillors elected each year was growing steadily. It had taken the Labour party at the beginning of the century nearly thirty years to realign the party system, when the conditions were unusually favourable. What the Alliance needed, ran the argument, was a similar length of time in which the SDP and the Liberals together could erode the harsh terrain of the British electoral system.

This proposition probably deserves little credence. The Conservative and Labour sea-walls in the late 1980s and early 1990s were still too strong, and Labour's, in particular, were constantly being reinforced. But precisely how much credence it deserves will never be known, because, as the concluding chapters relate, after the 1987 general election the Alliance partners finally lost patience with one another.

Part IV

• • • •

MATURITY AND DEATH

17

••••

The Owen Ascendancy I:
1983–1985

The 1983 election took place on Thursday, 9 June, and the following day, within hours of the final result being declared, David Owen in an interview in *The Times* refused to rule out the possibility that he might challenge Roy Jenkins for the SDP leadership.[1] That weekend he went further, phoning Jenkins at home and telling him bluntly that, unless he resigned the leadership immediately, he, Owen, would declare his intention to stand against him. Jenkins had originally intended to soldier on until at least the autumn, but on Monday, 13 June, at a private lunch party for the Gang of Four and a few others who had been prominent in the campaign, he announced he was going. He said he hoped that Owen would succeed him without a contest.[2] When the six surviving SDP MPs met for the first time on 15 June, no one emerged to challenge Owen, and he formally became leader a week later.[3]

Jenkins subsequently said that he had probably made a mistake in resigning so precipitously, but in fact he had little choice. A contest for the leadership would have lasted for several months and produced deep divisions in a party that was already deeply demoralized; and in the end he would almost certainly have lost. Compared with Owen, he had not been an impressive leader during the campaign, and one of the main arguments that had been used in his favour a year earlier—that he, unlike Owen, could be presented to the public as a serious contender for the prime ministership—no longer applied. The choice facing Jenkins was between going at once with dignity or going later amidst a great deal of acrimony. He chose to go immediately.

For the ensuing four years, between the 1983 and 1987 general elections, David Owen *was* the SDP and the SDP *was* Owen. Hardly anyone else spoke for the party in public, and he totally dominated its inner councils. He was the party's leader in fact as well as in form. Few challenged his authority.

But Owen was a strange man, even by the standards of a profession dominated by strange men and women. He appeared constantly to need to prove himself. Risk-taking was central to his nature. He once set sail on the English Channel in a

Force 9 gale with one of his sons—and boasted of it afterwards. On another occasion, following a meeting in Cambridge, he was driving back to London with an SDP candidate. The night was dark, it was raining heavily, and the windscreen wipers were not coping. Owen at the wheel could hardly see, but he drove faster and faster. He sensed his passenger was nervous. 'You're frightened, aren't you?' he said gleefully. 'You're frightened!' And, as he said it, he pressed hard on the accelerator.

A love of 'sheer devilment', as one of his colleagues put it, went with this love of physical danger. Ian Wrigglesworth, the party's economics spokesman, liked to tell the story of how Owen insisted that the two of them gatecrash a party given by Jeffrey Archer, the novelist and Conservative vice-chairman (whom Debbie Owen, a literary agent, happened to have as one of her clients). 'Come on,' said Owen, taking him up in the lift to the Archers' penthouse flat. When they were admitted, Owen proceeded to greet the startled Archer in his most charming manner; but he declined Archer's offer of a glass of champagne, asking, 'Now you wouldn't expect me to sup with the devil, would you?' Archer's Conservative guests were visibly shocked. Owen loved it.

The new SDP leader was also an extremely macho man—not in the sense that he regarded women as his inferiors (on the contrary, he respected them and enjoyed their company), but in the sense that he relished conflict and looked down on anyone whom he regarded as being weak or indecisive. His principal adjectives of praise were 'tough', 'strong', 'challenging' and 'determined'. His principal adjectives of disdain were 'gutless', 'feeble', 'pathetic' and 'wet'. His ultimate put-down was to say of a man 'He hasn't any balls.' According to colleagues, he got 'a positive charge' out of Dennis Skinner, the vociferous Labour backbencher who had made life so difficult for Jenkins.

Owen was often assertive to the point of being aggressive, and he sometimes gave the impression that if he lost an argument he would lose some part of his inner self. He wanted, as one acquaintance put it, 'to be omnicompetent, omniscient and omnipotent'. His assertiveness was often mistaken for ambition; but in fact he was not especially ambitious: he was too concerned to be right, and he lacked the truly ambitious person's ability to manœuvre and compromise. Shortly before he left the Labour party, he chided John Smith, a former cabinet colleague, for the latter's 'fudging and mudging'—one of Owen's favourite phrases—in order to hold the Labour party together. Smith replied that Owen would realize sooner or later that fudging and mudging were an essential part of politics.

Like many macho men, Owen was determined to be entirely his own man, and he gave the impression of preferring to be wrong in his way rather than right in anybody else's. He seemed always to want to say, in the words of the Frank Sinatra song, 'I did it *my* way.' He appeared to see life as necessitating a continuous assertion of will: his will. He was far from being, in any ordinary sense, self-centred; his concern for groups like the homeless, NHS patients and the unemployed was real, and so was his love of his family. But he seemed quite unable ever to submerge his own identity in that of a larger group. Perhaps he feared that, if he did, his own identity would somehow be swallowed up. The self must, at almost any cost, be protected.

Owen largely lacked the gift of colleagueship. As someone who knew him well remarked:

David is one of those people who can be a father or a son, but never a brother. He can work for somebody else; look at how well he got on with Barbara Castle at the DHSS [Department of Health and Social Security]. Or he can be the boss himself; he liked being in charge as foreign secretary. But he's completely incapable of working with others on a basis of equality. It was lucky for him that when he was foreign secretary he was in a department that was out on a limb. He wasn't constantly having to go to meetings and deal with other departments.

The fact that he refused to accept Jenkins as a 'father' when Jenkins was leader led to Owen's being somewhat isolated in the party before the 1983 election; and, once he became leader himself, he was content with nothing less than a position of total dominance. With very few exceptions, those closest to him were dependants rather than associates. Most of them were employees or people attracted to him by his celebrity and strength of character, rather than fellow politicians.

Owen did have a sense of fun, if of a somewhat roguish character. It came out with his family and in episodes like his gatecrashing of the Archer party; his smile on a good day could be as sunny as anyone's. But underneath the fun and the smile his underlying disposition seemed to incline towards pessimism (or, as he would call it, 'realism'). The opposite of one of nature's 'happy warriors', he appeared always to assume that anything he wanted to achieve in politics would come only after years of struggle. His sense of humour, while real enough, was sardonic rather than jovial. He reminded many others in the SDP of historical would-be messiahs: men like Savonarola. Robespierre or, closer to home, Tony Benn. At one party meeting, Owen was delivering himself of one of his doom-and-gloom monologues when Shirley Williams intervened to say, only half-jokingly: 'You shouldn't talk like that: people will think we're just waiting for the Great Dictator.' His nickname, used occasionally by almost everyone in the party, was Dr Death, and, although no one ever suggested that he was violent, let alone that he wanted to kill anyone, he did have an undeniable air of menace about him.

The self-doubt that always appeared to lurk beneath Owen's surface confidence expressed itself, as self-doubt often does, in the form of doubts about others. Sometimes his judgements about other SDP politicians could be both perceptive and affectionate; but frequently they were tinged with suspicion. What *were* Shirley, Bill and Roy up to? He seemed to think that what they were up to much of the time was plotting against himself. The fact that there was no evidence of plotting—or indeed that there was evidence that there was probably no plotting—only made the alleged conspiracies that much more sinister. Even his greatest admirers admitted that there was a streak of paranoia in his character. The word was frequently used. Owen was obsessed with loyalty; and disagreement, except from among his most trusted confidants, was easily construed as disloyalty. Owen in any case had a somewhat Manichaean view of the world: he seemed almost to need to divide the world into those who were for him and those who were against him. In the course of the 1987 parliament, he even began to ask Margaret Thatcher's famous question: 'Is he one of us?'

Two features of the new leader's personality had already impinged, and were to impinge even more, on those who worked with him. One was his moodiness. 'As soon as he walked in the door,' one member of the Cowley Street staff said, 'you knew what kind of day it was going to be, either reasonably agreeable and businesslike or *very* stormy.' And Owen seemed to make little or no effort to damp down his moods. If, for whatever reason, he was in a bad mood, he let everyone around him know it; they were to adapt to him, not the other way round. At a particularly difficult meeting with the Liberals, he tapped his foot more and more impatiently and, as someone present put it, 'glowered like a Welsh hillside'. Another member of the Cowley Street staff likened working with Owen to listening to a performance of Beethoven's Pastoral Symphony: 'You know the storm is coming, but you're never quite sure when.' The same person added: 'When he's in one of his moods, he thinks everyone is against him.'

The other feature of his personality that all those who came into contact with him had to reckon with was his extraordinary capacity for rudeness. Owen was a man wholly lacking in pomposity or side. If the phone rang, he picked it up. If a table needed to be cleared after a dinner, he helped to clear it. If boxes needed to be loaded on to a lorry after a party conference, Owen would quite unselfconsciously help with the loading. (No one could imagine Jenkins doing any of these things.) And he was undoubtedly capable, when the occasion required, of disciplining himself in his dealings with others, especially if he needed them or believed that they might be able to harm him. He was especially circumspect in his dealings with journalists and television presenters.

But his rudeness towards everyone else could be breathtaking. He did not seem positively to enjoy being rude; he was not obviously malicious. He just could not be bothered not to be rude. If he felt scornful, he expressed his scorn. If he felt impatient, he expressed his impatience. Like many thin-skinned people, he seemed to assume that everyone else had the hide of a rhinoceros. His mother said that Owen had been 'a spoiled brat' as a child.[4] A good many in the SDP thought he still was.

People wore memories of his rudeness like battle honours; and they traded them, as though trying to reassure themselves that they had not been singled out personally. A man others described as being one of Owen's acolytes conceded readily that he was 'brutish, insensitive and impatient'. Another laughed as he said: 'David is a true egalitarian: he treats everyone awfully.' A member of the SDP National Committee remembered an occasion when the committee was discussing who should speak on its behalf at a coming Council for Social Democracy. Owen was sardonic at the expense of everyone whose name was put forward. Shirley on inner cities? 'Sure. That's a good subject for bleeding hearts.' Roy on law and order? 'Fine. Otherwise no one will realize he's still a member of the party.' Lord Harris, one of the Jenkinsites? 'No. We can't have both him and Roy. It would be too much like the master and his master's voice.' The tone was humorous, but no one doubted that he meant what he said. Another person described the experience of writing speeches for Owen during an election campaign: 'I wouldn't have minded if he hadn't used the speeches. I wouldn't even have minded if he'd torn them up. But what I did object to was his throwing them in the waste-basket while I was still in the room.'

Owen's style as leader of the SDP was all of a piece with the man. Indeed, unlike Harold Wilson, Margaret Thatcher and many other political leaders, Owen almost certainly did not consciously choose a leadership style: he just allowed himself to be himself. Leadership, like life, involved for him a continuous assertion of will. He consulted widely and loved to argue with those who tried to influence him; and he retained the disconcerting habit of often changing his mind—sometimes several times, in the course of a single conversation. But, once his mind was made up on an issue, especially an issue that was important to him, he was immovable. He would consult, but he would not, or could not, compromise. If he appeared to compromise, it was only because he had persuaded himself that he himself had changed his mind or, alternatively, that the issue was no longer important. Once he had made up his mind, he was less concerned to persuade others of the correctness of his view than to make sure that the votes he needed were on his side—that he would get his way. Most of the time, other members of the SDP did agree with him and he had little difficulty in getting his way, but before the 1987 election there was to be one very loud and damaging explosion.

Owen brought to the job of being leader fierce determination, immense energy and an extraordinary capacity for hard work. If Jenkins' leadership style had been laid back, Owen's was up front. Whereas Jenkins had been content to delegate, Owen insisted on being in effective charge of the party machine and also on having a good grasp of every major political question on which he might be asked to express a view. The fact that there were now only six SDP MPs made it even more imperative than before that the leader master not just two or three policy briefs but dozens across the entire policy range. A parliamentary colleague described with admiration how Owen had been determined to understand all the implications of a set of social-security reforms being proposed by the government. He had sat up till 4 o'clock in the morning wading through an enormous pile of documents and then the next day had made a much better speech on the subject in the House of Commons than Neil Kinnock, the Labour leader, who had been 'blundering and confused'.

One of Owen's greatest assets, in the eyes of both his party and the general public, was his directness and manifest sincerity of purpose. He was the opposite of phoney. He said what he thought and expected others to do the same. He was even capable of praising his political opponents and saying that he agreed with them. In responding to interviewers' questions, he sounded natural, and he was seldom, if ever, evasive. What you saw (as the Americans say) was what you got. He was not an especially good platform performer, lacking a gift for words and being somewhat wooden, but in face-to-face encounters on television he excelled. His strengths in many ways were the opposite of Jenkins'. The older man, a considerable orator, seemed most at ease on a public platform; the younger man evidently felt more comfortable in front of a television camera, especially when he was being interviewed.

Not surprisingly, a man of Owen's undoubted force and stature had little difficulty inspiring loyalty. Those closest to him—his wife, Debbie, his personal assistant Maggie Smart, and one or two MPs—were totally devoted to him. They admired his integrity, his political vision and his sense of purpose; they were prepared to put up with his rudeness (which was anyway mainly directed at others); and they probably sensed, and responded to, the element of vulnerability in his make-up. They and a wider circle of admirers were in no doubt that Owen was a real man, possibly a great man, just conceivably Britain's man of the future. In addition, Owen's hold on the party's membership in the country was virtually total. The party's members, like those closest to him, were attracted by his integrity and vision; and they, like the general public, were continually impressed by him on television. Owen's greatest difficulties were with those in the party who had power bases and strong political views of their own and who had already seen too much of politics to be over-impressed by a moody 45-year-old who had once had the good luck to be foreign secretary for a couple of years. Even they took him seriously, both as a man and as their party's leader; but their view of him was more mixed—and more detached—than that of his perfervid admirers. His fellow politicians were prepared to do business with him; they were not prepared to kneel before him.

Owen brought another important quality to the party leadership: a total devotion to the SDP and its continued existence as an independent political force. Quite apart from his mistrust of the Liberals, he seemed to regard the SDP almost as though it were a part of himself. To lose it would be like losing a limb. For the rest of the Gang of Four the party was a means to an end; for Owen it almost seemed to be an end in itself. The party's very name, SDP, seemed, in his eyes, to have almost mystic properties. It is not clear why he felt so strongly about the party. Perhaps he saw it as a kind of altar on which he had sacrificed his previous political career. Perhaps he saw it as *his* party. Perhaps he just needed something to cling on to. Whatever the explanation, Owen was determined from 1983 onwards that the SDP was going to continue to exist and that no one was going to be allowed to separate him from it.

The outcome of the 1983 election, although depressing for the SDP and the Alliance as a whole, had a tonic effect on Owen personally. He had held his seat in Plymouth Devonport despite stiff competition from both the major parties; and he was apparently able to command a personal vote in the constituency of at least 20 per cent.[5] He was now an SDP member of parliament in his own right, no longer merely a renegade from Labour. More than that, he was now the SDP's leader and could mould the party in his own image. He had come well out of the last election campaign; he proposed to come even better out of the next one. His personal triumphs in 1983 confirmed him in the view that he knew better than anyone else how the party should move forward.

The 1983 election also confirmed his view that it was idle—and always had been idle—for the SDP and the Alliance to talk as though they were in a position, by themselves, to form a government. He believed such talk was unrealistic; he thought it gave voters the impression that the Alliance parties and their leaders were living in a dream world; and he also thought that talk of 'going for government' undermined one key element in the Alliance's appeal to voters: its emphasis on the desirability of different parties working together. If the SDP and the Liberals aimed to work together with other parties, why pretend (especially since it would only be a pretence) that their aim was to triumph over all the other parties, with a view to excluding them from power? From the outset of his leadership, David Owen indicated in all his speeches and public statements that the way ahead for the SDP would be long and hard and that the most the party could realistically hope for was to share power in some future coalition. He did not make a dramatic public announcement saying he was abandoning the 1983 Jenkins–Steel 'go for government and go for it now' strategy; but he was abandoning it all the same.

Owen's first tasks in the new post-1983 situation were, as he saw it, to secure the independence of the SDP and to define its relationship with the Liberals.

Securing the independence of the SDP ought, on the face of it, to have been easy. The party in 1983 was only two and a half years old, it had a large corps of enthusiastic members, in June it had helped the Liberals to secure a record third-party vote and, despite everything, it still had six members of parliament, as many as the Liberals on their own had had throughout the 1950s. The reality, however, was more complicated.

For one thing, the psychological balance within the Liberal–SDP Alliance, having favoured the SDP prior to the election, was now heavily tilted in favour of the Liberals. Whereas before the election the SDP had had nearly thirty MPs and the Liberals thirteen, the Liberals now had seventeen to the SDP's half-dozen. The Social Democrats were no longer 'big brother' inside the House of Commons. Moreover, the SDP's tacit (and sometimes not so tacit) claim that it and it alone could do what the Liberals had always failed to do—namely, destroy the existing two-party system—had proved to be hollow. The Liberal party had been in a small minority in parliament before the SDP was ever thought of. Two years and oceans of media-hype later, it still was. A few Liberals believed that they would have done better on their own in the election, without the SDP. Many more believed that they would have done better with the SDP, but without Roy Jenkins. At the Liberals' election-night party at the National Liberal Club there was a certain amount of *Schadenfreude* as news of the SDP's continuing misfortunes was flashed up on the television monitors. There were ill-concealed smiles of satisfaction when the news came through that Mike Thomas, the Liberals' scourge in the pre-election seats negotiations, had finished third in Newcastle East. How were the mighty—and the cocky—fallen. It was clear to Owen that in this changed situation the SDP was going to have to be, not less assertive in its dealings with the Liberals than in the past, but, if anything, even more so.[6]

Owen's own views on the matter were straightforward. He was passionately devoted to the SDP, and he held the Liberal party in considerable contempt. He admired the Liberals for their fortitude in managing to keep a minority party alive over a period of many decades, and he was sympathetic towards their emphasis on pluralism and decentralization; but at the same time he thought the Liberals were soft on issues like defence, nuclear power and the environment, and he regarded the Liberals' internal decision-making procedures as being utterly ill-disciplined and chaotic. He seemed to feel an almost physical repugnance at the thought of becoming bogged down in the Liberals' quagmire. He wanted to be free to determine his own and his party's destiny; the Liberals, given half a chance, would crawl over him like ants. The conclusion was obvious: the SDP should maintain its independence and should resist every move that might lead, however indirectly, to the SDP's merging its identity with the Liberals'. Owen's view of the Liberals closely resembled, in both tone and substance, Margaret Thatcher's view of the European Community: co-operation, by all means; integration, never.

Owen's view was shared by his closest political allies, notably John Cart-wright, Mike Thomas and Christopher Brocklebank-Fowler. Indeed, being a passionate believer in the SDP's independence was a necessary, if not quite a sufficient, condition of being admitted to the leader's inner circle. The leader's view was not shared, however, either by the other members of the old Gang of Four, Jenkins, Rodgers and Williams, or by the other SDP members of parliament, Kennedy, Maclennan and Wrigglesworth. It was also not shared by many SDP candidates, supporters and activists in the country. Those who dissented from Owen did not so much disagree with him intellectually, though they did disagree: it was more a matter of their having an altogether more relaxed attitude towards the entire issue. Wrigglesworth cheerfully described himself as an 'agnostic' on relations with the Liberals.[7] Anne Sofer, an SDP member of the Greater London Council, wrote that her heart went out to a rank-and-file party member who, having listened to an earnest local debate on SDP–Liberal relations, said at the end: 'I came to this meeting with a completely open mind and nobody yet has said anything to change it.'[8]

Owen at some later stage seems to have persuaded himself that there had all along been a Jenkinsite conspiracy to merge the SDP and the Liberals, but he does not appear to have believed this in 1983. If so, he was quite right not to: there was no conspiracy. What there was instead was a widespread feeling in the SDP that the status quo in SDP–Liberal relations was inherently unsatisfactory, that closer relations between the two parties were desirable and that, whether they were desirable or not, they were almost certainly going to develop as Liberal party members and members of the SDP worked together increasingly amicably on the ground.

The arguments in favour of closer co-operation between the two parties, possibly leading to an eventual merger, were mainly practical and matter-of-fact.[9] No one wanted a mystical union with the Liberals: Owen was quite wrong to project his own virtually mystical view of the SDP on to other people's views of the Liberals. All that those who disagreed with him wanted was a more efficient use of scarce resources. The two parties had similar, if not quite identical, policies, so why have two parties? The existence of separate parties imposed heavy human costs: hours—indeed, days and weeks—of valuable time were devoted to the two parties meeting first separately and then together to hammer out agreements that could more easily and expeditiously have been hammered out within a single party. It also imposed heavy financial costs: two party headquarters instead of one, two chief executives instead of one, two press and publicity departments instead of one, and so on. The phone bill between the Liberal and the SDP headquarters alone ran into many hundreds of pounds.

Those who favoured closer co-operation between the two parties were also worried about the political costs. The existence of two separate parties had the effect of multiplying, in a seemingly artificial way, the disagreements within and between them. The Liberals had an internal argument over, say, defence or the negative income tax. Then the SDP had an internal argument over the same topic. Then the Liberals and the SDP, at a joint meeting or a whole series of joint meetings, went on to have yet another argument, still on the same topic. Three or more arguments instead of one—and at each stage the chances of new issues being raised, and of tempers being inflamed, increased.

The potential for discord was still further ratcheted up by the fact that, when the two parties met, they did not always have a comradely discussion. Rather, they very often conducted 'negotiations', rather in the style of management and unions in industry. These interminable arguments and negotiations not only seemed to many in the SDP (and in the Liberal party) to be debilitating in themselves; they gave political journalists endless opportunities for making trouble. The press loved to write about splits, and it seemed that two parties were not twice as likely, but at least three times as likely, to split as one. Those who favoured eventual merger also maintained that, because it was composed of two separate parties, the Liberal–SDP Alliance was liable to confuse ordinary voters, many of whom could not see the logic of its claiming to have one policy but two leaders and two sets of candidates. There was no hard evidence supporting the notion that a merged party would gain more votes than a two-party alliance, but the view was passionately held all the same.[10]

Arguments like these were reinforced by developments that were taking place in the SDP's area parties and in the constituencies, often at a considerable distance from London. The fact was that in many parts of the country local Social

Democrats and local Liberals were working more and more closely together, not as the result of any formal debates and decisions, but in response to good personal relations and the two parties' success in working together during the 1983 campaign. Presented with the possibility of closer association, they did not ask 'Why?' They asked 'Why not?' There was much talk in the months after polling day of each party's members having 'associate membership' of the other, of the formation of local 'Alliance clubs' and of the possibility that a merger of the two parties at the grass roots might take place 'organically'.[11] The *Guardian* published a report, headed 'Alliance merger gathers appeal', based on conversations with prominent Liberal and SDP figures in the West Country. The feeling appeared to be widespread there that the experience of fighting the campaign together had cleared away mutual misunderstandings and weakened the case for having two separate parties. Some of the *Guardian*'s informants suggested that a merged party might be called the 'Liberal Democrats'.[12]

One specific problem soon dominated the discussion. Local political parties in Britain exist for all kinds of reasons: to provide forums for political discussion, to provide milieux in which people with similar political views can meet socially and to elect candidates to the local council. But above all they exist to nominate and campaign for a local member of parliament. If the SDP and the Liberals were to remain separate parties, what was to happen to the local Liberal association in a constituency where, as under the pre-1983 seats allocation, the SDP had a monopoly of choosing the parliamentary candidate? And what was to happen to the local SDP in a constituency where the candidate was a Liberal chosen by Liberals? Separate parties with independently chosen candidates seemed to mean that in every constituency in the country the members of either the Liberals or the SDP would become in effect onlookers, mere second-class citizens. The danger was that in every constituency one or other of the two Alliance parties would simply atrophy. As a result, neither the SDP nor the Liberals would any longer be a genuinely national party; both would become half-national parties, with the geographical boundaries between them permanently frozen. The problem had, of course, been mentioned during the pre-1983 seats negotiations, but it had never really been faced: electoral success, it was thought, would somehow make it go away. But now, in the aftermath of electoral failure, the issue had clearly, in some manner, to be resolved.

In the summer of 1983 David Owen's leadership of the SDP began well. Both Owen and David Steel believed that the most immediate threat to co-operation between their two parties came from within the Liberal party, from men like Cyril Smith, David Alton and Simon Hughes who had succeeded on their own in capturing seats from Labour in by-elections and who often gave the impression of regarding the Social Democrats as an unnecessary, even undesirable, intrusion.[13] Owen and Steel, whatever their views on broader questions, both recognized that co-operation in some form between the parties would have to continue and they met at Owen's house in rural Wiltshire in late June to compare notes. Afterwards they let it be known that the Liberal–SDP Alliance would remain in being at least until the 1984 elections to the European Parliament. Steel would ideally have liked to begin moves towards an eventual merger, but he knew that Owen was opposed and the matter was allowed to rest. It was later claimed that Steel in Wiltshire had agreed that he would never say 'merger now' if Owen would resist the temptation to say 'merger never'.[14] The meeting between the two men was a considerable media success. In a scene reminiscent of the David Steel–Shirley Williams tryst on the lawn of Dean's Yard, Westminster, two years before, the two were photographed, wreathed in smiles, leaning on a five-barred gate.[15]

Owen spent the rest of the summer stamping on anyone and anything that seemed to threaten, however remotely, the SDP's independence. A number of pro-merger voices were raised on both sides of the Liberal–SDP divide. Dick Taverne of the SDP and William Wallace of the Liberals wrote articles advocating an eventual merger, and Roy Jenkins in a speech to an SDP conference in London said that, while there were good reasons not to plunge immediately into merger discussions, no one should 'clang gates for the future'.[16] In early September two dozen Liberal and SDP parliamentary candidates issued a call for the parties to develop closer links—links that 'could lead, if both parties wished it, to eventual union'.[17] Bill Rodgers in the *Political Quarterly* likewise emphasized that rejection of an instant merger was 'quite different from a deliberate attempt to frustrate the organic growth of the Alliance':

Although the SDP was launched from the top by the Gang of Four, it has made a virtue of one man, one vote and established a Constitution designed to enable its regional membership to have a major say in running the party. As for the Liberals, local autonomy has always been a virtue. If members of both parties at local level wish to turn a loose Alliance into a close day-to-day relationship, speaking as one and jointly selecting candidates, it would be foolish to resist such pressure on the grounds that premature merger might result.[18]

Probably more worrying from Owen's point of view than mere speeches and newspaper articles was the evidence beginning to accumulate that local Liberal and Social Democratic parties were not merely talking about merger in the abstract but were behaving in ways that seemed on the face of it to make mergers at the constituency level almost inevitable. Someone remarked that relations between the two parties were 'much more cordial in the country than among the leaders and MPs'. In Cambridgeshire (to take the extreme case) 90 per cent of those taking part in a postal ballot among SDP members declared themselves to be in favour of joint selection with Liberals of local, parliamentary and European candidates.[19] Other area parties in places as far apart as Bath, Chelmsford and Derbyshire were setting up joint Liberal–SDP organization groups, and by the end of the summer of 1983 several joint selections of council candidates had already taken place in south London.[20]

But Owen was adamant. 'They shall not pass,' he seemed to say. His private feelings about the Liberals he kept mostly to himself, but in a newspaper article he set out a long list of reasons why, in his view, the SDP ought to remain an independent party.[21] Making a virtue of the 'diversity of views between the parties' in the Alliance, he maintained that the joint election manifesto had benefited considerably from the SDP's distinctive input on defence and the Liberals' on industrial policy and co-ownership. He referred to 'a definable philosophy of Social Democracy', a philosophy that separated the Social Democrats from the Liberals as well as from the Conservatives and Labour. The special appeal of this philosophy had brought large numbers of new people into politics for the first time; nearly 60 per cent of those who had joined the new party during its first year had never previously belonged to any party. Owen reminded his readers that, at the time of the SDP's launch, there had never been any suggestion that the SDP's MPs should merely join the Liberals or that the SDP was being founded merely as a prelude to the formation, at some later date, of a unified 'Alliance party'.

Owen had no time for the idea that the existing Alliance, consisting of two separate parties, confused and alienated the electorate. On the contrary, he argued that large numbers of voters found the spectacle of two separate parties working together instead of cutting each other's throats positively refreshing. The Alliance in its present form had won the support of one-quarter of the electorate in the recent campaign. Why put at risk such a substantial achievement? If the two parties did try to merge, there would be endless constitutional wrangles of the kind that had recently done so much damage to Labour.

Owen advanced a further argument, of a different character. He pointed out that the Alliance's declared aim was to achieve proportional representation and that proportional representation was meant to lead—and undoubtedly would lead—to coalition governments becoming the norm in Britain as they were on the Continent. What better way was there, he suggested, to accustom people in Britain to the idea of inter-party co-operation and coalition government than to see the Liberals and the SDP remaining separate but 'working together across the party political divide'? The existing Liberal–SDP Alliance was, in itself, the best possible advertisement for the new style of politics that would follow the introduction of proportional representation, and the continued existence of the Alliance would, Owen suggested, stimulate public backing for the cause.

These arguments were to remain the bedrock of David Owen's resistance to merging the SDP with the Liberals for as long as the SDP survived. Underlying them were three assumptions. One was stated explicitly in Owen's 1983 article. The other two were not.

One of the unstated assumptions was that neither the SDP nor the Liberals, nor the two of them together, could realistically hope to win a general election outright and go on to form an Alliance government. Although he did not say so in so many words, Owen in his article was already abandoning what he believed to be his predecessor's, and David Steel's, ludicrously over-ambitious strategy. The image in his mind was different. It was of a hung parliament—possibly after the next election, possibly at some more distant date—in which a relatively small Liberal parliamentary party and a relatively small (possibly even smaller) contingent of SDP MPs would manœuvre with and between the two major parties in order to achieve proportional representation and, with it, the new style of politics that was his aim. Jenkins had sought to break the mould of the British party system; but he had also sought to win an overall parliamentary majority within the existing electoral arrangements. Owen was more cautious than his predecessor, but also more radical: he wanted to break both the mould of the existing party system and also the mould of the existing system of government. Jenkins was in some ways the prisoner of the very political system that, verbally, he rejected. When Owen spoke of coalition politics—and coalition politics more or less in perpetuity—he really meant it.

The other unstated assumption in Owen's article was implicit in his references to electoral reform and coalition politics and, in particular, to the specific system of proportional representation that the Alliance had earlier decided to advocate: the single transferable vote. The point about the single transferable vote (as distinct from, say, the German form of proportional representation) is that it positively invites a large number of political parties to fight one another constituency by constituency, even if these same parties then go on subsequently to form a coalition government.[22] Owen pointed out in his article that the single-transferable-vote system requires the abandonment of Britain's existing single-member constituencies and their replacement by an arrangement under which each constituency has several MPs. What Owen did not go on to point out, but undoubtedly had in mind, was that under the single-transferable-vote system the SDP would no longer have any electoral incentive to ally itself with the Liberals or any other political party. On the contrary, every party could, and would, go its own way. In other words, the long-term purpose of the Liberal–SDP Alliance, in Owen's view, was to create a situation in which the Alliance would no longer be necessary. Under the single-transferable-vote system the SDP would no longer have to tie itself to the Liberals; it would be wholly independent, and SDP and Liberal candidates could oppose each other in the new multi-member constituencies (even if they subsequently chose to work together in the parliament that resulted from any given election). Owen in 1983 clearly wanted to maintain the SDP's independence against the day when it could fight elections on its own and under its own banner. On the very day that proportional representation was adopted, Owen and the SDP could jettison the Liberals and cry for all the world to hear, 'Free at last!'

The third assumption in Owen's article was stated explicitly, even if its full implications were not. Owen argued that the electorate would not be happy with a choice in which the Alliance, taken as a whole, was forced to choose between having either the Labour party or the Conservative party as potential coalition partners. If the Alliance were seen to be likely to choose Labour, Conservative-inclined voters would be put off; if it were seen to be likely to choose the Conservatives, Labour-inclined voters would be put off. Better, he suggested, the prospect of a situation in which there would be a three-party coalition—either SDP–Liberal–Conservative or SDP–Liberal–Labour—and in which therefore the SDP and the Liberals would have the maximum opportunities for manœuvring and bargaining to the SDP's and the Liberals' advantage.

But this line of argument, which was stated in the article, had two implications which were not stated. One was that, since the Liberals were known to be much more inclined towards Labour than towards the Conservatives, the SDP would be the Conservative-leaning party in either type of coalition government: if Labour was the largest party, the SDP would keep a Labour-led coalition 'honest' from Conservative voters' point of view; if the Conservatives were the largest party, the SDP would prevent a Conservative-led coalition from being broken up by the Liberals' miscellaneous and generally left-wing enthusiasms. Either way, the SDP would be the party of good order, good sense and political stability.

The second implication, also unstated but obvious to anyone who stopped to think about it, was that, if the SDP remained independent of the Liberals, it would be able, in any negotiations leading up to the formation of a coalition or minority government, *in extremis* to part company from the Liberals. Election partners they might have been; coalition partners they need not necessarily be. Independence as a political party had as a logical consequence the possibility of independent political action. At every stage between 1983 and 1987, as well as afterwards, David Owen sought to pursue a policy that would leave the SDP—i.e. himself—with the maximum possible freedom of manœuvre. His party might be small, but—who could possibly say?—it might have enormous clout when, if ever, the time came. Owen was absolutely determined to retain that clout—far more determined than most people realized.

He was not, in fact, especially secretive. Anyone could infer his line of reasoning from his published speeches and statements. But few actually did so. Even the most suspicious-minded Liberals, while detecting that Owen was anti-Liberal and somewhat Conservative-inclined, failed to detect the extent to which he was prepared, if need be, to distance himself from his Liberal allies. Owen's line was increasingly resented by Liberals and by many in the SDP; but most of his critics seemed not to appreciate the full implications of what he was saying. If they had, they would have been even more critical. For Owen the alliance with the Liberals was not, to use Roy Jenkins' pre-1983 phrase, 'a partnership of principle'. Rather, it was a political tool, to be used when it was apt for the task in hand, to be discarded if ever it ceased to be. A puckish subeditor on the *Guardian*, the newspaper that published Owen's 1983 article, must have been conscious of the deep irony in Owen's position. He put a headline on the article that read: 'Divided we stand for coalition'.

The SDP leader did not restrict himself to newspaper articles in his efforts to prevent any kind of merger with the Liberals, whether 'organic' or not. He took more concrete steps. At meetings of the SDP's National Committee, he and his allies took the line that, even if the SDP wanted to permit joint selection with the

Liberals of 'Euro-candidates' and parliamentary candidates, such a course was precluded by the party's constitution, which required that SDP candidates be chosen by SDP members in one member-one-vote postal ballots. There was no provision allowing others to participate. Legal advice was sought from William Goodhart, one of the constitution's original authors, and he confirmed that the constitution did not allow for across-the-board joint selection, though he added that the National Committee could authorize the use of joint selection in specific constituencies 'in exceptional circumstances'.[23]

Owen also took steps to ensure that the first post-election gathering of the Council for Social Democracy, whatever else it did, would assert the SDP's determination to continue to work within its existing constitution and to maintain its independent existence as a party, at least till the next election. In mid-August 1983 Christopher Brocklebank-Fowler, an Owen supporter, tabled a motion for the CSD conference due to be held at Salford University in September. Supported by thirty-two other CSD members, the motion declared:

This Council for Social Democracy reaffirms its strong support for our Alliance with the Liberal Party, calls on the National Committee, while preserving the separate identity of the SDP, to deepen and strengthen the arrangement for working together between the two parties, within the context of the present Constitution of our party, and asks the National Committee to reach an agreement with representatives of the Liberal Party on both the seat allocation for the 1984 European Elections and for the next General Election as soon as possible so that the two parties can most effectively campaign together and maximize their voting potential.

One amendment to the Brocklebank-Fowler motion called on the National Committee to invite the Liberals to join in establishing machinery to maximize the Alliance's effectiveness 'at every organizational level'. Another read:

The option of a full merger between the Liberals and the SDP cannot be properly discussed until the two parties have more experience of working together and until they have established the machinery for full co-operation. Therefore this Council rejects the option of an outright merger until at least after the General Election.[24]

The language of the Brocklebank-Fowler motion and the two amendments was often tortuous, but its meaning was clear: no merger, a new seats allocation but on the old basis, no joint selection, the Liberals to be kept at arm's length, business as usual.

By the time of the 1983 Salford conference, only three months after the election, tempers were beginning to fray. The Owenites suspected the judgement and sometimes the motives of those who could not be got to see that the SDP must at all costs retain its independence and that joint candidate selection in any form would undermine that independence. The pro-Liberals and many of those who were agnostic on the issue were increasingly repelled by what they perceived as the Owenites' arrogance and their stubborn refusal to contemplate practical measures that, common sense seemed to dictate, would enable the SDP and the Liberals to work together more effectively, especially at the grass roots. Ominously, Owen was more and more on one side of the argument, all the other members of the old Gang of Four on the other. Liberals meanwhile noted with dismay and sometimes anger the increasingly anti-Liberal noises emanating from the Owen camp. Rank-and-file party members on both sides disliked the bickering and found it hard to see what all the fuss was about. At a difficult meeting on the eve of the conference, the SDP's National Committee agreed by thirteen votes to twelve to ask Brocklebank-Fowler to remit his business-as-usual motion. Were he to refuse, the committee further agreed by seventeen votes to ten to give the motion their collective support. The closeness of the votes accurately reflected how deep the divisions had become.[25]

The conference itself, coming so soon after the disappointments of the election, was a subdued affair, a sharp contrast to the ebullient rolling conferences of 1981 and 1982. At times there were scarcely a hundred people in the hall, and Salford University's bleak functionalism contrived to make the proceedings even more sombre than they would have been in any case. Frank Johnson in *The Times* paid tribute to the sacrifice being made by the party's former leader:

As yet another service to his country and his party, Mr Roy Jenkins yesterday spent a Sunday in Salford.

He peered down from the platform as the Social Democratic Party's annual conference got under way at Salford University. The thoughts of all Kensington were with him in this hour. He was almost completely cut off.

The nearest decent restaurants lay a mile and a half to the south [in] Manchester city centre. For anything other than Chinese or Indian, Mr Jenkins, his party, and indeed the British people, would have to show a still greater breadth of vision, and willingness to go out and meet their joint destiny, by looking more southerly still to the fat commuter country of Cheshire, and the Good Food Guide lands beyond.[26]

The debate on merger and joint selection took place on the first day, and it was clear from the beginning that, irrespective of the arguments, the great majority of delegates were content to give the party's new leader—who at this stage had been in post for only a few weeks—the benefit of any doubt. If he did not want merger, they did not want it either. Tom McNally, one of the MPs who had lost his seat, declared that the Limehouse Declaration had not been a half-way negotiating package but a declaration of principle: 'Big Cyril [Smith] said he would have liked to strangle us at birth. Being smothered by him at three years of age would be no less disagreeable.'[27] Owen ensured that there would be no doubt in anyone's mind that he regarded the merger issue as one of confidence by stating, in an interview published as the conference began, that if the Liberals and the SDP merged before the next election he would stand down as leader in favour of David Steel.[28]

In the event, motions calling for joint selection of both Euro-candidates and Westminster candidates were heavily defeated and the Brocklebank-Fowler motion and its amendments were carried overwhelmingly. Owen had won. He was concerned, however, that the SDP's declaration of independence should not be construed as a declaration of war on the Liberals, and he concluded his own speech in the same debate with a personal tribute to Steel, who had decided shortly after the election to take a three-month 'sabbatical' from politics:

Friendship holds the key to it all. That is why I will never allow the press and media, who only want to report division, to drive a wedge between David Steel and myself. I say to David how much I know every single SDP member wants him back on the British political scene.[29]

The remark was greeted with cheers.

The Salford decisions settled the merger issue for the remainder of the 1983 parliament. The SDP, as the Owenites put it, had 'survived', and it had also asserted its bargaining rights *vis-à-vis* the Liberals. The Social Democrats might now, following the election, be the junior partners in the Alliance, but they were going to be full partners all the same. At the same time, however, the Salford decisions, and Owen's statements and speeches during the summer of 1983, raised a tantalizing possibility. Owen had apparently agreed with Steel that he would 'never say never' so far as merger was concerned, and every time he spoke, although he dashed any prospect of merger in the short term, he simultaneously made a merger sound a distinct possibility in the long term. Here are some of the phrases he used:

I am not prepared to act as a stalking horse for a merger *before the next election*.[30]

I think we're wiser to stick to two parties working together *up to the next election*. After that, who can tell?[31]

I do not think a single fused Alliance party *at this stage in our development* would be as successful as if we stayed as we are *for this Parliament* . . .[32]

I am not opposed in principle to a merger. After the next election, it might be the right thing to do, who knows?[33]

It would be an extremely foolish fellow who took a position never to agree to a merger.[34]

The anti-merger amendment to the Brocklebank-Fowler amendment contained similar language: 'Therefore this Council rejects the option of an outright merger *until at least after the next General Election*.'

Owen went on using phrases like these for the next four years. But they were ambiguous. Owen probably intended them to mean only that he wanted to reserve his position; but it is hardly surprising that others took him to be saying that his mind in fact was open and that he was perfectly prepared to consider merging the two parties at some later date. Owen probably had no choice but to use such language: it would be ridiculous to say that the two parties should *never* merge, and any principled declaration against a merger in the future would only cause an unnecessary row now. Nevertheless, by using such phrases, and by going on using them, Owen was storing up false expectations, and trouble, for the future.

The Salford conference settled the issue of merger for the time being. It did not, however, settle the issue of joint selection. Joint selection was by far the more complicated issue of the two, and deciding what to do about it caused a great deal of aggravation in the party, although an amicable settlement was reached in the end.

Owen's initial position was clear. He wanted all parliamentary constituencies to be allocated to either the Liberals or the SDP as they had been prior to the 1983 election, and he wanted the Liberal candidates to be selected only by Liberals and the SDP candidates to be selected only by SDP members. The only element of formal grass-roots co-operation he was prepared to envisage had to do with short-listing: he was prepared to allow the possibility that local Liberals might veto the name of anyone on a proposed SDP short list to whom they took particular exception. He also had to acknowledge that, if the Liberals in Liberal-led constituencies wanted to involve local SDP members in the selection of Liberal candidates, there was not much the SDP could do about it.

Those who, unlike Owen, wanted closer co-operation with the Liberals at the local level sought to avoid a repetition of the seats-allocation exercise if they could and, failing that, to involve members of both parties in as many selections as possible. There were two possibilities. One—the less attractive from this point of view—was 'joint closed selection'. Seats would be allocated as in the past, and every seat would be Liberal-led or SDP-led; but Liberals would be able to participate in the selection of SDP candidates and vice versa. The other possibility—more attractive from the co-operationists' point of view—was 'joint open selection'. A seat or seats would not be allocated to either party. Instead Liberal and SDP would-be parliamentary candidates would compete locally for the support of both Liberal and SDP party members. The two local parties would in effect merge, at least for the purpose of selecting the candidate. The majority of Liberals, being co-operationists, naturally favoured joint open selection.

It might have been expected that Owen would be strongly opposed to joint open selection—and, to begin with, he was. He feared, not least, that, since the Liberal party had far more rank-and-file members than the SDP, the Liberals would swamp most joint open selections and nominate their own candidates. The SDP might wind up fighting many fewer than half the seats in the country (including fewer than half the winnable seats), with devastating consequences for the SDP's standing within the Alliance. To Owen, proposals for joint open selection seemed, initially, to amount to a Liberal takeover bid for his own party. He was not having it.

Following negotiations between John Roper for the SDP and Russell Johnston for the Liberals, outline agreement on a procedure for dealing with the allocation of seats for the European elections was reached fairly quickly. There was to be no national allocation. Instead, regional negotiators were to allocate seats to one or other of the parties on a regional basis, with each party to be given its fair share of all seats and also of the most winnable seats. With varying degrees of reluctance on the part of its members, the SDP's National Committee agreed that, while the party's constitution formally required SDP candidates to be chosen as the result of a ballot restricted to SDP members, joint selection was not to be ruled out 'in exceptional circumstances . . . for the purpose of expediting the selection process'.[35] The Liberal party, while objecting to the 'exceptional-circumstances' formula, was ready to acquiesce. In the event, despite a number of local rows in places as far apart as the West Country, London and Yorkshire, the regional negotiations proceeded reasonably smoothly, and the SDP and the Liberals wound up dividing Britain's seventy Euro-constituencies evenly between them.[36]

A deal over Europe, however, was always likely to be relatively easy to strike: time in the European case was pressing (the elections were to be held in June 1984), and the stakes were not high (no one imagined, given the first-past-the-post electoral system, that the Alliance could win more than one or two Euro-seats). But a satisfactory deal over Westminster was going to be a much harder nut to crack: the stakes were much higher, and, however much Liberals and Social Democrats might profess their 'Europeanness', members of both parties actually cared far more about Westminster than about Strasbourg.

Most people in the SDP, whatever their views about joint selection and the long-term future of Liberal–SDP relations, were SDP patriots in the sense that, like Owen, they thought that, as in 1983, the SDP should fight roughly half the 633 seats in Britain at the next election and that the SDP should also fight roughly half the seats that seemed winnable from the Alliance's point of view. Shirley Williams, speaking as a guest from the platform at the 1983 Liberal assembly, reminded Liberals that opposition to joint selection was not just David Owen's view but a collective view of his party;[37] and a year later Bill Rodgers, also speaking on the SDP's behalf, urged Liberals to accept that the pre-1983 allocation of seats should form the basis of any new round of negotiations between the two parties.[38]

But satisfying the claims of rough parity between the Liberals and the SDP and also, at the same time, the claims of joint open selection, which were still being pressed by the Liberals and many Social Democrats, was not going to be easy. The difficulties were compounded by the fact that the Liberals appeared to the SDP to be adopting a highly aggressive stance. In terms of parliamentary seats, the SDP merely wanted to hold on to what it already had. The Liberals, on the other hand, were already indicating that they wanted to reclaim for themselves many seats that had been SDP-led in 1983; and, by proposing widespread joint open selection, they also appeared to want to be in a position to use their greater weight of numbers to dislodge SDP candidates from still more seats. Owen's views on the matter were more extreme than many others', but he was not alone in wanting to defend what the Social Democrats saw as their legitimate claims.

Liberal and SDP negotiators first had to work out for Westminster, as they had for the European elections, a set of agreed national guidelines. The Liberals, in accordance with their party's constitution and traditions, wanted the allocation of seats between the two parties to take place at the local level, and they also wanted as many joint open selections as possible so that seats would not really be 'allocated' at all. The SDP negotiators, led by Mike Thomas, wanted whatever decisions were taken locally to be vetted and approved nationally, and they also wanted to retain the formula that joint open selection should be permitted only in exceptional circumstances. The agreement finally reached, in mid-January 1984, provided that Liberals and Social Democrats in groups of parliamentary constituencies (corresponding roughly to the areas covered by the SDP's area parties) should meet locally and decide which party should fight which seats and also how the two parties' candidates should be chosen. Local autonomy, however, was not to be complete. At the SDP's insistence, all proposals that deviated, or might seem to deviate, from the provisions of the national parties' constitutions would have to be approved by the national parties' governing bodies—in the SDP's case, the National Committee—before the selection of any candidate could take place. Both sides were happy. The Liberals achieved a measure of local decision-making and moved away from the nationally dominated negotiations that had marked the period before 1983; the SDP got the degree of ultimate national control that it, and especially its leader, required.[39]

The key phrase in the Westminster agreement, as in the earlier European Parliament agreement, was the phrase, used in connection with joint selection, 'in exceptional circumstances'. It was clear from the beginning that most Liberals, and many SDP supporters, wanted to interpret the phrase broadly, so that it covered more or less every situation in which the local Liberals and the local SDP either could not agree on the allocation of a seat or else decided for some other reason that they wanted to select their local candidate jointly. It was equally clear that Owen and his supporters on the National Committee would want to interpret the phrase much more narrowly, so that 'exceptional' actually meant exceptional and joint selection would be used only where there was a serious danger of local relations between the two parties breaking down—and possibly not even then. For the Liberals, in other words, the phrase was a lever; for the SDP it was a lid. The January 1984 agreement thus settled little. Everything would turn on how the SDP National Committee responded, case by case, to local requests that joint selection of a candidate in this or that constituency should be permitted.

Because of the involvement of the two parties' national governing bodies, this new round of negotiations regarding the allocation of seats and candidate selection was even more complicated than the one before 1983 had been.[40] National officials met national officials; local party activists met other local activists (and pretty much made up the rules as they went along). Party members in the constituencies grew increasingly frustrated at the delays being imposed by the centre. Headquarters staff were irritated by many local activists' seemingly wilful ignorance of the national guidelines that had been agreed upon.[41] Hardly surprisingly, the necessary agreements, which had to be arrived at area by area and seat by seat, took a great deal of time. Only 285 had been come to, or were even well under way, by the autumn of 1984. Only 336, out of the 633 that were needed, had been negotiated by the end of that year.[42]

And, sure enough, requests to hold joint selections began to come forward to the National Committee, first in a trickle, then in a steady stream. By October 1984 forty-three applications for joint open selection and thirteen for joint closed selection had been received by the SDP's Cowley Street headquarters.[43] In some cases the local SDP genuinely saw joint selection as the only way out of a local impasse; but in others it was clearly seen as being positively desirable in itself or else as a sensible and relatively easy way of reaching a compromise with the local Liberals. The behaviour of many area parties suggested that they did not share their leader's preoccupation with maintaining the SDP's independence at all costs: if the Social Democrats were supposed to be the Liberals' allies, why should they spend so much time fighting them, or at least haggling with them? Labour and the Conservatives, after all, were the real enemy.

Some of the requests for joint selection were bizarre. In connection with Saffron Walden in Essex, where the 1983 SDP candidate was standing down, the local area party met no fewer than four times before deciding to recommend joint open selection or, failing that, that the seat be handed back to the Liberals (who were stronger than the SDP in that part of the county).[44] In other words, the local party was recommending that, if the compromise of joint selection was not accepted, the Social Democrats should simply capitulate. The National Committee in this case was unhappy and it eventually voted by a majority of fourteen to eight to reject joint open selection ('it did not appear that exceptional circumstances applied'). The seat therefore reverted to the Liberals. In other cases, the committee somewhat gloomily accepted whatever the local parties were proposing, including joint selection.[45]

The Saffron Walden case was admittedly somewhat extreme, but during 1983, 1984 and 1985 the National Committee spent hours of its time debating the principles of joint selection and responding, constituency by constituency, to dozens of joint-selection requests. For the first year or so, the problems posed, while vexatious, were not particularly serious; relatively few requests were coming forward, and difficult decisions could be postponed. But from the autumn of 1984 onwards, following the party's second post-election conference, it was clear the issue had to be faced. The pace was forced partly by odd instances like that of Saffron Walden, but chiefly by the actions of the SDP Council in Wales, which, under the leadership of Gwynoro Jones, the former MP, and without any reference to the National Committee, proceeded to strike a comprehensive deal with the Welsh Liberals under which, out of the thirty-eight seats in Wales, no fewer than eight would be the subject of joint selection. The first that many in the national party heard of the Welsh arrangement was when they read about it in the national newspapers.[46]

Owen by now had had enough. The Liberals were constantly carping and demanding that the SDP make concessions; far too many SDP area parties seemed ready to acquiesce in joint selection of one kind or another; the Welsh were behaving abominably; and, worst of all from his point of view, it was not clear that he could rely any longer on a majority of the National Committee. He had been defeated over the granting of joint open selection in two Euro-constituencies; he had won only narrowly on several other occasions; and now it looked as though the new National Committee, elected at the 1984 conference, might be more open-minded on joint selection than its predecessor. At the regular National Committee meeting in November 1984, he blew up. He maintained that for many in the party joint selection was no more than an excuse for not standing up to the Liberals; joint open selection would make it impossible for the SDP to maintain parity with the Liberals in terms of the number of seats that each side fought; joint closed selection threatened to jeopardize the party's integrity. In his view, the alliance with the Liberals was like a marriage. He wanted to maintain it, but 'he had to accept that sometimes there were divorces'.[47] Several members of the National Committee came away from the November meeting convinced that Owen had hinted that he would resign if he did not get his way.[48]

For the next few months, with feelings running high, almost every proposal for joint selection was considered in detail and on its merits. Contested votes were the norm. In December 1984, for example, the National Committee agreed by fifteen votes to eleven to accept the Welsh Council's proposals as a *fait accompli*, voted by a majority of fifteen to ten not to accept proposals for three joint selections in Cambridgeshire and agreed by eighteen votes to five that joint open selection should be permitted in the exceptional circumstances prevailing in Salisbury.[49]

Gradually, however, the issue began to seem one of practicalities not of principles, the discussions became cooler, and contested votes became fewer. Not least, David Owen's opposition to anything that smacked of giving in to the Liberals began to abate. 'There was', said a close friend, 'a time when he made you wash your mouth out with soap if you so much as mentioned the word "Alliance". Now he himself often talks about "the Alliance parties".' The breakthrough came in July 1985 when a negotiating group led by Bill Rodgers presented the National Committee with a complicated package of local deals and told the committee, in so many words, that the package 'reflected a complex balance of judgement' and that it had to stand or fall as a whole. Despite the fact that the package contained no fewer than twenty joint open selections, the committee accepted it almost without demur. Several other proposals for joint selection were accepted at the same meeting.[50]

What caused Owen, so passionate on the issue in November 1984, to have become much less passionate, even agnostic, by the middle of the following summer?

Part of the answer is that, to a large extent, he had won: he had got his way. Owen undoubtedly disliked joint selection for its own sake; he did not want the Liberals interfering in the SDP's internal affairs. But his real fear was that the Liberal party and the pro-merger forces in the SDP would succeed in obtaining such a large number of joint selections that the balance of power in the Alliance would be tipped decisively in the Liberals' favour. He feared a gradual Liberal takeover, with formal merger to follow. By the summer of 1985, that fear had largely receded. By taking such a strong line in opposition to joint selection, Owen had ensured that, although it would take place, it would take place on only a relatively small scale. His efforts, in other words, ensured that the famous phrase 'in exceptional circumstances' did serve as a lid and not a lever. At the same meeting that accepted the Rodgers group's elaborate seats package, Rodgers was also able to announce that, as a result of his negotiations, the SDP would almost certainly contest more than 300 seats at the next election—that rough parity with the Liberals, including among the most winnable seats, would be maintained.[51] The pressure was off.

Once it was clear that rough parity with the Liberals would indeed be maintained, Owen had another incentive for backing off: the trench warfare over joint selection was proving politically very costly—costly in terms of personal relations among the Social Democrats, costly in terms of SDP–Liberal relations, costly in terms of adverse publicity in the media (the typical Alliance-related headline during this period read 'Alliance constituency wrangle continues') and costly, not least, in terms of the SDP leadership's relations with its own supporters in the constituencies, where annoyance with both Owen and the National Committee was rife. For Owen to have gone on resisting joint selection on grounds of principle would have been to risk alienating all but a handful of his staunchest supporters. It would also have meant risking defeat, since he could not count on a majority on the National Committee to back him on individual cases that seemed to have intrinsic merit.

Owen's change of mood probably owed something, too, to the fact that by the summer of 1985 his personal dominance of the SDP was unquestioned and the SDP's status as an equal partner in the Alliance was also unquestioned. He was more relaxed because he could afford to be. Even the process of joint open selection was not proving to be the Liberal ramp he had feared. Salisbury in Wiltshire was one of the most promising seats in the south of England from the Alliance's point of view. It had been Liberal-led in 1983, and there were far more Liberals in the constituency than SDP members; but in March 1985 the Salisbury Liberals and the SDP voted together to adopt as their candidate Parry Mitchell of the SDP, a wealthy businessman who was also a strong Owen supporter.[52] Perhaps the Liberals were not so bad after all.

The final outcome of the post-1983 seats negotiations was quite satisfactory so far as Owen and the SDP were concerned. Rodgers and Andy Ellis for the Liberals made sure that, from early 1985 onwards, the discussions, however decentralized, were conducted in a more workmanlike and politically sensitive way. Instead of merely accepting the outcomes of local deliberations, they intervened—or got others to intervene—to identify log-jams in individual areas and to suggest what one Liberal called 'sideways views' of possible solutions, involving a number of different areas. Difficulties were thus turned into opportunities. Fortunately for both Rodgers and Ellis, and despite the best efforts of Owen and those around him, the relations between the Liberals and the SDP on the ground were by now considerably more easy-going and tolerant than they had been three years earlier. The two sides had got to know one another well in the interim, and they had worked well together during the 1983 campaign. In the end, the SDP in 1987 fought 306 seats, only five fewer than in 1983. The combination of area-by-area seats allocation and joint open selection caused a total of seventy-eight seats to change hands between the two elections; but the net turnover between the two parties was minimal. Given the SDP's weakened position following the 1983 election, it had held its ground well.[53]

The SDP more than held its ground in another respect. During the years when the seats negotiations were at their most intense, David Owen was performing one of the most remarkable conjuring tricks in the history of modern British politics. As someone who was not otherwise an admirer of Owen put it at the time, 'David is pulling himself up by his bootstraps; but the amazing thing is: he doesn't *have* any bootstraps!' Between 1983 and 1985 the leader of a party that had only six seats in the House of Commons and had been all but obliterated at the previous general election established himself as one of the central figures in British public life, the sort of figure whose opinion is sought on every imaginable topic, who is constantly seen on television and heard on radio and who is talked of endlessly as a future prime minister. Owen also established himself in the House of Commons as one of the very few MPs who could draw members into the chamber and whom occupants of both front benches stayed on to listen to. There are not, and never have been, many stars in British politics. Owen had not been one before. Now, in the mid-1980s, he became one—or, more precisely, he turned himself into one.

Owen made headlines out of all proportion to his party's real significance. When he was denied an invitation to the annual Remembrance Day service at the Cenotaph, his angry letter to the prime minister about her 'petty and partisan' snub was reported in almost every newspaper and was made the subject of leading articles in several.[54] (The publicity was bad for the government, and Thatcher subsequently relented.) Shortly after the 1984–5 miners' strike began, Owen made a speech at a Liberal summer school in which he urged the government to stand firm and declared in the most uncompromising terms that the miners under Arthur Scargill must be beaten 'in the name of economic and political sense'.[55] The *Sun* headlined the story: 'Miners must be beaten, says Owen'. The headline in the *Sunday Express* read: 'Owen: I'm backing Maggie'. Throughout the parliament, despite the SDP's complaints against the BBC described in Chapter 14, Owen contrived to ensure that he—and therefore to a considerable extent his party—maintained a high media profile.

Nor did his success lie merely in headline-catching; journalists and politicians in other parties often commented on his courage and sureness of touch:

In politics, as in racing, a special aura hangs about the man in form. For the moment, however brief, he seems to have some kind of unique insight into the secrets of the universe, which causes other superstitious mortals to crowd in behind him in the hope of picking up the odd grain of fortune, but at a slightly respectful distance, for fear of breaking the spell.

The man in political form at present is Dr David Owen . . .[56]

Dr Owen . . . has won widespread acclaim as the most formidable leader of any Opposition party in the present Parliament.[57]

If David Owen has succeeded in anything in the past year, it is in persuading influential people of differing political outlooks that he really has the potential to play a messianic role in British politics. 'He is the only person with anything approaching the qualities of Thatcher.'[58]

Owen did not owe his achievement merely to fluency. On the contrary, he lacked a gift for phrase-making and his delivery was often wooden. Rather, he took himself seriously, demanded that others do the same and was sufficiently intelligent, tough-minded and determined that, sometimes to their own surprise, they did take him seriously. His ideas were fresh at a time when both Thatcherism and the Labour party's thinking seemed stale, and he was far less predictable than most of the other parties' leading figures; he would appear 'right wing' on one issue but 'left wing' on another. His combination of fierceness and boyish good looks set him apart from the more stolid figures who occupied most of the front benches, and he had the inestimable advantage of being the dominant figure in a minuscule party: he did not have to clear his speeches with others, and he could say more or less whatever he liked—on whatever subjects he liked—without fear of being contradicted. Above all, Owen worked terribly hard—far harder than his predecessor, Jenkins, had done. He even installed a Press Association wire immediately outside his office so that he could issue statements within minutes of news appearing on the tape. The flow of press releases from his office was prodigious. Many of them were used.

On a much smaller scale, Shirley Williams, as president of the party, and the tiny contingent of SDP MPs, performed a similar feat. There were hardly any of them; they could not look for any favours to the broadcasting authorities, especially the BBC. But they managed nevertheless to make themselves heard. Jenkins played a smaller part than in the previous parliament, especially in the first two years; but Ian Wrigglesworth, Robert Maclennan and John Cartwright, in particular, asked questions and spoke frequently in the House and were constantly available for radio and television interviews. An analysis by *The Times* of the Hansard indices for one year, 1984, showed that two-thirds of the SDP and Liberal MPs had above-average workloads in the House of Commons. Seventy-one per cent of Alliance MPs had a heavy workload, compared with 44 per cent of Labour backbenchers and only 27 per cent of Conservatives.[59] Asked how the SDP's half-dozen MPs contrived to give the impression of being a substantial parliamentary force, John Cartwright, the chief whip (and David Owen's closest parliamentary friend and ally), laughed and replied: 'It's a matter of ring-mastering with mirrors.' The SDP's parliamentary performance reminded him of one of those old cinema spectaculars in which the extras are killed off in one scene but somehow miraculously come back to life again in time for the next.

Owen's reward for his force and assiduity was a consistently high rating in the opinion polls. During the four years that the 1983 parliament lasted, the Gallup Poll found in every month that more people thought Owen was 'proving a good leader of the SDP' than thought he was not. The proportion who approved of his leadership never fell below 45 per cent, and the ratio of those who approved to those who disapproved was usually two-to-one or more. In some months, despite the SDP's minority status, more than one voter in five told the polls they believed Owen would make a better prime minister than any other party leader.[60] The contrast between Owen and Jenkins was stark—and must have been painful for the older man.

An unintended by-product of Owen's success during these years was that he eclipsed to a considerable extent the man who had previously been the dominant figure in the centre of British politics: his Liberal opposite number, David Steel. Owen's grasp of the details of policy was always greater than Steel's, and he was now consistently the tougher, more incisive performer both in the House of Commons and on television. A constant refrain in the newspapers was that 'Steel is not as sharp as he once was', and there was speculation that he had never fully recovered from a viral infection that had kept him out of politics during the summer of 1983.[61] Steel's poll ratings remained high, and in most months more people thought he was proving a good leader of the Liberals than thought Owen was proving a good leader of the SDP; but the gap between them narrowed, and during 1986–7, in the run-up to the 1987 general election, Owen's rating as a potential prime minister was higher than Steel's in more months than not. Conscious that many of his Liberal followers were unhappy at the way Owen was upstaging him, Steel felt constrained to say at one point that it was not in his 'nature to play second fiddle to anyone'.[62]

The electoral fortunes of the Alliance as a whole fluctuated over almost as wide a range between 1983 and 1987 as between 1981 and 1983. After the disappointing 1983 results, there could never really be 'glad confident morning again'. Even so, periods when the Alliance was in the doldrums were punctuated by moments of considerable elation. Figure 6 sets out the three main parties' standings in the Gallup Poll, quarter by quarter, between the two elections. As can be seen, the Liberals and the SDP trailed badly in third place during most of 1983 and 1984, though with levels of support not substantially lower than the 25.4 per cent they had achieved at the 1983 election. Their fortunes then improved between the second quarter of 1985 and the second quarter of 1986, with the Alliance as a whole sometimes moving into second place or even in two or three months taking a small lead. But from the spring of 1986 onwards the Alliance fell back to third place, with levels of support a little improved on those of 1983–4, but not much.

There was no golden age for the Alliance and the SDP during the 1983

1 The hard left's political style. Jenkins hit by a flour bomb while speaking on Reg Prentice's behalf at Newham, September 1975.

2 An isolated figure. David Owen waits to speak at the special Labour party conference at Wembley, January 1981.

3 A question from the gentleman at the back. The Gang of Four launch the SDP at the Connaught Rooms, London, March 1981.

4 'Like two young lovers'. David Steel and Shirley Williams launch the first Liberal–SDP joint policy statement, 'A Fresh Start for Britain', at Dean's Yard, Westminster, June 1981.

5 On the stump. Shirley Williams campaigns for a bemused Roy Jenkins in Warrington, July 1981.

6 Roy Jenkins leans in a forward direction to converse with a Warrington voter, July 1981.

7 Already the elder statesman. Roy Jenkins sits down to acclamation after speaking at the SDP's consultative conference, Perth, October 1981.

8 Roy Jenkins at Central Hall, Westminster, October 1981.

9 On her way to victory. Shirley Williams campaigns from the back of a van in Crosby, November 1981.

10 After the count. Shirley Williams with exuberant supporters at her victory party, Crosby by-election, November 1981.

11 Not claret, Sainsbury's Bergerac Rouge. Rodgers, Owen and Jenkins discuss the seats row with the Liberals at Rodgers' house, January 1982.

12 Shirley Williams shields her eyes from the television lights, SDP constitutional conference, Kensington town hall, February 1982.

13 Roy Jenkins returns to the
House of Commons from
Hillhead in March 1982
after a six-year absence.

14 Bill Rodgers ponders a point
at the SDP's consultative
conference in Derby,
October 1982.

15 The Gang of Three. Shirley
Williams, David Owen and Bill
Rodgers in consultation,
February 1983.

16 Shirley Williams addressing
the SDP Conference, Salford,
September 1983.

17 David Steel, September 1984.

18 'Ringmastering with mirrors': the SDP in Parliament in 1986. John Cartwright sits on David Owen's right with Robert Maclennan on his right. On Owen's left is the winner of the Portsmouth South by-election, Mike Hancock.

19 In Owen's pocket. Spitting Image squeaky dolls of the two Davids, on sale at the 1986 SDP Conference.

Britain United
—The time has come—

SDP Liberal ALLIANCE

20 (*above*) David Owen and David Steel launch the Alliance's manifesto, 1987 general election.

21 (*below*) Not waving but drowning. Steel and Owen greet supporters and photographers at the end of the election campaign, Richmond, June 1987.

22 Bob Maclennan seeks to stiffen his party's resolve, SDP conference, Portsmouth, September 1987.

23 Putting on a brave face. David Steel and Bob Maclennan tell journalists that the merged party's policy programme is not quite ready. January 1988.

24 Still determined. David Owen addresses members of his 'continuing SDP', May 1989.

25 A grim-faced David Owen arrives at Broadcasting House in June 1990 to announce the imminent demise of his 'continuing SDP'.

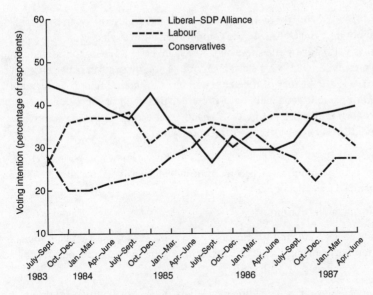

Fig. 6 The standing of the parties in the Gallup Poll, 1983–1987

parliament, but there was a sort of silver age lasting roughly from May 1985, shortly after the end of the miners' strike, until May 1986, when Thatcher and her government were beginning to recover from the Westland affair. The Alliance did not do well in the June 1984 European Parliament elections, winning no seats and only 19.1 per cent of the popular vote, but the county-council elections in May 1985 were a considerable success.[63] The Alliance gained more than 260 seats and found itself holding the balance of power on more than a dozen councils, including Devon, Hertfordshire, Oxfordshire, East Sussex, Essex and North Yorkshire. The extent of the Alliance triumph was at first exaggerated, and subsequent vote tallies showed that since 1983 it had really done little more than hold its own (the true victors being Labour).[64] Nevertheless, the Alliance's new local-government power was real enough, and so was the boost to Alliance morale.

During this brief silver age, the Liberals gained Brecon and Radnor from the Conservatives in a by-election in July 1985, and in July and September of that year the Liberals and SDP together led both major parties in the opinion polls. Indeed, in the twelve months from May 1985 to April 1986 taken as a whole, the Alliance, with the backing of 32 per cent of the electorate in the Gallup Poll, led the Conservatives, with 31 per cent, and was only three points behind the Labour party, with 35 per cent. In May 1986 the Liberals followed up their Brecon and Radnor victory by winning Ryedale in north Yorkshire from the Conservatives, and on the same day another Liberal candidate nearly gained West Derbyshire. Talk of the Liberals and the SDP holding the balance of power in a hung parliament

329

suddenly revived, and there was a good deal of learned discussion in the broadsheet press about how the Queen should comport herself in such a situation.[65]

It was also during the silver age, in December 1985, that the comedian John Cleese presented what must have been one of the most successful party political broadcasts in the history of the genre—in terms of both audience enjoyment and the resulting public good will. It was presented on behalf of the SDP, and its subject was proportional representation. It began with Cleese sitting in a conventional party political broadcast set, yawning and saying:

I am sorry, but this is a party political broadcast, and you know how boring *they* are. This one, I'm afraid, promises to be quite outstandingly tedious, because it's all about proportional representation.

Yawning again, he continued:

And don't complain to me it's boring, because I know in advance what I am going to say. So the level of boredom I shall experience during the next ten minutes will be really appalling, compared even with yours.[66]

There followed a rapid-fire exposition of the mechanics of proportional representation and the case for it, interspersed with ironic remarks to the effect that, while, of course, the Norwegians, Swedes, Finns, Danes, Irish, Dutch, Belgians, Germans, French, Italians, Portuguese, Spaniards and Greeks had no trouble in operating a proportional-representation system, the British were probably too stupid to. At any rate, that is what their politicians kept telling them. The SDP received 6,000 phone calls and 1,500 letters following the broadcast, and a private Gallup survey, commissioned by the SDP, reported that support for proportional representation had risen sharply, especially among working-class voters and the young.

But the silver age came to an end, as had the golden age before it. The Alliance remained what it had always been: largely a refuge for those voters—and there were often large numbers of them—who were temporarily disenchanted with the major parties. The Alliance lost support the moment Neil Kinnock replaced Michael Foot as Labour leader in 1983. It began to gain strength during the violent phase of the miners' strike, when many voters were alienated both by the government's intransigence and by Kinnock's apparent reluctance to distance himself from the miners' leader, Arthur Scargill. But then decline set in again when the Conservatives began to recover from the Westland débâcle and the resignation of Michael Heseltine. The Alliance itself had limited appeal; it benefited largely from rejection of the other parties.

As during the 1983 parliament, the Alliance's political fortunes in general seemed to ebb and flow with the SDP's and the Liberals' performance in by-elections. Victories brought media attention and often a considerable boost in the polls; defeats caused the curtain to come down again. Sixteen by-elections were held during the 1987 parliament. The Alliance gained seats in four of them and moved up from third place to second in another four; it only once failed to increase its share of the vote. Indeed, its share of the vote in all sixteen by-elections, 39 per cent, was higher than that of either the Conservatives, 30 per cent, or Labour, 28 per cent. But the Alliance's actual performance was considerably patchier than the overall figures suggest. In July 1983 the Liberals came within 553 votes of capturing Penrith and the Border, the seat vacated by the Conservative deputy leader William Whitelaw, and Thatcher never again elevated a sitting MP to the peerage; a year later, in June 1984, an unknown Social Democrat local councillor named Mike Hancock startled the political world—and also strengthened the SDP's position within the Alliance—by capturing the previously safe Conservative seat of Portsmouth South. The Portsmouth South victory was followed a year later by the Liberals' success in Brecon and Radnor and, nearly a year after that, by their even greater success in Ryedale. But the Alliance's candidates were comprehensively beaten in several by-elections in safe Conservative and Labour seats, and, worse, it was Labour rather than the Alliance who won the only classic Conservative–Labour inner-city marginal fought during the parliament: Fulham in west London, where Roger Liddle, Bill Rodgers' former assistant, was disappointed not to increase the SDP share of the vote by more than a trivial 0.5 per cent.

By the end of the silver age in the spring of 1986 there were still a number of by-elections to be fought, including one that was to cause a sensation. But one thing was already clear—and becoming clearer. Whatever the fine points of difference among its original founders, the SDP had been set up to replace, or at least challenge, the Labour party as the principal party of the left in Britain. It had been intended to be a party that would appeal to the liberal-minded middle classes, but also, and overwhelmingly, to working-class voters alienated by Labour's extremism, the idea being that the SDP would target, and in due course capture, large numbers of Labour-held seats. But, as we have seen already in earlier chapters, that was emphatically not what was happening. Certainly, the SDP and the Alliance as a whole had considerable appeal to many former Labour voters and to voters who, in the absence of an Alliance candidate, would probably still have voted Labour (the Alliance cut quite heavily into the Labour vote in 1983); but it was clear that it had an even greater appeal to former Conservative voters and to voters who, in the absence of an Alliance candidate, would probably have voted Conservative. The Alliance was going down reasonably well on working-class council estates, but it was going down much better in rural areas and comfortable suburbs.[67]

The experience of the 1983–7 by-elections rammed home the point. In the presence of an Alliance candidate, Labour's share of the vote actually rose, or else fell by fewer than ten percentage points, in every one of the sixteen by-elections fought during the period; the Conservatives' share of the vote, however, fell in all sixteen by-elections, in eleven by more than ten percentage points, in another two by more than twenty points. The implication was obvious: the SDP and the Alliance had turned out to be more successful as exploiters of Conservative unpopularity than as exploiters of Labour unpopularity. There were more votes to be won on the right than on the left. The SDP needed perhaps to rethink its electoral strategy.[68]

David Owen was in no doubt that it needed to; and he responded following the 1983 election by substantially reorienting the SDP's ideology and propaganda. Electoral considerations apart, he was also persuaded that many of the ideas he and others had inherited from the Labour party—ideas about Keynesian fine-tuning, public ownership, state planning of the economy and co-operation between the government and the trade unions—were no longer intellectually sustainable and so should be abandoned. Like Mikhail Gorbachev in the Soviet Union, Owen set out to bring 'new thinking' to the SDP—and also, if they cared to pay attention, to the Liberals. He developed his thinking, and also signalled his determination to change many of the SDP's ideas, in an Institute of Economic Affairs article published as early as October 1983, in his 1984 Hoover Address at Strathclyde University, in his 1985 Gaitskell Memorial Lecture at Nottingham University, in all his speeches to the Council for Social Democracy and in the two books he somehow found time to write during this period, A Future that will Work and A United Kingdom.[69]

The range of subjects covered in his lectures, speeches and books—technology, public expenditure, the environment, tax credits, unemployment, the health service, European security, constitutional reform, incomes policy, incentives in industry, urban regeneration, education—was prodigious, but underlying all of them were four themes.

One was patriotism and the need for a strong national defence. He had no time for anyone who would sell Britain short; he had no time, either, for the woolly-minded people who seemed somehow to imagine that, if only Britain abandoned its nuclear weapons, others would do the same. He once described the effect that working one summer as a manual labourer on a construction site had had on him:

For the first time I mixed with people outside my usual circle. In 1956, when the Suez crisis broke, there was Gaitskell on television and in the House of Commons criticizing Eden, and here were these men working alongside me, who should have been his natural supporters, furious with him. The Daily Mirror backed Gaitskell, but these men were tearing up their Daily Mirrors every day in the little hut where we had our tea and sandwiches during our break. The main subject of conversation was 'this bloody rag, the Mirror', and the Mirror writers were 'bastards, Commie-lovers!' It was not only that they taught me how people like them think; they also opened my eyes to how I should think myself.[70]

Owen as SDP leader did not necessarily agree with people like these; but he did identify with them. Equally important, he knew a great deal about defence, having been a junior defence minister in the 1960s and foreign secretary in the 1970s and having written a book on the subject.[71] The combination of his personal commitment and his considerable expertise made him impatient with those whom he believed were not thinking clearly enough on the issue or who seemed prepared to compromise for the sake of short-term political advantage. He was adamant that 'objective political and strategic considerations continue to reinforce the view that Britain should remain as long as financially feasible a nuclear-weapon state'.[72]

A second theme was constitutional reform. Owen wanted open government, decentralization and an extension of civil liberties, but above all he wanted proportional representation and coalition governments. His espousal of electoral reform had something to do with fairness, but it had more to do with his conviction that in the post-war period British-style strong governments had too often in practice been bad governments. Policies, especially economic and industrial policies, had been changed too often. The Conservatives had been too solicitous of the interests of their business allies; Labour had been too solicitous of the interests of its union allies. Both parties had fallen into the hands of ideological zealots. 'Proportional representation and the coalition governments that ensue', he wrote, 'are . . . necessary to provide the cohesion and stability that come from governments that represent at least half the electorate.'[73] He added:

Coherence [of policy] demands also that any political party should be very reluctant to implement structural industrial changes which appear to have no long-term hope of being accepted by the other parties and [are] virtually certain to be reversed if the government changes. That is not to exclude imposing structural changes which are politically controversial, but it is to argue that the onus of proof should be shifted for making industrial changes in a way that gives a far higher priority to them having a reasonable chance of lasting.[74]

Owen's model was that of countries on the continent of Europe, especially Germany.

His third theme, developed mainly after the 1983 election, was the superior efficiency and effectiveness, for most purposes, of the free market. He believed that a careful distinction should be drawn between the service-oriented and profit-oriented sectors of the economy, but that, the distinction having been drawn, the profit-oriented sector should be encouraged and should be left largely free of state control. In his Institute of Economic Affairs article he wrote:

We must be prepared to use the term 'market' openly and unashamedly. Britain cannot recover its economic strength without a far stronger emphasis on winning markets and without a clearer recognition of the commercial and competitive imperatives on which our prosperity depends.[75]

Owen was concerned about ownership; he wished to encourage industrial democracy, profit-sharing, co-ownership and co-operatives. But he was principally concerned about competition. There was a good case to be made for privatization, but not if it consisted merely of transforming state monopolies into private monopolies. Government industrial policy should consist largely of competition policy. This free-market theme was new and in some ways unexpected. Not surprisingly, it attracted the most attention.

Owen's fourth theme was the need to create a classless, more equal and more humane society. Because Owen's views on the free market and defence aroused more controversy, they were usually more widely reported, but he actually devoted considerably more space in his speeches and writings to matters of social concern. The chapter titles of his books capture both the content and the tone: 'Towards Green Growth', 'Responsibilities to the Unemployed', 'Social Responsibilities', 'Caring for the Whole Person', 'Industrial Partnership', 'Industrial Regeneration', 'Urban Regeneration', 'Educational Standards', 'Health Care'. Owen wanted to relieve poverty and create a more humane society for its own sake, but he also believed that only if the country were more equal and more humane could it grow and prosper. Consent was required for economic adaptation and change. If there were too many losers, the losers would succeed in blocking further adaptation and change. In his speech to the Salford party conference, he said that the SDP had to persuade the bulk of the people who had a job and who were relatively prosperous that they had responsibilities towards those who were less fortunate, that the achievers in society should not just shut themselves off from reality, that there were some who would always be dependent on others. 'We must not shy away', he said, 'from talking about values, love, charity, altruism, call it what you may.'[76]

In advocating nuclear weapons and a strong national defence, Owen was, or appeared to be, aligning himself with the Conservative party. In advocating constitutional change, he was clearly aligning himself with the Liberals. In propounding the virtues of the free market, he was again aligning himself with the Conservative party. In advocating a classless, more equal and more humane society, he was, or appeared to be, aligning himself with both the Liberals and Labour. Owen, needless to say, was conscious of the confusion that this unexpected combination of views might cause. 'What is needed', he wrote in *A Future that will Work*, 'is a new synthesis, a combination of what are too often wrongly assumed to be incompatible objectives.' 'It is not', he added, 'an easy balance to achieve.'[77] In order to try to achieve his new synthesis he introduced into many of his writings and public pronouncements a series of dichotomies that were meant to suggest the compatibility of incompatibilities, the need to adopt a philosophy of 'both . . . and' instead of 'one or the other':

'tough and tender'
'competitiveness and compassion'
'social concern and market realism'
'profit and service'
'the social market and also social justice'.

Owen believed that many European societies had achieved these twin objectives. He did not see why Britain should not achieve them too.

Owen's ideas taken separately were not new, but they were new in combination, and Owen increasingly championed them in a rhetoric that laid heavy emphasis on credibility, determination and discipline, on the need to make hard choices and difficult decisions and on the need also to accept the reality of many of the Thatcher government's achievements. It was arguable whether Owen's ideas deserved to be called right wing or not, but a lot of his rhetoric undoubtedly *sounded* right wing. Owen was said to be Margaret Thatcher's favourite opposition politician; she occasionally sounded like *his* favourite prime minister. Temperamentally, the two had much in common.

Many members of the SDP were dismayed by the unexpected direction in which their leader was taking them. Gone was any idea that the SDP might be a Labour party Mark II. Gone, too, was the Gaitskellites' old belief in state centralism. A large element of radical idealism did remain in Owen's new conception, but for many it seemed to be overlaid by his passion for hard-line defence policies and his willingness, even eagerness, to accept large chunks of Thatcherism as the new conventional wisdom.[78]

Among those who were most unhappy were the remainder of the old Gang of Four. As so often, the tensions between Owen and them were partly political but also partly personal. Bill Rodgers lacked a truly fulfilling role following his defeat in the general election; Roy Jenkins still resented the brutal way in which Owen had treated him following the election; Shirley Williams, although she had a central role to play in the party as its president, objected to, and was sometimes thrown off balance by, Owen's hectoring and dismissive manner (she always called him 'fierce David'). All three deeply disliked Owen's constant belligerence, his free-market rhetoric and his scarcely concealed admiration for Margaret Thatcher. All of them felt excluded—because they were excluded—from the leader's inner circle.

Bill Rodgers responded by giving a Tawney Society lecture entitled 'My Party—Wet or Dry?' in which he insisted that the SDP's natural province was not in the centre of British politics, let alone on the centre right, but 'unequivocally [on] the centre left'. He added, in a not very coded message to Owen:

The antithesis of 'tough and tender' brilliantly encapsulates the social market approach, but 'tough' is the dominant mood and can elbow 'tender' out of the way. It is time to talk more of our tender dimensions and to make it better known that we are a party of social reform, deeply concerned with the welfare of our people.[79]

Jenkins for his part responded publicly by warning Social Democrats against adopting a 'sub-Thatcherite posture'—and privately by likening David Owen to the Japanese upas tree, which is alleged to poison all life around it.[80] Williams as the party's president had to be more restrained, but she shared the others' doubts and in private did her best to persuade Owen to stick to the Limehouse Declaration's centre-left spirit. Asked at about this time to describe relations among the members of the Gang of Four, a member of the Cowley Street staff laughed and said that they were 'impossible—at best'.

Matters came to a head at the party's regular autumn conference in September 1985, held in Torquay. A small Limehouse Group had been formed to try to keep the party on the left, and the Stevenage area party, one of the largest and most successful in the country, put down a motion for the conference calling 'for greater attention on policy presentation in the coming year to promote ourselves as a party of radical social and constitutional reform, deeply concerned with the well-being of the people, the evil of unemployment and the need for a caring society'. Specifically, the Stevenage motion called on the SDP to confirm its 'original objective to become, on the centre-left of politics, the . . . main challenger to the Conservatives, taking over many of the traditional values (and voters) of the Labour party'.[81] Owen probably welcomed the tabling of the Stevenage motion, with its reference to 'traditional Labour values'. It provided him with a symbolic opportunity to distance himself from what one of his allies called 'yesterday's men and yesterday's measures' and another called 'the continuation of old Labour party disputes by other means'.

The Torquay debate, held only a few weeks after the Liberals' success in the Brecon and Radnor by-election and at a time when the Alliance was riding high in the opinion polls, was a triumph for Owen and those who wanted to set the Social Democrats on a new course. So overwhelming was the opposition to the Stevenage motion that, by prior agreement, its mover, Ben Stoneham, withdrew its more controversial passages in favour of an Edinburgh amendment that rejected right, left and centre labels in favour of the SDP's being seen as a radical party in its own right, combining economic realism with social compassion. The mover of the Edinburgh amendment, Keith Smith, said that to talk of Labour values without spelling out what they were would be to play into the hands of the party's opponents, especially the Conservatives: 'To hell with arguments about labels,' he said. 'Let's get out and prove our determination to tackle the abuses which remain in our society. That is what matters and what we must do to win the next general election.'

Derek Scott, the Swindon parliamentary candidate, said to loud applause that the Stevenage motion was 'muddled, politically inept and obscured the SDP's position': 'We are not a mark II Labour party. The values of social compassion and social justice are Social Democratic values and are our values.' Sue Slipman, once a Communist but now one of Owen's most fervent supporters, emphasized from the platform that the National Committee was happy to accept those parts of the Stevenage motion that referred to the SDP as being 'a party of radical social and constitutional reform, deeply concerned with the well-being of the people'; but it was not happy to accept the others. In her presidential address Shirley Williams ruefully conceded that the desire she shared with Bill Rodgers to associate the SDP with traditional Labour values had not gone down very well. She had to acknowledge that the phrase 'traditional Labour values' had no echoes and provided no reference point 'for the principles that you and we share': 'The Labour party of those values, you said, was sick thirty years ago and died five years ago.' She tacitly admitted that the SDP's umbilical ties with its Labour past had, at last, been broken.[82]

The 1985 Torquay conference was a considerable success. More than 1,400 delegates attended, and the atmosphere, while optimistic, was less febrile than it had been at the time of the first rolling conference four years before. The party had survived the 1983 defeat, it was in good heart, and it had good reason to think that, together with the Liberals, it might well hold the balance of power in the next parliament. Owen had won his victory partly because he was the party's unchallenged leader but also because most of those present genuinely wanted to make a fresh start and welcomed a chance to declare their independence of the older parties. In any case many had never belonged to either. The debate on the Stevenage motion cleared the air. The phrase 'traditional Labour values' was rejected; but at the same time the party reasserted its objective of creating a more equal, more caring society. More than one leading figure in the party subsequently described Torquay as a 'watershed'. Peter Riddell wrote in the *Financial Times* the day after the debate on the Stevenage motion: 'The Social Democratic Party has found itself at Torquay . . . There is now a self-confidence and cohesion about the SDP which was not apparent even at Buxton a year ago.'[83] The SDP probably felt happier with itself during and immediately after the Torquay conference than at any other time in its brief life.

18
····

The Owen Ascendancy II:
1985–1987

The afterglow of the successful Torquay conference lingered on for several months. Between a quarter and a third of the electorate continued to tell the opinion polls that they would vote for the Alliance at an early election, and personal relations among the old Gang of Four, while still strained, gradually became less fraught and more businesslike. Moreover, despite the disagreements within the SDP that surfaced at Torquay and despite Owen's apparent shift to the right, relations between the SDP and the Liberals improved and showed every sign of going on improving.

David Owen seemed to worry less about the Liberals as he became more confident of his own party and also of his personal standing with the public. Any thoughts he may once have had of abandoning the Alliance had receded, and he appeared to accept that, if he were going to have to live with the Liberals, he might as well put his relationship with them on a reasonably amicable footing. It probably helped, too, that the Liberals themselves showed signs of becoming more ambitious for power. Most of the Liberal MPs made a favourable impression on their SDP opposite numbers, and they were no longer just good constituency members; they were effective in parliament. In addition, the Liberals, following the 1985 local elections, had a record number of local councillors, and Liberal parliamentary candidates took themselves, and were taken, more and more seriously. As a mordant Liberal put it, there had been a time when 'anybody other than a convicted rapist' was acceptable as a Liberal candidate; but local associations were now being, and could afford to be, a good deal fussier.[1]

Moreover, although few seem to have noticed it at the time, the potentially difficult question of the Alliance leadership had already been settled. Owen and Steel each had reasons for thinking that the 1983 'prime minister-designate' experience had been a disaster, and neither intended to repeat it. The obvious alternative was to elect a single Alliance leader, who would both lead the Alliance in the election campaign and then go on to become prime minister if the two parties won. But Owen was not having any of that: it would mean, in effect, the merger of the two parties; and, since Liberals greatly outnumbered Social Democrats in the country, it would also mean that the single Alliance leader would almost certainly be Steel rather than himself. Steel thought it would probably be a good idea if there were a single Alliance leader, but he knew it would be both useless and damaging to press the point in the face of Owen's opposition, so the two of them agreed on a third course of action, which they announced at a press conference at the end of the Liberal assembly in Harrogate in September 1983.

Asked by a reporter how the Alliance would choose a prime minister if the Liberals and the SDP went into the next election with two separate leaders, Owen replied:

The country has to know who will be the prime minister in the situation following an election. The proper constitutional position would be that whoever had the largest number of MPs would be the person called upon by the Queen to form a government.[2]

Steel indicated his agreement, and that was that. During the next three years, dissident Liberals pressed constantly for the election of a single leader, but so long as Owen and Steel stuck to their agreement—and they did—there was little the dissidents could do.

The two leaders took additional steps to improve their own and their parties' working relationship. As early as July 1984, well before all the differences over parliamentary seats had been resolved, it was agreed that by the summer of 1986, at the latest, the two parties should produce a joint policy document which would form the basis of the next election manifesto. After the document had appeared, neither party would issue any further policy statements and the manifesto would not simply be cobbled together as it had been in 1983.[3] In November 1984, only a few days after Owen's outburst at the National Committee over the seats negotiations (and possibly partly because of it—several newspapers had reported Owen's alleged threat to resign), the two leaders met and agreed on a kind of peace treaty, which was also meant to be a blueprint for their future co-operation. Owen conceded that henceforth the Alliance should be conceived of as 'a lasting partnership' and not just as a temporary marriage of convenience (with or without divorce); Steel for his part conceded that the partnership would be a partnership of equals. The two leaders also announced that theirs would be a 'tandem leadership' and that in future they intended to appear more often together both at Alliance meetings and on television. They also intended to establish a joint leaders' office well in advance of the election.[4]

A few months later, in July 1985, the Joint Leaders' Advisory Committee, which had been meeting since shortly after the previous election, turned itself into the Alliance Strategy Committee (the change of name was significant), and it was announced that Owen and Steel would in future address each others' party conferences as a matter of routine.[5] Joint meetings of Alliance candidates and eventually some kind of joint conference would be held. The two parties' headquarters were working increasingly closely together, and the SDP even agreed to the making of a joint Liberal–SDP appointment: that of Bill LeBreton to service Alliance groups on county councils. Such a development would have been unthinkable two years before. As a Cowley Street official said in late 1985, 'We're working so closely together you can't see the seams.'

More stitching was required, however, before decisions could be reached about who, apart from the two leaders, should be designated as 'official Alliance spokesmen'. Owen initially—and predictably—did not want any such spokesmen. In his eyes, the appointment of joint spokesmen nationally would be the equivalent of the joint selection of parliamentary candidates locally. If the two parties spoke with one voice, they would no longer be two parties; another step towards merger would have been taken. In the early years of the parliament, Owen resisted pressure from Steel to appoint joint spokesmen in the House of Commons, mainly because such a move would be a step towards merger but also because the Liberals had so many more MPs than the SDP, especially with both Rodgers and Williams out of the House. Owen was also conscious that, if ever the Liberals and the SDP no longer had separate parliamentary spokesmen, there was a danger that Alliance MPs as a whole would be called upon less frequently to speak in debates.

But Steel persisted, agreeing that there should be joint spokesmen rather than joint *parliamentary* spokesmen and making the point that joint spokesmen would be desirable during the coming election campaign to minimize the chances of Liberals and members of the SDP contradicting each other in public. The appointment of joint spokesmen, especially if they were not required to be MPs, would have the additional advantage of being a means by which Rodgers and Williams could be given more prominent and regularized public roles. Jenkins, who had been relatively inactive since his loss of the leadership, could also be given a substantial job to do. Steel warned publicly that the Alliance had to be seen to be about teamwork 'or it will fail to change politics in the way we all want'.[6]

Owen gradually relented. He could see the force of Steel's arguments and was genuinely anxious to concede a somewhat larger role to Jenkins, Rodgers and Williams, whom he knew he had neglected and to a considerable extent alienated: if the Alliance were to do well in the election, it needed all the troops it could muster. However, just as soon as the discussions began about who the joint Alliance spokesmen should be, Owen must have begun to have doubts about whether he had done the right thing. Even pro-Liberals in the SDP described the subsequent negotiations as 'awful':

Every last Liberal [one of them said] thinks he should be a spokesman, but only about a third of them are any good. Steel wants to keep everybody sweet. He simply isn't strong enough to say to them: 'You bloody well aren't good enough . . .' Our David is being amazingly patient.

The discussions dragged on for months, one round being held on the railway journey from Truro to London following the memorial service for David Penhaligon, a Liberal MP who had been killed in a car accident. But in the end agreement was reached, and the Alliance team was announced in January 1987. Jenkins became Treasury spokesman, Williams Home Office spokeswoman and John Cartwright spokesman on defence. Rodgers was to shadow the Department of Energy, a significant appointment in view of the differences between the Liberals and the SDP over nuclear power. The SDP had done well overall.[7]

Formally and organizationally, the Alliance was thus functioning increasingly effectively. But the potential for disagreement, possibly disastrous disagreement, still existed, both within the SDP and between the SDP and the Liberals. Approximately a year before the appointment of the joint spokesmen, in March 1986, the authors of this book had interviewed a leading member of the Liberal party. He had seemed sanguine about the Alliance's electoral prospects, and we therefore pressed him about what, if anything, might go wrong. He had seemed genuinely puzzled by the question and replied that, so far as he could tell, there was no reason why things should not continue to go well. But then a cloud passed over his face. 'Of course,' he said nervously 'defence is still a problem. I don't think it will go wrong—but it might.'

It did—and the issue that had disrupted the Labour party for so much of the post-war period now proceeded to disrupt the Liberal–SDP Alliance.

The dispute over defence that broke out in 1986 had two sources. One was rational and practical and had to do with the future shape of British defence policy and with how the Alliance should present itself to the electorate on defence. The other was sub-rational and emotional and had to do with pride and the desire to dominate. The reasoned arguments were concerned with high technology, the evolution of superpower relationships and the future of Europe; the emotions were those of the primary-school playground. The accumulation of irritations, grievances and resentments that had found partial expression over David Owen's seizure of the party leadership and his subsequent shift to the right now found full expression over the issue of the future of Britain's nuclear deterrent. Owen as leader had so far fought his political battles mainly with the Liberals. Now he took on both the Liberals and also many prominent figures in his own party.

The potential for disagreement between the SDP and the Liberals on defence had always existed. Both parties were committed to Britain's continued membership of NATO and also to NATO's and therefore Britain's continued reliance on the American nuclear shield. Both parties were also anxious to increase the influence within NATO of its European member countries, ideally by means of the development of a common European defence strategy. Thus, neither the Liberal party nor the SDP was unilateralist in the sense that it wanted, as the Labour party then wanted, to require the United States to remove its nuclear weapons from British soil and to close its nuclear bases.

But from that point onwards the two parties' policies—and, perhaps more important, their instincts and outlooks—quickly diverged. Putting it crudely, the Liberals were inclined to be soft on defence; the SDP was inclined to be hard. The Liberals were opposed to the deployment of American cruise missiles in Europe;

the SDP was, however reluctantly, prepared in the end to accept them as part of NATO's 'dual-track' strategy. Both parties believed that the government's programme to purchase submarine-launched Trident nuclear missiles from the United States should be cancelled; but, whereas the Liberals wanted to cancel it on grounds of principle, the SDP merely claimed the programme was too expensive. (Moreover, the SDP was ready to reconsider its position if, at some later stage, it turned out that it would be more expensive to cancel it than to carry on with it.) With regard to Britain's existing fleet of Polaris submarines, the Liberals wanted to scrap it, while the SDP believed it should be retained for as long as possible or until it was negotiated out of existence as a result of some future arms-control agreement. At bottom, the Liberals wanted Britain, while remaining in NATO, to abandon its independent nuclear deterrent; at bottom, the SDP thought Britain should retain the deterrent for the foreseeable future. Owen, in particular, felt strongly that the nations of Europe could not rely indefinitely on the United States to provide Europe with its nuclear defence, and he disliked the idea that France might become Europe's only nuclear power. He was therefore convinced that Britain should remain more or less indefinitely 'a nuclear-weapon state' (his phrase). It was a view he frequently expressed and never wavered from.

David Owen and David Steel agreed soon after the 1983 election that their two parties needed to have an agreed policy on defence as soon as possible. They were acutely aware of the damage that had been inflicted on the Labour party during the 1983 campaign by its public disagreements on defence, and they did not want the same thing to happen to them in 1987 or 1988. They also knew that agreement between their two parties would not come easily. It would have to be worked for. Accordingly, they set up in the summer of 1984 a Joint Commission on Defence and Disarmament charged with preparing detailed proposals for consideration by the parties in time for their conferences in the autumn of 1986. The commission was intended to function rather in the style of a royal commission. Its members included John Cartwright, Owen's principal parliamentary lieutenant; Bill Rodgers, a former defence minister and passionate anti-unilateralist; Richard Holme, one of Steel's main political advisers; and Paddy Ashdown, the new Liberal MP for Yeovil, who had led the opposition inside his party to the deployment of cruise missiles and who had recently published a pamphlet with Holme advocating a policy of 'no first use' of nuclear weapons. The commission's chairman, John Edmonds, had once led the British delegation to the comprehensive nuclear test-ban negotiations in Geneva.[8]

Many acknowledged that the motive behind the setting-up of the commission was mildly cynical. It was, as one commission member put it, 'to kick the ball into touch'—to buy the two parties time in which they could try to figure out what to do. As if to drive home the point that the parties did need time, the Liberals at their annual assembly in Bournemouth in September 1984—only a few weeks after the setting-up of the commission—voted, despite an eloquent appeal from the floor by Steel, for a motion calling for the immediate withdrawal of cruise missiles from

British soil. Steel was irritated but at the same time firm: 'We are not going into an election on this policy,' he said on television that night. 'There is a lot more work to be done.'[9]

Despite this new rift between the Liberals and the SDP, Owen for the time being remained relaxed about defence. He knew what his own position was, he knew he was not going to budge from it, and he knew that he had the broad support of his party. He was also aware that, partly because Steel was not an expert on defence and did not have strong views on the subject, he could count on bringing the Liberals round sooner or later to his point of view. At the Torquay conference, for instance, three motions critical of the leadership's defence policy—one calling for 'no first use', one calling for Trident to be cancelled immediately in the event of an Alliance government and a third calling for drastic cuts in defence spending—were all defeated.[10] The Liberals might not be sound on defence. The SDP was. Or so, at any rate, it seemed.

The Joint Commission was meanwhile quietly going about its work—as one of its members put it, 'lumbering away'. Edmonds, the chairman, wanted to avoid controversy and believed that knotty problems could best be resolved if wide areas of agreement were first established on other issues. Most members of the commission apparently saw themselves as acting independently; they did not see themselves as either party representatives or the mere agents of their leader. They were there to give their own best advice. But there was some misunderstanding on this point. John Cartwright felt that he did not have to play a central role on the commission because Bill Rodgers was there to defend David Owen's interests, but Rodgers, on the contrary, thought that that was why Cartwright was there. Similarly, Cartwright thought Rodgers was keeping in touch with Owen while Rodgers assumed that Cartwright was and that Cartwright would never agree to anything of substance without Owen's approval. It turned out that both men were wrong.

In the course of the commission's deliberations, its Liberal members moved much further towards the SDP's position than its SDP members moved towards the Liberals'. That was probably why neither Cartwright nor Rodgers, nor anyone else on the SDP side, had any inkling of the trouble to come. The commission made no concessions to the Liberals' pacifist and unilateralist wings. On the contrary, it came out firmly in favour of Britain's continued membership of NATO and a continued American military presence in Europe. It expressed alarm about the weakness and underfunding of Britain's armed forces. It accepted the continuing presence of United States' bases, including nuclear bases, in Britain. It did not call for the withdrawal of cruise missiles from the US base at Greenham Common. It did call, as David Owen had done on many occasions, for the defence of Europe to be given a larger European dimension. Paddy Ashdown, having led the Liberal opposition to the deployment of cruise missiles, now shifted his position significantly towards that of the SDP, and the Liberal Campaign for Nuclear Disarmament signalled its strong disapproval of the commission's main proposals as reports of them began to appear in the press.

By this time, however, the main issue was no longer cruise missiles (which by 1985 had been stationed on British soil for more than two years). Rather, it was the future of Britain's own independent deterrent. The commission left this decision, which it thought to be the most difficult, to the last. However, once the commission's members began to address the issue directly, agreement among them came much more easily than expected. Edmonds' tactics as chairman were paying off. The commission first agreed that Britain's existing fleet of Polaris submarines should not be scrapped—in other words, that Britain should retain its independent deterrent, at least for the time being. That decision having been taken, however, the commission then had to decide what should be done about an eventual replacement for Polaris when it came to the end of its natural life in the late 1990s or the early 2000s. Should there be a replacement at all? If so, what form should it take?

One option was to decide that Polaris should *not* be replaced, whatever the circumstances (by Trident or anything else); another was to decide that it *should* be replaced, again whatever the circumstances (perhaps by submarine-launched cruise missiles, which Owen tended to favour, or by some kind of Franco-British missile system or possibly by an up-dated version of Polaris itself). But the commission decided not to adopt either of these options. Instead it decided to take the view that, since Polaris would not have to be replaced, if at all, until at least the mid- or late 1990s, a decision on the issue could be, and should be, deferred. There was no overriding need to take a decision immediately, and circumstances in the late 1980s or early 1990s would be likely to indicate, at that time, whether an independent British deterrent was still required. The commission's members believed that deferring a decision would also have the political advantage of preventing any Liberal–SDP split; but the great majority of them, possibly all of them, also felt that they could make such a recommendation in good conscience. They believed that a decision could only sensibly be taken at a considerably later date. The commission thus initially agreed to recommend that a decision on 'whether, and if so how' Polaris should be replaced should be postponed till 'after the election'.

With the commission due to publish its recommendations in June 1986, most senior Liberal party and SDP politicians by early May had a pretty good idea of the general lines along which it was thinking. No one said anything. Nothing seemed amiss. But then in mid-May David Steel happened to have a relaxed lunch with Martin Dowle, the lobby correspondent of the *Scotsman*, the most important paper north of the border. Dowle asked him whether the commission's report committed the Liberals to replacing Polaris. 'No, it doesn't,' Steel replied. Dowle suggested that Owen might be disappointed as a result. Steel, it seems, did not disagree.

Within hours Steel's relaxed lunch had become the *Scotsman*'s lead story. Under the headline 'Alliance report rejects UK deterrent: Owen's nuclear hopes dashed', Dowle wrote:

Dr David Owen's attempts to commit the Alliance to a policy of replacing Polaris with a new independent nuclear deterrent have been dashed by a joint SDP–Liberal policy commission.

The Alliance commission on defence has unanimously rejected his suggestion that Britain should purchase a new nuclear deterrent at the end of the Polaris life-span in the 1990s.

The unanimity of the finding by the commission, which is drawn equally from the SDP and the Liberals, means that the SDP leader's favoured policy has been rejected by the specialist nominees of his own party.

The finding will strengthen the hand of Mr David Steel, the Liberal leader, in the difficult negotiations of ironing out the two parties' differences on nuclear defence policy and help him to confront the large number of Liberal activists in favour of scrapping Polaris immediately.[11]

The *Scotsman*'s report, with its seriously misleading headline and its broad hint that the canny Steel had gained the upper hand over the obstreperous Owen, appeared on 16 May. The Council for Social Democracy was due to begin its annual spring meeting in Southport the next day. Owen, not normally a *Scotsman* reader, did not at first see the report, but he heard about it on his car phone on the way up to Southport. He was incandescent with rage—angrier than at any time since the National Committee row over joint candidate selection eighteen months earlier. He knew that the source of the *Scotsman* story must be Steel, and it looked as though Steel were trying to humiliate him by claiming that in the Joint Commission's discussions the Liberals had gained a glorious victory over the Social Democrats. The headline—'Alliance report rejects UK deterrent: Owen's nuclear hopes dashed'—was insupportable. And, as though all this were not enough, the *Scotsman* report also gave the impression that Owen had been betrayed by his own side, that he had been deserted by Rodgers and Cartwright in the face of the enemy. The phrase 'the SDP leader's favoured policy has been rejected by . . . his own party' could bear no other construction.

Owen's response was immediate. He had intended in his Southport speech to concentrate on the issue of nuclear power. Instead, without consulting any of the Social Democrat members of the commission (John Cartwright was only just returning from a visit to the United States), he rewrote his speech and on 17 May 1986 publicly threw down the gauntlet to Steel, to the whole Liberal party and to any Social Democrat who might dare even to consider accepting the commission's report as it then stood:

I have not seen the joint document yet, but the SDP's policy on this is perfectly clear . . . I must tell you bluntly that I believe we should remain a nuclear weapon state.

If we are to carry conviction in our decision to cancel Trident after an election, we ought to be prepared to say that we will find a replacement for Polaris, unless there has been such a massive reduction in nuclear warheads on the part of the Soviet Union and the United States that we would feel it right in negotiations to give up our nuclear weapons.

He added:

Certainly you should know quite clearly that I definitely do not believe that I would carry any conviction whatever in the next election were I to answer—on your behalf—on the question of the replacement of Polaris, that that would have to depend on the circumstances of the time. That would get, and would deserve, a belly laugh from the British electorate. That sort of fudging and mudging was what I left behind in the Labour party.[12]

So much for the Joint Commission. So much, by implication, for Rodgers—and even Cartwright.

Afterwards, seeking to account for Owen's outburst, even some of his friends acknowledged that prior to the Southport meeting he had been 'in a fragile mood'. The Liberals had won Ryedale and nearly won West Derbyshire, whereas the SDP had been badly beaten in Fulham; and in recent weeks the Alliance had been going through a phase in which Steel, however briefly, seemed to be gaining the upper hand over him. Owen also apparently felt that Rodgers, Williams and Steel (and possibly also Jenkins) were plotting against him, not only over defence but over the whole direction in which the SDP was going. His old fears of merger, and of plots of merger, resurfaced. One member of the defence commission said: 'It was a case of mild paranoia. David thinks people are ganging up on him so he behaves in ways that lead them to do precisely that.' Owen in this frame of mind could not believe that Steel's casual remarks to Dowle were anything other than a conscious effort to demean him. His suspicions were reinforced the day after his Southport speech when the *Sunday Telegraph* quoted a 'leading Liberal MP' as saying, 'Liberals are wreathed in smiles as we have ruled out a Polaris replacement.'[13]

Owen, convinced he was right on the substance of the issue and convinced also that the Social Democrats, at least, must be unambiguous in what they said to the electorate about defence, persisted with his campaign. 'Britain should continue as a nuclear weapon state with the French,' he wrote in the *Observer* on 1 June. 'For the present, we should be ready to replace Polaris with a minimum deterrent.'[14] He dismissed the Joint Commission as a mere advisory body with no status and, having previously insisted, with David Steel, that the SDP and the Liberals should have an agreed defence policy, he now backtracked. 'I have never believed', he told the *Today* newspaper, 'it is absolutely vital to agree on everything. I would not mind going into an election on different sides on this.'[15] In case anyone missed the point, Owen reiterated his position in a carefully prepared speech to the Anglo-German Society in Bonn. Britain's contribution to strengthening the European pillar of NATO was important, he declared, and it had to include, at least for the present, a minimum nuclear deterrent. *The Times* headlined its front-page report of the speech: 'Owen splits Alliance on defence'.[16]

Up to this point, most people in both Alliance parties had been fairly muted in their public response to Owen's various pronouncements; they had no desire to isolate Owen or split the Alliance further. Steel indicated that he was 'not wildly happy' with the Southport speech, and someone in the SDP commented that Owen increasingly reminded him of Joseph Chamberlain, who had succeeded in splitting two parties in the space of twenty years. But remarks like these were made in private.[17] However, with the Bonn speech the dam burst. For the first time in the SDP's history the public was treated to the spectacle, not of the Liberals and the SDP attacking each other, but of the SDP leadership at war with itself. The Gang of Four had long since ceased to exist as a collective decision-making body; now it ceased to exist even as a façade.

Shirley Williams, interviewed on *The World at One*, said acidly, having read the text of the Bonn speech: 'It does not follow that what the leader says is the same and identical with the policy of the party.'[18] Jenkins remarked, even more acidly, that with Owen's speeches there was 'a danger of theatre taking over from valour': 'Custer's Last Stand should not be a nightly event.'[19] For his part, Rodgers began by being gentler—'David is expressing a personal view . . . This is a difference between friends, but it is a matter of concern, and we are all anxious to find a way to heal the wounds'[20]—but he added, in an obvious reference to his leader: 'Certainty is not always a virtue. Nor is conviction by itself evidence of truth.'[21] From the outside, Steel wrily remarked that his relationship with the SDP leader reminded him of Dame Sybil Thorndyke's comment on her long marriage. She had contemplated 'divorce never, murder frequently'. He would not go quite that far: with Owen it was only a matter of 'murder occasionally'.[22]

Amidst this commotion, the Joint Commission quietly concluded its work. Relations among its members were good and remained so even as relations among the erstwhile Gang of Four worsened. Indeed, had it not been for Owen's intervention, Cartwright and Jim Wellbeloved, another Owenite on the commission, might well have signed the report in its original form; but at the very last minute they were prevailed upon to press for a number of changes in its wording and also to find a way of distancing themselves from the conclusions of the majority. They considered issuing a formal note of dissent, but it was evident that this would be highly divisive and further prolong the controversy, and in the end Edmonds agreed to make it clear in his preface to the report that different members of the commission held different views about the desirability of replacing Polaris. In addition, and out of deference to Owen, the phrase 'after the election', which had appeared in an earlier draft of the report, was dropped, and the commission merely said that the Polaris submarines did not need to be replaced 'now'.[23]

The report was launched on 11 June 1986 at a press conference attended by most of the commission's members, including Cartwright. It caused little stir. As predicted, it indicated (though not in so many words) that a final decision on a Polaris replacement did not need to be taken for several years, since Polaris submarines would remain in service 'well beyond the end of the next Parliament'.[24]

When the time finally came, the decision, in the commission's view, should be guided by a number of considerations: the progress of arms control and disarmament, the European–American balance within NATO, the technical range and costs of potential Polaris replacements and the views of Britain's European allies. Edmonds added, as agreed, a paragraph to his preface:

Since we completed our work, there has been a lot of misleading speculation about the Report's conclusions. As a result, certain members of the Commission wish it to be made clear that in their view Britain should in present circumstances remain a nuclear weapon state and that they are willing to replace Polaris. Some other members believe that present circumstances do not justify the replacement of Polaris. I must stress, however, that all members agree that a decision on whether, and if so how, to replace Polaris should be made on the basis of the criteria we have set out.[25]

Edmonds' repeated use of the phrase 'in present circumstances' reinforced the report's principal point.

Later that day Owen and Steel began the process of restoring their personal and political relations by holding a joint press conference. Owen pointedly refrained from rubbishing the commission's report (he had done that *in extenso* already), but he insisted that the issues that the commission had left unresolved would have somehow to be settled before the next election, adding: 'I think it is necessary to say you wish to keep your existing nuclear capability unless there has been some dramatic unprecedented change in the arms control climate at the time of the election.' Steel, while agreeing with the commission's broad approach, appeared to concede Owen's point that the Alliance could not go into the election saying that it would cancel Trident but refusing to say what, if anything, it would put in its place: 'I believe when the next election comes we have to have specific answers to these questions. The election is not on us yet.' It would be quite wrong to take up 'cast-iron attitudes' now.[26]

Steel and Owen were both acutely conscious of the damage the controversy was doing. Accordingly, they agreed that from now on they should air their differences in private and not in public and they began to look around for a solution to their problem that would not compromise Owen's declared position and would not embarrass Steel with his party, but at the same time would enable the two partners to present a united front. As always, Steel was more concerned that the Alliance should have an agreed policy than with what the details of that policy should be. In view of the troubles he had had over many years with his Liberal followers, it must have given him considerable amusement that the imperious Owen was now having similar problems with *his* followers. For once, the shoe was on the other foot.

One possible way out of the impasse, if a highly circuitous one, seems to have occurred fairly quickly to the two leaders (or possibly to their aides).[27] Owen was adamant that Britain should remain a nuclear-weapon state; France was going to remain such a state; the Joint Commission's report and both the Alliance parties favoured an enhanced European role in Europe's defence. So why not explore the possibility that Britain and France might somehow combine their nuclear-weapons efforts (thereby, among other things, saving a great deal of money)? The idea was to use the Alliance's broad agreement on Europe to circumnavigate its deep disagreements on nuclear weapons. Different figures in the two parties took the idea of Anglo-French co-operation with differing degrees of seriousness. Owen seems genuinely to have believed that an Anglo-French nuclear force was a realistic possibility and that meaningful conversations could take place between the leaders of Europe and the leaders of the Alliance. Some Liberals, more cynically, regarded the whole exercise as a pure public-relations effort, 'an absolute snow job'. But that was all right so long as it got them out of the deep political hole they were now in.

Whatever their private views, Owen and Steel met on several occasions during June and July 1986, including a day at Ettrickbridge, and agreed to explore the possibility of a European, as distinct from an exclusively British, deterrent. They also agreed to conduct their exploration partly in Britain but also partly on the Continent, in the form of meetings with French, German and NATO leaders. In July they met Hans-Dietrich Genscher, the West German foreign minister. In early September they visited Brussels, where they talked to General Bernard Rogers, the American Supreme Allied Commander in Europe, and later Paris, where they were entertained by President François Mitterrand and the French prime minister, Jacques Chirac. All the foreign dignitaries treated them extremely politely and at least affected to take the two leaders seriously (the French were said to be keen on building up a closer Anglo-French relationship as a counterpoise to the Franco-German relationship). And Steel's and Owen's travels yielded a rich harvest of photo-opportunities. The two leaders were widely presented in the media as genuine, if somewhat small-scale, world leaders. In the meantime, the Alliance published its pre-election joint policy document, *Partnership for Progress*. The document noted that NATO would continue to depend in part on nuclear weapons and declared the two parties' joint determination to explore the possibility that Britain's nuclear capability might make a contribution to European deterrence. But on the issue of a replacement for Polaris *Partnership for Progress* was necessarily silent. Agreement was still some way off.

A combination of Owen's firmness on defence and the SDP activists' personal loyalty to their leader got the party through its 1986 autumn conference at Harrogate without any difficulty. It was a somewhat grim occasion, with many delegates privately unhappy about both the defence row and Owen's high-handed style of leadership, but Owen himself had no desire, or need, to stir up any further trouble, and both he and the other platform speakers presented themselves as reasonable people seeking a way out of a genuine difficulty. They also concentrated on issues other than defence (notably the party's radical proposals for relieving poverty by reforming the tax and benefits system). Owen opened the conference by indicating what the Alliance's new line on defence was to be:

The concept of a European minimum deterrent, respecting the political structures of the French and British nations, makes sense. It leaves Britain not wholly dependent on the US nuclear guarantee, but nor does it pretend to a wholly British independence which in 1986 makes neither political nor military sense.[28]

At Owen's instigation, the National Committee prevented Rodgers from opening the debate on defence, but Charles Kennedy, chosen to speak in his stead, went out of his way to say that the SDP was not committing an Alliance government to replacing Polaris 'come what may', and John Cartwright likewise conceded that the party's defence policy was not 'engraved on tablets of stone'.[29]

In this less highly charged atmosphere, the Harrogate conference officially welcomed the Joint Commission's report while reaffirming that the resolution it had passed at Torquay a year before still formed the basis of the party's policy. To Owen's delight, a North Glasgow motion that would have tilted the SDP's policy some way away from a Polaris replacement was defeated by a margin of four to one. 'I've got what I wanted,' Owen triumphantly declared, 'the freedom to go for the Labour party's jugular on the crucial question of defence at the next election.'[30] The SDP phase of the Alliance's two-party conference season was thus safely over.

The trouble started all over again, however, when the Liberals' assembly convened at Eastbourne a few days later. The build-up to the Liberals' defence debate was very carefully contrived. Steel appeared with Owen on television to restate his personal commitment to a European nuclear deterrent and he made the same point at a meeting of Liberal MPs and candidates. Owen, in a dignified and well-received speech, took great pains to lay greater stress on disarmament than on nuclear defence. The Liberals' steering committee deliberately chose to point up the issue by choosing for the debate only two motions, one straightforwardly welcoming the Joint Commission's report as a basis of Liberal policy in its negotiations with the SDP, the other calling for a strengthening of European defence—but only provided it was non-nuclear. One motion was clearly pro-leadership and pro-Alliance; the other was equally clearly anti-leadership, anti-Alliance and unilateralist. The idea was that the delegates, faced with a straightforward choice between these two motions, knowing that a general election was in the offing, and knowing, too, how much damage the defence row had already inflicted on the two parties, would vote overwhelmingly for the motion supported by Steel and the rest of the leadership. Certainly that was what everyone expected to happen. The *Guardian*'s headline read: 'Liberal leaders outflank CND on evening of crucial defence debate'.[31]

But then, on 23 September 1986, the whole elaborate edifice collapsed. The Steel camp, over-confident, had no idea that it might be defeated and as a result did not bother to consider carefully who ought to speak in the debate and what they ought to say. Unknown to the leadership, there was also a widespread feeling in the hall, shared by both pro-leadership delegates and unilateralists, that Owen's and Steel's so-called European minimum deterrent was in fact a nonsense. At best, such a deterrent would be impossible to organize; it was no more than a device for preventing an Alliance split. At worst, it might actually be organized, in which case there would soon exist a veritable 'Euro-nuclear bomb mountain—with twelve fingers on the button'.[32] Many on both sides believed the European deterrent idea to be at least a delusion, quite possibly a dangerous delusion. In addition, a great many of the Liberals at Eastbourne wanted to cock a snook at Owen and at the same time, by showing that the Liberal party could not be taken for granted, strengthen Steel's hand in his dealings with Owen. It was not only unilateralists among the Liberals who felt that Owen's behaviour earlier in the summer—at Southport and later in Bonn—had been totally outrageous and that the SDP leader needed to be taken down a peg or two. Asked afterwards what the message of Eastbourne had been, one of Steel's allies replied: 'That's easy. The message of Eastbourne was: fuck Owen.'

In the event, the actual debate appears to have determined the outcome. Had the debate gone differently, the vote would have gone differently too. For the leadership, Paddy Ashdown and Richard Holme spoke hesitantly and badly. Alan Beith spoke better (and with considerable humour). Steel did not speak at all. For the opposition, Simon Hughes, the victor of Bermondsey, spoke with passion and conviction and was seconded by Michael Meadowcroft, the MP for Leeds West, who insisted, first, that the Liberal assembly should bear in mind that its only duty was to determine Liberal policy and, second, that Liberal policy should be intellectually sustainable and rooted in Liberal values, which the Owen–Steel line on defence patently was not. When the votes were taken, acceptance of the Joint Commission's report was carried overwhelmingly; but the non-nuclear motion was also carried by 652 votes to 625—a margin of only twenty-seven. Several hundred delegates to the conference were either absent or abstained. Some who did vote undoubtedly supported the non-nuclear motion only because they wanted to make some kind of anti-leadership, anti-Owen gesture and in the belief that the motion had no chance of passing.

The result was a bolt from a clear sky, especially coming after a display of good feelings towards the Liberals at the SDP's conference and Steel's efforts, sustained over many weeks, to come to an agreement with Owen. When the result was announced, many in the hall were stunned, realizing immediately that the Liberals had now compounded Owen's sin of dividing the Alliance and realizing also that the electoral consequences of the decision were likely to be dire. Several delegates wept as they left the hall, and many Liberal candidates in winnable constituencies were aghast as they saw their chances of victory evaporating in the late-afternoon Eastbourne air. Some who had voted for the anti-nuclear motion desperately wished they had not.

Predictably, the vote had the effect of putting the Alliance back in the headlines—in the most unwelcome possible way. Steel's defeat was the main political item on most television news bulletins that night, and the headline on the front page of *The Times* the next morning proclaimed: 'Steel defeat puts Alliance in disarray'. The headline in the *Guardian* read: 'Liberals rebuff Steel over nuclear policy'. Steel's reaction was pained but, as usual, philosophical. He had suffered much at the hands of the Liberals. Eastbourne was nothing new. He gave the impression that he did not mean to quarrel with his party openly but that, at the same time, he had no intention of abandoning his efforts to reach an accommodation with Owen. 'It is an irritant,' he said of the vote, 'but not a set-back.'[33]

The sequel was strange. Eastbourne seems to have acted as a kind of catharsis for both the Liberals and the SDP. Emotionally exhausted, and having got a lot of bad blood out of their systems, they could now start behaving reasonably. Owen, in particular, perhaps feeling just a little guilty, knew that Steel was now in real political trouble, and he responded rather in the manner of a big boy whose younger brother has been given a bloody nose in a playground fight. Far from taking advantage of Steel's difficulties, he became positively protective towards him, defending him both privately and publicly and showing a new willingness to make at least a few compromises in order to reach a Liberal–SDP agreement. When the two leaders were interviewed on television together towards the end of the Eastbourne conference, Owen went out of his way to play down the significance of the defence vote and, turning to Steel, said at one point: 'What is important to the people of this country is that we two are united.'[34] Still, David Owen, with one part of himself, must have enjoyed the whole Eastbourne spectacle, which totally vindicated his view of the Liberals, demonstrating to the whole world just what a laughable crowd they were. No one could possibly want to merge with *them*.

The Liberals for their part closed ranks. Many of those who had voted for the offending motion could see the damage they had caused and were exceedingly contrite. Simon Hughes was visibly shaken by the amount of hostility he encountered from his fellow MPs, and Archie Kirkwood, a friend of Steel's who had not spoken for the anti-nuclear motion but had been seen to vote for it, was said to be 'shattered' by the negative publicity it had given rise to. Considerable numbers of the activists who had been present at Eastbourne and had voted for the anti-leadership motion similarly received a hostile reception from ordinary party members when they got home. Their fellow Liberals asked: 'What the hell were you playing at?'

Steel subsequently changed his mind on the question of whether or not to quarrel openly with his party and, in his leader's address to the closing session at Eastbourne, accused delegates of having shown 'breath-taking misjudgement' in supposing that a vote for the non-nuclear motion would strengthen his hand in dealing with Owen.[35] But at the same time he was aware that he had been defeated partly because he had not taken enough trouble to carry his party with him, and in the weeks following Eastbourne he set about getting every wing of the party— the Policy Committee, the national executive, the parliamentary party, the Liberal Council, even the Association of Liberal Councillors—used to the idea that the Liberals and the SDP must have a single defence policy at the coming election and that it must include a commitment to some form of minimum British nuclear deterrent.

With Owen now willing to make compromises and with the Liberals in their newly chastened mood, the task of achieving agreement proved easy. In private talks immediately following the Eastbourne conference Steel and Owen quickly reached agreement on the line that Steel would take in dealing with the Liberals and that Owen would back him in taking. Steel conceded (although for him personally it was not much of a concession) that the Alliance's new policy statement on defence should contain an explicit commitment to a minimum deterrent (that is, that the Joint Commission's proposal to defer a decision should be abandoned); Owen conceded that the statement should contain no mention of the precise form that any Polaris replacement might take and agreed also that the statement should emphasize that, whatever form Britain's new nuclear deterrent eventually took, it would not be on a bigger scale than Polaris. In view of the hostility and incredulity it had aroused at Eastbourne, Steel and Owen, while they continued to talk about European defence co-operation in general terms, were happy to suppress any further mention of a minimum European deterrent.[36]

Between late September 1986 and the end of the year Steel consulted—and made sure the newspapers reported that he was consulting—every section of his party. He also took the trouble to secure formal approval for the statement he had negotiated with Owen from the party's national executive and the parliamentary party. With this strong backing, the two leaders launched the new Alliance defence statement at a press conference in mid-December 1986. 'This is the text', Steel announced proudly, 'on which we will base the Alliance programme for government.' He added, with evident relief: 'It puts the defence debate, internally, to bed.'[37] The statement's words were repeated, almost verbatim, in the Alliance manifesto for the 1987 election a few months later:

In government we would maintain, with whatever necessary modernisation, our minimum nuclear deterrent until it can be negotiated away, as part of a global arms negotiation process, in return for worthwhile concessions by the USSR which would enhance British and European security. In any such modernisation we would maintain our capability in the sense of freezing our capacity at a level no greater than that of the Polaris system . . . We would assign our minimum deterrent to NATO and seek every opportunity to improve European cooperation on procurement and strategic questions.[38]

Owen had won and won decisively. Some in the Liberal party were unilateralists, and many would have been content with a fudge. The Joint Commission had recommended delaying a decision—a course of action that would undoubtedly have laid the Alliance open to the charge of dithering and of not being able to reconcile the two parties' conflicting views. The effect of the post-Eastbourne agreed statement was to ensure that such charges could no longer be made to stick. The statement also meant that a minimum British deterrent was, beyond any doubt, official Alliance policy. Individual parliamentary candidates might dissent, but they would be dissenting from a clear rather than an ambiguous statement.

The question, therefore, is not whether Owen won: he did. The question is whether he might not have won at considerably less cost to himself, his party and the Alliance. The answer is that he almost certainly could have: he could almost certainly have got everything he wanted far more easily and at a far smaller political cost.

An alternative scenario is easily sketched. (It was urged on Owen at the time, but not before a good deal of damage had already been done.) The SDP leader was in a very strong position. He knew his own mind: he believed that in a dangerous world Britain must retain a realistic minimum nuclear deterrent; and he further believed that the Alliance must tell the electorate in unambiguous terms that an Alliance government would retain such a minimum deterrent. Not to do so would be dishonest and would result in the Alliance's losing votes to the Conservatives. Moreover, his position on the issue was well known: he had been stating it and restating it for years. And he had the broad backing of his party. Against that background how should he have responded when he learnt that the Edmonds commission was proposing that the Alliance should say it intended to defer a final decision on a Polaris replacement?

The answer seems obvious. In public, he should have welcomed the commission's findings as a useful contribution to an ongoing debate but at the same time restated, in sober and measured terms, his own view that Britain should remain a nuclear-weapons state. Meanwhile, in private, he should have warned Steel that he was not going to budge on the issue and that the Alliance would not have an agreed defence policy in time for the election unless Steel and the Liberals came round to his way of thinking. Had Owen followed this strategy, he would almost certainly have got his way. Steel himself had no conscientious objection to what the SDP leader was proposing; indeed he probably agreed with it. Moreover, Steel was well aware that, Owen being Owen, there would be no agreed Alliance policy before the election unless it was an Owen-approved policy. Owen had, in other words, a total veto. And Owen's position was further strengthened by the fact that, whereas Steel was desperate to have an agreed policy before the election, he, Owen, was completely agnostic on the matter. In fact, he was by no means averse to the SDP's having a tougher policy than that of the Liberals; different policies would underline the fact that they were different parties. In other words, Owen not only had a total veto; he was perfectly prepared to use it—and Steel knew it, and was appalled at the thought that he might.

That being so, Owen did not need to cause a public row. All he needed to do was apply pressure on Steel. The problem would then have been Steel's, and Steel would almost certainly have solved it. Apart from the Liberal Campaign for Nuclear Disarmament, a small minority group, most members of the Liberal party were either positively in favour of retaining a minimum British deterrent or else not strongly opposed to it. All Steel would have had to do was carry the Liberal assembly with him in welcoming the Joint Commission's report and in not passing a unilateralist motion. Then, having privately conveyed his own views—and the strength of Owen's—to the Liberal MPs and the Liberals' main committees, he could have used his constitutional control over the Liberal party's manifesto to see to it that the terms of the Alliance's joint manifesto met the SDP leader's requirements. The final outcome on this scenario would have been much the same as it was in reality.

Owen, however, appears not to have given any thought to the possibility of pursuing any such softly-softly strategy. He did not sit down and ask himself (or anyone else) how he could best get the Alliance from point A (the commission's report) to point B (acceptance by the Alliance that Britain should remain a nuclear-weapons state). Instead he allowed himself the luxury of exploding in rage at a story in a Scottish newspaper about an (admittedly ill-advised) lunchtime conversation that his Liberal opposite number happened to have had with several lobby correspondents—and then by carrying on with his crusade long after his initial outburst had served its purpose. Owen responded like a man in a weak position; he should have responded like a man whose position was impregnable. It cannot be said that the SDP leader miscalculated—because he did not calculate. He merely lashed out blindly at the forces of his seen and unseen enemies (of whom there were so many). He would probably have got his way considerably sooner—as well as at much less cost—had his Southport and Bonn speeches not angered so many Liberals that they voted, in many cases against their own better judgement, for the calamitous Eastbourne motion.

The costs of the Southport and Bonn outbursts were considerable. In the short term, the row cost the two Alliance parties a good deal of electoral support. As Figure 6 shows, the Alliance began 1986 with the support of approximately a third of the electorate; in January the figure was 35 per cent, fractionally ahead of both the other parties. In the second quarter of the year, despite the Liberals' success in Ryedale and their near-success in West Derbyshire, support for the Alliance dipped to below 30 per cent. Then, in the third quarter, following the initial Southport–Bonn phase of the defence row, it slipped further. Finally, in the fourth quarter of 1986, following the Eastbourne débâcle, it slipped further still, from a third of the electorate at the beginning of the year to less than a quarter at the end. The 35 per cent of January 1986 fell to a figure of only 23.5 per cent in December (and even less immediately after Eastbourne).[39] Not all the Alliance's slide could be attributed to the defence row, of course; as usual, the performance of the economy and of the Labour and Conservative parties was important. But some of it could be attributed to the row—and the slide badly dented the Alliance's confidence.

The row also affected relations between the two Alliance parties. Steel and Owen in their different ways were both professionals, able to keep their personal relations on a reasonably even footing whatever their political differences; but large numbers of others in both parties could not preserve such a high level of detachment. Many Liberals at all levels, already suspicious of Owen because of his increasingly right-wing views and the difficulties he was constantly making in SDP–Liberal relations, came now to dislike him intensely. He might be grand and impressive; but they thought he was also a wrecker, a man who had no time for anyone's opinion except his own. These Liberals thought less well of the SDP as a consequence. The débâcle at Eastbourne had a similar effect on many in the SDP. Owen had warned members of the SDP that, when it came to the crunch, the Liberal party was not to be trusted, and now, after Eastbourne, they could see what he meant. Liberal–SDP relations at the local level did not deteriorate markedly following Eastbourne, but in many areas there was a certain coolness for a time.

The defence row was, if anything, even more divisive within the SDP (though after the brief outbreak of public squabbling in June—'Custer's Last Stand should not be a nightly event'—the Social Democrats were more successful than the Liberals in keeping their differences behind closed doors). The Cowley Street meetings of the National Committee were fraught and occasionally acrimonious for several months following Southport and Bonn, with many members of the National Committee badly disaffected and David Owen increasingly taking the line 'You're either for me or against me'. One woman member of the committee voted against Owen at an early meeting following the Southport row, and other members of the committee noted that Owen seemed to hold it against her for several months afterwards. Rodgers for his part felt wholly betrayed. In 1986 the SDP was polarized in a way that it had never been polarized before, and the source of the trouble was personal rather than ideological.

By the summer of that year the members of the old Gang of Four had relearnt how to behave towards one another reasonably politely in public; but Owen had nevertheless contrived to create, in effect, a new Gang of Three. The old Gang of Three had consisted of him, Rodgers and Williams. The new one consisted of Rodgers, Williams and Jenkins. The three seldom, if ever, met as a group; they certainly did not plot. But they increasingly, if largely independently, were of the view that Owen was personally impossible and that sooner or later both the party and the Alliance would have to be put on a new basis. Owen knew, whether he liked it or not, that he had to work with the others; Williams was the party's elected president and a friend of Rodgers and Jenkins, and all three were essential to the party's appeal to the public. But Owen increasingly dismissed them all as unsound, has-beens, people of little account. He maintained his majorities on the National Committee and in the House of Commons on the strength of his public standing, his personality and his intellect and on the basis that, on almost all substantive issues, including the need for a minimum British deterrent, the great majority of the SDP agreed with him. Indeed, one odd feature of the SDP during this period was that it was largely, if not wholly, agreed on most of the essentials: foreign policy, defence, European integration, the tax and benefits system, education, devolution, transport, industrial policy and most elements of macro-economic policy. Its internal differences as a consequence were almost wholly tactical and temperamental. But they went deep—and were increasingly hard to contain.

The defence row also had the effect of planting doubts about Owen in many of his followers' minds. Some concerned his judgement. The Southport speech apart, many people wondered why Owen had agreed to the setting up of the Joint Commission in the first place if he was prepared to rubbish its conclusions. After all, the commission's whole purpose had been to produce some kind of compromise formula. Owen had rebuked it for doing precisely what it was intended to do. Other doubts concerned the transparent disjunction between Owen the advocate of coalition politics and Owen the practiser of conviction politics. If this was coalition politics à la Owen, what would confrontation politics be like? The verb 'to coalesce' means 'to fuse', 'to unite into a whole'. If the defence row was Owen's idea of how to pursue the politics of fusion and unity, it was by no means most people's. Owen's style persistently contradicted his stated views.

But perhaps the most profound doubts spreading in the party concerned the degree of Owen's commitment to the political left, to traditional British-style progressive politics. Owen not only sounded more and more right wing, but his Southport speech and subsequent statements seemed to open up the possibility that in the end Owen's natural political home might actually be in the Conservative party. On 24 July 1986 Hugo Young wrote a column in the *Guardian*, published under the headline: 'Why David Owen might want to keep his options open'. Young began by describing the party's internal tensions:

The SDP is becoming significantly more divided: over style, over policy, over post-election tactics, over the very nature of the Alliance. Personal relations have never been worse. At the top they range from Mr Rodgers, Mrs Williams and Mr Roy Jenkins on one side, Dr Owen on the other. Lower down, the factions are reproduced. Sober members of the SDP believe that what is at stake is the future leadership role of three of the four people who set the party up.

At the centre of the argument, Young continued, was Owen's towering personality:

With brief lapses into collegiate mode, this has become ever more dominant, ever more impatient, and ever more convinced that hardly anyone else in the party is worth a row of beans. One of the most formidable and most spaciously knowledgeable men in politics, Owen exhausts himself in the task of knowing everything about everything and declining to trust almost anyone with anything.

Having drawn this unflattering personality sketch, Young went on to ask why Owen seemed so intent on registering, at every point, his disapproval of the Joint Defence Commission's report. Why did he seem so anxious to distance himself not only from the Liberals but also from many, including Rodgers, in his own party? Young noted that many in the SDP were perplexed by Owen's behaviour and could not understand his motives, so he offered an explanation, one that had the virtue of at least fitting the facts:

Maybe Dr Owen wants to be, above all, free. If a hung parliament is returned, he would like to be unencumbered by the Liberals. He has always found many of their attitudes uncongenial, and has the old Labour man's contempt for their nagging individualism. But far more important than that, in a certain configuration of seats, he would want to keep open the Tory option: do a deal with a new Conservative leadership as the last hope of precluding what would be, for Owen personally, the ruin of his political life—the installation of Neil Kinnock in Downing Street.

Young admitted that this particular parliamentary scenario was improbable and that his notion of Owen's joining the Conservatives might be 'merely a fantastic speculation'. Nevertheless, he was giving vent to thoughts that were beginning to form in many people's minds. Was Owen possibly another Ramsay MacDonald, ready to sell out his party to gain office in a Conservative-dominated government? Several of Owen's confidants dismissed the idea with scorn, but it clearly tweaked a nerve. In 1986 for the first time, considerable numbers of people in the SDP began to contemplate the possibility that their leader, who had been proud to describe himself as a socialist only five years before, and had been the radicals' standard-bearer in the 1982 leadership election, had become a closet Conservative. One member of the SDP National Committee, a man by no means hostile to Owen, observed ironically: 'If Owen joined a Tory government, I could write the speech now: "We shall not turn our back on the nation, etc., etc.".' The thought persisted, and it drove a deeper wedge between Owen and many of his followers than Owen himself may have realized.

The defence row did the Alliance considerable electoral damage in late 1986, and there was a widespread fear that it might do more; pessimists spoke of the row's having cost the Liberals and the SDP 'a million votes', and one senior Cowley Street official, someone who normally looked on the bright side, was convinced that any recovery would be both 'slow and protracted'. In fact, the Alliance's leaders, like most politicians, tended to exaggerate the amount of attention the non-political public paid to short-lived political crises, and the Alliance's performance in the polls began to improve from December 1986 onwards as Labour's fortunes slumped. The Alliance parties succeeded for a considerable period in avoiding damaging public rows, and a big Alliance rally at the Barbican Centre in London at the end of January 1987 was a success. The Liberals and the SDP adopted a common gold logo and livery and also a common theme tune, Purcell's *Trumpet Tune in D* (played with gusto at the Barbican rally by the Rothwell Temperance Band). In the opinion polls, the Liberals and the SDP showed every sign of edging into second place past Labour. Steel and Owen worked increasingly effectively together and were increasingly frequently photographed together.

The Alliance's progress at the beginning of 1987, however, was gentle, and, while it owed something to the ending of the defence row, it undoubtedly owed even more to the troubles of the Labour party (arising from its continuing associations with extremism, especially in the big cities). But there then occurred one of those events in the SDP's short history that suddenly captured the public's attention and made the party seem once again a serious contender for power: the February 1987 Greenwich by-election.

All three of the SDP's by-election gains since 1981—Crosby, Glasgow Hillhead and Portsmouth South—had been at the expense of the Conservatives, but Greenwich was a Labour-held seat. Like Woolwich, John Cartwright's seat to the east, and Bermondsey, Simon Hughes' to the west, Greenwich was a largely working-class constituency on the south bank of the Thames in London. It was also, somewhat incongruously, the home of the Royal Naval College. Historically Greenwich had been a safe Labour seat, but a combination of social change and Labour's long-term national decline was taking its toll of Labour's Greenwich majority. Guy Barnett had held the seat in 1983 with only 38.2 per cent of the vote. The Conservatives, with 34.8 per cent, had come second. The then SDP candidate, with 25.1 per cent, had finished third. It was not a seat that the Alliance could normally have expected to win.

But in 1987 every circumstance was to conspire in the Alliance's favour.[40] Guy Barnett, the sitting Labour MP, died on Christmas Eve 1986. His successor as Labour candidate was Deirdre Wood, a woman who might almost have been invented by the tabloid press to symbolize the London Labour party's 'loony left'. Standing far to the left of Neil Kinnock and the Labour party's desperate-to-be-moderate national leadership, she was, in political terms, a sort of female Peter Tatchell, in favour of forming black sections in the Labour party and of inviting Sinn Féin speakers to come and speak in London and with a hard-left voting record on both the Inner London Education Authority and the Greater London Council. Partly because the Greenwich by-election happened to occur in the midst of a tabloid campaign, already under way, attacking the loony left, Wood seemed precisely the sort of candidate who would cause marginal Labour voters to desert the Labour party and also cause wavering Conservatives to try to figure out which candidate was most likely to keep Labour out. Shortly before Wood was adopted, a *Guardian* reporter described her as being 'the first choice of the Tories and the Alliance as an opponent'.[41]

If Deirdre Wood was an archetypal representative of the hard-left wing of the Labour party, Rosie Barnes, her Alliance opponent, was an archetypal member of the SDP. She might well have been chosen to exemplify 'the growing "service class" of highly qualified managers and specialists' we described in Chapter 15. The daughter of working-class parents, she had gone to a grammar school and Birmingham University and now at the age of 40 was the mother of three children with a job in market research. Her husband was an SDP member of the Greenwich council and a successful investment analyst. More to the point, Rosie Barnes was, as it turned out, a born political campaigner. Like Shirley Williams, she seemed nice because she was nice, and within days of the beginning of the campaign the polls were reporting that her soft North Country accent and her air of being a down-to-earth sort of person, not at all a politician, were making a very favourable impression on Greenwich voters.[42]

The voters knew a good deal about her, partly because the national media, believing Greenwich would be a pointer to the timing and outcome of the next general election, descended on the constituency in force, but also because Alec McGivan, the SDP's national organizer, used Greenwich as a test-bed to perfect the local campaigning techniques that he had imported from the United States and had developed in previous by-election campaigns. A substantial influx of SDP and Liberal workers into the constituency enabled him to exploit the new techniques to the full. Some 70 per cent of Greenwich's voters were canvassed, and specific groups like policemen and head teachers received personal letters outlining the SDP's policies in their special fields of interest.[43] (McGivan won £1,500 in bets on the result.) Labour also mounted a considerable effort during the campaign, but the Conservatives, probably suspecting from the beginning that they were going to do badly whatever they did, decided to do little. From the beginning, the media and the parties both treated the by-election as though it were not, as it had been in 1983, a Labour–Conservative contest but, as it now appeared to be, a Labour–SDP contest.

Partly for that reason, the election came to hinge on tactical voting—specifically on how the supporters of whichever party found itself in third place in the opinion polls would ultimately decide to vote. The Warrington and Crosby by-elections had resembled carnivals. Glasgow Hillhead had resembled a Gladstonian crusade. Greenwich was more like an elaborate exercise in calculus. A BBC *Newsnight* poll, published three weeks before polling day, suggested that Labour was losing support because of its selection of Deirdre Wood and, more significantly, that the SDP had overtaken the Conservatives and was now in second place.[44] The poll was given wide publicity, partly because its results were attacked by the Conservatives. For the next fortnight, support for both Labour and the Conservatives declined very slowly and somewhat erratically with Rosie Barnes slowly gaining support; but then, in the last few days of the campaign, thousands of Greenwich voters suddenly changed sides. Desertions from Labour took place on a large scale and so, on an even larger scale, did tactical switching from the unfortunate Conservative candidate, a young merchant banker named John Antcliffe, to the Social Democrats.

On the day, the turn-out on a new register was 68.4 per cent, higher than at the general election, and Rosie Barnes romped home, taking 53.0 per cent of the vote, more than double that of her SDP predecessor four years before. Labour's share of the vote, 33.8 per cent, fell only slightly (it should have increased substantially given Labour's poor showing in 1983 and its subsequent national recovery), but the Conservatives' vote collapsed, from more than a third of the total, 34.8 per cent, at the general election, to less than one-eighth, 11.6 per cent, at the by-election. The Alliance had won a great victory, and the SDP, once thought of as a party that would eventually replace the Labour party, had won, after six years, its first-ever Labour-held seat. With the Thatcher government still widely unpopular and Labour again in disarray, it seemed to many in the party that the great days of 1981 might be about to return, that a new golden age might be about to dawn. Rosie Barnes immediately became one of David Owen's most loyal supporters in the House of Commons. He had campaigned hard for her (even cancelling a family holiday in India to do so), and many of her most enthusiastic workers during the campaign had come over the border from the neighbouring constituency of Woolwich, whose MP, John Cartwright, was also one of Owen's closest allies.

Greenwich, unlike most by-elections, was a real political event, with real political consequences. Neil Kinnock's position as Labour leader was badly shaken by the loss of a safe Labour seat and by his apparent inability to control his own party, and Labour slumped to below 30 per cent in a series of national polls. The Alliance moved into second place in many polls, with the support, again, of nearly a third of the electorate. Labour's poor performance, and widespread Conservative fears that a new Alliance bandwagon might be starting to roll, revived speculation that Thatcher might well go to the country sometime in 1987 and not in 1988 as had previously been supposed—speculation that was further fuelled when, a fortnight after Greenwich, the Liberals easily held on to Truro, the seat left vacant by the death of David Penhaligon. The Liberals' share of the vote rose in Truro, despite the party's loss of a popular local MP; Labour's rose only slightly; and the Conservatives' fell by less than might have been expected.

This post-Greenwich Alliance surge, together with Labour's post-Greenwich slump and the fact that the Conservatives remained in the doldrums—seldom able to push their standing in the polls above 40 per cent—had the additional effect of making it seem possible again that the next election would produce a hung parliament in which the Liberals and the SDP might conceivably hold the balance of power. Owen and Steel in the spring of 1987 began to be pressed to say what they would do in that event. Which of the two major parties would they throw their weight behind?[45]

Before the early months of 1987, Owen and Steel had devoted a certain amount of time, though not much, to thinking about how they would behave in the event of a hung parliament, one in which they held the balance of power—and also to thinking about the more important question of what they would say ahead of time about how they proposed to behave in such an eventuality. It was not actually very likely that there would be a hung parliament with the Alliance holding the balance of power; but it was certain that Owen and Steel would be asked what they intended to do if there were. Journalists knew that the Alliance leaders were potentially vulnerable—or at least capable of being greatly embarrassed—on this subject and they were therefore bound to raise it. Many journalists also believed that voters who were thinking of voting Alliance had a legitimate right to know whether an Alliance vote would, in the event of a hung parliament, be more likely to result in the formation of a Conservative–Alliance government (possibly led by Margaret Thatcher) or a Labour–Alliance government (possibly led by Neil Kinnock). It would be strange for voters *not* to want to know.

The two leaders had little difficulty in reaching broad agreement on the general line they intended to follow. Their position was similar to that adopted by Steel and Jenkins in 1983.[46] The Alliance would negotiate as a unit, not as two separate parties. It would be prepared to negotiate with either the Conservatives or Labour, but the initial approach would be to whichever party had won the most votes in the election. The Alliance partners would probably not seek to join a coalition, but they would be prepared to support a minority government. A necessary condition of their support, however, would be agreement on a detailed programme for government and an explicit understanding that the agreement should run for at least two or three years. The other parties must be prepared to talk, and there would be no *ad hoc* deals of the kind that had led to the Lib–Lab pact in 1976; any deal would have to have some quality of permanence about it and also the formal backing of both the Liberal and Social Democratic parties. If either the Conservatives or Labour refused to talk to the Alliance but attempted to form a government all the same, the Alliance MPs would immediately vote them out of office and force a second general election. On one occasion, Owen was asked what the Alliance would do if a Conservative or Labour minority government published a Queen's Speech without consulting the Liberals and the SDP. He replied tartly: 'We won't read it.'[47]

Owen and Steel never spelt out in any detail what the terms of a programme for government acceptable to them would be. It would have been strange if they had, since they would not have wanted to show their hand before entering into negotiations. But it was clear that they would have demanded from the Conservatives mainly a programme to combat unemployment and the abandoning of Trident and from Labour the abandonment of most of that party's more extreme left-wing policies. Labour would have had to agree to maintaining a minimum British nuclear deterrent, to remaining in Europe, to abandoning its pledge to repeal all of the Thatcher government's trade-union legislation, to dropping its plans for further nationalization and also to rescinding its pledge to try to repatriate British investment capital from overseas. The two Alliance leaders disagreed on only one major point. Steel wished to insist on the introduction of proportional representation as the Alliance parties' price for supporting a minority government. Owen, however, believed that a major constitutional change like the introduction of proportional representation should not—and could not—be forced down the throats of reluctant MPs and that the issue ought to be settled in a national referendum. Only in that way could the Alliance parties be sure that proportional representation, once introduced, would stick and not be repealed by some later administration.[48] Owen introduced the idea of a referendum on proportional representation into the debate without having gone through any of the Alliance's or the SDP's formal policy-making machinery, and many Liberals were extremely annoyed both by the substance of his proposal (they wanted parliament to decide the issue) and also by Owen's seeming high-handedness; but Owen had taken the trouble to consult Steel beforehand, and the two men subsequently seemed content to agree to disagree on this one point.[49]

The formalities of any Alliance negotiations with the other parties had thus largely been settled. In May 1986 the two leaders even wrote a letter to the two parties' parliamentary candidates telling them what they should say and not say if they were asked during the coming election campaign about Alliance policy in the event of a hung parliament.[50] But, although the formalities were agreed, the underlying politics were not. There were two problems. One existed only as a worry in the minds of some Alliance politicians. The other was ventilated frequently on television and in the national press.

The lingering worry in some Alliance politicians' minds was the one that Hugo Young had raised in his *Guardian* column during the defence row: that, whatever he might say in advance, Owen might be prepared, given a hung parliament, to sever his links with the Liberals and do a deal on his own with the Conservatives. Owen denied adamantly that he had any such intention. In his joint letter with Steel to the two parties' candidates, for example, he wrote: 'We must all make it plain that Liberals and Social Democrats will be indivisible in all stages of the negotiations after the next election.'[51] But doubts persisted. They were widespread among Social Democrats as well as among Liberals, and Steel occasionally found himself being asked about them on television. 'I cannot see any circumstances in which it would happen [i.e. that Owen would defect],' he said in the course of one interview; but he was forced to add that in politics one could never say never. He maintained that the two parties would have to work together if they held the balance of power because otherwise they would be betraying the whole basis on which they had fought the election.[52] Owen took the same line, but he never managed to dispel entirely the idea that he might abandon his Liberal allies after the election if he wanted to—and if he thought he could get away with it.

These doubts persisted only partly because some of his fellow politicians believed Owen was not entirely to be trusted. They persisted chiefly because the two Alliance leaders, however hard they tried, could not conceal either from each other or from the general public that they would approach the inter-party negotiations in a hung parliament in completely different frames of mind. This was the second of the two problems.

Steel, politically a product of the 1960s and early 1970s, still saw himself very much in traditional left-of-centre terms. He had worked reasonably satisfactorily with the Labour leadership in the course of the 1970s Lib–Lab pact, and he personally liked a number of senior Labour politicians. All his instincts and his political experience inclined him towards Labour and the left and away from the Conservatives, especially the Conservatives under Margaret Thatcher. Steel was in no conceivable sense a socialist, but his themes tended to be Labour themes: the evils of poverty and unemployment, the need for greater social equality and the virtues of neighbourliness and mutual care, including state care. Steel even wrote articles for the left-wing *New Statesman*.

Owen, however, had by now distanced himself much further from his old party. Impatient with what he saw as the 'old politics' of Steel and his generation, he wanted to move the SDP and British politics generally on to a new, post-Thatcher basis, one in which, as we saw in the last chapter, a high level of social concern would be allied to an emphasis on competition, the free market and free enterprise. Far more than Steel or the other members of the Gang of Four, he had come to loathe the Labour party and almost everything it stood for. It, and particularly its leadership, stood in his eyes for inefficiency, for failure and for national decline.[53] The whole Labour spectacle revolted him.

Even before the 1987 election was announced, Owen and Steel were already differing in their approach to the two other parties and were also feeling the need to respond to each other's discrepant views. Throughout the 1983 parliament, but particularly as the election approached, Owen vented his dislike of Labour, and of Neil Kinnock personally, in terms that were frequently contemptuous:

Mr Kinnock's Labour party is so buckled and bent by the hard left that it can neither walk nor think straight.[54]

There is probably no other politician with the exception of Mr Tony Benn who has done more harm to Anglo-American relations and to NATO than Mr Kinnock.[55]

[On the poor reception that Kinnock had got on a pre-election visit to the United States:] He got his comeuppance and fully deserved it.[56]

We have yet to finish the job of demolishing the Labour party.[57]

Owen similarly made it clear that, while he was prepared to work with Labour if Labour radically changed its defence and foreign policies and abandoned many of its other pledges, he thought this was extremely unlikely to happen and therefore that co-operation with the Conservatives in any hung parliament was much the more likely of the two alternatives. Asked by the *Independent* whether he would find it easier to do a deal with the Conservatives than with Labour, Owen made no effort to conceal where his preferences (or at least his expectations) lay:

The rebels in the Conservative party—pretty mild rebels, the wets—are at least basically arguing for the things we want. There's common ground. The rebels in the Labour party are arguing for things we find a total anathema, so there's the difficulty we have.[58]

On a later occasion, when Owen had given a television interview at the end of which he was forced to agree that an SDP–Conservative deal might 'bring out the best in both parties', Steel felt constrained the next day to balance his SDP partner by insisting in another interview: 'We are prepared to work with the Conservative party or the Labour party so long as the programme is right.'[59]

Steel attacked Labour as frequently as did Owen, but unlike Owen he seemed to speak more in sorrow than in anger. The ire in his speeches and writings was directed almost entirely at the Conservative party and, especially, its then leader:

You cannot get rid of Thatcherism without getting rid of Thatcher.[60]

The cost of Thatcherism is not just to be counted in lost jobs and missed opportunities but in a loss of civic virtue, less neighbourliness and mutual care, more intolerance and naked greed.[61]

I think that the whole tone of Mrs Thatcher's government is deeply repugnant, and I do not see how we could retain our self-respect and serve in a government over which she presides.[62]

Owen frequently criticized the Conservatives, but he seldom used such strong language and he very seldom used the term 'Thatcherism'. His response to Steel's suggestion that the Alliance parties could not serve under Thatcher was to say, with Steel present, that the Alliance should not 'get into the business of telling other parties who is to be their leader'.[63] Nor were the two men engaged in some kind of complicated double-act, with 'nice Mr Steel' taking on the Tories while 'nasty Dr Owen' savaged the Labour party. On the contrary, each of them spoke from the heart.

The result was, or should have been, ominous for the Alliance partners. On the eve of the 1987 general election, it was clear to everyone with eyes to see that, in the event of a hung parliament in which the Alliance parties held the balance of power, David Steel would prefer to do a deal with the Labour party and would find it almost impossible to work with Margaret Thatcher, while David Owen would prefer to do a deal with the Conservatives and would find it almost impossible to work with Neil Kinnock. The two leaders had agreed on terms for the conduct of formal negotiations, but there had not been anything like a true meeting of minds. It was going to be a miracle if, under the pressures of the election campaign, this fundamental disagreement were not to be further, and damagingly, exposed.

19

• • • •

Humiliation: June 1987

The SDP had entered the 1983 election campaign with trepidation. It approached the 1987 campaign with some optimism. Everything appeared to have turned out surprisingly well since the Barbican rally at the beginning of the year. The issue of what, if anything, should replace Polaris, which had caused such bad blood within both the SDP and the Liberals, had been successfully resolved. Rosie Barnes' victory in Greenwich had restored the SDP's morale. Relations between David Owen and the rest of the Gang of Four, while far from warm, had thawed somewhat, especially after Owen had agreed to Jenkins being brought in as the Alliance's spokesman on the economy.

The Barbican rally also seemed to mark a turning-point in relations between the SDP and the Liberals. Leading members of both parties detected a new 'Alliance spirit'. In particular, Owen and Steel were getting on better, at least on the surface. The improvement in their relations was partly in response to the imminence of an election and the alertness of the media to any tension between them; but it was also the paradoxical result of Steel's defeat in the Eastbourne defence debate. Following Eastbourne Owen had taken a sympathetic and constructive line which benefited both leaders. Steel was relieved that Owen had not exploited the defeat to widen the rift between the SDP and the Liberals, while Owen enjoyed his new role as Steel's adviser and protector on defence. Owen gained the psychological upper hand. Paradoxically, the relationship between the two leaders became more co-operative precisely because it became less equal.

Co-operation between the two parties had come to fruition in other respects. The seats negotiations were virtually complete by the autumn of 1986 and this time, unlike in 1982–3, there were no public rows, no break-offs in negotiations, no constituencies in which a disgruntled Liberal (or SDP) candidate stood against the official Alliance candidate. The final stages of the negotiations in fact went almost unreported in the media. The SDP and the Liberals had also reached agreement on policy. After twelve months of tortuous discussions in joint committees ('a balls-aching exercise'), the two parties published a 128-page joint policy document, *The Time has Come*, early in 1987.[1] On the ground, where the Alliance had always been a reality, relations between the parties were, despite Eastbourne, usually close. Liberal activists had flocked in large numbers to Greenwich, where they had worked happily under the SDP's by-election organizer, Alec McGivan. It was the first by-election in which Liberal and SDP helpers were properly integrated into an Alliance team. Tom McNally, a full-time member of the team, remembered walking home in the early morning after the victory party, seeing the sun rising as he emerged from Woolwich tunnel and thinking 'All's well with the world. The Alliance is going to work after all.' However, Greenwich, as it turned out, was the Alliance's high watermark.

The by-election victories at Greenwich and then at Truro led to a surge of Alliance support in the opinion polls. The three parties' support in the nine polls conducted in February, before the Greenwich by-election, averaged out at Conservatives 38 per cent, Labour 36 per cent and Alliance 23 per cent. In the six polls conducted during the fortnight between the Greenwich and Truro by-elections, the Conservatives remained at 38 per cent, but Labour dropped to 32 per cent and the Alliance rose to 29 per cent. Then, in the six polls taken in March after the Truro by-election, the Conservatives rose a point to 39 per cent, Labour dropped a point to 31 per cent, while the Alliance remained steady at 29 per cent—only 2 per cent behind Labour. Some polls showed the Alliance level-pegging with Labour, and a few put it fractionally ahead, attracting headlines suggesting that Labour might actually go into the election campaign in third place.[2] Although Alliance support gradually subsided towards the end of April, the Alliance's local election performance in May again revived the possibility that it might overtake Labour. The Alliance gained over 450 seats (Labour, by comparison, lost 230 and the Conservatives gained only 75) and won control of six more councils. Psephologists estimated that the local results were the equivalent of a national vote of Conservatives 40 per cent, Labour 31 per cent and Alliance 27 per cent.[3]

The Liberal–SDP Alliance's local-election vote in May 1987 was the highest base from which any third party had launched itself into a general-election campaign since the 1920s. Moreover, the records showed that centre parties usually increased their support over the four-week campaign because during that period they received much more media coverage than normal.[4] In 1983 the Alliance's vote had dropped from the 22 per cent in the local elections to an average of 18 per cent in the first week of the general-election campaign before rising to 26 per cent by polling day. The Alliance had started fourteen percentage points behind Labour in 1983 and ended up only two points behind. Now the gap was much smaller, and Labour was again being damaged by its hardliners (especially on local councils), by its unilateralist defence policy and by its interminable internal ructions. It was at this time that the *Sun* newspaper popularized the phrase 'loony left'.

Almost everyone in the two Alliance parties therefore assumed that the 1987 campaign would be a rerun of 1983 except that this time the two parties, starting from a higher base, had a much better chance of making a breakthrough. Most people took it for granted that the Conservatives would win; but they were also convinced, especially after the broadcasting authorities had granted them equal time with the two big parties, that as the campaign progressed their vote would rise with the inevitability of an incoming tide. They further assumed that the Labour party would self-destruct, as it had in 1983. They could easily imagine the Alliance overtaking Labour early in the campaign, thereby persuading voters that Labour was doomed and then squeezing the Labour vote much as Labour had squeezed the Liberals' vote in the past. The Alliance's leaders knew that the Alliance could not beat the Conservatives, but they hoped that the interaction of the opinion polls, the media and tactical voting would trigger a big shift of votes towards the end of the campaign, just as it had in Greenwich. Fifty or even a hundred seats were not, they reckoned, entirely beyond reach.

The SDP's spirits were high for another reason: the party believed it was well prepared. In 1983 there had not been enough time to plan. The election was called when the party had been in existence for little more than two years; most active members, including many of the staff at Cowley Street, had no campaigning experience; most candidates had been in place for only a few months; and policy had not been co-ordinated in detail with the Liberals. The SDP approached the 1987 campaign confident that in the main its planning was thorough and professional. Unlike in 1983, it felt in control, capable of handling whatever was thrown at it. The SDP believed, firstly, that its candidates were better trained and briefed than before. After taking the expensive advice of an American campaign consultant, Matt Reese, Cowley Street reallocated its limited resources to election preparation at the expense of policy-making and the servicing of committees. In October 1985 a General Election Unit was set up under Dick Newby, who was relieved of the more routine parts of his job as national secretary. Alec McGivan acted as his deputy. The Unit proceeded to identify sixty 'target seats' of which twenty-one were 'top grade'. The latter included Cambridge and Milton Keynes, where Shirley Williams and Bill Rodgers were standing, both of them having concluded that the chances of regaining their old seats of Crosby and Stockton North were slim.

The Unit's aim was to generate an above-average swing in the target seats so that, even if the party's overall vote declined, it could still gain seats against the national trend and build up a viable base in the House of Commons. The Unit's ethos was professional and high-tech, and it put an enormous amount of time and effort into the seats-targeting exercise. The sixty target seats were provided with advice, training and grants for computers and agents. Candidates and local parties were issued with a tightly phased programme of tasks, targets and deadlines. Although the responsiveness of local parties to the constant prodding from the Unit varied, Cowley Street was optimistic about the chances of improving on the national swing in most of the sixty seats.

Advance preparation of the Alliance's policies had been equally thorough.

They had already appeared in *The Time has Come*, which would be holy writ when it came to drafting the joint manifesto and to issuing policy statements during the campaign. The risk of electorally damaging deviations from disgruntled minorities in either party had thus been reduced as far as was possible. Moreover, as we saw in the last chapter, the two parties had also prepared carefully—or thought they had—for the question of what they would do if the election produced a hung parliament.[5] Owen and Steel had agreed that they would resolutely refuse to express a preference between the Conservative and Labour parties as possible coalition partners. This approach worked well in a *Weekend World* programme on 12 April, before the election was announced, when Brian Walden grilled David Owen at length on his position in a hung parliament. Owen skilfully refused to be drawn on which of the two parties he preferred.

The SDP was not, in fact, as well prepared as Cowley Street imagined. Campaign-planning was thorough and well integrated between the Liberals and the SDP in both the country and at party headquarters, and two-way communications between London and the constituency parties had improved considerably since 1983; but planning and communications were inadequate where they mattered most—at the top. In November 1986 the parties established an Alliance Planning Group to prepare and direct the Alliance campaign. It was designed to be a small executive body, consisting of people who, apart from the two leaders, were not standing as candidates. The SDP members were David Owen, Lord Harris of Greenwich, Polly Toynbee and Roland Freeman, a former Conservative GLC councillor and public-relations consultant. The Liberal members were David Steel, John Pardoe, the former Liberal MP, the Liberals' president, Des Wilson, and Paul Tyler, a former MP and recent chairman of the party. At first Owen resisted the Liberals' proposal to put the president and general secretary of both parties on the committee, because he regarded both Shirley Williams and Dick Newby as politically unsound. He relented on Des Wilson's membership (while still vetoing Williams' on the ground that she was a candidate); and eventually, in March 1987, he did allow Dick Newby from the SDP and Andy Ellis from the Liberals to join. None the less, there was resentment in both parties that experienced professionals such as these had originally been excluded.

The group did not work well either personally or organizationally. The two sides were each suspicious and dismissive of the other. The SDP team regarded Steel as lazy and indecisive, incapable of taking responsibility or planning ahead and unwilling to attend to the details of policy-making and public relations. The Liberals regarded Freeman and Toynbee as mediocre timeservers, put there for their political loyalty to Owen rather than for any campaign expertise. The party secretaries aside, the only member to command cross-party respect was John Pardoe, who was Liberal by affiliation but Owenite in his tough, no-nonsense style. Moreover, he was independent of Steel, his former rival for the Liberal leadership.

The group was always a joint committee of the two parties and never became an integrated Alliance body. Its weekly meetings after November 1986 were chaired alternately by the two party leaders until the election was announced, when, by agreement, Pardoe took over not only as chairman but as campaign director, while Harris, his SDP deputy, was given a formal 'right of appeal'. The group's pre-election budget was a minuscule £85,000, which was spent on the Barbican rally and two party political broadcasts; its campaign budget was a wholly inadequate £250,000. The bulk of the spending decisions were made independently by the two separate parties, each of which jealously guarded its own budget.

Because the group never jelled, its preparatory work was narrowly organizational rather than political. The group delegated the drafting of the manifesto to Alan Beith, the Liberals' deputy leader. Beith invited the group to propose some new ideas for the manifesto, going beyond *The Time has Come*, and that was the extent of its involvement. It appointed David Abbott of the Abbott Mead Vickers advertising agency to take control of the Alliance's advertising on the recommendation of David Sainsbury ('Abbott is in a class of his own'), but made very little use of his talent. It also decided on the structure and mechanics of the daily campaign routine. The Planning Group had to address one particularly tricky issue: how would the Alliance campaign with two separate leaders? The group resolved to make a virtue of necessity. The Alliance would not repeat the mistake of implying that one of the two parties' leaders was also leader of the Alliance: that way might only lead to another Ettrickbridge showdown. Nor would it allow the two leaders to follow quite separate campaign itineraries and risk the hit-and-miss media coverage that Steel and Jenkins had suffered from in 1983.[6]

Rather, Owen's and Steel's equal status would be underlined by ensuring that they appeared together on television and at public meetings as much as possible. Indeed this political togetherness would be turned into the Alliance's 'unique selling point'—a way of hammering home to voters the message that the Alliance stood for co-operation among parties as well as competition between them. When combined with the theme of electoral reform, the tandem leadership would, with luck, personify the advantages of multi-party politics and coalition government. Most important of all, it would also ensure, or so the group hoped, that any real or alleged disagreement between Owen and Steel would be sorted out straightaway by the leaders themselves. When explaining why they should be yoked together, 'we told them', said Pardoe, 'that it was because they were so good together. The truth is that we were terrified of what they would say apart.'[7]

The daily structure of the leaders' campaign was worked out accordingly. Steel and Owen would both attend the early morning press conference at 8.30 a.m. before going their separate ways during the day, Steel on the Liberals' 'battlebus' and by helicopter, Owen by plane. While apart, they would keep in touch constantly by radio and car telephone. They would then rejoin each other in the early evening in time for photo-calls and joint interviews on regional television stations. Finally, they would appear together at a regional 'Ask the Alliance' meeting, each speaking briefly and then answering questions informally from the audience, before returning to London in the late evening.

But the Planning Group rarely discussed and never determined an overall theme or plan for the campaign, largely because neither party leader believed in overall themes or plans. Steel and Owen both regarded electioneering as a form of tactical warfare, consisting of lightning strikes and mobile defence, not of set-piece battles. And both fancied they were good tacticians. The result was that some fundamental strategic questions were never addressed.

These questions of strategy arose from the same dilemmas that faced the Alliance in 1983.[8] Should the Alliance say it was aiming for outright victory or for a share in a coalition government? Should it target Conservative voters or Labour voters? Should it concentrate its fire on the Conservative government or the Labour opposition?

The first of these dilemmas was raised at a meeting of the Joint Strategy Committee (the parent body of the Planning Group) on 7 April 1987, when a number of Liberals voiced their worries about Owen saying in public that the only realistic objective for the Alliance was to hold the balance in a hung parliament.[9] This, they argued, was not so much realistic as defeatist; people did not vote for hung parliaments or second place; such a tactic would only persuade sympathizers that a vote for the Alliance was a wasted vote. To encourage tactical voting for, rather than against, the Alliance, its prospects had to be talked up. But Owen, with Steel's concurrence, resisted. The polls, he pointed out, showed that only one in six voters, even in the Alliance's strongest areas, thought it could win nationally. Talk of outright victory was therefore utterly implausible. The issue was left unresolved, and the committee came to no decision about the line that should be taken by candidates in the constituencies or by the two leaders. The dilemma of whether to attack the Conservatives or Labour was never analysed properly, let alone confronted and resolved. The Campaign Group failed to disentangle two separate issues. The first concerned ends: should the Alliance target Conservative or Labour voters? To most members of the group it seemed obvious that, if the Alliance's objective was to replace the Labour party—and if, in addition, Labour support looked fragile—it was Labour voters the Alliance should go for. But a minority led by Owen (who certainly wanted the SDP to supplant the Labour party) pointed out that the Alliance's best prospects of gains were in Conservative seats where the Labour vote had already been squeezed. To win these seats the Alliance needed to convert disillusioned Conservatives, not Labour loyalists.

The second issue concerned means: having identified its target voters, should the Alliance try to win them over by attacking their existing party or by attacking their 'enemy' party? Some in the group, mainly Liberals, assumed that the best way of attracting disillusioned Conservatives was to assail Thatcher; others, like Owen, assumed that it was better to establish the Alliance's anti-Labour credentials in areas such as defence and privatization. Similarly, there was disagreement over the best means of attracting Labour voters: some advocated broadsides against the Labour party, others broadsides against Thatcher. With no hard evidence to rely on, both tactics seemed equally plausible. As a result the Alliance tacked first one way, then the other, with a rationale that was persuasive at each separate turn but lacked consistency or coherence.

On 11 May the date of the forthcoming election was announced: it was to be on Thursday, 11 June. The Conservative and Labour parties planned to wait until 19 May to launch their manifestos. The Alliance Planning Group decided to begin campaigning before the other parties in order to maximize the Alliance's chances of overtaking Labour early in the campaign.

The daily routine at Alliance headquarters in London was similar to that in 1983.[10] John Pardoe and Lord Harris arrived at Cowley Street shortly after 7 a.m. to be briefed by Des Wilson on the overnight news, the morning papers and breakfast television, and the theme of the day. They then repaired to the National Liberal Club a mile away to brief Owen and Steel in time for the press conference at 8.30 a.m.. The Planning Group held the first of its two daily meetings at 10.15 a.m. to discuss the tasks for the day, media coverage, the polls and the other parties' tactics. Liberal and SDP staff crammed into Cowley Street's small offices to prepare briefings, issue press releases, deal with the media and organize the leaders' tours. (They got on well. The rows were not between the two parties working in Cowley Street but, as we shall see, between Cowley Street and the two leaders touring the country.) At 10 p.m. Des Wilson would begin the night shift, co-ordinating a team of six to prepare material for the morning press conference, speeches and media briefings.[11] On Sundays the Planning Group met in full, with the two leaders present, to discuss strategy.

At its first Sunday meeting, on 17 May, Owen proposed that the Alliance should launch the campaign by attacking the Conservatives and not Labour, a reversal of the tactics agreed, or so many thought, at the 7 April meeting of the Joint Strategy Committee. Owen was insistent. Labour should be dismissed as irrelevant, as no-hopers, and the Alliance should project itself as the one force capable of preventing a further four years of uninterrupted Thatcherism. He pointed to the variety of tactical advantages. The Alliance's best prospects of gains were in Conservative seats where it was already the clear challenger. In these seats the Labour vote had already been compressed to a hard core and it was disillusioned Conservative voters whom the Alliance had to win over. An onslaught on the government would both bring down the Conservative vote and encourage those Labour supporters who could still be detached to vote tactically for the Alliance. Moreover, according to Owen, it would enable the Alliance to fight a positive campaign, putting forward its own alternatives to the government's policies.

Everybody else present was sceptical. If the Alliance's objective was to supplant the Labour party, it needed to push Labour into third place early in the campaign, and this could not be done without a concentrated attack on Labour. Some of the sceptics suspected that Owen's real but unstated objective was to hold the balance of power ('he was desperate for power'), which could only be achieved if the Conservative vote was brought down to below 40 per cent and if the Labour vote was not pushed down too far. But the sceptics also recognized that attacking the Conservatives would nail the impression that Owen was closer to the Conservatives than to Labour. In reality Owen was in a minority of one, but nobody had the stomach for a row so he got his way.[12]

In the week before campaigning formally began, Owen and Steel visited every regional media centre and the Alliance brought out its programme in four instalments in an attempt to maximize publicity. On 12 May it released a report by Coopers & Lybrand, the accountants, on the cost of the Alliance programme. The next day it launched its 'Great Reform Charter', consisting of a bill of rights, a freedom of information act, electoral reform, elected regional assemblies, fixed-term parliaments and an elected House of Lords. On the 15th it announced its 'rent-a-room' scheme, devised by Des Wilson and Polly Toynbee in response to Beith's call for new ideas. Intended to deal with housing shortages, especially the plight of the homeless, the scheme allowed householders to rent out a room on a short tenancy tax free. On the 18th the Alliance finally launched its full manifesto, *Britain United—The Time has Come*.

The main themes of the manifesto were a united Britain, constitutional reform and policies for employment and public services. The opening sentences set the theme of unity:

The Alliance's vision is of a Britain united, a Britain confident, compassionate and competitive. We know that it is possible to unite our country. We know the British people want greater unity. But we also know the task of drawing Britain together again can only be achieved through political, economic and social reform on a scale not contemplated in our country for over forty years.

This hint of fundamental reform was largely confined to the Great Reform Charter, which took up the first section of the manifesto. The Alliance's macro-economic strategy consisted of new capital investment in the national infrastructure, an 'incomes strategy' backed by a counter-inflation tax on companies and membership of the European exchange-rate mechanism. The short section on defence, tucked away at the back, laid most stress on disarmament but promised to 'maintain with whatever necessary modernisation our minimum nuclear deterrent until it can be negotiated away . . . in return for worthwhile concessions by the USSR', to 'maintain our capability in the sense of freezing our capacity at a level no greater than that of the Polaris system' and to 'cancel Trident'.

The manifesto had been carefully drafted and survived the media's search for gaffes and ambiguities. At its press launch Owen and Steel concentrated their attack, as planned, on the Conservatives. The Labour party, Owen stated, 'was unelectable but that cannot mean that the Conservatives are irreplaceable'. Talking to journalists later that day Steel said 'we don't see any reason to pay much attention to Labour. What's the point of going on and on about what a Labour government might do when there is not going to be one?'[13] But the manifesto itself received a poor press. Conservative newspapers predictably described it as 'a document with a strong scent of the 1970s about it' (*Daily Telegraph*), 'a plastic key to a bounteous togetherness where the waiting is taken out of wanting' (*Daily Mail*) and 'having your fudge and eating it' (*Daily Express*). But sympathetic and non-partisan newspapers were scarcely more enthusiastic. The *Guardian* called upon the Alliance to come off the fence about which party it would support in a hung Parliament. *The Times* commented sourly that 'the Alliance have never lacked for theme tunes. What they have lacked is a theme. "Britain United" is a theme of sorts, but the manifesto still lacks a philosophical base.' The media's general view was that the manifesto was serious and worthy—but also bland and dull. 'As a rallying cry,' the *Independent* concluded, 'moderate dirigisme is not frightfully inspiring.'

Coverage of the Alliance manifesto made the front page of only three newspapers, all of them quality broadsheets, and probably had a negligible impact on the public. But on the same morning, Tuesday, 19 May, another story about the Alliance did hit the front page in seven of the ten national dailies: the Alliance's decline in the opinion polls. As soon as the election had been called, the Alliance vote had begun to drift down while the Labour vote had begun to climb (see Table 19.1 in Appendix 5). There was a false dawn on 14 May when the *Daily Telegraph* published a Gallup survey putting the Alliance two percentage points ahead of Labour.[14] But thereafter the polls consistently showed the Alliance in third place, trailing Labour by an ever-widening gap. On the 15th three polls put Labour ahead of the Alliance, in one case by as much as nine points;[15] on Sunday the 17th the *Observer*'s Harris poll put Labour ten points in front; on Tuesday the 19th, the day the Alliance hoped for favourable coverage of its manifesto, three more polls were published, all placing Labour between eight and nine points ahead of the Alliance. A chorus of dispiriting headlines enhanced Labour's credibility and undermined the Alliance's: 'Labour Leaps in Poll' (*Daily Mirror*), 'A Goliath Task for Davids as They Slump in Polls' (*Daily Express*) and 'Alliance Losing Ground in Polls' (*Daily Telegraph*).[16] Readers were left in no doubt that Labour was better placed to challenge the Conservatives and that it was the Alliance who were the also-rans.

This disappointing news came in the first week of the campaign; but in Cowley Street people kept their spirits up by recalling that the Alliance had dropped four points in the first week of the 1983 campaign, only to surge (and almost overtake the Labour party) in the final ten days. The polls, they reasoned, were registering the shift from protest voting to choice-of-government voting that normally occurs at the start of a campaign. There was plenty of time for the Labour campaign to disintegrate and for the Alliance to pick up the pieces.

But that week the Labour campaign did the opposite of disintegrating. To everyone's surprise, the Labour campaign turned out to be polished, punchy and professional. Of the three parties' campaigns, Labour's made by far the most favourable impression on the media and therefore, it was assumed, on the voters. On 21 May a Labour party broadcast probably attracted more attention than any party election broadcast had ever attracted before. It focused on Neil and Glenys Kinnock, skilfully linking Kinnock's rise from working-class boy to party leader with his party's claim to represent the aspirations of ordinary people. The broadcast won Labour few extra votes, but it boosted Kinnock's personal ratings, buoyed up Labour's activists and impressed the political commentators enormously.

The Alliance's electioneering, by comparison, seemed uninspired. For most of the first week, coverage of the Alliance campaign focused on a row between Thatcher and Owen about the Alliance's defence policy. The Conservative manifesto, published on 19 May, described it as 'one-sided disarmament by default or inadvertence', differing from Labour's outright unilateralism only on timing: 'Labour would scrap Britain's deterrent immediately on entering office. The Liberals and SDP would allow it to wither on the vine.' The Alliance would take the country 'down the same disastrous road as the Labour Party towards a frightened and fellow-travelling Britain'. Owen wrote an open letter to the prime minister protesting at 'this foul smear' and demanding a retraction. There was genuine outrage behind his letter, but also a wish to reassure potential defectors from (or to) the Conservatives about the Alliance's defence credentials. Thatcher's reply the next day deliberately exploited the Alliance's vulnerability on defence: 'there is only one reason why you are so vague on this crucial defence question. It arises from the need to present a semblance of unity between the SDP and the unilateralists of the Liberal party.'

Owen returned to the fray on 21 May, telling journalists that this was 'a far more potent libel for me than being accused of having it off with someone . . . Hell's teeth—that is the issue on which I broke with the Labour party.' By prolonging his row with Thatcher, the issue of the Alliance's defence policy made the news from the Tuesday to the Friday of the first week. But the tactics were bad. Owen won some headlines, but unhelpful ones. It seems unlikely that the Alliance lost many votes as a result, but they wasted an opportunity. The original plan had been for the Alliance to begin the campaign on its own distinctive issue, constitutional reform. Instead it found itself campaigning on what Owen had always feared would be its most vulnerable issue, defence. He had fallen into a Conservative trap.[17]

The Alliance's early campaigning also suffered from looking lacklustre on television. Its first party election broadcast, the day after Labour's, bemused the media. Rosie Barnes, the victor of Greenwich, sat in a garden with her small daughter and the family's pet rabbit, talking to an invisible and edited-out interviewer about parents' worries about the world their children were growing up into, the failure of the old parties to address modern problems and the need for new solutions from a new party. She was filmed throughout the ten minutes in soft focus, and from time to time was faded out and then faded in again. It came over as a cross between a soap commercial and Private Eye's *Bores of Today*. Party workers, especially Liberals, thought it a hopeless flop: they complained that it reinforced the stereotype of the Alliance as nice, but mushy and amateurish.[18]

The 'Ask the Alliance' sessions in the evenings had a similar effect. The

Planning Group had chosen this format, ostensibly because it projected the Alliance as the 'thinking person's party', in reality because Owen and Steel found the format easier to handle than big set-piece speeches, at which neither was especially adept. Moreover, question-and-answer meetings appeared to have worked well in recent by-elections, where they had attracted big audiences. But it turned out that they did not make good television. When Thatcher and Kinnock addressed large all-ticket rallies of the party faithful, television showed thundering applause from overflowing halls. When Owen and Steel chaired 'Ask the Alliance' meetings, television showed desultory question-and-answer sessions in half-empty halls. There was no excitement or sense of occasion. The format made the Alliance look like a small grouping with no hope of winning. 'It did wonders for our soul,' a sympathetic journalist concluded, 'but was no good for our standing in the polls.'[19]

The Alliance's evening meetings not only served to remind viewers that the Alliance was a minor party. Steel's and Owen's dual appearances also reminded viewers that the Alliance was actually not one minor party but two. Cowley Street soon concluded that all their dual appearances, whatever the format, looked wrong. One reason was technical: some regional studios trained a single camera on both leaders so that their shoulders were centre screen while their heads tended to exit right and left. Another was presentational: whenever one leader answered a question put to him, it was a problem for the other to know what to do. A pose of rapt attention looked false; anything more casual gave the impression of boredom. More important, both leaders found the dual appearances uncomfortable. Each felt inhibited by the other's presence, with the result that both came over as stilted and wooden. It was a special problem for Steel. On the one hand, he knew the importance of avoiding even a hint of disagreement with Owen; on the other, he was acutely conscious of the popular impression that he was David Owen's stooge.

The satirical television show, *Spitting Image*, in particular, portrayed Steel as a little mouse of a man, with a quivering high voice, popping in and out of Owen's top pocket. In a characteristic scene, both are in bed:

STEEL [*high quivering*]. David, after we have merged what shall we call our new party?

OWEN [*deep and gruff*]. I propose we take one part of your party's name and one part of my party's name.

STEEL [*expectantly*]. What bit of your party's name will you take, David?

OWEN [*drawling*]. Social Democratic.

STEEL [*his little brow furrowing*]. Then what part of my party's name will you take, David?

OWEN [*smirking*]. Party.

STEEL [*disappointed*]. Very well, David.

On 23 May, to Cowley Street's consternation, Steel let slip to accompanying journalists that the joint interviews made him and Owen look like Tweedledum and Tweedledee and should stop. The phrase was a gift to the Sunday press, who treated it as a panic response to the Alliance's poor poll showing. That weekend the newspapers' leaders and feature articles were full of references to the Alliance's flagging campaign ('staggeringly inept', 'uninspiring').

The second week proved as dispiriting as the first. On the Wednesday it emerged that no script or film had been prepared for the party election broadcast scheduled for the Friday. Communications between David Abbott and Roland Freeman, who was dogged by illness, had broken down. It was a particularly damaging example of the way mutual suspicions between the two sides on the Planning Group meant that organizational problems were hidden until the last moment. An old-fashioned broadcast with David Steel talking straight to camera had to be improvised at the last minute.

Owen remained convinced, however, that the Alliance could detach some anti-Thatcherite Conservatives so long as it took a tough line on defence and did not align itself too closely with Labour. On 26 May he and Steel did a lengthy interview on *Panorama*. At the very end Sir Robin Day asked Owen: 'If either Labour or the Conservatives were to have a majority, which would you regard as the lesser evil?' With characteristic honesty Owen replied that, if pushed, he would have to say that the security of the country came first and that on that score 'Labour's position is unacceptable'. After Steel had said that he saw no reason why the country should have to choose between two evils, Owen, realizing his mistake, tried to repair the damage: 'David is much wiser in dealing with these questions.'

The incident went almost unreported in the next day's papers; but commentators belatedly noticed the first crack in the Alliance façade. From then on, it became even clearer than before the campaign that Owen was much readier than Steel to do business with the Conservatives while Steel was much happier than Owen to negotiate with Labour. The worst fears of Alliance politicians prior to the campaign—that Owen and Steel, under pressure from the media, would expose their fundamental political disagreements—were well founded. The carefully worked-out formula for an agreed approach to the issue of a hung parliament could not mask the fundamental disagreement between the two men.

Owen's apparent preference for a Conservative over a Labour government did not square easily with his earlier insistence on attacking the Conservatives. It was not strictly illogical, but all but the most sophisticated voters must have wondered why he was prepared to negotiate terms with a party which only a week earlier he had accused of being uncaring and of issuing 'a foul smear'. In the constituencies, Liberal workers complained that Owen's remarks undercut their efforts to persuade Labour sympathizers to vote tactically for the Alliance.

A chastened campaign committee met on Sunday, 31 May. There had still been no hint of a revival in the polls. A succession of press headlines told readers that the Conservatives enjoyed a comfortable lead and that Labour was closing the gap with the Alliance in third place:

Tories Hold on to their 13% Lead as Alliance Slips (*Sunday Times*, 24 May)

Kinnock Charisma Gives Labour a Lift (*Sunday Times*, 24 May)

Labour Overtakes Tories in Marginal Seats Poll (*Independent*, 25 May)

5%: The Gap Closed: Thatcher Lead is Sliced in Half (*Daily Mirror*, 27 May)

Tory Lead is Halved (*London Daily News*, 27 May)

Alliance Support Drops to All Time Low (*Daily Telegraph*, 28 May).

Most of those at the 31 May meeting called for more passion and bite in the Alliance campaign and for a greater emphasis on the Alliance's own policies. But they thrashed around for a theme. It was agreed that Steel would spell out the disastrous consequences if either the Conservatives or Labour won on their own, while Owen would concentrate on six Alliance commitments: reducing unemployment, spending more on education, maintaining Thatcher's trade-union legislation, upholding the rule of law, reducing hospital waiting lists and retaining a minimum nuclear deterrent.

Owen's and Steel's different preferences as between a Conservative and a Labour government, first uncovered in the *Panorama* interview on 26 May, turned into open confusion and contradiction on 3 June when Steel appeared on the BBC's live phone-in programme, *Election Call*. Asked whether he would support Thatcher in a hung parliament, Steel replied: 'I find it unimaginable that there would be any circumstances in which a minority government led by Mrs Thatcher could be sustained in office by us.' What Steel had meant to convey was that in a hung parliament Thatcher's position in her own party would be untenable and she would almost certainly prefer resignation to the humiliation of negotiating with the Alliance;[20] but he seemed to be vetoing support for a minority Conservative government only a week after Owen had vetoed support for a minority Labour government.

During the rest of that day Steel appeared to harden his line, while Owen, on tour elsewhere, argued that it was not for one party to choose the leader of another and that the real issue was one of forming a government on agreed policies. By late afternoon, after frantic discussions by mobile telephone, the two leaders felt they had to issue a joint statement setting out in detail the Alliance's position if it held the balance of power. But the statement made no difference. The next day the press seized on the divisions between the two.[21] The lead story in the *Independent* ('Alliance Split over Coalition with Thatcher') pointed out that Owen and Steel not only disagreed on whether they could do business with Thatcher but on whether a hung parliament was likely to arise. In answer to a question about the gap between the Conservative and Labour parties, Steel answered: 'It is not likely to close to the extent where, with a small number of MPs, we would hold the balance.'[22] Owen, however, was publicly insisting that the Alliance actually had good prospects of holding the balance of power. Confusion deepened on 4 June when Owen again appeared to rule out support for a Labour government while Steel told a meeting at St Andrews University that he would not work with Thatcher.[23] Owen and Steel never contradicted one another directly, and certainly they sought agreement; but the overall impression conveyed was one of division and muddle.

The Alliance limped gamely on through the campaign's final week. There was not a flicker of a revival in the polls. In public, Owen and Steel talked confidently of a late surge of support. Steel's speeches were directed at persuading Labour supporters to cast a tactical vote, while Owen continued to predict a hung parliament in which the Alliance could block a Thatcherite programme. There seemed little else for them to say. In private, they clung to the hope of picking up some tactical votes and 'don't knows' in the final forty-eight hours and of bucking the national trend in individual constituencies (where some local polls had been encouraging).

On the day, 11 June, the Conservatives were comfortably re-elected with an overall majority of 102, winning 376 seats to Labour's 229. There was no last-minute miracle for the SDP. The result was a humiliation: its already small parliamentary strength was reduced from eight to five. In the early hours of 12 June Roy Jenkins lost Glasgow Hillhead to a Labour left-winger, and Ian Wrigglesworth, who had been lucky to hang on to Stockton South in 1983, narrowly lost to a Conservative.[24] The SDP held Greenwich, where Rosie Barnes was re-elected with a much smaller majority than at the by-election, but it lost its other by-election gain in Portsmouth South, where Mike Hancock went down by a mere 200 votes. David Owen held Plymouth Devonport with a slightly increased majority, while John Cartwright clung on to Woolwich by a margin of under 2,000.[25] The SDP's two Highlands MPs, Robert Maclennan and Charles Kennedy, increased their majorities spectacularly. Shirley Williams in Cambridge and Bill Rodgers in Milton Keynes improved marginally on the SDP's 1983 vote but were comfortably beaten by the sitting Conservatives. The Liberals' parliamentary strength remained at seventeen.[26]

For the Alliance as a whole, the result was not quite the catastrophe that many had privately feared. It won 23.1 per cent of the popular vote in Great Britain, doing slightly better than the final polls had forecast, probably because of last-minute tactical switching among Labour supporters.[27] This was the second-best performance by a centre party since 1929 and only 2.9 percentage points less than the Alliance's showing in 1983. The Alliance fell back furthest where it had no chance of winning, such as in Conservative–Labour marginals, but almost held its vote in suburban and rural seats where it was clearly the challenger to the Conservatives.[28]

But, given the two Alliance parties' high expectations a month earlier, the result was an acute disappointment. For the first time since the 1950s the centre had lost support during the course of a campaign. Fourteen of the Alliance's twenty-two MPs now represented the rural periphery, compared with eleven out of the twenty-three elected in 1983. Like the old Liberal party, the Alliance had become a party of the Celtic Fringe.

For the SDP specifically, the result was little short of a disaster. The party failed to gain a single seat. Its change of leader, its repositioning on the ideological spectrum, its local election advances and its by-election victories had all counted

379

for nothing. The target-seats exercise, on which so much effort and money had been lavished, had proved futile: although the SDP did marginally better in its target constituencies than elsewhere, the difference was not enough to win extra seats (or to save Wrigglesworth in Stockton South).[29] Most demoralizing of all, the Alliance completely failed to squeeze the Labour vote in the dozen three-way marginals in which it had finished second in 1983,[30] and it faded particularly badly among working-class voters—the group that the SDP had originally set its sights on.[31] The result squashed any lingering hopes that the SDP might replace Labour as the main opposition to the Conservatives.

In terms of seats the SDP was back where it had been in June 1983. But, for most of the Social Democrats' founders, the 1987 election represented the end of the political road. Only one of the Gang of Four remained in the House of Commons. The political careers of Shirley Williams and Bill Rodgers were effectively over, as was that of Roy Jenkins. Most of the other former SDP MPs who were standing again, including those who had lost only narrowly in 1983, found that their personal vote had disappeared and that they could not win additional tactical votes. They fell back badly.[32] Of the twenty-eight SDP members in parliament in 1982–3, only three—Cartwright, Owen and Maclennan—remained.

'The most dispiriting experience of my political life' was John Pardoe's verdict on the Alliance campaign.[33] Most other Liberals and Social Democrats agreed. Frustrated by four weeks of flat polls, their post-mortems pinned the blame on the campaign. In retrospect, most of the criticisms seem overdone. For example, the manifesto was criticized as too bland and middle of the road: for Pardoe it was 'the least exciting, least stimulating, least credible document it has ever been my misfortune to campaign on . . . if you read it you have a damned hard job finding anything positive in it'.[34] This overstates the shortcomings of the manifesto—and its importance. It was more detailed but no duller or less radical than the 1983 manifesto. The press was lukewarm about it but not persistently disparaging (as it was, for instance, about the 1983 Labour programme); and in largely ignoring Alliance policies it was behaving no differently from how it had behaved in previous elections.

A second criticism, not wholly consistent with the first, was that the leaders should have stuck more closely to the manifesto, stressing the Alliance's more distinctive and positive policies, in particular the Great Reform Charter. Had they concentrated on their theme of constitutional reform, some argued, they could have made their position on the balance of power both clearer and more attractive. But polling evidence clearly indicates that most voters were unconcerned about constitutional issues. The Alliance's problem was that, like the old Liberal party, it was not judged by journalists or voters in terms of its programme: nobody expected it to be in a position to puts its programme into effect. Irrelevant policies did not lead to the Alliance's poor vote; the Alliance's poor vote made its policies irrelevant.

Some blamed Alliance tactics. 'It was criminal not to attack Labour in the first week, push it into third place, declare it unelectable and go for Conservative votes towards the end,' said one Liberal official, echoing the view of many Liberal candidates. This criticism, too, was exaggerated. It is unlikely that an onslaught against the Labour party would have knocked it into third place. Almost the whole of Labour's rise in the polls occurred between 9 May and 15 May, before the first week of campaigning when the Alliance decided to turn against the Conservatives. Moreover, Owen and Steel did not stick to their original tactic for long; at the beginning of the second week Owen turned his fire on Kinnock's defence policy and Steel on Labour's extremists. They were joined by the Conservatives and their supporting press, who throughout the week attacked Labour where it was most vulnerable, on defence. Yet the result of this combined onslaught was a tiny and temporary dip in Labour's support. Labour support in 1987 was already at bedrock level and, short of a dramatic rift among Labour's leaders, it was very unlikely either to erode or crack.[35]

Some critics, especially among the Liberals, pinned the blame on Owen's strategy of aiming for the balance of power rather than all-out victory. In their view the strategy was risky and unrealistic. By conceding that outright victory was unlikely, they argued, it may have convinced potential sympathizers that a vote for the Alliance would be wasted; at the same time, the concept of holding the balance of power was too abstract for many ordinary voters to grasp, let alone to embrace. Moreover, to talk of the balance of power was to raise the prospect of a coalition government, which was electorally unpopular and which exposed the Alliance leaders' differences over the issue of coalition partners.

This criticism, like the others, overestimates the electoral impact of campaign strategies. It is unlikely that Owen's balance-of-power strategy did appreciable damage to the Alliance vote. Although it was the rationale behind his insistence on attacking the Conservative party in the first week, it did not figure prominently in his public speeches until the final week; and during that week support for the Alliance in the polls did not budge.[36] Moreover, the differences about coalition tactics between Owen and Steel would have been exposed in any case. After the publication of polls suggesting that Labour was narrowing the gap and could just possibly deprive the government of its majority, the coalition question would have been raised no matter what Owen said.

The commonest and most plausible explanation for the Alliance's poor result was the 'two-leader problem'.[37] But critics differed on what the problem was. For crisis-managers like Pardoe it was a problem of personality and discipline: the Alliance's campaign problems arose from Steel's and Owen's indiscretions to journalists.[38] 'Two leaders thinking aloud on two different buses in two different parts of the country is a recipe for disaster,' Des Wilson confided to his diary.[39] For most critics, however, it was the disagreement between Owen and Steel about whether the balance of power was a primary objective, and, if so, how the Alliance should behave if it found itself in that position, that did the Alliance most electoral damage. As far as they were concerned, the Alliance was working well on the ground, and would have done considerably better on polling day, if only the two leaders had not ruined things by failing to co-ordinate and agree on such basic issues. Roped together like mountaineers, 'the two Davids could either assist each other towards the peak—or at least camp one—or drag each other, and the Alliance, to certain death'.[40] Yet the serene stability of the Alliance's position in the polls during and after the period of greatest confusion about coalition partners suggests that the leaders' disagreements on the issue did not lose votes; at most they stopped the Alliance from achieving the centre party's usual campaign lift-off.[41]

For other critics, the problem was not the behaviour or views of Owen and Steel but the very existence of a dual leadership. So long as there were two leaders, the media and the opposition would find (or invent) differences and would proceed to inflate them. And, however united a front the two leaders presented, voters would always ask 'Who is really in charge?' and 'Who would be prime minister in an Alliance government?' For as long as the two parties maintained their separate identity within the Alliance, the dual-leadership problem would remain. The idea of two parties working in partnership under a joint leadership, some critics concluded, was too bizarre for voters accustomed to single-party governments. It was an experiment that had failed administratively, politically and electorally. The obvious solution was to take the idea of an alliance to its logical conclusion and merge the two parties. Before the campaign, feeling optimistic about the result, only a few Social Democrats would own to holding such views, even in private. By polling day, stunned and angry, many more were convinced that merger was the only way forward.

20

. . . .

The SDP Disintegrates:
1987–1988

Politicians are seldom at their best following election defeats. They are tired and disappointed and their thoughts almost inevitably turn to the question of who or what was to blame. The leaders of the Liberal–SDP Alliance—especially the leaders of the SDP—had additional reasons for despair on 12 June 1987. In the pale light of that summer morning, with television screens still flickering manically in the background, all their dreams of forming an Alliance government, of holding the balance of power, of replacing Labour as the main opposition to the Conservatives, even of gaining a significant number of seats in the House of Commons, were coldly revealed as having been only dreams. The great SDP project had failed. The mould of British politics remained unbroken.

For six years the party's leaders had worked hard and risked their political careers for the party's success—and now it seemed that little, if anything, had been accomplished. Not unnaturally, they were frustrated, angry and even bitter. Their frustration, anger and bitterness led in the following nine months to the SDP's complete disintegration. In a grotesque parody of the celebratory spirit that had attended the party's launch in 1981, the SDP's leaders now engaged in an orgy of name-calling, mutual recrimination and abuse. Personal relations in some cases were severed altogether. To the onlooker, the sight of all these earnest and well-meaning persons, formerly friends, solemnly trying to destroy one another politically was somewhat comic. To those involved, it was a nightmare. Years later passions in a few cases had still not cooled.

What happened to the SDP in 1987–8 owed much to simple post-election depression, but it also arose as a result of less ephemeral factors. The issue of a possible merger between the SDP and the Liberals had been with the party from the beginning. It would never go away. Despite David Owen's repeated utterances prior to polling day, which implied that he would be ready to consider a possible merger once the election was out of the way, he had in fact no intention of ever surrendering the SDP's independence.[1] He was never going to allow himself and his beloved party to be separated. Alan Watkins, writing in the *Observer*, read Owen's mind perfectly. The SDP leader, Watkins wrote, as the merger crisis intensified, had never been wholly frank:

Dr Owen was rather like a man whose wife wanted to go on holiday to Greece. He did not wish to go, was determined not to, hated the place, preferred France instead. But, to make life easier at home, he said: 'Of course we shall go to Greece, darling, but not this year. Let us look at some brochures and not hurry our decision.' And all the time he did not have the slightest intention of going to Greece—or forming a merged party.[2]

If anything, Owen's contempt for the Liberals and his determination to go his own way had been reinforced by the 1987 campaign. It was Steel who had caused so much trouble by introducing the unfortunate phrase 'Tweedledum and Tweedledee', and it was Owen's joint appearances with Steel that had contrived to convey a sense of Alliance disunity. Owen was furious at having to defend the Alliance's cobbled-together defence policy against Thatcher's assaults, and the outcome of the election further convinced him of the need to position the SDP in such a way that it could appeal successfully to wavering Conservatives. In his view, a merged party, in which former Liberals would be in a majority, would inevitably be a Labour-inclined rather than a Conservative-inclined organization. He was simply not prepared to lend himself to such an enterprise.

Those in the SDP who were already inclined to favour a merger with the Liberals drew the opposite conclusions from the campaign. In their eyes, the 1987 election—not only the result, but the way in which it had been fought—demonstrated the utter futility of having two parties and two leaders. The alliance of two separate parties was costly, inefficient and prone to precisely the kind of accident that had overcome Owen and Steel in their television interview with Sir Robin Day. Moreover, their experience during the campaign told them that the continued existence of two separate parties confused and alienated potential Alliance supporters.[3] For all these reasons, they were keener than ever to merge with the Liberals—to go on holiday to Greece. Like Owen, they, too, were aware that, whatever their protestations of neutrality during the election campaign, most of them were considerably more anti-Conservative than they were anti-Labour (especially now that Labour under Neil Kinnock was showing signs of reform). A merged party, they thought, would be a left-of-centre party. That was what they wanted. During the campaign they had taken exception to Owen's demonstrative wooing of potentially dissident Conservative voters.

These political disagreements were genuine enough; but, as always in the SDP's short history, personal tensions and animosities were never far beneath the surface. The blunt fact was that by the summer of 1987 David Steel, Shirley Williams, Roy Jenkins, Bill Rodgers—and many others in both the Liberals and the SDP—had had more than enough of David Owen. They disliked him and they found him domineering and impossible to work with. On top of all that, they increasingly suspected him of being a closet Tory. It is impossible to prove—but also impossible not to believe—that the 1987–8 merger row took the form it did partly because Steel and the others were consciously or unconsciously out to 'get' the SDP leader. They would either tame him by forcing him to help merge the two parties; or they would break with him completely. In the case of many of them, dislike and impatience had long since given way to something approaching hatred.

It was Owen in the event who made the first move. He knew, in any case, that Steel, Jenkins and probably Williams were bound to press for a merger once the election was over, and he had also got wind of a telephone conversation that had taken place the day before polling day between his ally David Sainsbury and Dick Newby, the SDP's national secretary. Newby had advocated a post-election merger and poured scorn on the notion of a federation between the two parties. Suspecting a merger plot involving Cowley Street officials, including Newby, Owen decided to give a press conference in Plymouth the day after the election, within hours of the final results being declared.[4]

The occasion was somewhat chaotic. The SDP leader refused to be interviewed in the lobby of his hotel and insisted instead that the assorted journalists and TV cameramen follow him outside. There, in response to reporters' questions, he proceeded to make it clear that he was opposed to any merging of the two parties: 'I knew [when the SDP was launched] that we needed a fourth party, and I think that everything that has happened since has justified that decision'; and he also hinted broadly that, if the two parties did merge, he would not be interested in being the new party's leader.[5] The next morning's *Independent* gave considerable prominence to its report of the Plymouth press conference, and the paper's reporter had no doubt about the message Owen intended to convey: 'David Owen yesterday fired the opening shots in his campaign to resist demands for the merger of the SDP and Liberal parties in the aftermath of the Alliance's poor general election performance.'[6] Owen was, of course, quite right to anticipate that there would be pressure for a merger. Within forty-eight hours Jenkins and Williams, and Paddy Ashdown and Alan Beith of the Liberals, were all calling publicly for a merger to take place.[7]

Owen's remarks at the Plymouth press conference came as a considerable surprise to David Steel, relaxing after the rigours of the campaign at his home in Ettrickbridge. The two leaders had spoken on the phone in the early hours of Friday morning. What passed between them is unknown, but Steel had got the impression that Owen was not adamantly opposed to merger. On the contrary, Steel—and many others who favoured such a move—had listened over the years to Owen's pronouncements on the subject, had taken them at their face value and had assumed that, while Owen was certainly not positively in favour of uniting the two parties, he was not adamantly opposed either.[8] They thought he would probably be guided in the end by the wishes of the SDP membership. Steel, in particular, recalled a warm and enthusiastic 'Ask the Alliance' rally in Edinburgh, when Owen had actually appeared ready to embrace the idea of merger. For months afterwards, Steel carried round with him a crumpled sheet of paper on which were typed a large number of Owen's allegedly pro-merger—or, at any rate, not anti-merger—statements.

Thus, when Steel opened his copy of the *Independent* on the Saturday morning after the election, he got a considerable shock. There was Owen publicly denouncing the idea of merger even before the most informal of preliminary consultations between the two leaderships had taken place. Steel knew that the SDP's National Committee was due to meet on the following Monday—in roughly forty-eight hours' time—and he assumed, given Owen's Plymouth declaration, that the purpose of the meeting was to persuade the National Committee to come out immediately in opposition to merger. In 1983–4 Owen had devoted the first few months of his leadership to opposing merger; it now looked as though he were about to do the same thing again. Telephone enquiries by other Liberals elicited the fact that several of Owen's closest associates—notably, they suspected, Mike Thomas—were briefing the media 'madly' against any possible merger deal.

Steel responded at once. There were now no signs of the physical and emotional lethargy that had led to his sabbatical following the 1983 election. Owen, in Steel's view, had attempted a pre-emptive strike; Steel would demonstrate that he could not be pre-empted. The initiative would be his. Television cameras were in attendance within hours as Steel drafted a memorandum to the officers of the Liberal party advocating 'democratic fusion' of the two parties, the phrase 'democratic fusion' being used to avoid the suggestion that the Liberals intended simply to take over the SDP. Steel in a press statement made it clear that he wanted the two parties to progress towards merger talks as rapidly as possible. 'I have told David Owen', he said with studied correctness, 'that I shall make a copy [of my memorandum] available to him so that he and his colleagues may be fully aware of my views.'[9] Owen had sought to take merger off the agenda. Steel now put it back on. Owen's supporters subsequently accused Steel of having acted with undue haste in issuing his weekend statement; but in fact it was Owen who had spoken out first.

If Steel's mood immediately after the election was remarkably buoyant under the circumstances, Owen's was the opposite. The weeks between June and August 1987 must have been among the blackest of Owen's life. All his friends agreed that he was tired and unhappy—'very, very low'. The self-made man of the 1983 parliament had been abruptly unmade by the humiliating election results. The man of the future now seemed to have no future. He had held his own seat in the House of Commons, but his tiny parliamentary group had been reduced to five. All hopes of wielding power, of influencing great events, had been dashed. At the age of only 49, Owen was suddenly in danger of becoming yesterday's man—a has-been before his time. The expenditure of energy—and of self—had been so great. The results were contemptible.

Nor could the SDP leader see any way out of the impasse he was in. He may at odd moments have toyed with the idea of acquiescing in merger; but all his instincts rebelled against that option, and his instincts were reinforced constantly by the advice of his wife and his other close friends and colleagues. If he found himself inside a merged party, he would be like a caged animal, even assuming he agreed to join. Moreover, he might well not be elected any new party's leader after the previous year's defence row and in the light of the deep-seated antipathy that had developed between him and many Liberals. Even if he were elected leader, he would still find himself at the head of a party that he could not control and that would almost certainly treat him in the same way that the Liberals had so often treated Steel—casually and disrespectfully. Owen knew the kind of party he wanted. It existed already. It was called the SDP. He was its leader.

But, if not merger, what? The status quo, it was clear, was no longer sustainable. The Alliance of two separate parties had not made a breakthrough in 1983. It had not made a breakthrough in 1987. And there had been real practical and political difficulties before, as well as during, those two campaigns. Moreover, it was clear that the Alliance in anything like its present form no longer had the support either of the Liberals or of a substantial faction within his own party. The Alliance was an idea whose time had come, but gone.

But, yet again, if not the Alliance, what? One option was to seek a closer relationship with the Liberals than had hitherto prevailed but one that stopped short of total merger—in other words, a close federation. It was a federation of this kind that Dick Newby and David Sainsbury had discussed briefly on the day before the election. Owen and most of those around him were attracted by the idea of some sort of federation short of merger; and they were to pursue this option with considerable vigour during the coming weeks. But it actually had several flaws from their own point of view.

In purely practical terms, a federation would either be tantamount to a full merger or else would fail to address the numerous difficulties—over membership, candidate selection, policy-making, headquarters organization and so on—that were universally recognized to exist and that had occasioned so much discontent with the existing arrangements. In broader political terms, it was also not clear how a federation would work. Once again, either a federation would be a merger in all but name or the Liberals and the SDP would retain a degree of real autonomy. If the former, why stop at federation? If the latter, how would a federation differ, in reality, from the existing Alliance?

More fundamentally still, Owen and his advisers soon recognized that there was something inherently false in their claim that they wanted a closer relationship with the Liberals—as all talk of a federation implied—when that was not what they really wanted at all. What they really wanted was to have as little to do with the Liberals as possible. In other words, the underlying logic of Owen's position pointed not towards federation with the Liberals but, on the contrary, towards breaking with them completely (though possibly with a view to recreating some sort of loose electoral pact with them at a later stage).

It took a little time for the basic logic of Owen's position to surface. Not only was he himself initially distraught and not thinking clearly (several of his friends thought that for some time after the election his judgement was seriously impaired); but, unlike Steel, he could no longer be confident of his political base. The great majority of Liberals were known to favour merger; but no one could know for sure how the rank-and-file members of the SDP would respond to the merger calls, and all the other members of the old Gang of Four were now on the other side. (Bill Rodgers soon joined Jenkins and Williams in calling for the two parties to fuse.) The only people Owen felt he could rely on absolutely were his wife, his constituency supporters, a few close friends such as Mike Thomas, Polly Toynbee and Ian Wrigglesworth, and the other SDP members of parliament. John Cartwright, his closest parliamentary lieutenant, was utterly loyal; Rosie Barnes could similarly be relied upon; Charles Kennedy, still the baby of the party, as yet showed no signs of wanting to untie Owen's apron strings; and Robert Maclennan was speaking out more vigorously against merger than anyone else. It was a comfort for Owen to know that, with the political ground otherwise shifting almost hourly under his feet, he could at least count on the backing of his parliamentary colleagues. They might differ about tactics, but they all wanted the SDP to remain independent.

One measure of Owen's unhappiness and disorientation at this time was the extent to which he withdrew, physically as well as emotionally, into his inner circle. After giving his June press conference outside his Plymouth hotel, the SDP leader for weeks afterwards scarcely spoke to journalists or appeared on radio or television. Hitherto an avid publicity-seeker (for his party if not for himself), he now became publicity-averse. Apart from attending SDP committee meetings and performing his parliamentary duties, he became a virtual recluse. Like Richard Nixon in the last stages of his presidency in America, Owen increasingly made his views known through surrogates. The words were the words of Owen; the voices were the voices of others. Friends said he was in a state of shock and, as party leader, did not want to make the party's difficulties even greater than they were. Enemies increasingly objected to the fact that he 'got others to do his dirty work for him'.

Owen isolated himself, in particular, from the other members of the Gang of Four. He refused to see them; he refused to talk to them on the phone. Shirley Williams, in her role as party president, was desperately anxious to see him to find out whether some accommodation could be reached, if not over the merger issue itself, then over the arrangements for a ballot of the party's members. She phoned repeatedly requesting a meeting, but her calls were never returned. She went round to his office but was told he was not available even though she could clearly see his silhouette behind the door. Finally, she rang David Sainsbury to say that the party would split disastrously if she could not talk to Owen to try to find a way out. Sainsbury rang back a few hours later with a blunt message: 'He won't see you and I can't do anything. You're on your own.'

The National Committee held its first post-election meeting on 15 June. David Steel had supposed that the meeting had been called for the purpose of putting obstacles in the way of merger. In fact, Shirley Williams, the party's president, had called it partly because there had been no meeting of the full committee since the previous April and partly to initiate a discussion of the election campaign. Although the merger issue was raised and discussed briefly, the mood of the meeting was more subdued than acrimonious, and it was agreed to postpone discussion of future relations with the Liberals for a fortnight—until 29 June, when a special meeting would be held.[10] Briefing the press afterwards, Williams said she regretted that the committee had not opted for an immediate ballot of the SDP's members on the issue of merger, but added that it had been 'silly' of David Steel to try to 'bounce' Social Democrats into a decision on the matter before they were ready.[11] The tone of the comments emanating from both the pro- and anti-merger camps after the meeting was, on the whole, conciliatory.

One excuse for delaying discussion of merger was that members of the committee had not yet received copies of the document that David Steel had drafted for the Liberal officers over the weekend. Everyone knew it called for 'democratic fusion' because Steel had told the press it did; but it was addressed formally to the Liberals' officers and no Social Democrat had yet seen it. When it arrived the next day, it turned out to consist of a general discussion of Liberal–SDP relations setting out three broad options. The first was 'separate parties', but with friendly relations between the two and local electoral pacts; the second was 'growing together', along the same lines that the Alliance had been developing since 1981; the third was 'democratic fusion', which, if it took place, would follow negotiations between the two parties and ballots of their members.[12]

Steel made it clear that he was opposed to the separate-parties option, which would undo all the Alliance's work over the previous six years; and, in view of all the familiar practical difficulties, he saw little point in the growing-together option. His preferred option, by a wide margin, was democratic fusion. A united party would be more efficient, and it could project itself more clearly. In his only allusion to the deeper differences underlying his strained relations with Owen, he noted that, if either of them had run the recent election campaign on his own, the Alliance would probably have had a sharper image: 'David Owen, I think, would have wished a more assertive balance-of-power coalition focus, while I would have preferred a clear anti-Thatcher, non-socialist alternative.'[13]

The SDP's parliamentary party first met two days after the National Committee, on 17 June. By this time Owen, working largely alone, thought he had found a way out of his impasse. In a secret memorandum to his parliamentary colleagues, he made one of the most extraordinary proposals that can ever have been made by the leader of a serious British political party. He proposed, as leader, that his own party should split. Those who wished to remain members of the SDP should be encouraged to do so. Those who wished to merge with the Liberals should be encouraged to do that. The SDP's physical and financial assets should be divided proportionally between the two groups. No effort should be made to hold the party together. On the contrary, an amicable divorce should be arranged as quickly as possible.

The secret memorandum took the form of a draft resolution which Owen wanted his parliamentary colleagues to support at the forthcoming National Committee meeting. Its key passages read:

profoundly aware of the dangers of a deeply divisive debate being undertaken in which members of the party explain why they do or do not believe that a merger of the party is desirable against a background of 'winner takes all' . . . an immediate consultative ballot [should be held] of all members of the SDP so as to allow for an amicable settlement between those SDP members who wish to open negotiations with the Liberal Party and those members who do not wish to do so and want to remain members of the SDP.

Do you want your membership registration to remain with the SDP as a separate party? YES / NO

Do you want your membership registration to be transferred to an SDP group who will go into negotiation with the Liberal Party with the aim of forming a merged party? YES / NO

If you do not register your vote on this ballot paper, your membership will remain registered with the SDP as a separate party.

The resources of the SDP, its financial and physical assets, will be split fairly on a proportional basis between those who decide to transfer their membership and those who remain members of the SDP. The National Committee will appoint an independent arbitrator to preside over such an allocation. The Electoral Reform Society will supervise the ballot. An independent returning officer will be appointed by the National Committee.

. . . it is vital that there is no personal acrimony between Social Democrats and our Liberal partners and that we retain the spirit of partnership that has been a feature of the Alliance in the past and will be important for the future.[14]

Owen's reasoning was straightforward. Given the tensions among the old Gang of Four, and between himself and many Liberals, he had concluded that any prolonged controversy about merger and the future of the SDP was bound to become acrimonious and that the acrimony was certain to damage both the SDP and the Alliance. Better, therefore, to acknowledge the depths of people's differences right at the beginning and arrange for a friendly parting of the ways. Afterwards those who merged with the Liberals and those who chose to remain in the SDP could resume their normal political collaboration. The Alliance could, albeit in a somewhat different form, be reborn.

But Owen's proposal ran into a blank wall of opposition from his parliamentary colleagues. According to one MP who was present, there was 'a sharp intake of breath' when it was revealed. The same MP described Owen's document as 'chilling'. The parliamentary group—including Jack Diamond and Alastair Kilmarnock from the House of Lords—were united in being opposed to merger, but precisely because they were devoted to the SDP they were aghast at the idea of splitting it, especially in this premeditated, cold-blooded, almost clinical manner. They insisted that some other, less brutal way forward could and should be found; or at least they ought to do their best to find one. Owen must have known the document would be controversial (and potentially highly damaging if it leaked out): he took care to number all the copies and collect them up after the meeting. The document's existence was publicly revealed only in his memoirs.[15]

The idea of an amicable settlement was to resurface later in the summer, but for the time being the parliamentary group confined itself to taking two decisions, which on the face of it—a measure of the prevailing confusion—pointed in opposite directions. One was to suspend the arrangement, dating from the 1983 parliament, under which the Liberals and the SDP as a matter of routine appointed joint parliamentary spokesmen. The initiative for breaking this particular tie apparently came from Robert Maclennan. The Liberals were amazed. But at the same time the SDP MPs, with Owen's somewhat reluctant acquiescence, decided to pursue the growing-together option raised in David Steel's memorandum. Steel himself had indicated that this was an option. As a means of maintaining the SDP's continued existence, it seemed worth taking up.

On the face of it, the growing-together option might have been expected to become the basis of a possible compromise between Steel and Owen and the pro- and anti-merger factions. Before the publication of Steel's memorandum, Owen's spokesmen were already indicating to journalists that, in the light of recent experience, the Liberals and the SDP did need to grow closer together and that some kind of federal structure might be appropriate for this purpose. A single Alliance leader at some time in the future, perhaps before the next election, was also not beyond the bounds of possibility. Ian Wrigglesworth said he was 'in favour of federation rather than merger', and John Cartwright said he thought a federal solution was 'worth considering'.[16]

Federalism, however, turned out to be a blind alley. Three developments quickly ensured that the idea of a Liberal–SDP federation, far from providing a basis for compromise, would become no more than a tactic in the Owenites' campaign to thwart an outright merger at almost any cost.

One of these developments was the line taken by Steel himself. The list of options contained in his memorandum to the Liberal officers did indeed include 'growing together'; but scarcely had the memorandum been published than Steel took steps to distance himself totally from this option. He had not been very keen on it in the first place and other senior Liberals advised him that, in the light of the Alliance's experience, it was simply not workable. Steel, in addition, must have realized that, by mentioning the growing-together option at all, he was placing a potentially potent weapon in the hands of the anti-merger campaigners, who could claim that, if growing together was possible, merger was unnecessary. In an article in the *Guardian*, published only a few days after his memorandum, Steel tacitly disowned growing together and posed the choice much more starkly—between 'one campaigning entity, looking outward' and 'two parties by another name, locked together in a state of perpetual inward negotiation'.[17] A few days after that, he was talking of 'merger or bust'.

The second development arose from the Owen camp. Steel was not the only one to have supposed that Owen, while certainly not keen on a merger, would eventually go along with a merger if that was what his party's members wanted. Almost everyone in the SDP, apart from Owen himself, operated on that assumption. After all, Owen was the one who, while still a member of the Labour party, had staked his all on 'one member, one vote'. Those who favoured a merger believed that there would eventually be a ballot of members, and they took the view that, if the ballot went against them, they would be bound by the members' verdict: they would remain in the SDP and neither join the Liberals nor quit politics. And they took it more or less for granted that Owen's response would be the same. If he won in an anti-merger ballot, fine. If he lost, they assumed that he would, at best, remain a member of the merged party and possibly contest its leadership or, at worst, stand aside from politics or possibly, like Steel after the 1983 election, take a sabbatical. It never occurred to most leading figures in the SDP, apart from Owen's intimates, that, if Owen lost, he would have nothing to do with the new party and might even go into opposition to it. They had no inkling of his 'chilling' secret document.

The first intimation that they might be wrong came in Owen's Plymouth press conference, where he spoke of two separate strands in British politics, social democracy and liberalism, and alluded to the continuing need for a separate fourth party;[18] but his remarks at Plymouth were somewhat veiled, and most of the mergerites do not seem to have regarded them as being especially significant. Owen, however, soon enormously increased the stakes. Returning from a conference in Oslo, he said bluntly (in one of his rare comments to reporters): 'I have made up my mind. A merged party is not for me'; and, in a letter sent to rank-and-file Social Democrats who sought his views about Steel's merger proposals, he went still further. He described Steel's document as 'hasty'. He spoke of the Alliance's splitting apart 'in a mood of despair and self-indulgence'. He also spoke of the need for a quick decision from the membership. But, above all, he went out of his way to distance himself from the mergerites and from anything they might manage to put together in the future:

Obviously as a democrat I will accept the judgement of the members of the party. There are some on the national committee who sincerely wish to merge our two parties; indeed some of them have wanted to do so from the beginning. If they win the ballot it will, I imagine, be for them to negotiate with the Liberals.

I for my part will remain a member of the SDP as long as it exists, but I have no intention of being persuaded to become a member of a merged party.[19]

Owen's reference to his remaining a member of the SDP 'as long as it exists' seemed to underline earlier newspaper suggestions that finance might be available for a breakaway SDP if the Owen camp were to lose the merger battle.[20]

Steel's increasing insistence on merger or bust (he probably could not have carried the Liberal party for anything less), together with Owen's declaration that he would have nothing to do with any merged party, completely transformed the situation. What had been a reasonably fluid situation, with talk of 'getting together' and 'federation', suddenly became rigid. Three options were narrowed to two, and a strange asymmetry now dominated the scene. The mergerites operated on the basis of one principle: abide by the will of the majority, whatever it is. But Owen and his followers operated on the basis of another, different principle: abide by the will of the majority, but only if you get your way; otherwise keep your options open. The mergerites were surprised, and considerably rattled, by this completely (to them) unexpected turn of events.

The third development was probably an inevitable consequence of the first two: all the antipathies and antagonisms that had been building up ever since the launch of the SDP in 1981—but especially since the defence row of the previous year—suddenly exploded. Every insult was remembered, every slight repaid, every wrong revenged. In public, the relations among former colleagues were venomous. In private, they were, if anything, worse. Political journalists, who had little else to write about in the immediate aftermath of the general election, reported with gusto and at length the SDP's precipitous descent from niceness into nastiness.

As early as 18 June, only a week after polling day, John Cartwright wrote in the *Guardian*, obviously referring to Steel, Jenkins and Williams: 'Those responsible for the current pro-merger Blitzkrieg in the Alliance seem to have combined the sensitivity of Genghis Khan with the strategic genius of Ethelred the Unready.'[21] On the following day, the front page of the *Social Democrat*, edited by an Owen supporter, was dominated by a photograph of Owen and Steel that had been torn down the middle; the *Social Democrat* predicted 'a battle royal' on the merger issue.[22] A week later, following the publication of Owen's anti-merger letter to rank-and file SDP supporters, Shirley Williams warned of 'a war to the death' between the two SDP factions, and David Marquand compared Owen to 'Napoleon at St Helena, divorced from reality'.[23] Someone at about this time suggested that, if a separate Owenite party were formed, it would have to be called the 'Monster Raving Ego Party'.[24] By the time the National Committee reconvened on 29 June, the atmosphere was poisonous.

At first, Owen and his supporters were adamant that any decision on merger should be delayed at least until the autumn, possibly until the following year. They wanted time to think, and they were genuinely angry at being bounced by Steel. But within a few days they turned through 180 degrees and joined the mergerites in advocating an immediate ballot. The Owenites were worried that the pro-merger forces would have a majority at the forthcoming SDP conference, due to be held at Portsmouth at the end of August; and they were also worried that, as during the 1983 parliament, local mergers would start to take place on the ground in the absence of any moves to stop them.[25] More important still, the widespread anger in the SDP at Steel's hastily prepared memorandum, and the expressions of support for the SDP's continued independence that were pouring into Owen's office from all over the country, appear to have convinced him and those around him that, if there were an early ballot, and if the issue put to the membership were sufficiently starkly posed, the anti-merger forces would win; the SDP's rank-and-file membership would rally to the leader in order to keep the SDP flag flying—and Owen could then go on to lead the party on his own terms. For all these reasons, the Owenites dropped their initial opposition to an early ballot and, on the contrary, began to press for the members to be consulted during the coming few weeks, in advance of the Portsmouth conference.

Since the pro-merger forces, for their part, were already in favour of an early ballot, the only remaining question concerned the actual form the ballot would take. Both sides believed that, with the party's leadership split, many ordinary party members—not well informed on the substance of the issue and greatly confused by the conflicting signals emanating from the pro- and anti-mergerites—would not be sure how to vote and would respond to the clearest and most unambiguous signal they got. The precise wording of the options on the ballot paper, therefore, might well determine the outcome. The wording had to be got right.

The anti-merger forces were quick to grasp this point, and Robert Maclennan, on Owen's behalf, was commissioned to draft a series of ballot propositions that the Owenites could recommend to the National Committee. When published, his proposals provoked howls of protest from the mergerites. With the backing of his fellow MPs, Maclennan suggested that one of the options on the ballot paper should read: 'Do you want the national committee to seek a total merger of the SDP with the Liberal Party which involves the abolition of the SDP?' The proposition was literally correct—a merger with the Liberals *would* involve the abolition of the SDP—but Shirley Williams objected vehemently that the wording did not give full weight to the case of those who favoured merger, and Bill Rodgers said he was 'disappointed at such an obvious attempt to manipulate the ballot and prejudice the outcome'.[26] Accusations of attempted ballot-rigging were still flying about when the National Committee reconvened on 29 June. The general election had been held only three weeks before, but already the six-year-old Liberal–SDP Alliance, which had come to seem such a permanent part of British politics, lay in ruins. Humpty-Dumpty had had a great fall. There was no way in which anyone could put him back together again.[27]

Williams was convinced that, when the National Committee met on the 29th, the Owenite majority would misrepresent the views of party activists in the country and claim that they had a large majority opposed to merger behind them. Thwarted in her attempts to see Owen, she spent an entire day before the meeting ringing round all of the SDP's regional chairmen and also a considerable number of other regional officers and candidates. Many of them were in favour of merger themselves and thought that a majority of their members were. Most said they objected to the proposed wording on the ballot paper.

Perhaps because so much bad blood had been spilt in public by then, the committee, when it reconvened on 29 June, was in a somewhat chastened mood, and the meeting itself, although strained, was less heated than many had feared. As

Williams had expected would happen, one of Owen's supporters began the relevant part of the discussion by insisting that his own members were strongly opposed to merger and would support Maclennan's draft wording of the ballot paper. He and other Owenites were clearly surprised when Williams riposted by reporting, in detail and naming names, the results of her survey of the regions. In the event, Maclennan himself withdrew his proposed wording, with its offending phrase 'the abolition of the SDP', and it was agreed instead that the party's 58,000 members should be asked to choose between two options:

Option 1   Do you want the National Committee to negotiate a closer constitutional framework for the Alliance, short of merger, which preserves the identity of the SDP?

Option 2   Do you want the National Committee to negotiate a merger of the SDP and the Liberal Party into one Party?[28]

It was further agreed that the party's national officers should play no part in the campaign, that neither side should be allowed to make use of the party's membership lists, that the editorials in the *Social Democrat* should be neutral and—a little triumph for the anti-merger forces—that area parties 'should not hold meetings with local Liberal Associations to discuss [the ballot] and should not invite individual members of the Liberal Party to take part in discussions of the matter at SDP meetings'.[29] The ballot papers were to be sent out on 18 July and returned by 5 August.

How would the committee recommend that the party's members should vote in the ballot? In view of his dominance of the party over the previous four years, Owen was confident that a majority of the committee would back him in opposing merger and in recommending Maclennan's formula of 'a closer constitutional framework' for the Alliance. His confidence was borne out. The committee endorsed the Owen–Maclennan view by eighteen votes to thirteen. As in the past, the closeness of the vote reflected how evenly—and deeply—the party was split.

The Owenites, however, were shaken by one incident that occurred during the meeting. Up to this point, the five SDP MPs had stood shoulder to shoulder in opposition to merger; and they had also agreed without difficulty to withdraw from the scheme for joint Liberal–SDP spokesmen in the House of Commons. But at the 29 June meeting, to the considerable surprise of everyone in the room, Charles Kennedy broke ranks. He had come to the meeting more or less expecting to vote with Owen and Maclennan in support of Option 1; but Option 1 envisaged closer co-operation with the Liberals, and closer co-operation implied, in Kennedy's view, both a willingness on the Liberals' part to bring the two parties closer together without their actually merging but also a willingness on Owen's part to work together with the Liberals in such a way that the two parties might eventually merge at some indefinite time in the future.

But by the time of the 29 June meeting the Liberals had indicated that, for them, it was now merger or bust, and at the meeting itself Owen, in response to a question from Kennedy, reiterated even more forcefully than before that he would never join a merged party—not now, not ever. Owen's adamant and blanket rejection of any possible merger, even at some distant future date, convinced Kennedy, who was already having his doubts, that Option 1 did not mean what it said and that the practical effects of passing it would be to rule out a genuinely closer relationship with the Liberals and also to make any eventual merger of the two parties impossible. 'In that case,' Kennedy said, 'I shall vote for Option 2.' Maclennan afterwards tried to talk him round. Owen just smiled sardonically. But the five anti-merger MPs were now down to four.

Kennedy was, of course, quite right about Option 1's implications. Its words pointed to closer co-operation with the Liberals; but its logic, and the motives of those who supported it, pointed in the opposite direction. Owen in his letter to rank-and-file Social Democrats had already gone out of his way to underline the policy differences that separated the SDP from the Liberals (and had done so in such a way as to leave the clear impression that the alliance with the Liberals had never been a partnership of principle but only a not-very-happy marriage of convenience):

[The] truth is that without the SDP the Alliance would never have been able to maintain the policy stand that we did over the Falklands, over the miners' dispute, over the right-to-buy council house legislation, over the market economy, over the Prevention of Terrorism Act, over deployment of cruise missiles . . . over the integration of tax and social security and over maintaining the minimum nuclear deterrent. There are a host of other policy areas where the SDP voice has been crucial . . .[30]

In case that was not enough, Owen, in his press statements following the National Committee meeting, went even further, criticizing the Liberal leadership more openly than at any time in the past and giving the impression that he would really prefer to wash his hands of the entire Alliance concept:

There is [he said] an element in the Liberal Party that believes you . . . negotiate under threat and under bounce.
The history of our relationship is that you have got to be prepared to stand up to anarchic forces.

He added that perhaps his strong stand against the Liberals might help his colleagues, 'if they ever get into negotiations on a merger, to stand a bit firmer'.[31]

The ballot, held between 18 July and 5 August, was thus a rather curious affair. The mergerites said what they meant and meant what they said; the anti-mergerites did neither. The mergerites wanted merger; the anti-mergerites said they wanted closer relations with the Liberals but actually wanted relations that were less close. Later many of the Owenites were happy to concede that their position in the ballot had been, at bottom, a false one. One said that the Option 1 position was basically 'dishonest' and that it had been no more than a 'rallying compromise' in order to try to muster the largest possible anti-merger vote.

Another remarked that the anti-merger option was both immoral and politically implausible—'a hopeless fudge and mudge'. He personally would have preferred a straightforward go-it-alone option and knew that Owen felt the same; but they recognized that they could not carry enough party members with them on that basis. If ordinary members of the SDP during the ballot showed signs of perplexity at the strange and contradictory signals emanating from some of their leaders, it was hardly a wonder. It seemed strange to spend most of one's time abusing the Liberals—'you have got to stand up to anarchic forces'—while claiming at the same time that one wanted closer relations with them.[32]

The pro-mergerites organized their forces under the banner 'Yes to Unity'. At the launch of their campaign on 2 July, Roy Jenkins was insistent: 'The logic now points inexorably either to separation, or to union, not to a fudged compromise.' 'Separation', he added, 'means impotence.' The 'Yes to Unity' statement to the party's members, to be sent out with their ballot forms, maintained that the growing-together or partnership option—the one being recommended by the anti-mergerites—had 'even less chance of working after recent disputes with, within, and between the two parties than it did up to June 11'. 'The real choice', the statement said, 'is unity or bust.' Bill Rodgers, the campaign's chairman, insisted at the opening press conference that David Owen's preferred option, federation, 'could only be a recipe for adversarial politics within the Alliance of the kind that we have deplored outside'.[33]

According to the mergerites, the electorate had decisively rejected the Alliance approach at the June election; a merged party would be more efficient organizationally and would have a much sharper campaigning image; and a new federal structure would solve few or none of the practical problems that the Alliance in its existing form had thrown up. In addition, the mergerites stressed two further points. One was that any new party would be a genuinely new one, incorporating the best features of both the Liberals and the SDP; it would not be a takeover by the Liberals of the SDP.[34] The other was that in any merger negotiations the SDP's representatives would be in a position to insist that all the SDP's reasonable demands be met; the present ballot was purely consultative, and any final merger agreement would have to be submitted to the membership in a second ballot for formal ratification. Underlying much of the mergerite propaganda, though seldom expressly stated, was the view that a merged party, with or without Owen, would be a more left-wing, more anti-Thatcher party than the SDP had recently become.

The headquarters of 'Yes to Unity' was located at 43 Campden Hill Square, the elegant Holland Park home of Celia and William Goodhart, both of whom had been SDP candidates at the election. A landing was cleared to make space for a secretary and a word processor. Five extra telephone lines were installed. A portrait of Gladstone gazed down on the activity in the mail room. At first the campaign was co-ordinated by Martin Beecroft, who had resigned from the party's Cowley Street headquarters in protest against the Owenites' efforts to thwart merger.[35] Later Beecroft worked with Alec McGivan, formerly the SDP's national organizer, who had also resigned from the Cowley Street staff. It was estimated that 'Yes to Unity' might spend about £20,000 in the course of the month-long campaign.

The anti-mergerites' campaign did not have a name. Instead it had a slogan: 'Vote for the SDP'. Those wanting to oppose merger were invited to write to Rosie Barnes at her modest SDP headquarters in Greenwich. At the first anti-mergerite press conference she and Owen were joined on the platform by John Cartwright and Robert Maclennan. They also had the backing not only of a majority of the SDP National Committee but also of Sir Leslie Murphy and David Sainsbury, the party's financial trustees, both of whom declared their opposition to merger. As it seemed that a large proportion of those who cast their ballots would do so early on, those opposed to merger chose 10 July, the day after most party members would have received their ballot papers, to publish full-page advertisements in the *Guardian* and the *Independent*, two papers with large SDP readerships. The advertisements featured prominently a copy of an SDP membership card. Underneath it the text read:

Once merged, the SDP with its distinctive policies and appeal would be lost for ever. The Alliance and the country would be much poorer as a result.

So, to the SDP's members we say, the future is now in your hands. Please support the National Committee recommendation for option one on your ballot paper.

You can vote for the SDP or you can vote for merger. You can't vote for both.

The anti-merger statement sent out to the party members with their ballots developed the same theme. It reminded the SDP's members that two-thirds of them had never before belonged to any party and asked them not to be too down-hearted by the results of the June election. After all, under proportional representation the SDP would have won sixty-three seats and the Liberals eighty-three. The SDP was sound both financially and organizationally, and 650 SDP councillors were working effectively alongside their Liberal colleagues. The statement emphasized once again the considerable policy differences that separated the SDP from the Liberals—over defence, the right to buy and the Prevention of Terrorism Act—and then claimed that the SDP had 'evolved a distinctive political philosophy':

tough on economic issues, tender on social issues; strong on defence, serious about disarmament; concerned about individual liberties, conscious of society's larger obligations; in favour of a welfare state and a wealth-creating economy.

The document also contained an appeal that was at once accurate and somewhat disingenuous:

We are disturbed by the number of members of the SDP who do not wish to become members of any merged party. We cannot see any sense in dividing our party. The time may well come when it is right to merge our two parties, but that will be when we know 80–90 per cent of our members are enthusiastic to merge. A successful merger cannot be half-hearted, nor forced by an unacceptable ultimatum that there is a simple choice—merge or separate.[36]

The appeal was accurate in that by this time it was clear that substantial numbers of Social Democrats would indeed refuse to join a new party. It was somewhat disingenuous in that it was the signatories to the statement themselves who were threatening not to join a merged party and encouraging others to do the same. Owen and his allies were not at all 'disturbed by the number of members of the SDP who [did] not wish to become members of any merged party'. They rejoiced at it.

Much of the emphasis of the Owenite campaign in 1987 lay, as in 1986, on the issue of defence. Speaking at a meeting in Pinner, John Cartwright reminded party members that the Alliance had fought the June election on a pledge to maintain Britain's minimum nuclear deterrent, but he then went further, warning the pro-merger faction that by the time of the next election, in 1991 or 1992, some 80 per cent of the government's investment in replacing the Polaris system with Trident would have been spent or contractually committed. It would still be possible to cancel Trident, but only at vast cost. He concluded: 'At the next election, there will be no middle course. The stark choice for Britain will be Trident or nothing.'[37] David Steel riposted that it was far too soon to be taking decisions about Trident, and he accused Cartwright of 'tearing up' the Alliance's existing defence commitments.[38]

The arguments on both sides were powerful and skilfully deployed; but there was no possibility that the debate could remain on a high intellectual level. Far from it: it was apparent from the beginning that the actual campaign would be every bit as choleric as the pre-campaign had been. The summer of 1981 had seen the ferocious Benn–Healey contest in the Labour party. The summer of 1983 had seen the battle between Neil Kinnock and Roy Hattersley for the Labour leadership. Now it was the SDP's turn 'to lay on this sort of summer entertainment'.[39]

For one thing, procedural wrangling continued well beyond the 29 June meeting of the National Committee. The anti-mergerites and their allies decided it would be a good idea to print the committee's recommendation in favour of Option 1 on the same sheet of paper as the ballot form. 'Yes to Unity' said it was 'amazed and saddened by a second destructive attempt to rig the ballot'; and Bill Rodgers on behalf of 'Yes to Unity' took the issue to the Electoral Reform Society, the neutral body running the poll. After a hastily arranged four-hour hearing, the Electoral Reform Society upheld Rodgers' complaint.[40] For their part, the Owenites demanded an enquiry into allegations that the pro-merger forces, in direct contravention of the party's constitution and resolutions of the National Committee, were making illicit use of the party's confidential membership lists.[41]

Accusations of sharp practice were accompanied by harsher-than-ever language and fresh charges of bad faith. The relatively small size of the party, and especially of its leadership group, contrived to make the battle all the more clangorous—like the sound of gun fire in a closely confined space.

Dick Taverne warned David Owen that he risked becoming 'a sort of Napoleon figure—a leader without a party' and likened Owen's resistance to merger to 'the path of perdition'.[42] Voicing his resentment at the Liberals' continuing pressure for merger, Owen insisted that he was 'not about to be rolled over by the Liberals'.[43] Relations between Owen and Williams were said to be so bad that Owen cancelled a BBC appearance when he heard that his party president was also to appear.[44] Owen wrote to Dick Newby, the SDP's national secretary, telling him he should resign in view of his private support for merger. Newby declined.[45] When Alec McGivan did resign, John Cartwright wrote to him accusing him of 'cynical motives' in the timing of his departure and adding: 'I would have hoped that you would have treated yourself and the party with more respect than to allow yourself to be used by a factional group within the SDP for its own purposes.'[46] McGivan observed that Cartwright was obviously 'in an intemperate mood'.[47] A few days later McGivan responded to the Owenites' full-page anti-merger advertisements, estimating that they must have cost at least £25,000 and adding: 'They have gone over the top if they imagine our members can be bought for a 50p piece.'[48] The allusion to Judas Iscariot was unmistakable—and typical.

Journalists clearly found the whole thing a hoot. Robert Harris in the *Observer* remarked of the SDP's leaders: 'They are breaking the mould at last—over one another's heads.'[49] A headline in the *Guardian*, punning on the title of the Alliance's election manifesto, read: 'The time has come—to let mud fly'.[50] Anthony Bevins noted in the *Independent*: 'The delight of the current power struggle for the soul of the Social Democratic Party is the sheer openness of the process. Back-stabbing has been replaced by front-stabbing.'[51]

The campaign reached its acrid climax in mid-July when the two forces met head on at a meeting of the Association of Social Democratic Councillors (ASDC) in Nottingham. Shirley Williams, hitherto somewhat embarrassed by being the SDP's president (and therefore National Committee chairman) as well as a strong mergerite, chose the occasion to speak out more forcefully on the topic than ever before, claiming that Owen's opposition to merger amounted to 'a pointless act of vivisection' on the Liberal–SDP Alliance.[52] Owen objected to the phrase and warned her, and also the councillors present, 'not to use language about each other that will make it difficult to work together again'. He conceded that the Alliance was now split 'from top to toe'.[53] Williams and Owen spoke separately and behind closed doors, but Dick Taverne and Rosie Barnes debated the issue more formally and in the open. Barnes spoke of 'the dotty things' Liberals do, while Taverne rebuked the Owenites for their party chauvinism:

What is regrettable is the public abuse there has been over the Liberals and the contempt which has been shown for them. There has been constant reference to the Liberals in the way Rommel might have referred to his Italian allies during the desert war.[54]

The assembled councillors were horrified by the tone of the exchanges and by the damage being inflicted on the SDP's reputation and its ability to fight and win elections, including local elections. Serge Lourie, a Richmond councillor, intervened to say: 'If these people are typical of the SDP, then I don't want to know.

For Christ's sake, control yourselves.'[55] The ASDC executive rebuked both sides in the controversy:

We are very concerned about the effect that this public argument may have on the running of town halls and county halls, on Alliance council groups up and down the country, on our ability to gain and defend council seats in by-elections, and the eventual performance of Alliance candidates in the May 1988 local elections. We call upon all members of the Gang of Four and all SDP MPs to get together the day after the ballot is counted and to work together in a spirit of unity to implement the wishes of the party as expressed in that ballot without delay.[56]

But more significant than the councillors' unhappiness about the tone of the merger debate was the fact that a large proportion of them also indicated that they were not happy about losing their separate SDP identity. When Taverne suggested that party members should unite in abiding by the result of the ballot, there were shouts of 'No' followed by a heckler's jibe: 'You didn't accept Labour party decisions when you were a member.' It had been supposed that the SDP councillors, accustomed to working with Liberal colleagues on local councils up and down the country, would be almost unanimously in favour of merger; but the *Guardian*'s reporter at the Nottingham meeting formed the impression that, among the eighty-odd councillors present, 'there was a strong majority for Dr David Owen and for keeping the party separate'.[57]

Something else emerged as the campaign progressed. The mergerites had undoubtedly seen the holding of a membership ballot as a clean, almost surgical way of deciding the outcome. The members would vote. The result would go one way or the other. The great bulk of the party would abide by the majority's verdict. And that would be that. It gradually became clear, however, that it was not going to be at all like that: the outcome of the ballot, whatever it was, was going to produce neither a clean nor a surgical result but, instead, a complete mess. Owen said that he would not join a merged party. Others said the same. Williams now said that she would probably have to resign as SDP president if the anti-merger option were carried.[58] It was impossible to predict how many in the SDP would join a merged party, or how many would not join, or how many, disgusted, would abandon politics altogether. It was also impossible to predict precisely what the anti-mergerites would do if they lost. Abandon the struggle? Form a new party? Or, just possibly, try to keep the existing Social Democratic party going on some new basis? The outcome of the ballot, it was clear by the end, was going to be important in determining the SDP's ultimate future, but hardly decisive.

Balloting closed on 5 August, and the Electoral Reform Society announced the result the following day. Turn-out had been high—fully 77.7 per cent of the SDP's 58,509 members voted—and Option 2 had been carried, by a margin only slightly smaller than the 60–40 margin predicted by 'Yes to Unity':

Option 1	19,228	42.6%
Option 2	25,897	57.4%

If the ballot had been any ordinary election, the result would have been easy to interpret: Option 2 would have won. But in the circumstances of August 1987 it was at least as significant that less than half the total membership (44.6 per cent) had voted for merger and that, of those who had voted, as many as 42.6 per cent had 'voted for the SDP'. The result was thus far less lop-sided in favour of merger than the mergerites had hoped and probably expected. There were, it seemed, out in the country nearly 20,000 potential Owenite dissidents.

Three factors undoubtedly underlay the anti-mergerites' considerable success. One was loyalty to the SDP. Many members *were* proud of their party. They did *not* think of themselves as Liberals. They thought the existing Alliance, all things considered, had not worked *that* badly. A second was personal loyalty to Owen. He was the party's leader; he was in favour of Option 1; a large proportion of members clearly thought he deserved their backing. Finally, many members' loyalty to Owen was almost certainly reinforced by the fear that, if Option 2 were carried, Owen and the majority of the SDP MPs might go their own ways. By announcing in late June that he was not prepared to join a merged party, Owen had effectively turned the ballot into a vote of confidence in himself: a vote for merger would be, in effect, a vote against himself. Even some of those who favoured merger in the abstract must have been deterred from voting for merger by the fact that, if merger took place, Owen might be lost to the new party. Better, they thought, the existing arrangement, however unsatisfactory, with Owen at its head than some theoretically better arrangement without him.

Whatever the motives of those who voted against merger, Owen's reaction to the result was instant. On 6 August, less than an hour after the declaration of the result, he resigned as leader of the party. His resignation statement said:

Ours is a democratic, one-member one-vote party. The members have decided, as they have the right to do, to seek a merger with the Liberals against my advice, and in the circumstances I do not believe I should continue as their leader during the period of negotiations.[59]

He went on to say that he and those on his side of the argument, while they would not participate in any merger negotiations, would at the same time not put any obstacles in their way. In a television interview that evening, Owen reiterated that those who wanted to merge were entitled to do so. He added, harking back to his secret memorandum, that he hoped there would be an 'amicable settlement' between the two sides.[60]

The suddenness of Owen's resignation seems to have taken the mergerites totally by surprise. David Steel, from Ettrickbridge, issued a statement expressing regret at Owen's decision but accepting that it was 'logical' under the circumstances.[61] Shirley Williams, on holiday in Wyoming, expressed the hope that 'David Owen and those who support him will once again join with us, for we believe Britain badly needs the voice of the Alliance'.[62] Roy Jenkins—who, having lost his Hillhead seat at the election, had recently been ennobled—admitted that the split

Source: *Guardian*, 7 August 1987

Merger

had taken 'the gilt off the gingerbread of the [ballot] result' and stressed that one of the main aims of the merger negotiations would be 'to try to set at rest some of the doubts which made 42 per cent vote the other way'. He said it was now time to bind up wounds and bring the party together.[63]

Owen did not, however, stop at resigning. He issued a number of broad hints that he had no intention of standing aside and merely serving out his time as MP for Plymouth Devonport. He insisted, rather, that the campaign for social democracy would go on: 'Don't write me off, or the party, or the SDP or social democracy.'[64] He effectively invited Social Democrats in parliament and outside to join him in a new venture; and, when he referred to an 'amicable settlement', he seemed to be referring (as indeed he was) to some kind of division of the Social Democrats' assets. Owen's colleagues were quoted as saying that a settlement would leave them with the structure and framework of the existing party.[65] David Steel at Ettrickbridge was one who took the hint. 'I wish', he said, '[Owen] were with us in forming this new third force rather than, as it sounds, going off into a semi-wilderness to form a less effective fourth force.'[66] A Gibbard cartoon in the *Guardian* showed a submarine named Son of SDP, with a grim-faced Owen on the bridge, preparing to torpedo the good ship Merger.[67]

If Owen was portrayed as grim faced at this stage, it was because his feelings were grim. On the one hand, he was increasingly conscious of what he wanted; on the other, he was not at all sure he could get it. What he wanted was, in effect, to start all over again: to turn the clock back to 1981 and to re-found the SDP as the kind of party he had wanted right from the beginning. His new SDP would be a genuine fourth party, with its own philosophy and its own policies; and it would be a fiercely independent party, not entangled in any permanent alliance with the Liberals or anyone else. Owen's ideal, relaunched SDP might negotiate *ad hoc* electoral pacts with the Liberals or others, but it would be prepared to do so only from a position of strength, after it had clearly demonstrated its own vote-winning potential. It still rankled with Owen that the original SDP had not taken on the Liberals at either Warrington or Croydon North-West. Owen's new SDP would have the additional advantage that it would be led by him and would consist exclusively of those who supported his strategy.

But could such a party be created? Owen appears to have spent much of the summer of 1987 debating this question in his own mind. A victory for Option 1 in the ballot would, of course, have delivered the existing SDP into his hands and would have obviated any need for a new party; but Option 1 had been defeated. Against that, as many as 42 per cent of the party's members had backed Option 1, and Owen had been greatly heartened by the positive response to the anti-mergerites' two 'Vote for the SDP' advertisements and also by the loyalty to the party shown by many of those present at the ASDC meeting in Nottingham. It began to look as though an independent Social Democratic party might just possibly, by some means or other, be kept going. As soon as the result of the ballot was known, Rosie Barnes addressed a circular letter to SDP members in which, under the heading 'Campaign for Social Democracy', she appealed for the names of individuals who wished 'to remain a member of the SDP', asked for donations to a 'Support the SDP Fund' and urged supporters of Option 1 to attend a 'Grassroots Uprising' meeting to be held on the eve of the party's Portsmouth conference.[68]

The mergerites now had to face up to the real possibility that Owen and his followers might not merely refuse to join a merged party but might actually set up a breakaway party in opposition to it. They were appalled, with the result that their denunciations of Owen became even more angry and bitter than in the past.

The mergerites deeply resented the Owenites' apparent willingness to defy both the SDP's constitution and the majority verdict of the party's members as recorded in the ballot. Alec McGivan said on behalf of himself, Jenkins, Rodgers and Williams: 'We consider it outrageous that within hours of a democratic decision to opt for merger negotiations with the Liberals, this group should start setting up the mechanics for creating a new political party.'[69] Shirley Williams accused Owen of seeking to 'negate' the result of the ballot and later of 'sabotaging' it.[70] Roger Liddle, Bill Rodgers' former aide, published an article in the *New Statesman* under the heading: 'Democracy David Owen style: Heads I win, tails I split the party'.[71] Rodgers himself insisted that the Owenites had no right to either the SDP's name or any part of its organization. If the Owenites chose to form a new party, it would not be the SDP; it would be a breakaway.[72] Both the mergerites in the SDP and many Liberals, led by David Steel, insisted repeatedly that, if Owen did start a relaunched SDP, the merged party would be bound to fight it. There could be no question of electoral pacts or a new alliance. Only the sitting SDP MPs might possibly be given a clear run at the next election.

Now that the ballot was over, the mergerites, for the first time, felt really free to vent their personal loathing of Owen and his entire political approach. One of them told the *Sunday Telegraph*:

All he wants is a David Owen party. All this row is bound up in the personality of David Owen.

The SDP does not belong to anyone but the membership of the party. David Owen has no ability to be a team-player and he does not want other people around him.[73]

Roy Jenkins, writing in the *Observer*, dismissed the idea of a new fourth party as being no more than 'a piece of political self-indulgence'. Alluding to Owen's growing enthusiasm for Trident, Jenkins observed loftily: 'I have never heard of a political party founded upon a weapons system.'[74]

But it was left to David Marquand, in another article in the *New Statesman*, to say at length what most of the others were thinking and feeling.[75] Predicting that the Owenites had embarked on a course that would lead them 'either to oblivion or to the Tory party', Marquand savaged them for claiming that they were campaigning for closer relations with the Liberals when actually they were campaigning for the reverse:

Well before the votes were counted, the dirty little secret which had always lain at the heart of the anti-merger position came out into the open. Dr Owen and his closest supporters made it plain that they are separatists on principle: that their attitude to the Liberal Party is one of lordly contempt, tinged with paranoid suspicion; and that they had joined in an Alliance with the Liberals, not because they believed in it, but only because the exigencies of electoral arithmetic had given them no alternative.

Though this, Marquand continued, became clear during the campaign, it was not at all clear at the beginning: 'The separatists set sail under false colours: only when battle was joined did they hoist the Jolly Roger.' As a result, those who had voted for Option 1 undoubtedly included many who were by no means opposed to merger on principle and, unlike the Owenites, actually did want closer relations with the Liberals. Yet, despite the large majority in favour of merger, the separatists now refused to accept the verdict of their own ballot: 'To use H. N. Brailsford's famous phrase about Mussolini, they now appear like knights clad in shining blackmail.' Why?, asked Marquand. What drove the Owenites?

The answers are rooted in the extraordinary, brilliant, tormented personality of David Owen. For the opposition to merger can be understood only as an emanation of his over-mastering Ego. It exists because he exists, and because he has taken the line he has; had he taken a different line it would long ago have disappeared. There may be a certain wistful charm in the notion that Mr Edward Lyons or Dr Dickson Mabon or Ms Sue Slipman or even Ms Rosie Barnes might have led a campaign against merger if he had been in favour of it, but it has no toehold in reality.

The question therefore, according to Marquand, was not what drove the Owenites but what drove Owen. Not, he maintained, ambition (conventional ambition pointed not against merger but towards it) and not any comprehensible matter of political principle (on any reasonable definition, the other members of the Gang of Four were just as good Social Democrats as Owen, and most Liberals, like Owen, believed in the social market). Rather, the key, Marquand insisted, lay in the fact that Owen himself was not in fact a Social Democrat: he was an Owenite:

In spite of his extraordinary capacity to pick up the latest political ideas and run with them, in spite, for that matter, of his marvellous command of the details of policy, there is no evidence that he has a coherent, thought-out philosophy. What he has are demonic energy, a quick intelligence, enormously powerful instincts and a driving Will. What he craves—what he must have in order to cope with the tensions which have aged him ten years in the last five—is the psychic space in which to follow that Will wherever it may take him.

As, however, this gigantic Will could not operate entirely on its own, Owen needed 'a sounding board, a vehicle, an instrument'. That, in Owen's eyes, was the SDP's function: 'Its destiny is to be the violin to his Paganini: the Old Guard to his Napoleon.' Marquand concluded that Owen was a profoundly, instinctively illiberal person—with a small 'l' as well as a large—and that 'an Owenite rump party could move only to the right'. Marquand's article was widely quoted—and, among the mergerites, widely approved of.

As for Owen himself, when he resigned on 6 August he seems to have assumed that, with his departure, the leadership would remain vacant. The party's constitution required that the leader be an MP. Only one of the five MPs, Charles Kennedy, was not backing him; and it seemed improbable that Kennedy, still only 27 and a relative newcomer to the House of Commons, would put himself forward for the leadership at such a difficult moment and at such an early stage in his career. Owen's calculation seems to have been that Kennedy would not stand and that, if the merger talks failed or if any merger deal with the Liberals were rejected by the SDP's membership, then he could simply resume the leadership. After all, he had said in his resignation statement only that he was 'standing aside' for the duration of the talks. Alternatively, he could become the leader of a new party if that turned out to be the upshot of the crisis.

If that was Owen's calculation, he reckoned without Robert Maclennan, the MP for Caithness and Sutherland. Maclennan was one of the least visible of British politicians. First elected for his sprawling and isolated Scottish constituency in 1966, he had resigned from the Labour front bench over Europe in 1972 and later had served for five years, during the Wilson and Callaghan governments, in the lowly position of parliamentary undersecretary at the Department of Prices and Consumer Protection (the first two years under Shirley Williams). He had become disillusioned with the Labour party long before many of his colleagues, had kept in touch with Roy Jenkins at the European Commission in Brussels and had been one of the first Labour MPs to announce his support for the Gang of Four. He held his seat easily in 1983 and 1987. Despite voting for Jenkins in the 1982 leadership election, he managed to work well with Owen throughout the 1983 parliament. Owen thought of him as loyal and as a safe pair of hands. A modestly successful London-based barrister, Maclennan was, as we saw in Chapter 12, the principal author of the SDP's constitution, including its provisions for 'one member, one vote'.

It was hard to imagine Maclennan as the leader of any political party—which is probably why Owen, and not only Owen, did not imagine him in that role. Maclennan's father was an ambitious Scottish gynaecologist with an extensive network of business and civic interests. Maclennan's intelligent and forceful wife, Helen, the daughter of a Massachusetts judge, likewise gave the impression of being ambitious, on her husband's behalf if not her own. He would probably have been most at ease in an essentially private occupation. Instead, he first read for the bar and then moved on to a career in politics. An extraordinarily nervous and hesitant public speaker, he frequently looked on public platforms and in the House of Commons as though he might break down. It seemed that sheer determination and will-power were seeing him through. With all that, Maclennan was a transparently honest person as well as a highly intelligent one, and he had few, if any, enemies.

Despite his limitations, Maclennan was a shrewd politician, and it is arguable that he was one of the few people in the SDP to foresee the disaster that might follow if the pro-merger forces were foolish enough to try to push Owen further and faster than he was prepared to go. Maclennan's belief immediately following the election was that the ensuing summer should be spent relaxing, recovering and contemplating the future in as calm and reflective a way as possible. He regarded the calls for the holding of an early ballot in advance of the Portsmouth conference as 'insensate'. He genuinely wanted closer relations with the Liberals. In his view, the two parties should move towards joint open selection of candidates, a single leader and a single annual conference, though with separate policy committees. Option 1, with its reference to 'a closer constitutional framework for the Alliance', was his doing, and, unlike most of the Owenites, he actually voted for it in good faith. He believed that, if the two parties succeeded in working together within a new framework, then a merger between them would take place almost imperceptibly. The separate structures would in time simply 'wither away'.

Maclennan was thus by no means opposed to merger in principle. But he was strongly opposed to merger in the specific circumstances of 1987. He had two reasons for his opposition. Both related to Owen. In the first place, Maclennan was prepared to go to almost any lengths to keep Owen inside the SDP—or, as he put it, 'on board'. He knew as well as anyone that Owen could be difficult to work with ('He ignores everyone who doesn't play the role of Little Sir Echo'); but he also believed that Owen was one of the Alliance's greatest assets. His standing with the public was high. He had a firm grasp of policy. Not least, he had made a major contribution in transforming the SDP's and the Liberals' policies from 'soggy centrism' into something much more robust. Many in the Liberal party, as well as members of the SDP, were grateful. To lose such a man would be deeply damaging.

Secondly, Maclennan, having observed Owen at close quarters for more than twenty years and especially during his four years as party leader, had a vivid sense of Owen's 'capacity for destruction'. Owen in good humour was already a force of nature. Owen angry was capable of almost anything, including splitting the SDP and going off to found a new party. Maclennan was convinced that Jenkins, Rodgers, Williams and the other mergerites had simply failed to take the measure of the havoc Owen could wreak. He was also convinced that they underestimated 'the degree of institutional loyalty to the SDP among the members'. Early in the summer of 1987 he spent four hours at East Hendred trying to impress on Jenkins, his former mentor, the need to exercise caution in pressing for merger and warning him of the damage Owen might do. But in his view 'Roy never took the measure of the problem'. Indeed Maclennan concluded that Owen's old comrades in the Gang of Four would not be in the least bit sorry to see the back of him.

All of Maclennan's worst fears were confirmed by the two opposing sides' conduct during the membership ballot. On the one hand, the mergerites scarcely attempted to conceal the depths of their animus against Owen. On the other hand, the Owenites' publicly declared contempt for the Liberals completely undercut Maclennan's own Option 1, which called for a closer relationship between the two parties. He regarded the Owenites' campaign as being 'unpleasant and dishonest', and long before the campaign was over he was indicating to journalists that, although he was opposed to merger and would vote for Option 1, he was not disposed to go down the road of separation. A great admirer of Owen, he was nevertheless no Owenite.

Once the result of the ballot was known, Maclennan was clear what his own views were. He was the principal author, and felt himself to be one of the custodians, of the SDP's constitution. The party's members had voted for merger in a democratic ballot under the constitution. Maclennan felt strongly that the members' wishes should be respected. At the same time, he also felt that the SDP should bargain hard in the merger negotiations and that, if the negotiations succeeded more or less on the SDP's terms, then every effort should be made to persuade Owen and his followers that, whatever their initial and understandable reservations, they should change their minds and join the new party. The new party should be made to resemble the tough-minded Owenite SDP more than the traditional beards-and-sandals Liberal party. Either that, or the negotiations should fail. In other words, were Maclennan to participate in the negotiations, it would be as a committed and sceptical hawk. He would negotiate as Owen himself might have negotiated. With luck, even the Doctor might be persuaded to see that a good deal had been struck.

Holding these views, Maclennan began by trying to dissuade Owen from resigning as leader. He spoke to him on three occasions and at length, both before and after the ballot result was declared. He believed that if, even at this juncture, Owen were to relent and accept the result of the ballot he would be 'the hero of the hour' and would be in a very strong position both to conduct the negotiations with the Liberals in a tough-minded way and also, eventually, to become the new party's leader. But Owen was implacable. He would go. The party would—or should— remain leaderless.

How much of Maclennan's thinking was known to the pro-merger campaigners is not clear. Initially, probably not a lot. After all, Maclennan and the others had been on opposite sides in a peculiarly hard-fought campaign. It was going to take a little time for Maclennan and them to re-establish personal relations and a degree of mutual trust. In addition, the business of re-establishing personal relations was considerably complicated by the fact that by the second week of August 1987 all the leading figures in the SDP, far from being together in London, had gone on holiday. Williams had already disappeared to the United States. Jenkins was in Italy, Rodgers in Greece, Owen in France and Kennedy in Turkey. Maclennan, like Williams, soon departed for America. There followed a somewhat bizarre period of what the *Guardian* dubbed 'Ambre Solaire politics', with Kennedy, in particular, running up enormous phone bills at his hotel on a Turkish beach.[76]

The victorious mergerites were determined that the new leadership vacancy should be filled if at all possible; and Alec McGivan, one of the few principals left in London, mounted a well-publicized mini-campaign in favour of the absent Kennedy; a *Guardian* headline read: 'Kennedy ready to lead SDP into merger'.[77] But Kennedy insisted he was not interested, and attention immediately switched to Maclennan. Shirley Williams, in the peripatetic tradition of her party, had meanwhile flown east from Wyoming to Cape Cod where she arranged a meeting with Maclennan and his wife. Maclennan, a naturally diffident man, was initially reluctant to stand; he seemed not entirely confident of his ability to handle the pressures of the job. But Williams was adamant that he could do it and that, without a leader, the party was in imminent danger of drifting on to the rocks; and finally Maclennan was won round. It remained only to inform Owen that his place was going to be taken after all. The ensuing transatlantic telephone conversation between Maclennan and Owen was said to have been 'cool'.

Maclennan then issued a statement from his holiday home in New Hampshire announcing that he would be standing for the leadership. 'The party', he said, 'has signalled in the result of the ballot the need for a wholly new party organization with the Liberals to advance our objectives. The SDP must therefore enter in good faith into constructive discussions to try to give effect to this purpose.'[78] A few days later, on 18 August, Maclennan and Williams met again on Cape Cod and agreed that the merger negotiations should deal not just with the new party's constitution but should, in addition, include a substantial policy element. 'Issues of policy', Maclennan and Williams said, and in particular defence and the economy, 'are central'.[79] Their insistence that any merger agreement must cover policy as well as constitutional matters was intended to reassure those who had hitherto been opposed to merger. As events transpired, it was to be a central feature of the negotiations between the two parties during the next few months. As events also transpired, it was to be a source of enormous grief.

21

• • • •

Of Merger and a Dead Parrot

The unexpected defection of Robert Maclennan from their ranks meant that the Owenites in parliament were now reduced to three members: Owen himself, John Cartwright and Rosie Barnes. The party's autumn conference was due to begin in Portsmouth in less than a fortnight's time and merger would be high on the agenda. For all practical purposes it would be the only item on the agenda. In the meantime, Maclennan's defection had the effect of confronting the Owenites with a new problem and forcing them to give further thought to an old one.

The new problem was whether Cartwright or Barnes should stand for the now vacant leadership or whether the Owenites should stand aside, allowing Maclennan to be returned unopposed. 'Stop Maclennan' feeling ran high in the Owenite inner group. Maclennan was seen as an inconsiderable person, someone beneath the Owenites' dignity. He was also seen as a traitor, a deserter from the cause; one Owenite angrily quoted him as having said earlier in the summer, 'I'll quit politics before merger.' For nearly ten days, although pressed repeatedly to do so, Cartwright and Barnes each refused to deny that they would allow their names to be put forward.

But good sense eventually prevailed. If either Cartwright or Barnes did contest the leadership, the membership would have to be balloted, and forcing a ballot at this time would be seen as unnecessarily divisive. Moreover, whoever stood against Maclennan would almost certainly lose. It seemed to the Owenites more prudent to make a virtue of not standing and of being able to say that a pro-merger leader —Maclennan—should be allowed to conduct the merger negotiations. At a two-hour meeting of the five SDP MPs on 27 August, Owen, Cartwright and Barnes tried to talk Maclennan out of standing ('they produced all kinds of threats and blandishments'), but he would not be dissuaded and was duly elected leader, unopposed, two days later.

The remaining problem for the Owenites was what line they should take in response to the mergerites' victory in the ballot. There were two possibilities. One was to fight merger every inch of the way, fighting on the National Committee, fighting in the area parties, fighting in the Council for Social Democracy, all the while taking advantage of every available constitutional and procedural device, notably the provision that one-third or more of the members of the Council for Social Democracy—the party's supreme governing body—could block any proposed amendment to the constitution. The other possibility was, in effect, to disengage: to say to the mergerites, almost in so many words, 'Erring sisters, go thy way in peace.' On this scenario, the mergerites would be left to get on with merger and those opposed to merger would be left to get on, undisturbed, with the business of setting-up a new social-democratic organization.

The fight-them-all-the-way strategy had obvious attractions. The Owenites were in a fighting mood. If Steel and the other members of the Gang of Four were out to get Owen, Owen and many of his followers were by this time out to get their Liberal and Social Democrat opponents. As one member of the Cowley Street staff put it, 'David [in the late summer of 1987] was in one of his purgative moods.' It would also seem odd if the Owenites did *not* fight merger by every available means. If the Owenites wanted to keep the Social Democratic flag flying, how could they justify—to themselves, let alone to anyone else—not fighting to retain control of the Social Democratic flagship, the SDP itself? In particular, how could they justify a strategy of disengagement to their own followers in the country, people who had voted for Option 1 and who, more than anything else, wanted to stay inside the existing party? To disengage would be to appear to surrender, to admit tacitly that one had lost the argument as well as the vote. Not least, disengagement might be very hard, in practical terms, to organize. Even if Owen and those closest to him had no intention of fighting to the finish, it might be difficult to send the appropriate signals to the anti-mergerites in the country and then to ensure that they acted on those signals. Like isolated Japanese platoons after the Second World War, the Owenite troops in the country might just fight on.

Nevertheless, despite all these disadvantages, the case in favour of standing aside—for not continuing to oppose the merger—was just as strong. Owen and others around him did indeed wish to 'purge' the mergerites, to be shot of them completely. What better way to be shot of them than to stop having anything to do with them? Fighting, after all, implies a certain respect; by contrast, refusing to fight implies a certain disdain. Owen was also conscious that, if a continuing SDP were to be established, it would sooner or later have to come to some sort of electoral arrangement with the Liberals or with the new party (albeit an arrangement far short of the now defunct Alliance). A fight to the finish within the existing SDP would make such an arrangement much more difficult, perhaps impossible, to achieve.

Still more persuasive as a factor pointing towards disengagement rather than combat was the reality of the situation in which the Owenites now found themselves. Although it was just possible that at some time in the future the anti-mergerites might obtain a majority in the Council for Social Democracy or among the party's membership in the country, it seemed far more probable that they would lose whenever and wherever they fought and that they could hope only, at best, to amass a blocking third in the council. Even that blocking third, were it to be obtained, would not be at all satisfactory, as it could only be used to prevent the majority from doing what the majority wanted to do—namely, merge with the Liberals. How could the anti-mergerites claim the right not to be forced into joining a party that they did not want to join, while at the same time seeking to prevent the pro-mergerites from forming the new party that they clearly wanted to form? 'Dog in the manger' would not be a comfortable position.

Faced with these finely balanced arguments, the Owenites initially resolved their dilemma by not resolving it. On the one hand, they fought to maintain their grip on the National Committee, put pressure on members of the Cowley Street staff, hurled abuse at their opponents and continued to threaten to mobilize a blocking third on the CSD. On the other hand, Owen, in particular, repeatedly reiterated that all he wanted was 'an amicable settlement', 'an amicable divorce'.[1] This inconsistency baffled and infuriated the pro-mergerites and seemed to justify David Marquand's use of the phrase 'knight in shining blackmail'. It took the Owenites several weeks to work out what they really wanted to do.

In the meantime, one rather poignant piece of business was attended to. On 26 August 1987 David Steel and David Owen met for a 'private and pleasurable' lunch in London and agreed to go their separate ways. It was the formal end of the six-year-old Liberal–SDP Alliance.[2]

The Portsmouth conference a few days later was a bitter, but also a sad, occasion. Owen's dignified speech winding up the debate on the general election campaign—'This is one general who will not blame the poor bloody infantry'—brought tears to many delegates' eyes; Roy Jenkins was warmly applauded when he said that he for one would not be a party to any attempt to deprive Owen, Cartwright and Barnes of their seats in parliament ('The memories of the last six years belong to all of us'); and Owen went so far as to shake Robert Maclennan's hand after the new leader, overcoming his habitual nervousness, issued a fervent appeal to Social Democrats to put an end to their 'midsummer madness'.[3] Everyone knew that the SDP as they had known it was dying. For much of the time, the tone was valedictory rather than angry.

But the rancour remained and frequently broke surface. When Shirley Williams, in her presidential address, urged Owen to think again about forming a new party ('We need him, but I also believe he needs us'), she was loudly heckled from the back of the hall, and at the end of her speech several Owenite members of the National Committee ostentatiously walked off the platform.[4] That evening, at the anti-mergerites' Grassroots Uprising rally, Owen's speech was frequently interrupted by pro-mergerites in the hall. One of them shouted: 'This looks like a party within a party. I feel very upset and let down by you, David.'[5] When the conference was over, Owen, no longer needing to be polite, accused his opponents of having 'chickened out' by advocating merger with the Liberals.[6] Shirley Williams—already infuriated by the Owenites' behind-the-scenes attempts to prevent her from speaking her mind as president—retorted angrily: 'I have never chickened out of anything.'[7] Almost the only moment of light relief came when John Bancroft, an Edinburgh delegate, said that he did not normally admit to being a psychiatrist but in the present situation he thought he ought to. He had come to Portsmouth with his 'family therapy emergency kit' but had discovered that what was needed was more drastic: 'mouth to mouth resuscitation'.[8]

The main thrust of the Owenites' argument at Portsmouth was that, while they respected the result of the merger ballot, they could not, as individuals, be bound by it. When hecklers at the Grassroots Uprising meeting shouted that the party had democratically voted to merge, Owen shouted back: 'It's quite clear tonight that you cannot incorporate everybody.'[9] John Cartwright said he was a member of the SDP because that was where he felt 'comfortable and at home', and no ballot, however democratic, could deprive him of that home: 'No ballot gives anybody the right to tell me which political party I should be a member of.' The anti-mergerites, he said, were 'flesh and blood human beings' and could not be coerced.[10]

For their part, pro-merger speakers insisted—sometimes to noisy barracking —that Owen and his followers should abide by the result of the ballot; and they protested at the Owenites' claim to be the real SDP even though the majority of the SDP had voted against them. Bill Rodgers derided the Owenites' position as being one of 'heads I win, tails you lose'.[11] But the mergerites' main claim—charges of sharp practice apart—was that a continuing SDP, once the majority of the old party had merged with the Liberals, simply had no future. 'It will be a very long time', Shirley Williams said, 'before some fragment of the SDP on its own, albeit led by one of the most towering people in politics [in] this generation, could hope to have a real effect on the political process.'[12] Roy Jenkins was equally forthright, dismissing the belief that a fourth party could survive under Britain's electoral system as 'an immensely dangerous fantasy'.[13] Charles Kennedy concurred: 'Under our present political arithmetic and system, the accommodation within British politics is already fully booked and there is no room at the inn for further parties.'[14]

The set-piece debate on merger exposed the precariousness of the Owenites' position in the party. Charles Kennedy moved a resolution calling for the creation of a new party 'incorporating the SDP and the Liberal party', with a constitution based on 'one member, one vote', a common set of principles, a single leader, a single democratically elected policy-making body and a national membership list. The resolution was carried easily. Then came the Owenites' turn to gauge their strength. Sally Malnik, one of the SDP's original full-time employees, moved a resolution which did not actually oppose merger but which, in line with the Owenites' call for 'an amicable divorce', suggested that, in the event of a merger taking place, the SDP's assets should be divided proportionally between the two factions and that those who wished to remain members of the SDP should be free to do so. But her motion was defeated by 228 votes to 151.

It was probably at that precise moment that Owen finally decided that, short of retiring from politics, he had no option from then on but to bypass the SDP's existing structures and to found, in effect, a new party. Both he and Cartwright at Portsmouth strongly advised their followers not to act precipitously and to await the outcome of the merger negotiations and the second membership ballot.[15] But, short of the merger negotiations collapsing, Owen must have known that it was now his turn to be on his own. A *Guardian* reporter described how the former leader received the result of the vote on Malnik's motion:

There was grief and desolation . . . yesterday as the Malnik amendment—the last hope of the anti-mergerists, though that was not how they presented it—went down by a 3–2 margin.

David Owen, who had been lurking in the dark recesses at the back of the platform all day, had come to the front to hear his party's verdict. As Shirley Williams announced it, he slowly, disconsolately, and then with a gesture of great finality, clipped his pen back into his pocket.[16]

By contrast, Maclennan, Owen's successor, was not prepared to accept that anything final had happened. On the contrary, Maclennan was now a man with a mission—and he was determined to prove to his party, to his detractors and, not least, to himself that he was capable of carrying his mission out. As Maclennan saw it, he had two main tasks in the weeks ahead. One, the easier, was to conduct the negotiations with the Liberals in such a way that his own social-democratic beliefs and those of the majority of his party were embodied in the policies and structure of a merged party. The second, much more difficult, was to be so successful in the negotiations as to convince the Owenites—including, ideally, Owen himself—that the new party would not be some soggy Liberal mishmash but would, in effect, be the old SDP writ large. Maclennan was determined to vindicate both himself and his decision to assume the party leadership. Throughout the subsequent negotiations, he found himself playing to an audience that consisted partly of himself but mainly of Owen and all those who had voted with him for Option 1. Owen, everyone knew, was a tough operator. Maclennan was anxious to prove that he was just as tough.

In his main leader's speech at Portsmouth, and in a subsequent address to parliamentary candidates, Maclennan set out in broad terms what he hoped the negotiations would achieve. He was determined to provide the new party with an acceptable 'policy stance' as well as a democratic constitution. 'We shall', he predicted, 'have far fewer problems on the shape of the constitution than in resolving questions about our policy stance.'[17] He was particularly concerned that the new party's policies should include commitments to the social market and the 'retention of a nuclear element in Britain's defence capability'.[18] Far from taking it for granted that the talks with the Liberals would go well, he hinted on several occasions that they might not. 'I shall negotiate in good faith,' he said, but added that he could not promise a favourable outcome. Moreover, any agreement that the negotiators arrived at would have to have the support of the overwhelming majority of both parties: 'Anything less than that would fail to achieve the purpose of the talks.'[19] So far as he was concerned, the purpose of the talks was to try to deliver the great majority of the SDP—in effect, a reunited party—into a merged party. Only in that way was there a chance of dissuading David Owen, even at the last moment, from setting up on his own.

The formal negotiations began in late September 1987 and lasted until mid-January 1988. In the event, they resembled a cross between the Twilight of the Gods and a Feydeau farce, with the farcical element increasingly to the fore as time went on. One Social Democrat, who had participated in all the negotiations with the Liberals since the SDP had been formed, described the ones that took place in 1987–8 as 'awful', 'all over the place', 'appalling' and 'the most dreadful we have ever had'. A Liberal called them 'toy-town negotiations'.

Ideally the negotiations would have been conducted by a small number of people—say, three or four on each side—who would have assumed that they could complete their work quickly and would have seen themselves, not as official representatives of the Liberal and Social Democratic parties, but as practical politicians carrying out a specific task in an efficient and expeditious way. David Steel was always convinced that, if the negotiations had been conducted in that way, they could have been successfully concluded within weeks. He was not alone in that belief.

That, however, was not what happened. The two negotiating teams were vast: not three or four on each side but seventeen, making a total of thirty-four negotiators altogether (in addition to the two parties' legal advisers and the secretaries, Dick Newby for the Social Democrats and Andy Ellis for the Liberals). The Liberals took the lead in electing a huge negotiating team (to satisfy all shades of party opinion and a variety of regional interests); and the Social Democrats, not to be outnumbered, were forced to follow suit.

In addition to being huge, the Liberal team was divided and essentially leaderless. Ever suspicious of the party's leadership, the Liberal activists at Harrogate had elected a team that included such practical and conciliatory figures as Tim Clement-Jones (the chairman of the party's executive), Alan Beith and Des Wilson, but also Tony Greaves, the heaviest cross that every modern Liberal leader had had to bear, and the Young Liberals' equally impassioned and assertive Rachael Pitchford.[20] Clement-Jones and the majority of the Liberal team rather liked the SDP's constitution, with its deliberative policy-making structures combined with a substantial element of one-member-one-vote democracy; but Greaves, Pitchford and others insisted on trying to retain a large role in the new party for the traditional Liberal activists, those who showed up, unelected and unannounced, at Liberal Council meetings. In the SDP team's eyes, Greaves was the Liberals' Tony Benn—just as fanatical, just as wild, just as committed to 'participationist democracy' of a fundamentally undemocratic kind.[21]

Steel was the Liberal side's nominal leader, but protracted negotiations of this kind were not his style; he attended meetings only sporadically and did not always take the trouble to brief himself properly. In practice, the Liberal team had no leader. One of its members, when asked who was in charge on his side, replied vaguely, 'That's an interesting question', adding only that Clement-Jones some-times took the initiative when the matter under discussion was one on which he felt particularly strongly. SDP negotiators felt that the absence of leadership among the Liberals was no accident. The Liberals seemed not to understand what leadership was, let alone the need for it. One SDP negotiator complained that the Liberals constantly strove for consensus among themselves; but consensus, in practice, often meant giving way to a few aggressive and outspoken individuals. According to the same person, the Liberals refused to recognize that in politics one occasionally had to have rows and that, once the row was over, it had to be seen that one side or the other had won.

The SDP negotiators were more disciplined than the Liberals and grew more so as the negotiations proceeded. Anne Sofer and Ben Stoneham, it was said, occasionally sided with the Liberals, and Shirley Williams sometimes disrupted proceedings because she appeared not to have read the papers properly; but Maclennan grew more and more anxious that the Social Democrats should present a united front and, according to one participant, was apt to 'deliver a bollocking' to anyone who stepped out of line. Maclennan remained consistent in his deter-mination to conduct the negotiations in such a way that as many as possible of the Option 1 supporters could be brought back on board. As one of his Liberal critics put it, 'He seemed determined to out-Owen Owen.' This approach irritated the Liberals and undoubtedly made the negotiations more difficult; but it also greatly strengthened the SDP's hand. The Liberals could not help having at the backs of their minds the thought that, if Maclennan was pressed *too* hard, he might suddenly abort the entire process.[22]

One feature of the talks that contributed to their farcical quality, especially towards the end, was their formality. Instead of simply sitting around a table, the two parties' teams began most sessions by meeting separately—and then, if a new issue or unexpected difficulty arose later in the session when they were together, one or other of them, usually the Liberals, would call for a time-out so that they could go away and huddle in private. At one all-day session, held at the Reform Club in London, it was alleged that the time-outs took up more time than the actual meetings. At least a dozen formal disagreements were registered on that occasion, with increasingly harassed runners dashing up and down the stairs of the Reform Club trying to keep the two sides in communication. Shirley Williams at one point had to be extricated from the gentlemen's loo, which she had blundered into while trying to find where the SDP team was caucusing. Ordinary members of the club, trying to read a newspaper or waiting for a luncheon guest, must have wondered whether they had wandered into a madhouse. It was like the original seats negotiations all over again.

The amount of time, energy and paper consumed by the whole process was prodigious. Several of the meetings, having begun early in the evening, went on till 2 o'clock in the morning. Dick Newby and Andy Ellis were reckoned to be working a hundred hours a week. As early as mid-December—well before the process was complete—John Carvel of the *Guardian* estimated that the full negotiating teams had devoted 200 hours to the discussions and that, if the meetings of the various subgroups were included, the total might even rise to 700.[23] The negotiations cannot have consumed many fewer than 6,000 man and woman hours altogether. Maclennan looked at the agenda and the pile of papers for one meeting and said he knew what the dinner arrangements were but he wondered what was being done about breakfast.[24]

The two parties' negotiators fought over almost every clause of the new party's constitution. The SDP side, fearful of the influence of an aggressive minority of activists (and mindful of their own previous experiences inside the Labour party), wanted the new party's whole membership to be balloted on major issues; some of the Liberals were insistent instead that the party conference, and not the entire membership, should be supreme. The Social Democrats wanted the conference itself to be a fairly compact body; many Liberals wanted it to resemble a mass meeting. The SDP wanted the new party to be essentially a national institution, though with regional forums; the Liberals demanded that Scotland, Wales and the English regions should not only have a good deal of autonomy within the new party's structure but should constitute its basic building blocks. The SDP reckoned that it would be enough to have the new party's conference meet twice a year; the Liberals, with their suspicion of their own leadership and their passion for 'accountability', wanted in addition a body that would meet more or less every month, along the lines of the Liberal Council.

Nevertheless, despite these differences and despite some initial wariness on both sides, the negotiations did make slow if fitful progress throughout October, November and early December; by mid-December the broad outlines of a proposed constitution were in place. With its wide range of checks and balances and its emphasis on cautious and consensual policy-making, the new constitution on the whole resembled the SDP's more than the Liberals'. The new party was to have a federal structure, with 'state' parties in England, Wales, Scotland and possibly, eventually, Northern Ireland. Constituency parties would elect members every two years to the party's conference, which would meet twice each year, once for a week in the autumn and once for a weekend in the spring. Responsibility for policy-making was divided, along SDP lines, between the conference and a specially constituted policy committee, partly elected by the conference but also comprising representatives of the parliamentary party, local government and the 'states'. A federal executive would administer the party and have the power to organize consultative ballots of the party's membership on issues deemed fundamental. The leader was to be elected by the entire membership, on the basis of the single-transferable-vote method of proportional representation. In a pre-Christmas letter to the members of the Council for Social Democracy, Maclennan maintained that the new constitution was wholly in line with the wishes expressed at the Portsmouth conference. The conference had wanted a constitution similar to that of the SDP. 'In my view,' Maclennan wrote, 'that is exactly what we have achieved.'[25]

Broad agreement on the new party's constitution, however, left three other issues unresolved: what the new party's name should be; whether specific commitments such as Britain's membership of NATO should be written into the constitution's preamble; and what form the new party's 'policy stance' should take. (Maclennan at Portsmouth had insisted that a policy stance must form an integral part of the total merger package.) In mid-December all three of these issues were still in dispute.

In September, before the negotiations even began, an unidentified Liberal hazarded the guess that 'the name of the new party might actually take us as long to agree as everything else put together'.[26] He (or she) was right. On the one hand, the Liberals (not just Greaves and Pitchford but virtually the entire Liberal team) were desperately anxious that the word 'Liberal' should figure prominently in the new party's name; Alan Beith, in particular, insisted that he had been born a Liberal and meant to die one. On the other hand, the Social Democrats were equally anxious that the words 'Social Democratic' should remain in the name. This was partly for sentimental and propagandistic reasons, but partly also to make it more difficult for the Owenites to lay claim to the Social Democratic label.

But any name that incorporated both 'Liberal' and 'Social Democratic' posed problems. 'Liberal and Social Democrats' sounded all right, but the SDP negotiators pointed out that the initials 'LSD'—the name of a hallucinatory drug—would make the party look ridiculous. 'Social and Liberal Democrats' was said to give too much prominence to the Social Democrats (and could be shortened to 'Salads', though no one seemed to notice it at the time). Other possible names—the Union of Social Democrats and Liberals, the United Liberal and Social Democratic party and the New Liberal and Social Democratic party—were far too cumbersome and would have to be accompanied by some agreed short title. The Liberals liked 'Liberal Democrats', but for obvious reasons the Social Democrats were unenthusiastic. The Social Democrats liked simply 'the Democrats', but for obvious reasons the Liberals were not enthusiastic. Some in both parties were keen on retaining 'Alliance'—after all, a quarter of the electorate had voted for the Alliance at both the 1983 and 1987 elections and the term 'Alliance' ought by now to have acquired a good deal of brand loyalty—but many on the Liberal side objected to the loss of 'Liberal' and also insisted that the merger was taking place precisely because the Alliance in its previous form had failed. The word 'Alliance', for them, had too many negative connotations.[27]

The debate dragged on for weeks, becoming increasingly heated as time went on. The Liberals at first pressed for 'Liberal Democrats'. Maclennan suggested 'Union of Social Democrats and Liberals' ('the Democrats' for short). The negotiators by early December appeared to be agreed on 'the Democrats', but Liberal protests forced them to think again, and at a meeting on 10 December they finally settled on 'New Liberal Social Democratic party' or 'Alliance' for short. It was thought that 'Alliance', being well established and familiar, would appeal to both parties' candidates; but again there were howls of protest, mainly from outraged Liberals, and the debate went on into the New Year.

Similar ructions were caused by the debate over the constitution's preamble. Led by Maclennan, the SDP negotiators were adamant that an explicit commitment to continued British membership of NATO (as well as the United Nations, the European Community and the Commonwealth) should be written in at some point. They feared that in the absence of such a commitment the strong unilateralist wing of the Liberal party would agitate endlessly on the issue and might even succeed in forcing the party to go unilateralist. Steel and most of his fellow negotiators were happy to include a reference to NATO in the preamble—they, too, were opposed to unilateralism—and the draft constitution agreed to in mid-December duly contained such a reference. But, as in the case of the new party's name, the debate was by no means over.

Whatever they disagreed about, everyone involved in the negotiations readily accepted that the constitution, including the new party's name and the preamble, were appropriate matters to be dealt with by the negotiators. It was less clear, however, how the merged party's initial policy stance should be handled. Maclennan insisted on having one, and Steel agreed (albeit somewhat reluctantly as he knew a potential source of trouble when he saw one). But both men were afraid that, if the drafting of a policy document got caught up in the full merger negotiations, the negotiations themselves might go on forever. There was also the danger that disagreements over policy, especially over defence policy, might derail the entire merger process (as they had very nearly derailed the Liberal–SDP Alliance in 1986). They therefore decided that the initial policy document would be drafted by themselves and their advisers. It would be their document and would be presented to the two teams of negotiators and their parties pretty much on a take-it-or-leave-it basis. At Maclennan's insistence, he and Steel further agreed that the policy document would be put to both parties' memberships, together with the proposed constitution, as a single package. Anyone in either the Liberals or the SDP who voted for the merger would also be voting for the document.[28]

As time went on, the issue of whether there should be an 'initial policy stance' and, if so, what it should contain became more and more identified with Maclennan personally. In late October he warned at a press conference that he would recommend his party to vote against merger unless he could negotiate a policy agreement that would secure Social Democratic values. 'I do not underestimate for one minute', he went on, 'the difficulty of getting agreement on this, nor can I underrate the importance of getting it right.'[29] He and Steel let it be known in mid-November that the two of them would in due course hold a 'mini-summit' to agree on the final terms of the document.[30]

As, however, Steel was not greatly interested in the details of policy and was apt to be out of the country, it fell largely to Maclennan to draft the document, or at least to supervise its drafting. To assist him the SDP leader recruited Hugo Dixon, a writer on the *Financial Times*, and later Andrew Gilmour, a researcher on loan from a strategic studies institute in Washington. So long as the main negotiations proceeded, the activities of the three of them attracted little attention. They were drawing up the policy statement behind the scenes, and anyway there did not seem to be any great hurry about it: it did not have to be produced until the full negotiations had been completed. Nevertheless, it was the policy document that in the end caused a massive, and nearly fatal, explosion.

The SDP's negotiators throughout this period were left mercifully free from interference by the rest of their party. Unfortunately for them, their Liberal opposite numbers were less lucky. As a result of leaks and the various press conferences that were held from time to time as the negotiations proceeded, one or more sections of the Liberal party were more or less continuously in uproar. The rebels were seldom numerous, and they appear to have represented few but themselves; but they made a great deal of noise, and they also made some of the Liberal negotiators distinctly uneasy.

The trouble began at the Harrogate assembly in September, with the election to the negotiating team of people like Greaves and Pitchford. Then in November the ever-troublesome Liberal Council, at its monthly meeting in York, tried to instruct the Liberal negotiators to renegotiate those sections of the draft constitution that dealt with the party conference, on the grounds that they unduly restricted the rank and file's influence in policy-making.[31] A few weeks later, a group of Liberal activists announced that they were placing a full-page advertisement in the *Liberal News* to protest about the negotiators' proposals for consultative membership ballots.[32] Shortly after that, in mid-December, the Liberal Council, this time meeting in Northampton, voted to reject the inclusion of a reference to NATO in the constitution's preamble and also, by a margin of more than nine to one, to reject 'the Alliance' as the new party's name.[33] The council's decisions were not binding, and Steel dismissed these last resolutions as merely 'an irritant';[34] but the Liberal activists' moves contributed to creating a general air of uncertainty.

This sense of uncertainty, which tended to grow rather than diminish as the talks went on, was reinforced by the fact that no one knew who might lead the new party if and when it was formed—or indeed at what stage its new leader would be chosen. David Steel, the obvious choice, appeared to be in two minds about whether to stand or not and resolutely refused to commit himself one way or the other. If he stood down, it was not clear who else was available. Beith seemed too dull, Ashdown too inexperienced and unpredictable ('an unguided missile') and Maclennan—by now known derisively at Westminster as 'Big Mac'—altogether too fragile and lacking in confidence.[35] On the issue of timing, Steel all along wanted any leadership contest to take place within a few weeks of the new party's being launched—as soon as the new constituency organizations were in place— but Maclennan believed that the merger would take considerably longer to become effective and wanted any election postponed until after the new party's inaugural conference.[36] This question, like so many others, had not been resolved when the merger discussions were suspended for the Christmas and New Year break.

By this time, the numerous tensions and uncertainties—over the leadership, over the new party's name, over the preamble and over the still unpublished policy document—were beginning to accumulate and tempers were starting to fray. Steel at one point described the whole negotiating process as 'exceedingly boring' and, when interviewed on television about the dissidents' *Liberal News* advertisement, was visibly annoyed.[37] The SDP negotiators, for their part, were increasingly irked by the inability of the Liberals to agree among themselves. One of them told the *Independent* in mid-December: 'The indiscipline on the Liberal side, at times, has frankly tried the patience of most of us excessively'; and John Grant, another member of the SDP team, resigned, denouncing the 'idiocy' of the Liberal Council. 'Liberals', he declared, 'are simply not ready to move from the politics of pro-test towards the politics of power.'[38] Not to be outdone, Greaves and Pitchford inti-mated that they, too, were thinking of quitting. They complained that the draft constitution in its existing form was too centralist, too inward-looking and too élitist.[39]

Whether or not the constitution was too inward-looking, the negotiators, by this time, certainly were. They took themselves more and more seriously just as the outside world—in so far as it was aware of them at all—took them less and less. A *Guardian* headline in December read: 'Allies in navel engagement'.[40] Peter Jenkins in the *Independent* wrote icily:

For a moment, at the beginning of the decade, the possibility may have existed for a realignment in the centre-left. If so, that moment has passed. The Owenite cause is a lost cause. The cause of the new Liberal and Social Democratic Party is likely to be the futile one of perennial protest. Liberal revivals have come and gone since Orpington in 1962 and will come and go till kingdom come. The fights within the Alliance are fights about nothing. The protagonists are engaged in tearing apart the stuff of a dead dream.

The headline on the article read: 'Third party's pantomime of hot air'.[41]

While the negotiations with the Liberals were proceeding, the mergerites and the Owenites continued to coexist—with difficulty—within the existing SDP. Following the Portsmouth conference, Owen was determined to maintain in being an independent party with the name 'SDP', and towards that end he established what was, in effect, a party in waiting, with its headquarters in a suite of offices in Buckingham Gate, only a few yards from Buckingham Palace. The new grouping retained for the time being the name adopted over the summer, 'Campaign for Social Democracy'. Owen himself chaired the campaign, John Cartwright was in executive charge, David Sainsbury provided the office space, and the six-person full-time staff were all recruited from Cowley Street. The campaign's principal means of propaganda comprised extensive direct mailings, a full schedule of speaking engagements by Owen and a modest newsletter-cum-newspaper. Cartwright, Mike Thomas and other CSD spokesmen made large and impressive claims about the numbers of supporters that Owen was attracting to his cause. The figures given rose from 7,000 in late November, to 10,000 a few days later, to 15,000 at the end of December, to 16,000 by mid-January.[42] Virtually no one outside Buckingham Gate believed the figures—how, for instance, did someone qualify as 'a supporter'?—but none outside was in a position to check.

Owen meanwhile, in speeches and two pamphlets published at this time, staked out his claim to the slice of political territory wedged between the extreme left of the Conservative party, on the one hand, and the extreme right of the Liberals and the old SDP, on the other. In a speech to the American Chamber of Commerce in London, he committed his new party to the Trident missile system and to the 'popular economic achievements of the Conservatives'. Turning his back on the style and policies of the Alliance, he went on: 'The SDP will not, as it rebuilds in the aftermath of the merger debate, risk ever again the charge of playing a fuddled fiddle in the muddled middle.' Thatcherism, he said, should not be a term of adoration, but neither should it be a term of abuse. The rebuilt SDP would have 'a full-blooded commitment to make the market economy succeed'. However, he attacked the Conservatives' narrow conception of capitalism: 'In their approach to health, child benefit, education and research, unemployment and the elderly, they will, unless checked, sooner or later give wealth creation a bad name.'[43] More pragmatically, he told a North London audience that he believed that he, Cartwright, Rosie Barnes and others had a better chance of holding and winning seats in parliament as members of the SDP than as members of the new merged party.[44]

The Owenites were still having some difficulty deciding whether they wanted to go on fighting within the existing SDP or whether they wanted to disengage completely; but gradually over the autumn they evolved a two-track strategy that seemed to make sense. On the one hand, the Owenite faction would not resist merger in any way; in particular, the Owenites let it be known in late November that they would not attempt to mobilize a blocking third on the Council for Social Democracy.[45] On the other hand, they would continue to participate in the affairs of the existing SDP—especially the National Committee, on which they still had a slender majority—and, in particular, they would use their position within the existing party to try to strengthen their hand against the day when they eventually left. Their situation bore a striking resemblance to that of Rodgers, Williams and Owen on the eve of their quitting the Labour party.

Initially, during the weeks following the Portsmouth conference, relations between the mergerites and the Owenites, having previously been bad, got worse. Perhaps the most unpleasant meeting of all took place at the National Committee on 21 September. The Owenites had earlier accused the mergerites of illicitly using the SDP's membership list to canvass support during the pre-Portsmouth ballot. Now they insisted that the Electoral Reform Society's investigation of the incident vindicated their claim; and towards the end of the 21 September meeting Mike Thomas, on behalf of the Owenites, moved that the party's full national membership list should be made available on equal terms to both the pro- and anti-merger forces. Access to the membership list would obviously greatly assist the Owenites either in continuing to resist merger (if that was what they decided to do) or in setting up their own party (if that was the road they finally chose to go down).

Shirley Williams, in the chair, refused to put Mike Thomas' motion, arguing that it contravened an earlier decision that the committee had taken and making the point that the use of the membership list by the two factions might contravene the Data Protection Act. Thereupon, Thomas, seemingly by prior arrangement, moved that Williams should leave the chair. His motion was, in effect, a motion of no-confidence in Shirley Williams as president of the party. When the vote was taken the result was a fourteen-all tie, and Williams was forced to use her casting vote to protect her own position. The brutality of the Owenites' attack on the party president, a founder member of the Gang of Four and one of the best-liked members of the party, staggered the mergerites. After the meeting, Bill Rodgers told the press: 'It was the ugliest meeting I have ever been to. We had two hours of the most vicious mistrust.' 'It was', he added, 'very well planned.'[46]

The atmosphere at the National Committee's next meeting a month later was little better, though on this occasion it was the mergerites who went on the attack, accusing the Owenites of organizing 'a party within a party'. Maclennan, normally reticent, startled many of those present by remarking that Owen's organization, which had 'suddenly sprung into existence in Buckingham Gate', struck him personally as being 'about as free standing as Mr Derek Hatton's Militant Tendency'.[47] Maclennan and Williams both suggested that the Owenites' activities would normally call into question their continued membership of the party, and after the meeting Williams suggested that actual expulsions could not be ruled out.[48] In an almost uncanny echo of what Tony Benn and Neil Kinnock had been saying about them six years before, Williams and Maclennan said that the honourable course for the Owenites would be either to cease building up the Campaign for Social Democracy or else to resign. It was said afterwards that Owen himself had scarcely spoken during the meeting. He had confined himself to agreeing with everything John Cartwright said.

Perhaps because both sides realized that matters were getting out of hand, or perhaps because the Owenites were becoming clearer about the course they wanted to pursue, relations from about mid-October onwards became a little less fraught, although both sides still manœuvred to place themselves in the most advantageous position for when the split finally came. Following a meeting of the National Committee at the end of November, Owen and the fourteen other committee members who intended to remain 'loyal' to Social Democracy issued a statement confirming their intention to disengage totally from the merger process:

We have no wish [the statement said] to turn the next few months into a family feud between anti-merger and pro-merger factions. We are not prepared, therefore, to block or vote against a merger at any stage.

The Campaign for Social Democracy was formed immediately after the members' ballot, not to oppose the merger, but to promote the continuation of the SDP. We are a positive force and we intend to remain so.[49]

At a subsequent press conference—attended, unusually, by both Cartwright and Williams—Cartwright said that both camps were 'beginning at last to realise that it makes no sense to scratch each other's eyes out'.[50] At the end of the year the Owenites indicated that, if the merger went ahead and did so more or less on schedule, their continuing version of the SDP would come into existence on 1 March 1988. (It would not be 'launched', however; the Owenites insisted that they were merely keeping the existing SDP alive.)

If there was still doubt about the precise timing, it was because it was still not clear whether the merger between the Liberals and the SDP was going to take place on schedule. The timetable was a tight one. The mergerites on both sides had hoped to complete the negotiations before Christmas so that there would be ample time for the members of the two parties to consider the new constitution and the total merger package before the two parties held special conferences in the New Year. The Liberals were due to meet in Blackpool on 23 January 1988, the Council for Social Democracy in Sheffield on 30–1 January. But it was clear well before Christmas that a pre-Christmas deadline for concluding the negotiations could not be met: there were too many issues still outstanding, and the policy document had still not been produced. Moreover, the two negotiating teams could not easily be got together again until parliament reassembled in January.

Even so, those who favoured merger were still confident that concrete proposals could be put to the two parties at their conferences and that full membership ballots could be held, as planned, in February. A final meeting of the negotiators was arranged for Tuesday, 12 January. The two leaders would present their policy document that same day. And then, on Wednesday, 13 January, Maclennan and Steel would triumphantly announce at a specially organized press conference in the Jubilee Room at the House of Commons that full and final merger terms had, at last, been agreed upon. Although time was short, with only ten days remaining between January and the Liberals' assembly, all those involved were quietly confident that the outcome would be favourable and that everything would go according to plan.

But at this point the whole proceeding, hitherto so solemn and portentous, finally degenerated into total farce. Parts of the script had to be rewritten. The actors quarrelled. The lights went out. And the scenery collapsed. The poor audience did not know whether to laugh or cry—or simply dismiss the whole spectacle as absurd. The episode became known as 'the dead parrot' after a bird of that description in a Monty Python sketch. It looked at one stage as though it might prevent a merger between the two parties from taking place at all.[51]

The dead parrot in question was the policy document, and the trouble to come was inherent in the way the drafting of the document was organized. Right from

425

the beginning, the party leaders insisted that the initial policy document (or 'stance' or 'prospectus') was to be *their* document. Steel seems to have agreed to a very leisurely timetable for drafting it in the belief that, if it were presented to the two parties' negotiators and his own party's policy committee at the very last moment, none of them would be in a position to object. They would have to take it or leave it—and, in the interests of allowing the merger to proceed, they would take it.

Steel was not in a hurry, and he was, notoriously, not interested in policy. He was also, as it happened, due to spend a fortnight immediately after Christmas on a charity fund-raising visit to Kenya (where he had lived for several years as a child). Steel was therefore happy to hand over the main—almost the sole—responsibility for drafting the document to Maclennan. Under the circumstances Maclennan, not unnaturally, came to see the document as *his* document; *he* would write it with the aid of his two advisers, Dixon and Gilmour. Steel's job was merely to make sure that whatever Maclennan and the others wrote was saleable to the Liberal party. Maclennan throughout assumed, again not unnaturally, that whatever Steel agreed to would also be acceptable to the Liberals. Either Steel would have con- sulted other senior Liberals to ascertain their views, or he would know his party well enough to know what it would—and would not—accept.

Maclennan seems to have become more and more emotionally engaged in the whole policy enterprise. The document was his. He was putting a lot of thought and work into it. He seems to have seen it as his unique contribution to the formation of the new party. It would give the new party a sense of direction and, with luck, a distinct ideological identity. Equally important, if the document turned out to be both radical and tough-minded, the Owenites would be prevented from dismissing the new party out of hand as a vehicle for old-fashioned woolly Liberalism. Many of those who had voted for Option 1 might even be induced to join. It was the policy document that was going to ensure that the new party really was new.

Maclennan, Dixon and Gilmour began work on their own in late November, and on 22 December Maclennan and Steel held their 'mini-summit' at Ettrick- bridge. Maclennan brought with him his two advisers. Both were in their 20s; neither was a politician. Steel had with him Alan Beith, in his role as Liberal deputy leader and chairman of the party's policy committee, and Alec McGivan, who, having been for years the SDP's national organizer, had recently been appointed political adviser to the Liberal leader (a transmogrification that he himself viewed with considerable amusement). The meeting at Ettrickbridge was meant to be only preliminary. Beith was carefully introduced to Dixon and Gilmour but claimed later that he was not clear who they were.

Because the Liberals regarded the document as being Maclennan's respons- ibility, they had given the matter little thought and did not feel it was up to them to prepare anything in advance. They were there to respond to Maclennan's initiatives. The SDP leader brought with him two papers. One was a fairly detailed draft of a possible section of the document on defence. The other was a four-page outline, consisting of headings and subheadings on such themes as 'market democracy' and 'social entitlements'. The three main features of the final document were meant to be defence, Europe and policies for the elimination of poverty. The discussion at Ettrickbridge was general. No final decisions were taken. It was agreed that Dixon and Gilmour would go away and continue their drafting under Maclennan's supervision. The Ettrickbridge meeting was the two leaders' first meeting during the drafting of this crucial document. More ominously, it was also very nearly their last.

Maclennan's two young assistants worked hard over Christmas. They enjoyed being in a position to break new policy ground. As they produced draft passages, they faxed them to Steel at Ettrickbridge and Maclennan in New Hampshire, where the SDP leader had gone to spend the holiday with his wife's family. From the United States Maclennan relayed his ideas back to Dixon and Gilmour in England. The summer's Ambre Solaire politics was now earmuff politics; Robert Harris in the *Observer* referred acidly to 'the fine old Alliance tradition of never letting anything interfere with a foreign trip'.[52] On New Year's Day Steel, on his way through London to Nairobi, left his copy of the draft material, together with a few marginal comments, with Alan Beith. Beith was supposed to take charge while he was away.

Beith's interest in the document was, at best, semi-detached. No one had ever suggested that the document was his or that he was supposed to be centrally involved in drafting it. On the contrary, the leaders had insisted it was their document; Maclennan, in particular, did not seem to want outsiders interfering. Beith's approach to the document while Steel was away was thus rather casual. He read two-thirds of a preliminary draft faxed to him on New Year's Eve, found he did not like some parts of it and conveyed his anxieties to Steel. Still in possession of only two-thirds of the draft, Beith then spent a day working on it during the first week of January, later going through his comments with Dixon over the phone. He assumed that Dixon would do the necessary redrafting and, as he was busy, asked Dixon to take the initiative in clearing the various sections of the draft with the relevant Liberal spokesmen.

Afterwards Beith's role in the whole episode was the subject of considerable controversy. Beith maintained that the responsibility was Steel's and that, even though he, Beith, was chairman of the Liberal party's policy committee, his role had been peripheral throughout; but several on the SDP side were insistent that Beith knew perfectly well what was in the document and had deliberately set a trap for Steel in order to further his own leadership ambitions.[53] One Social Democrat called it a calculated double-cross. This interpretation seems altogether too Machiavellian. It seems more probable that Beith, irritated by having the draft document suddenly dumped on him as Steel departed for Africa, responded by doing as little work on it as he felt he decently could. After all, Steel was supposed to be the wily one, the great fixer. If the document needed fixing, let *him* fix it.

The policy document produced by Maclennan, Dixon and Gilmour was indeed

radical and tough-minded. Entitled *Voices and Choices for All*, it made no concessions either to Liberal susceptibilities or to any effects it might have on public
opinion. It identified problems and, in the style of modern policy analysis, set about
providing the 'best'—that is, the most equitable and efficient—solutions to them.
Its approach was wholly consistent with Maclennan's purpose: to strike out boldly,
posing hard choices, breaking new ground.

On defence, *Voices and Choices* asserted that in a dangerous world Britain
should continue to retain and control its own nuclear weapons. In the circumstances of the 1990s, that would mean, in practice, retaining Trident. Research
and development should likewise be continued in the field of civil nuclear power.
Under the headings 'liberal democracy', 'market democracy' and 'social democracy', the document gave prominence to tax reform, to the need for 'a crusade
against poverty' and to the completion of the Single European Market. In order to
make resources available for combating poverty, *Voices and Choices*, as it emanated
from the Maclennan–Dixon–Gilmour team, proposed the extension of value added
tax (VAT) to food, children's clothing, newspapers, domestic fuel and financial
services, the rapid phasing-out of mortgage tax relief and the abolition of universal
child benefit. As well as raising additional revenue, the extension of VAT would
bring Britain's tax regime more closely in line with that of its European partners.
The document also proposed that rent controls on new lettings should be abolished
in order to encourage a revival of the private rental housing market.[54]

It was this document—written with a minimum of discussion or consultation, but with Maclennan's strong personal backing—that awaited Steel when he
returned from his Kenyan trip late on Sunday, 10 January. The next morning he
and Maclennan met to go through *Voices and Choices* in detail. Steel, still tired from
his journey, could see nothing wrong with it. On the contrary, he said he thought it
was a bold and imaginative document, and he congratulated Maclennan and his
advisers on the work they had put into it. Beith, for his part, was still unhappy
about some of the passages on defence, and Steel later agreed to a certain amount
of redrafting of that section. However, Steel at this stage appeared determined to
retain the references to extending VAT. The time for any substantial redrafting of
the document was in any case rapidly passing: the scheduled press conference in
the Jubilee Room was only forty-eight hours away. At the end of the Monday
meeting, it was agreed that—as had happened earlier in the year in connection
with the Alliance election manifesto—copies of *Voices and Choices* would be left in
the anteroom to Steel's office for Liberal MPs to peruse, if they wanted to, in the
course of the next day. So far nothing seemed amiss.

Meanwhile, the two parties' teams of negotiators were preparing to meet for
their final session, which they knew would be a long one. They were concerned
only peripherally with the policy document; but they still had to settle the name of
the new party and the preamble to the constitution as well as a whole host of more
technical matters.

The negotiations resumed on Tuesday, 12 January. As usual, the two teams met separately before coming together at 2.30 p.m. in the upstairs conference room at Cowley Street. Everyone knew it was going to be a long, hard session—probably the hardest yet—but there was a general sense of relief that it would all soon be over. The two sides quickly agreed to slog through a long series of amendments to the constitution before they tackled the big issues: NATO and the name. There were no rows at first, and early in the evening Charles Kennedy, Tony Greaves and two other negotiators retired to a pizza restaurant around the corner from Cowley Street to work on the preamble.

At about 8 o'clock, before the two-party negotiations recommenced, the Liberals met separately to try to sort out their internal disagreements. Many of the Liberals were not keen on NATO appearing in the preamble; most felt very strongly about the name. The SDP wanted Social and Liberal Democrats (Democrats for short, 'Alliance' having by this time been abandoned); the majority of Liberals wanted Liberal and Social Democrats (with, ideally, Liberal Democrats for short). After nearly an hour of increasingly heated argument, the chairman, Tim Clement-Jones, proposed a straightforward compromise: the Liberals would accept NATO if the SDP would accept Liberal and Social Democrats. By the narrowest of margins, seven votes to six, the Liberals agreed to negotiate on the basis of this compromise. However, one of the team, Michael Meadowcroft, refused on principle to accept any mention of NATO in the preamble and immediately left.

While the Liberal negotiators were having so much trouble making up their minds, the increasingly impatient SDP negotiators were waiting outside. It was getting late, they were bored, and they wanted the plenary discussions to resume. At one point, someone on the SDP side banged on the door and said that, if the Liberals could not come to a decision within five minutes, the entire SDP team would walk out. Five minutes passed with the Liberals still arguing; but eventually they reached their compromise. It was rejected by the SDP. Maclennan, despite an effort by Anne Sofer to find a middle way, pounded on the table and, 'white in the face', according to one Liberal, threatened that, if the Liberals did not accept both NATO and the SDP's preferred name within five minutes, the SDP would abandon the negotiations entirely and the merger would be off. He then rose and left the room, followed by his visibly startled SDP colleagues. One newspaper report said that, as Maclennan delivered his ultimatum, his voice was 'quivering with emotion'.[55]

The Liberals were understandably annoyed at being treated in this fashion, especially as many of them, possibly a majority, had already decided that, if need be, they would give way on the name as well as NATO. Partly to indicate their displeasure, they again allowed this new five-minute deadline to pass. But in the end they reluctantly conceded all the SDP's demands; and shortly before midnight the Liberal–SDP merger negotiations, which had lasted for fifteen weeks, finally came to an end. The Liberal team's concession on the new party's name, Social and Liberal Democrats, was, however, too much for three more of the Liberal negotiators. Tony Greaves and Rachael Pitchford had hinted before Christmas that they might resign. They now did so. They were joined by another Liberal, Peter Knowlson, someone whom the SDP had all along thought might bolt.

Many of both sides' negotiators went home that night fondly imagining that the final obstacles in the path of a merger between the two parties had at last been cleared and that, almost as a matter of routine, the negotiations' successful outcome would be announced at Maclennan's and Steel's press conference the next day.[56] They were wrong. They had reckoned without the Maclennan–Steel policy document.

The plan was for the document to be shown to the two parties' negotiators at about lunchtime on the Tuesday, with a meeting of the Liberals' policy committee to follow at 6.30 that evening. The negotiators' initial responses to it seem to have ranged all the way from the positively enthusiastic to the extremely apprehensive. On the SDP side, there was a strong disposition to trust Maclennan, and most of the negotiators skimmed through the document rather than reading it carefully. They were reassured to be told that its bolder and more radical passages had Steel's backing as well as Maclennan's. A senior member of the SDP team reported afterwards that 'people didn't recoil in horror'. One did say doubtfully, 'I can just see the headline "Tax children's clothing and food to pay for Trident"', but another described it as 'the most courageous policy document I've ever seen'. On the Liberal side, however, doubts were more widespread; Tony Greaves kept muttering 'This is terrible', and Des Wilson claimed that his 'hair stood on end'. But most of the Liberal negotiators were preoccupied with the negotiations and were anyway conscious that the full Liberal policy committee would be dealing with the matter in a few hours' time. If anything were seriously wrong, it could be put right then.

It was at the Liberals' early evening meeting of their policy committee that the trouble really began. Alan Beith, the chairman, made no attempt to defend the document, even though he had played a role in preparing it; according to some accounts, he actually opened the meeting by distancing himself from it. As the discussion proceeded, it was evident that the Liberals objected not only to specific passages on defence, civil nuclear power and the extension of VAT but also to the document's whole tone, with its Thatcherite ideas (or so it seemed to the Liberals) and its seemingly deliberate desire to provoke. It was radical but also, they thought, naïve. Baroness Sear gave it a mark of 'beta-double minus' and Des Wilson complained that it was 'a gratuitous insult' to the Liberal party.

David Steel arrived at the meeting with the discussion already well under way and was evidently taken aback by the scale of the opposition. 'Is it really that bad?', he asked somewhat plaintively. He was told firmly that it was. But the majority of the committee did not seem disposed to reject it entirely out of hand—after all, the scheduled press conference was only eighteen hours away—and Steel, Beith, Des Wilson and William Wallace were given permission to go back to Cowley Street to try to persuade Maclennan to accept substantial drafting amendments that night.

On the Liberals' return to Cowley Street, Maclennan was called out of the negotiating session and bluntly told that the policy prospectus in its existing form was unacceptable to the Liberal party. Steel informed him that it would have to be revised and that the next day's press conference had therefore to be postponed. Des Wilson warned the SDP leader that, apart from anything else, his own 'reputation as an intellectual' would be irreparably damaged if he insisted on going ahead with the document as it stood. Maclennan at first was adamant. It was his and Steel's document. They had worked on it. They had agreed on it. It could not be changed. If the Liberals would not accept it, he would publish it on his own. After a few moments, however, he gave a little ground, though not much. The next day's press conference, he insisted, would have to go ahead as planned; but once the formal negotiating session was over in a few hours' time he was prepared to stay behind and have a shot at revising the document with a view to meeting some, at least, of the Liberals' complaints.

While Steel, Maclennan and the others were haggling outside, the two parties' negotiators inside were still debating the twin issues of NATO and the new party's name. Beith apparently tried to convey to the Liberal negotiators the extent of the crisis over the policy document, but they were too tired and too preoccupied to pay much attention. Once the negotiations had been successfully completed later in the night, and the issues of NATO and the name had been resolved, most of those involved went happily if wearily home to bed.

A few, however, remained behind, to put in further work on *Voices and Choices*. Maclennan was accompanied by his personal aide, Simon Coates, and the document's two principal authors, Dixon and Gilmour. Beith and Wallace joined Steel. By 4 a.m. the group, which also included Dickson Mabon and Ian Wrigglesworth, had succeeded in making considerable changes. A new introduction made it clearer that the document was only the leaders' and that it was, of course, open to further consideration and discussion. The defence section was toned down, although the reference to Trident remained; the anti-poverty programme also remained, but the proposals to extend VAT in order to fund the programme were given significant 'green edges'. Most of those present apparently returned home in the small hours believing that the document was now much better worded and that the Liberals would accept it. The next day's press conference would therefore go ahead as planned. The final piece of the great jigsaw puzzle was now, at last, in place.

What the late-night negotiators did not know, however, was what the Wednesday morning newspapers would say. During most of Tuesday the unrevised version of *Voices and Choices* had lain in the anteroom to Steel's office, available to be consulted by any Liberal MPs who chose to do so. Apparently few, if any, did; or, if they did, they gave it no more than a cursory glance. Certainly none of them complained. But some time on the Tuesday evening, while the negotiations on the constitution were still in progress, someone leaked some of the document's more contentious passages to one of the provincial press agencies, and the next morning, the day of the scheduled press conference, Liberal MPs and activists awoke to be confronted for the first time with the details of what Maclennan and Steel were proposing—and also with the treatment that the press could be expected to give it. The *Guardian's* report, in particular, emphasized all the features of the document that were likely to be most offensive to Liberals and quoted one Liberal activist as saying that many of the ideas being advanced were 'unbelievable': 'They will cause a furore in the party.'[57]

They did. When David Steel arrived at his office on Wednesday morning, having had only a few hours' sleep and with the press conference due to be held at noon, he found that virtually the whole of the Liberal party, with Liberal members of parliament in the vanguard, was in a state of uproar. Liberal MP after MP phoned Steel's office or called in to say that *Voices and Choices* was totally unacceptable; Alan Beith threatened to resign as the party's treasury spokesman; and the Liberals' president and chairman, Adrian Slade and Tim Clement-Jones, arrived with Richard Holme to say that publication of the document must at all costs be postponed. Otherwise Clement-Jones himself would summon a meeting of the party's national executive later in the day for the sole purpose of disowning it. It did not matter in the least that most of the Liberals' responses arose out of press reports of a version of the document that had already been substantially revised. It was clear to Steel that, so far as the Liberals were concerned, any document remotely resembling *Voices and Choices* was dead. Or, more precisely, if *it* was not dead, *he* was. No explicit threats were made; nothing untoward was said. But it was beyond any doubt that Steel had lost his party's confidence on the issue and that, if he did not withdraw his signature from the document at once, his leadership of the party would be at an end—probably within hours.

Confronted with this unpleasant situation, Steel called Maclennan shortly after 11 a.m., with the press conference now less than an hour away. 'I've got a major problem,' he told him over the phone. 'I'd rather tell you face to face.' Until that moment, Maclennan had apparently no inkling that anything serious was amiss. According to one Liberal, he arrived at Steel's office ten minutes later 'looking rather chipper'. He appeared to be under the impression that Steel's major problem concerned nothing more than the precise line the two of them should take at the impending press conference.

If so, he was immediately disabused. By the time he arrived, virtually the entire Liberal establishment—and an increasing proportion of the Social Democrats'—was milling around Steel's office and the anteroom outside. Steel, Alec McGivan and Alan Beith were all there. So were Slade, Clement-Jones and Holme, who had stayed on after their meeting with Steel. The SDP's Tom McNally at this point happened to drop in to see Steel about an unrelated matter. Sizing up the situation, McNally at once rang Charles Kennedy and told him, too, to come round to Steel's office at once: there were '*big* problems'.

Everyone present that gloomy January morning agrees that Steel was 'absolutely shattered'. He had worked towards a realignment of the centre-left in British politics for more than a decade. He had taken the initiative after the general election in calling for a merger between the Liberals and the SDP. As recently as

4 o'clock that morning he had believed—or at least had had good grounds for hoping—that the revised version of *Voices and Choices* would be acceptable to his party. But, with scarcely half an hour left before the press conference, it now seemed that the merger might not go ahead after all. He had been totally repudiated by his colleagues, and his very leadership was under threat. More than that, he had (as he must have known) been made to look a complete fool. Much of his reputation was founded on his being a consummate political operator. It appeared that over *Voices and Choices* his much vaunted skills had deserted him. He was supposed to be a magician, and he had lost his magic.

The newcomers who joined the growing crowd in and around the Liberal leader's office were amazed by the spectacle. Everyone in the suite of rooms looked, according to one late-comer, 'absolutely ashen-faced, sandbagged'. Steel's secretaries were in tears. Beith, looking 'awfully depressed', was heard to say, 'David's in real trouble—and he knows it.' But no one was more completely shattered, as the bad news was broken to him, than Maclennan. Bringing about the Liberal–SDP merger and gaining acceptance of his 'initial policy stance' were the most important things Maclennan had ever undertaken, and now both were threatened —for reasons that he may not initially have understood. Like Steel, Maclennan must have known that, almost no matter what now happened, he too would look a fool. In political and journalistic circles, the view was widely held that Maclennan, however honest, was out of his depths as a party leader. Now the failure of his plans—if they did fail—would prove that his severest critics had been right all along.

As soon as Maclennan appeared, Steel came to the point. The Liberals would not accept the policy document. The merger was in mortal danger. Even at this last minute, the press conference *must* be postponed. 'The document', Steel said, 'has been rejected by my colleagues. I can't deliver my party.' But Maclennan, angry as well as badly shaken, refused to budge. 'Come on,' he told Steel, 'be a leader. You've got to be tough.' Maclennan refused absolutely to consider postponing the press conference, saying that, if it was postponed, he would have no choice but to abandon the negotiations and call off the whole merger deal. He even considered going to the press conference and launching the document by himself. He was tempted to say to the assembled journalists: 'You have the document before you. It has been agreed by the two leaders. But Mr Steel seems to have been delayed.'

After a few minutes of polite but increasingly passionate argument, with both men refusing to budge from their positions, Steel took the initiative. Shooing everyone else out of his inner office, he spent ten minutes alone with his SDP opposite number. The position, as Steel saw it, was stark. He, Steel, had lost the support of his party. If he went to the press conference with Maclennan and tried to introduce the policy document as though nothing had happened, he would be forced to resign as party leader, probably by 10 o'clock that night. If Maclennan wanted to hold the press conference by himself, then so be it: there was nothing Steel could do to stop him, but, equally, there would then be no way in which

Maclennan could put the pieces of the shattered deal back together again. If Maclennan did insist on going it alone, they would both face a major catastrophe, not just for themselves but for the cause of progressive politics. If, however, Maclennan would agree to postpone the press conference, then they might possibly be able, even now, to patch something up. At first Maclennan protested that there could be no merger between the parties without the document. But in the end he gave way. The force of Steel's logic was too great. No one who was not present that morning in Steel's office knows precisely what was said; but when the two men emerged Maclennan looked as though he had been crying and both men, according to one witness, were 'as white as corpses'.

No one as yet had the faintest idea what the next positive steps should be; but it was agreed that the press conference should be postponed till 5 o'clock that afternoon and that in the meantime Maclennan and Charles Kennedy would meet the Liberal MPs. McGivan and Maclennan's aide, Simon Coates, raced through the corridors from Steel's office to the Jubilee Room to announce the postponement of the press conference and to try to prevent the by-now highly embarrassing policy document from being circulated to reporters. But they were too late. With their customary efficiency, Dick Newby, the SDP's secretary, and Sarah Holmes, a press aide, had already handed out some fifty copies of the revised statement. Newby was in the midst of telling Peter Riddell of the *Financial Times* how well it was all going when McGivan and Coates, both out of breath, burst into the room. To the assembled journalists' (and Newby's and Holmes') astonishment, McGivan announced that both the launch of the document and the press conference were being postponed 'pending further consultations with party colleagues'.[58]

Postponing the press conference for a few hours was one thing; deciding what to do about the now-endangered merger was quite another. Amidst the pandemonium in Steel's office—almost none of those who had been present earlier in the morning had left, and McGivan and Coates soon returned—no one had any idea what the new game plan should be. Maclennan was still insistent on his document. The Liberals were adamant in opposing it. There was only one point on which all seemed agreed: that the merger process must, somehow or other, be carried forward. After all that they had already accomplished, no one was prepared to contemplate turning back.

The Liberal parliamentary party and the two pro-merger SDP MPs, Maclennan and Kennedy, met in Committee Room Six in an upstairs corridor at the House of Commons at 1 o'clock. What followed has variously been described by those present as 'shocking', 'harrowing' and 'deeply embarrassing'. The SDP leader, pale and trembling, rose to speak but could not get his words out. He began to sob, tears streaming down his cheeks. Unable to compose himself, he made to leave, but Liberal MPs restrained him, pointing out that, if he did leave, he would have to run a gauntlet of reporters waiting outside. Simon Hughes, the victor of Bermondsey, put a consoling arm around his shoulders. Eventually Charles Kennedy led him over to a window, and, with their backs to the others, the two men talked in low voices for nearly twenty minutes. The other people in the room affected to continue their deliberations.[59]

It was now the Liberal MPs' turn to be seriously shaken. There had been something more than a little cavalier about their off-hand, instantaneous dismissal of the two leaders' document. Now, from what they had heard of the press conference fiasco and from what they could see of Maclennan's and Steel's state, they seemed to wake up to the enormity of what they had done. The stakes were much higher than they had realized: not only were Maclennan and Steel both seriously damaged, but the merger, which all of them wanted, might actually fall apart. In some cases their own seat in parliament suddenly seemed vulnerable. Several of the MPs, including Simon Hughes, tried to insist that the policy document could be salvaged, and Hughes set about redrafting it then and there; but time was running out, and both Steel and Maclennan left well in advance of the reconvened press conference. Steel's wife, Judy, flew down from Scotland to be with her beleaguered husband. His daughter, Catriona, joined him at the House of Commons for tea.

At the press conference there seemed to be nothing that could be said apart from giving some account, however lame, of what had taken place. The two leaders had drawn up the policy document and agreed on it; the Liberal party had rejected it; it was not clear what was going to happen next. As the two leaders answered reporters' questions, the chastened ranks of the entire Liberal parliamentary party stood behind them in support. Maclennan, shaken but still stubborn, continued to insist on *Voices and Choices*. 'The document is here,' he said. 'It's been published and these are our views. We are not unsaying them. We have no intention of unsaying them.' When a journalist asked the Liberal MPs whether any of them supported the document, Maclennan intervened to say, with strained humour: 'They will not be allowed to open their mouths.' Asked whether he was prepared to contemplate any changes to the document, he gave only a little ground, saying that he would not reply 'no' because that would give the impression that he was not prepared to listen.

Steel summed up the situation. Asked whether the rejection of the document meant that the whole merger deal was now off, Steel replied: 'No, it doesn't mean it's all off; it means that we do not see a way forward at the moment. But give people three or four days, give people some sleep and there may be a way forward.'[60] The Liberal executive confirmed that night that, despite the document, it still wanted a merger between the two parties to take place.

Only one person could now decide whether the merger would indeed take place and whether there actually was a way forward. That person was Maclennan. On the one hand, his personal commitment to *Voices and Choices* was unwavering; it was his document and he believed in it. On the other hand, if he continued to insist defiantly on 'the document, the whole document and nothing but the document', then the merger would not proceed and he would be—and be seen to be—the sole author of an extraordinary débâcle, one that would set back the cause of centre-party politics for years, perhaps decades. The pressure on the Wednesday night and the Thursday morning was on Maclennan and on no one else. If he did not shift his position, the whole carefully constructed merger edifice would collapse into rubble.

Overnight Maclennan spoke to several of the SDP negotiators, and he must gradually have recognized the impossibility of his position, because, by the time he bumped into the Liberals' Des Wilson in the make-up room at TV-am the next morning, he had softened his line considerably. He was, he told Wilson, 'not inflexible'. Wilson put it to him that a new, much shorter policy document could be drafted, based on the 1987 Alliance election manifesto, *The Time has Come*, and also on *Voices and Choices*. In that way, Maclennan's document would at least inform the thinking that went into the new document. Maclennan seemed taken with the idea, and Wilson, to keep up the pressure, leaked the fact that a deal along these lines might be in the offing to Chris Moncrieff of the Press Association. That same day, Thursday, 14 January, SDP headquarters was inundated with phone calls from perplexed and irate SDP supporters, many of them complaining, like the Liberals, about the contents of *Voices and Choices*, others insisting that the merger itself was far more important than any mere policy document.[61]

Maclennan's climb-down, when it came, was total. On the afternoon of the 14th he and Steel issued a joint statement in which they formally withdrew *Voices and Choices for All* and announced that they had established a new six-member team to draft a shorter policy statement which would be put to the two parties' teams of negotiators on the following Monday. If the negotiators gave the new statement their approval, it would be put to the special Liberal and SDP merger conferences over the two following weekends. The new policy statement's starting-point would be 'the wide range of policies evolved by the two parties over the last few years'. Maclennan and Steel noted ruefully:

We accept that some of the thought-provoking ideas we raised in our joint paper are not suitable for the initial policy stance of the new party, but are happy to accept the suggestion of colleagues that they will, more appropriately, be put into the democratic policy-making process of the new party, together with the ideas of others.[62]

The leaders' new six-member team was easily agreed upon and consisted solely of experienced politicians, people who knew what needed to be done. The Liberals were represented by Des Wilson, Jim Wallace and Alan Leaman, vice-chairman of the party's policy committee, the SDP by Tom McNally, David Marquand and Edmund Dell, who had served for a time in the last Labour cabinet. Working mainly on the basis of the 1987 election manifesto, the six had little difficulty over the next three days in drafting a new document, one considerably shorter than *Voices and Choices*. The new document dropped all of its predecessor's proposals which had caused the Liberals such offence—introducing means-tested child benefit, abolishing the married man's tax allowance and extending VAT to children's clothing—and, with regard to the two other most contentious issues, Trident and the future of civil nuclear power, left the final decisions to be taken by the new party under its own policy-making procedures. In view of the fiasco over

Source: *Independent*, 21 January 1988

'*This parrot is definitely deceased. It has passed away. It has ceased to be.*
It is no more. It's a stiff. He's snuffed it, bereft of life, indubitably extinct.
This is an ex-parrot!' (Monty Python)

Voices and Choices, the Liberal MPs, in particular, made sure that they read the new version extremely carefully; but they could find little fault with it, and it was accepted with alacrity, and more or less unanimously, by both the Liberal parliamentary party and the two negotiating teams. A much-relieved David Steel commended the new document as 'sound and sensible'. Shirley Williams for the SDP said simply, 'I'm happy.'[63]

The Owenites meanwhile had been beholding the *Voices and Choices* débâcle with a joy that was unconfined. The Maclennan–Steel shambles appeared to confirm everything they had come to believe about Maclennan's ineptitude and also about the Liberals' unreliability. The whole episode also seemed certain to get the merged party off to the worst possible start—a substantial bonus for Owen's continuing SDP. On the Wednesday, as the scheduled launch of *Voices and Choices* first descended into chaos and then was cancelled, Owen himself sat ostentatiously in the chamber of the House of Commons reading the offending document and smiling from ear to ear. The following day, as he left for a meeting in Edinburgh, he tried, but largely failed, to conceal his jubilation. 'I must look sombre,' he muttered half-jokingly to aides: 'I don't want to be photographed grinning.'[64] He reiterated that there was still a home in his new Campaign for Social Democracy for anyone in the SDP who, even at this late stage, wanted to reject the merger; and John Cartwright a few days later declared that the chaos over *Voices and Choices* had led to an 'avalanche' of SDP members wanting to register their support for the anti-merger campaign.[65]

At about this time there occurred one of the oddest incidents in what had, all along, been a thoroughly odd episode. Even at the last moment, Maclennan was still not absolutely convinced that the merger should go ahead—'My head was at war with my heart'—and at the same time he was determined that, if it did go ahead, every effort should be made, despite everything Owen had said and done, to persuade Owen that the merged party was not in fact a sell-out to the Liberals and was worth joining. Failing that, Maclennan wanted to demonstrate to the media and to the SDP's rank and file, including those still loyal to Owen, that he had done everything that anyone could possibly do to keep Owen on board.

Accordingly, on Monday, 18 January, as the two teams of negotiators were preparing to approve the successor to *Voices and Choices*, he initiated a series of telephone calls to John Grant, who had resigned a few weeks earlier as one of the SDP's negotiators but was not adamantly opposed to merger and had remained close to Owen. Maclennan wanted to keep his options open. If he decided at the last minute to reject the merger, he wanted to be in a position to try to persuade Owen to join him in mounting a 'no' campaign (rather than a 'divorce' campaign) within the SDP. If, on the other hand, he decided (as was probable) to go ahead with the merger, he wanted to be in a position to be seen to be making a last-minute appeal to Owen. Either way, it was important to find out where Owen was and to open up the possibility of a meeting with him.

It was on this basis that Maclennan phoned Grant. He was, however, deliberately vague about his intentions—because, as yet, he did not know for sure what they were. Perfectly naturally, Grant took him to be saying that he was now inclined to reject merger and to urge a 'no' vote on the party's members and that he wanted to find out whether Owen might still be prepared to join him in an anti-merger 'no' campaign. Grant accordingly made urgent attempts to reach Owen, finally succeeding only late in the evening after Owen had returned from a trip to Paris.[66] Owen at this point made it clear that, while he was more than ready to welcome Maclennan back as a member of the continuing SDP, he was not ready to join him in voting 'no' and opposing merger, if that was what Maclennan intended. Owen was more convinced than ever that, whichever side Maclennan was on, 'amicable divorce' was the only way forward.

By this time—at about 8 p.m. on the evening of the 18th—Owen was convinced, or at least half-convinced, on the basis of his conversations with Grant, that Maclennan was about to turn his back on the whole merger enterprise. He was also expecting, or at least half-expecting, to receive a call from Maclennan announcing that, so far as he was concerned, the deal between the two parties was off. Maclennan was meanwhile concluding, however, that the merger deal was in fact acceptable, possibly partly because Owen, through Grant, had made it so clear that he still wanted a divorce and was still not prepared to do anything to keep the existing party together.[67] Shortly after his last telephone conversation with Grant, at about 8.30 p.m., Maclennan and his SDP colleagues finally shook hands with the Liberals and the deal was done.

438

At this point the SDP leader, seemingly on the spur of the moment, phoned Owen at home and said, 'I want to see you—urgently, ideally now.' Owen at once agreed, evidently imagining that, as Grant had told him, Maclennan was on the point of rejecting the merger. But then, a few moments after the call came through, Maclennan emerged on the steps of the SDP's Cowley Street headquarters to announce that he and his colleagues had actually accepted the new document and that he was on his way to Limehouse in an eleventh-hour bid to win over Owen. The scene was broadcast on the BBC's *Nine O'clock News*, and Owen, sitting at home watching, was livid: he concluded that Maclennan was simply trying to exploit him in some pro-merger publicity stunt. When Maclennan eventually arrived at Owen's house in Narrow Street at about 9.30 p.m., he received a frosty reception. Maclennan put in his plea; Owen rejected it; after about ten minutes Maclennan left. Owen publicly registered his displeasure; but Maclennan's post-bag made him feel that, on balance, the trip had been worthwhile.

Once the two parties had agreed on the new policy document, the rest was anticlimax. Despite the efforts of a vociferous anti-merger minority in the Liberal party, led by Tony Greaves and Michael Meadowcroft, the special Liberal assembly in Blackpool on 23 January 1988 voted by an overwhelming majority—2,099 votes to 385—to approve the merger, thereby bringing to an end the Liberal party's long and distinguished history as a fully independent organization. David Steel paid tribute to the Social Democrats' 'freshness of approach' and the 'strength of their ideals'. 'The assets of the two parties taken together', he maintained, 'will provide the basis for a truly formidable force.'[68] Asked a few weeks later why, after all the fuss of the negotiations, the merger at Blackpool had gone 'like cream down a cat's throat', Steel laughed and replied: 'Because the cat was petrified.' A ballot of the party's rank-and-file membership subsequently confirmed the assembly's decision, though on a relatively low turn-out.[69]

Predictably, the SDP's Sheffield conference a week later was more fractious. The new SDP leadership tried to prevent the Owenite faction from using the main conference hall for a Saturday night rally and only backed down when the Owenites began court proceedings to take out an injunction. Shirley Williams from her presidential chair accused Owen of impetuosity and quoted Robert Browning's 'The Lost Leader': 'Never glad confident morning again.' Owen at his rally warned that the merged party would either have to reach an accommodation with the continuing SDP or else face the certainty of an electoral confrontation: 'No one should doubt our resolve or our commitment.'[70] Apart from appearing at his own rally, Owen refused to speak at the Sheffield conference, instead stalking the tea rooms and corridors 'like', as someone put it, 'a spectre at a feast'. He wanted to be seen to be at the proceedings but in no way part of them.

The Owenites, having had such difficulty in deciding what their line at any merger conference should be, nevertheless did succeed at Sheffield in acting more or less in unison. When the vote was finally called at about midday on the Sunday, almost all the Owenites present abstained, others having deliberately stayed away.

Partly as a result, the merger motion was carried overwhelmingly, by 273 votes to 28, with 47 registered abstentions. Merger supporters chanted 'Easy, easy' as the result was announced, and Williams and Maclennan insisted afterwards that the vote represented an overwhelming endorsement of their merger policy. But the Owenites, for their part, claimed that only 57 per cent of those eligible to vote at the conference had supported merger and continued to insist that, if they had wanted to, they could have mustered the necessary blocking third.[71]

In the subsequent ballot of the SDP's membership, held to coincide with the Liberals' ballot, merger was approved by 18,722 votes to 9,929, but, as in the case of the Liberals, on a low turn-out. The low turn-out and the actual result—only 35.9 per cent of the SDP's membership finally voted for merger—were a measure of the party's collective deflation, disillusionment and alienation from the leadership.[72] So much hope; so little to show for it; such total chaos. Whatever else it was, support for merger with the Liberals among the SDP's rank and file was neither overwhelming nor enthusiastic. Clearly many in the SDP, including many who actually voted for merger, were in a state of deep mourning for their old party.

The name 'SDP' continued to be used, however. David Owen launched his new party with the same name shortly after the final merger vote. It fought the Kensington by-election in July 1988, winning only 5.0 per cent of the vote, and the Epping Forest by-election in the following December, winning only 12.2 per cent. The merged Social and Liberal Democrats also did badly, if not quite so badly, on both occasions. But a few weeks later, in February 1989, Owen's party secured its one partial success, winning 32.2 per cent of the vote in a by-election in Richmond in Yorkshire. Although the Conservatives won, the 'SDP' succeeded in driving the Social and Liberal Democrats into third place. The partial Richmond dawn turned out, however, to be a false one, and during the remainder of 1989 the Owenites were badly beaten in all the by-elections they fought, and they seldom rose above about 4 per cent in the opinion polls.

The end of the continuing SDP finally came in May 1990. In a routine by-election in the safe Labour seat of Bootle in Lancashire, the Owenite candidate, Jack Holmes, finished seventh in a field of eight candidates. He secured a risible 155 votes compared with the 418 cast for Lord David Sutch, campaigning on behalf of the Monster Raving Loony Cavern Rock Party. A few days later Owen and his colleagues, humiliated, announced that the continuing SDP was being wound up. It was perhaps appropriate that what one journalist had dubbed 'the Monster Raving Ego Party' should in the end have been destroyed by the Monster Raving Loony Party.

22
• • • •

Who Was to Blame?

One thing was clear by the time the Liberals and Social Democrats finally merged in March 1988 and became still clearer during the ensuing years. Whatever else the debate over merger and the subsequent negotiations had done, they had inflicted substantial damage on the cause of British centre-party politics. The farce of the dead parrot was merely the final episode in a process that had already gone badly wrong.

The opinion polls between 1988 and 1992, culminating in the results of the 1992 general election, tell the story. During the whole of the 1983 parliament, when David Owen was leader of the SDP, the average standing of the Liberal–SDP Alliance in the Gallup Poll was no less than 26.9 per cent. Between March 1988 and the time of the 1992 election the merged party's average standing, according to Gallup, was a mere 11.7 per cent, less than half of what it had been before. Similarly, the Liberal–SDP Alliance at the 1987 general election, led by David Owen and David Steel, won 22.6 per cent of the popular vote and twenty-two seats in the House of Commons. At the 1992 general election the merged party—by now known as the Liberal Democrats and led by Paddy Ashdown—won only 17.8 per cent of the popular vote and twenty seats. The Liberals on their own would almost certainly have done as well.

In other words, the merger was a failure in its own terms. Its undoubted gains in bureaucratic efficiency were more than offset by the enormous political costs inflicted by the process of bringing the merger about. Instead of being a bold step forward, the merger, when it finally came, turned out to be a substantial step backward. The last two chapters have told the story of the events of 1987–8. In this chapter we try to make sense of what went wrong. Who or what was to blame?

Part of the blame undoubtedly attaches more or less equally to both the mergerites and their opponents. The summer of 1987, following the general-election defeat, called for a period of quiet reflection, a period in which the lessons of the election (and of the previous six years) were mulled over calmly and in which

441

nothing was said or done in haste. Instead, David Owen insisted on putting down his marker within hours of the polls closing, and two days later David Steel was to be seen in his garden coolly composing a memo advocating merger, which he must have known would infuriate his SDP opposite number. Owen made no attempt whatever to get in touch with Steel; Steel made only half-hearted attempts to get in touch with Owen. Both men seemed to operate on the principle: better to row in public than to talk in private—and their example was immediately taken up by most of their followers.

The subsequent lack of self-restraint on both sides was astonishing (and deeply damaging to the causes of both Liberalism and Social Democracy). The reasons for it are easy to understand and even to sympathize with: the mergerites by 1987 believed that Owen was someone with whom no one could co-operate, and Owen was similarly convinced that the mergerites were trying to take his party— his pride and joy—away from him. But the more strongly the two sides felt, the more they should have tried to restrain themselves from expressing their feelings in public. Like the civil war in the Labour party in the early 1980s, that in the SDP in 1987–8 was fought out without the benefit of any kind of Geneva Convention or even of occasional truces. The senior figures in the party more and more resembled frustrated politicians in a small country's government-in-exile arguing over whether their country should be a monarchy or a republic. The more they argued, the less the chances of their actually returning to their homeland became.

So much blame attaches to both sides. But the mergerites and the anti-mergerites both contributed their own special mistakes and miscalculations. Both acted before they thought. Both seemed to act almost entirely on instinct and impulse.

The mergerites made six principal errors. The first was greatly to exaggerate the importance—and therefore the desirability—of creating a single party under a single leader. On balance, and other things being equal, merger was probably a good idea. It would save administrative costs; it would save endless haggling over which party should fight which seat; it would avoid needless duplication of effort over party policy-making; and it might, with luck, enable the united party, as David Steel hoped, to present a somewhat clearer image to the electorate.

All these benefits were worth having; but they were not enormous benefits, and they were worth having only on condition that the price was right. Contrary to what the mergerites repeatedly claimed, there was, as we saw in Chapter 19, no really hard evidence that large numbers of voters had been put off voting for the Alliance by the fact that it consisted of two parties with two leaders; the Owenites could claim equally plausibly that some voters, at least, were positively attracted to the Alliance by the different appeals of its two constituent parts—and, furthermore, that many voters quite liked the spectacle of two separate parties co-operating instead of competing. After all, the Alliance in both 1983 and 1987 had won the support of a quarter of the electorate—much the best third-party performances for more than half a century. Five years later, in 1992, a single party under a single leader did not do nearly so well. Certainly, the Liberal Democrats' indifferent performance in the 1992 election could be attributed in part to the reinvigoration of the Labour party and the rows surrounding the merger; but it also suggested that the mergerites had pitched their claims for the benefits of merger far too high—and the possible costs of achieving merger far too low.

The mergerites, in addition, exaggerated the extent to which creating a single party would, in and of itself, eliminate the political and policy differences that had bedevilled the old Alliance. The mergerites somehow seemed to imagine that creating a single party would automatically create a united party. But the experience of the Labour party in the 1970s and 1980s—and the experience of the Liberal party at Eastbourne in 1986—should have suggested that this was not necessarily so. Even if David Owen had agreed to participate in a merged party, it is hard to believe that that party would not have been just as internally divided as the old Alliance had latterly become.

The mergerites' second principal mistake was greatly to underestimate the degree of loyalty to the SDP both as a symbol and as a cause. The founding of the SDP in 1981 drew into politics tens of thousands of 'political virgins', people who were interested in politics but had never before been actively involved. Also attracted were thousands of disillusioned ex-Labour supporters. What the great majority of these people had in common was a desire to create and to sustain something entirely new. The SDP *was* new; and it was *theirs*. They identified with it, not with anything else; and they certainly did not identify, in the great majority of cases, with the Liberal party. If they had originally been attracted to the Liberals, they could easily have joined them. But they had not. The mergerites sought to portray merger as an act of creation; but, as the result of the first merger ballot in 1987 made clear, many in the SDP saw it, rather, as an act of destruction. Even many of those who finally voted for merger did so with a heavy heart.

The mergerites' third mistake was of a piece with their second: they under-estimated the degree of loyalty inside the party to David Owen personally. The leading mergerites—Jenkins, Rodgers, Williams and Steel—knew Owen well and had worked with him—or, rather, had tried to work with him—for years. They thought he was impossible. So far as they were concerned, one of the principal aims of the entire merger exercise by the summer of 1987 was either to tie him down or else to get rid of him. Owen, in their eyes, was a large part of the problem.

But that was not the way the majority of rank-and-file SDP members saw him. They had not been personally slighted or insulted by Owen; they had not themselves experienced his irascibility and his insistence on always getting his own way. At most, they had seen occasional references in the newspapers to his strained relations with his senior colleagues. The Owen whom most SDP members knew was the Owen who appeared on television, who played a prominent role in the House of Commons and who spoke so authoritatively at SDP conferences and meetings. The Owen whom they saw was dogged, intelligent and almost absurdly brave. He had kept the SDP alive after 1983. For many of them by 1987 Owen *was* the SDP. If, therefore, he opposed merger, as he vehemently did, many rank-and-file party members were certain to take his opposition seriously and to be swayed by it. If, furthermore, he announced, as he did, that he would play no part in any merged party, the doubts in the minds of many party members about the wisdom of a merger were still further reinforced. Loyalty to Owen might be misguided; it might be sentimental. But it existed, and the mergerites were wrong not to give it sufficient weight in their calculations.

The mergerites' fourth main mistake was the one that Robert Maclennan had warned Roy Jenkins about: they grossly underestimated both the probability that Owen would damage the merger process and also the amount of damage that he could cause. It did occur to them that he would oppose merger (indeed his anti-merger comments on the day after the general election had provoked David Steel's pro-merger memorandum); but it never occurred to them that he would carry his opposition to the lengths that he did (including contemptuously slagging off his former Liberal allies), and it certainly never occurred to them that, if defeated inside the SDP, he would not only remain active in politics but would go off and set up his own party.

Yet all these actions were wholly in character—and Steel and the rest of the old Gang of Four claimed by this time to be close students of his character. It is hard to escape the conclusion that his former colleagues had by now ceased to care what Owen said or did; they were so fed up with him that they could no longer bring themselves to think rationally about him and to factor his probable future behaviour into their present calculations. They said they wanted to keep him on board; but, Shirley Williams and Robert Maclennan apart, they took no practical steps towards that end. But the consequence of creating a merged party without Owen, given Owen's national standing and the fact that he was the only one of the Gang of Four left in the House of Commons, was to create a party that was, at least in the short term, considerably weaker than the old Alliance had been. And, in the event, Owen not only absented himself from the new party but for a time actively opposed it. The mergerites should have seen and accepted that, whether they liked it or not, Owen had an effective veto on the success of their venture, a veto that he was not only capable of imposing but was very likely to impose. For their lack of foresight, they—and centre-party politics—paid a heavy price.

The mergerites' fifth mistake was an understandable one and stemmed from the fact that most of the leading mergerites were politicians operating in London rather than at grass roots. In so far as Jenkins in Hillhead, Rodgers in Milton Keynes and Williams in Cambridge had grass-roots connections, they were with local Social Democratic parties that had excellent fraternal relations with the Liberals. The trouble with this kind of close relationship was that it provoked in the mergerites the question 'Why should we *not* merge?' whereas it could equally plausibly have led to the question 'If our relations with the Liberals on the ground are so good, why should we *bother* to merge?' The quality-of-local-relations argument cut both ways. As was pointed out at the time, there was in fact scarcely any relationship between how well local SDP area parties and local Liberal associations got on and local SDP enthusiasm, or the lack of it, for merger.

The mergerites' sixth and final mistake was equally important but was of a different order. The mergerites believed in the principle of 'one member, one vote'; but they neglected to notice a crucial difference between most votes based on this principle and the ballots on merger that took place in 1987 and 1988. Most ballots—whether in general elections or elections in the local cricket club—do not require the great majority of those who participate in them to do or to become anything. The person who votes in a general election casts his or her ballot, watches the results on television (or not, as the case may be) and then goes to bed. The result of the election may be pleasing or disappointing; but it does not require the voter to *do* anything.

But the ballots on whether or not to merge the Liberals and the SDP were of a different character. The members of the two parties were being asked, in effect, whether they wanted to change their 'citizenship'—to cease to be members of one political party and to become members of another. The results of the ballots were intended to have, and were bound to have, a significant effect on the lives of the members of both parties, an effect made greater by the fact that almost all the members of the two parties were politically interested citizens who had elected, voluntarily, to take up membership in one party or the other—and in one party *rather than* the other. Their political participation was active and deliberate. It was not passive or casual.

The unusual circumstances of the merger ballots thus greatly increased the stakes. If the results went against merger, nothing happened; but, if they went in favour, every member of the two parties had to make an individual decision about whether or not to transfer his or her membership—or to permit his or her membership to be transferred—to the new party. And there was no way of coercing or cajoling anyone who refused to agree to the transfer. Some were bound to decline, thus weakening from the outset the new party's strength, and among those who did decline would almost certainly be a significant number of the former parties' most committed members, people who would be losing not only their former party but also their standing and their offices within it. The stakes being thus high, the resistances to merger were bound to be great. The mergerites seem simply to have assumed that, if a democratic ballot produced a majority in favour of merger, virtually all the members of the SDP, including those who had voted against merger, would almost automatically wheel about and—in obedience to the one-member-one-vote principle—join the new party. In this they were profoundly, and predictably, mistaken.

To repeat: the mergerites exaggerated the benefits of merger and miscalculated the costs of bringing a merger about. Or, rather, they did not miscalculate: they did not calculate at all: they simply plunged in. The mergerites found themselves at point A, with, as they saw it, an unsatisfactory Alliance. They wished to reach point B, with a 'democratic fusion' between the two parties. And they spent almost no time, if any, thinking through the political logic of how they might get from A to B. It was not an impressive performance.

But, if the foolishness and lack of foresight of the mergerites were considerable, that of the Owenites bordered on the transcendental. Many of those closest to Owen attributed to him almost God-like qualities of farsightedness, vision and strategic grasp. They saw him as, in effect, a supremely gifted military commander. In fact, he was nothing of the sort. He was an incompetent. If there was a shell-crater full of water anywhere on the battlefield, Owen unerringly led his dwindling band of troops directly into it. No wonder that in the end they all drowned.

One of Owen's problems by the summer of 1987 was that he had largely cut himself off from his former colleagues, people with independent political standing and weight. Steel, Jenkins, Rodgers and Williams had gone. So had Charles Kennedy. Robert Maclennan was about to go, and so was Ian Wrigglesworth, one of Owen's closest collaborators throughout the 1983 parliament. John Cartwright could still be counted on to give him disinterested advice, but his advice was that of a loyal lieutenant rather than a genuine equal. For the rest, Owen's associates—his increasingly isolated inner circle—consisted almost entirely of non-politicians—people like Debbie, his wife, David Sainsbury, the supermarket tycoon, and Eric Woolfson, another financial contributor to the Owenite cause—or else of political neophytes, like Sue Slipman, Polly Toynbee and Rosie Barnes. Collectively they functioned less as a sounding-board, more as an echo-chamber.

Owen's and the Owenites' growing isolation manifested itself in a number of rather strange ways. Not the least was the extent to which members of the inner circle not only took an identical political line but used identical words with which to describe it. Their opponents' activities were invariably 'disgraceful' or, worse, 'outrageous'. They themselves, in response, were inevitably 'bitter'. They were united in attributing the mergerites' current machinations to plots laid long ago. 'Now it can be told!' was a constant refrain. The Owenites' language was increasingly that of a messianic—and apocalyptic—religious sect.

Unlike the mergerites, who frequently admitted to being baffled by the Owenites' actions and the reasoning that lay behind them, the Owenites always claimed to know exactly what their opponents were doing and, moreover, exactly what their motives were in doing it. If they were feeling charitable, they ascribed their opponents' behaviour to physical or mental illness (or possibly drunkenness): 'Bill has never been the same ever since he left the Labour party'; 'That tobogganing accident [at Christmas 1981] must have done something to Shirley'; 'You could tell [at the 29 June 1987 National Committee meeting, when Charles Kennedy changed sides] that he had had too much to drink over lunch.' If, however, they were feeling uncharitable, they attributed their opponents' behaviour to dishonesty, treachery or bad faith. Roy Jenkins, for example, and a large part of the Cowley Street staff, notably Dick Newby and Alec McGivan, were accused of having secretly—and, worse, from inside—plotted the SDP's downfall. The possibility that the differences between the Owenites and the mergerites might have stemmed straightforwardly from honest political disagreements was never entertained.

But the principal manifestation of Owen and the Owenites' increasing political isolation was an increasing clouding of their political judgement. As Owen's vision of the future became clearer and clearer, his hold on the reality of the political situation in which he found himself became more and more infirm. Clarity was undoubtedly achieved, but only at the price of the purest fantasy. The logic of the Owenites' position was impeccable; the empirical foundations on which it rested were virtually non-existent. Against the catalogue of the mergerites' mistakes can be set an equally long catalogue of the Owenites' mistakes—and the Owenites' were more serious.

In the first place, the Owenites were quite wrong to attribute to the mergerites a pro-merger fanaticism comparable to their own fanaticism against merger. For the mergerites, almost without exception, merger with the Liberals was not a cause, an end in itself, an intrinsic good; it was merely a pragmatic means of improving the electoral chances of what David Steel called Britain's 'radical non-socialist alternative'. The Liberals and the SDP agreed on almost everything; maintaining two separate parties was costly; in so far as the Liberal party did contain a dotty element, fusion with the SDP would serve to contain it; so why not merge? Many—most—of the mergerites did not actually feel very strongly about the matter—until, that is, they ran up against the blank wall of Owen's adamant and unreasoning response to any hint or suggestion of merger.

Jenkins and the Jenkinsites, notably Dick Taverne, were undoubtedly keenest on the idea—Jenkins reckoned that a separate Social Democratic party had probably served its purpose after the Alliance's failure to break through in the 1983 election—but even the Jenkinsites were fairly relaxed. Rodgers and Williams were agnostic on the issue, though increasingly inclined towards merger as time went on. David Steel was similarly agnostic until after the 1987 election. Indeed, Steel and Owen had more in common than probably either realized. Neither of them really liked the Liberal party or felt comfortable with it; it was altogether too anarchic and irresponsible. But, whereas their common discomfort led Steel to favour merger, it led Owen to oppose it. The one saw a merged party as a refuge, the other as a prison.

The mergerites' pragmatism, however, was never understood by the Owenites, who succeeded in convincing themselves, first, that the mergerites were as implacably pro-merger as they were implacably opposed to it and also, second, that almost from the launch of the SDP—in Jenkins' case from even before the launch— the mergerites had been engaged in a subtle, insidious, carefully thought-out campaign to undermine the SDP's independence. The Owenites were wrong on both counts. In particular, the notion that the post-1987 mergerites had all along been engaged in some deep-laid plot to submerge the SDP's separate identity was pure fantasy: why should Jenkins *et al.* have been engaged in such a plot? What would have been the point? But, of course, anyone disposed to believe in the existence of a conspiracy can always, if he looks hard enough, find evidence to support his belief. In the Owenites' case, the walk in the woods at Königswinter described in Chapter 10—when Rodgers, Williams, Steel and Holme met for the first time—was thought to have been especially suspicious.

Unfortunately for them, the Owenites' fantasy was not merely a fantasy: it had consequences. It caused suspicion and mistrust. It led the Owenites to retreat further and further into themselves and to treat the alleged conspirators as though they were conspirators even when they were not. Above all, it led to a hardening of attitudes, especially the attitude of 'merger or bust'. If Rodgers, Williams and the others were going to be accused of working towards merger no matter what they said or did, they might as well actually work towards it. One early casualty of this kind of thinking, on both sides, was the possibility of a serious federal solution to two parties' problems.

The Owenites' second mistake, more prosaic, was to do a volte-face in 1987 and to agree to an early merger ballot. The National Committee was divided, but Owen and his allies had a clear majority on it. They could have used this majority to capitalize on the feeling, widespread in the party, that David Steel was trying to bounce the SDP into merger and to insist on a summer-long period of reflection and stock-taking. Such a period, extending through and beyond the Portsmouth conference, could have been used to build up support in the party among people who were not opposed to merger in principle and who believed that it would probably have to come eventually but who at the same time wished to remain loyal to the SDP and who could see the advantages of closer co-operation between the two parties some way short of their merging at once. Had such a body of opinion been built up in the party—it would have included, for example, Charles Kennedy, Robert Maclennan and Ian Wrigglesworth—merger would probably have been blocked and in a reasonably amicable fashion. A federal solution could have been presented as a reasonable compromise and, to the mergerites, as a temporary resting place on the road to a merger eventually.

Instead the Owenites played into the hands of those who favoured immediate merger by accepting the holding of a ballot prior to Portsmouth. They probably thought they could win. Perhaps they did not care whether they won or not (as the mergerite said, Owen was 'in one of his purgative moods'). Either way, the Owenites' agreement to an early ballot was a serious tactical blunder. Instead of fighting what might well have been—indeed, probably would have been—a successful rearguard action, they chose to do battle at once and were defeated at once. Owen himself was said to have been distraught at the outcome.

The Owenites' defeat in the pre-Portsmouth ballot was rendered more probable by their third mistake: their decision (if decision is not too strong a word) to fight the ballot campaign in the way that they did. Had the Owenites, first, refrained from attacking the Liberals and, secondly, patiently made out the positive case for a federal solution via Option 1 (which is what they claimed to be advocating), they might well have won. At the very least, they would have narrowed the margin. Instead, they chose to fight on the ground chosen by Steel: 'merger or bust' in his case, 'independence or bust' in their case. They thereby alienated many of their potential supporters at the top of the party, notably Kennedy and Wrigglesworth, and probably many thousands of ordinary rank-and-file party members as well. Perhaps the Owenites did not consciously decide to fight the campaign that way; perhaps they just blundered into fighting it that way. If so, their mistake was the more egregious.

The Owenites' fourth mistake, possibly specific to Owen personally, was to assume that the five SDP MPs would remain a solid bloc. It obviously was in Owen's interests to maintain the unity and support of the MPs, especially during the period of the ballot. It was also obviously in Owen's interests, therefore, to keep in close touch with the MPs and to adjust his own tactics with a view to meeting their individual concerns. Instead, Owen seems to have taken the MPs almost entirely for granted, indeed to have run risks in alienating them. The loss of Kennedy, and the subsequent loss of Maclennan, dangerously exposed his flank. Owen's approach to both men seems to have been one of 'take it or leave it'. They soon decided to leave it—and him.

Owen's fifth mistake, also relating to the MPs, concerned the party leadership. When he resigned the leadership in early August 1987, he seems to have assumed that the post would remain empty, that no one would wish, or dare, to step into his shoes—or that, if they did both wish and dare, he could somehow stop them. The empty chair at the head table would then stand as a silent rebuke to the party for having voted for merger and would also serve as a reminder of the quality and integrity of the leader they had lost. The only trouble was that the leadership did not remain vacant. It could have been foreseen that the mergerites were most unlikely to allow it to remain so. Owen's apostasy was Maclennan's opportunity—and, as a result, Owen's parliamentary supporters were reduced to two. Instead of spending the summer and autumn of 1987 gathering support, Owen spent his time alienating it. Perhaps he wanted fewer supporters. The smaller a sect, the purer its devotion to its leader is likely to be.

But Owen's sixth mistake was the most serious—and the most remarkable. The fact that he could make it provides the final indictment of his political judgement. His sixth and greatest mistake was to suppose that he could establish a 'continuing SDP' and that such a party could possibly succeed.

It is important to understand what Owen thought he was doing. When the SDP was launched in 1981, Owen had a clear—and characteristically belligerent —idea of what he wanted to happen. He made it clear what it was. It was his col-leagues' fault if they did not listen. Owen from the beginning wanted the SDP to act completely independently, to assert itself as a major political party in the making, to contest all by-elections in this guise and to do a deal with the Liberals, if at all, only after the SDP had demonstrated its superior vote-winning capacity (and, presumably, trounced the Liberals in a number of electoral contests). The SDP was to be independent. It was also to be the senior partner—neither the junior partner nor an equal—in any electoral deal with the Liberals or anyone else.

In the early 1980s Owen had been frustrated in his desire to pursue this strategy because almost no one in the SDP agreed with him. But now, in the late 1980s, he thought he could start again. No longer restrained by Jenkins, Williams and other fainthearts—indeed no longer restrained by anybody—he would press the rewind button, spool back to 1981 and re-launch the SDP as though none of the events in the intervening years had ever occurred. The new-born SDP would build up a mass membership. It would fight by-elections—if need be against the new merged party. It would win some of these by-elections. It might or might not negotiate an electoral pact with the merged party; but, if it did, it would negotiate it from strength and it would be no more than an electoral pact. And then, by the time of the next election, in 1991 or 1992, the Mark II SDP would be in a position to win twenty or thirty parliamentary seats and with any luck hold the balance of power in the House of Commons. Serious multi-party politics would then commence. The new merged party would appeal to the left-leaning portion of the centrist electorate; the continuing SDP would appeal to its more right-leaning portion. The two parties, remaining separate, would have a useful division of labour between them.

This strategy appealed to the Owenites, and they adopted it. It can only be described, however, as being completely potty. First, a continuing SDP had no chance of building up a mass membership: the politically active segment of the right-leaning portion of the centrist electorate was far too small. Secondly, in any prolonged contest between the merged party and a continuing SDP the continuing SDP was bound to lose: the merged party would have superior organization and far greater credibility, based on its origins in the long-established Liberal party. Thirdly, after all that had happened, there was no way in which the merged party—by now an anti-Owenite party, whatever else it was—was going to agree to an electoral arrangement. Fourthly, the subtlety of the distinction between the left-leaning merged party and the right-leaning continuing SDP would be lost on all but a tiny handful of voters (the existing Alliance arrangement was already hard enough to understand). Fifthly, the Owenite scenario assumed, in effect, that a multi-party system, and a system of proportional representation to underpin it, already existed and that the continuing SDP—as though it were operating in Italy, Israel or the Netherlands—could manœuvre and bargain amongst and between all the other parties.

But above all, sixthly, the Owenite scenario assumed, given that the existing British electoral system was in place, that there was a place for the Owenites within it, that their particular brand name and form of niche-marketing could enable them to capture a small but politically significant sector of the market. But, for all the reasons just given, this belief was completely illusory. Given the British electoral system and given the majority of voters' predisposition to vote for either the

Conservatives or Labour, there was scarcely room for a third party, let alone a fourth. Any Liberal could have told Owen that. As Charles Kennedy had put it at Portsmouth, there was no room at the inn: all the available accommodation was already taken. Even in the improbable event that the continuing SDP managed to win a significant number of votes, its chance of actually winning seats approached zero.

In other words, the Owenite enterprise did not merely fail in the event: it was always doomed to fail. No rational politician would have undertaken it or even dreamt of undertaking it. The launch of the original SDP in 1981 had been rash enough, and it had failed. The launch of the continuing SDP in 1987 was rash to the point of absurdity. David Owen began as Napoleon and ended up as Baron Munchausen.

Who, then, was ultimately more to blame? Both sides in the merger dispute undoubtedly behaved badly and short-sightedly—and without due regard for the legitimate concerns of the other—but David Owen's sins were undoubtedly the greater. By his wilfulness, recklessness and lack of judgement he inflicted a substantial set-back on the cause of centre-party politics in Britain and destroyed the political careers of both himself and his two closest colleagues, John Cartwright and Rosie Barnes (both of whom, unlike Charles Kennedy and Robert Maclennan, lost their seats at the 1992 election). There is no point today in looking around for David Owen's monument: there is none. Owen might respond that 'he did it his way' and that he would not have felt comfortable anywhere except in the SDP. To that one can only reply that his way was the wrong way and that personal comfort is not the purpose of serious politics.

Part V

....

OBITUARY

23
....

The SDP: A Study in Failure

The brief history of the British Social Democratic party is one of failure. Roy Jenkins' experimental plane began by soaring into the sky, then glided for a time, then crash-landed in a very muddy field. That was even before the crew bailed out and started fighting among themselves. The new party barely dented, let alone broke, the mould of British party politics. It did not obtain power on its own or hold the balance of power in a hung parliament. It did not displace the Labour party, or usher in multi-party politics, or bring electoral reform to the statute book, or even permanently alter the political agenda. The party system of today scarcely differs from that of the 1960s and 1970s, before the new party was formed.

It is tempting on these grounds to dismiss the SDP as merely an aberration, a historical curiosity, possibly interesting in itself and even entertaining, but of no broader historical or political significance. But such a temptation should be resisted. The SDP was more than an aberration. The implications of its failure are far-reaching.

We need to remind ourselves, in the first place, that the SDP, in alliance with the Liberals, succeeded in mounting by far the most serious challenge to the existing two-party hegemony for more than sixty years. Unlike earlier breakaway parties, such as Oswald Mosley's New Party in the early 1930s or the short-lived Scottish Labour party in the 1970s, the SDP was a genuinely national party.[1] In the space of two years it established a large national membership, local branches throughout the country, regional offices, a democratic constitution, an elected leader, a national executive and deliberative assembly, a small but professional central headquarters, a viable financial base and detailed policy positions on almost all aspects of public concern. Together with the Liberals, the SDP contested every parliamentary seat in Great Britain. It took the Labour party nearly three decades to build up a national organization on a comparable scale. The SDP was the first breakaway party in the twentieth century to play in the big league.

Secondly, the SDP's founders could not have chosen a more promising time to launch their assault on the existing two-party system. In 1981 the British public was less enamoured of the two main parties than at any time since the Second World War. The worst recession since the 1930s had alienated voters from the Conservatives; the most bitter left–right battles since the 1950s had alienated them from Labour. The retreat from consensus by both parties, personally symbolized by the ideological gulf between Thatcher and Foot, appeared to vacate the middle ground of politics, leaving room for a new party of the moderate centre. By the closing months of 1981, the Conservative and Labour parties were each supported by scarcely more than a quarter of the electorate. Never before had the standing of either major party, whether in government or in opposition, fallen so low.

This immediate opportunity was, thirdly, reinforced by the longer-term 'partisan dealignment' that was taking place in the British electorate.[2] The proportion of the electorate turning out to vote for the Conservatives or Labour, the proportion of voters identifying with the Conservative and Labour parties, the proportion of Conservative and Labour identifiers with strong attachments to their party and the number of signed-up members of the two parties were all in decline. More and more voters were restless and on the move.

These ideal circumstances for a third-party breakthrough were reflected in the Alliance's electoral achievement, which far outclassed that of any previous breakaway grouping. The Alliance's performance in the 1983 and 1987 general elections established new records in Britain, while on the European continent no liberal or centre party has been remotely so successful since the war. In large parts of Britain the Alliance either began to compete on more or less equal terms with both the Conservatives and Labour or more commonly, as in the West Country and in large parts of East Anglia, replaced the old Conservative–Labour two-party system with a new Conservative–Alliance two-party system. The Alliance terrorized the Conservatives in many parts of the country. It could not be ignored altogether by the Labour party.[3]

Yet, although the circumstances of the early 1980s were unusually propitious, and although the Alliance's electoral achievements were considerable, the SDP in the end was a failure. It fell far short of transforming the existing party system. It failed to achieve a parliamentary breakthrough: a couple of dozen MPs, representing two separate parties, are unlikely to be able to participate seriously in a coalition government or wield the balance of power effectively in a hung parliament. Not least, it failed to make a breakthrough in local government. Whatever their progress in terms of votes and seats in town halls, the Alliance parties in the 1980s rarely exercised real power. Following the 1987 local elections—after the SDP had gained seats for four consecutive years and the Liberals for nine—the Alliance parties together still ran only fifteen district and borough councils, most of them with only a minority of seats.[4]

The question therefore arises: why did the Gang of Four's project fail? What went wrong? Did their fault lie in their stars or in themselves that they were laid so low? There are no certain answers to these questions, but some answers are more plausible than others.

We begin by considering those explanations of the SDP's failure that attribute it to strategic and tactical errors made either by the party's founders or by its rank-and-file members. Explanations of this kind figure largely in many contemporaneous accounts of the SDP and also in David Owen's most recent volume of memoirs. In addition, an American political scientist, Patricia Lee Sykes, emphasizes the price that the SDP paid for its internal disunity in her book, *Losing from the Inside*.[5]

One possible error that the Gang of Four made was to found the SDP in the first place. The social democrats in the Labour party, so the argument goes, might have fared better if they had never launched the SDP at all but had instead joined the Liberal party straightaway, perhaps persuading the Liberals to change their name. This was the position of many leading Liberals (though not David Steel) in 1981. They thought, in Cyril Smith's words, that the SDP 'should have been strangled at birth'. The formation of a second centre party, with its own membership, organization, leadership and programme, was bound to lead to wrangling between the two parties, at a considerable cost in terms of votes. Had the Labour defectors instead joined an enlarged Liberal party, there would have been no squabbling over the seats share-out in 1982, no defence row in 1986 and none of the problems with Steel's and Owen's joint leadership during the 1987 election campaign.

This argument falls on two counts. First, there was never any chance of the Gang of Three and most of the other Labour defectors joining the Liberal party. Offered the choice of becoming Liberals or staying in the Labour party, most of them would have stayed—or left politics altogether. Switching to the Liberals would have meant joining an alien party, one that had been a historic failure, and accommodating all manner of Liberal suspicions and prejudices. By contrast, creating a new party meant a fresh start. Roy Jenkins and at most four Labour backbenchers might have joined the Liberals. Any impact on the general public would have been small and transient.

Secondly, even if the rest of the Gang of Four had joined the Liberals, it is doubtful whether the enlarged Liberal party would have lifted off in the way that the Alliance did in 1981–2.[6] At least in 1981 the SDP attracted voters and members in a way that an enlarged Liberal party could never have done. It was the SDP's very freshness and novelty that beguiled thousands of voters into thinking that it stood for new ideas and a new politics. The SDP's lack of a clear identity enabled voters to convince themselves that it stood for whatever they stood for. Nor would the Liberal party have been universally hospitable to an influx of ex-Labour Social Democrats. The stubborn resistance of local Liberals in Greenock, Hackney, Liverpool and elsewhere to the nomination of SDP MPs as Alliance candidates suggests that there would still have been rows about seats.

Would a single party, whatever it was called, have done better than an alliance of two parties at a general election? The answer seems to be: not in 1983 and to only a limited degree in 1987. According to the survey evidence, the two-party format cost the Alliance, at most, 1 per cent of the vote in 1983.[7] In 1987 having two leaders probably cost the Alliance more dearly, conceivably as much as 6 per cent of the total vote—enough, perhaps, to win another ten seats, though not enough to overtake Labour.[8] But the strains between Steel and Owen would almost certainly have emerged even if Owen had, however improbably, joined the Liberals.

Another possible error made by the Gang of Four was to enter into discussions with the Liberal party almost as soon as the new party was formed. Although David Owen never pressed his case formally on the National Committee or at an annual SDP conference—he frequently contented himself with muttered asides—this was the line that he took in 1981–2, and it is one that he sets out at some length in his memoirs.[9]

In Owen's view, the SDP would have fared better if it had refused to enter into any alliance with the Liberals in 1981 or much of 1982 and had instead fought the Liberals both at the local level and in parliamentary by-elections. Had the SDP determined to fight both Warrington and Croydon North-West, the Liberals might have withdrawn their candidates; even if they had insisted on standing against Roy Jenkins in the one and Shirley Williams in the other, they would almost certainly have come bottom of the poll. Whether or not the Social Democrats actually won the two by-elections, they would have polled well and convinced the Liberals that the SDP was now the major party of the centre and that their own existing seats and other good prospects were therefore under threat. Going on to negotiate with the Liberals from a position of strength, the SDP would have unequivocally dominated any alliance that the two parties formed, putting its leader at its head, fighting the lion's share of seats and stamping its policies on any joint programme. In all probability, given the new situation, some Liberal MPs and many rank-and-file members of the Liberal party would actually have changed sides and joined the Social Democrats.

Although Owen believed in it passionately, this go-it-alone strategy was not remotely credible. It might have worked in a country that already had proportional representation and a multi-party system, but it was utterly unsuited to the realities of Britain's first-past-the-post system. It is inconceivable that the Liberals would have taken Owenite bullying lying down. For them, of all parties, bottom place and lost deposits in by-elections held no terrors; they had been there too often before. The outcome in 1981–2 would have been what it was in fact after the merger fiasco: two centre parties competing for the same vote and denying each other victory as a consequence. Probably the SDP would have come out ahead of the Liberals in many by-elections, but probably, too, it would have failed to win any of them—and would thereby have forgone the electoral momentum, media coverage and the influx of new members that occurred between the summer of 1981 and the spring of 1982. Once the decision was taken to establish a separate party, the logic of the first-past-the-post system required an electoral pact with the Liberal party and therefore *ipso facto* an agreed policy programme. And, given the need for an alliance, it would have made no sense to delay negotiations until 1982–3, when relations between the two parties would probably have cooled to freezing point and when the Liberals would already have adopted candidates in all their winnable seats.

Another possible error, this time perpetrated by the SDP's rank and file, was the election of Jenkins rather than Owen as leader in July 1982. Jenkins proved an unsatisfactory leader, especially for a fledgling political party desperate for publicity. He was ill at ease in parliament, long-winded and obscure on television, uninspiring to party activists, bored with the details of party organization and uncomfortable on the campaign trail. Most seriously of all, he failed to find a coherent theme for the Alliance's policies, relying instead on traditional centrist phrases like 'divided Britain' just when the Falklands War made such rhetoric seem outdated. As a consequence, his standing with the voters was low, whereas Owen's, to judge from his poll ratings after 1983, would almost certainly have been higher. As leader between 1981 and 1983, Owen would have caught the shifting national mood better than Jenkins and given the SDP's policies a sharper cutting edge.

Against these probable benefits, however, must be set the near certainty that under Owen's leadership relations with the Liberals in 1982–3 would have been every bit as fraught as they in fact became later. After all, Jenkins won the party leadership partly because the SDP's members, taking a broad hint from David Steel, thought he would get along better with the Liberals. Owen's views on relations with the Liberals were well known before the leadership election—indeed they were at the forefront of Owen's campaign—and from the beginning the Liberal party saw him as a hostile element. Under Owen a row with the Liberals like the 1986 defence row would probably have occurred sooner rather than later.

In addition, Jenkins' electioneering in 1983, although it was undoubtedly lacklustre, was well down the list of reasons given by potential Alliance voters for preferring another party. Only 9 per cent of potential Alliance supporters claimed that Jenkins had put them off.[10] It seems unlikely that the net gain to the Alliance in 1983 from electing Owen rather than Jenkins would have been more than 2 or 3 percentage points, and it might have been less or even negative (especially if Steel and Owen had fought publicly over the Alliance leadership). Even on the most optimistic scenario, the Alliance in 1983 would have done no more than nose ahead of Labour in the popular vote and possibly gained a few more seats. But even the benefit of this outcome to the Alliance would have been doubtful. Labour would still have had far more seats than the Alliance in the House of Commons, and the Conservatives would still have had a large overall majority. The post-1983 campaign for electoral reform would have started with a bigger head of steam, but it would soon have run out of steam. The quality press would have published indignant letters from 'Disgusted, Hampstead' about the iniquities of the electoral system, but the system would have remained unreformed all the same.

Another possibility is that the SDP would have fared better if it had aimed to supplant the Labour party in a reconstituted two-party system rather than strengthen the centre in a realigned three-party system. This argument was often made in the Conservative press, but it was also popular in the SDP's early days among the Gang of Three, who saw the Social Democrats as a left-of-centre party, and among defecting Labour MPs hoping to be re-elected in their old constituencies.[11] Such a strategy implied targeting disaffected Labour voters in Labour areas where Liberal competition was weak and the electoral system might have been expected to work in the SDP's favour. It further implied that the SDP should turn itself into a modern, moderate social democratic party in the European tradition: a party of the welfare state, good public services, responsible trade unionism and full employment, but at the same time, unlike Labour, one opposed to large-scale nationalization, centralized economic planning, unilateral nuclear disarmament and withdrawal from the EEC. In a short time, it was hoped, the SDP could take over Labour's existing electoral base, with its deep social foundations and cultural roots, much as the French Socialists had replaced the Communists as the dominant left-wing party in France during the 1970s.

However, the idea that the SDP faced a stark choice between two incompatible strategies (and opted for the wrong one) is misconceived. The objectives of the two strategies were different, but in terms of the SDP's policy appeals they largely overlapped. Almost all the positions that the SDP adopted in order to mobilize the broad centre of the political spectrum were the same as those it would have adopted had it decided to focus its appeal on traditional Labour voters—who were, after all, part of the 'moderate majority'. The only issue on which some traditional Labour voters differed from the centrist consensus was trade-union rights, but even here the SDP's position of 'returning trade unions to their members' was in line with the wishes of most ordinary Labour supporters. It was not until 1984–5, when Owen took a tough stand against the miners' strike, that the SDP could be portrayed as in any way 'anti-union'; and even then, since Labour voters were themselves divided over the strike, it is unlikely that the SDP forfeited much support as a result. There was, therefore, no need to tailor the details of policy to attract the traditional Labour voter: that was being done already.

At the same time, it would have made little sense to concentrate resources overwhelmingly in Labour seats. Some resources were indeed concentrated in Labour-held seats; but all the evidence suggested that levels of potential centre-party support were generally higher in Conservative than in Labour seats, and it would therefore have been foolish for the SDP to neglect the Conservative heartlands by, for example, leaving them to Liberal candidates.

In addition, the SDP had no roots to speak of in working-class communities or in the trade unions. Its members were mainly middle-class residents of middle-class areas; in most working-class constituencies the party had fewer than thirty members. No trade unions supported the party, few active trade unionists joined as individual members, and none of the tabloid newspapers read by the working classes supported the party or gave it much coverage following the launch. The result was that the SDP had virtually no presence in inner cities, on council estates or in the industrial heartlands and, moreover, no obvious means of establishing one. In the longer term, the SDP might have built up visibility in traditional Labour areas by pursuing some variant of Liberal-type community politics; but Liberal advances by these means had been limited, patchy and slow, and a new party like the SDP, if it were to succeed at all, had to succeed quickly. Targeting Labour seats would have been a feasible option only if a much larger segment of the labour movement—including entire trade-union branches and constituency Labour parties—had come over.[12]

Another possible error made by the SDP was its failure to merge with the Liberals after the Alliance's failure to break through in 1983. Certainly some pro-merger Social Democrats, notably Roy Jenkins, believed, following the 1983 election, that the SDP had missed its historical opportunity and that a merger between the two parties was now the only sensible course. A post-1983 merged party, on this argument, might well have elected Owen rather than the demoralized David Steel as its leader and a unified centre party would have been able to fight the 1987 campaign unburdened by divisions over defence, the two-leader problem and the endless joint policy discussions.

This line of argument, however, has two drawbacks. One is that there is very little evidence that such divisions as there were between the Liberals and the SDP actually did the Alliance serious damage in 1987. The defence row in May 1986 undoubtedly cost the Alliance some support, as did the Liberal assembly's subsequent split over defence four months later; but the two parties' position in the polls had been restored by the time of the general election and there is little reason to think that, in the absence of the rows and the split, the Alliance would have fared significantly better.

The other drawback to the 1983 merger argument is that any such idea is totally fanciful. Owen would not have allowed a merger to take place, as his determination to stamp out talk of a merger at the 1983 Salford Council for Social Democracy amply demonstrated. If a majority for merger, or even a substantial pro-merger faction, had emerged at that time, Owen would have reacted no less vigorously—and probably with greater support—than he did in 1987. If Jenkins had decided to try to stay on as leader and had somehow managed to be re-elected, the result, if he had chosen to press for merger, would have been the same. The split over a merger would simply have been brought forward by four years, with disastrous consequences.

Finally, David Owen's critics insist that the SDP and the Alliance would have fared better after 1983 if Owen had been more emollient in his dealings with the Liberals. Non-Owenite Social Democrats and Liberals alike maintain that, if Owen had been readier to compromise with the Liberals over such matters as joint open selection and defence and had been more committed to working out an agreed line over Alliance tactics in a hung parliament, the two parties would have won more votes and seats in 1987. They may be right, but there is little evidence that they are. As we have noted, the famous defence row in fact did little long-term damage, and the electoral consequences of the Alliance's uninspired campaign in 1987 have been greatly exaggerated. Even if Steel and Owen had collaborated perfectly throughout the campaign, the gain in votes to the Alliance would not have been substantial—no more than a percentage point or two. It would certainly not have been enough to take the Alliance ahead of the Labour party.[13]

Some of the arguments just outlined have greater validity than others. Jenkins probably was something of a liability as leader in 1983, and closer Liberal–SDP co-operation might well have produced a fractionally better result in 1987. It is probably also the case that, on balance, the SDP suffered from bad luck. If Benn had defeated Healey in Labour's 1981 deputy-leadership contest, more Labour MPs would probably have defected to the SDP, Labour's lurch to the left would have accelerated, and the civil war within the Labour party would have been fought with renewed ferocity. The wholly fortuitous Falklands War, and Britain's victory in that war, was an even more serious set-back. The war saved Thatcher and her government and caused Alliance support to fall within a few months from nearly 40 per cent to less than 25 per cent. The SDP and the Liberals never really recovered.[14]

But, all that said, it is still hard to escape the conclusion that the SDP's failure lay far more in the institutional and structural obstacles it confronted than either in ill luck or in the misguided tactics and actions of its leaders. For reasons to be explained shortly, there is a sense in which the SDP was fated to fail. The political environment into which Roy Jenkins launched his experimental plane in 1981 simply proved to be too hostile, as Jenkins himself always expected it might.

The central problem, already referred to in Chapter 16, is that the first-past-the-post electoral system, wherever it operates, makes it almost impossible for a third party, especially a nationally based third party like the Liberals or the SDP, to dislodge either of two existing parties. The system fails to turn a minority party's share of the popular vote into a proportional share of seats. Because it fails to turn votes into seats, it has the further effect of discouraging people from voting for the party at all (because they do not want to 'waste their votes'). On top of all that, the first-past-the-post system, by slowing up any process of change that may be taking place in the party system, gives the existing two parties, if they are threatened by a third party, invaluable time—years, maybe decades—in which to change their leaders, revise their policies and adapt their tactics to meet the new situation. In all countries at all times, the first-past-the-post electoral system is a formidable obstacle to fundamental change.

With a single exception, the historical experience of breakaway and other third parties in the Anglo-American democracies is uniformly bleak. Since the beginning of the twentieth century breakaway parties in Australia, Canada, New Zealand and the United States have not secured more than 10 per cent of the vote or more than a handful of seats, and centrist third parties have never taken or shared office or come close to doing so.[15] By the standards of other countries with a first-past-the-post system, the electoral performance of the Alliance, far from being feeble or derisory, was a historical record. The wonder is not that the Alliance won so few seats but that, despite everything, it won so many votes.

The single exception to the general rule that new parties in countries with first-past-the-post electoral systems find it almost impossible to dislodge either of the existing parties is, of course, well known: the rise of the Labour party in Britain and its displacement of the Liberal party as the main opposition to the Conservatives between 1900 and the late 1920s. There is a sense in which the Liberals and the SDP were trying to reverse this very process.

The Labour party's rise is a complicated phenomenon to analyse, and historians are by no means agreed on all the details; but they do agree that three factors were of overwhelming importance—and all three factors throw light on why, a half-century later, the Liberal–SDP Alliance was destined to fail.[16]

The first was simply the fact that the Labour party in its early decades had a specifically class-based appeal, and the class to which Labour appealed, the manual working class, was the largest in the country. Labour's historic project was quite straightforward: to mobilize the manual working classes and to cause them to come to identify their interests and aspirations with those of 'their' party, the Labour party. Capturing large numbers of working-class votes enabled Labour to overtake the Liberals as early as the late 1920s. The Labour project reached its culmination with the party's stunning victory in 1945. Needless to say, the British Labour party's success in appealing to manual working-class voters was paralleled by the rise of political parties with similar class appeals throughout most of the industrial world.

By contrast, the Liberals and Social Democrats in the 1980s had no such appeal. Unlike their Conservative and Labour rivals, they were not, as Sir Ian Gilmour put it, 'interest-based'.[17] They did not appeal to any specific social class, or religious denomination, or ethnic group, or region, or small nation. Almost no one in Britain felt that the Alliance uniquely represented the interests that were most important to him or her personally and that it was imperative, therefore, for them to vote for the Alliance on those grounds. On the contrary, the Alliance's leaders deliberately eschewed class-based and other similar appeals, which they regarded as socially divisive and inappropriate in an increasingly classless and multicultural country. The one social class to which the SDP did make a special appeal, the public-sector salariat, was much too small to constitute, by itself, an adequate base.

The second factor in the Labour party's rise was the enormous expansion in the size of the British electorate that took place between 1918 and 1929, with the enfranchisement for the first time of women and the whole of the male manual working class. At the last general election fought before the First World War, that of December 1910, the total number of adults eligible to vote was 7,709,981. At the first general election after the war, that of 1918, the total was 21,392,322— nearly three times as many. By 1929, following the enfranchisement of all women aged 21 and over, the eligible electorate had grown to no fewer than 28,850,870—

little short of a fourfold increase in the course of a single generation.[18] The Labour party, then still in its infancy, was doubly advantaged. The majority of the new voters were manual workers, members of 'its' class. In addition, Labour, in appealing to those millions of new voters, did not have to sever existing bonds of partisan loyalty and commitment. Far fewer new voters than old ones had formed a stable identification with either of the existing two parties. The new voters were, so to speak, clean slates on which Labour could write.

The Liberals and the SDP in the 1980s had no such luck. There was no dramatic increase in the size of the electorate during the 1980s. The Alliance, therefore, had to try to woo millions of voters away from pre-existing Conservative and Labour loyalties. Their success in doing so was remarkable; but it was not enough. The only substantial group of new voters to whom the Alliance might have been expected to make a special appeal was the young: 18–24-year-olds who had not previously voted. But, while young voters have fewer partisan attachments than their elders, they are also less interested in politics and politically less knowledgeable. The SDP and the Alliance probably never impinged at all on many young people's consciousness. The niceties of Alliance politics were far removed from the world of the apprentice garage mechanic in Bolton or the trainee hairdresser in Southend.

But it was the third factor that was probably the most important in the rise of the Labour party. Indeed some historians believe it was crucial: without it, Labour, despite its class appeal and the extension of the franchise, would probably never have broken through. That factor was the quite fortuitous disintegration of one of the two existing political parties, the old Liberal party. The Liberals split in 1916 when Lloyd George displaced Asquith as prime minister. The party's two wings then put up candidates against one another at the general elections of 1918 and 1922. Although the two parts of the party came together again following the 1922 election, by this time it was too late: the Liberals had been relegated to third place behind Labour in terms of both votes and seats. The Liberals' subsequent decline— as the first-past-the-post electoral system began to do its work—was precipitous.[19]

It is clear in retrospect that those who founded the SDP in 1981 did so on the basis of two beliefs (or at least hopes). One was that the Labour vote would simply implode, given Labour's internal bickering and its evident determination to adopt policies further and further removed from the interests and aspirations of ordinary Labour voters. The other belief (or at least hope) was that the Labour party, like the Liberals in an earlier era, would simply disintegrate, with the traditionalists and modernizers no longer able to coexist in the same party with Foot, Benn and the hard left. It was this belief that underlay David Steel's comment when Healey narrowly defeated Benn in the 1981 deputy-leadership election: 'Denis Healey looks like being leader of half the Labour party for no more than a year.'[20]

In the circumstances of the early 1980s, both of these beliefs were not unreasonable. The Labour vote was haemorrhaging fast (already down to less than 37 per cent at the 1979 general election), and it seemed a distinct possibility that, quite apart from the setting-up of the SDP, Labour could no longer contain its internal divisions and contradictions. But in the event the forces of inertia within the Labour party, and within the political system more generally, proved too strong. The Labour vote did indeed continue to decline, from 36.9 per cent in 1979 to 27.6 per cent in 1983; but the 27.6 per cent of 1983—Labour's lowest share of the total vote since 1918—was nevertheless still large enough to return 209 Labour members of parliament, 186 more than the Liberals and the SDP combined. And, just as important, Labour neglected to fall apart. Despite the depths of their policy disagreements with Foot, Benn and the hard left, most Labour right-wingers— people like Denis Healey, Roy Hattersley and Peter Shore—retained a strong loyalty to Labour as an institution; and, moreover, they did not want to lose their seats. The resulting amalgam of traditional loyalty and political expediency constituted a glue that was more than strong enough to hold the Labour party together.

What the first-past-the-post electoral system did—by depriving the Alliance of a significant number of votes and seats and by enabling more than 200 Labour MPs to be returned on the basis of a much-reduced popular vote—was to give the Labour party time, time in which it could replace Michael Foot by Neil Kinnock and then by John Smith and Tony Blair, and time in which it could rethink its approach to both foreign and domestic policy and abandon its commitments to whole-sale nationalization, centralized economic planning, overweening union power, unilateral nuclear disarmament and hostility to the European Community. Successive electoral defeats provided the impetus for change; the workings of the first-past-the-post electoral system provided Labour with the time in which to change.

In short, it was the combination of the workings of the British electoral system together with the failure of the Labour party to fall apart that ultimately doomed Roy Jenkins' experimental plane. There was little or nothing that Jenkins or any other member of the crew could have done about it. Their fate was really sealed, as Jenkins himself was among the first to realize, by the Alliance's failure to break through in June 1983. The history of the SDP after the 1983 general election, though full of colour and incident, was essentially anticlimactic.

However, the fact that the SDP failed to achieve what it set out to achieve does not necessarily mean that it had no consequences for British politics. Even if it fails to attain office, a new party brings new people and new ideas into political life and may affect the balance of power among the other parties. In its six years on the British political stage, the SDP played a major role, if not quite a starring one. The media lavished attention on it at the moments of its greatest success and gave it equal or near-equal coverage with the other parties at election time. Twenty-nine MPs knowingly risked, and in most cases forfeited, their political careers. Many thousands of ordinary men and women gave up a large amount of their time and energy to a new political commitment. What legacy—in terms of people, ideas and the wider political system—did they bequeath to their successors, beyond the political grave?

Sadly, the SDP's contribution to the country's pool of political talent was almost wholly negative. The whole episode put an end to far more political careers than it created—notably those of Bill Rodgers, Shirley Williams and David Owen and also those of the great majority of Labour backbenchers who defected. Had they remained in the Labour party, each of the Gang of Three would almost certainly have been opposition frontbenchers in the 1980s and cabinet ministers in any subsequent Labour government. Many of the backbenchers would also have been certain to rise through the ranks. The destruction of talent was not on an enormous scale, but it was not trivial. Charles Kennedy, alone among the newly elected SDP MPs, remains a member of the House of Commons in 1995.

In the constituencies, the SDP brought tens of thousands of hitherto uncommitted citizens, most of them young and well-educated professionals, into party politics for the first time. It politicized the new meritocracy—the emerging 'service' class created by the twin expansions of higher education and the public sector in the 1960s and 1970s. Here was a fresh source of political ability—articulate, enthusiastic, capable of organizing and free of ideological orthodoxies. But, when the SDP died, its rank and file dispersed, and most were lost, probably permanently, to party political life. Large numbers quit politics altogether to concentrate on more rewarding non-political careers. Of the rest, the largest single group, but a minority of the total SDP membership, was absorbed into the Liberal Democrats. The wave of political mobilization generated by the SDP left, in the end, only the faintest of tidemarks.[21]

The SDP's contribution to the realm of political ideas was also negligible. The party throughout its life engaged in feverish policy preparation, but its dozens upon dozens of policy statements, documents and pamphlets were ultimately, as we remarked earlier, beads without a string. Most were distinctly old-fashioned and Fabian in style—detailed, incremental, managerial and addressed to policy professionals rather than the general public. The SDP's think-tank, the Tawney Society, was too small and too new to exert any substantial influence outside the party's ranks.

It could be argued that, especially under Owen's leadership, the SDP did develop two distinctive themes: constitutional reform and the social market economy. But as a contribution to British political debate neither was particularly original. The SDP's Great Reform Charter—comprising a bill of rights, devolution, proportional representation and freedom of information—was the standard Liberal package, most of it dating from well before the SDP was born. The most that can be claimed is that the SDP gave these old ideas a new respectability. The fact that men like Roy Jenkins and David Owen embraced the constitutional-reform agenda merely made it seem less cranky. The notion that capitalism could be combined with redistribution and the welfare state was also not new. It had been a constant preoccupation of left-wing Conservatives and Labour revisionists since the war, and elements of it can easily be traced back to Iain Macleod's 'One Nation' conservatism and Tony Crosland's revisionist socialism.[22]

The Social Democrats did have an ideal opportunity to develop and popularize those ideas when the Conservative and Labour parties abandoned the ideological centre ground in the early and mid-1980s. But they largely failed to do so. At the intellectual level, little progress was made towards establishing principles for determining when governments should apply market criteria and when they should apply social criteria. At the popular level, the language of 'tough and tender' never caught on. The idea of the social market economy likewise failed to register with the great majority of voters. Other minor parties have forced at least one major item onto the political agenda—a Scottish parliament, Welsh language rights, the environment—and have obliged the Conservative and Labour parties to respond. With the best will in the world, the same cannot be said of the SDP.

Denis Healey advanced a different argument. The SDP's 'most important effect', he wrote in his memoirs, 'was to delay the Labour Party's recovery for nearly 10 years, and to guarantee Mrs Thatcher two more terms in office'.[23] This argument too, however, does not stand up. The evidence suggests that, on the contrary, if the SDP and the Alliance had not existed in 1983 and 1987 or if they had not appeared to offer a genuine alternative to the two older parties, the Conservatives under Thatcher might well have done even better at both elections and would almost certainly not have done worse. The truth is that the existence of the SDP did not materially affect the outcome of either election. In its unreformed, divided, antediluvian state, the Labour party was doomed to defeat in both 1983 and 1987, no matter what the SDP or anyone else said or did.

The argument that the SDP delayed the Labour party's recovery also hinges on the probable consequences for the Labour party if the Gang of Three and their followers had decided to stay on and fight inside their old party rather than leave and form a new one. The departure of twenty-eight right-wing MPs in 1981–2 did indeed tilt the political balance in the parliamentary Labour party further towards the left, but this shift in itself made very little difference to the party overall, because it was the party in the country—notably the constituency Labour parties—that was making most of the running. The SDP breakaway did result in the loss of two right-wingers from Labour's National Executive Committee—Shirley Williams and Tom Bradley—but they had been in a tiny minority on most contentious issues and both, as it happens, were replaced by moderates. Had the Social Democrats not defected, Benn would still have challenged Healey for the deputy leadership (and would have lost by a fractionally larger margin). Most of the left wing's key advances, such as the mandatory reselection of MPs, an electoral college for the election of the leader and the adoption of the 'alternative economic strategy' as official party policy, occurred before, not after, the SDP was formed, while the 1981–2 conference votes in favour of a unilateralist defence policy were so overwhelming, thanks to the trade-union bloc vote, that a decision by the Social Democrats to remain in the party would have made no difference.

Indeed the civil war in the Labour party would probably have raged with even greater intensity if the Social Democrats had decided to stay and fight on. The Gang of Three had become hate figures to the Labour left after they published their open letter in the *Guardian* and the *Daily Mirror*, while, among both the mainstream in the parliamentary party and the rank and file outside, they were seen as rockers of the boat, not as rescuers. It is inconceivable, too, that Rodgers or Owen would have responded passively to the inclusion of unilateralism in Labour's 1983 manifesto. The muddle and divisions over defence that in any case wrecked Labour's 1983 campaign would have been even more serious if Rodgers and Owen had still been party members. The likely outcome of the Social Democrats remaining in the Labour party is that they would have lost all their policy battles, Labour would have continued to lurch further and further to the left, and the turmoil in the party would, if anything, have been still further intensified.

But an argument directly contradicting that of Healey can also be developed. One of the Gang of Three, Bill Rodgers, subsequently argued that, far from delaying Labour's recovery, the SDP breakaway actually accelerated it: that

the threat from the Alliance was the main reason for the modernisation of the Labour party . . . Over a wide spectrum the Labour party has been remade in the image of the SDP. If Her Majesty's Opposition is now in serious business again as a potential government of Britain, it is because the SDP showed the way.[24]

It is true that the Labour party's comprehensive policy review after the 1987 general election effectively ditched old-fashioned socialism, abandoned the contents of the 1983 and 1987 manifestos wholesale and substituted for both of them a new programme that was virtually indistinguishable from the SDP's programme in 1987. Under Neil Kinnock's leadership after 1987, Labour replaced the rhetoric of class with the rhetoric of citizenship and adopted as its underlying theme, ironically, the social market economy. On price and import controls, a wealth tax and unilateralism, the party executed a 180° turn. Renationalization was ruled out if it required 'substantial resources' (as it inevitably would), and almost none of the trade unions' traditional legal privileges was to be restored. There would likewise be no return to high marginal rates of income tax; and, far from remaining resolutely anti-European, Labour now came out in favour of the European social charter (later the social chapter) and also the European exchange-rate mechanism.[25] Tony Blair's 'new' Labour party from 1994 onwards went still further down the same road.

Yet this wholesale recasting of Labour policy owed almost nothing to the SDP. Most of it occurred after 1987, by which time the SDP had effectively ceased to exist. Moreover, the driving force behind it was not the right wing of the Labour party but Neil Kinnock and his colleagues on the so-called soft left, who had never been close personally or politically to the Social Democrats. The impetus came, as we have seen, from Labour's devastating 1983 and 1987 election defeats—which would have occurred whether or not the SDP had been formed—and also from the sheer passage of time. By the late 1980s the reversal of Thatcher's privatization programme would have been prohibitively expensive, the restoration of the unions' traditional prerogatives would have been politically and electorally impossible, and a wholesale withdrawal from the European Community would have been impracticable. Similarly, Kinnock renounced his lifelong commitment to unilateral nuclear disarmament partly for electoral reasons but partly because of the super-power accord on nuclear-weapons reductions negotiated in 1988.[26]

New Labour policy thinking was thus internally generated, not plagiarized from the SDP. Many social-policy proposals drew on the Labour party's experience in local government, and the ideas on taxation came from a Fabian research group. Even Labour's partial acceptance of constitutional reform owes little to the SDP or the Liberal Democrats. The Labour party initially rejected a bill of rights and proportional representation, and its commitment to Scottish and Welsh devolution was primarily a response to the electoral threat of the two nationalist parties. The SDP did not teach the Labour party to be a modern centre-left party. Neil Kinnock did—assisted, if indirectly, by Margaret Thatcher.

As for the Conservatives, they were almost wholly unaffected by the SDP. Their vote in 1983 and 1987 barely slipped. They lost only one backbench MP and a very small number of local activists to the new party. Government policy did not change one iota, even when the SDP was at the height of its popularity and gaining safe Conservative seats such as Crosby and Portsmouth South in by-elections. Under Margaret Thatcher, the Conservative party sailed on regardless. Thatcher finally went, but by that time the SDP had also gone.

The SDP did transform the politics of the centre during its brief existence, but even here its long-term impact was remarkably slight. It helped to mobilize the largest centre vote for sixty years, but, as we saw in an earlier chapter, it largely failed to realign the electorate's underlying loyalties. Scarcely more voters iden-tified with the Alliance parties in 1987 than had identified with the Liberals on their own in 1979, and the attachment of Alliance voters and Alliance identifiers to their party remained far weaker than in the case of either of the other parties. Not surprisingly, this weak support for the two centre parties largely collapsed as soon as the SDP started its own civil war in 1987.[27] In 1991, a year after the Owenite continuing SDP breathed its last, the size and geography of support for the centre looked very similar to what they had been in 1979–80, a year before the SDP was launched.[28]

The only visible monument to the SDP is the Liberal Democratic party, formed by the union of the Liberals and the pro-merger Social Democrats. As the limited change of name suggests, the Liberal Democratic party differs very little from the old Liberal party. Its leader, Paddy Ashdown, is a former Liberal, and the majority of its MPs, most of its leading members and its rank and file are also former Liberals. Its most distinctive policy positions—constitutional reform, closer Euro-pean integration, environmental protection and the extension of individual liberties and rights—are a direct inheritance from the old Liberal party. The only discontinuities in policy are the Liberal Democrats' much firmer commitment to the free-market economy (and to making it freer still), the renunciation of corporatist and Keynesian macro-economic strategies and the acceptance of multilateral rather than unilateral nuclear disarmament; but these discontinuities probably owe more to the Thatcherite revolution in political economy and the end of the Cold War than to the Liberals' merger with the Social Democrats.

The SDP's influence is more evident in some aspects of the new party's organization. The Liberal Democrats' constitution closely resembles that of the SDP—David Steel's hated Liberal Council has gone—and their party organization has acquired some of the SDP's hi-tech professionalism. The Liberal Democrats, like the SDP, have a centralized membership list and raise funds via computerized direct mail. Compared with the old Liberal party, the new party's ethos is also altogether more managerial and disciplined, less eccentric and anarchic, more geared to power and less to protest. Partly as a result of their success in local elections—a development that does owe something to the SDP—the Liberal Democrats are a considerably more responsible, government-oriented party than the old Liberals were.

That said, someone who returned to Britain in the mid-1990s after having lived abroad (and been out of touch) throughout the 1980s would find very little difference in the British party system—and almost no trace of the SDP. There has been no partisan realignment in the electorate, no enduring shift in the balance of power among the three main parties, no sustained growth of centre-party support, no hung parliaments or coalition governments, no alteration in the electoral system, no major redesigning of the nation's political agenda. The Conservative and Labour parties represent the same coalitions of interests and dispute the same issues of economic management and the quality of public services as they did in the 1960s and 1970s, even though the terms and axes of the debate have inevitably evolved with the passage of time. The one genuinely significant change, the replacement of the old state-control/free-market polarization of the 1970s and 1980s with a new two-party acceptance of the market, is the achievement, in their different ways, of Margaret Thatcher, John Major, Neil Kinnock, John Smith and Tony Blair, not of the SDP or of anyone associated with it.

It is a measure of the British party system's resilience, and of the power of the first-past-the-post electoral system, that the most serious challenge to the system in half a century ended in such total failure, making no discernible impact. Those who founded the SDP and were committed to it throughout its life may rejoice in the fact that the beliefs of the new Labour party under Tony Blair are far closer to their own beliefs than were the views of either the Conservatives or the Labour party in the 1970s and 1980s. Otherwise they are left with only their memories.

• • • •

Epilogue

Nearly a decade after the demise of the SDP, where are its leading figures now?

Roy Jenkins, who became a life peer after losing his seat in 1987, was chosen a year later to be the new merged party's first leader in the House of Lords—a post he still held in 1995. But at another election, also held in 1987, he was more successful, defeating two Conservatives, Robert Blake and Sir Edward Heath, for the chancellorship of Oxford University. Jenkins as chancellor has been in the forefront of raising funds for the university and in raising its public profile. His autobiography, *A Life at the Centre*, was published in 1991. *The Economist* described the book as 'truly distinguished' and 'a model of what a modern politician's autobiography should be'.

David Owen, after a good deal of semi-public agonizing and in the wake of persistent rumours that he might join John Major's Conservative government, announced in September 1991 that he intended to stand down as MP for Plymouth Devonport, severing an association with that city that had lasted for a quarter of a century. In an article for the *Mail on Sunday* published on the eve of the 1992 election, he endorsed the premiership of John Major and castigated Neil Kinnock for 'his record of political misjudgements', but at the same time he went out of his way not to endorse the Conservatives as a party. The article made little impact. Later, rumours that he was about to be made governor of Hong Kong also proved unfounded (the Foreign Office reportedly feared the damage he might do Sino-British relations), and in August 1992 he was appointed instead the European Community's peacemaker in the Bosnian conflict—a task he pursued indefatigably over the next three years. The fact that he failed was hardly his fault. He accepted a life peerage in 1992 but holds the House of Lords in considerable contempt and seldom goes there. When he does, he sits on the cross benches.

Bill Rodgers, having failed to win Milton Keynes in 1987, left politics later that year to become director-general of the Royal Institute of British Architects, a post he held for seven years. On retiring from the RIBA, he became part-time chairman

471

of the Advertising Standards Authority. In 1992 he joined the Liberal Democratic group in the House of Lords, taking the title of Lord Rodgers of Quarry Bank after the Liverpool school that he attended. When Tony Blair was elected Labour leader in 1994, Rodgers shocked many of his Liberal Democrat colleagues by declaring that Blair was the right man to lead Britain in the second half of the 1990s.

Shirley Williams also now sits in the House of Lords, as Baroness Williams of Crosby. She divides her time more or less equally among the John F. Kennedy School of Government at Harvard University (where she was appointed professor of elective politics in 1988), her home in rural Hertfordshire and the world's airlines. Since the fall of the Berlin Wall in 1989 she has been heavily involved in Project Liberty, an American-based organization devoted to promoting democracy in central and eastern Europe. She took her peerage in 1993. Like Rodgers, she greeted Tony Blair's election as Labour leader with considerable enthusiasm, arguing that closer co-operation between Labour and the Liberal Democrats was now essential.

David Steel—who was such a leading figure in the history of the SDP, if not in the SDP itself—greatly disappointed those who hoped in 1988 that he would stand for the leadership of the merged party. He probably felt by then that he had been a party leader for quite long enough (twelve years), and he must also have been bruised by the dead-parrot episode. Instead he became the new party's foreign-affairs spokesman, thus putting himself in a position to take advantage of still further opportunities for foreign travel. In 1989 he polled more than 15,000 votes as a candidate for one of the Italian seats in the European Parliament. In 1990 he was knighted. In 1994 he announced that, after more than thirty years in parliament, he would not be standing for re-election.

Rosie Barnes and John Cartwright, the two remaining Owenites in the House of Commons apart from Owen himself, both fought the 1992 election as Independent Social Democrats. Both were defeated. Barnes in Greenwich lost to Labour by 1,357 votes; Cartwright in Woolwich lost to Labour by 2,225 votes. Neither faced opposition from the new merged party, and Shirley Williams spent a day campaigning for Cartwright, who was an old friend. Barnes is now the director of Wellbeing, a charitable trust for research into the health of women and children. Cartwright joined the Police Complaints Authority shortly after losing his seat, later becoming its deputy chairman.

Unlike Barnes and Cartwright, Robert Maclennan and Charles Kennedy, who both joined the Liberal Democrats, are still MPs. Maclennan held Caithness and Sutherland at the 1992 general election by 5,365 votes; Kennedy held Ross, Cromarty and Skye by 7,630 votes. Kennedy was elected as president of the new merged party in 1990. Maclennan succeeded him in 1994, easily defeating two candidates from the former Liberals. Kennedy speaks for his party on European affairs. Maclennan, as well as being president, is the party's spokesman on the national heritage.

Among the other former SDP MPs, Christopher Brocklebank-Fowler stayed for a time with David Owen's continuing SDP but eventually joined the Liberal Democrats and unsuccessfully contested Norfolk South in 1992 against the Conservative cabinet minister John MacGregor. Ian Wrigglesworth, having reluctantly come round to the view that the Liberals and the SDP should merge, then served for two years as the new party's president, putting it (not without some difficulty) on a secure financial footing. He was knighted in 1991 and, although still active in the Liberal Democrats, has largely moved from the political world into the world of business. He is a director of a number of industrial companies and deputy chairman of the northern machine-tool and engineering group, the Livingston Group. Mike Thomas had already moved into the world of business even before he 'retired hurt' from David Owen's continuing SDP when it collapsed. In 1988 he established his own business, Corporate Communications Strategy, of which he is still chairman and managing director. Since 1990 he has also been chairman of an advertising consultancy, Media Audits.

John Horam—the man who first planted doubts in Bill Rodgers' mind about the future of the Labour party—also built up his own business, the Commodities Research Unit. He joined the Conservatives shortly before the 1987 election and, after several unsuccessful attempts to secure Tory nominations, was finally elected for the safe seat of Orpington in 1992. In early 1995 he was appointed junior minister in the Office of Public Service and Science, thus becoming only the second person in history to have served in both a Labour and a Conservative administration (he had been a junior transport minister under Rodgers in the 1970s). On joining the government, Horam dismissed his time in the SDP as having been merely a 'stage in my political development when I was rejecting Labour'.

Among the senior members of the Cowley Street staff, Bernard Doyle, the party's first chief executive, left in 1983 to become chief executive of the Welsh Water Authority and subsequently held a number of senior management posts in the private sector. His Cowley Street successor, Dick Newby, resigned as soon as the new party was formed and served as director of corporate affairs for the property developers Rosehaugh until shortly before that company collapsed. In 1992 he and a colleague set up their own firm, the Matrix Communications Consultancy, which now operates in eastern Europe as well as Britain. Still active in politics, Newby will serve in 1996 or 1997 as deputy to Richard Holme, the chairman of the Liberal Democrats' next general-election-campaign committee. Alec McGivan, formerly the SDP's national organizer, remained on David Steel's staff until the latter decided not to stand for the new party's leadership. Since then he has held a number of posts in the public-relations world (including fund-raising for the projected Globe Theatre on the South Bank). He is now employed by the Football Association, organizing media relations for the 1996 European football championships.

What happened to the ordinary members of the SDP? Roughly two-fifths of them joined the merged party when it was first formed; one-fifth joined Owen's continuing SDP; the remainder refused to have anything to do with either party. By the time of the 1992 election, there had been a still further drifting-away from active politics: one in four of those who had joined the merged party had left without going anywhere else. On polling day in 1992 the great majority of former SDP members appear to have supported either the Liberal Democrats or Labour. The number who, like Owen, flirted with the Conservatives was small.

The new merged party itself suffered initially from a serious identity crisis. Very few knew what it amounted to. Very few could even remember its name. Social and Liberal Democrats (SLD) was generally agreed to be too cumbersome, but the approved shorter version, the Democrats, failed to catch on. Eventually, in October 1989, the party's rank-and-file members voted by a wide margin to call themselves the Liberal Democrats.

The immediate effects of the merger row and the dead parrot were devastating. Between 1988 and 1990 support for the party in the polls frequently fell below 10 per cent, and Liberal Democrat support in by-elections fell sharply compared with that of the old Alliance. But gradually the position righted itself, especially after the disappearance of the continuing SDP, and in 1990–1 the new party gained three Conservative seats in by-elections—Eastbourne, Ribble Valley, and Kincardine and Deeside. The Liberal Democrats also began to make substantial progress in local elections. They made 520 net gains in 1991, 308 in 1992, 341 in 1993 and 388 in 1994. Following the 1995 local elections, the Liberal Democrats held a total of 5,043 seats in local government and controlled no fewer than fifty-one county and district councils.

The 1992 general election, however, came as yet another disappointment. The party's share of the vote fell to 17.9 per cent (18.3 per cent on the British mainland)—lower than the Liberals' share in 1974. Despite a widely applauded campaign, the Liberal Democrats won only twenty seats (compared with the Alliance's twenty-three in 1983 and twenty-two in 1987). They forfeited all three of their gains in by-elections.

The new party's first leader, Paddy Ashdown, initially declared that the Liberal Democrats' aim was the same as that of the SDP and the Alliance: namely, to replace Labour as the principal opposition to the Conservatives. But that claim seemed increasingly implausible as Labour's electoral fortunes gradually recovered (and as Ashdown was reminded that most Liberal Democrat target seats were Conservative held, not Labour held). Especially after Tony Blair's election as Labour leader in July 1994, it was clear that the Liberal Democrats—like the Liberals and the SDP—were fated to remain a third party and that the only real question was how they should position themselves in relation to the other parties. In the mid-1990s it looked as though their only real option was to lean towards Labour.

Looking forward to the next general election, the Liberal Democrats' hope was that in 1996–7 enough former Conservative supporters would be sufficiently hostile to the Tory government—and sufficiently reconciled to Labour—to vote for the Liberal Democrats in seats where they were second. Their fear was that Labour would mount such an effective national campaign that Labour supporters and former Conservatives would fail to do the sensible thing and vote tactically in seats where the Liberal Democrats were second but would instead vote for no-hope Labour candidates, thereby depriving the Liberal Democrats of victory in many seats and enabling incumbent Conservatives to win on minority votes. Either way, the Liberal Democrats in the 1990s—apart from their very real successes in local government—seem not to have progressed very far beyond where the Liberals were a generation before.

Appendix 1

• • • •

Former Labour MPs, Not Elected to the 1979 Parliament, who Joined the SDP

Austen Albu[†]	(Edmonton, 1948–Feb. 1974)
Michael Barnes[1]	(Brentford and Chiswick, 1966–Feb. 1974)
Herbert Bowden*	(Leicester, South-West, 1945–67)
George Brown*	(Belper, 1945–70)
Elaine Burton	(Coventry South, 1950–9)
Edmund Dell*	(Birkenhead, 1964–79)
John Diamond*	(Manchester, Blackley, 1945–51; Gloucester, 1957–70)
William Edwards	(Merioneth, 1966–Feb. 1974)
Hugh Gray	(Yarmouth, 1966–70)
William Hannan	(Glasgow Maryhill, 1945–Feb. 1974)
Roy Jenkins*	(Southwark Central, 1948–50; Birmingham Stechford, 1950–76; Glasgow Hillhead, 1982–7)
Gwynoro Jones	(Carmarthen, 1970–Oct. 1974)
Dick Leonard	(Romford, 1970–Feb. 1974)
Evan Luard[†]	(Oxford, 1966–70, Oct. 1974–9)
Roderick MacFarquhar	(Belper, Feb. 1974–9)
David Marquand	(Ashfield, 1966–76)
Edmund Marshall[2]	(Goole, 1971–83)
Eric Moonman	(Billericay 1966–70; Basildon, Feb. 1974–9)
Francis Noel-Baker[3]	(Brentford & Chiswick, 1945–50; Swindon, 1955–69)
Derek Page	(King's Lynn, 1964–70)
Colin Phipps	(Dudley West, Feb. 1974–9)
Paul Rose	(Manchester Blackley, 1964–79)
Hartley Shawcross*	(St Helens, 1945–58)
John Stonehouse*	(Wednesbury, 1957–Feb. 1974; Walsall North, Feb. 1974–6)
Dick Taverne[†]	(Lincoln, 1962–73; 1973–Oct. 1974 as Democratic Labour)
Michael Ward	(Peterborough, Oct. 1974–9)
John Watkinson	(Gloucestershire West, Oct. 1974–9)
William Wells	(Walsall, 1945–55; Walsall North, 1955–Feb. 1974)
Alan Lee Williams	(Hornchurch, 1966–70, Feb. 1974–9)
Shirley Williams*	(Hitchin, 1964–Feb. 1974, Stevenage, Feb. 1974–9; Crosby, 1981–3)
Ian Winterbottom[†]	(Nottingham Central, 1950–5)

*   Cabinet member.
†   Junior minister.
¹   He rejoined the Labour party in autumn 1983.
²   He remained a Labour MP throughout the 1979–83 parliament, failed to be
     nominated as a result of constituency boundary changes, and joined the SDP in
     1984. He was a Liberal candidate for Louth in 1964 and 1966.
³   He joined the Conservative party in 1984.

Appendix 2

• • • •

SDP Peers

(Any former party affiliation is in parentheses.)

Lord Ashby
Earl Attlee
Lord Aylestone (Labour)*
Lord Bullock
Baroness Burton (Labour)*
Lord Chandos
Lord Cudlipp
Duke of Devonshire (Conservative)
Lord Diamond (Labour)*
Lord Donaldson of Knightsbridge (Labour)
Viscount Falkland
Lord Flowers
Lord Grenfell
Viscount Hanworth
Lord Harris of Greenwich (Labour)
Lord Henniker
Lord Hunt of Llanfair Waterdine
Lord Hutchinson (Labour)
Lord Kahn
Lord Kennet (Labour)
Lord Kilmarnock
Lord Kirkwood

Lord Lindsay
Lord McGregor (Labour)
Lord Morris of Kenwood
Lord Parmoor
Lord Perry
Marquess of Queensbury
Lord Raglan (Labour)
Lord Rathcreedan
Lord Roberthall
Lord Sainsbury (Labour)
Baroness Sharpe
Lord Shawcross *
Baroness Stedman (Labour)
Lord Taylor of Gryfe (Labour)
Lord Tedder
Lord Vernon
Lord Walston (Labour)
Lord Weidenfeld (Labour)
Lord Whaddon (Labour)*
Lord Wilson of Langside (Labour)
Lord Winterbottom (Labour)*
Lord Young of Dartington (Labour)

* Former Labour MP.

Appendix 3

• • • •

Potential Recruits to the SDP who Remained in the Labour Party

EEC REBELS

Leo Abse (Pontypool)
Peter Archer (Rowley Regis and Tipton)
Joel Barnett (Heywood and Royton)
Tam Dalyell (West Lothian)
Ifor Davies (Gower) (d. June 1982)
Dick Douglas (Dunfermline)*
Jack Dunnett (Nottingham East)
Andrew Faulds (Warley East)*
Ben Ford (Bradford North)*
Roy Hattersley (Birmingham Sparkbrook)
Denis Howell (Birmingham Small Heath)
Alex Lyon (York)
Roy Mason (Barnsley)
Arthur Palmer (Bristol North-East)*
Robert Sheldon (Ashton-under-Lyne)
Sam Silkin (Dulwich)
John Smith (Lanarkshire North)
Phillip Whitehead (Derby North)*
Fred Willey (Sunderland North)

MENTIONED AS A POTENTIAL RECRUIT IN THE PRESS OR OUR INTERVIEWS

Donald Anderson (Swansea East)
Betty Boothroyd (West Bromwich West)
Ian Campbell (Dunbartonshire West)
Stanley Cohen (Leeds South-East)
Donald Dewar (Glasgow Garscadden)
Alan Fitch (Wigan)
George Foulkes (Ayrshire South)
Harry Gourlay (Kirkcaldy)

Brynmor John (Pontypridd)
Jimmy Johnson (Hull West)
Walter Johnson (Derby South)
Harry Lamborn (Peckham) (d. Aug. 1982)
Giles Radice (Chester-le-Street)
Albert Roberts (Normanton)
George Robertson (Hamilton)
Shirley Summerskill (Halifax)
Tom Urwin (Houghton-le-Spring)
Ken Weetch (Ipswich)
James White (Glasgow Pollok)
William Whitlock (Nottingham North)
Alan Williams (Swansea West)

* Also mentioned as a potential recruit in the press or in our interviews.

Sources: On the October 1971 EEC vote: Philip Norton, *Dissension in the House of Commons, 1945–1974* (London: Macmillan, 1975), 397–8. The other potential recruits are names mentioned in our interviews; the twelve signatories of the statement in *The Times* of 22 Sept. 1980 calling for reforms in the party's structure; and the MPs listed in Peter Rose, '12 Labour MPs Set to Join SDP', *Sun*, 27 July 1981. These names largely overlapped.

Constituencies are those represented by the MP in 1981, which in a few cases differ from those represented at the time of the EEC debate (October 1971).

Appendix 4

• • • •

Liberal–SDP Alliance Guidelines for the Allocation of Seats in the 1983 General Election

1. It is the objective of the two parties to fight the next general election in alliance. It follows that they should not fight each other in any parliamentary seat. Together the parties intend to fight every seat in England, Scotland and Wales. The aim will be rough parity in the total number of seats each party fights.

2. Each party will fight seats throughout the country and support the other in so doing. The aim will be a spread of seats between the parties in every nation and region of Great Britain. The disparity in favour of either party in any negotiating unit should not normally exceed 3 : 2.

3. Each party will fight a substantial number of seats differing in their economic, social, environmental and political characteristics. Each will fight rural and industrial seats; suburban and inner-city seats; Labour and Conservative seats; preferred and less promising seats in each negotiating unit. The aim is not to 'cluster' Liberal and Social Democratic seats.

4. In negotiating which seats either party should fight, weight will be given to local opinion, taking into account the relative strengths of the local parties, their campaigning record and potential and the particular electoral appeal of prospective candidates and the respective parties insofar as this can be ascertained.

5. Negotiations to give effect to these considerations shall take place within negotiating units, agreed between the parties. Each party's local representation shall be supported by members of the National Negotiating Teams and, if appropriate, by its regional leadership. Our parties in Scotland and Wales are proceeding on a similar basis.

6. The National Negotiating Teams shall number six-per-side plus a senior executive from each party and meet regularly during the negotiations. Together they will constitute the Joint Negotiating Group and will take responsibility for the general oversight of these negotiations and any conciliation that may be necessary. There may be circumstances when a matter in dispute cannot thus be resolved. Consideration will therefore be given to the establishment of an independent arbitration panel to assist in the implementation of this agreement.

7. At the beginning of the negotiations in each negotiating unit, sitting MPs of both parties in each unit shall be recognised as the Candidates in their existing constituencies provided that they are members of their respective parties by 1 January 1982 and that they may be re-adopted in the form prescribed by their respective party rules.

The seats of these members shall be counted towards the ratios referred to in paragraphs 1 and 2 above. In the case of such a Member of Parliament whose seat may disappear or be substantially changed by boundary proposals, he/she will be given special priority and consideration in finding a new seat.

8. The division of seats between the parties shall proceed on existing constituency boundaries, and on such new boundaries as have been recommended by the Boundary Commission, in parallel. This will be amended in the event of revised or final proposals from the Boundary Commission.

9. Following the choice of a candidate by the party to which the seat has been allocated, it is anticipated that he/she will wish to seek the endorsement of the other party at local level. In all cases both parties should be fully involved in the campaign. This could be achieved by the use of the formula 'with Liberal support' or 'with Social Democratic support', but it is recognised that endorsement may not be universal. A formula incorporating the expression 'Alliance' may be favoured as the two parties' election campaigns come together in a more integrated way. 'Joint selection' will not be the normal method of selection. The National Negotiating Teams will, however, consider the practicality and constitutionality of this procedure further.

10. It is proposed that negotiations on the allocation of seats shall begin not later than 31 October 1981, and be concluded by 31 March 1982. During these negotiations, neither party should adopt any further prospective parliamentary candidates other than in a by-election, save where the two parties have properly agreed in a negotiating unit to the satisfaction of the Joint Negotiating Group.

11. Each party will continue to recruit members wherever and in whatever ways it wishes. However, deliberate recruitment of each other's membership or the holding of dual membership will be discouraged.

12. The implementation of this agreement shall be effected within the constitutions and rules of the respective parties.

Appendix 5

• • • •

Tables

Table 1.1. The major parties' electoral decline, 1959–1979

Year	% of popular vote cast for either Conservative or Labour party	% of electorate identifying 'very strongly' or 'fairly strongly' with either Conservative or Labour party
1959	93.2	n.a.
1964	87.5	74
1966	89.8	74
1970	89.4	71
Feb. 1974	75.0	63
Oct. 1974	75.0	61
1979	80.8	60

n.a. = not available.

Sources: David Butler and Gareth Butler, *British Political Facts 1900–1985*, 6th edn. (London: Macmillan, 1986), 227–8; Ivor Crewe, Anthony Fox and Neil Day, *The British Electorate, 1963–1987* (Cambridge: Cambridge University Press, 1992), table 2.1, p. 47.

Table 6.1. Actual and potential defectors, by CLP vote for deputy leader

Potential defector's action	CLP voted for			
	Benn		Healey	
Switched to SDP	(22)	55%	(4)	20%
Stayed Labour	(9)	23%	(14)	70%
Was deselected or retired	(9)	23%	(2)	10%
TOTAL	(40)	100%	(20)	100%

Note: The table examines the twenty-eight Labour MPs who defected plus the forty 'potential defectors' listed in Appendix 3. It excludes the eight CLPs that voted for Silkin, changed votes between rounds or abstained.

Sources: Labour Party, *Annual Report*, 1981, 345–55; *The Times Guide to the House of Commons, June 1983*, 287; Byron Criddle, 'Candidates', in David Butler and Dennis Kavanagh, *The British General Election of 1983* (London: Macmillan, 1984).

Table 6.2. The deputy-leadership vote by the CLPs of actual or potential defectors

CLP vote	CLPs of potential defectors who						All CLPs	
	joined SDP		did not join SDP					
			EEC rebels		Others			
Voted Benn	(22)	85%	(11)	61%	(8)	47%	(443)	80%
Voted Healey	(4)	15%	(7)	39%	(9)	53%	(108)	20%
Did not vote	(2)		(1)		(4)		(49)	
Silkin/other*	—		—		—		(23)	
TOTAL	(28)		(19)		(21)		(623)	

* Switched from Healey to Benn between first and second rounds.

Sources: As for Table 6.1.

Table 6.3. Defection and loyalty, by age

Age in 1981	Defected to SDP	Stayed Labour	% who stayed Labour
Under 40	2	2	50
40–49	8	10	56
50–59	15	15	50
60 and over	3	13	81
All	28	40	59

Source: Who's Who, 1981.

Table 6.4. Defection and loyalty, by class and prospects

Class and prospects	(N)	Defected to SDP (%)	Stayed Labour (%)	Total (%)
Occupational class*				
Manual,[†] clerical, technical	(25)	36	64	100
Professional, business	(42)	45	55	100
Financial prospects[‡]				
Prospect of earning at least equal income shortly after losing seat:				
Probable	(32)	53	47	100
Improbable	(23)	48	52	100

* Based on occupation prior to entering parliament. In one case the information was not obtainable.

† Only six MPs were manual workers, two of whom defected.

‡ This section of the table excludes the eleven potential defectors who retired in 1983 and two for whom the financial implications of electoral defeat were unclear.

Sources: Dod's Parliamentary Companion, 1980; *The Times Guide to the House of Commons, May 1979; Who's Who,* 1981.

Table 6.5. Defection and loyalty, by different connections to the labour movement

Connections to labour movement	(N)	Defected to SDP (%)	Stayed Labour (%)	Total (%)
Trade-union connections				
No trade-union connections	(21)	57	43	100
Trade-union member	(47)	34	66	100
Sponsored by a trade union*	(28)	29	71	100
Held trade-union office	(10)	10	90	100
Local-government service				
Had never been a councillor	(39)	51	49	100
Served as a local councillor	(29)	28	72	100
Residence in constituency[†]				
Lived away from constituency	(25)	56	44	100
Lived in or close to constituency	(29)	28	72	100

* Another seven MPs were sponsored by the Co-operative Movement, of whom four defected to the SDP.

[†] This section of the table excludes fourteen MPs whose home address was not available.

Sources: As for Table 6.4.

Table 6.6. Defection, loyalty and roots in the labour movement

Roots in labour movement	Defected to SDP	Stayed Labour
	(28)	(40)
Trade-union *and* local-government involvement*	1	5
Trade-union involvement only	—	3
Local-government involvement only	7	16
Neither trade-union *nor* local-government, of whom	20	16
live in/near constituency	4	6
live away from constituency	12	4
home address not known	4	6

* Trade-union involvement is defined as holding a local, regional or national office in a trade union. Local-government involvement is defined as election as a local councillor.

Sources: As for Table 6.4.

Table 10.1. Estimated number of Liberal and SDP MPs at different levels of Alliance vote in the 1983 election

Alliance vote (%)	Number of MPs elected			SDP as % of Alliance
	Lib.	SDP	Total Alliance	
If Alliance takes votes equally from both Con. and Lab.				
28	21	8	29	28
30	25	14	39	36
32	28	19	47	40
34	39	26	65	40
36	54	54	108	50
38	76	77	153	50
If Alliance takes all extra votes from Con.				
28	20	11	31	35
30	25	14	39	36
32	37	21	58	36
34	54	44	98	45
36	76	71	147	48
38	116	110	226	49
If Alliance takes all extra votes from Lab.				
28	21	8	29	28
30	23	15	38	39
32	27	19	46	41
34	32	36	68	53
36	48	52	100	52
38	64	74	138	54

Source: Authors' calculations.

Table 12.1. Membership ballot on method of electing party leader, April 1982

Method	1st round (distribution of preferences)			2nd round (elimination of 'election by MPs only' option and redistribution of its supporters' second preferences)			
	Votes	%		Votes		Total votes	%
Election by ballot of members	16,186	43.5	+	432	=	16,618	51.5
First election by ballot of members; subsequent elections by MPs only	12,560	33.7	+	3,110	=	15,670	48.5
Election by MPs only	8,500	22.8		Eliminated (4,968 did not express a second preference)			
TOTAL	47,246	100.0					

Source: SDP Archives.

Table 12.2. The composition of the National Committee

Section of National Committee or position	Who could stand for election?	Who could vote?
President	Any member	Party membership
Leader	SDP MP nominated by at least 15% of SDP MPs	Party membership
Parliamentary		
10 SDP MPs (or all SDP MPs, if fewer than 10 returned to Commons)	SDP MP	SDP MPs
2 SDP peers	SDP peer	SDP peers
1 SDP Member of the European Parliament	SDP MEP	SDP MEPs
Local councillors		
3 SDP local councillors	SDP members of local council (other than town/parish council)	Council for Social Democracy
Council		
12 area Council members, elected from each of 12 regions	Area Council member from region	Area Council members for the region
Nationally elected members		
4 men and 4 women	Any member except for MPs	Party membership by STV in a postal ballot
Young member		
1 member of Young Social Democrats or SDP Students	SDP member under 26	Council for Social Democracy
Co-opted members (non-voting)		
up to 3	SDP member	National Committee

Table 12.3. Originators of policy motions at SDP Councils, October 1982–September 1986

Originator	7 councils Oct. 1982–Jan. 1985		4 councils Sept. 1985–Sept. 1986*		All councils	
	Number	%	Number	%	Number	%
Policy Committee[†]	(39)	66	(22)	47	(61)	58
Regional council	(9)	15	(7)	15	(16)	15
Council members	(11)	19	(7)	15	(18)	17
Area parties[‡]	(n.a.)	—	(11)	23	(11)	10
TOTAL	(59)	100	(47)	100	(106)	100

Notes: Policy motions exclude emergency motions.

n.a. = not applicable.

* The May 1985 Council was devoted to revisions to the party constitution.
† Includes one motion submitted by the president.
‡ Area parties were not entitled to submit policy motions until September 1985.

Source: Council for Social Democracy, Minutes.

Table 12.4. Amendments to policy motions at SDP Councils, October 1982–September 1986

Date	Council	Number of debated policy amendments submitted by area parties*	% carried
Oct. 1989	Great Yarmouth	(14)	50
Jan. 1983	Newcastle	(38)	58
Sept. 1983	Salford	(11)	9
Jan. 1984	Aston	(39)	46
May 1984	Edinburgh	(11)	55
Sept. 1984	Buxton	(38)	71
Jan. 1985	Birmingham	(24)	63
Sept. 1985	Torquay	(36)	58
Jan. 1986	Bath	(22)	86
May 1986	Southport	(25)	72
Sept. 1986	Harrogate	(41)	73

* Excludes tabled amendments that were withdrawn or ruled out of order.

Source: Minutes of SDP Council meetings, SDP Archive.

Table 13.1. SDP membership, 1981–1987

Date	Number
June 1981	54,000
June 1982	64,000
June 1983	54,000
June 1984	45,000
June 1985	52,000
June 1986	58,000
June 1987	58,000

Note: Figures exclude the category of 'supporters', i.e. sympathizers, who, in return for a donation, are invited to SDP activities but have no voting rights.

Sources: President's Reports to Council for Social Democracy and Consultative Assembly, 1982/3–1986/7; SDP Archive.

Table 13.2. Regional distribution of SDP membership, May 1981

Region	Number of constituencies	Number of members per constituency
South & Wessex	42	134
Eastern	45	134
South East	40	125
Greater London	92	116
South West	34	106
East Midlands	40	70
Yorkshire & Humberside	54	69
North	37	65
North West	76	65
Midlands	56	59
Wales	36	40
Scotland	71	33

Notes: There were fifty-seven members in Northern Ireland in 1981. The number of parliamentary constituencies in each region refers to the position prior to the 1983 boundary revisions.

Source: Richard Evans, 'SDP Getting Most Members in the South', *The Times*, 22 May 1981.

Table 13.3. The ten strongest SDP area parties, October 1986

Area party	Parliamentary constituencies comprising area party	Members in area party*	Members per constituency*
Camden	Hampstead & Highgate Holborn & St Pancras	851	426
South Cambridgeshire	Cambridge Cambridgeshire South-East Cambridgeshire South-West	964	321
Kensington & Chelsea	Chelsea Kensington	568	284
Richmond & Twickenham	Richmond & Barnes Twickenham	528	264
Oxford & Abingdon	Oxford East Oxford West & Abingdon	492	246
East Berkshire	Berkshire East Slough Wokingham Windsor & Maidenhead	868	217
Mid-Hampshire	Eastleigh Hampshire North-West Winchester	644	215
Barnet	Chipping Barnet Finchley Hendon North Hendon South	706	177
Wandsworth	Battersea Putney Tooting	528	176
Plymouth	Plymouth Devonport Plymouth Drake Plymouth Sutton	522	174

* Excludes 'supporters'.

Source: Private communication from Dick Newby.

Table 13.4. Central income of SDP, 1981/2–1986/7*

Source of income	1981/2 £000	%	1982/3 £000	%	1983/4 £000	%	1984/5 £000	%	1985/6 £000	%	1986/7 £000	%
Membership subscriptions	760	89	584	60	424	60	381*	57	486	58	469	50
Donations†	53	6	364	38	236	33	217	33	298	36	457	49
Profits on sales of merchandise	15	2	3	—	5	1	18	3	9	1	(–11)	n.a.
By-election fund‡	—	—	5	1	28	4	19	3	19	2	(–6)	n.a.
Miscellaneous (interest, letting, *Social Democrat*, etc)	28	3	12	3	14	2	28	4	25	3	9	1
Total routine income (at March 1982 prices)	855 (855)	100	968 (872)	100	707 (606)	100	663 (541)	100	837 (647)	100	918 (722)	100
Donations to general election fund	50		152		928		103		55		60	
Total income	905		1,120		1,635		766		892		978	

Notes: General election funds are excluded. 'Short' money for opposition parties and grants from the European Parliament towards the costs of the 1984 European election campaign are excluded.

n.a. = not applicable. A dash indicates less than 0.5.

* In 1984–5 a scheme for subscription by instalments was introduced; the comparable figure with previous years is therefore somewhat higher.

† Excludes donations to the general election fund.

‡ Remitted by area parties.

Source: SDP Annual Reports.

Table 13.5. Company donations to the SDP and the Alliance, 1981–1987

Financial year of donations	Number of donor companies	Total value of donations (£000)	Recipient
1981/2	1	5.0	SDP
	1	5.0	Joint Lib.–SDP Commission
1982/3	n.a.	n.a.	n.a.
1983/4*	6	12.3	SDP
	4	15.5	Alliance
1984/5	4	12.0	SDP
	8	16.3	Alliance
1985/6	6	21.3	SDP
	16	33.6	Alliance
1986/7	7	23.3	SDP
	14	35.1	Alliance
1987/8	11	57.0	SDP
	14	57.0	Alliance

Notes: This table is based on surveys of the 3,000 leading public companies undertaken by *Labour Research*. It excludes contributions of under £200, which do not have to be disclosed in company accounts, and contributions made by private companies, and thus underestimates the total amount donated by companies. It also excludes payments by the Joseph Rowntree Social Service Trust of £29,100 in 1981/2, £13,400 in 1983 and £105 in 1987, made mainly to the Alliance.
n.a. = not available.

  * Election year.

Sources: *Labour Research*, July 1983 (166), Aug. 1984 (204–7), May 1985 (117), Dec. 1986 (7–11), May 1987 (12–13), Dec. 1988 (7–10); David Worsfold, 'Not Left, but Right and Maybe Centre', *Guardian*, 25 May 1985; Michael Pinto-Duschinsky, 'British Political Funding, 1979–1983', *Parliamentary Affairs*, 38 (1985), 328–47, at 338.

Table 13.6. Election expenditure by local parties, 1983 and 1987

Election	Conservative	Labour	Liberal	SDP	Lib.–SDP Alliance
1983 election					
Number of candidates	633	633	322	311	633
Average expenditure per candidate	£3,320	£2,297	£2,282	£2,777	£2,525
Total local expenditure	£2.102m.	£1.853m.	£0.735m.	£0.864m.	£1.599m.
Central and regional grants to local parties	£0.062m.	£0.500m.	£0.140m.	£0.380m.	£0.520m.
Local expenditure minus central/regional grants	£2.040m.	£1.353m.	£0.595m.	£0.484m.	£1.079m.
% of local expenditure based on local revenue	97%	73%	81%	56%	67%
Amount of locally raised revenue spent per candidate	£3,222	£2,137	£1,847	£1,556	£1,705
Locally raised local expenditure, per party member (est.)	£1.77	£4.58	£3.31	£9.31	£4.65
1987 election					
Number of candidates	633	633	327	306	633
Average expenditure per candidate	£4,423	£3,949	£3,472	£3,416	£3,445
Total local expenditure	£2.80m.	£2.50m.	£1.14m.	£1.05m.	£2.19m.
Central and regional grants to local parties	£0.14m.	£0.42m.	—	£0.62m.	£0.62m.
Local expenditure minus central/regional grants	£2.66m.	£2.08m.	£1.14m.	£0.43m.	£1.57m.
% of local expenditure based on local revenue	98%	83%	100%	41%	72%
Amount of locally raised revenue spent per candidate	£4,202	£3,286	£3,472	£1,405	£2,473
Locally raised local expenditure, per party member (est.)	£2.31	£7.56	£7.60	£7.41	£7.55

Sources: M. Pinto-Duschinsky, 'Financing the British General Election of 1983', in Crewe and Harrop (eds.), *Political Communications* (1986); Pinto-Duschinsky, 'Trends in British Political Funding, 1979–1983', *Parliamentary Affairs*, 38 (1985). 328–47; Pinto-Duschinsky, 'Financing the British General Election of 1987', in Crewe and Harrop (eds.), *Political Communications* (1989); Pinto-Duschinsky, 'Trends in British Party Funding, 1983–1987', *Parliamentary Affairs*, 42 (1989).
197–212; David Butler and Dennis Kavanagh, *The British General Election of 1987* (1988), 249.

Table 13.7. SDP, Liberal and Alliance central expenditure on general elections, 1983 and 1987 (£000)

Party	1983	1987
SDP		
Before campaign		
(e.g. billboard poster campaign in 1983)	467	217
During campaign		
Grants to constituencies	380	617
National advertising (mobile poster campaign, ethnic press, share of Alliance party election broadcasts)	181	33*
Private opinion polling	48	102
Leaders' tours	39	72
Printing and publications (net of receipts)	130	
Additional staff	111	
Permanent staff salaries	65	
Additional office space and equipment	39	250
Election organizers	20	
Miscellaneous	59	
TOTAL	1,072	1,074
Liberal party[†]		
Party leaders' tours	20	80
Grants to constituencies	168	—
Joint publicity with SDP	57	
General headquarters expenditure	120	200
TOTAL	365	280
Liberal–SDP Alliance fund		
Party election broadcasts	—	100
'Ask the Alliance' rallies	—	50–65
Advertising	—	20–25
Press conferences	—	25
Manifesto and materials	—	15–20
Regional offices	—	10–15
General	47	—
TOTAL	47	250
OVERALL TOTAL	1,951	1,821

* These categories are not directly comparable because most national advertising was separately funded by each party in 1983 but jointly funded through the Alliance Fund in 1987.

† These figures combine the Liberal Party Organization's budget with the separate Liberal leader's account.

Sources: M. Pinto-Duschinsky, 'Financing the British General Election of 1983', in Crewe and Harrop (eds.), *Political Communications* (1986); Pinto-Duschinsky, 'Trends in British Political Funding, 1979–1983', *Parliamentary Affairs*, 38 (1985), 328–47; Pinto-Duschinsky, 'Financing the British General Election of 1987', in Crewe and Harrop (eds.), *Political Communications* (1989); Pinto-Duschinsky, 'Trends in British Party Funding, 1983–1987', *Parliamentary Affairs*, 42 (1989), 197–212.

Table 13.8. Candidates' general-election expenses, 1983 and 1987

Party	1983 (June 1987 prices)			1987		
	Candidates' expenses (mean)	% of legal maximum	Number of candidates	Candidates' expenses (mean)	% of legal maximum	Number of candidates
Conservative	£4.008	72	633	£4.423	78	633
Labour	£3.534	63	633	£3.949	70	633
Liberal	£2.753	50	322	£3.472	60	327
SDP	£3.353	62	311	£3.416	61	306
(Alliance)	(£3.048)	(55)	(633)	(£3.445)	(61)	(633)

Sources: David Butler and Dennis Kavanagh. *The British General Election of 1983* (1984), 266–7; Butler and Kavanagh. *The British General Election of 1987* (1988). 235–6; R. J. Johnston, private communication.

Table 14.1. Liberal–SDP Alliance support in opinion polls before and after heavily publicized by-elections (%)

National polls conducted *before* by-election					By-election (and date)	National polls conducted *after* by-election			
29–35 days before	22–8 days before	15–21 days before	8–14 days before	1–7 days before		1–7 days after	8–14 days after	15–21 days after	22–8 days after
27	28	—	—	27	Warrington (16 July 1981)	—	31	—	32
30	29	—	—	—	Croydon NW (22 Oct. 1981)	40	—	42	—
40	—	—	42	—	Crosby (26 Nov. 1981)	44	—	51	—
29	—	—	30	30	Glasgow Hillhead (23 Mar. 1982)*	34	32	33	31
21	21	20	22	21	Bermondsey (24 Feb. 1983)	34	31	27	28
n.a.[†]	34	31	27	28	Darlington (24 Mar. 1983)	22	23	23	20
—	31	30	27	—	Brecon and Radnor (4 July 1985)	34	33	31	31

Notes: Entries are percentage who said they intended to vote SDP, Liberal or 'Alliance' at the next election. in published opinion polls. The by-elections listed are those given unusually heavy attention by the media. In periods with more than one poll, the average is taken.

* Polls conducted after 2 Apr. 1982 recorded the impact of the Falklands crisis on public opinion.

† Not applicable. The Bermondsey by-election took place at end of this week.

Source: Authors' private files.

Table 14.2. Electoral support for the Alliance, by newspaper readers, 1983 and 1987 (%)

Newspaper	1983	1987
Conservative press		
Sun	26	19
Daily Mail	26	34
Daily Express	22	18
Daily Star	—	16
Daily Telegraph	12	21
The Times	33	28
Labour press		
Daily Mirror/Record	23	18
Mixed/non-partisan press		
Daily Star	31	n.a.
Guardian	41	37
Independent	—	35
Does not read daily newspaper	43	n.a.

Note: n.a. = not available.

Sources: Recalculated from Patrick Dunleavy and Christopher T. Husbands, *British Democracy at the Crossroads* (London: George Allen & Unwin, 1985), table 5.16, p. 113; and Brian MacArthur, 'The National Press', in Ivor Crewe and Martin Harrop (eds.), *Political Communications: The General Election Campaign of 1987* (Cambridge: Cambridge University Press, 1989), 104.

Table 14.3. Vote in 1983 by whether or not influenced by a party election broadcast

1983 vote	All voters		New voters		Late deciders		Vote switchers	
	No (%)	Yes (%)	No (%)	Yes (%)	No (%)	Yes (%)	No (%)	Yes (%)
Con.	50	35	48	29	28	21	30	19
Lab.	32	20	34	19	28	18	18	10
Lib–SDP	19	45	18	59	45	61	52	71
TOTAL	100	100	100	100	100	100	100	100
Category as a % of all voters for Con., Lab., Lib.–SDP	78	22	7	4	4	4	16	9
Number of respondents	(2,399)	(671)	(229)	(112)	(109)	(126)	(504)	(261)

Notes: Respondents categorized as 'influenced by a PEB' are those who gave a Conservative, Labour or Liberal–SDP party-election broadcast as one of the reasons that applied when they 'finally decided which way to vote'. Nationalist and other minor party voters are excluded. *New voters* are those who were too young to vote in 1979, but who voted in 1983. *Late deciders* are respondents who said they did not decide how to vote until the last week of the campaign. *Vote switchers* are 1983 voters whose vote differed in 1979, or who, although old enough, did not vote in 1979.

Source: BBC TV–Gallup survey, 8–9 June 1983.

Table 14.4. Public awareness of party leaders on television and in the press, September 1984 (%)

Awareness of party leaders	Thatcher	Kinnock	Steel	Owen
Saw something on television				
In last week	60	25	9	9
Between week and month ago	25	38	29	22
Longer ago	16	36	62	68
Saw something in the newspapers				
In last week	68	33	11	11
Between week and month ago	16	33	28	22
Longer ago	16	33	61	67

Source: *Gallup Political Index*, No. 300, Aug. 1985, 11. The question was: 'About how long ago is it that you saw anything about Mrs Thatcher (Mr Kinnock, Mr Steel, Dr Owen) in the newspapers? And on television?'

Table 15.1. Party activists, social profile

Social profile	SDP members	SDP activists	Conservative activists	Labour activists	Liberal activists	GB population
Male percentage	67	72	76	86	76	48
Age						
Under 35	33	25	24	29	41	32
35–60	52	66	58	55	47	42
Over 60	15	9	17	15	13	26
Occupation*						
Professions, senior management,	} 77	46	33	18	32	} 29
Intermediate professions, junior management		36	46	42	48	
Clerical and office workers	14	14	15	12	14	19
Foremen, skilled workers	7	3	6	22	5	} 52
Semi and unskilled manual	3	1	1	5	—	
Sector of employment						
Public	64	54	23	60	35	35
Private	36	46	78	40	65	65
Father's occupation						
Higher white-collar	} 47	19	26	6	24	n.a.
Intermediate white-collar		18	40	17	40	n.a.
Lower white-collar	} 54	21	4	8	9	n.a.
Blue-collar		42	30	68	27	n.a.

Table 15.1. (Cont.)

Social profile	SDP members	SDP activists	Conservative activists	Labour activists	Liberal activists	GB population
Social Mobility[†]						
Upwardly mobile	n.a.	65	43	54	44	n.a.
Non-mobile	n.a.	24	34	34	36	n.a.
Downwardly mobile	n.a.	13	23	13	21	n.a.
Education: type of school						
Elementary only	n.a.	1	6	29	2	⎫ 70
Secondary modern/comprehensive	n.a.	15	18	31	16	⎭
Grammar school	n.a.	60	44	35	51	26
Independent fee-paying	n.a.	23	33	6	31	5
Higher education						
Completed education over the age of 18	46	65	27	25	53	10

Note: n.a. = not available.

* Excludes the unemployed, retired and housewives.

† Based on a comparison of the respondent's occupational status with that recalled of the respondent's father.

Source: SDP members: Data made available from the *Weekend World* survey, except for 'sector of employment', which is taken from the Newcastle survey. *Activists*: Herbert Doring, 'Who are the Social Democrats?', *New Society*, 8 Sept. 1983, pp. 351–3, and Terry Barton and Herbert Doring, 'Social Mobility and the Changing Party System'. Doring's data on Conservative, Labour and Liberal activists were in turn taken from surveys of delegates to the three parties' annual conferences conducted by Gordon and Paul Whiteley in 1978 and 1979. *GB population*: A. H. Halsey (ed.), *British Social Trends since 1900* (London: Macmillan, 1988), 105 (age), 164 (occupation); Ivor Crewe, Neil Day and Anthony Fox, *The British Electorate, 1963–1987* (Cambridge: Cambridge University Press, 1991), 40 (school); Social and Community Planning Research, *British Social Attitudes Cumulative Sourcebook: The First Six Surveys* (Aldershot: Gower, 1992), table G.1–31 (sector of employment), table I–4 (school leaving age).

Table 15.2. The policy views of SDP members, 1981

Policy item*	For (%)	Against (%)	Don't know (%)	Are majority of members closer to Con. or Lab. party on issue?
Withdrawal of Britain from EEC[†]	5	95	(5)	Con.
Proportional representation[‡]	95	5	(5)	Neither
Compulsory secret ballots in trade-union elections[‡]	95	5	(5)	Con.
Remain in NATO[‡]	93	7	(7)	Con.
Incomes policy[†]	91	9	(2)	Neither
Reflate economy through public spending[‡]	88	12	(18)	Lab.
Reduce parliament to Commons only[‡]	14	86	(14)	Con.
Government aid rather than open market as source of finance given to certain industries[†]	81	19	(2)	Lab.
Positive action to give women equal opportunities[‡]	79	21	(20)	Lab.
Abolish tax relief on mortgages[‡]	21	79	(20)	Con.
Unilateral nuclear disarmament[†]	22	78	(2)	Con.
The right of council tenants to buy their homes[‡]	76	24	(13)	Con.
Legislation placing employees on companies' boards of directors[‡]	75	25	(2)	Lab.
Curtailment of trade unions' immunities against legal action[†]	75	25	(4)	Con.
Retaining current frontier between nationalized and private industry[†]	74	26[§]	(2)	Neither
Leave private schools as they are[†]	28	72[¶]	(–)	Lab.
Outlaw the closed shop[†]	68	32	(2)	Con.
Autonomous assemblies for English regions[†]	32	68	(2)	Both
Control prices by government action[‡]	67	33	(24)	Lab.
Introduce a wealth tax[†]	65	35	(3)	Lab.
Base an incomes policy on the taxation of above-average wage increases rather than voluntary co-operation with trade unions[‡]	63	37	(4)	Neither

Table 15.2. (Cont.)

Policy item*	For (%)	Against (%)	Don't know (%)	Are majority of members closer to Con. or Lab. party on issue?
Substantially reduce unemployment even at risk of noticeable increase in inflation†	63	37	(4)	Lab.
Withdraw British troops from Ulster‡	38	62	(18)	Both
Consider voluntary repatriation under some circumstances, as solution to racial tensions‡	40	60	(18)	Lab.
Establish separate national assemblies for Scotland and Wales†	58	42	(3)	Lab.
Raise income tax and/or VAT to pay for more social services and benefits†	57	43	(4)	Lab.
Abolish state-assisted places at private schools‡	53	47	(19)	Lab.
Restore death penalty for certain categories of murder‡	48	52	(11)	Lab.

* The policy items are listed in order of consensus of view among SDP members. The wording is abbreviated from the original survey, but the essential phrasing is retained. To make it easier to compare policy items, members' views are expressed as dichotomized percentages, after excluding 'don't knows', which are listed in a separate column. The number of 'don't knows' in the *Weekend World* survey is very small because the self-administered questionnaire posted to SDP members did not contain a 'don't-know' box for them to tick. The right-hand column indicates whether the majority of SDP members were closer to the policy thinking and direction—which was not necessarily official policy—of the Conservative party or the Labour party.

† *Weekend World* national survey of 5,568 area party members, 13–24 Nov. 1981.

‡ Survey of 283 members of Newcastle-upon-Tyne area SDP, Nov.–Dec. 1981.

§ Of whom 21% favoured some privatization and 5% favoured some further nationalization.

¶ Of whom 54% favoured the abolition of their charitable tax status and 18% favoured their integration into the state system.

Sources: As in Table 15.1.

Table 15.3. Parliamentary candidates, by social background, 1983 and 1987

Social background	Con.	Lab.	Lib.	SDP	All*
Percentage women	7%	14%	12%	17%	12%
(number)	(86)	(171)	(77)	(103)	(437)
Median age (years)	44	41	40	40	42
Type of occupation	%	%	%	%	%
Professions	44	48	53	54	48
Business	36	11	24	23	23
Miscellaneous[†]	19	22	22	20	21
Manual workers	2	20	1	4	8
Education	%	%	%	%	%
Elementary only/Elementary[†‡]	—	5	—	1	1
Secondary only	8	15	11	8	11
Secondary[†‡]	11	21	15	14	15
Secondary and university	23	45	39	49	38
Fee-paying only/Fee-paying[†‡]	14	1	6	3	7
Fee-paying and university	44	12	29	26	28
% attending fee-paying schools	58%	13%	35%	28%	34%
% attending university	67%	57%	69%	74%	65%
% attending Oxbridge	37%	13%	21%	28%	25%
% Asian or Afro-Caribbean	1%	2%	1%	2%	1%
(number)	(10)	(20)	(6)	(10)	(46)

* Conservative, Labour, Liberal and SDP candidates.

† Includes farmers, journalists, housewives, students and political organizers.

‡ Further education short of university/polytechnic.

Sources: These figures are derived from Byron Criddle, 'Candidates', in David Butler and Dennis Kavanagh, *The British General Election of 1983* (London: Macmillan, 1984), tables 10.1 and 10.3, pp. 232 and 235–6; and Byron Criddle, 'Candidates' in David Butler and Dennis Kavanagh, *The British General Election of 1987* (London: Macmillan, 1988), tables 9.1 and 9.3, pp. 200 and 202. Owing to rounding, percentages do not always add up to 100.

Table 15.4. Parliamentary candidates, by occupational background, 1983 and 1987 (%)

Occupational background	Con.	Lab.	Lib.	SDP	All*
Professions					
Barristers and solicitors	18	6	11	12	12
Doctors and dentists	1	1	2	3	1
Architects, surveyors, civil and chartered engineers	3	1	4	2	2
Accountants, chartered secretaries	5	1	3	2	3
Civil servant, local government official	3	6	6	4	5
Armed services	3	—	—	1	1
Total non-educational professions	34	15	26	24	23
Education and research					
University teachers	1	4	4	6	4
Adult education	1	11	8	8	7
School teachers	6	17	10	12	11
Scientific research/other	2	2	4	3	2
Total education/research	10	33	27	30	24
Total professions	44	48	53	54	47
Business					
Company director or executive	25	2	14	14	14
Commerce/insurance	6	2	4	3	4
Management/clerical	2	5	4	3	3
General business	2	1	2	2	2
Total business	36	11	24	22	23
Miscellaneous					
Journalist, author, publisher	5	4	5	8	6
Farmer	4	—	2	2	2
Various white collar	2	12	8	6	7
Political organiser/full-time politician	5	4	4	2	4
Other (housewife, student, local administration)	2	3	3	2	2
Total	18	22	22	20	21
Manual workers	2	20	1	5	8
TOTAL[†]	100	100	100	100	100

* Conservative, Labour, Liberal and SDP candidates.
† Owing to rounding, column totals do not always add exactly.

Sources: As in Table 15.3.

Table 16.1. Identification with Liberal party, 1964–1979, and with Liberal–SDP Alliance, 1983–1987

Strength of identification	1964	1966	1970	Feb. 1974	Oct. 1974	1979	1983	1987
Percentage of respondents identifying with Liberals/Lib.–SDP Alliance								
Very strongly	4	4	2	2	2	2	2	2
Fairly strongly	6	6	5	8	9	6	7	8
Not very strongly	3	2	2	5	6	5	6	10
TOTAL*	12	10	8	14	15	13	14	19
Percentage of Liberal/Lib.–SDP Alliance identifiers with a								
Very strong identification	30	33	25	11	13	13	12	10
Fairly strong identification	47	53	52	52	53	47	46	41
Not very strong identification	23	14	23	37	34	40	42	49
TOTAL	100	100	100	100	100	100	100	100

* The total percentage of Liberal/Lib.–SDP Alliance identifiers is less than the sum of the column owing to rounding.

Source: Ivor Crewe, Neil Day and Anthony Fox, *The British Electorate, 1963–1987* (Cambridge: Cambridge University Press, 1991), table 2.1. All the data are taken from the British Election Studies.

Table 16.2. Where the SDP and Liberal vote came from, 1983 and 1987 (%)

	1983 vote			1987 vote		
	SDP	Lib.	Lib.–SDP Alliance[‡]		SDP	Lib.	Lib.–SDP Alliance[‡]
Party identification, 1983*				**Party identification, 1987**			
Conservative	12	13	14	Conservative	16	11	15
Labour	24	18	25	Labour	16	10	16
Liberal–SDP	50	57	52	Liberal–SDP	56	68	59
Other	1	1	1	Other	1	1	1
None	13	11	8	None	11	11	10
Total[‡]	100	100	100	Total	100	100	100
Vote in 1979[§]				**Vote in 1983[§]**			
Conservative	21	20	20	Conservative	26	11	18
Labour	40	19	32	Labour	14	8	12
Liberal	25	48	39	Liberal	49	76	63
Other	8	6	2	Other	3	2	1
Did not vote	7	7	7	Did not vote	9	3	6
Total[‡]	100	100	100	Total[‡]	100	100	100
(Too young)	(13)	(8)	(10)	(Too young)	(11)	(5)	(8)
(N)	(376)	(236)	(730)	(N)	(252)	(159)	(842)

* The party identification question was 'Leaving aside this particular election, would you say you generally think of yourself as Conservative, Labour, Liberal, SDP or what?'

[†] Includes all respondents who said they voted SDP, Liberal or 'Alliance'.

[‡] Because of rounding, columns do not always total 100%.

[§] Because respondents' recall of their vote at a previous election can be unreliable, the figures have been weighted by the actual vote in Great Britain in that year.

Source: BBC/Gallup election surveys, 10–11 June 1983 and 8–9 June 1987.

Table 16.3. The party leanings of different categories of Alliance voters, 1983 and 1987

	1983				1987			
	Con.	Lab.	Lib.–SDP	(N)	Con.	Lab.	Lib.–SDP	(N)
Which party has the best policies?								
Lib.–SDP voters	11	5	77	(804)	8	9	74	(897)
'Not very strong' Lib.–SDP identifiers	18	2	67	(206)	16	8	63	(250)
All Lib.–SDP recruits	14	5	74	(460)	14	10	66	(404)
Lib.–SDP recruits from Labour	9	8	71	(219)	4	23	64	(145)
Which party has the best leaders?								
Lib.–SDP voters	25	2	69	(804)	n.a.	n.a.	n.a.	
'Not very strong' Lib.–SDP identifiers	35	3	56	(206)	n.a.	n.a.	n.a.	
All Lib.–SDP recruits	27	3	68	(460)	n.a.	n.a.	n.a.	
Lib.–SDP recruits from Labour	21	5	71	(219)	n.a.	n.a.	n.a.	
Which party should the Alliance join in a coalition?*								
Lib.–SDP voters	n.a.	n.a.	n.a.		35	27	n.a.	
'Not very strong' Lib.–SDP identifiers	n.a.	n.a.	n.a.		40	17	n.a.	
All Lib.–SDP recruits	n.a.	n.a.	n.a.		39	25	n.a.	
Lib.–SDP recruits from Labour	n.a.	n.a.	n.a.		12	48	n.a.	

Note: n.a. = not available.

* Permitted answers also included 'form minority government' and 'hold fresh elections'.

Source: BBC–Gallup election surveys. 10–11 June 1983 and 8–9 June 1987.

Table 16.4. Voters' social profiles, by party, 1983 and 1987 (%)

Profile	All electors	Con. voters	Lab. voters	Alliance voters	'Liberal' voters	'SDP' voters
1983						
Men	47	49	48	44	36	46
Women	53	51	52	56	64	54
18–24	12	11	11	13	10	15
25–44	40	39	39	42	41	44
45–64	30	31	28	32	31	31
65+	19	20	22	13	19	9
AB	20	28	8	20	17	20
C1	24	30	17	22	17	27
C2	28	24	33	28	35	24
DE	28	18	41	29	31	29
(N)	(4,141)	(1,567)	(1,024)	(915)	(236)	(376)
1987						
Men	47	49	50	46	40	48
Women	53	51	50	54	60	52
18–24	13	11	11	10	6	13
25–44	41	37	42	49	40	56
45–64	26	31	24	24	25	21
65+	20	21	22	18	29	10
AB	15	22	7	19	16	16
C1	25	31	17	28	14	30
C2	30	28	31	30	31	31
DE	31	19	45	24	38	22
(N)	(4,885)	(1,577)	(1,024)	(915)	(236)	(376)

Source: BBC–Gallup election surveys, 8–9 June 1983 and 10–11 June 1987.

Table 16.5. Alliance voters, by social background, 1983 and 1987

Social category	(% electorate)	1983 % vote for Alliance	1983 Deviation from GB average	1987 % vote for Alliance	1987 Deviation from GB average	Change 1983–7
All (Great Britain)		26	0	23	0	–3
Men	(47)	24	–2	22	–1	–2
Women	(53)	28	+2	24	+1	–4
Age						
18–22	(13)	29	+3	20	–3	–9
23–44	(39)	27	+1	27	+4	0
45–64	(29)	27	+1	20	–3	–7
65+	(19)	19	–7	20	–3	+1
Social Class						
A	(3)	19 ⎫26	–7 ⎫+2	26 ⎫27	+3 ⎫+4	+7 ⎫+1
B	(16)	28 ⎭	0 ⎭	27 ⎭	+4 ⎭	–1 ⎭
C1	(23)	24	–2	25	+2	+1
C2	(28)	26	0	24	+1	–2
D	(18)	29 ⎫27	+3 ⎫+1	21 ⎫19	–2 ⎫–4	–8 ⎫–8
E	(11)	25 ⎭	–1 ⎭	17 ⎭	–6 ⎭	–8 ⎭
Other factors						
Trade-union member	(35)	28	+2	25	+2	–3
Non-member	(65)	25	–1	22	–1	–3
Unemployed	(9)	25	–1	17	–6	–8
No further education	(54)	25	–1	19	–4	–6
Some further education	(40)	26	0	26	+3	0
University	(6)	31	+5	36	+13	+5
Black	(3)	12	–14	5	–18	–7

Table 16.5. (Cont.)

Social category	(% electorate)	1983 % vote for Alliance	1983 Deviation from GB average	1987 % vote for Alliance	1987 Deviation from GB average	Change 1983–7
Housing tenure						
Middle-class owner-occupiers	(32)	27	+1	27	+4	0
Working-class owner-occupiers	(25)	30	+4	24	+1	−6
Working-class council tenants	(26)	25	−1	18	−5	−7
Occupation						
Middle-class, private sector	(23)	23	−3	21	−2	−2
Middle-class, public sector	(15)	28	+2	31	+8	+3
Working-class, private sector	(34)	27	+1	23	0	−4
Working-class, public sector	(18)	26	0	19	−4	−7
Social class/union membership						
AB, non-union	(14)	24 ⎱ 22	−2 ⎱ −4	23 ⎱ 23	0 ⎱ 0	−1 ⎱ +1
C1, non-union	(16)	21	−5	23	0	+2
C2, DE, non-union	(33)	29	+3	21	−2	−8
AB, union member	(5)	36 ⎱ 32	+10 ⎱ +6	37 ⎱ 31	+14 ⎱ +8	+1 ⎱ +1
C1, union member	(7)	28	+2	29	+6	+1
C2, DE, union member	(23)	25	−1	22	−1	−3

Source: BBC–Gallup election surveys, 8–9 June 1983 and 10–11 June 1987.

Table 16.6. The vote of the salariat, 1983 (%)

Divisions within the salariat	(% of electorate)	Con.	Lab.	Lib.–SDP	Other		(N)
Educational divisions within the salariat							
Degree	(4)	42	16	41	1	100	(131)
'O' level or above	(17)	54	12	33	1	100	(501)
Below 'O' level	(8)	60	17	22	2	100	(231)
Sectoral divisions within the salariat							
Private sector	(15)	62	9	28	1	100	(441)
Nationalized industries	(3)	47	23	30	—	100	(78)
Government sector	(11)	46	18	35	2	100†	(323)
Occupational divisions within the salariat*							
'Line' occupations	(3)	68	12	20	1	100†	(102)
'Staff' occupations	(10)	44	19	35	2	100	(302)
Trade-union divisions within the salariat							
Trade-union members	(5)	40	23	36	1	100	(210)
Non-members	(14)	68	8	24	—	100	(569)

* The distinction between 'staff' and 'line' occupations is based on the Office of Population Censuses and Surveys' distinction between 'managers in small establishments' and 'ancillary workers'; these form only a sub-set of the salariat.

† Because of rounding, rows do not always sum to exactly 100 per cent.

Sources: Anthony Heath, Roger Jowell and John Curtice, *How Britain Votes* (Oxford: Pergamon Press, 1985), 60, 61 and 67; and, for trade-union divisions, BBC–Gallup survey, 8–9 June 1983.

Table 16.7. The policy beliefs of Alliance voters (%)

Policy*	Voters†			Distance of Alliance voters from		Consensus among Alliance voters?‡
	Con.	Lab.	Alliance	Con. voters	Lab. voters	
CLASSIC LEFT–RIGHT SOCIO-ECONOMIC ISSUES						
Public expenditure and welfare						
Increase public expenditure to reduce unemployment[a]	26	3	9	17	**6**§	Yes
Redistribute income and wealth in favour of poorer people[a]	46	7	22	24	**15**	Yes
Tackle unemployment by leaving it to private companies, or to government?[c]	81	25	46	35	**21**	No
Cut down public spending to reduce inflation[a]	73	61	61	12	**0**	No
Trade unions						
Restore right to secondary picketing[c]	95	54	87	**8**	33	Yes
Introduce stricter laws to regulate trade unions[a]	88	43	79	**9**	34	Yes
Nationalization/privatization						
Sell off British Steel and British Leyland[b]	83	24	49	34	**25**	No
Return British Gas and British Telecom to public ownership[c]	75	25	57	**18**	32	No
Will privatization spread prosperity or concentrate wealth?[c]	83	22	37	46	**15**	No
Taxation						
Replace local rates by a standard charge levied on every adult[c]	66	33	42	24	**9**	No
Reverse the recent 2p cut in income tax[c]	80	37	51	29	**14**	No
THE PROGRESSIVE AGENDA						
Various issues						
Send coloured immigrants back to their own country[a]	55	45	47	8	**2**	No
Give more aid to poorer countries in Africa and Asia[a]	56	42	43	13	**1**	No
Bring back death penalty[a]	82	70	75	7	**5**	Yes

Table 16.7. (cont.)

Policy*	Voters†			Distance of Alliance voters from		Consensus among Alliance voters?‡
	Con.	Lab.	Alliance	Con. voters	Lab. voters	
Take measures to reduce the amount of sex and nudity on TV and in films and magazines[a]	77	70	76	1	6	Yes
Make abortion widely available on the National Health Service[c]	52	45	40	12	5	No
Set up a Ministry for Women[c]	48	24	41	7	17	No
Constitutional issues						
Withdraw from the EEC (% against)[b]	87	33	72	15	39	Yes
Take Britain out of the Common Market (% against)[a]	79	42	46	31	4	No
Shift power from London to the regions and local authorities (% against)[a]	34	16	23	11	9	Yes
Withdraw British troops from Northern Ireland immediately (% against)[a]	52	33	49	3	16	No
Change present system of voting to proportional representation (% disagreeing)[c]	55	36	16	39	20	Yes
Inflation						
Establish a Prices Commission[b]	29	10	18	11	8	Yes
Government should set firm guidelines for wage and price increases[a]	19	15	16	3	1	Yes
Levy tax on firms paying too big wage rises[b]	49	51	50	1	1	No
Universal v. selective education						
Re-establish grammar schools as an alternative to comprehensive schools[a]	84	51	70	14	19	Yes
Allow state schools to opt out of local authority control and set their own entry tests[c]	70	25	36	45	11	No
Withdraw tax exemptions from private schools[b]	60	27	34	26	7	No

Table 16.7. (Cont.)

Policy*	Voters†			Distance of Alliance voters from		Consensus among Alliance voters?‡
	Con.	Lab.	Alliance	Con. voters	Lab. voters	
Defence issues						
Allow cruise missiles on British soil?^b	83	26	45	38	**19**	No
Give up the Polaris missile^b (% against)	92	60	79	**13**	19	Yes
Give up Britain's nuclear weapons, whatever other countries decide^a (% against)	89	44	64	25	**20**	No
Remove US nuclear weapons from British soil^c (% against)	83	19	46	37	**27**	No
Spend as much money as is necessary to maintain a strong defence for the Falkland Islands^a	66	34	34	32	**0**	No

* Issues on which there was an overwhelming consensus among voters of all three parties are excluded from the table. These include 'Putting more money into the National Health Service', 'Spending more money to tackle pollution of the air and rivers', 'Giving council tenants the right to buy their houses', 'Increase measures to promote equal opportunities for women' and 'Keep up government services like health, education and welfare even if it means that taxes cannot be cut' (as distinct from 'Cut taxes even if it means some reduction in government services like health, education and welfare').

† The entries record the percentage giving the right-wing response. Respondents answering 'Don't know' or giving a neutral or intermediate response. e.g. 'It doesn't matter either way', were omitted from the percentage base; thus the proportion giving a left-wing response always equals 100 minus the proportion giving a right-wing response.

‡ A 'consensus' is defined as a division of opinion of at least 67 : 33.

§ The emboldened figures indicate whether Alliance voters are closer in their views to Conservative or Labour voters.

Sources:

^a Unpublished tabulations of a Gallup poll conducted 19 Jan.–3 Feb. 1986. The wording of the question was: 'I am going to read out a list of things that some people believe a government should do. For each one can you say whether you feel it is very important that it should be done. fairly important that it should be done. it doesn't matter either way. fairly important that it should not be done or very important that it should not be done.'

^b BBC–Gallup election survey, 8–9 June 1983.

^c BBC–Gallup election survey, 10–11 June 1987. The wording of the question in the BBC–Gallup survey was: 'I am going to read out some proposals that the parties have put forward in this election. Please say whether you think the proposal is a very good idea. a fairly good idea. a fairly bad idea or a very bad idea.'

Table 16.8. Voters' preference for their own party in different policy areas, 1979, 1983 and 1987 (%)

Would you tell me which party you think would be best at . . .*	1979			1983			1987		
	Con. voters	Lab. voters	Lib. voters	Con. voters	Lab. voters	Lib.–SDP voters	Con. voters	Lab. voters	Lib.–SDP voters
Reducing unemployment	80	87	39	71	90	58	73	93	48
Making Britain more prosperous	94	81	46	97	77	60	98	77	51
Cutting income tax	93	55	29	80	71	43	95	48	25
Reducing crime and vandalism	88	53	27	79	67	50	76	71	51
Cutting down strikes	75	78	33	89	63	41	96	54	34
Furthering cause of world peace/ bringing about disarmament	n.a.	n.a.	n.a.	88	80	61	51	91	36
Providing properly for the National Health Service	n.a.	n.a.	n.a.	66	95	59	67	96	59
Ensuring that Britain is properly defended	n.a.	n.a.	n.a.	97	58	50	98	58	46
Average (first five)	86	71	35	83	74	50	88	69	42
Average (all eight)	n.a.	n.a.	n.a.	83	75	53	82	74	44

Note: Entries are the percentage of each party's voters who chose their own party. n.a. = not available.

* 'Don't knows' are excluded from the percentage base; the small proportion answering 'no difference' are included.

Sources: BBC–Gallup election surveys, 2–3 May 1979, 8–9 June 1983, 10–11 June 1987.

Table 16.9. The parties' images, 1983 and 1987 (%)

Image	1983			1987		
	Con. party	Lab. party	Lib.–SDP Alliance	Con. party	Lab. party	Lib.–SDP Alliance
Extreme	49	49	6	49	47	5
Moderate	40	37	74	41	39	73
Neither/both/don't know	12	14	20	11	14	21
Good for one class	58	54	8	67	50	11
Good for all classes	35	34	64	27	37	67
Neither/both/don't know	7	12	28	7	12	21
Has clear policies	76	35	30	71	38	39
Has vague policies	17	56	50	22	52	44
Neither/both/don't know	7	9	20	7	10	18

Note: The wording of the questions was 'On the whole would you describe the Conservative party as extreme or moderate? And the Labour party, is it extreme or moderate? And the Alliance, is it extreme or moderate?' 'Would you describe the Conservative party as good for one class or good for all classes? And the Labour party, is it . . . etc. etc.' 'Do you think the Conservative party has clear policies or vague policies? And the Labour party, does it have . . . etc. etc.'

Sources: 1983 British General Election Study, quoted in *Gallup Political Index*, No. 306 (Feb. 1986), 5; *Gallup Political Index*, No. 321 (May 1987), 7.

APPENDIX 5

Table 16.10. General-election results, 1983 and 1987

Party	MPs elected	Total vote (UK)	% vote (UK)	% vote (GB)	Change in % vote (GB)
9 June 1983					
Conservative	397	13,012,316	42.4	43.5	−1.4
Labour	209	8,456,934	27.6	28.3	−9.5
Liberal	17	4,210,115	13.7	14.1	
SDP	6	3,570,834	11.7	11.9	
(Total Liberal–SDP)	(23)	(7,780,949)	(25.4)	(26.0)	+11.9
SNP/Plaid Cymru	4	457,284	1.5	1.5	−0.6
Irish parties	17	764,925	2.5	n.a.	n.a.
Others	0	198,729	0.6	0.7	−0.4
TOTAL	650	30,671,137	100.0	100.0	
11 June 1987					
Conservative	376	13,760,583	42.3	43.3	−0.2
Labour	229	10,029,807	30.8	31.5	+3.2
Liberal	17	4,173,450	12.8	13.1	−1.0
SDP	5	3,168,183	9.7	10.0	−1.9
(Total Liberal–SDP)	(22)	(7,341,633)	(22.5)	(23.1)	−2.9
SNP/Plaid Cymru	6	540,072	1.7	1.7	+0.2
Irish parties	17	730,152	2.2	n.a.	n.a.
Others	0	127,331	0.4	0.4	−0.3
TOTAL	650	32,529,578	100.0	100.0	

Note: n.a. = not applicable.

Source: F. W. S. Craig, *Britain Votes 4* (Aldershot: Gower, 1988), 185, 191.

519

Table 16.11. Local-election results, 1982–1987

Year	(Number of seats at stake)	Con.	Lab.	Lib.	SDP	Lib. + SDP
1982	(5,361)					
% of seats contested		80	86	n.a.	n.a.	n.a.
No. of seats won		n.a.	n.a.	n.a.	n.a.	n.a.
% of seats won		n.a.	n.a.	n.a.	n.a.	n.a.
Net gains/losses		+18	−51	+160	−49	+111
% of GB vote (est.)		42	31	n.a.	n.a.	26
1983	(12,458)					
% of seats contested		70	69	30	23	53
No. of seats won		n.a.	n.a.	n.a.	n.a.	n.a.
% of seats won		n.a.	n.a.	n.a.	n.a.	n.a.
Net gains/losses		+128	+37	+118	−8	+110
% of GB vote (est.)		41	35	n.a.	n.a.	22
1984	(3,982)					
% of seats contested		n.a.	n.a.	n.a.	n.a.	n.a.
No. of seats won		n.a.	n.a.	390	n.a.	n.a.
% of seats won		n.a.	n.a.	9.8	n.a.	n.a.
Net gains/losses		−131	+46	115	+28	+143
% of GB vote (est.)		37	38	n.a.	n.a.	22
1985	(5,361)					
% of seats contested		83	89	48	26	74
No. of seats won		1,360	1,263	536	109	645
% of seats won		38.2	35.5	15.1	3.1	18.1
Net gains/losses		−55	−32	+105	+24	+129
% of GB vote (est.)		32	37	n.a.	n.a.	27
1986	(5,319)					
% of seats contested		87	92	45	39	84
No. of seats won		1,574	2,550	676	173	849
% of seats won		29.6	47.9	12.7	3.3	16.0
Net gains/losses		−729	+493	+189	+98	+287
% of GB vote (est.)		34	37	n.a.	n.a.	27
1987	(11,219)					
% of seats contested		77	72	40	29	69
No. of seats won		n.a.	n.a.	n.a.	n.a.	n.a.
% of seats won		n.a.	n.a.	n.a.	n.a.	n.a.
Net gains/losses		+75	−227	+249	+204	+453
% of GB vote (est.)		40	31	n.a.	n.a.	27

Notes: Row percentages do not total 100 because information about Independents and other parties is omitted. Net gains/losses exclude the small number of local authorities in which ward boundaries had changed since the previous local elections.

n.a. = not available.

Sources: Number of seats at stake: F. W. S. Craig, *British Electoral Facts* (Aldershot: Parliamentary Research Services and Gower, 1989), 135–42; net gains/losses and % of GB vote: BBC TV, *Local Election Handbook* for 1983, 1984, 1985, 1986, 1987 and 1988.

APPENDIX 5

Table 16.12. By-election results, 1981–1987

Result	Con.	Lab.	Lib.	SDP	Lib.–SDP Alliance
July 1981–March 1983 (13 seats)					
Mean % vote	27.5	34.7	28.0	33.7	31.1
Change in % vote since 1979	−12.2	−14.0	+27.0	+23.2	+24.6
Number of gains	1	1	2	2	4
Number of losses	4	2	0	0	0
July 1983–March 1987 (16 seats)					
Mean % vote	29.0	32.0	41.7	31.8	36.5
Change in % vote since 1983	−14.4	+0.2	+14.8	+9.7	+12.9
Change in % vote since 1979*	−14.7	−8.6	+22.1	+23.4	+22.6
Number of gains	0	1	2	2	4
Number of losses	4	1	0	0	0

* These figures omit constituencies which the Liberal party did not contest in 1979: Coatbridge and Airdrie, Glasgow Queens Park and Cynon Valley. Because of constituency boundary changes between 1979 and 1983, comparison is made with the notional 1979 'result' for the new boundaries, estimated in the *BBC/ITN Guide to the New Parliamentary Constituencies* (Chichester: Parliamentary Research Services, 1983).

Source: F. W. S. Craig, *Chronology of British Parliamentary By-elections, 1833–1987* (Chichester, Sussex: Parliamentary Research Services, 1987).

Table 16.13. Party support in the opinion polls, 1981–1987

Year: quarter	Number of polls	Con.	Lab.	Lib.–SDP Alliance	Lib.	SDP	Con. majority over Lab.
1981: 1	10	33.6	38.2		17.6	n.a.	−4.6
1981: 2	8	32.0	37.7	27.7	15.5	12.2	−5.8
1981: 3	9	30.5	38.7	28.6	13.1	15.5	−8.2
1981: 4	7	26.8	28.9	42.1	14.4	27.7	−2.1
1982: 1	8	30.9	31.9	34.8	14.9	19.9	−1.0
1982: 2	23	44.4	28.8	25.3	—	—	+15.7
1982: 3	12	44.1	31.6	22.1	—	—	+12.5
1982: 4	12	42.7	33.2	22.0	—	—	+9.4
1983: 1	20	43.9	30.5	24.0	—	—	+13.4
1983: 2	12	45.0	31.2	21.9	—	—	+13.8
1983: 3	9	45.6	26.4	26.6	—	—	+19.2
1983: 4	11	43.1	35.8	19.6	—	—	+7.3
1984: 1	14	41.6	37.8	18.9	—	—	+3.8
1984: 2	16	39.9	37.4	21.2	—	—	+2.6
1984: 3	15	38.5	38.0	21.6	—	—	+0.5
1984: 4	16	42.3	33.6	22.2	—	—	+8.7
1985: 1	22	38.1	35.5	24.5	—	—	+2.6
1985: 2	14	3.8	36.2	28.4	—	—	−2.4
1985: 3	20	30.9	34.7	32.6	—	—	−3.8
1985: 4	17	34.8	35.4	28.0	—	—	−0.6
1986: 1	19	31.3	35.6	31.3	—	—	−4.3
1986: 2	19	31.9	37.9	27.6	—	—	−6.0
1986: 3	19	33.8	38.8	25.2	—	—	−5.0
1986: 4	22	39.2	37.9	20.6	—	—	+1.3
1987: 1	28	38.7	34.7	24.8	—	—	+3.9
1987: 2	41	43.1	31.5	23.0	—	—	+11.6
1987: 3	15	48.0	33.3	16.2	—	—	+14.7
1987: 4	16	47.8	34.8	14.5	—	—	+13.0

Notes: The figures for each quarter are the mean of the national poll of polls, which are the mean of the national polls conducted each month. From April 1981 to March 1982 most polls reported separate figures for the Liberals and the SDP; thereafter, most polls combined respondents' intention to vote Liberal, SDP or Alliance into a single 'Liberal–SDP Alliance' category.
n.a. = not applicable. A dash = not available.

Source: Authors' files of published national polls.

Publication date	Fieldwork date	Polling company	Newspaper/ TV programme	Con.	Lab.	Lib.–SDP	Vote intention for Lab. over Lib.–SDP
Thursday, 14 May	7–11 May	Gallup	Daily Telegraph	39	28	30	−2
Thursday, 14 May	8–12 May	Marplan	Guardian	43	29	25	+4
Friday, 15 May	6–11 May	NOP	Evening Standard	46	28	25	+3
Friday, 15 May	13 May	Marplan	Daily Express	41	30	26	+4
Friday, 15 May	11–13 May	MORI	Times*	43	32	23	+9
Sunday, 17 May	8–12 May	MORI	Sunday Times	44	31	23	+8
Sunday, 17 May	11–14 May	MORI	Sunday Times (panel)	44	30	25	+5
Sunday, 17 May	13–15 May	Harris	Observer	42	33	23	+10
Sunday, 17 May	13–15 May	Harris	Weekend World*	40	34	25	+9
Tuesday, 19 May	16–17 May	Harris	TV-am	42	32	24	+8
Tuesday, 19 May	18 May	Marplan	Today	41	33	24	+9
Tuesday, 19 May	14–17 May	Newsnight	Newsnight	40	34	24	+10
Thursday, 21 May	19 May	NOP	Independent*	42	34	23	+9
Thursday, 21 May	19–20 May	Gallup	Daily Telegraph	42	33	23	+10
Friday, 22 May	21 May	Marplan	Guardian	41	33	21	+12
Friday, 22 May	18–21 May	Harris	TV-am	43	36	20	+16
Sunday, 24 May	20–21 May	MORI	Sunday Times (panel)	44	31	24	+7
Sunday, 24 May	20–21 May	Harris	Observer	41	34	22	+12
Sunday, 24 May	20–22 May	Gallup	Sunday Telegraph (panel)	42	33	23	+10
Sunday, 24 May	20–22 May	Harris	Weekend World*	42	35	22	+13
Wednesday, 27 May	22–25 May	Harris	TV-am	42	37	21	+16
Wednesday, 27 May	26 May	Marplan	Today	42	35	20	+15
Thursday, 28 May	26 May	NOP	Independent*	42	35	21	+14
Thursday, 28 May	26–27 May	Gallup	Daily Telegraph	44.5	36	18	+18

* Poll of marginals, adjusted to reflect the whole country.

Source: Authors' files of published national polls.

Notes

• • • •

Chapter 1

1. For an account of the 1964 election campaign, and for an evocation of the mood of that time, see David Butler and Anthony King, *The British General Election of 1964* (London: Macmillan, 1965), esp. chs. 1–6.
2. There is no really good history of the 1964–70 Labour government. Its stumbling progress can be traced, however, in Clive Ponting, *Breach of Promise: Labour in Power 1964–1970* (London: Hamish Hamilton, 1989), and Harold Wilson, *The Labour Government 1964–1970: A Personal Record* (London: Weidenfeld & Nicolson, and Michael Joseph, 1971). See also Ben Pimlott, *Harold Wilson* (London: HarperCollins, 1992), chs. 15–24.
3. Economic data for the 1964–70 period are set out in David Butler and Gareth Butler, *British Political Facts 1900–1985*, 6th edn. (London: Macmillan, 1986), 382; David Butler and Michael Pinto-Duschinsky, *The British General Election of 1970* (London: Macmillan, 1971), 24; and Paul Whiteley, *The Labour Party in Crisis* (London: Methuen, 1983), 133.
4. The Heath government has attracted oddly little interest from political scientists and historians; but see David Butler and Dennis Kavanagh, *The British General Election of February 1974* (London: Macmillan, 1974), ch. 2; Anthony King, 'The Election that Everyone Lost', in Howard R. Penniman (ed.), *Britain at the Polls: The Parliamentary Elections of 1974* (Washington, DC: American Enterprise Institute, 1975), 3–15; Douglas Hurd, *An End to Promises: Sketch of a Government 1970–74* (London: Collins, 1979); Kenneth O. Morgan, *The People's Peace: British History 1945–1989* (Oxford: Oxford University Press, 1990), ch. 9; and John Campbell, *Edward Heath; A Biography* (London: Jonathan Cape, 1993), pt. IV.
5. On the 1974–9 Labour governments, see David Butler and Dennis Kavanagh, *The British General Election of 1979* (London: Macmillan, 1980), esp. chs. 1–2; Anthony King, 'Politics, Economics and the Trade Unions, 1974–1979', in Howard R. Penniman (ed.), *Britain at the Polls, 1979: A Study of the General Election* (Washington, DC: American Enterprise Institute, 1981); Harold Wilson, *Final Term: The Labour Government 1974–1976* (London: Weidenfeld & Nicolson, and Michael Joseph, 1979); Pimlott, *Harold Wilson*, chs. 26–8; and James Callaghan, *Time and Chance* (London: Collins, 1987), pt. V.
6. The best single account of the rise of trade-union militancy during these years is Robert Taylor, *The Fifth Estate: Britain's Unions in the Modern World*, rev. edn. (London: Pan Books, 1980). See also Robert Taylor, 'The Trade Union "Problem" in the Age of Consensus 1960–1979', in Ben Pimlott and Chris Cook (eds.), *Trade Unions in British Politics: The First 250 Years*, 2nd edn. (London: Longman, 1991).
7. Butler and Butler, *British Political Facts*, 373.
8. The story is told in Peter Jenkins, *The Battle of Downing Street* (London: Charles Knight, 1970).
9. See Michael Moran, *The Politics of Industrial Relations: The Origins, Life and Death of the 1971 Industrial Relations Act* (London: Macmillan, 1977).
10. See e.g. Anthony King (ed.), *Why is Britain Becoming Harder to Govern?* (London: British Broadcasting Corporation, 1976).

11. Much the best account of the breakdown of the post-war consensus (though the author himself rejects this specific term) is contained in Peter Jenkins, *Mrs Thatcher's Revolution: The Ending of the Socialist Era* (London: Jonathan Cape, 1987), esp. pt. I.

12. On the Labour party's internal battles over Europe in the early 1970s, see Anthony King, *Britain Says Yes: The 1975 Referendum on the Common Market* (Washington, DC: American Enterprise Institute, 1977), esp. ch. 3.

13. Taverne, one of the original founders of the SDP, was calling as early as 1974 for the creation of 'a new radical or social democratic party'; see Dick Taverne, *The Future of the Left: Lincoln and After* (London: Jonathan Cape, 1974), 159.

14. The literature on voters' responses to the politics of the 1960s and 1970s is huge. For a summary, see David Denver, *Elections and Voting Behaviour in Britain* (Hemel Hempstead: Philip Allan, 1989).

15. The Liberals' electoral fortunes can be traced in Butler and Butler, *British Political Facts*, 226–8. See also John Curtice, 'Liberal Voters and the Alliance: Realignment or Protest?', in Vernon Bogdanor (ed.), *Liberal Party Politics* (Oxford: Oxford University Press, 1983).

16. Quoted in Butler and King, *British General Election of 1964*, 103.

17. On the history of the Labour party in the late 1960s and the 1970s, see, among many other works, Dennis Kavanagh (ed.), *The Politics of the Labour Party* (London: Allen & Unwin, 1982); Whiteley, *The Labour Party in Crisis*; Geoff Hodgson, *Labour at the Crossroads: The Political and Economic Challenge to the Labour Party in the 1980s* (Oxford: Martin Robertson, 1981); Patrick Seyd, *The Rise and Fall of the Labour Left* (London: Macmillan, 1987); Eric Shaw, *Discipline and Discord in the Labour Party: The Politics of Managerial Control in the Labour Party, 1951–1987* (Manchester: Manchester University Press, 1988); Lewis Minkin, *The Labour Party Conference: A Study in the Politics of Intra-party Democracy* (London: Allen Lane, 1978); and Lewis Minkin, *The Contentious Alliance: Trade Unions and the Labour Party* (Edinburgh: Edinburgh University Press, 1991).

18. This sense of betrayal is well captured in Hodgson, *Labour at the Crossroads*, ch. 6, and David Coates, *Labour in Power? A Study of the Labour Government 1974–1979* (London: Longman, 1980). The Coates book maps out in some detail the discrepancies between Labour's 1974 manifesto commitments and its actual performance in office.

19. On the tensions that the Labour government's economic failures set up within the party, see Minkin, *The Labour Party Conference*, 330; David Coates, *The Labour Party and the Struggle for Socialism* (Cambridge: Cambridge University Press, 1975), ch. 5; and Whiteley, *The Labour Party in Crisis*, passim.

20. Butler and Butler, *British Political Facts*, 152.

21. See Michael Pinto-Duschinsky, *British Political Finance, 1830–1980* (Washington, DC: American Enterprise Institute, 1981), 156–7 n. 6.

22. For evidence bearing on these points, see Paul Whiteley and Ian Gordon, 'The Labour Party: Middle Class, Militant and Male', *New Statesman*, 11 Jan. 1980, 41–2; Paul Whiteley, 'The Decline of Labour's Local Party Membership and Electoral Base, 1945–79', in Kavanagh (ed.), *The Politics of the Labour Party*; and Whiteley, *The Labour Party in Crisis*, ch. 3.

23. No really satisfactory account of the changes in the character of Labour's grass roots has ever been provided, but see Henry Drucker, *Doctrine and Ethos in the Labour Party* (London: Allen & Unwin, 1979), and David Howell, *British Social Democracy: A Study in Development and Decay* (London: Croom Helm, 1976). On the struggle between right and left in the inter-war period, see David Marquand, *Ramsay MacDonald* (London: Jonathan Cape, 1977), passim.

24. On the abolition of the list of proscribed organizations, see Paul McCormick, 'The Labour Party: Three Unnoticed Changes', *British Journal of Political Science*, 10 (1980), 381–7. On the far left in Britain during the 1970s and 1980s, see John Callaghan, *The Far Left in British Politics* (Oxford: Basil Blackwell, 1987); Blake Baker, *The Far Left: An Exposé of the Extreme Left in Britain* (London: Weidenfeld & Nicolson, 1981); and John Tomlinson, *Left–Right: The March of Political Extremism in Britain* (London: John Calder, 1981).

25. On the rise of what later became called the 'hard left' in the Labour party, see Seyd, *The Rise and Fall of the Labour Left*, *passim*; Michael Cocks, *Labour and the Benn Factor* (London: Macdonald, 1989); Hugh Jenkins, *Rank and File* (London: Croom Helm, 1980); Peter Tatchell, *The Battle for Bermondsey* (London: Heretic Books, 1983); and Paul McCormick, *Enemies of Democracy* (London: Temple Smith, 1979). The books by Cocks, Jenkins, Tatchell and McCormick all relate to a single constituency Labour party and are all written from a committed rather than a detached point of view. Cocks and McCormick are anti-left, Jenkins and Tatchell pro-left. But, although the shadings are different, the pictures they paint are consistent with one another and portray CLPs as having changed radically in their social composition, their ideological orientation and their ways of conducting their internal politics.
26. A Labour MP, normally of a charitable disposition, told one of the authors that he sincerely wished, because of what Benn had done to the Labour party, that he had dropped dead sometime in the early 1970s. The MP spoke with great vehemence; he clearly meant it. Benn's own day-to-day account of events in the party during these years can be found in Tony Benn, *Out of the Wilderness: Diaries 1963–1967* (London: Hutchinson, 1987), *Office without Power: Diaries 1968–72* (London: Hutchinson, 1988), *Against the Tide: Diaries 1973–1976* (London: Hutchinson, 1989) and *Conflicts of Interest: Diaries 1977–1980* (London: Hutchinson, 1990). Benn looms large in Mark Hatfield, *The House the Left Built: Inside Labour Policymaking, 1970–75* (London: Victor Gollancz, 1978), and in Austin Mitchell's angry account of Labour party politics in the years after its 1979 defeat: *Four Years in the Death of the Labour Party* (London: Methuen, 1983). Benn's central importance in left-wing politics in the 1970s and early 1980s is recognized by Seyd in *The Rise and Fall of the Labour Left*, esp. 95–9. Seyd notes (p. 98) that Benn stood either second or third in the ballot for constituency places on Labour's National Executive in all but two of the twelve years between 1962 and 1973 and that he stood first in every year between 1974 and 1984.
27. On the Newham North-East affair, see Seyd, *The Rise and Fall of the Labour Left*, 60–2, 114; Shaw, *Discipline and Discord in the Labour Party*, 186–92; McCormick, *Enemies of Democracy*; and Roy Jenkins, *A Life at the Centre* (London: Macmillan, 1991), 428–9.
28. See the works referred to in n. 6.
29. Samuel H. Beer, *Britain against Itself: The Political Contradictions of Collectivism* (London: Faber & Faber, 1982), ch. 4.
30. See Hugh Berrington, 'The Labour Left in Parliament: Maintenance, Erosion and Renewal', in Kavanagh (ed.), *The Politics of the Labour Party*.
31. Oddly, no one seems ever to have analysed in detail the National Executive Committee's shift to the left between the early 1960s and the early 1980s; but the calculations are easy to make on the basis of the published lists of NEC members; and, with minor perturbations (such as the election of Healey referred to in the text), they show a steady and large-scale leftwards shift.
32. 'Let Us Work Together—Labour's Way Out of the Crisis', reprinted in F. W. S. Craig, *British General Election Manifestos 1959–1987* (Aldershot: Parliamentary Research Services, 1990), 191–8.
33. For example, in *Arguments for Socialism* (London: Jonathan Cape, 1979), Benn wrote: 'Whatever the merits of these arguments [for extending public ownership] may be, some people assumed automatically that if the Labour Party put them forward at a general election we would be heavily defeated. In 1974 we did put them forward and we won—twice' (p. 54). Made without qualification, this assertion is, to say the least of it, disingenuous.
34. There is an excellent book on the history of the Campaign for Labour Party Democracy: David Kogan and Maurice Kogan, *The Battle for the Labour Party*, 2nd edn. (London: Kogan Page, 1983). On the struggle for constitutional reform in the party, see also Seyd, *The Rise and Fall of the Labour Left*, esp. ch. 5.
35. On the leftward migration of the GMWU, see Minkin, *The Contentious Alliance*, *passim*.

36. Susan Crosland, *Tony Crosland* (London: Jonathan Cape, 1982), 250–3.
37. On the success of the Campaign for Democratic Socialism and Gaitskell's approach to Labour party leadership, see Stephen Haseler, *The Gaitskellites* (London: Macmillan, 1969); Philip M. Williams, *Hugh Gaitskell: A Political Biography* (London: Jonathan Cape, 1979), esp. pts. V–VII; and Philip Williams, 'Changing Styles of Labour Leadership', in Kavanagh (ed.), *The Politics of the Labour Party*.
38. The allusion is to Hugh Gaitskell's 'fight and fight and fight again' speech, attacking the unilateral nuclear disarmers, at the 1960 Labour party conference. See Williams, *Hugh Gaitskell*, 610–12.
39. Quoted in Ian Bradley, *Breaking the Mould? The Birth and Prospects of the Social Democratic Party* (Oxford: Martin Robertson, 1981), 62. Bradley provides a brief but useful history of CLV at pp. 61–3.

Chapter 2

1. For accounts of Benn's influence on the Labour party during this period, written from widely differing viewpoints, see Patrick Seyd, *The Rise and Fall of the Labour Left* (London: Macmillan, 1987), and Michael Cocks, *Labour and the Benn Factor* (London: Macdonald, 1989). For Tony Benn's version of events, see Tony Benn, *Conflicts of Interest: Diaries 1977–1980* (London: Hutchinson, 1990), and *The End of an Era: Diaries 1980–1990* (London: Hutchinson, 1992).
2. On the Campaign for Labour Party Democracy, see David Kogan and Maurice Kogan, *The Battle for the Labour Party*, 2nd edn. (London: Kogan Page, 1983). The term 'constitution' is used loosely here to refer to all of the party's rules relating to its structure and organization.
3. See Kogan and Kogan, *The Battle for the Labour Party*, 29–30, and Paul McCormick, 'The Labour Party: Three Unnoticed Changes', *British Journal of Political Science*, 10 (1980), 381–7.
4. The resolution is reprinted in full in F. W. S. Craig, *Conservative and Labour Party Conference Decisions 1945–1981* (Chichester: Parliamentary Research Services, 1982), 382.
5. Actually Clause V of the party's constitution refers only to a joint meeting between the National Executive Committee and 'the Parliamentary Committee of the Parliamentary Labour Party'; but in practice the latter phrase is taken to mean the cabinet when Labour is in power. Labour's constitution throughout bears the hallmarks of having been written for a party in opposition rather than a party in government.
6. Craig, *Conservative and Labour Party Conference Decisions*, 385.
7. Although the left's theory was seldom spelt out in detail, it amounted to saying that the Labour party should allow itself to be led by its activist minority and that this activist minority's views should determine government policy if and when Labour came to power—on the grounds that, if a Labour government were elected, the activist minority's views would, by definition, have received a mandate from the people. Echoes of this line of reasoning can be found in Tony Benn, *Arguments for Democracy*, ed. Chris Mullin (London: Jonathan Cape, 1979).
8. Denis Healey admits as much in his memoirs. Referring to CLPD and other left-wing and Trotskyite organizations, he says: 'It was all too easy for the Labour Party leadership to dismiss these little groups as no more than alphabet soup' (*Time of my Life* (London: Michael Joseph, 1989), 469). That was indeed the way most right-wingers saw them, in so far as they saw them at all.
9. *Report of the Seventy-eighth Annual Conference of the Labour Party* (1979), 185.
10. Ibid. 189.
11. Ibid. 186.

12. Peter Jenkins, *Guardian*, 2 Oct. 1979.
13. Craig, *Conservative and Labour Party Conference Decisions*, 246, 420.
14. Quoted in Kogan and Kogan, *Battle for the Labour Party*, 70.
15. *Guardian*, 25 Oct. 1979.
16. On the Daly article, see Ian Bradley, *Breaking the Mould? The Birth and Prospects of the Social Democratic Party* (Oxford: Martin Robertson, 1981), 62.
17. In the right's defence it should be said, first, that some moderates had always been unhappy about the bloc vote system and about the power of minorities in the party (though they had never previously done much about it) and, secondly, that after 1979 the gap between the views of Labour voters (not to mention potential Labour voters) and Labour party members was probably greater than it had ever been in the past. This last point was important electorally, but it cut little ice in the party's internal debates.
18. William Rodgers, *The Politics of Change* (London: Secker & Warburg, 1982), 4.
19. Ibid. 170.
20. *The Times*, 1 Dec. 1979.
21. The Underhill report and its fate were reported in *The Times*, 24 Jan. 1980. Typical of the press exposés was one that appeared in the *Sunday Times* on 20 Jan. Benn, Brown and Heffer were all quoted in the *Sunday Times*, 3 Feb. 1980.
22. *The Times*, 2 Feb. 1980. The Social Democratic Alliance was a relatively small group of Labour party members vehemently and vociferously opposed to the Trotskyites' entryist tactics and to the increasingly anti-democratic, anti-majoritarian thrust of much Labour policy-making. Some of its members bore a striking resemblance to the pro-welfare state but strongly anti-communist wing of the Democratic party in the United States, some of the intellectual supporters of which defected to the Republicans before and during the 1980s. On the SDA see Bradley, *Breaking the Mould?*, esp. chs. 1–2. Following Roy Jenkins' delivery of the 1979 Dimbleby Lecture (see ch. 3), members of the SDA, including Douglas Eden and Stephen Haseler, made contact with the emerging Jenkinsite group.
23. The opinion poll in *The Times* was published on 17 Jan. 1980. The CLV manifesto was reported in the same newspaper on 7 Feb., the backbenchers' appeal in the *Sunday Times* on 2 Mar.
24. *The Times*, 24 Nov. 1979.
25. *The Times*, 11 Jan. 1980.
26. David Owen, never one to do things by halves, has written his memoirs twice, in *Personally Speaking to Kenneth Harris* (London: Weidenfeld & Nicolson, 1987), and *Time to Declare* (London: Michael Joseph, 1991). *Personally Speaking* tells the story of his early years in politics and his role in the original SDP. *Time to Declare* is a more detailed and personal memoir and takes the story up to the demise of the Owenite SDP in 1990. Owen is often accused of rewriting history, but to us he seems no more open to that charge than most memoir-writers. He is undoubtedly paying a price for having often kept his own counsel, especially before 1987. The views he now claims he held at any given time are in fact usually the views he was expressing privately, if not necessarily to his SDP colleagues, at that time.
27. *The Times*, 24 Nov. 1979.
28. *Report of the Annual Conference and Special Conference of the Labour Party* (1980), 274–6, 271, 247 and 251. The shouts of 'Out, out' were reported in the *Sunday Times*, 1 June; Frances Morrell's remarks in *The Times*, 2 June.
29. *Annual Conference Report* (1980), 249–50.
30. See Owen's account in *Personally Speaking*, 166–7. Owen notes (p. 167): 'It was the turning point for me personally.'
31. While Labour was still in power in the mid-1970s, Williams caused considerable surprise by making speeches in which she quoted Trotsky to demonstrate that, far from being a democratic socialist, he was an advocate of violence and dictatorship.
32. *The Times*, 9 June 1980.

33. 'Under-50s' should strictly read 'under-52s'. Owen Williams, Hattersley and Smith were all under 50 when the Callaghan government left office in 1979, but Rodgers was born in 1928.
34. For Healey's speech, see *Annual Conference Report* (1980), 259.
35. The public history of the Bishops Stortford meeting and its aftermath can be traced in *The Times* of the following dates: 16–19 June 1980, 21 June, 28 June and 1 July. There is also a report in the *Observer*, 22 June.
36. *Guardian*, 1 Aug. 1980.
37. *The Times*, 2 Aug. 1980.
38. The full text was published in *The Times*, 22 Sept. 1980.
39. *Labour Weekly*, 26 Sept. 1980.
40. On the dilemma, see e.g. William Rodgers in the *Sunday Times*, 15 June 1980.
41. *Annual Conference Report* (1980), 31–2.
42. *The Times*, 30 Sept. 1980.
43. Ibid.

Chapter 3

1. For an account of Jenkins' career up to and including his time as leader of the SDP, see John Campbell, *Roy Jenkins: A Biography* (London: Weidenfeld & Nicolson, 1983). Chs. 28–31 of Jenkins' autobiography *A Life at the Centre* (London: Macmillan, 1991) deal with the formation and history of the SDP.
2. Jenkins' semi-detached tone can be detected in, for example, a volume of speeches he published in the early 1970s, *What Matters Now* (London: Collins/Fontana, 1972). Its appeal throughout is to 'radicals as well as socialists' (p. 17).
3. For a description of the grand style of the Britain in Europe campaign in 1975, see Anthony King, *Britain Says Yes: The 1975 Referendum on the Common Market* (Washington, DC: American Enterprise Institute, 1977), 106–7.
4. The 'nice to see you here' remark was quoted in a profile of Jenkins, *Observer* magazine, 8 Mar. 1981, 48. The 'I must be off now' story is told in Simon Hoggart, *Back on the House* (London: Robson Books, 1982), 29–30. Neil Kinnock told the 'No lad. We're all Labour here' story at the 1978 Labour party conference, where it was greeted with gales of laughter (Campbell, *Roy Jenkins*, 177).
5. To repeat: the truth about Jenkins was in some ways less important than what people believed about him. To take a trivial instance, he had a reputation for being a lover of good claret whereas he was not especially fond of claret; but the claret association gave him an irretrievably upper-class air. Susan Crosland conveys vividly the impression that Jenkins made on his enemies in *Tony Crosland* (London: Jonathan Cape, 1982); see esp. pp. 250–3.
6. On the early history of Jenkins' devotion to the European cause, see Campbell, *Roy Jenkins*, ch. 3.
7. The speeches were published as *What Matters Now*. The first of them, drafted by David Marquand, was more outspoken than the others, but Jenkins did not want to be provocative and after the first speech his tone became considerably more orthodox and cautious.
8. Jenkins quotes the phrase on p. 208 of his biography *Asquith* (London: Collins, 1964), adding, somewhat prophetically: 'He used the phrase in no apologetic or hesitant way, but rather as a threat . . . It was a use for which he was to pay dearly in the last years of his premiership when the phrase came to be erected by his enemies as a symbol of his alleged inactivity.'
9. By 1979–80 almost none of the Jenkinsites was a member of the House of Commons, Taverne and Barnes having lost their seats; but in the late 1960s and 1970s the Jenkinsite group had been largely centred in parliament. Both David Owen and Bill Rodgers had been

Jenkinsites at that stage, though Shirley Williams never was. Probably the only other modern British politician to have had a similar entourage for a time is Tony Benn.

10. *The Times*, 23 Nov. 1979. The lecture is reprinted in Wayland Kennet (ed.), *Rebirth of Britain* (London: Weidenfeld & Nicolson, 1982), 2–29. Jenkins gives his account of the preparation and delivery of the lecture—and of the thinking behind it—in *A Life at the Centre*, 414–20.

11. David Owen accused Jenkins of not wanting to soil his hands, in the Wolverhampton speech quoted above, p. 38.

12. For Steel's own reflections on pacts and pact-making, see David Steel, *A House Divided: The Lib–Lab Pact and the Future of British Politics* (London: Weidenfeld & Nicolson, 1980). Steel's political career can be followed in Peter Bartram, *David Steel: His Life and Politics* (London: W. H. Allen, 1981), and David Steel, *Against Goliath* (London: Weidenfeld & Nicolson, 1989).

13. Steel, Jenkins and the other Jenkinsites were acutely conscious of the unhappy Mayhew precedent, though they seldom referred to it publicly, perhaps out of deference to Mayhew himself. Mayhew tells the story of his departure from the Labour party in *Time to Explain: An Autobiography* (London: Hutchinson, 1987), chs. 15–17.

14. The course of the Jenkins–Steel discussions can be followed in Roy Jenkins, *European Diary 1977–1981* (London: Collins, 1989). The most important entries are those for 14 June 1979 (p. 460), 7 Jan. 1980 (p. 553), 13 Apr. 1980 (p. 587) and 3 Nov. 1980 (p. 643). The entry for 7 Jan. 1980 contains the following passage: 'He [Steel] perfectly understands that there is no question of me or anybody else joining the Liberal Party. He equally is anxious to work very closely, and possibly, if things went well, to consider an amalgamation after a general election. He would like the closeness at the time of the election itself to take the form not merely of a non-aggression pact, but of working together on policy and indeed sharing broadcasts, etc.' (p. 553). See also Jenkins, *A Life at the Centre*, esp. pp. 513–14. Steel's account of his discussions with Jenkins in *Against Goliath* (pp. 215, 217–18, 220) consists largely of reproducing passages from Jenkins' diaries.

15. The only Jenkinsite who straightforwardly offered to join the Liberals—'He was ready to sign on the dotted line'—was David Marquand; but Steel discouraged him.

16. *Guardian*, 29 Sept. 1979.

17. *Sunday Times*, 3 Feb. 1980.

18. *Guardian*, 8 Aug. 1980.

19. *Observer*, 13 Jan. 1980. The report referred explicitly to 'the future of a new Social Democratic party', using the phrase 'Social Democratic'.

20. *Sunday Times*, *Observer*, 8 June 1980.

21. *The Times*, 10 June 1980.

22. On the closeness of Jenkins' and Owen's relationship in the early 1970s, and its subsequent deterioration when Jenkins was president of the European Commission and Owen was British foreign secretary, see David Owen, *Personally Speaking to Kenneth Harris* (London: Weidenfeld & Nicolson, 1987), ch. 6, and also a number of entries in Jenkins' *European Diary*. Owen tells the story (pp. 114–15) of how he favoured Jenkins' attendance at European summits but how his refusal to write a formal minute to this effect got back to Jenkins and appeared to rankle with him. Jenkins in his diary recorded (p. 55) his first encounter with David and Debbie Owen after Owen became foreign secretary: 'There was undoubtedly a slight problem of adjustment, perhaps more on my part than on theirs. When somebody has been a loyal, young, junior supporter for a long time, it is a little difficult to get used to his suddenly being Foreign Secretary.' See also Jenkins, *A Life at the Centre*, 527–8, and David Owen, *Time to Declare* (London: Michael Joseph, 1991), 279–81. 'Slowly,' Owen writes of the period when he was foreign secretary and Jenkins president of the European Commission, 'our friendship ebbed away' (p. 279).

23. Jenkins in *European Diary* recorded (pp. 532–3) that Rodgers struck him 'as being emotionally committed to a break', whereas Williams, who had always, in Jenkins' view, been more

intellectually open to the idea than Rodgers, had 'not yet passed over the sort of watershed' that Rodgers seemed to have. 'But', Jenkins concluded, 'who can say what will happen?'
24. *Sunday Times*, 14 Sept. 1980.
25. The interview was quoted in *The Times*, 9 June 1980.
26. *Guardian*, 9 Aug. 1980.
27. Ibid.
28. *The Times*, 13 June 1980.

Chapter 4

1. Almost every history of the Labour party or volume of memoirs by a Labour leader testifies to the party's church-like qualities. James Callaghan actually describes how the Labour party and the Baptist church warred for his soul in *Time and Chance* (London: Collins, 1987), 40. 'I wanted', he says, 'to tell everyone about my discovery of socialism and must have been a very trying young man.' Even more vividly, Roy Hattersley describes in *A Yorkshire Boyhood* (London: Chatto and Windus and The Hogarth Press, 1983) how in 1950 he 'had never been so happy. For I was sixteen, with the hated fourth form behind me, I had something approximating to a girlfriend, and I had discovered the great excitement of my life. It was called the Labour Party. The party had claimed and caught me long before that year. But until 1950 I was a member in the same way that I was a Hattersley—naturally, inevitably, and without a thought of why it should be so. It was in my sixteenth year that I began to understand the reason, and I also began to understand the excitement of commitment to a great cause' (p. 174).
2. *Sunday Times*, 5 Oct. 1980. Owen's own account of the period between the Blackpool and Wembley conferences can be found in David Owen, *Personally Speaking to Kenneth Harris* (London: Weidenfeld & Nicolson, 1987), 168–80.
3. *The Times*, 17 Oct. 1980.
4. *The Times*, 13 Oct. 1980.
5. *The Times*, 22 Oct. 1980. Denis Healey gives his account of the leadership election in *The Time of my Life* (London: Michael Joseph, 1989), 476–9.
6. *The Times*, 22 Oct. 1980.
7. Healey, *The Time of my Life*, 477. David Owen contests this view in *Time to Declare* (London: Michael Joseph, 1991), 458.
8. See above, pp. 45–6.
9. *The Times*, 6, 12, 14 Nov. 1980. Details of the Hattersley compromise can be found in 'Shadow Cabinet Adopts Hybrid Poll Scheme', *The Times*, 12 Nov. See also Owen, *Time to Declare*, 459–60.
10. Degrees of animus against Roy Hattersley varied, but in some cases it was considerable. Right-wingers believed that Hattersley agreed with them about almost everything. They also believed that he was driven by personal ambition and by almost nothing else. In the first case they were almost certainly right, in the second case almost certainly wrong—as even casual reading of *A Yorkshire Boyhood* ought to make clear. Hattersley was like a Catholic curate during the Protestant Reformation. He did agree with most of the Protestants' aims, and, yes, he did very much want to be a bishop, a cardinal or even pope. But his loyalty to the Labour party, like the Catholic curate's loyalty to the Church, was of a much more emotional, deep-rooted kind. It was an elemental part of his being. To have deserted the Labour party would have been to desert himself. There was never any chance of this happening. Some of those who joined the SDP appreciated this, without necessarily having thought it through. Others did not.
11. *The Times*, 22 Nov. 1980.

12. Thomas on 30 October issued a vigorous statement on behalf of CLV denouncing the NEC for circulating to the party only its own proposals for an electoral college and putting forward CLV's own proposals for the election of the party leader by a secret ballot of all individual party members. 'It is monstrous', Thomas said, in the kind of language for which he was to become well known in the SDP, 'that the NEC should take it upon themselves to circulate only one model constitutional amendment—the one they prefer' (*The Times*, 31 Oct. 1980). Reports of the Owenite meetings appeared sporadically in the newpapers during December 1980. See also David Owen, *Personally Speaking*, 175–6, and *Time to Declare*, 472–3.
13. The results of the shadow cabinet election were reported in *The Times*, 5 Dec. 1980. It was a largely right-wing outcome. Benn lost his seat. The only left-wing newcomer was Neil Kinnock, who received the lowest number of votes, 90, among those elected. On the mis-understanding between Rodgers and Owen, see Owen, *Personally Speaking*, 172–3.
14. Some of all this surfaced publicly; see *The Times*, 8, 9, 12 Dec. 1980.
15. *The Times*, 29, Nov. 1980.
16. *Observer*, 30 Nov. 1980.
17. *The Times*, 2 Dec. 1980.
18. For the details, see *The Times*, 3 and 12 Dec. 1980, and then on a considerable number of dates in Jan. 1981.
19. William Sheridan Allen, *The Nazi Seizure of Power: The Experience of a Single German Town, 1930–35* (Chicago: Quadrangle Books, 1965).

Chapter 5

1. Roy Jenkins, *European Diary, 1977–1981* (London: Collins, 1989), 650.
2. David Owen, *Personally Speaking to Kenneth Harris* (London: Weidenfeld & Nicolson, 1987), 177.
3. Owen repeats and expands his account of the 29 November meeting in *Time to Declare* (London: Michael Joseph, 1991), 464–5. He adds that his wife, Debbie, agreed with him in the car afterwards that Jenkins must have 'registered that this pledge [on 'one member, one vote'] was crucial to me and other MPs' (p. 465). Jenkins in his memoirs describes the 29 November meeting at considerable length; and it is somewhat suspicious that—even though Jenkins' memoirs were published some four years after Owen's *Personally Speaking*, in which Owen states explicitly that Jenkins at the meeting accepted the principle of 'one member, one vote'— Jenkins himself still makes no mention of the subject, not even to refute the account given by Owen. See Jenkins, *A Life at the Centre* (London: Macmillan, 1991), 531–2.
4. *The Times*, 12 Dec. 1980.
5. *The Times*, 15 Jan. 1981.
6. Ibid.
7. 'Is there such a Place as the Centre?' *Sunday Times*, 30 Nov. 1980.
8. 'The Plunge into an Intellectual Vacuum', *Guardian*, 30 Dec. 1980.
9. An ORC poll for *Weekend World*, quoted in *The Times*, 19 Jan. 1981.
10. *Observer*, 18, Jan. 1981.
11. 'Roy and Gang of Three in Summit', *Observer*, 18 Jan. 1981.
12. Quoted in Andrew Stephen, 'The Kicking, Squealing Birth-pangs of the SDP', *Sunday Times Magazine*, 27 Sept. 1981, 84. Stephen's article is much the best newspaper account of the SDP's origins and early history. It captures the flavour of the time perfectly.
13. *Observer*, 25 Jan. 1981.
14. The machinations that led to the outcome at Wembley are described briefly in Patrick Seyd, *The Rise and Fall of the Labour Left* (London: Macmillan, 1987), 118–21.
15. *Sunday Times*, 25 Jan. 1981.

16. The Limehouse Declaration was published in *The Times* on 26 Jan. 1981 and is reprinted in Hugh Stephenson, *Claret and Chips: The Rise of the SDP* (London: Michael Joseph, 1982), 185–6.
17. *The Times*, 17 Mar. 1981.
18. Another was Clive Wilkinson, a prominent local politician in Birmingham. Members of the SDP ascribed Wilkinson's decision to his (natural) desire to maintain his position in Birmingham politics and to the fact that the Labour party in Birmingham was not nearly so left wing as in some of the other large cities. Chapple's decision tended to be put down to personal eccentricity.
19. *Observer*, 22 Mar. 1981.
20. The survey in the eleven MPs' constituencies was carried out by MORI for Granada's *The World in Action* programme and reported in *The Times* on 3 Feb. 1981. The Gallup Poll, in its regular survey in Feb. 1981, found that, of those who said that they felt 'very close' to the political party of their choice, as many as 46% were Labour supporters and 32% were Conservatives, while a mere 18% were supporters of a Liberal–social democratic alliance; see 'Battle for the Melting Icebergs', *Observer*, 22 Mar. 1981.
21. *The Times*, 2 Feb. 1981.
22. *The Times*, 31 Jan. 1981.
23. *The Times*, 10 Feb. 1981.
24. *The Times*, 31 Jan. 1981. In fact, Owen suggests in his memoirs (*Time to Declare*, 490–2) that he was anxious that the SDP MPs should fight by-elections. Either they should all resign their seats and fight, or else he 'should fight one symbolic by-election [in Plymouth] on behalf of all SDP MPs' (p. 481). He expresses his regret that, partly because Bill Rodgers argued strongly to the contrary, the SDP collectively did not take this line.
25. In a way that somewhat contradicts his insistence that the SDP should have fought by-elections (see n. 24), Owen in *Time to Declare* (p. 212) notes that, when Dick Taverne resigned his Lincoln seat in October 1972, the resulting by-election was not held until nearly five months later, in early March 1973. Owen emphasizes the enormous advantage that delay can give the incumbent party: 'Delay can give a massive advantage to the party defending the seat, for allowing the party whose MP had resigned to fix the by-election date keeps the former MP in limbo for five or six months without pay or influence.'
26. *The Times*, 13 Jan. 1981.
27. *Observer*, 18 Jan. 1981; *The Times*, 21 Jan. 1981.
28. *The Times*, 29 Jan. 1981.
29. *Sunday Times*, 8 Feb. 1981; *Guardian*, 23 Feb. 1981.
30. *The Times*, 28 Feb. 1981.
31. *Observer*, 18 Jan. 1981.
32. The SDP was the first new *national* party since 1900. It sought to establish itself in all parts of the country and, possibly in alliance with the Liberals, to contest every parliamentary constituency. None of the other new parties of the twentieth century—Oswald Mosley's New party, the Liberal Nationals and National Labour after 1931 and Common Wealth during the Second World War—had any such ambitions or prospects. None contested more than fifty seats at any election. Most contested fewer.
33. *House of Commons Debates*, 48th Parliament, 2nd Session, vol. 1, 26 Mar. 1981, col. 1074. The prime minister taunted Thomas, suggesting that the SDP was indeed going to be a centre party and quoting Shirley Williams' well-known views on the subject. Thomas and Wrigglesworth together were spectacularly successful in persuading the media to portray the new party as 'modern' and 'professional'. They not only projected an image of the party: they drew attention to the fact that that was what they were doing, and the press accounts of the 26 March launch contained full details of which advertising agency had managed it (Dewe Rogerson), who had designed the SDP logo (Dick Negus of Negus and Negus) and which

advertising executive had helped prepare the party's initial advertisement (David Abbott of Abbott, Mead & Vickers/ SMS Ltd). See, in particular, Andrew Stephen, 'Admen Give the Gang a PR Gloss', *Sunday Times*, 29 Mar. 1981. Stephen's account of the launch in the article cited in n. 12 above is also worth going back to.

34. *The Times*, 27 Mar. 1981. The party also issued a broad policy statement, based largely on the Limehouse Declaration, called 'Twelve Tasks for Social Democrats'. Its first paragraph was headed 'Breaking the mould'; 'Britain needs a reformed and liberated political system without the pointless conflict, the dogma, the violent lurches of policy and the class antagonisms that the two old parties have fostered.'

35. 'Why People are Hungry for this New Beginning', *The Times*, 26 Mar. 1981.

Chapter 6

1. The only other party split of a comparable magnitude was in October 1931 when twenty-three Liberal MPs broke away to form the Liberal National party. Unlike the SDP, the Liberal Nationals limited themselves to contesting only a few constituencies—forty-one in 1931, forty-four in 1935 and fifty-one in 1945—but as a result of being unopposed by the Conservatives were returned to parliament in much larger numbers.

2. The thirty-one ex-Labour MPs include six of the peers.

3. A quite different indicator produces a similar number. There remained in the 1979 parliament 118 MPs who in July 1975 had signed a letter of support for Reg Prentice when he faced deselection by his local party in Newham North-East. See Chris Mullin, 'How the SDP Tried to Provide the Sunday Times with a New "Hit List" ', *Tribune*, 11 Dec. 1981.

4. Of course, not all Healey voters were committed right-wingers. But even the 'firm right' embraced many more loyalists than defectors. The Manifesto Group, which organized the right-wing slate in the annual shadow-cabinet elections, could count on a core of eighty. In the 1976 leadership contest the combined first-round vote for the two indisputably right-wing candidates, Jenkins and Healey, was eighty-six, although this was in the previous parliament when the PLP was larger and more right wing in its make-up.

5. Dickson Mabon, Horam, Sandelson and Mike Thomas.

6. Bradley and Wrigglesworth had served as a PPS for Jenkins, and Ginsburg was an old friend from Oxford student days. Horam was a junior minister under Rodgers for whom both Ellis and Lyons had at some time been a PPS. Maclennan served under Shirley Williams as under-secretary for prices and consumer protection from 1974 to 1976. Mitchell was her PPS from 1974 to 1976 and Cartwright from 1976 to 1977. Wellbeloved was Owen's PPS.

7. The rule required the government to repeal the Scotland Act if the Act failed to secure the support of '40% of those entitled to vote' in the proposed referendum. Cunningham's amendment in fact superseded one calling for a one-third threshold, which was tabled by another defector, Bruce Douglas-Mann. See David Butler and Dennis Kavanagh, *The British General Election of 1979* (London: Macmillan, 1980), 125–6, and Tam Dalyell, *Devolution: The End of Britain* (London: Cape, 1977).

8. Peter Jenkins, *Mrs Thatcher's Revolution: The Ending of the Socialist Era* (London: Jonathan Cape, 1987), 137.

9. Tony Benn, *Office without Power: Diaries 1968–72* (London: Hutchinson, 1988), p. xiii. Benn wrote his commentary in July 1988.

10. The most famous case was Dick Taverne in Lincoln, who resigned and won a by-election on the issue (see p. 9). He joined the SDP in 1981 and was a member of its National Committee. Others include Colin Phipps (Dudley West) and Neville Sandelson (Hayes and Harlington), both of whom joined the SDP in 1981.

11. The picture is the same if the fourteen abstainers are added to the thirty October 1971

pro-EEC rebels. Of the forty-four rebels and abstainers, thirteen defected to the SDP; thirty-one stayed in the Labour party.

12. Of the six Labour defectors who entered parliament after 1971 three (Magee, Mike Thomas and Wrigglesworth) were convinced Europeans—the same proportion as for those defectors who voted in the October 1971 debate.

13. In addition to Roy Hattersley's autobiographical *A Yorkshire Boyhood* (London: Chatto and Windus and The Hogarth Press, 1983), see also his article, 'Why I will Stay on and Fight', *Observer*, 25 Jan. 1981: 'I accept that part of my inability to contemplate leaving the Labour Party is emotional rather than rational—the product of upbringing and personal gratitude.'

14. See also Radice's explanation ('Labour is Still the Most Effective Vehicle for Change', *Guardian*, 14 Dec. 1981), in which he argued that the SDP did not belong to the European social demo-cratic tradition.

15. See p. 90.

16. A number of the loyalists whom we interviewed thought that the right might well lose and that they would find themselves forced to leave the party within the foreseeable future. One suggested to us that the 1981 split was going to be by no means the last.

17. Of the other seven, Cunningham deliberately waited until after he had succeeded in being reselected before defecting; and Crawshaw, Ellis, Lyons and Sandelson would have defected whatever the outcome: they were in the original tranche of SDP MPs and switched long before their reselection conferences took place. Their quarrels with their local party encompassed far more than their own position.

Magee's late defection was not timed in relation to his reselection. An academic and writer with more interest in the arts than parliamentary politics, he was not unduly concerned at the prospect of being deselected and joined the SDP as a gesture of principled defiance, not of personal desperation.

McNally's case is the most marginal. His defection was unexpected, and it took place almost exactly a month before his constituency's selection conference. But his action was not that of someone calculating his prospects for survival: his chances of reselection were certainly good enough to make it worthwhile to stay on and fight; and, given the timing of his selection conference, if he had lost there still would have been time enough for him to switch to the SDP before the January 1982 'reselection deadline'—the deadline agreed by the SDP and Liberal party by which potential defectors had to join the SDP if they wanted backing from the headquarters of both parties (and thus a virtual guarantee) for selection as the Alliance's general-election candidate.

18. After his deselection, which he had expected, he announced his intention of standing as a 'Labour candidate seeking re-election', but was then persuaded by Michael Foot to appeal to Labour's National Executive. Only after his appeal was rejected did he talk to local Liberals about the possibility of standing as the Alliance candidate in his seat. See Ian Aitken, 'Rejected MPs Face New Snub by Labour', *Guardian*, 9 June 1981.

19. Two others, Stanley Cohen (Leeds South-East) and Ray Fletcher (Ilkeston), announced at the time of their reselection difficulties that they were considering standing as Social Democrats, but changed their minds. Arthur Lewis (Newham North-West) and Ben Ford (Bradford North) stood as Independent Labour candidates in the 1983 election; John Sever (Birming-ham Ladywood) soldiered on as a Labour candidate in the safely Conservative seat of Meriden; and Fred Mulley (Sheffield Park) retired. Ben Ford later joined the SDP.

20. He faced an overwhelming challenge from Ken Livingstone, the left-wing leader of the GLC, but was saved by the early calling of the general election, which prompted Labour party head-quarters to intervene.

21. These considerations applied with particular force to those who lost out in the round of selec-tions for the new merged constituencies—such as Stanley Clinton Davis in Hackney and Charlie Morris in Manchester—which was delayed until Mar.–Apr. 1983.

22. Grant and McNally were particularly anguished at leaving; Grant out of loyalty to his union, the Electrical Trades Union (ETU), McNally out of devotion to his Labour parents.

23. *The Times*, 1 Dec. 1981.

24. The pull of moderate CLPs on potential defectors' loyalty was probably even stronger than the figures suggest. Eighteen of the potential recruits with Bennite CLPs did not switch. But, as Table 6.1 shows, only nine of these 'loyalists' were reselected. Two were formally deselected (Ford and Cohen), one was squeezed out (Barnett), and six retired: Jack Dunnett, Jimmy Johnson, Arthur Palmer, Alfred Roberts, Sam Silkin and Fred Willey. Of these six, Dunnett, Roberts and Silkin were widely tipped for deselection: rather than jumping before they were pushed, they stood aside. There was no parallel retirement pattern, however, among those whose CLPs voted for Healey. If reselection rates are compared, therefore, the impact of having a right-wing rather than a left-wing party stands out: among potential defectors with Bennite CLPs, only 23% stood as Labour candidates in June 1983; among those with Healeyite CLPs, the figure was 70%.

25. The suggestion that right-wing Labour MPs were less likely to switch if they came from Labour's traditional strongholds because local parties in these areas tended to be more moderate was only partly borne out. It is true that only two of the eleven potential defectors from Scotland and three of the eleven from Wales actually joined the SDP; had these defection rates matched those for England (51%) the numbers would have been six from each. The SDP's recruitment of all but two of the eleven potential defectors from London reflects the much sourer atmosphere in the London Labour party. However, four of the six potential defectors from the north-east did join the SDP. Moreover, Scotland's CLPs were not moderate, judging by the 83% that voted for Benn as deputy leader.

26. See also p. 86.

27. Another particle of evidence supports this view. Had fear of defeat and a subsequent loss of income been a crucial factor, one would have expected the defection rates to have been lower among sitting Labour MPs than among those Labour MPs who had retired or been defeated in 1979. This latter group, after all, had little to lose financially by joining the SDP, yet the defection rate among the 1981 PLP (10%) was virtually identical to that among Labour MPs who had been defeated (11%) or had retired (12%) in 1979.

28. Alan Bullock, *The Life and Times of Ernest Bevin*, ii. *Minister of Labour, 1940–45* (London: Heinemann, 1967), 178.

29. Tom Bradley (President of TSSA, 1964–7); Andrew Faulds (council member, Equity); Alan Fitch (secretary, Golborne Trades and Labour Council); Ben Ford (shop stewards' convenor, AUEW); Denis Howell (president, APEX); Walter Johnson (treasurer, TSSA and NFPW); Albert Roberts (area organizer, NUM); George Robertson (Scottish organizer, GMWU, 1970–8); Tom Urwin (organizer, Amalgamated Union of Building Trade Workers); William Whitlock (area organizer, USDAW; president, Leicester District Trades Council).

30. However, the SDP victor at the Portsmouth South by-election in 1984, Mike Hancock, was an AUEW convenor.

31. Bradley was a Northamptonshire county councillor and alderman for over twenty years; Cartwright led Greenwich Council in the early 1970s; Crawshaw was a local councillor in Liverpool and continued to immerse himself in local politics after being elected to parliament; Mitchell was deputy leader on Southampton council; and Wellbeloved was at one time leader of Bexley council. Another three—Ogden, O' Halloran and Sandelson—had served as local councillors but only for short periods.

32. The exceptions were: Humphry Berkeley (Lancaster, 1959–66), who joined the Labour party before switching to the SDP, and William Shepherd (Bucklow, 1945–50; Cheadle, 1950–66). Aubrey Jones (Birmingham Hall Green, 1950–65), a minister of supply in the Macmillan government, joined the Liberal party in 1980. William Morgan (Denbigh, 1959–83), who was unamicably bundled out of his seat after the boundary revisions, joined the Liberals in

1984. The only other group of any significance to join from the Conservatives were a number of senior Young Conservatives who later stood as SDP parliamentary candidates.
33. For Brocklebank-Fowler's own account of his switch to the SDP, see 'On Joining the SDP from the Right', in Wayland Kennet (ed.), *The Rebirth of Britain* (London: Weidenfeld & Nicolson, 1982).
34. See Fred Emery, 'Search for "defecting Tory 20" ', *The Times*, 30 Jan. 1981.
35. For an attempt by *The Times* to smoke his intentions out, see Charles Douglas-Home, 'Will Ted Heath be the Gang's Biggest Catch?', *The Times*, 24 Apr. 1981. See also Julian Haviland and George Clark, 'Heath Hints he might Join a Tory–SDP Coalition', *The Times*, 30 Nov. 1981. It reports Heath as saying that he had no intention of leaving the Conservative party but, he continued, 'I'm prepared to help my country wherever I think I can be of service. There might be invitations . . . which might be acceptable.' Referring to the Labour party's insistence in 1940 that as a condition of their joining a war-time coalition government the Conservatives drop Chamberlain as leader, he went on 'it has happened in the past and it could happen again'. See also Adam Raphael, 'Tories may Defect', *The Observer*, 6 Dec. 1981.
    Other names mentioned in our interviews or in press reports were Peter Bottomley (Eltham), Julian Critchley (Aldershot), Alan Haselhurst (Saffron Walden), James Lester (Beeston), David Madel (Bedfordshire South), Charles Morrison (Devizes), Christopher Patten (Bath), Cyril Townsend (Bexleyheath) and John Watson (Skipton). Their mention as potential defectors probably owed more to wishful thinking in the SDP than to any serious intention on their part.
36. Julian Critchley, *A Bag of Boiled Sweets: An Autobiography* (London: Faber and Faber, 1994), 195. Gilmour made the same point to Roy Jenkins when commenting on his Dimbleby Lecture. See Roy Jenkins, *European Diary, 1977–1981* (London: Collins, 1989), 551.
37. Critchley, *A Bag of Boiled Sweets*, 195.

Chapter 7

1. The War of Jenkins' Ear (1739–41) actually arose out of commercial rivalry between England and Spain, but it was precipitated by Robert Jenkins, a ship's master, recounting to the House of Commons how the dastardly Spanish had cut off his ear (or so he claimed). The war did not amount to much, apart from a few minor engagements at sea, but it led to the more substantial War of the Austrian Succession. The war can be looked up in any good encyclopedia.
2. See e.g. Patrick Seyd, *The Rise and Fall of Labour Left* (London: Macmillan, 1987), esp. ch. 3, and David Kogan and Maurice Kogan, *The Battle for the Labour Party*, 2nd edn. (London: Kogan Page, 1983). Similar conclusions are suggested by two contemporary accounts of Labour politics at the grass roots, both by left-wingers: Hugh Jenkins, *Rank and File* (London: Croom Helm, 1980), and Peter Tatchell, *The Battle for Bermondsey* (London: Heretic Books, 1983). Putting it crudely, Labour's problems in the 1970s and early 1980s were probably 90% Tony Benn and only about 10% Leon Trotsky.
3. If the analysis in the text is correct, and if the Labour party was moving to the left because the majority of its members at that time wanted it to, then the introduction of 'one member, one vote' in 1981 would have had an unexpected and undesirable consequence from the right's point of view. A Labour leadership election held in the early 1980s under 'one member, one vote' would probably have given the leadership to at least Foot, quite possibly Benn. Would those who in the event defected to the SDP have been content with such an outcome, however democratic? It seems improbable. Of course, it is possible that in 1981 moderate rank-and-file party members were still in a majority in the party but that they were not on the whole very active and that their voice was persistently drowned out by the clamour of the more active

and vocal left. In that case, Healey or someone like him might possibly have won. There is no direct evidence bearing on the political views of ordinary Labour party members as distinct from activists at that time, so no one will ever know.

4. For two of the principal protagonists' own views on these matters, see David Owen, *Personally Speaking to Kenneth Harris* (London: Weidenfeld & Nicolson, 1987), 169–71, and Denis Healey, *The Time of my Life* (London: Michael Joseph, 1989), 479–80.

5. Our verdict is 'unfairly': see above, ch. 4 n. 10.

6. One of the original defectors said emphatically that Jenkins was irrelevant to the split and that if Jenkins had formed a new party without the Gang of Three almost no Labour MPs would have gone with him. Jenkins was, in this man's view, simply 'not rated'. This was—or appeared to be—the view of the majority. Almost no one we talked to contradicted it.

7. See p. 67.

Chapter 8

1. On the extraordinary political history of 1981, see Anthony King, 'Margaret Thatcher's First Term', in Austin Ranney (ed.), *Britain at the Polls, 1983: A Study of the General Election* (Durham, NC: Duke University Press/American Enterprise Institute, 1985); David Butler and Dennis Kavanagh, *The British General Election of 1983* (London: Macmillan, 1984), chs. 1–5; and Austin Mitchell, *Four Years in the Death of the Labour Party* (London: Methuen, 1983).

2. For a summary of the Gallup Poll's data, see King, 'Margaret Thatcher's First Term', table 1.3, p. 23. James Callaghan's rating as leader of the Labour party fluctuated between about 60% and about 45%. In the last four months of his leadership, July–Oct. 1980, 49% of the British public, on average, thought that he was 'proving a good leader of the Labour party'. Foot's ratings for the four quarters of 1981 were: 24%, 25%, 25%, 21%. His rating for the first quarter of 1982 was 19%—and it fell even lower later in the year. Nothing like it had ever been seen before; but then nothing like Foot had ever been seen before.

3. The decisions of the 1981 conference are contained in *Report of the Annual Conference of the Labour Party* (1981), esp. app. 2.

4. The Labour party's descent, as well as Michael Foot's, can be traced in the table referred to in n. 2 above as well as in the monthly *Gallup Political Index*. Following the 1981 conference, 86% (*sic*) of respondents told the Gallup Poll they thought Labour was divided. Regardless of their own views, a majority thought that most British people did not hold a favourable view of the Labour party. *Gallup Political Index*, Report No. 254, Oct. 1981, 11, 15.

5. King, 'Margaret Thatcher's First Term', table 1.2, p. 11.

6. In October 1981 only 24% of the Gallup Poll's regular monthly sample were satisfied with Thatcher as prime minister. For the full historical record, see Norman L. Webb and Robert J. Wybrow (eds.), *The Gallup Report* (London: Sphere Books, 1981), 167–85, and Norman Webb and Robert Wybrow, *The Gallup Report: Your Opinions in 1981* (London: Sphere Books, 1982), 191–2.

7. The Liberals on their own had occasionally got above 20% in the Gallup Poll (for several months in 1962 and again in 1973 and 1974), but they had never succeeded in pulling ahead of either of the other parties, let alone both of them. See the first *Gallup Report* cited in n. 6 above, pp. 167–85, and also the tables in David Butler and Gareth Butler, *British Political Facts 1900–1985*, 6th edn. (London: Mcmillan, 1986), 254–64.

8. Frank Johnson, *The Times*, 27 Jan. 1981.

9. *Private Eye's Bores 3*, with illustrations by Michael Heath (London: Private Eye, 1983).

10. *A Fresh Start for Britain*, Statement of Principles Commended by a Joint Working Party of Liberals and Social Democrats, David Steel and Shirley Williams, Joint Chairmen (London: Poland Street Publications, 1981). Alan Cochrane captured the flavour in the *Daily Express* of

17 June 1981: 'A betrothal between Mrs Shirley Williams and Mr David Steel leading to the wedding of their parties by the next General Election was announced yesterday.'

11. The poll, conducted by Gallup, suggested that, if Jenkins were the candidate, the SDP would get 26% of the vote; if Williams were the candidate, it would get 35%. The figure for the 'unnamed Social Democrat with Liberal support' was 29% (i.e. more than for Jenkins).

12. Owen recalls his dismay at Williams' refusal to stand in *Personally Speaking to Kenneth Harris* (London: Weidenfeld & Nicolson, 1987), 211–12, and also in *Time to Declare* (London: Michael Joseph, 1991), 519–22. He describes her decision as 'the worst decision Shirley has ever made in politics' (*Time to Declare*, 520) and expresses the belief that with Williams as the candidate the SDP would have won in Warrington (a view widely held in the SDP at the time). As Owen reports in *Time to Declare* (p. 520), Williams maintained her refusal despite receiving advance notice of a *Sun* poll showing her winning the seat with 55% of the popular vote. The *Sun* published the poll on 4 June 1981 under the headline 'You Can Do It Shirl'.

13. 'Declined to Take up the Challenge', *Sunday Telegraph*, 7 June 1981; 'flinched', *The Times*, 11 June 1981.

14. *Daily Telegraph*, 12 June 1981.

15. 'The Cracks in the Mould Open Wide', *Guardian*, 18 July 1981.

16. *Daily Mail*, 20 July 1981. She was quoted under the headline 'Plain Bill Pitt keeps fighting'.

17. Quoted in Hugh Stephenson, *Claret and Chips: The Rise of the SDP* (London: Michael Joseph, 1982), 84.

18. Shirley Williams nearly missed the train. She arrived at King's Cross only seconds before the train pulled out. Members of the Cowley Street staff were pleading with British Rail officials to hold the train for her.

19. David Cowling, then working as an assistant to the Labour party's Peter Shore, kept track of the three main groupings' percentage share of the vote in local by-elections during this period. The figures bear witness to the Alliance's spectacular rise—and subsequent decline. For example, in July 1981 the Alliance's share was 26%. In January 1982 it was 44%, but by June 1982 it had fallen to 28%.

20. *Observer*, 25 Oct. 1981.

21. 'We in this party have to scale unscalable heights. We have to take impossible risks' (*The Times*, 7 Oct. 1981). David Owen gives a slightly different account (*Time to Declare*, p. 535).

22. *Financial Times*, 20 Oct. 1981.

23. *The Times*, 27 Nov. 1981.

Chapter 9

1. The quarterly figures for inflation and unemployment, and also for the Gallup Poll standings of the government, the parties and the party leaders, can be found in Anthony King, 'Margaret Thatcher's First Term', in Austin Ranney (ed.), *Britain at the Polls, 1983: A Study of the General Election* (Durham, NC: Duke University Press/American Enterprise Institute, 1985), 10–11, 33.

2. David Sanders, Hugh Ward and David Marsh (with Tony Fletcher), 'Government Popularity and the Falklands War: A Reassessment', *British Journal of Political Science*, 17 (1987), 281–313. The view of Sanders and his colleagues that the Thatcher government's victory in the 1983 election was primarily economic in origin—and owed little, if anything, to Britain's victory in the Falklands War—has long been held in the Conservative party and is supported by Patrick Cosgrove in *Thatcher: The First Term* (London: Bodley Head, 1985), 145–6. For a critique of the Sanders thesis, see Harold D. Clarke, William Mishler and Paul Whiteley, 'Recapturing the Falklands: Models of Conservative Popularity, 1979–83', *British Journal of Political Science*, 20 (1990), 63–81.

3. It is intriguing to speculate what would have happened to the Labour party if Benn had defeated Healey and if the right's defeat in the party had turned into a rout. More Labour MPs would probably have defected to the SDP, and it is widely believed both in the Labour party and among those who belonged to the SDP that a number of major trade unions, notably the Amalgamated Engineering Union, might well have disaffiliated from Labour. If that had happened, then Labour might well have gone into a downward spiral from which it could never have recovered. The Liberal–SDP Alliance would almost certainly have outpolled Labour in the 1983 general election. Since Healey defeated Benn by only 0.85% of the electoral college vote, it is arguable that Labour owes its continued existence as a major party in the 1990s to any one of the MPs who voted for Healey rather than Benn in 1981 or any one constituency Labour party or any one trade union (say, the tiny National Union of Footwear, Leather and Allied Trades) that did the same. The margin was that fine.
4. For a more detailed account of the Rodgers episode, see pp. 180–1 and 545 n. 39.
5. See Hugh Stephenson, *Claret and Chips: The Rise of the SDP* (London: Michael Joseph, 1982), 153–8. In his account of the SDP's split over the Tebbit bill, David Owen stresses the importance of the SDP's need to distinguish itself from Labour: 'That the original founders [of the SDP] voted for the legislation was very important for the party. It averted what might have been a fatal danger to it: that we might appear to be *not* a new political force after all, but mutton dressed up as lamb. There was a danger that some of the old lags who had come or might come to us from the Labour Party would dominate our new party and would attempt to justify all their old Labour Party attitudes. We could not have that, and the best way to prevent it happening was to make it absolutely clear where we the leaders stood on this issue of trade union legislation . . . The problem of Labour members of parliament coming to us later was that they had not been with us in the early discussions about the nature of the party. They, understandably, hadn't thought through their position. They weren't sufficiently changed; they weren't thinking afresh'. See David Owen, *Personally Speaking to Kenneth Harris* (London: Weidenfeld & Nicolson, 1987), 211. See also David Owen, *Time to Declare* (London: Michael Joseph, 1991), 539–41.
6. The Labour party at almost all stages of its history (though not to the same degree in the mid-1990s) has been divided into easily identifiable left-wing and right-wing factions, with individual politicians being readily classifiable as left-wingers or right-wingers and with people who hold left- or right-wing views on one issue almost invariably holding left- or right-wing views on all the others. The party has effectively been two parties in one. By contrast, the Conservative party during most of its history (though less so in the mid-1990s) has been characterized by 'cross-cutting cleavages', with no stable factional structures and with opponents on one issue frequently becoming allies on the next. The effects on the unity of the two parties can be imagined.
7. The Gang of Four took turns chairing the sessions of the constitutional conference, and Owen probably did his leadership prospects no harm by turning out to be a considerably tougher, more decisive chairman than Jenkins. A fuller account of the debate over the method of electing the leader, and of the development of the SDP's constitution generally, can be found in Ch. 12. For the formal record of the debate at the Steering Committee, see Minutes of the Meeting of the Steering Committee on the Constitution held at 10.00 a.m. on Tuesday, 8 Sept, at 3 Dean's Yard. The debate at the constitutional conference is reported in *The Times*, 15 Feb. 1982. David Owen in *Time to Declare* (p. 531) describes Jenkins' manœuvre at the Steering Committee as 'the shabbiest act [in politics] that I have ever witnessed.' Owen in his memoirs takes it for granted—and took it for granted at the time—that Jenkins was personally behind this change of front. According to some Jenkinsites, however, the original pressure to have the leader elected only by MPs did not come from Jenkins. Rather, it is said, it came from a number of his supporters, and Jenkins backed what they were doing partly out of personal loyalty and

partly on the merits of the argument, not because he necessarily thought he would do better in an election held under an MPs-only system.

8. The results of the postal ballot are given in *Social Democrat*, May 1982, 1. The correlation between support for Jenkins and support for the election of the leader by MPs alone was high but not absolutely perfect. Robert Maclennan, for example, was pro-Jenkins but also pro-OMOV; Christopher Brocklebank-Fowler was anti-Jenkins but also anti-OMOV. But Maclennan and Brocklebank-Fowler were among the small number of exceptions.

9. Ivor Crewe, 'Everything that Roy should Know about his New Patch', *The Times*, 15 Jan. 1982.

10. The Hillhead by-election is described in detail in John Campbell, *Roy Jenkins: A Biography* (London: Weidenfeld & Nicolson, 1983), 214–18; Stephenson, *Claret and Chips*, 149–53, 164–7; and Edinburgh University Politics Group, 'Learning to Fight Multi-Party Elections: The Lessons of Hillhead', *Parliamentary Affairs*, 35 (1982), 252–66.

11. See e.g. Ivor Crewe, 'Good for the Alliance, Better for Labour', *The Times*, 27 Mar. 1982.

12. *The Times*, 26 Mar. 1982.

13. David Loshak wrote in the *Daily Telegraph*, 19 May 1982 ('Shirley Williams Opts Out'): 'Mrs Williams's decision not to stand is entirely practical. Although the most electorally appealing of the party's 29 MPs, she would never have enjoyed their confidence as leader, and thereby putative prime minister, if elected by the membership, and had she sought nomination would have been unlikely to gather the necessary five nominations from among her colleagues.' The latter statement was simply untrue: more than five MPs had already told Williams they would nominate and support her. Not all the Jenkinsites who said Williams would make a natural party president were being patronizing. Some genuinely believed that Jenkins would make a better leader in the House of Commons while Williams was more likely to be an effective campaigner—and arouser of the party faithful—in the country.

14. *Guardian, Daily Telegraph*, 27 May 1982.

15. *Guardian*, 1 Apr. 1982.

16. David Steel on *Panorama*, quoted in *Scotsman*, 30 Mar. 1982.

17. Alan Watkins wrote in the *Observer*, 18 Apr. 1982 ('Who is Doing Well out of the Crisis?'): 'Dr Owen . . . gives the impression that he could take on the entire Argentine fleet single-handed and give a good account of himself.' *The Economist* of 15 May, under the heading 'Winners in the War at Westminster', wrote: 'Among opposition politicians, Dr David Owen has gained more than most out of the crisis . . . He has clearly upstaged his rival for the SDP leadership, Mr Jenkins, only a month before the first leadership elections begin.'

18. The two candidates' lists of backers were published in full in the *Financial Times*, 12 June 1982. Those declaring their support for Jenkins were Tom Bradley, Tom Ellis, David Ginsburg, John Horam, Dickson Mabon, Robert Maclennan, Bill Rodgers, John Roper, Neville Sandelson, Jim Wellbeloved, Ednyfed Hudson Davies, Bryan Magee, Jeffrey Thomas and Ian Wrigglesworth. Owen's backers among the MPs were Shirley Williams, Christopher Brocklebank-Fowler, Ron Brown, John Cartwright, Richard Crawshaw, James Dunn, John Grant, Edward Lyons, Tom McNally, Bob Mitchell, Eric Ogden and Mike Thomas.

19. The denials came, not least, from Owen. For example, he wrote in the *Observer*, 20 June 1982 ('The SDP I would hope to lead'): 'We sprang from the collapse of the coalition that once made the Labour Party a great party. To forget that is to fly in the face of reality. But that reality does not mean we must be a Mark II Labour Party. It would be folly to attempt to be so . . .'

20. David Watt, *The Times*, 5 Feb. 1982, 'Roy Jenkins: the ayes have it'.

21. 'Why I am Standing for Leader—David Owen Talks to Alliance', *Alliance*, No. 2 (July 1982), 5–6.

22. The two statements were published in *The Times*, 18 June 1982.

23. The two headlines quoted both appeared on 7 June 1982. There were many more like them.

24. 'Poll Shows Owen in Shock Lead', *Observer*, 27 June 1982.
25. *Daily Telegraph*, 3 July 1982.
26. Quoted in *Daily Mail*, 3 July 1982.
27. *Daily Mail*, 3 July 1982; *Daily Telegraph*, 3 July 1982.
28. The results were reported in *Social Democrat*, 24 Sept. 1992, p. 1. Stephen Haseler, the author of several books on politics, was a former Labour member of the Greater London Council. He helped found the Social Democratic Alliance in 1975 and stood as an independent Social Democrat in the 1981 local elections. He contested the presidency against Williams and Rodgers on the grounds that the office should be held by a rank-and-file party member, close to the grass roots, rather than by a parliamentary grandee.
29. The Great Yarmouth debate was reported in *The Times*, 16 Oct. 1982. The official party newspaper, *Social Democrat*, noted laconically: 'Dr Owen emphasised to the Council his own unequivocal personal support for Mr Jenkins' Leadership' (22 Oct. 1982, p. 1). Owen concedes in his first volume of memoirs that he was 'foolish' in allowing Levitt to speak, adding that 'Shirley was quite correct in privately tearing me off a strip' (*Personally Speaking*, 218); see also *Time to Declare*, 565–6.
30. For the details of the by-elections, see Table 16.12, in App. 5.
31. Frank Johnson, 'Jenkins Rolls a Jowl at the Falklands', *The Times*, 21 Apr. 1982. Jenkins acknowledges that he was less good in the new-style House of Commons—and gives his account of why he thinks the House of Commons has changed—in *A Life at the Centre* (London: Macmillan, 1991), 564–6.
32. The Gallup Poll from time to time asked voters whether they had seen each of the four parties' leaders on television recently and, if so, whether they thought their television appearance had or had not increased support for their party. In early June 1983 fewer voters remembered seeing Jenkins than remembered seeing any of the other three leaders (even though the great majority of them probably had seen him) and nearly twice as many voters replied 'did not increase support for the SDP' as replied the opposite. The contrast was striking between the responses about Jenkins (No, did not see, 35%; Did increase support, 15%; Did not, 26%; Made no difference, 18%; Don't know, 5%) and those about David Steel (23%, 49%, 8%, 15%, 5% respectively). See *Gallup Political Index*, Report No. 274, June 1983, 30.
33. The *Gallup Political Index* each month reported the pattern of responses to the question: 'Do you think that Mr Jenkins is or is not proving a good leader of the SDP?' Gallup's findings bear witness to Jenkins' failure to make his mark and, worse, his actual decline in public esteem. The proportion replying 'Don't know' to the question never fell below 21% and on several occasions rose above 30%. The proportion who thought he would prove a good SDP leader in July 1982 was 50%. The proportion who thought he was actually proving a good leader had fallen by the time of the general election to 30%.

Chapter 10

1. In addition, Sandelson, Maclennan and Crawshaw each had exploratory talks with Steel.
2. Shirley Williams, interviewed on BBC Radio's *The World at One*, 8 June 1980. See p. 68.
3. See 'The Two Davids Find Hope for Agreement', *The Times*, 24 Mar. 1981.
4. Owen describes his mother as 'if anything, a Liberal' (David Owen, *Personally Speaking to Kenneth Harris* (London: Weidenfeld & Nicolson, 1987), 25). He claims to have formed an early suspicion of the Liberal party when he fought his first parliamentary contest in Torrington in 1964. He disapproved of its commitment to a federal Europe and of the Liberal candidate's attempt to water down the party's federalism when it proved unpopular locally. See David Owen, *Time to Declare* (London: Michael Joseph, 1991), 75. But as foreign secretary in

1977–8 Owen appears to have reconciled himself to the Lib–Lab Pact with better grace than some of his cabinet colleagues.

5. David Owen, speech to West Cheshire SDP, Chester, 17 July 1981.

6. This definition of a party of the left was adopted by Owen, more than once, in his discussions with Jenkins before the breakaway. See Roy Jenkins, *European Diary, 1977–1981* (London: Collins, 1989), 639, 650.

7. Roger Pincham, the Liberal party chairman, reported to Jenkins' supporter, Clive Lindley, that, at their Kiddington Hall conference, Liberals 'had resolved to fight [a Social Democratic party] tooth and nail since it must intend to appeal to their own area of support. He agreed that this would be a tragedy but in the absence of a new realignment of the centre it would be inevitable' (Clive Lindley, unpublished diary, p. 11).

8. Some were even less ambitious. In January 1981 Tom Ellis wrote in the Welsh current-affairs magazine *Arcade* that any new party should fight no more than, say, thirty or forty seats: 'The greatest threat to the embryonic party would be over-ambition. If it were, for example, to over-reach itself by fielding 300 candidates, it could not possibly enter into an electoral pact with the Liberals' (cited in *The Times*, 9 Jan. 1981). Steel at this time was anticipating the Liberals making way for the SDP in about 100 seats. See David Steel, *Against Goliath* (London: Weidenfeld & Nicolson, 1989), 224.

9. See pp. 64–6.

10. 'It was impossible to correct Bill in public on the platform, and Mike and I hoped no one would notice. But key Liberals noticed, and we were never able to recover the concept . . . that we might, by our standing in the polls and by our newness, have developed the strength justifiably to claim to fight the largest number of seats' (Owen, *Personally Speaking*, 206–7).

11. *The Times*, 11 June 1980.

12. See *The Times*, 29 Dec. 1980, and 'Liberal "Wets" attacked by Mr Smith', *The Times*, 26 Mar. 1981.

13. *Daily Telegraph*, 2 Apr. 1981.

14. See Ivor Crewe, 'Is Britain's Two-party System Really About to Crumble?', *Electoral Studies*, 1 (1982), 275–314; table A.1 on p. 306 shows that support for an alliance of the two parties was consistently larger, by one or two percentage points, than the combined support for the Liberals and SDP.

15. For true Liberals, 'the key political spectrum runs from diffusion of power to corporatism—private or public—[not] . . . from public ownership to private ownership' (Michael Meadowcroft, *Social Democracy—Barrier or Bridge?* (London: Liberal Publication Department, 1981), ch. 6).

16. See 'Steel Presses Liberal–Social Democrat Link', *Guardian*, 5 Feb. 1981.

17. See 'Liberals Step up Pressure for Pact', *Sunday Times*, 22 Mar. 1981.

18. Five SDP MPs voted against the Tebbit bill in February 1982 and another five abstained; the Liberals all voted in favour. See pp. 148–9.

19. Social Democrats were called upon to speak in the chamber much more frequently than Liberals, not only because there were more of them, but because they numbered five privy councillors (the Gang of Four and Dickson Mabon) to the Liberals' two (Steel and Grimond). By tradition the speaker gives privy councillors priority.

20. The lunch was engineered by Holme and Marquand. At Holme's suggestion, a few days earlier, Marquand lobbied Rodgers and Williams to use the opportunity of Königswinter to talk to Steel about future SDP–Liberal relations.

21. One significant point of disagreement was over the number of seats in which the Liberals would stand down for the SDP. Steel and Holme were still thinking in terms of 100 seats, whereas Rodgers repeated his launch press conference aim of a 50% share-out. See Steel, *Against Goliath*, 224.

22. Owen, *Personally Speaking*, 208.

23. Owen took a balanced line at both the Steering Committee meeting on 6 April and the joint meeting with the Parliamentary Committee the next day, suggesting that movement on policy discussions should be postponed until after Easter (i.e. for a month) while urging the party to reach agreement with the Liberals as soon as possible on an arbitration system for selecting by-election candidates, because 'it would be greatly damaging to fight each other'. He does not at that time appear to have believed that crucial principles in SDP–Liberal relations were at stake. See Minutes of Steering Committee, 6 Apr. 1981, and Minutes of the Meeting of the Parliamentary Committee and the Steering Committee, 7 Apr. 1981. See also Owen, *Personally Speaking*, 209. However, after 1983 his opposition to what took place at Königswinter turned into bitterness. A senior SDP officer was flabbergasted to witness in his own office Owen accusing Shirley Williams 'in the most brutal terms' of 'selling the SDP down the river at Königswinter'.

24. For the argument that the outlook of most Liberals and Social Democrats was rooted in one and the same tradition—the socially progressive 'New Liberalism' of 1884–1914—see Peter Clarke, *Liberals and Social Democrats* (Cambridge: Cambridge University Press, 1978), and S. J. Ingle, *The Alliance: Piggy in the Middle or Radical Alternative?* (Hull Papers in Politics, No. 38; Hull: Department of Politics, 1985), esp. pp. 15–24.

25. David Owen, *Face the Future* (London: Jonathan Cape, 1981).

26. The drafting was left to the SDP and Liberal press officers, John Lyttle and Paul Medlicott, using notes sketched by Holme and Marquand on a Euston Station beer mat.

27. This group was influenced, too, by the local-election results in May 1981, when the Liberal performance was lacklustre and unofficial SDP candidates (the SDP did not formally contest the elections) generally outpolled the Liberals in four-cornered contests. For example, in the GLC elections the Social Democratic Association's candidate pushed the Liberal candidate into fourth place in six of the seven seats the Association contested.

28. In August and September 1981 Gallup asked the somewhat leading question, 'If an election were to take place tomorrow and a candidate from the new Social Democratic Party stood, how would you vote?' Averaging the two polls, the result was: Conservative 27%, Labour 33%, Liberal 9%, SDP 31%. Thomas, and other sceptics about collaboration with the Liberals, took these figures as evidence that the SDP could, if necessary, stand against Liberals and win. They ignored the results of the conventional 'unprompted' vote-intention question, which showed the SDP preponderance over the Liberals to be a much more modest 18–13%. See *Gallup Political Index*, Nos. 252 and 253 (Aug. and Sept. 1981).

29. *The Times*, 24 July 1981.

30. See the letter of Roger Pincham, the Liberal party chairman, to *The Times*, 6 June 1981: 'it must be absolutely clear that the national leadership cannot and will not try to dictate local decisions. We can do no more than offer guidance, if asked, and seek to establish a framework of nationally acceptable procedures within which local decisions can be made . . .'.

31. Jeffrey Roberts, the candidate for Hackney South and Shoreditch, declared that he would not stand down 'even if David Steel asks me nicely'. Steel did; he didn't.

32. See 'Alliance States its Terms on Recruits', *Guardian*, 17 Sept. 1981, p. 1. Beith was referring to Michael O'Halloran, the MP for Islington North.

33. Michael Steed, 'The Alliance: A Critical History', *New Outlook*, 22 (1983), 3–45, at 12.

34. See 'Rapturous Welcome for SDP Leaders on Eve of Alliance Debate', *The Times*, 16 Sept. 1981.

35. See William Rodgers, 'The Alliance's Electoral Arrangements', memorandum submitted to the SDP Steering Committee, 4 Sept. 1981.

36. See n. 29.

37. The Liberals objected on the grounds that it was unconstitutional for non-Liberals to participate in the selection of Liberal candidates while the SDP assumed that it would be outnumbered locally by Liberals.

38. The Liberals had gradually built up a substantial local base in Greenock; they had increased their local vote against the national trend, had controlled the local council from 1977 to 1980 and came second in the 1979 general election. Their success was largely based on a community-politics campaign against a West of Scotland Labour machine that was symbolized by Mabon himself.

39. The SDP and Liberal teams agreed to a division of the ten Derbyshire seats at one meeting. The SDP assumed the agreement was final, subject only to formal national ratification; the Liberals assumed it was provisional, subject to the agreement of individual associations, because constitutionally the national party could not prohibit a local association from contesting a seat. The Derbyshire South association was unhappy at being one of the three neighbouring seats allocated to the SDP and proposed that either it or Erewash be returned to the Liberals in exchange for Amber Valley. There was no reason to think that the SDP would object as none of the seats in question was regarded as winnable; nothing momentous was at stake. Viv Bingham, who led the Liberal negotiating team, tried to telephone Rodgers, but finding that he was out left an unelaborated message. Irritated at an apparent reneging on a deal, Rodgers contacted Steel, who declined to become personally embroiled, arguing that such a small issue should be left to the local parties to sort out. Rodgers thereupon instructed his national negotiating team to postpone new negotiations until the Derbyshire problem was resolved, followed up by a letter to Steel which the latter interpreted as notice of a stalemate, not suspension. There followed conciliatory conversations between Rodgers and both Steel and Bingham. After Christmas, Steel issued a New Year's message to Liberal candidates which contained the following passage: 'I am concerned that in some cases the SDP is asking well organised Liberal associations, with a good record and hundreds of experienced campaigners, to stand aside for them, with a relatively untried membership. That is not the way to enhance the prospects for the Alliance. It is perfectly possible to achieve both rough parity of seats and rough parity of good prospect seats, without doing that. Equally there have been cases where Liberals have approached local negotiations with excessive demands. Both sides must avoid bluster and arrogance'. Rodgers interpreted the passage, especially the final remark, as a jab at him; Steel, not believing that negotiations had been frozen, saw it as a legitimate and even-handed public warning. The best detailed account is Peter Kellner, 'An Everyday Story of Breaking the Mould', *New Statesman*, 8 Jan. 1982.

40. 'I judged that an early row would clear the air and give an impetus to progress, while a later one, well into 1982, would be profoundly damaging' (quoted in Steel, *Against Goliath*, 229).

41. See, in particular, William Wallace, 'Stop the Squabbling and Get Down to a Real Alliance', *The Times*, 4 Jan. 1982, and Mike Thomas, 'A Crisis of Credibility for David Steel', *The Times*, 5 Jan. 1982.

42. Quoted in Hugh Stephenson, *Claret and Chips: The Rise of the SDP* (London: Michael Joseph, 1982), 121.

43. Robin Oakley, 'Even the Angels can Squabble!', *Daily Mail*, 5 Jan. 1982.

44. The slippage began well before the Rodgers–Steel row, which broke out on 3 January. A Gallup poll conducted 9–14 December put support for the Alliance at 50.5%, but an ORC poll for *Weekend World* conducted 15–22 December put it at only 38%. In the next two polls, taken after the row broke out, the level of support was 39.5% (Gallup, 13–18 January) and 40% (MORI, 21–2 January).

45. Mabon eventually agreed to move to the neighbouring seat of Renfrew West and Inverclyde, which he lost to the Conservatives by a narrower margin (3%) than the Liberals lost to Labour in Greenock (11%). Had he stood in Greenock, with active Liberal support, he would probably have done better than the Liberals (their share of the vote increased by less than the regional average) but not well enough to win.

46. There is absolutely no evidence for Owen's assertion that, in return for pressurizing the

Liberals into stepping aside in Hillhead for Jenkins, Rodgers' negotiating position was 'badly eroded', and the SDP paid 'a heavy price . . . in terms of surrendering chances of a fair allocation of seats' (Owen, *Personally Speaking*, 216). The Liberals were more conciliatory than before the row and the SDP were more resistant; moreover, those concessions made by the SDP in the course of bargaining were not connected in terms of timing, motive or location to Jenkins' candidature in Hillhead. Jenkins himself was not involved in the seats negotiations at this stage and his close ally, Matthew Oakeshott, was the toughest member of the SDP's negotiating team.

47. The three associations were Liverpool Broadgreen, Hackney South and Shoreditch, and Hammersmith. In each case both the Liberal and SDP candidates did poorly. Detailed accounts of the situation in the three constituencies can be found in Steed, 'The Alliance: A Critical History', 28–33. No SDP area party rebelled.

48. A non-party academic observer at the first round of negotiations for South Yorkshire revealed the flavour of the meeting: 'The presence of prospective parliamentary candidates on the Liberal team further complicated the process of negotiation . . . In particular, the chairman of the South Yorkshire Liberal group was the chosen candidate for Hillsborough, the most winnable seat in the region . . . The Liberal prospective candidate was willing to concede a great deal to maintain his district [*sic*], but the other Liberals were not. Because each Liberal had an equal say and opposing interests, members of the Liberal team failed to agree on a single plan' (Patricia Lee Sykes, *Losing from the Inside: The Cost of Conflict in the British Social Democratic Party* (New Brunswick, NJ: Transaction Books, 1988), 118).

49. See Peter Kellner, 'SDP Sunk in Private Gloom', *New Statesman*, 12 Nov. 1982. A particularly tendentious attack on the seats deal, containing all the Owenites' wildest suspicions, was made by Jenkins' one-time supporter Colin Phipps, in 'Saving the SDP from the Alliance', *The Times*, 9 Oct. 1982. Owen himself did not raise the issue at the time but took the same line retrospectively. See Owen, *Personally Speaking*, 216–17.

50. See John Curtice and Michael Steed, 'Turning Dreams into Reality: The Division of the Constituencies between the Liberals and the Social Democrats', *Parliamentary Affairs*, 36 (1983), 166–82, at 170.

51. Calculations based on more elaborate assumptions come to similar conclusions. See e.g. Curtice and Steed, 'Turning Dreams into Realities', 178, and Steed, 'The Alliance: A Critical History', 20–1.

52. Some Liberals cited the relatively untroubled share-out of wards for the 1982 local elections in support of their argument for wholly local negotiations. But the local elections were a misleading parallel. Co-operation in them was much easier to achieve because of the multiplicity of seats to be distributed and the existence in many boroughs of multi-seat wards, allowing both parties to share a single ward. Moreover, the Liberals' retention of the great majority of promising local-government wards suggests that, without national control, they would have contested an even larger proportion of the best parliamentary seats too. See Steed, 'The Alliance: A Critical History', 26.

53. One national negotiator described the 'complex evolution' of his thinking as follows: 'In my own case I went through the following sequence: (1) intense exasperation with the Liberals on Mike Thomas-ish grounds; (2) intense exasperation with the Mike Thomases in the SDP as it became clear that the deal was in fact quite good and that SDP anti-Liberals were continuing to bellyache when they had nothing to bellyache about; (3) a massive feeling of time and energy wasted and a conclusion that it would be insane to go through this sort of exercise ever again.'

54. 'I was against going to bed with the Liberals from the beginning. We should have run against them in the early by-elections and beat them into the ground. Then we would have had more clout in the negotiations' (quoted in Sykes, *Losing from the Inside*, 113).

NOTES

55. See David Owen's speeches at Southampton, 27 May 1981; Chester, 17 July 1981; Andover, 4 Sept. 1981; Milton Keynes, 6 Oct. 1982; Galashiels, 11 Dec. 1982; Luton, 20 Apr. 1983.

56. 'We are committed to demonstrating to the British people that in a partnership of principle we can form a coalition government with the Liberals' (speech at Milton Keynes, 6 Oct. 1982). Roy Jenkins referred to a 'partnership of principle' in a speech to the National Liberal Club on 31 Mar. 1981: 'If we are proposing an arrangement purely of convenience, even of opposites . . . that would seem to me rather discreditable, and would be seen as such by many people. How much better that we should be able to envisage a partnership of principle . . .'.

57. Those present were the Gang of Four, John Roper (the SDP whip), David Steel and five Liberal MPs: Alan Beith, Cyril Smith, Richard Wainwright, David Penhaligon and Russell Johnston.

58. A MORI poll for BBC's *Panorama* on the eve of the 1982 SDP conference reported that voters would prefer Steel to Jenkins as Alliance prime minister by a margin of 61 to 25% and it found a narrow majority for Steel (49 to 47%) even among the SDP's supporters. See Market & Opinion Research International, *British Public Opinion*, No. 9 (Sept. 1982), opinion poll 2080, p. 24. An earlier MORI poll, published shortly after Jenkins' election as party leader, reported that voters preferred Steel to Jenkins as Alliance prime minister by 55 to 27% (see *Daily Express*, 5 Aug. 1982).

59. According to Gallup polls, Steel was preferred to Jenkins as the Alliance *leader* by a 61 to 21% margin in March and by 65 to 19% in April. When the same polls asked who would make the better *prime minister*, Steel led by 57 to 24% in March and by 61 to 23% in April. In other words, the projection of Jenkins to the electorate as a prime minister-designate made little difference. See *Gallup Political Index*, nos. 271 and 272, Mar. and Apr. 1983.

60. The pretentious title was not used by Jenkins or Steel but had been coined earlier by Social Democrats and was taken over by the media. Despite the Alliance's slide in the polls, it stuck, to both parties' discomfiture.

61. The main exceptions were in a few urban areas like Liverpool and West Yorkshire where community-politics Liberals had built up support by campaigning against the local Labour machine and rejected MPs and members who had defected from it.

62. The 1886 pact between the Conservatives and Liberal Unionists was confined to seats represented by Liberal defectors, where the Conservatives stood down. The 1903 Gladstone–MacDonald agreement between the Liberal party and the Labour Representation Committee was limited in 1906 to thirty-two constituencies; in another eighteen Labour candidates were opposed by Liberals. In the 1931 election the coalition National government led by MacDonald tried to ensure that it was represented by only one of the coalition parties—the Conservatives, Liberal Nationals, Liberals or National Labour—but in eighty-eight constituencies two or more of the coalition partners fielded candidates. In 1951 and 1955 the Conservatives stood down in five constituencies to give the Liberals a clear run against Labour, as a result of locally initiated agreements. See Vernon Bogdanor, 'Electoral Pacts in Britain since 1886', in Dennis Kavanagh (ed.), *Electoral Politics* (Oxford: Clarendon Press, 1992), 165–87.

63. Ivor Crewe, 'Is Britain's Two-Party System Really about to Crumble?', *Electoral Studies*, 1 (1982), 275–313.

64. i.e. medium-sized, semi-isolated towns with a marked sense of community, usually reinforced by strong local media, e.g., York, Swindon, Carlisle and Peterborough.

65. In the small number of seats allocated to the SDP despite a relatively high Liberal vote in 1979 (over 20%) a Liberal candidate would probably have polled slightly better, especially in rural areas such as Bridlington, Ludlow, Saffron Walden, and Somerton and Frome, where the traditional Liberal vote does not appear to have converted fully to the SDP. However, an SDP candidate would probably have won a slightly higher vote than a Liberal candidate in urban working-class seats where the Liberal vote was particularly poor in 1979 (less than 10%). See

John Curtice and Michael Steed, 'An Analysis of the Voting', in David Butler and Dennis Kavanagh, *The British General Election of 1983* (London: Macmillan, 1984), 351.
66. It is arguable, but improbable, that the Liberals would have won Liverpool Broadgreen if the SDP had not insisted on fielding their defector, Richard Crawshaw, there.
67. For evidence on this point, see pp. 294–5.

Chapter 11

1. The Labour party in Bermondsey had all but fallen apart. It was a classic instance of a run-down, boss-ridden inner-city Labour party waiting to be taken over by the hard left, especially if the latter was well organized. When the hard left took over in Bermondsey, a number of Southwark councillors defected from the party, one of them, John O'Grady, standing against Tatchell in the by-election as 'Real Bermondsey Labour'. O'Grady and the other rebels had the support of the outgoing MP, Bob Mellish. Foot said at first that Tatchell would never be endorsed as the official Labour candidate because of his support for extra-parliamentary action, but then both he and Labour's National Executive were forced to back down in the face of the local party's insistence on standing by their chosen candidate; Foot was even photographed shaking hands with Tatchell towards the end of the campaign. The Bermondsey episode—both the nomination of Tatchell and Foot's maladroit handling of it—seemed to symbolize everything that was wrong with the Labour party at that time. Tatchell wrote a book about his political history and also about the by-election: *The Battle for Bermondsey* (London: Heretic Books, 1983). For an account of the by-election portrayed as a clash between two opposing cultures, that of the traditional British working class and what the writer called 'Tatchellism or radical post-materialism', see Laurie Taylor, 'Tatchell Man's First Test', *The Times*, 22 Feb. 1983.
2. The poll, conducted by NOP, appeared in the *Mail on Sunday* on 27 Feb. 1983. It gave the Social Democrats 38%, the Conservatives 37% and Labour only 25%. That there were left-wingers in the Labour party even in Darlington is attested to by the fact that Ossie O'Brien's runner-up for the Darlington nomination was Chris Mullin, a hard-left supporter and close associate of Tony Benn.
3. Liberal critics of the SDP campaign in Darlington also complained that the SDP's postal-ballot method of selecting parliamentary candidates (see ch. 12) might almost have been calculated to reward celebrity over ability and that Cook's political empty-headedness accurately reflected the political immaturity of the SDP's membership as a whole. See Peter Hetherington's post-mortem on the campaign, 'Alliance Campaign Bungling Leaves Cook the Scapegoat', *Guardian*, 26 Mar. 1983.
4. On this phase of the two parties' discussions about their joint leadership, see Peter Riddell, 'Alliance Leaders Try to Head off Row over Election Defeat', *Financial Times*, 26 Mar. 1983; Julian Haviland, 'MPs to Hold Talks on Alliance Leadership', *The Times*, 28 Mar. 1983; Peter Riddell, 'SDP and Liberals Postpone Decision on Alliance Leader', *Financial Times*, 29 Mar. 1983; and Peter Riddell, 'No Decision on Leader', *Financial Times*, 31 Mar. 1983.
5. See pp. 185–7.
6. See David Steel, *A House Divided: The Lib–Lab Pact and the Future of British Politics* (London: Weidenfeld & Nicolson, 1980), esp. ch. 11. Steel believed that the pact had been put together too hastily in 1976, that it had not really won the consent of either the Labour party or the Liberal party as a whole ('It wasn't so much a Lib–Lab pact as a Steel–Callaghan pact' (p. 153)) and that the two party leaders therefore found it difficult, if not impossible, to deliver their own followers.
7. For more detailed accounts of the drawing up of the manifesto, see David Butler and Dennis

Kavanagh, *The British General Election of 1983* (London: Macmillan, 1984), 79–80, and Jorgen Rasmussen, 'The Alliance Campaign, Watersheds, and Landslides: Was 1983 a Fault-line in British Politics?' in Austin Ranney (ed.), *Britain at the Polls, 1983: A Study of the General Election* (Durham, NC: Duke University Press/American Enterprise Institute, 1985), 90. The manifesto itself is reprinted in *The Times Guide to the House of Commons: June 1983* (London: Times Books, 1983), 334–50. A considerable number of Liberals complained about the haste in which the document was produced as well as about the lack of consultation. Tony Greaves of the Association of Liberal Councillors went further and characteristically complained that the manifesto contained nothing at all that was Liberal.

8. Altogether seven 'Ask the Alliance' rallies were held: in Glasgow, Stockport, Bristol, Edinburgh, Birmingham, Plymouth and London. David Steel was present on all seven occasions, Roy Jenkins on three, David Owen on two (including the Plymouth rally) and Bill Rodgers and Shirley Williams on one each (see Holi A. Semetko, ' "Working Together"?: Decision-Making, Coordination and Strategy in the Liberal–SDP Alliance Campaign', paper delivered at the Conference on Political Communications, the Media, the Parties and the Polls in the 1983 Election, University of Essex, Jan. 1984, 16 n. 2). The Semetko paper provides a detailed (and critical) account of the nuts and bolts of the Alliance campaign.

9. Semetko, ' "Working Together"?', 1.

10. Not everyone was happy about the composition of the joint campaign committee or about the little groups around Jenkins and Steel who were clearly going to dominate the running of the campaign. With the exception of Bernard Doyle and the partial exception of Lord Diamond, those most centrally involved in planning the campaign were members of either the 'Jenkins mafia' or the 'Steel machine'. Those who had hitherto supported Owen or Williams, or Liberals from outside the Steel circle, were largely excluded. For an account of Steel's personal campaign organization, see *The Times*, 18 May 1983.

11. For a detailed account of the 1983 campaign, see Butler and Kavanagh, *The British General Election of 1983*, ch. 6.

12. 'The occasionally fulsome presentation [of this first Alliance election broadcast] led one critic unkindly to liken the programme to a commercial for a gay dating agency' (Martin Harrison, 'Broadcasting', in Butler and Kavanagh, *The British General Election of 1983*, 154). The programme was nevertheless widely judged a success, including within the Alliance.

13. These weekly averages are calculated from the table of opinion polls during the campaign on p. 125 of Butler and Kavanagh, *The British General Election of 1983*. The dates of publication rather than the dates of interviewing in the surveys were what mattered: they were the dates on which Alliance workers saw the results.

14. Quoted in *Daily Star*, 23 May 1983.

15. *Daily Express*, 13 May 1983.

16. Reported in the *Observer*, 22 May 1983.

17. Reported in *The Times*, 25 May 1983.

18. *Observer*, 22 May 1983. The headline on Laurence Marks' article accurately summed up the feeling in the Alliance at that stage of the 1983 campaign: 'The Alliance Awaits a Miracle'.

19. *Daily Telegraph*, 23 May 1983.

20. *The Times*, 25 May 1983.

21. *The Times*, 28 May 1983.

22. The account below of the Ettrickbridge meeting is largely based on interviews with a majority of those who were present. David Owen gives a brief description of the meeting and the events leading up to it in *Personally Speaking to Kenneth Harris* (London: Weidenfeld & Nicolson, 1987), 219–21. He describes the episode as 'the worst part of the general election', adding: 'In all my years in the Labour Party I had never seen such a ruthless and savage deed' (p. 219). See also David Owen, *Time to Declare* (London: Michael Joseph, 1991), 577–82.

David Steel is extremely coy—'Judy had laid on a superb buffet'—in *Against Goliath: David Steel's Story* (London: Weidenfeld & Nicolson, 1989), 245–6; his account of the meeting itself is confined to one short paragraph. Roy Jenkins—the intended Duncan of the piece—is wry and largely forgiving in *A Life at the Centre* (London: Macmillan, 1991), 575–7. Jenkins writes nevertheless (p. 575): 'I did not enjoy the 1983 campaign. This was because of the so-called Ettrick Bridge Summit and the events leading up to it.'

23. The first public reference appears to have been Peter Jenkins, 'Nearly Everyone Recognizes that the Alliance cannot be Expected to Survive by Standing Still', *Guardian*, 12 Sept. 1983.

24. See Butler and Kavanagh, *The British General Election of 1983*, 125. Of the twenty polls conducted during June, i.e. during the last ten days of the campaign, five showed the Alliance ahead of Labour and one showed the Alliance and Labour tied. The five polls showing the Alliance ahead were conducted by three different polling organizations: Marplan, Harris and Audience Selection. The Audience Selection polls, published in the *Sun* newspaper, gave the Alliance its largest leads over Labour and occasioned a good deal of scepticism—on grounds of the telephone-interviewing methods that Audience Selection was using—within the polling industry. For Audience Selection's reply to its critics, see John Clemens, 'The Telephone Poll Bogeyman: A Case Study in Election Paranoia', in Ivor Crewe and Martin Harrop (eds.), *Political Communications: The General Election Campaign of 1983* (Cambridge: Cambridge University Press, 1986).

25. Quoted in *The Times*, 17 May 1983.

26. Quoted in *Financial Times*, 21 May 1983.

27. *The Times*, 3 June 1983.

28. In their analysis of the 1983 voting John Curtice and Michael Steed state: 'The four Alliance by-election victors all held substantial personal votes; that for Shirley Williams would probably have been enough to re-elect her but for adverse boundary changes'. See Curtice and Steed, 'An Analysis of the Voting', in Butler and Kavanagh, *The British General Election of 1983*, 346–7.

29. John Horam joined the Conservative party in 1986 and became the Conservative member for Orpington in 1992 and a junior minister in 1995.

30. According to Martin Harrison in his chapter ('Broadcasting') in Butler and Kavanagh, *The British General Election of 1983* (p. 160), Jenkins was quoted on seventy-seven occasions on the BBC *Nine O'clock News*, whereas Owen was quoted on only twenty-four occasions and Williams on only seventeen; likewise Jenkins was quoted fifty-six times on ITN's *News at Ten*, while Owen was quoted twenty-six times and Williams thirteen. This outcome, of course, was not just a consequence of Alliance strategy but reflected the television networks' predilection for focusing on 'the leader'. As it was, Jenkins and Steel between them, being the leaders of two parties, were quoted far more often than either Thatcher on her own or Foot on his.

31. An alternative criticism of the Alliance's 1983 campaign theme was that, whether or not national unity was more or less present in 1983 than it had been before, the country was by now looking for something different: decisiveness, a willingness to confront opposition, a desire 'to see things through'. If this were so, then for the Alliance to emphasize, as it did, the themes of national unity and consensus was to appear somewhat wet and feeble. Whichever view is preferred, the Alliance's 1983 campaign seemed to many to be somewhat irrelevant to the circumstances in which it was fought.

Chapter 12

1. According to a November 1981 *Weekend World* survey of party members, preferences for the party leader broke down as follows:

	Jenkins	Williams	Owen/Rodgers/others
Men	56	22	23
Women	45	36	19
18–34	44	30	27
35–54	56	25	19
55 +	57	24	20
Non-manual	55	25	20
Manual	37	32	32
Ex-Con. member	67	17	17
Ex-Lib. member	46	29	25
Ex-Lab. member	48	36	15
Not previously a member	51	27	22

2. David Owen is the partial exception. Since the early 1970s he had intermittently campaigned for the reform of the bloc vote and the candidate selection procedures.

3. In late 1979 and 1980 Williams, with the support of Bryan Stanley and Tom Bradley, tried on a number of occasions to move a proposal for union executives to split their bloc votes at Labour party conferences on the basis of a formally conducted ballot of affiliated members' preferences. The attempts got nowhere.

4. Between March 1981 and March 1982 the Steering Committee was convened on ten occasions to deal solely with the writing of the constitution. There were nine drafts.

5. Maclennan saw himself that way. See his references to the Philadelphia Debate and the Founding Fathers in 'Settling the constitution', in *The Social Democrat, The First Five Years* (London: SDP, 1985). Not inappropriately, the draft constitution presented to the Steering Committee in September was written in Massachusetts, where both Goodhart and Maclennan were staying with their relatives on holiday.

6. The parallel was misleading because the German SPD makes provision for *three* leaders: a president of the party, a leader in the Bundestag and, if successful, the Chancellor. Unlike the SDP's proposal the same person can (but need not) occupy more than one of the offices.

7. See, in particular, Robert Maclennan, 'Constitution: Some Questions of Principle' (unpublished paper, Feb. 1981), and 'The Constitution of the SDP' (memorandum submitted to the Steering Committee of 12 June), and notes taken by William Goodhart in February 1981 at a meeting of the SDP's legal advisers to draw up the Interim Rules.

8. The following extract from the unpublished June 1981 draft gives a flavour of these provisions: 'There will be twenty-four elected members of the Regional Steering Committee. Not more than four may be MPs. Not more than eight may be Councillors. Not more than two may be MEPs. Not more than two thirds may be of the same sex. In regions where there are substantial ethnic minorities the membership of the Regional Steering Committee should reflect this. At least two members of the Committee must be under the age of 26.'

9. Robert Maclennan, 'The SDP Draft Constitution Explained' (discussion paper at 1981 rolling conference).

10. Goodhart, Notes on Interim Rules. The Rules themselves included the following revealing section on the constitution:

'The terms of the draft constitution will reflect the following principles of the Party organisation:

NOTES

a) all voting within the Party will be on the principle of 'one member, one vote';
b) postal voting and secret ballots will be used whenever appropriate to ensure that everyone who has a vote can use it;
c) any associated organisations will have no votes as such;
d) there will be no block votes or card votes;
e) all elected members will be representatives, not mandated delegates;
f) all elected representatives of the Party will have freedom of conscience;
g) candidates for public election, parliamentary, local and European, will normally be directly selected by all the Party members in the relevant electoral areas;
h) the organisation of the Party will be as decentralised as practicable.

11. In the first months Maclennan was particularly exercised by potential infiltration and subsequent expulsions of the kind that destroyed the Scottish Labour party in 1978. In the event, expulsions were confined to a few infiltrators from the National Front.
12. See pp. 151–3.
13. The amended clause was permissive, not mandatory. The original 'no Area shall consist of a single Parliamentary constituency or more than seven' was changed to 'an Area shall consist of one or more Parliamentary constituencies up to a maximum of seven'. After the convention the party's Organization Subcommittee sought to minimize its impact. The right of a single constituency organization to form its own area party would not be automatic but subject to the approval of the proposed National Committee. It would require the area party to form a coherent social and geographical unit and to have a minimum membership of about 250.
14. See pp. 152–3.
15. This argument was not supported by some early surveys of ordinary members. The one conducted for the *Weekend World* television programme found that members preferred election by SDP MPs (with the Council 'having the power to endorse or reject the MPs' choice') to 'one member, one vote' by 53 to 45%. A survey of Newcastle upon Tyne members reported that they preferred election by SDP MPs to a ballot of the whole membership by 59 to 39%. None the less the abandonment of 'one member, one vote' would undoubtedly have disillusioned many members, even if not the majority.
16. The full result was: election by 'one member, one vote', 164 (with no formal review subsequently, 81; and a compulsory review after three years, 83); first election by 'one member, one vote'; subsequent elections by MPs only, 73 (after general election, 62; once 100 SDP MPs elected, 11); election by MPs only, 63 (with no additional ratification, 37; with ratification by the full membership, 6; with ratification by the Council, 17; with reversion to a ballot of the membership, if Council fails to ratify MPs' choice, 3).
17. Ironically, a majority of the supporters of 'MPs only' failed to express any second preference at all. Had more of them done so—another 1,200 would have been enough—the compromise proposal would have been carried in the second round and election of the party leader would have reverted eventually to the MPs. There turned out to be a second twist to this tale. In the leadership election later that summer, Jenkins, the champion of parliamentarianism, was comfortably elected by the mass membership—more comfortably, in all probability, than if the election had been confined to MPs (at the time of the election fourteen MPs declared themselves for Jenkins, twelve for Owen). And in the subsequent leadership election in June 1983, Owen, the tribune of 'one member, one vote', was unopposed by his five fellow MPs and thus became party leader without a membership ballot.
18. Provision was made for 'associated organizations' such as the Association of Social Democratic Lawyers, but their rights were restricted to the possibilty of places at meetings of the Consultative Assembly and of consultation on the preparation of draft policy documents.

Moreover, membership of the party was a condition for joining such groups and not, as in the Labour party, an automatic by-product.

19. This included the Liberal party. The idea of a double membership of both Alliance parties was mooted at the Steering Committee (by Shirley Williams, among others), but slapped down.

20. Non-voting members entitled to attend and speak included SDP MPs and MEPs, National Committee members not elected as area members, the trustees and co-opted members.

21. In this it largely succeeded. The four men directly elected by the membership in 1982 were the two former Labour MPs Dick Taverne and David Marquand, the well-known journalist and author, Anthony Sampson and Roy Evans, a black tax consultant. Only the latter was not a national figure. In 1984 Bill Rodgers and Mike Thomas, who lost their parliamentary seats in 1983, replaced Sampson and Evans. Marquand, Rodgers (far ahead of the others), Taverne and Thomas were all re-elected in 1986.

   The four women elected in 1982 were the *Guardian* journalists Polly Toynbee and Mary Stott, the GLC councillor Anne Sofer and a rabbi, Julia Neuberger. In 1984 Sue Slipman, a union official (and former president of the National Union of Students) replaced Mary Stott. Sofer and Neuberger had national profiles through their frequent writing for the press. Neuberger, Slipman, Sofer and Toynbee were all re-elected in 1986.

22. The proportion of registered members returning a postal ballot was 75.6% for the election of the leader and 46.3% for the election of the president.

23. There were regional councils for Scotland, Wales, London, Yorkshire and Humberside, the West Midlands, the North West and the North.

24. See, in particular, Henry Drucker, 'All the King's Horses and All the King's Men: The SDP in Britain', in William E. Paterson and Alastair H. Thomas (eds.), *The Future of Social Democracy* (Oxford: Clarendon Press, 1986), 108–26, especially pp. 119 ff.; and Vincent McKee, 'Factionalism in the SDP, 1981–87', *Parliamentary Affairs*, 42 (Apr. 1989), 165–79.

25. See p. 193. The party was fortunate to escape a similar embarrassment soon afterwards in Cardiff North-West, where its prospective parliamentary candidate resigned when the seat fell vacant because of a reluctance to deal with media enquiries about his private life. The scheduled by-election was overtaken by the dissolution of parliament.

26. See McKee, 'Factionalism in the SDP'. 169.

27. An area party could submit only one motion per Council. The motion had to be approved by a quorate general meeting of the area party and by the National Committee.

28. The constitution described such a ballot as 'consultative' (ch. 6, sect. A, cl. 2) but in effect it was mandatory: it would have been politically impossible for the Policy Subcommittee to overturn the result of a membership ballot.

29. See Geoffrey Pridham and Paul Whiteley, 'Anatomy of the SDP: Is the Party Structurally Top-Heavy?', *Government and Opposition*, 21 (1986), 205–17, which reports the findings of a survey of CSD members in the summer of 1983. Asked to say how much their area parties discussed policy green papers, 22% said 'extensively', 62% said 'selectively' and 26% said 'very selectively' or 'not at all'. In the typical party local and national politics were 'often' discussed, European and international politics 'rarely' or 'never'. (These answers, moreover, probably inflated the true degree of discussion.)

30. Policy initiatives were in fact concentrated among a small number of particularly active area parties. In the four Councils between September 1985 and September 1986 half of all the amendments and motions were submitted by thirty-seven area parties, and one-third by a mere eighteen.

31. For example, at the Newcastle Council a controversial policy paper on defence attracted fourteen amendments, all submitted by area parties. Only two were carried, and both involved minor drafting changes. At the same Council the white paper on trade-union reform

generated ten amendments, but only one of substance was passed. Most white papers attracted fewer amendments. At the Salford Council, for example, the Policy Committee's white papers on poverty and taxation (which contained radical proposals), Europe, education and training, and urban policy all passed unaltered.

32. The Council at Great Yarmouth passed an amendment which replaced the proposal for a statutory incomes policy with one based on a 'specific mandate from the electorate' and on wide consultations about 'the arrangements for the success of this policy'. At the Buxton Council an emergency motion calling upon the Government to suspend the use of plastic bullets in Northern Ireland pending an enquiry was passed against the advice of the Policy Committee. At the following Council, in Birmingham, the Policy Committee's report rejected the call for suspension of plastic bullets; an amendment to reinstate the policy was defeated, but Owen intervened in the debate to propose that in future disputes of this kind the Policy Committee should be obliged to explain its objections to Council. The constitution had always included a provision that 'the National Committee shall conduct . . . a ballot if required to do so by the Council in consequence of a deadlock between the Council and the Policy Committee on an issue of policy of major importance' (ch. VI, sect. A.2).

33. The SDP's active members included William Plowden, director-general of the Royal Institute for Public Administration; Keith Kyle, David Stephen and Lawrence Freedman, research fellows of the Royal Institute of International Affairs (whose research director, William Wallace, was a prominent Liberal close to David Steel), Lord Young and Eirlys Roberts (founder and chairman respectively of the Consumer Association), and Ushar Prashar of the race relations institute, the Runnymede Trust. The Institute of Fiscal Studies, which was founded by Dick Taverne, inspired many of the ideas and conducted most of the work for the radical proposals that emerged from the Poverty and Taxation Group. The party's strongest links of all were with the oldest and most wide-ranging of the research bodies, the Policy Studies Institute (formerly Political and Economic Planning), which accommodated Shirley Williams as a temporary fellow and numbered its chairman (Charles Carter), director (John Pinder) and three permanent fellows as members.

34. These included Robin Mathews, master of Clare College Cambridge, and chairman of the Bank of England's panel of academic consultants; Joan Mitchell, professor at Nottingham University, formerly a member of the National Board for Prices and Incomes and a special adviser to Shirley Williams when she was secretary of state for prices and consumer protection; Marcus Miller, professor at Warwick and a member of the Treasury's academic advisory panel; and Professor Richard Layard, director of the Centre for Labour Economics at the London School of Economics. A number of other major figures, who were SDP sympathizers but not members, contributed papers, including Alan Budd, professor at the London Business School and director of its economic forecasts; Sir Alec Cairncross, master of St Peter's College Oxford and a former government economic adviser; and Sir Bryan Hopkin, formerly head of the Government Economic Service and chief economic adviser at the Treasury. See Frances Williams, 'How the SDP's Leaders are Picking the Professors' Brains', *The Times*, 22 Jan. 1982.

35. Policy-making under Owen's leadership is discussed more fully in chapter 17.

36. Two of the SDA's leading members, Douglas Eden and Jim Daly, were co-opted on to the Steering Committee for a short time but then dropped from it when the SDA insisted on contesting the May 1981 local elections. The SDA recruited activists within the Labour party and trade unions committed to campaigning against the growing influence of the left. It was expelled by the Labour party for adopting candidates against left-wing official Labour candidates at the general election. It claimed to have 3,000 members but was barely active outside London and the East Midlands. Its president was Lord George-Brown, the former Labour foreign secretary and deputy leader, who was disappointed not to have been invited to join a Gang of Five.

37. 'Any organisation of persons having some common link of interest (as students, members of

a trade or profession ... or otherwise, membership of which is limited to ... SDP members and non-members who support its objectives' (ch. XIV, para. 1).

38. See McKee, 'Factionalism in the Social Democratic Party', 170–1. This section of the chapter is indebted in various ways to McKee's useful article.

39. The SDP Friends of Ireland successfully moved the resolution, at the Salford Council, on the total banning of plastic bullets in Northern Ireland, against the advice of the SDP's parliamentary spokesman on Northern Ireland, Robert Maclennan.

40. See n. 24.

41. For example, parliamentary candidate selection is subject to a form of 'one member, one vote' by single transferable vote (although representatives of locally affiliated trade unions can also cast votes) and the automatic inclusion of at least one woman on the short list is also standard practice.

Chapter 13

1. See p. 235.
2. See pp. 96–7.
3. As paymaster-general in the Callaghan government, Williams chaired the cabinet committee on devolution and reported in favour of a Scottish parliament with tax-raising powers.
4. See pp. 221–2.
5. Clive Lindley, one of the SDP's original trustees, was unceremoniously told to quit once it became clear that he had parliamentary ambitions.
6. A more detailed account of the SDP's computing troubles can be found in Hugh Stephenson, *Claret and Chips: The Rise of the SDP* (London: Michael Joseph, 1982), 94–7.
7. *The Times*, 5 June 1981.
8. Newby was formerly a civil servant in the Customs and Excise Department. In the early 1970s he had been general secretary of Young European Left, the small pro-European group of young Labour party members, and was a national committee member of the Labour Committee for Europe. He married the daughter of Lord Thomson, the Labour cabinet member and European commissioner, who also joined the SDP. For respite from the aggravations of Cowley Street he played the cornet in the Rothwell Temperance Band.
9. There are two exceptions. Since 1975 opposition parties have been allocated 'Short money' (named after the then leader of the House, Edward Short) for research and secretarial assistance to the parliamentary party. The SDP received an annual grant of £25,000 in 1983, £45,000 in 1984 and £63,000 in each of 1985 and 1986; the Liberals' share averaged £64,000 and Labour's £270,000. The differences in the amount arose from the grant formula, which was based on a combination of the total number of votes cast and the number of MPs elected for each party. The second form of 'state aid' is the grant made by the European Parliament towards the 'information' costs of the European elections. Most of the 1984 grant was distributed by the European Parliament's transnational party groups to member parties in proportion to their number of MEPs. Since the SDP had no MEPs and belonged to no European party group it received no grant before the election, but £89,345 after. The Conservative party received £4.4m., Labour £1.35m. and the Liberals £244,000. See David Butler and Paul Jowett, *Party Strategies in Britain* (London: Macmillan, 1985), 44–5.
10. See Michael Pinto-Duschinsky, 'Trends in British Party Funding', *Parliamentary Affairs*, 42 (1989), 197–212, for the source of revenue to the Conservative and Labour parties in the 1980s. He estimates that between 1983–4 and 1987–8 trade-union payments accounted for about 79% of the Labour party's central income (excluding the 'Short' money), whereas companies and other institutional sources provided between 43 and 52% of the Conservative party's central income.
11. Credit-card subscriptions averaged £17.

12. The SDP originally claimed a figure of 70,000 but this number included many duplicated names generated by the party's inadequate computing operation in its first year.
13. See pp. 224–5.
14. Dick Newby, quoted in Anthony Bevins, 'SDP Forced to Cut its Cloth', *The Times*, 7 May 1984.
15. A survey of the Newcastle upon Tyne area party reported that 'out of the total of 26 wards in the city, the 13 more middle-class wards contain 78% of membership, while the 13 more working-class wards contain only 22%. Fifty-four per cent of the membership, in fact, is concentrated in four of the most middle class wards'. See David S. G. Goodman and David Hine, 'The SDP in Newcastle-upon-Tyne: A Survey-based Analysis', (paper presented to the Workshop on Contemporary British Politics, Political Studies Association, University of Kent, April 1982), 4.
16. *Campaign*, 4 Sept. 1981.
17. They were nearly right. 'I have become convinced that we should move ahead as rapidly as possible to establish an operating company . . . to handle the whole of our trading and merchandising operations . . . we should [also] consider (a) insurance, (b) travel, (c) printing, (d) general household and personal goods of the Barclaycard/Scotcade mail-order type' (Clive Lindley to Ian Wrigglesworth, 14 Oct. 1981).
18. Others included Edmund Dell, chairman of Guinness Peat and former Labour minister of trade; John Hull, chairman of Schroeder Wagg; Sir Claus Moser, vice-chairman of the merchant bankers N. M. Rothschild; Sir Lesley Murphy, a director of the merchant bank Shroders and the former chairman of the National Enterprise Board; Lord Sainsbury, the joint president of Sainsbury's; Michael Shanks, a director of BOC Group Ltd., and Anthony 'Cob' Stedman, finance director of Unilever.
19. The only recorded company donations in 1981 and 1982 were £5,000 each from Thorn EMI and Marks and Spencer. The latter was earmarked for the Joint Liberal/SDP Commission on Employment and National Recovery. In 1981 Marks and Spencer also gave £5,000 to the National Committee for Electoral Reform, a group campaigning for proportional representation. See also 'Fundraising Strategy for the General Election' (Finance Committee Papers, Apr. 1983, SDP archives).
20. See Charles Nevin, 'Keeping Shop for the Doctor' [a profile of David Sainsbury], *Guardian*, 25 Sept. 1989.
21. See Pinto-Duschinsky, 'Trends in British Party Funding', esp. 197–204.
22. Altogether the number of full-time staff was halved from fifty-three to twenty-eight and all of the senior staff who left—Doyle, Smallwood, Roger Carroll (director of communications)— were replaced by lower paid staff or not at all. Other economies included the closing-down of three of the five regional offices and the letting of the upper floor of Cowley Street.
23. See 'The Doctor's Good Friends', *The Economist*, 20 July 1985.
24. See Kevin Swaddle, 'Ancient and Modern: Innovations in Electioneering at the Constituency Level', in Ivor Crewe and Martin Harrop (eds.), *Political Communications: The General Election Campaign of 1987* (Cambridge: Cambridge University Press, 1989), 29–41 (esp. 36–8).
25. The average donation was about £17, the same as the annual subscription. An additional £88,000 was raised by telephone canvassing and a further £25,000 came in small donations. Fund-raising costs were £115,000. See Fiona Wilson, 'Monies Raised for the 1987 General Election Campaign during the Period 18 May to 19 June' (23 June 1987, SDP Archives).
26. Pinto-Duschinsky, 'Trends in British Party Funding', 346.
27. The three exceptions were Lonrho, which owned the pro-Alliance *Today* newspaper, and whose chairman, Tiny Rowland, bore a grudge against the government for allowing Harrods to be sold to a rival bidder; United Leasing, whose chairman was an SDP candidate; and Laura Ashley, the manufacturer of fabrics and furnishings, whose wholesome, farmhouse style was especially popular with the educated middle classes and thus regarded as quintessentially SDP.

28. The Conservative : Labour : Alliance ratio of local campaign spending was about 1.3 : 1.2 : 1.0 in both 1983 and 1987. These figures provide only a rough comparison because it is not known how much of their general-election fund local parties left unspent. Moreover, the figures for the Liberal party and SDP do not reveal the spending patterns of local parties in constituencies contested by the other Alliance partner. Local Labour party income contains an institutional element because it includes contributions from locally affiliated trade unions.

29. Michael Pinto-Duschinsky, 'Financing the British General Election of 1987', in Crewe and Harrop (eds.), *Political Communications*, 15–28, at 25. His figures exclude central grants to local constituencies; if they and subsidies in kind are included the ratios narrow markedly, to about 10 : 6 : 4 in 1983 and 10 : 8 : 7 in 1987.

30. See David Butler and Dennis Kavanagh, *The British General Election of 1987* (London: Macmillan, 1988), 235–6, and R. J. Johnston, C. J. Pattie and L. C. Johnston, 'The Impact of Constituency Spending on the Result of the 1987 British General Election', *Electoral Studies*, 8 (1989), 143–55 (see p. 145).

31. In 1983 every SDP candidate received a grant of £2,000, except for SDP MPs who had their full costs met. In 1987 grants were targeted: the minimum was £1,000, the average just under £2,000 but most candidates in 'target' seats received considerably more.

32. In 1983 the Conservatives took out sixty-seven pages of advertising in the national press; Labour, twenty-seven pages; the Alliance, none. Support for the two major parties fell four percentage points each between the first week of the campaign and election day. The Alliance's support rose eight percentage points. According to the 1983 and 1987 BBC–Gallup election-day surveys, under 2% of respondents said they were influenced in their voting decision by either a Conservative or Labour poster or press advertisement.

33. There is statistical evidence that the more the SDP spent locally, the more votes it won (after controlling for the constituency's social characteristics and the Liberal or Alliance vote at the previous election). See R. J. Johnston, 'A Further Look at British Political Finance', *Political Studies*, 34 (1986), 466–73, and Johnston *et al.*, 'The Impact of Constituency Spending'. However, in 'A Further Look' (pp. 471–2), Johnston shows that, if all three parties had spent the legally permitted maximum in 1983, the SDP would not have gained a single seat (although the Liberals might have gained some).

34. See Dick Leonard, *Paying for Party Politics: The Case for Public Subsidies*, PEP Broadsheet No. 555 (London: Political and Economic Planning, 1975), 2–3; and *Report of the Committee on Financial Aid to Political Parties* (Houghton Report) (London: HMSO, Cmnd. 6601, Aug. 1976), 31–2; and for approximate but up-to-date membership figures, Michael Pinto-Duschinsky, 'Political Parties' in Catterall (ed.), *Contemporary Britain*, 29–45 *passim*.

Chapter 14

1. Hugh Macpherson, 'Can the Left ever be Impartial on the BBC?', *Tribune*, 26 Mar. 1982. The conspiracy view of the Dimbleby Lecture can be found in Harold Frayman, 'Myopia of the Media', *Labour Weekly*, 18 Dec. 1981.

2. The author of an early study of the SDP noted the political moderation of her media respondents and explained it in terms of their 'professional obligation to be objective'. A lobby correspondent for a popular Labour newspaper was quoted as saying 'our profession demands that we try to be objective. That places all of us at odds with any ideology or dogmatism.' Another reporter told her 'we're all sympathetic . . . We'd like to see the Alliance replace the Labour party because it is more moderate.' See Patricia Lee Sykes, *Losing from the Inside: The Cost of Conflict in the British Social Democratic Party*, 2nd edn. (New Brunswick, NJ: Transaction Books, 1988), 205.

3. See pp. 101–2.

4. In the Gallup Poll it rose from 14 to 19% between 12–17 Mar. and 25–31 Mar.; Liberal support stayed the same, at 18%.

5. See Holli Semetko, 'Political Communications and Party Development in Britain: The Social Democratic Party from its Origins to the General Election Campaign of 1983' (doctoral thesis, London School of Economics, June 1987, 139–40). But the arrangement only worked once. The following year the travel and disruption caused irritation. 'Rolling conferences gather no media' was one journalist's conclusion (Alan Watkins, *Observer*, 17 Oct. 1982).

6. Similar conclusions are reached in Colin Seymour-Ure in 'The SDP and the Media', *Political Quarterly*, 53 (1982), 433–42.

7. For an amusing account of this episode, see Jeremy Josephs, *Inside the Alliance* (London: John Martin, 1983), 179–82.

8. See pp. 142 and 192–3.

9. Martin Harrop, 'Press', in David Butler and Dennis Kavanagh, *The British General Election of 1983* (London: Macmillan, 1984), 179 and 186; Martin Harrop, 'Press', in David Butler and Dennis Kavanagh, *The British General Election of 1987* (London: Macmillan, 1988), 167–8.

10. See e.g. Anthony Bevins' lead story 'Jenkins and Steel Split on Deterrent', *The Times*, 8 June 1983.

11. Ironically, a notable exception was the socialist *New Statesman*, which listed the Conservative constituencies in which its Labour readers should switch to the Alliance. The logic of this tactic was blunted by the restriction of the list to constituencies in which the Alliance candidate was a Liberal.

12. Harrop, 'Press', in Butler and Kavanagh, *The British General Election of 1983*, 195.

13. But then he had not expected to be, for he told Harold Evans, the editor, in advance that 'they were all crap'. Moreover, 'nothing could propitiate' *The Times*' managing director, Gerald Long, who 'made the mistake of arranging lunch at a table long enough for a regiment, so that yards separated each person from the other; he filled the gaps with his bristling and glowering'. See Harold Evans, *Good Times, Bad Times* (London: Weidenfeld & Nicolson, 1983), 218–19.

14. A survey of Newcastle area party members found that the most popular national newspaper was the *Guardian* (45%), followed a long way behind by *The Times* and the *Daily Telegraph* (17% each). See David S. G. Goodman and David Hine, 'The SDP in Newcastle upon Tyne: A Survey-based Analysis' (unpublished paper, Political Studies Association, University of Kent, April 1982).

15. Recalculated from Patrick Dunleavy and Christopher T. Husbands, *British Democracy at the Crossroads* (London: George Allen & Unwin, 1985), table 5.16, p. 113, and Brian MacArthur, 'The National Press', in Ivor Crewe and Martin Harrop (eds.), *Political Communications: The General Election Campaign of 1987* (Cambridge: Cambridge University Press, 1989), 104.

16. See Martin Harrop, 'The Press and Post-war Elections', in Crewe and Harrop (eds.), *Political Communications*, 137–49, and William Miller *et al.*, *How Voters Change: The 1987 British Election Campaign in Perspective* (Oxford: Clarendon Press, 1990), 86–9.

17. Something of their flavour is revealed in the various proposals made to avoid too small an attendance at the Perth stage of the 1981 rolling conference. These included arranging whistle-stops at York and Leeds; organizing 'walks' to Perth from various parts of the country; inviting a hundred sixth-formers from Perth Academy; and conveying a multiracial band from Birmingham to Perth and then on to the special train to Bradford, where they could entertain the passengers. Occasionally, one of the committee's gimmicks worked. When David Steel and Shirley Williams sang a duet on the sparsely watched *Afternoon Plus* television programme ('If you were the only Shirl in the world, and I was the only boy . . .'), the 'story', with photograph, appeared in all the tabloids the next day.

18. John Lyttle, 'Communications Strategy' (15 Apr. 1982, paper SC 40/4/82, Communications Committee, SDP Archives). Lyttle had been Shirley Williams' political adviser from 1974 to

NOTES

1979. He resigned as chief press officer to head Roy Jenkins' private office from Apr. 1982 to June 1983. From 1987 until his death in 1991 he was secretary for public affairs to the Archbishop of Canterbury.

19. The figures in the mid-1980s were about 14.5 million for the early evening news and about 14.7 million for the national dailies. See Barrie Gunter, Michael Svennevig and Mallory Wober, *Television Coverage of the 1983 General Election* (Aldershot: Gower, 1986), 26 (table 3.2), and Butler and Kavanagh, *The British General Election of 1987*, 165–6.

20. For example, a week before polling day in 1983 more electors claimed that they had seen an Alliance party election broadcast (65%) than received an Alliance election leaflet (48%), met an Alliance party worker (18%) or heard an Alliance radio election broadcast (14%). The figures for the campaigning efforts of the two major parties were a little higher but the ordering was the same. See Ivor Crewe, 'How to Win a Landslide without Really Trying', in Austin Ranney (ed.), *Britain at the Polls, 1983* (Durham, NC: Duke University Press, 1985), 163.

21. See Gunter *et al.*, *Television Coverage of the 1983 General Election*, 84, and Robin McGregor, Michael Svennevig and Chris Ledger, 'Television and the 1987 General Election Campaign', in Crewe and Harrop (eds.), *Political Communications*, 179.

22. In the BBC's 1987 election-day survey, 19% of respondents said their final decision on how to vote was influenced by a party election broadcast whereas the proportions mentioning a poster, advertisement or newspaper article were, in each case, 5%.

23. The audience survey found a similar pattern for the influence of television coverage in general. See Gunter *et al.*, *Television Coverage*, 113.

24. This rule was applied for the first two years after a general election. Thereafter votes in by-elections held after the general election were also taken into account. The SNP was entitled to one ten-minute broadcast for every 200,000 votes and Plaid Cymru to one for every 100,000 votes.

25. Shirley Williams, speech at Unity Hall, Wakefield, 23 Apr. 1982.

26. Sect. 6(ii) of the 1947 *aide-mémoire* stated 'The BBC reserve the right, after consultation with the party leaders, to invite to the microphone a member of either House of outstanding national eminence who may have become detached from any party'. The *aide-mémoire* is set out in an appendix to Semetko, 'Political Communication and Party Development', 309–10.

27. In 1982 Channel 4 disavowed PPBs and instead offered a weekly three-minute 'Comment' slot to the parties in the ratio Conservative 10 : Labour 10 : Liberal 3 : SNP 2 : Liberal/SDP Alliance 1 : Plaid Cymru 1.

28. Martin Harrison, 'Broadcasting', in Butler and Kavanagh, *The British General Election of 1983*, 148.

29. The audience figures must be interpreted with care: those who watched two or more PEBs or interviews are counted twice or more. See Gunter *et al.*, *Television Coverage*, tables 3.1, 3.4 and 3.8. A MORI poll towards the end of the campaign (2 June) reported much narrower differences in the proportions claiming to have seen an Alliance PEB (65%) as opposed to a Conservative or Labour PEB (71 and 72% respectively). See Market & Opinion Research International, *British Public Opinion, General Election 1983, Final Report* (London: Market and Opinion Research International, 1983).

30. Our description of television news journalists' attitudes is indebted to the participant observation reported in Jay G. Blumler, Michael Gurevitch and T. J. Nossiter, 'Setting the Television News Agenda: Campaign Observation at the BBC', in Crewe and Harrop (eds.), *Political Communications*, 1986, 104–24.

31. Harrop, 'Press', in Butler and Kavanagh, *The British General Election of 1983*, 186.

32. Holli Semetko, 'The Impact of the Alliance in the Media: Television and the 1983 General Election Campaign' (paper presented to the annual conference of the Political Studies Association, Nottingham, 1986), 5–6. However, in other respects, such as 'visuals' and politicians' 'soundbites', the Alliance was not disadvantaged.

33. See pp. 206–10.
34. See Crewe, 'How to Win a Landslide without Really Trying', 164–5.
35. The 'appreciation score' they earned among viewers surveyed by the BBC and IBA was relatively high by past standards (55) but only marginally above that accorded to the Conservative PEBs (53) or to the Liberal PEBs in 1979 (49) and October 1974 (51). See Gunter *et al.*, *Television Coverage*, 48 (table 4.2). The method of constructing the appreciation index is described as follows: 'Television viewing diaries listing all programmes broadcast on all TV channels are sent to samples . . . respondents say how much they found each programme they watched interesting and/or enjoyable along a six-point scale. From these opinions, an appreciation score ranging from 0 to 100 is computed for each programme' (p. 17).
36. The exception was the election campaign of October 1974, during which Liberal support remained level. On the 1979 election, see Ivor Crewe, 'Why the Conservatives Won', in Howard Penniman (ed.), *Britain at the Polls, 1979* (Washington, DC: American Enterprise Institute, 1981), 272–3. The trend in Liberal support during the campaign is based on a comparison between its average standing in the first week's opinion polls and its eventual vote.
37. Strictly speaking the ratio was 5 : 5 : 2 : 2 (counting the SDP and Liberal party separately) compared with 12 : 12 : 4 : 1 before the election. The Alliance also obtained the right of reply to the chancellor of the exchequer's broadcast on the budget.
38. By chance this study coincided with the spectacular Liberal victory at the Bermondsey by-election and, for the sake of comparison with the follow-up study, the figures cited *omit* coverage of the by-election. If by-election news is included, the ratios are 4 : 4 : 1 on the BBC and 5 : 4 : 1 on ITN. Details are reported in Tony Flower, *Parties in the News* (London: Tawney Society, 1983) and there is a summary in Semetko, 'Political Communications and Party Development', 124–8 (Semetko undertook the content analysis). Although the study was commissioned by an interested party, the accuracy of the analysis was not disputed by the broadcasting authorities.
39. Semetko, 'Political Communications and Party Development', 291 and 306 n. 4.
40. Alastair Hetherington, 'Miners and the Media', *Listener*, 17 Feb. 1985, pp. 5–6.
41. Over the period January 1985 to April 1986, the ratio of coverage of the four parties was Conservative 18 : Labour 7 : Liberal 2 : SDP 1 in television news of House of Lords debates and 9 : 6 : 2: 1 in the special format programmes (the BBC's *The Lords Today* and ITV's *Their Lordships' House*). See Bob Franklin, 'Television and the House of Lords' (unpublished paper, Centre for Television Research, University of Leeds, 1986).
42. The same poll found that 60% could recall seeing something about Margaret Thatcher and 25% something about Neil Kinnock in the previous week. In July 1985, shortly after the Liberal victory in the Brecon and Radnor by-election, the Gallup Poll put the identical question about media prominence and found somewhat smaller—but still wide—differences between the four party leaders. The proportion saying they had seen nothing about them on television in the previous month was 9% for Thatcher, 19% for Kinnock, 35% for Steel and 41% for Owen. See *Gallup Political Index*, no. 300, Aug. 1985, 11.
43. However, the very success of the Alliance at by-elections (and of the Liberals and Nationalists before them) reduced their frequency. The annual number of by-elections fell from an average of eleven between 1945 and 1970, to seven in the 1970s and to four between 1979 and 1987. After the mid-1970s both government and opposition were less willing to risk by-election defeats by nominating their backbenchers for life peerages or for appointments requiring resignation from the House of Commons.
44. Quoted in David Watt, 'Alliance Show that Gets a Bad Review', *The Times*, 18 Jan. 1985.
45. Colin Munro, 'Legal Controls on Election Broadcasting', in Crewe and Harrop (eds.), *Political Communications*, 296.
46. See Alan E. Boyle, 'Political Broadcasting, Fairness and Administrative Law', *Public Law*

(1986), 562–96. See also Colin Munro, 'Party Politicals: Who Says they are Legal, and Why?', *The Times*, 12 Feb. 1982; and Munro, 'Legal Controls on Election Broadcasting'.

47. Semetko, 'Political Communications and Party Development', 297.

48. Barrie Axford and Peter Madgwick, 'Television News Monitoring Project, April–June 1986: Second Report' (unpublished paper, Oxford Polytechnic, September 1986). If references to the government are excluded, the Alliance parties accounted for 10% of all mentions.

49. Holli Semetko, 'Images of Britain's Changing Party System: A Study of Television News Coverage of the 1983 and 1987 General Election Campaigns' (paper presented to the annual meeting of the American Political Science Association, Atlanta, 1989).

50. Labour PEBs contributed an additional 1.0 percentage points to the Labour vote; Conservative PEBs a tiny 0.4 percentage points to the Conservative vote. See Ivor Crewe, 'Why Mrs Thatcher was Returned with a Landslide', *Social Studies Review*, 3 (1987), 2–9 (at p. 6).

51. See ch. 19.

Chapter 15

1. This and the following quotation come from Raphael Samuel, 'The SDP and the New Political Class', *New Society*, 22 Apr. 1982, 124–6. The article is a provocative but wholly unsubstantiated social analysis of SDP members.

2. Frank Johnson, 'A Happy Party, Fit for all Factions', *The Times*, 16 Sept. 1986.

3. Julian Critchley, 'The Yuppies of the SDP', *Observer*, 14 Sept. 1986.

4. This made no difference to the commentators: 'For much of last week Social Democrats kept coming up and protesting "We don't all have Volvos, you know" . . . so I explained that political parties . . . had a certain irreducible spirit which formed their timeless nature, and that even if it were true, which it was not, that no single Volvo survived in the SDP, those almost imperceptible forces which shape the historical perception of a party . . . had decreed that the SDP was iconographically identified with the Volvo as an almost Platonic essence' (Frank Johnson, 'Intruding in Life's Departure Lounge', *The Times*, 23 Sept. 1986).

5. This chapter draws on the following surveys of SDP members: (1) the *Weekend World* survey: a postal survey of 5,568 SDP members (response rate: 56%) conducted by Opinion Research Centre on behalf of *Weekend World* in November 1981 and reported in Ian Bradley, 'Socially Distinguished People', *The Times*, 30 Nov. 1981, and Peter Kellner, 'The Rabbit is in the Right-Hand Pocket', *New Statesman*, 4 Dec. 1981; (2) the Newcastle survey: a postal survey of 283 members of the Newcastle upon Tyne area SDP (response rate: 72%) conducted by David Goodman and David Hine in Nov./Dec. 1981 and reported in 'The SDP in Newcastle upon Tyne: A Survey-Based Analysis'; (3) the SDP membership survey: a postal survey in November and December 1984 on subscribing members of the SDP (response rate: 38%) commissioned by the SDP National Committee. Results are reported in Sarah Horack, 'Results of Membership Opinions Questionnaire', memorandum to National Committee, 20 Mar. 1985 (SDP Archive, University of Essex, paper N3 (85)); (4) the BBC *Newsnight* survey: a self-administered questionnaire returned to BBC *Newsnight* by 527 out of 994 participants (53% response) at the SDP rolling conference in Cardiff and Derby in Sept. 1982 and by 131 out of 372 delegates (35% response rate) to the October 1982 Council for Social Democracy at Great Yarmouth; (5) the Council for Social Democracy survey: a survey of 260 area party delegates (response rate: 62%) to the Council for Social Democracy at Great Yarmouth in October 1982, conducted by Herbert Doring and reported in 'Who are the Social Democrats?', *New Society*, 8 Sept. 1983, 351–3, in Terry Barton and Herbert Doring, 'Social Mobility and the Changing British Party System' (paper presented to the Political Studies Association Conference, University of Southampton, 1984, and in Terry Barton and Herbert Doring, 'The

Social and Attitudinal Profile of Social Democratic Party Activists: Note on a Survey of the 1982 Council for Social Democracy', *Political Studies*, 34 (1986), 296–305; (6) the Scottish survey: a survey of 184 participants (response rate: 67%) at the first Consultative Assembly of the Scottish SDP held in St Andrews in late February 1983. The survey was conducted by John Bochel and David Denver and reported in 'The SDP and the Left–Right Dimension', *British Journal of Political Science*, 14 (1984), 386–92.

Readers should bear in mind that the latter three surveys are of activists, whereas the first three are of ordinary, and typically non-active, members, and that the small sample numbers in all but the first and third survey means that percentages based on detailed analysis should be treated with caution.

6. The best sociological account of the service class is John Goldthorpe, 'On the Service Class, its Formation and Future', in Anthony Giddens and Gavin Mackenzie (eds.), *Social Class and the Division of Labour: Essays in Honour of Ilya Neustadt* (Cambridge: Cambridge University Press, 1982), 162–85.
7. The figure for Newcastle area SDP is very similar: 78% had not joined a party before and only 13% were former Labour party members. The proportion once belonging to the Conservative party was 7% in the *Weekend World* survey and 4% in the Newcastle survey.
8. The figures were: never joined another party, 65%; belonged to Labour party, 22%; belonged to Conservative party, 8%; belonged to Liberal party, 8%. (The total adds up to over 100 per cent because a few members had belonged to more than one other party in the past.) The higher proportion of ex-Labour members and the smaller proportion of 'virgins' compared with the *Weekend World* survey is as likely to reflect sampling error and low response rates as real change since 1981.
9. Only 33% of the delegates and 38% of the area party office holders attending the first Council for Social Democracy in October 1981 had once been Labour party members.
10. The 1979 vote among Newcastle upon Tyne members was further to the left (24% Conservative, 46% Labour, 29% Liberal, 1% other), but this probably reflects the Labour culture of a town like Newcastle.
11. Among those attending the first SDP Consultative Assembly in Scotland, the 1979 vote was even more favourable to Labour: 42% Labour, 16% Conservative, 23% Liberal, 13% SNP (see Bochel and Denver, 'The SDP and the Left–Right Dimension', 388).
12. The remaining 25% described themselves as plain 'left' (see Barton and Doring, 'Social Mobility and the Changing British Party System', 36).
13. Kellner, 'The Rabbit is in the Right-Hand Pocket', 5.
14. Analysis of the SDP's 1984 membership survey found more divisions between the generations and sexes than between those coming from different parties. There were no important differences between ex-Labour, ex-Liberal and previously unaffiliated members; and former Conservative members differed from other members on only three issues (out of seventeen): equal opportunity measures, worker participation and opposition to PWR reactors. See also Barton and Doring, 'The Social and Attitudinal Profile of SDP Activists', which shows that among delegates to the October 1982 Council for Social Democracy attitudes to the TUC and CBI did not differ between those who had once been members of the Labour party and those who had not.
15. On the thirty-three policy issues covered by the *Weekend World* and Newcastle surveys, the two groups took opposite sides on five: the death penalty, wealth tax, the abolition of state-assisted places to private schools, whether the government's first priority should be to cut unemployment or inflation and whether taxes should be raised to finance higher public spending.
16. The 1984 membership survey revealed a similar ambivalence about an inflation tax. See 'Results of Membership Opinions Questionnaire', 2.
17. E. E. Schattschneider, quoted in Austin Ranney, *Pathways to Parliament* (Madison: University of Wisconsin Press, 1965), 269.

18. See pp. 230–1 for a detailed description of the procedure for selecting parliamentary candidates.
19. See pp. 192–3.
20. The exception was Michael O'Halloran. He was squeezed out by his two fellow SDP MPs in Islington when the Boundary Commission reduced the borough's seats from three to two. Subsequently, he quit the SDP and fought Islington North as an Independent Labour candidate. One SDP MP, James Dunn, retired. Boundary revisions obliterated the seats of four others—Richard Crawshaw, John Horam, Hudson Davies and Jeffrey Thomas—but all succeeded in finding new seats to fight, but not win.
21. Bruce Douglas-Mann, Gwynoro Jones, Evan Luard, Rod MacFarquhar, David Marquand, Colin Phipps, Paul Rose, Dick Taverne and John Watkinson.
22. See p. 260.
23. David Denver, 'The SDP–Liberal Alliance: The End of the Two-Party System?', in Hugh Berrington (ed.), *Change in British Politics* (London: Frank Cass, 1984), 91.
24. This is brought out by a comparison of the median age of the four parties' unsuccessful candidates: Conservative 37, Labour 38, Liberal 40, SDP 40. See Byron Criddle, 'Candidates', in David Butler and Dennis Kavanagh, *The British General Election of 1987* (London: Macmillan, 1988), table 9.1, p. 200.
25. See Ian Bradley, 'The SDP Mould', *New Society*, 27 Jan. 1983. The article also reports that 10% of the sample were awarded a first-class degree.

Chapter 16

1. See p. 131.
2. See *Gallup Political Index*, Nos. 245, 246 and 247, Jan., Feb. and Mar. 1981.
3. In the Gallup poll for March 1981, 91% thought that the Labour party was divided and only 20% thought that Michael Foot was 'proving a good leader of the opposition'. Both figures set new records. See *Gallup Political Index*, No. 247, Mar. 1981.
4. For detailed evidence, see Ivor Crewe, Bo Särlvik and James Alt, 'Partisan Dealignment in Britain, 1964–1977', *British Journal of Political Science*, 7 (1977), 129–90, and Ivor Crewe, 'The Electorate: Partisan Dealignment Ten Years On', in Hugh Berrington (ed.), *Change in British Politics* (London: Frank Cass, 1984), 183–215.
5. The Liberals' share of the national vote was affected by their failure to contest every constituency before October 1974. Their average share of the vote in the constituencies they did contest was 16.9% in 1959, 18.5% in 1964, 23.6% in Feb. 1974 and 18.9% in Oct. 1974. Since the Liberal party generally contested those seats where it was electorally strongest, these figures almost certainly overestimate the support the Liberals would have received by fielding candidates everywhere.
6. For the most part, this chapter examines the electoral record of the Alliance rather than of the SDP alone and treats the Alliance as one rather than two parties. As this chapter shows (see in particular n. 22), voters made almost no distinction between the parties.
7. However, the Labour party was more likely to be the contender in the more marginal Conservative seats. In the 119 Conservative seats won with a majority of under 15% in 1983, Labour came second in 77, the Alliance parties in 37 (and the Scottish Nationalists or Plaid Cymru in 5). Of the 120 Conservative seats won with a majority of under 15% in 1987, Labour came second in 87, the Alliance parties in 30 (and the Scottish Nationalists in 3).
8. Except in the 1984 European elections, where, despite taking 18.5% of the UK vote, the Alliance parties failed to win a single seat.
9. See Table 16.11. These figures exclude town and parish councillors and are approximate. They are based on David Butler and Gareth Butler, *British Political Facts 1900–1984*, 6th edn

(London: Macmillan, 1986), 443–8, and on information kindly supplied by Colin Rallings and Michael Thrasher of the Local Elections Unit of the Polytechnic South West, Plymouth. The SDP suffered a small net loss of seats in 1982 and 1983, as a result of councillors who had defected (almost entirely from the Labour party) going down to defeat when seeking re-election under their new colours. The SDP did not contest the 1981 local elections; the Liberals made a net gain of 168 seats.

10. The Alliance won absolute control in the Isle of Wight and minority control in Cambridgeshire (until July 1986), Devon (until July 1987), Gloucestershire, Somerset and Wiltshire.

11. See Table 16.12.

12. See Table 16.13.

13. The Alliance also tended to do particularly well in local by-elections, where its vote typically ran 8% ahead of its support in the national polls and 7% ahead of its vote in the annual round of local elections. See Colin Rallings and Michael Thrasher, 'Party Competition and Electoral Volatility: The Case of Local By-elections, 1983–87', *Local Government Studies*, 14, No. 6 (1988), 67–76.

14. For a more detailed analysis of the Liberal vote, from which the next three paragraphs are drawn, see Ivor Crewe, 'Great Britain', in Ivor Crewe and David Denver (eds.), *Electoral Change in Western Democracies* (London: Croom Helm, 1985), 115–22.

15. See e.g. the results of the 1979 British Election Study, reported in Bo Särlvik and Ivor Crewe, *Decade of Dealignment* (Cambridge: Cambridge University Press, 1983), 290–3: 29% of Conservative voters and 28% of Labour voters said they were 'very likely' to vote Liberal if the party had looked like winning 'a lot more seats in Britain as a whole'. Had they all done so the Liberals would have taken 34% of the three-party vote. The potential Liberal vote was estimated to be well above 40% in surveys conducted between elections when the government was unpopular. See e.g. the Jan. 1973 and Sept. 1973 Gallup polls in George H. Gallup, *The Gallup International Public Opinion Polls: Great Britain 1937–1975* (New York: Random House, 1976), 1222, 1274.

16. In 1979, 68% of Conservative voters and 75% of Labour voters identified 'very' or 'fairly' strongly with their party; among the smaller number of Liberal voters the figure was only 42%.

17. See David Butler and Anthony King, *The British General Election of 1964* (London: Macmillan, 1965), 15.

18. The increase appears to have occurred in 1985. The annual *Social Attitudes Survey* reports the following proportions of Alliance identifiers: 1983, 15%; 1984, 13%; 1985, 18%; 1986, 17%. See John Curtice, 'Interim Report: Party Politics', in Roger Jowell, Sharon Witherspoon and Lindsay Brook (eds.), *British Social Attitudes: The 1987 Report* (Aldershot: Gower, 1987), 172. The measurement of party identification in the British Social Attitudes Survey differs slightly from that adopted in the British Election Study.

19. For example, when Alliance support was at 50.5% in the Dec. 1981 Gallup poll, 36% said they intended to vote SDP and 14.5% Liberal. Exactly a year later, when Alliance support had fallen to 22%, 10.5% said they intended to vote SDP, 9% Liberal and 2.5% 'Alliance'. See *Gallup Political Index*, No. 256 (Dec. 1981) and No. 268 (Dec. 1982).

20. In every year from 1981 to 1986, SDP support oscillated more sharply and (except for 1984) across a wider range than Liberal support did. The volatility of Liberal and SDP support—measured by the standard deviation of monthly support within each calendar year—was, respectively, 1981: 2.2, 7.7; 1982: 2.0, 4.9; 1983: 1.2, 2.5; 1984: 1.5, 1.9; 1985: 1.5, 2.4; 1986: 1.4, 3.3. The percentage point ranges for Liberal and SDP support in each year were, respectively, 1981: 6, 25; 1982: 7, 16; 1983: 5, 8; 1984: 6, 5; 1985: 5, 7; 1986: 6, 11.

21. In the BBC–Gallup election survey for 1983, 52% of those who voted for Alliance candidates said they voted 'SDP', 32% said 'Liberal' and 16% said 'Alliance'.

22. On the 1983 election see John Curtice and Michael Steed's psephological analysis in David

NOTES

Butler and Dennis Kavanagh, *The British General Election of 1983* (London: Macmillan, 1984), 351. On the 1987 election, see their analysis in David Butler and Dennis Kavanagh, *The British General Election of 1987* (London: Macmillan, 1988), 343. A neat illustration of the tendency for the two parties to attract and repel support in combination rather than separately occurred in the 1982 London borough elections, which were contested in multi-seat wards. Where candidates from both parties stood for the Alliance in a multi-seat ward, there was no evidence of the SDP candidates doing systematically better or worse than Liberal candidates in any type of ward. See John Curtice, Clive Payne and Robert Waller, 'The Alliance's First Nationwide Test: Lessons of the 1982 English Local Elections', *Electoral Studies*, 2 (1983), 3–22.

23. See Table 16.10.

24. The SDP appears to have been a somewhat stronger magnet than the Liberal party. In both 1983 and 1987 those who called themselves 'SDP voters' were far more likely to have switched from other parties or to be first-time voters than those who called themselves 'Liberal voters'. But the magnet pointed in different directions in the two elections. 'Liberal voters' were drawn in equal and relatively small proportions from the two main parties, whereas SDP voters in 1983 included twice as many Labour as Conservative defectors but in 1987 twice as many Conservative as Labour defectors. This switch may have had something to do with the SDP's rightward shift in tone and policy after Owen took over from Jenkins as party leader, but it probably also reflected the SDP's reputation as the more credible and dynamic element in the Liberal–SDP Alliance.

25. Raphael Samuel, 'The SDP and the New Political Class', *New Society*, 22 Apr. 1982, pp. 124–7.

26. But in fact self-proclaimed SDP voters in the 1980s were not an exact replica of self-proclaimed Liberals. They were somewhat less likely to be women and somewhat more likely to be young, middle-class and well educated. There is no reason, however, to suppose that the SDP drew its support from a markedly different social constituency than the Liberals. The age difference, for example, probably arose from the natural inclination of older Alliance voters to mention the name of a party that had existed throughout their lifetime (and for which some had voted in the past).

27. The Alliance did better among public-sector than private-sector employees in other social classes, too, although the difference was not as marked. See Anthony Heath, Roger Jowell and John Curtice, *How Britain Votes* (Oxford: Oxford University Press, 1985), 69.

28. According to a poll of 495 GPs in *General Practitioner* magazine, Conservative support fell from 65% in the June 1983 election to 44% in Mar. 1986, while support for the Alliance rose from 23 to 44%. A poll of 526 teachers in England and Wales for the *Times Educational Supplement* reported that Conservative support fell from 44% at the 1983 election to 24% in May 1987, while support for the Alliance rose from 18 to 46%. These Conservative-to-Alliance swings of, respectively, 21% and 24% are much higher than the swings over the same period among the electorate as a whole. See 'GP's Tonic for the SDP!', *Social Democrat*, 18 Apr. 1986, and *Times Education Supplement*, 29 May 1987.

Between 1983 and 1987 support for the Alliance increased in the public-service salariat in general when it was slipping almost everywhere else. Among non-manual workers in the public sector the Alliance vote rose from 28 to 31% and among graduates working in the public sector from 31 to 36%—thirteen percentage points above the national average.

29. According to an ORC survey for London Weekend Television's *Credo* programme in October 1982, the voting intentions of Church of England clergy were: Alliance, 54%; Conservative, 31%; Labour, 13% (at that time support for the Alliance in the national polls was 23%). In a Gallup survey of the voting intentions of 402 Church of England clergymen conducted in late 1985, voting intentions were fairly similar: Alliance, 49%; Conservative, 24%; Labour, 13% (at that time national polls put support for the Alliance at 29%). A *Times Educational Supplement*

survey (for details see n. 28) reported the 1987 voting intentions of teachers as Alliance, 46%; Labour, 28%; Conservative, 24%. A separate poll of 497 teachers in higher and further education found equal support for Labour and the Alliance (39% each), with the Conservatives on 17%. Among the 250 university teachers there was fractionally more support for the Alliance (40%) than Labour (39%)—a statistically insignificant difference. See 'Scathing Verdict from Lecturers on Government', *Times Higher Education Supplement*, 5 June 1987, 8.

30. This may well have included wine. According to an analysis of the census characteristics of constituencies, 'centres-of-learning' seats contained a particularly high proportion of the professional public-sector salariat. A marketing analysis summarized the consumer characteristics of such areas as follows: 'a highly educated, mobile population, with high proportions of single people, make this considerably the most important target market for the leisure industry. The propensity for these groups to wine, dine and take long and expensive holidays is unrivalled' (CACI Market Analysis Group, *ACORN: A New Approach to Market Analysis* (London: CACI Inc., n.d., c.1979), 55).

31. The public's view of the SDP's place in the party system does not appear to have changed over the 1981–7 period. Fig. 1, which is based on data for 1986–7, is almost identical to a figure constructed from 1981–2 data. See Ivor Crewe, 'Is Britain's Two-party System Really about to Crumble?', *Electoral Studies*, 1 (1982), 275–313, at p. 302.

32. Each member of the Gang of Three wrote a book which attempted to delineate a distinctive Social Democratic approach to politics. See David Owen, *Face the Future* (London: Jonathan Cape, 1981); Shirley Williams, *Politics is for People* (Harmondsworth: Penguin, 1982), and William Rodgers, *The Politics of Change* (London: Secker & Warburg, 1982). David Owen's later book, *A Future that will Work: Competitiveness and Compassion* (Harmondsworth: Penguin, 1984), sets out his revised view. Note the subtitle.

33. The views of 'Liberal' and 'SDP' voters were the same on most issues. However, 'SDP' voters were more liberal on the issues of repatriation of immigrants, foreign aid, the death penalty, abortion and the regulation of sex and nudity in the media. This difference probably arose from the younger age of 'SDP' than 'Liberal' voters (see n. 26).

34. Anthony Heath, Roger Jowell and John Curtice, *How Britain Votes* (Oxford: Pergamon Press, 1985), ch. 8. See also Anthony Heath, Roger Jowell and John Curtice, 'The Emerging Alliance Voter', *New Society*, 13 Sept. 1985, pp. 371–3.

35. David Owen and Clement Freud, 'Consultations on "Priorities for the 1990's"' (letter and draft papers), 27 Nov. 1985, SDP Archives.

36. Heath *et al.*'s argument suffers from two weaknesses. First, the east–west class axis is represented by the single issue of nationalization versus privatization and the north–south liberal axis by the single issue of nuclear weapons. The former is not a self-evident class issue nor the latter a self-evident liberal issue in the usual sense of the terms. Moreover, adoption of a single indicator for each axis leaves the results too reliant on the precise wording and timing of the issue question. For example, Table 16.7 shows that the views of voters for the Alliance on nuclear weapons depended on the exact nature of the issue (Polaris? cruise missiles?). The meaning of the liberal axis becomes even more confused by its representation elsewhere in the book by the issues of spending on social services (which one might have regarded as a model 'class issue') and by the death penalty.

Secondly, the north-east quadrant should not be described as an Alliance 'heartland'. Although the Alliance's share of the vote was higher in this part of the policy map than elsewhere, it was not the most popular party, and a substantial majority of voters residing in this policy quadrant voted for a party other than the Alliance. Nor did the majority of Alliance voters fall into this quadrant: voters for the Alliance were spread across the policy map more evenly than Conservative and Labour voters were, and barely more than a third (35%) occupied the north and north-east sectors.

37. The middling position of Alliance voters on this issue is demonstrated by their answers to a

trichotomous question on the Trident missile asked in the 1987 BBC–Gallup election survey: 24% wanted Britain to 'keep its Trident nuclear weapons system', 14% wanted Britain 'to get rid of all nuclear weapons' and 62% believed that 'Britain should scrap Trident but keep a minimal nuclear deterrent'. These figures compare with 73% of Conservatives who wanted to keep Trident and 45% of Labour voters who wanted to get rid of all nuclear weapons.

38. See Crewe, 'Is Britain's Two-Party System Really about to Crumble?', 304. 'SDP' voters were fractionally more liberal than Labour voters on immigration, but on no other issue.

39. Respondents probably interpreted the question as party-political rather than constitutional, i.e. as a shifting of power away from the Conservative government at Westminster.

40. This is reflected in the similar (and typically small) proportions of voters of all three parties who gave answers of 'don't know' or 'it doesn't matter either way'.

41. In a January 1981 poll, supporters of a putative SDP–Liberal Alliance cited as their reasons: 'to get a moderate, middle of the road government' (30%), 'to give a new party a chance' (17%), 'because it is led by intelligent and reasonable people' (16%). The answer 'because it has good policies for Britain' came only fourth (15%). See Audience Selection, 'Voters Verdict One', table 4 (unpublished report of telephone poll reported in *Sun*, 28 Jan. 1981).

42. Robert Worcester, 'Disillusioned from Warrington Votes SDP', *New Statesman*, 11 Sept. 1981 (a report of a MORI survey conducted for Granada Television; for fuller details, see MORI, *Public Opinion in Great Britain*, No. 4 (May–Oct. 1981).

43. See MORI, *Public Opinion in Great Britain*, No. 4.

44. Alliance voters displayed more confidence in their party on those issues the Alliance had tried to make its own: 82% said their party would be best at 'making government more democratic'; 70% chose their party to 'protect individual freedom and rights'; and 69% to 'provide children with better education'. But high though these levels of partisan faith were, they were higher still for the latter two policy areas among Conservative and Labour voters.

45. In 1983, 83% of Alliance voters chose either Steel (70%) or Jenkins (13%) as the leader who would make the best prime minister. By comparison, 85% of Conservative voters chose Thatcher and 44% of Labour voters chose Foot. In 1987 73% of Alliance voters chose either Steel (27%) or Owen (46%). Thatcher was chosen by 86% of Conservatives and Kinnock by 79% of Labour voters. The sources for these figures are the BBC–Gallup election surveys for 8–9 June 1983 and 10–11 June 1987.

46. The 1983 and 1987 BBC–Gallup election surveys asked respondents whether they voted out of like of their own party or dislike of the other(s); and whether they had specific reasons for their party choice or simply felt that 'it was time for a change' (or, in the case of Conservative voters, that 'there was no need for a change'). At both elections 22% of Alliance voters combined positive with specific reasons. The proportion combining a negative with a general reason was 40% in 1983 and 42% in 1987.

47. This is also apparent from Fig. 5. What distinguished SDP voters from others (including Liberals) was their positioning of the Conservatives and Labour. SDP supporters pushed both major parties out to the extremes: no other group of voters placed the Conservative party so far to the right; and only Conservative voters placed the Labour party (just) even further to the left.

48. These answers partly overlapped: some Liberal–Alliance respondents will have said that both Conservative and Labour extremism influenced their vote.

49. BBC–Gallup election surveys, 8–9 June 1983 and 10–11 June 1987. See Ivor Crewe, 'How to Win a Landslide Without Really Trying: Why the Conservatives Won in 1983', in Austin Ranney (ed.), *Britain at the Polls 1983: A Study of the General Election* (Durham, NC: Duke University Press, 1985), 155–96, at 194, and Ivor Crewe, 'Why Mrs Thatcher Was Returned with a Landslide', *Social Studies Review*, 3 (1987), 2–9, at 9.

50. Curtice and Steed, 'Analysis', in Butler and Kavanagh, *The British General Election of 1987*, 336–7.

51. See pp. 368 and 380 on the failure of the SDP's seats-targeting exercise in 1987. On the

campaign in favour of tactical voting, see Nina Fishman and Andrew Shaw, 'TV87: The Campaign to Make Tactical Voting Make Votes Count', in Ivor Crewe and Martin Harrop (eds.), *Political Communications: The General Election Campaign of 1987* (Cambridge: Cambridge University Press, 1989), 298–304. The campaign was endorsed by *Today*, the *Observer* and the *New Statesman*.

52. Curtice and Steed (in 'Analysis', 335–8) show that there was more tactical voting both for and against the Alliance in north and west Britain that in south and east Britain.

53. The Alliance's vote fell by 2.9 percentage points nationally but by 1.6 points in Conservative–Alliance seats and by only 1.1% where the third-placed Labour candidate had trailed the second-placed Alliance candidate by at least 15% in 1983.

54. The two seats which the Alliance came closest to winning in 1983 (and in which its candidate was not the former Labour MP for the seat) were Edinburgh West (Conservative majority 1.1%) and Stevenage (Conservative majority 3.3%). In Edinburgh West the Labour vote rose from 20.1 to 22.2% between 1983 and 1987 and in Stevenage the Labour vote rose from 24.0 to 25.4%. It was also noticeable that in those 'three-party' marginals where the lead of both the Conservatives over the Alliance and, in turn, the Alliance over Labour was small— Clwyd South West, Edinburgh South, Renfrew West and Inverclyde, and Strathkelvin and Bearsden—Labour came from third place to win, squeezing the Alliance vote (Curtice and Steed, 'Analysis', 336).

Chapter 17

1. *The Times*, 11 June 1983.

2. *The Times*, 14 June 1983. Jenkins and Owen give their accounts of the leadership change in Roy Jenkins, *A Life at the Centre* (London: Macmillan, 1991), 577–8, and David Owen, *Time to Declare* (London: Michael Joseph, 1991), 591–2.

3. *The Times*, 14 June 1983. In his earlier volume of memoirs, *Personally Speaking to Kenneth Harris* (London: Weidenfeld & Nicolson, 1987), Owen gives a distinctly bowdlerized account of his anti-Jenkins coup: 'Inevitably, for the SDP to survive as a separate party, it had to have a new leader and, if necessary, there would have to be an election. However, Roy decided to bow out gracefully and I was chosen unanimously as leader by the MPs' (p. 222).

4. Owen quotes his mother against himself in *Personally Speaking*, 3.

5. See John Curtice and Michael Steed, 'An Analysis of the Voting', in David Butler and Dennis Kavanagh (eds.), *The British General Election of 1983* (London: Macmillan, 1984), 346.

6. In fact anti-SDP feeling was not common among Liberals, but members of the SDP found out what rank-and-file Liberals were thinking (or supposed to be thinking) largely from the press, and newspapers were naturally most interested in reporting apparent tensions between the parties. For example, on 16 June 1983 the *Guardian* reported Cyril Smith as saying: 'I believe that most of the eight million people who voted for the Alliance in this election voted because of the Liberal influence and not the SDP influence. I believe that in future the Alliance has got to have a much greater Liberal input.'

7. *Guardian*, 7 July 1983.

8. *The Times*, 1 Aug. 1983.

9. See e.g. Dick Taverne, 'Double Talk', *Guardian*, 18 July 1983, and William Wallace, 'If we Share Objectives then we must Combine to Attain them', *Guardian*, 29 July 1983. The *Guardian* was used by both sides in the merger argument as a kind of noticeboard or Chinese-style wall newspaper.

10. For example, Taverne wrote in his 18 July *Guardian* article (see n. 9): 'I believe that in the last election the Alliance did worse than it might have done because it was composed of separate parties. Many people were confused.'

11. See e.g. 'Closer Ties for Alliance to Stop Short of Merger', *Guardian*, 16 June 1983. *The Economist* carried a similar report, 'Not so Pally Allies', 16 July 1983.
12. *Guardian*, 27 June 1983.
13. Smith's views are quoted in n. 6 above. Smith, Alton and Hughes were all campaigning actively for the Liberals to adopt a more collective style of leadership and for Steel to be forced to accept a deputy leader elected by the party. See 'Liberal MPs Want Steel to Find Deputy Leader', *Guardian*, 3 Aug. 1983. Smith, Alton and Hughes were the kind of people who typified the Liberals for David Owen and many others in the SDP.
14. Adam Raphael, 'Thin End of a Merger is Dilemma for Owen', *Observer*, 4 Sept. 1983.
15. Steel, having seriously considered resigning as Liberal leader, then went off on a three-month sabbatical. He was unhappy and ill and increasingly fed up with the attacks on his leadership from within his own party. See David Steel, *Against Goliath* (London: Weidenfeld & Nicolson, 1989), 250–5.
16. Dick Taverne, 'Double Talk', *Guardian*, 18 July 1983; William Wallace, 'If we Share Objectives then we must Combine to Attain them', *Guardian*, 19 July 1983; Roy Jenkins quoted in *Observer*, 11 July 1983.
17. *Observer*, 4 Sept. 1983. The group included Dick Taverne, David Marquand, Matthew Oakeshott and Richard Holme.
18. William Rodgers, 'The SDP and the Liberal Party in Alliance', *Political Quarterly*, 54 (1983), 354–62, at 357–8.
19. *The Times*, 2 Sept. 1983; *Observer*, 4 Sept. 1983.
20. *Observer*, 4 Sept. 1983.
21. David Owen, 'Divided we Stand for Coalition', *Guardian*, 4 July 1983.
22. For a brief introduction to the workings of electoral systems like STV and the German system, see Martin Harrop and William L. Miller, *Elections and Voters: A Comparative Introduction* (London: Macmillan, 1987), ch. 3.
23. *The Times*, 2 Sept. 1983.
24. The wording of the various pro- and anti-merger motions can be found in the Record of Decisions, Salford, 11–14 Sept. 1983, filed with the National Committee Minutes. As though to emphasize the party's independence, the anti-mergerites always liked to underline the initials 'SDP'.
25. National Committee Minutes, 10 Sept. 1983. In an article in the *New Democrat* (Sept.–Oct. 1983) Owen referred to 'certain anarchical tendencies in the Liberal party' (p. 12).
26. *The Times*, 12 Sept. 1983.
27. *The Times*, 12 Sept. 1983.
28. *New Democrat*, Sept.–Oct. 1983, 12; *Guardian*, 10 Sept. 1983.
29. *The Times*, 12 Sept. 1983. Some believed that Owen deliberately fostered a merger scare following the 1983 election in order to strengthen his hold on the party and to make it more difficult for a merger to take place in the future.
30. *Western Mail*, 27 June 1983.
31. LBC radio interview quoted in the *Guardian*, 30 July 1983.
32. *New Democrat*, Sept.–Oct. 1983, 12.
33. *New Democrat*, Sept.–Oct. 1983, 13.
34. *Guardian*, 12 Sept. 1983 (emphasis added).
35. Record of Decisions, Salford, 11–14 Sept. 1983, Emergency Motion 3; also *The Times* and the *Guardian*, 10 Sept. 1983.
36. Only two joint selections were held in the event. The SDP's National Committee, after a long discussion in December 1983, agreed by a vote of fourteen to ten that there were exceptional circumstances in the north-east of England and that joint open selection should be permitted in Tyne and Wear and in Durham. An SDP candidate eventually fought Tyne and Wear; a Liberal fought Durham. See National Committee Minutes, 5 Dec. 1983, item 5(*c*); *Daily*

Telegraph, 1 Mar. 1984; and David Butler and Paul Jowett, *Party Strategies in Britain: A Study of the 1984 European Elections* (London: Macmillan, 1985), 72–3.

37. *The Times*, 21 Sept. 1983.
38. *The Times*, 19 Sept. 1984.
39. Reporting the agreement on the guidelines on 22 Jan. 1984, the *Observer* quoted one Owen-ite as describing the agreement as 'an important victory'.
40. See pp. 181–4.
41. Merely keeping track of what was happening in 633 individual constituencies imposed heavy burdens on the staff. In a paper prepared for the National Committee in the autumn of 1984, Alec McGivan, the SDP's national organizer, conveyed a vivid sense of his staff's problems and frustrations and he pleaded with the committee to discuss overall strategy with regard to the interparty negotiations: 'In these deliberations it should be borne in mind that nationally we are now being inundated with calls and letters for advice. In order to draw up this paper we now have detailed notes on every area party and on most constituencies. All of this does, however, involve a vast amount of staff time. Even given this staff time, and the dropping of other projects, it is perhaps worth stressing what may appear obvious. With the best will in the world, it is extremely difficult to co-ordinate and negotiate successfully, from one central place, all the seats in the country.' See 'Westminster Seats: Liberal Negotiations', 9 Oct. 1984, NC/381084, 7.
42. 'Westminster Seats: Liberal Negotiations'; 6 Dec. 1984, NC/51/1294.
43. 'Position on Westminster Seats (13.7.84)'; 'Westminster Seats: Liberal Negotiations', 9 Oct. 1984, NC/38/1084, 2.
44. 'Saffron Walden: Request for Joint Open Selection', undated paper filed with 'Position on Westminster Seats (13.7.84)'.
45. In Bristol, to take another extreme case, it took the local Liberals and Social Democrats months to arrive at an elaborate compromise. It provided that four of the six seats in the area were to be fought by the party that fought them in 1983, but with members of both parties participating in joint closed selections. In the case of the other two seats, Bristol North-West and Bristol West, the candidates were to be chosen by joint open selection; but, in order to try to ensure that each of the two parties fought one of the two seats, the parties' members had to split their ballots so that, if they voted for an SDP candidate in one seat, they had to vote for a Liberal in the other. Hilary Long, who later became one of David Owen's strongest support-ers on the National Committee and who had fought Bristol North-West in 1983, was said to have walked out of the crucial meeting when the compromise was arrived at. See 'Bristol Dispute Threatens Alliance Prospects', *Guardian*, 25 Feb. 1985, and National Committee Minutes, 22 July 1985, item 5. On the final Saffron Walden decision, see National Committee Minutes, 15 Oct. 1984, item 7.
46. 'Alliance Agrees Seats Strategy in Wales', *Guardian*, 17 Sept. 1984.
47. National Committee Minutes, 12 Nov. 1984, item 5.
48. Owen had to go out of his way to dispel the impression during the next few days. The row was reported quite widely in the press. See Peter Kellner, 'With Enemies like These, who Needs Friends?', *New Statesman*, 16 Nov. 1984, and 'Owen and Steel to Pull Together', *Sunday Times*, 18 Nov. 1984.
49. National Committee Minutes, 10 Dec. 1984, item 6.
50. National Committee Minutes, 22 July 1985, item 5.
51. Ibid.
52. 'SDP Success in "Safe" Liberal Seat may Force Owen to Trim on Selection', *Guardian*, 14 Mar. 1985. There was probably yet another reason behind Owen's change of mood. Once the decentralized seats negotiations were well under way, and once, therefore, difficult cases began to come before the National Committee by the dozen rather than in ones and twos, there was no way in which Owen could continue to exercise personal control. He either had

to trust the Rodgers group (which included his allies Mike Thomas and John Cartwright) or else devote himself to the seats negotiations and to almost nothing else. With Rodgers on the scene, bearing the great bulk of the burden, Owen was probably relieved to be able to move off it. Although Rodgers was a Jenkinsite and a person who favoured 'organic' merger, he was also remembered, not least by Owen, as the man who had abruptly broken off the seats negotiations with the Liberals in January 1982. Whatever else he was, Rodgers was not a soft touch. One of the other negotiators described him as 'foolish but noble' in having agreed to take the negotiations on.

53. The full position was set out in a document presented to the National Committee a few weeks before the 1987 general election by Tony Halmos, the deputy national organizer, 'Parliamentary Seat Allocations and Selections'. With four candidate selections still in progress, Halmos reported that twenty seats that had been SDP-led in 1983 were now Liberal-led while twenty-three seats that had been Liberal-led four years before were now SDP-led. This tally comprised only those seats that had been allocated as a result of the seats-negotiations process. Among the eighty-three seats whose candidates had been chosen by means of joint open selection, twenty-one seats that had been SDP-led in 1983 had gone to the Liberals but fourteen seats that had been Liberal-led four years before had adopted as candidates members of the SDP. Overall there was little in it.

54. See the reports and leading articles on 25 Oct. 1983 in the *Daily Express, Daily Telegraph, Sun, Guardian* and London *Evening Standard*.

55. *Guardian*, 14 July 1984.

56. David Watt, 'The Hurdles Facing Tomorrow's Man', *The Times*, 16 Sept. 1983.

57. Geoffrey Smith, 'Commentary', *The Times*, 11 July 1984.

58. Patrick Bishop, 'Messiah without Disciples', *Sunday Times*, 6 Jan. 1985. See also Robin Oakley, 'Why Owen Keeps Getting it Right', *Daily Mail*, 23 June 1984, and Alan Watkins, 'Seasonal Advice for our Leaders', *Observer*, 18 Dec. 1983.

59. Anthony Bevins, 'Alliance Sets High Workload Pace in House', *The Times*, 21 Oct. 1985. The survey covered only backbenchers and excluded Owen and Steel.

60. The figures in the text are calculated from the *Gallup Political Index*.

61. It was also suggested that after nearly a decade Steel was simply bored with being Liberal leader. The 'not as sharp' quotation is taken from James Naughtie, 'The Fighting Fit Doctor', *Spectator*, 14 July 1984.

62. Interviewed on *Panorama*, quoted in *The Times*, 18 Sept. 1984.

63. On the European elections, see Butler and Jowell, *Party Strategies in Britain, passim*.

64. See 'Labour Real Winner, Local Vote Shows', *The Times*, 18 May 1985.

65. See e.g. Ronald Butt, 'If the House were Left Hanging', *The Times*, 30 May 1985, and Adam Raphael, 'Queen Acts to Head off Row over Election Tie', *Observer*, 15 Sept. 1985.

66. Quoted in *Sunday Times*, 1 Dec. 1985.

67. The SDP's failure to do better among working-class voters caused considerable concern in the party, especially among those who still thought of the SDP as the natural successor to Labour. Roger Liddle wrote a paper, 'The SDP and the Working-Class Vote' (NC/19/0785), that was discussed at the July 1985 meeting of the National Committee. See also Robert Taylor, 'SDP Struggles for Share of Blue Collar Vote', *Observer*, 4 Aug. 1985. Taylor pointed out that the party's membership was overwhelmingly middle-class, that the party's members were not very good at knocking on doors and that the party might have suffered from its strong stance in favour of trade-union reform. He suggested that it might do better if more were seen of Shirley Williams (and, by implication, less of David Owen).

68. In fact, the terms 'right' and 'left' rapidly became meaningless—if they had ever had any meaning—within the SDP. As always, personal loyalties cut across lines of ideological cleavage, lines of ideological cleavage cut across each other, and the party's official policies combined right- and left-wing elements. Owen was hardly a right-winger in any meaningful

sense. That said, Owen's instinct was clearly to appeal to voters who, if they did not vote for the SDP, would be likely to vote Conservative, while people like Rodgers and Williams wanted the party to appeal more to Labour-inclined voters.

69. Actually the two books were both largely compilations of his other writings and speeches. The main sources for the development of Owen's ideas during his period as SDP leader are the following (Owen is the author unless otherwise indicated): 'Agenda for Competitiveness with Compassion', *Economic Affairs*, 4 (Oct. 1983), 26–33; Fourth Hoover Address, University of Strathclyde (n.d.); 'Ownership The Way Forward', Gaitskell Memorial Lecture 1985, Open Forum No. 9; 'Electors will Yearn for us after Tory "Course in Survival", Owen Says' (report of speech to Council for Social Democracy, Salford, 12 Sept. 1983), *The Times*, 13 Sept. 1983; 'Social Market and Social Justice', Tawney Society Fifth Annual Lecture, 25 Jan. 1987 (published by the Tawney Society); *A Future that will Work: Competitiveness and Compassion* (Harmondsworth: Penguin Books, 1984) and *A United Kingdom* (Harmondsworth: Penguin Books, 1986). See also Alex de Mont, 'A Theory of the Social Market' (London: Tawney Society, 1984).

70. Owen, *Personally Speaking*, 17.

71. David Owen, *The Politics of Defence* (London: Jonathan Cape, 1972).

72. Owen, *A Future that will Work*, 154.

73. Owen, 'Agenda for Competitiveness with Compassion', 26.

74. Ibid. 28.

75. Ibid. 27.

76. *The Times*, 13 Sept. 1983.

77. Quoted on the cover of *A Future that will Work*.

78. Owen's willingness to accept much of Thatcherism as the new conventional wisdom was set out most fully—and more or less in so many words—in *Social Market and Social Justice*.

79. Rodgers, *My Party—Wet or Dry?*, Tawney Society Lecture, 16 May 1985 (London: Tawney Society, 1985), 6, 12. See also 'Show Tender Side, Rodgers Tells SDP', *The Times*, 17 May 1985. There were other coded messages. On defence, Rodgers in his Tawney Society lecture urged Owen not to 'try to win over the Alf Garnetts of this world' (p. 8).

80. See 'Jenkins and Owen "Role Reversal"', *The Times*, 12 July 1984, and George Brock, 'Count David's Gang of One', *The Times*, 25 Feb. 1985.

81. The Stevenage motion is reproduced in full in *Social Democrat*, 9 Aug. 1985, p. 5.

82. The above account of the debate on the Stevenage motion is based on reports in *The Times* and *Guardian*, 11 Sept. 1985, and *Social Democrat*, 20 Sept. 1985.

83. *Financial Times*, 11 Sept. 1985.

Chapter 18

1. For a wide-ranging assessment of the Liberal party's condition in the mid-1980s, see George Brock, 'Why Steel Stays Best Bet for Alliance Unity', *The Times*, 26 Feb. 1985.

2. *The Times*, 26 Sept. 1983.

3. *The Times*, *Financial Times*, 26 July 1984.

4. *Daily Telegraph*, *Guardian*, *Financial Times*, *The Times*, 21 Nov. 1984.

5. *The Times*, 10 July 1985.

6. *Guardian*, 28 July 1986. Steel was speaking at a joint Liberal–SDP candidates conference and could not resist a sly dig at Owen's leadership style: 'After the Thatcher years people want to see less autocracy and more collegiality.'

7. In addition to Jenkins, Williams, Cartwright and Rodgers, Robert Maclennan became spokesman on agriculture and fisheries, Charles Kennedy social security spokesman and Ian Wrigglesworth employment spokesman. The full list was published in the *Guardian*, 13 Jan.

1987. David Penhaligon was an extremely popular and influential West Country Liberal who had always been somewhat doubtful about the Alliance.

8. *Daily Telegraph*, 12 July 1984. The other commission members included Lord Mayhew for the Liberals and John Roper, the former MP, for the Social Democrats. Another Social Democrat, the former MP Jim Wellbeloved, was added later.

9. *The Times*, 21 Sept. 1984.

10. *Social Democrat*, 20 Sept. 1985, 6. In addition, John Cartwright accepted on behalf of the platform an amendment, moved by Tom McNally, urging the party to press for a policy of 'negotiated freeze' if a new round of Geneva negotiations failed to achieve any momentum in reversing the arms race. The amendment was intended to shift the SDP's defence policy towards that of the Liberals and was implicitly critical of the leadership; but in the circumstances of 1985 Owen and Cartwright, while putting their own gloss on it, felt confident enough of their position on the issue not to oppose it.

11. *Scotsman*, 16 May 1986.

12. *Social Democrat*, 30 May 1986, p. 1.

13. The *Sunday Telegraph*'s report was quoted in *Social Democrat*, 30 May 1986. The *Social Democrat*—clearly anxious to justify Owen's outburst and also, apparently, to show what perfidious people the Liberals were—also reprinted an exchange that appeared in the *Scotsman*. Steel wrote to the *Scotsman* acknowledging that he had spoken to Martin Dowle but saying that he would be very surprised if, when the commission's report finally appeared, it contained 'such a bald and unqualified statement' about the rejection of a Polaris replacement as Dowle had reported. The *Scotsman*'s editor appended to Steel's letter (20 May 1986) the bald statement: 'The story was based on unambiguous information given to our reporters.' In almost all the Owenite statements on the issue, the impression was given that the 'joint' commission had actually ruled out a Polaris replacement. In fact, it was in the course of doing no such thing; it was merely about to recommend that the relevant decision be deferred.

14. David Owen, 'Polaris must be Replaced', *Observer*, 1 June 1986.

15. *Today*, 2 June 1986.

16. *The Times*, 6 June 1986.

17. The remarks were quoted by Peter Riddell, 'Partnership at Odds over British Deterrence', *Financial Times*, 5 June 1986.

18. Quoted in *The Times*, 7 June 1986.

19. *Observer*, 15 June 1986.

20. *Sunday Times*, 8 June 1986.

21. William Rodgers, 'Keep the Defence Options Open', *The Times*, 12 June 1986.

22. *Weekend World* interview quoted in the *Guardian*, 9 June 1986.

23. *Defence and Disarmament*, Report of the Joint SDP–Liberal Alliance Commission (Hebden Bridge, West Yorks.: Hebden Royd Publications, 1986), 30.

24. Ibid.

25. Ibid., p. i.

26. *The Times*, 12 June 1986.

27. Some on the SDP side attributed the idea that emerged to John Roper, who by this time was a member of the senior staff of the Royal Institute of International Affairs at Chatham House.

28. *Observer*, 14 Sept. 1986.

29. *The Times*, 15 Sept. 1986.

30. Ibid.

31. *Guardian*, 23 Sept. 1986.

32. Simon Hughes quoted in Des Wilson, *Battle for Power* (London: Sphere Books, 1987), 51. The Eastbourne conference and the whole defence row from the Liberal side (and from Des Wilson's point of view) are described at length in *Battle for Power*, chs. 2–3.

33. *Guardian*, 24 Sept. 1986.
34. Thames Television's *This Week*, quoted in *Guardian*, 26 Sept. 1986.
35. *Guardian*, 27 Sept. 1986.
36. Adam Raphael, 'Steel's Defence Deal', *Observer*, 28 Sept. 1986.
37. *Guardian*, 18 Dec. 1986.
38. *Britain United: The Time has Come*, The SDP/Liberal Alliance Programme for Government (London: SDP, 1987).
39. The figures are taken from *Gallup Political Barometers: 1945–92* (London: Social Surveys Gallup Poll, 1992).
40. There is a full account of the Greenwich by-election in Pippa Norris, *British By-elections: The Volatile Electorate* (Oxford: Clarendon Press, 1990).
41. Andrew Rawnsley, 'City Shadow on Greenwich Tories', *Guardian*, 31 Jan. 1987.
42. See e.g. the MORI poll reported in *Sunday Times*, 22 Feb. 1987, 'Voters Warm to Barnes'.
43. Colin Brown, 'How the SDP Targeted the Greenwich Floating Voters', *Independent*, 2 Mar. 1987.
44. For full details and an analysis of the polls, see Norris, *British By-elections*, 89–107.
45. The discussion that follows deals only with Alliance thinking, such as it was, on this question. It does not deal with two related and important questions: first, the arithmetical likelihood of an election leading to a hung parliament in which the Alliance held the balance of power (which was in fact quite remote) and, secondly, the probable behaviour in such an event of the other parties, irrespective of what the Alliance might want. Peter Kellner of the *New Statesman* devoted a number of columns during these years to showing how unlikely a hung parliament in which the Alliance held the balance of power was and also to showing how unlikely it was that, in the event of a hung parliament, the two major parties, especially Labour, would play the Alliance's game. See e.g. 'No one Votes for Coalitions', *The Times*, 5 June 1985, and 'Powerful Dreams of the Two Davids', *Independent*, 27 Oct. 1986. Kellner did not seek to deny that a hung parliament was possible; indeed, at times during the 1983 parliament he thought one was probable. His point was that a hung parliament in the circumstances of the 1980s would be unlikely to be (though it might be) one in which the Alliance, and the Alliance alone, held the balance of power, being in a position by itself thereby to install either the Conservatives or Labour in power, Kellner was also insistent, rightly, that an Alliance-backed minority government or coalition would not come about because voters had deliberately voted for it but because the general election had produced one result rather than another and the Alliance parties had subsequently decided to behave in one way rather than another. Such a government would be an outcome of the election; it would not be the result of any conscious decision on voters' part.
46. See pp. 195–6.
47. David Owen interviewed by Andrew Marr, 'No Flinching at a Poll Rerun', *Independent*, 2 Apr. 1987.
48. Owen set out his terms in an article in *The Times*, 'PR: Let the People Decide', 30 Nov. 1985.
49. On Owen's consulting Steel and the response of some Liberals to the idea of a referendum, see John Carvel, 'Owen Upsets Partners with Referendum Call', *Guardian*, 30 Nov. 1985.
50. *The Times*, 16 May 1986.
51. Ibid.
52. Steel interviewed on *A Week in Politics*, quoted in *Guardian*, 1 June 1985.
53. The late Peter Jenkins was one of the first to note the fundamental difference between Owen's and Steel's political temperaments. He described the two men as being of two different political generations. They were not really, but they certainly seemed that way. See Peter Jenkins, 'Alliance on the March into a Defence Minefield', *Guardian*, 24 Sept. 1983.
54. *Independent*, 6 Mar. 1987.
55. *Observer*, 29 Mar. 1987.

56. *Observer*, 29 Mar. 1987.
57. Ibid.
58. *Independent*, 2 Apr. 1987.
59. Quoted in *Guardian*, 13 Apr. 1987.
60. *The Times*, 20 May 1985.
61. *New Statesman*, 30 Jan. 1987.
62. *Guardian*, 16 Feb. 1987.
63. Owen interviewed on TV-am, quoted in *Guardian*, 2 Feb. 1987.

Chapter 19

1. David Owen and David Steel, *The Time has Come: Partnership for Progress* (London: Weidenfeld & Nicolson, 1987).
2. Four successive polls conducted in late Mar. and published in early Apr. put the Alliance equal with or ahead of Labour. See *Daily Telegraph*, 27 Mar. 1987 ('Alliance Overtakes Labour as Kinnock Popularity Falls'); *Today*, 26 Mar. 1987 (the lead story begins: 'The Alliance are poised to smash Labour into third place'); *Sunday Times*, 5 Apr. 1987 and *Daily Express*, 6 Apr. 1987 ('Up, Up and Nearly Away! But Alliance is Holding Firm').
3. See David McKie, 'Tories Take Long Lead into Election but Rivals Keep them in their Sights', *Guardian*, 9 May 1987; and David Butler, 'Are the Tories Sure to Win?', *The Times*, 9 May 1987.
4. The Liberal vote (in 1983, the Alliance vote) was greater than Liberal (Alliance) support in the polls in the first week of the official campaign at every election since 1964, except for 1966 and October 1974, when it remained the same. The position in the 1950s cannot be judged because the Liberal party contested only a small number of seats.
5. See pp. 361–3.
6. See 'Two Davids to Perform Election Duet', *Sunday Times*, 21 Sept. 1986.
7. Quoted in Peter Kellner, 'Did the Campaign Make any Difference to the Result?', *Independent*, 26 Oct. 1987.
8. See ch. 11.
9. For an account of this meeting, see Des Wilson, *Battle for Power* (London: Sphere Books, 1987), 187.
10. See pp. 199–200.
11. Wilson, *Battle for Power*, 189.
12. On the early evening news that day, Steel, Owen and Pardoe were interviewed (in two cases before the meeting). 'Who', they were all asked, 'was to be the Alliance's principal target?' 'Labour,' said Steel; 'The Tories,' said Owen; 'Both,' said Pardoe. It was an eloquent portrayal of the Alliance's strategic confusion.
13. Wilson, *Battle for Power*, 219.
14. The figures were: Conservative 39%, Alliance 30%, Labour 28%.
15. A MORI poll of marginal seats in *The Times*.
16. An exception was the *Today* newspaper, which supported the Alliance, and led on 19 May with a story about the substantial vote the Alliance would win if voters 'thought they had a chance of winning in their constituency' ('Big Chance for Davids').
17. Owen later claimed that his row with Thatcher was a deliberate ploy to distance the Alliance from Labour and to get a difficult issue for the Alliance out of the way early in the campaign (see David Owen, *Time To Declare* (London: Michael Joseph, 1991), 690). If so, it failed. According to a daily survey of voters' perceptions of the campaign, the proportion who thought that the Alliance was stressing defence as its main issue jumped from 8% on 19–20 May to 16% on 21–2 May—the height of the row—after which the proportion settled at about 14% throughout the rest of the campaign. Moreover, in their impression of the three parties'

NOTES

defence policies (specifically defence spending), voters placed the Alliance closer to Labour than to the Conservatives. See William L. Miller *et al.*, *How Voters Change: The 1987 British Election Campaign in Perspective* (Oxford: Clarendon Press, 1990), 164, 174.

18. In fact the Alliance's private polls found no evidence that the election broadcast was badly received by ordinary viewers.

19. Roger Carroll, 'The Alliance's Non-advertising Campaign', in Ivor Crewe and Martin Harrop (eds.), *Political Communications: The General Election Campaign of 1987* (Cambridge: Cambridge University Press, 1989), 90.

20. See David Steel, *Against Goliath: David Steel's Story* (London: Weidenfeld & Nicolson, 1989), 280, and Owen, *Time to Declare*, 698–9.

21. See e.g. 'Alliance Split on Tory Coalition Deal', *Guardian*, 4 June 1987, p. 36; 'Alliance in Wonderland', *Star*, 4 June 1987, 8; 'Owen and Steel Split on Hung Parliament', *Daily Express*, 4 June 1987, 5.

22. *Independent*, 4 June 1987, 1.

23. See David Butler and Dennis Kavanagh, *The British General Election of 1987* (London: Macmillan, 1988), 115.

24. Wrigglesworth's 103-vote majority in 1983 was almost certainly due to the press revelation in mid-campaign that his Conservative opponent was formerly a parliamentary candidate for the National Front.

25. However, Owen's share of the vote fell from 44.3% in 1983 to 42.3% in 1987, while John Cartwright's share of the vote rose from 40.5% to 41.8%.

26. The tally of seventeen masked considerable turnover. The Liberals lost Colne Valley and the Isle of Wight, where the incumbent Liberal MPs were retiring, as well as Cambridgeshire North-East (Clement Freud's seat) and Leeds West (where Michael Meadowcroft went down). In compensation the Liberals captured Southport and two rural Scottish seats, Fife North-East and Argyll and Bute, and they just clung on to their by-election gain of Brecon and Radnor. In Ryedale they were comfortably beaten by the Conservatives.

27. See Miller *et al.*, *How Voters Change*, 258–9. There was a small increase in tactical voting in favour of the Alliance compared with 1983, but it was too limited and patchy to win it more than a single extra seat—Argyll and Bute, where the Liberal squeezed the Nationalist, not the Labour vote. However, many sitting Alliance MPs owed their re-election to the continuation of tactical voting from previous elections.

28. Butler and Kavanagh, *The British General Election of 1987*, 320, 329, 336–7.

29. In its twenty-one top priority target seats the Alliance's share of the vote rose on average by 0.7%, a fractional improvement on its nation-wide performance of −2.9%. In the other thirty-nine target seats the Alliance share of the vote fell by 2.0%.

30. See p. 299.

31. See Table 16.6; also Ivor Crewe, 'Why Mrs Thatcher was Returned with a Landslide', *Social Studies Review*, 3 (Sept. 1987), table 2.

32. For example, Jim Wellbeloved stood again in Erith and Crayford, which he had lost by only 920 votes in 1983. His vote slumped from 14,369 (34.9%) to 11,300 (25.3%). Similarly, Dickson Mabon stood again in Renfrewshire West and Inverclyde, which he had lost by 1,322 votes in 1983. His vote dropped from 12,347 (29.5%) to 9,669 (21.4%) in 1987. Both came third. The one exception was George Cunningham, who raised his vote from 35.3% to 38.1% in Islington South and Finsbury, partly by winning tactical support from Conservatives. But he failed, by two percentage points, to win the seat.

33. Crewe and Harrop (eds.), *Political Communications*, 54.

34. Crewe and Harrop (eds.), *Political Communications*, 55–6. David Owen later judged that 'it was not hard-hitting or dynamic enough', a fault he attributed to the constant need to compromise with the Liberals when making policy. See Owen, *Time to Declare*, 687.

35. It is worth noting that in the 1983 campaign Labour's support in the polls hovered around

the 33% mark until the Labour leadership's divisions over defence policy surfaced on 24–5 May. See the list of opinion polls in David Butler and Dennis Kavanagh, *The British General Election of 1983* (London: Macmillan, 1984), 125.

36. Owen had wanted to make it the main theme of the campaign from 1 June onwards but was persuaded to desist for a few days by the Campaign Committee. See Wilson, *Battle for Power*, 268.

37. Butler and Kavanagh's post-election survey of Alliance candidates found 'almost universal agreement . . . that the "dual leadership" was a disaster' (*The British General Election of 1987*, 232).

38. See his account in 'The Alliance Campaign', 57: 'I had lectured both leaders before the campaign about how to treat journalists, not that I thought it necessary. I had said, "journalists are not your friends. They are shits. Worse, they are professional shits: they are paid good money to be shits. So you must never, ever talk to them as though they are your lifelong buddies." '

39. Wilson, *Battle for Power*, 273.

40. Peter Jenkins, 'The Double Act that Polaris cannot Destroy', *Sunday Times*, 15 June 1986.

41. Support for the Alliance averaged 21% in polls conducted between 31 May and 2 June, just before the muddle about coalition emerged on 3 June. In polls conducted after 3 June, support for the Alliance averaged 21.5%. The proportion perceiving the Alliance as 'united' dropped suddenly on 21–2 May (when Owen and Steel were appearing together on television, but well before their public differences on coalition partners), but thereafter remained constant. See Miller *et al.*, *How Voters Change*, 157.

Chapter 20

1. See p. 319. David Owen sets out his own rationale for the SDP's continuing independence in his memoirs, *Time to Declare* (London: Michael Joseph, 1991), esp. 593–5.

2. 'Steel should Watch Shirley', *Observer*, 20 Sept. 1987.

3. In fact, as our analysis in ch. 19 suggests, there is no evidence to suggest they were right and a good deal to suggest they were wrong. The problems with the Alliance were problems within the Alliance, not in the relationship between the Alliance and the electorate.

4. Owen was wrong, as usual, to suspect (indeed be convinced of) the existence of a plot, but he was quite right to suppose that several senior Cowley Street officials, notably Dick Newby and Alec McGivan, were disposed to favour a merger of the two parties once the election was over. The origins of the Newby–Sainsbury phone call were straightforward. Newby had been told by John Pardoe, the campaign co-ordinator, that David Sainsbury had come to him to discuss the possibility of a federation of the two parties after the election. The idea was new to Newby and he thought it was awful: a Liberal–SDP federation would have the worst features of both a merged party and two non-merged parties. He phoned Sainsbury because he thought Sainsbury ought to be aware of his views. Had Newby been engaged in some deep-laid plot, it is unlikely that he would have alerted Sainsbury by making the call. Owen by the time of the 1987 election had developed a deep suspicion of some members of the Cowley Street staff and says of Newby in his memoirs (*Time to Declare*, 726) that 'for the last year or more I had virtually regarded [him] as a Liberal'. For Owen's account of the pre-polling day 'plotting', see *Time to Declare*, 697. For his account of the post-election Plymouth press conference, see pp. 707–8.

5. *Independent*, 13 June 1987.

6. Ibid.

7. Jenkins said: 'There is no alternative to a merger if the Alliance is to have a serious future.' He added: 'One leader is vital in any future campaign and two parties make it impossible to have one leader.' Williams called for an early ballot of the two parties' memberships and was said to favour Owen as the parliamentary leader of a merged party, with the Liberals providing a non-parliamentary president. Ashdown insisted the two parties could not continue 'this hybrid relationship without risking again the price we have paid'. Beith likewise maintained that a merged party must have one leader, one shadow cabinet and one principal policy-making body. See the reports in *Observer*, 14 June 1987.

8. For examples of the statements, see p. 319. A number of senior figures in the SDP insisted that they had heard Owen talking in similar terms on several occasions, even using the phrase 'when we merge' at private meetings.

9. *Guardian*, 15 June 1987.

10. National Committee Minutes, 15 June 1987.

11. *Independent, Guardian*, 16 June 1987.

12. *Independent*, 17 June 1987.

13. Ibid.

14. *Time to Declare*, 714. Owen says (p. 13) that in preparing his memorandum he 'consulted widely'; but he does not seem to have alerted his fellow MPs to the way his mind was working. Otherwise they would not have been so taken aback by the memorandum and so hostile to it.

15. At the 17 June meeting Owen also made a rather surprising concession. Presumably sensing that the mergerites' argument that the Alliance had suffered at the election from having two separate leaders was gaining ground, Owen agreed that at the next election the Alliance should have a single leader—provided that by that time the two Alliance parties had come to a full agreement on policy. See his account in *Time to Declare*, 715–16.

16. *Independent*, 16 June 1987.

17. David Steel, 'Joint Outlook', *Guardian*, 20 June 1987.

18. *Independent*, 13 June 1987.

19. *Sunday Times*, 28 June 1987.

20. See e.g. 'Owen Rules out Merger as Alliance Faces Split', *Sunday Times*, 21 June 1987: 'Finance is believed to be available for a breakaway SDP if the Owen camp loses the merger battle.'

21. John Cartwright, 'Shotgun Wedding Blues', *Guardian*, 18 June 1987.

22. Val Taylor, 'SDP MPs Hold back on Merger', *Social Democrat*, 19 June 1987.

23. *Sunday Times*, 28 June 1987.

24. Steve Bell depicted a continuing SDP as a 'Monster Raving Ego Party' in his strip cartoon in the *Guardian*, 29 June 1987.

25. For example, the *Independent* reported on 17 June 1987 that Liberals and Social Democrats in four Glamorgan seats, in Gravesend in Kent and in Bridlington in Yorkshire were forming single groups. In Wales there was already a joint Alliance headquarters in Cardiff.

26. *Guardian*, 25 June 1987.

27. Owen believed—and went on believing—that Humpty-Dumpty could be reconstructed. In his letter to rank-and-file Social Democrats he said that 'the Liberal–SDP Alliance must be preserved', and he concluded the letter by saying: 'I will remain a Social Democrat ready to work at some future date with Liberals to realign British politics' (*Sunday Times*, 28 June 1986). But the letter itself—which went on to insist that only Social Democrat pressure had prevented the Liberals selling the pass on such issues as the Falklands and the miners' dispute—caused considerable resentment and made it even less likely that the Liberal party would be prepared to work with him in the future.

28. National Committee Minutes, 29 June 1987.

29. Ibid.

30. *Sunday Times*, 28 June 1987. The SDP had taken a 'stand' over the Falklands in the sense that the party's MPs, including Jenkins and Williams, had followed Owen in backing Thatcher's

efforts to regain the islands from the Argentinians. In Owen's view, the Liberals had been more equivocal.

31. *Independent*, 30 June 1987.
32. In a sardonic column in the *Guardian* (30 June 1987) Hugo Young drew attention to the contradiction between Owen's insistence on 'the partnership approach' before and during the election campaign and the 'detestation of the Liberals and all they stand for' that he was now evincing. It was now emerging, Young wrote, that all of Owen's talk of partnership during the campaign had been not merely optimistic: 'It was a lie, perpetrated by a man who did not truly believe what he was saying.' Young continued: 'one look[s] back with gaping incredulity at the words he so piously said and the propaganda he was so willingly a part of for so long.' There was, he said, 'dishonesty at the heart of it'.
33. *Independent*, 3 July 1987.
34. David Steel, in all his public pronouncements at this stage, insisted that any party resulting from a merger between the Liberals and the SDP would be entirely new and that it would be the Liberals, with their long and distinguished history, who would, if anything, be making the greater sacrifice. See, for example, the reports of a press conference he gave on 1 July in the *Guardian* and the *Independent*, 2 July 1987.
35. On the 'Yes to Unity' campaign, see the detailed account in Robert Harris, 'The Doctor's Dilemma', *Observer*, 5 July 1987.
36. Both sides' statements were reprinted in full in *Independent*, 10 July 1987.
37. *Independent*, 9 July 1987.
38. *Independent*, 9 July 1987. Steel did everything within his power during this period to maintain the unity of his own party but also to influence developments within the SDP. He even used an Alliance party political broadcast for the purpose of urging rank-and-file SDP members to back a new merged party. The anti-merger forces were extremely displeased by Steel's readiness to intervene in another political party's internal affairs.
39. Robert Harris, 'The Doctor's Dilemma', *Observer*, 5 July 1987.
40. *Observer*, 5 July 1987.
41. *Independent*, 17 July 1987. The Electoral Reform Society produced a somewhat Delphic report on the matter, but it seemed to be clear that some area secretaries were co-operating with the 'Yes to Unity' campaign and were supplying it with the names and addresses of party members. Owen provides his account of these goings-on in *Time to Declare*, 725–6.
42. *Independent*, 1 July 1987.
43. Ibid.
44. *The Economist*, 4 July 1987.
45. *Independent*, 5 July 1987.
46. *Guardian*, 8 July 1987.
47. *Independent*, 8 July 1987.
48. *Guardian*, 10 July 1987.
49. *Observer*, 5 July 1987.
50. 10 July 1987.
51. 7 Aug. 1987.
52. *Guardian*, 11 July 1987.
53. *Observer*, 12 July 1987.
54. *Independent*, 13 July 1987.
55. Ibid.
56. Ibid.
57. Alan Travis, 'Charges Fly as SDP Debates Merger Issue', *Guardian*, 13 July 1987. With respect to this meeting and subsequent anti-merger rallies, the pro-mergerites suspected that anti-merger members of the party—and possibly non-members of the party—were being bussed in to swell the attendance.

58. Williams indicated that she would probably have to go at a pro-merger meeting in Nottingham (*Guardian*, 13 July 1987), but she did not indicate whether she would leave the SDP altogether if it refused to merge. Jenkins' remarks seemed to imply that he would leave and join the Liberals.
59. *The Times*, 7 Aug. 1987.
60. *Independent*, 7 Aug. 1987.
61. *Guardian*, 7 Aug. 1987.
62. *Independent*, 7 Aug. 1987.
63. Ibid.
64. *The Times*, 7 Aug. 1987.
65. *Independent*, 7 Aug. 1987.
66. Ibid.
67. *Guardian*, 7 Aug. 1987.
68. *Independent*, 8 Aug. 1987.
69. Ibid.
70. *Independent*, 14 Aug. 1987.
71. 21 Aug. 1987.
72. *Guardian*, 22 Aug. 1987.
73. 9 Aug. 1987.
74. *Observer*, 9 Aug. 1987.
75. 14 Aug. 1987.
76. *Guardian*, 14 Aug. 1987.
77. 10 Aug. 1987.
78. *Observer*, 16 Aug. 1987.
79. *Guardian*, 19 Aug. 1987.

Chapter 21

1. Owen in mid-August again called for an 'amicable separation'. 'I hope', he said, 'that the party will come to its senses and realise, sadly, that we are embarked on a divorce. There are those who are going to stay Social Democrats and those who wish to merge with the Liberals' (*Independent*, 21 Aug. 1987).
2. *Guardian, Independent*, 27 Aug. 1987. A brief statement issued afterwards said that the lunch had been pleasurable and that the two men intended to lunch together from time to time. They had no intention of allowing their personal relationship to be affected by what was happening between their parties.
3. Owen is quoted in *Independent*, 31 Aug. 1987, Jenkins in *Independent*, 1 Sept. 1987, Maclennan in *Independent*, 2 Sept. 1987.
4. *Guardian*, 1 Sept. 1987.
5. *Independent*, 1 Sept. 1987.
6. *Guardian*, 3 Sept. 1987.
7. *Guardian*, 1 Sept. 1987.
8. Ibid.
9. *Independent*, 31 Aug. 1987.
10. *Independent*, 1 Sept. 1987.
11. *Guardian*, 1 Sept. 1987.
12. *Independent*, 31 Aug. 1987.
13. *Independent*, 1 Sept. 1987.
14. Ibid.
15. At the Grassroots Uprising meeting Owen repudiated moves among his supporters to launch

a breakaway SDP immediately and urged all the party members to await the outcome of the merger negotiations and a second ballot before deciding whether to join the merged party or stay outside (*Independent*, 31 Aug. 1987). Cartwright the next day likewise insisted that nothing precipitate would be done and that the Owenites would await the outcome of the merger negotiations and the membership's verdict on them (*Guardian*, 1 Sept. 1987).

16. David McKie, 'Last Turn of the Knife for Disconsolate Owen', *Guardian*, 1 Sept. 1987.
17. *Guardian*, 2 Sept. 1987.
18. *Independent*, 2 Sept. 1987.
19. *Independent*, 2, 3 Sept. 1987.
20. The full teams comprised, for the Liberals, David Steel, Adrian Slade, Tim Clement-Jones, Alan Beith, Des Wilson, Michael Meadowcroft, Tony Greaves, Andrew Stunnell, Peter Knowlson, John MacDonald, Rachael Pitchford, Chris Mason, Sir Russell Johnston, Gwyn Griffiths and Geraint Howells and, for the SDP, Robert Maclennan, Shirley Williams, John Grant, Will Fitzgerald, Charles Kennedy, Dickson Mabon, Ian Wrigglesworth, Anne Sofer, Ben Stoneham, Frances David, Clive Lindley, Tom McNally, Lindsay Granshaw, Jane Padget and John Strak. The SDP team included five members who had voted for Option 1 and therefore against merger in the August ballot: Maclennan, Wrigglesworth, Grant, Mabon and Fitzgerald. For a collective profile of the two negotiating teams, see John Carvel, 'The Mixed Marriage Brokers', *Guardian*, 25 Sept. 1987. Tony Greaves and Rachael Pitchford have left their own account of the negotiations: *Merger: The Inside Story* (Colne: Liberal Renewal, 1989).
21. In a profile of Greaves published on 12 Sept. 1987 the *Independent* described him as having 'a notoriously bad temper' and as being 'very slow to praise and quick to criticise'.
22. On the one hand, the Liberals were convinced that Maclennan had nowhere else to go, that he had to agree to merger on whatever terms were on offer. On the other hand, Maclennan was evidently emotional and therefore unpredictable, and the Liberals knew it was in their interests to be circumspect and cautious.
23. John Carvel, 'Allies in Navel Engagement', *Guardian*, 17 Dec. 1987.
24. *Independent*, 4 Dec. 1987.
25. *Guardian*, 23 Dec. 1987. For a summary of the proposed constitution, see John Carvel, 'Dissent Mars Debut of Alliance Constitution', *Guardian*, 19 Dec. 1987.
26. *Independent*, 4 Sept. 1987.
27. For what it is worth, our view is that 'Alliance' would have been the best name. It was what the voters had grown used to; it had overtones of 'togetherness'; and it was appropriately vague (like the names of the Democratic and Republican parties in the United States). It even resonated with phrases like 'the Western alliance' and 'the Atlantic alliance'. The negotiators, however, do not appear to have been especially interested in mere voters. Their attention was turned inwards, into the two parties' internal politics. 'Alliance' would have had the additional advantage of being familiar yet at the same time connoting a clear break with the past.
28. The discussions over the initial policy document are reported in *Guardian*, 22 Oct. 1987, and *Guardian* and *Independent*, 29 Oct. 1987.
29. *Guardian*, 29 Oct. 1987.
30. *Independent*, 16 Nov. 1987.
31. *Guardian*, 24 Nov. 1987.
32. *Guardian*, 9, 10 Dec. 1987.
33. *Observer, Sunday Times*, 20 Dec. 1987. The Northampton meeting took place on the same day as Shirley Williams married Richard Neustadt, a professor at Harvard University. David Steel and all the other members of the original Gang of Four were invited to the wedding reception. The atmosphere was reasonably cordial, but the Owenites and mergerites sat somewhat self-consciously at separate tables.
34. Quoted in *Guardian, Independent*, 21 Dec. 1987, from an interview on BBC Radio 4's *The World this Weekend*.

35. Maclennan's 'Big Mac' nickname was reported in *Guardian*, 29 Oct. 1987.
36. Maclennan's views were reported in *Observer*, 13 Dec. He may still have been hoping that Owen could eventually be reconciled to a merged party. He may have wanted to ensure that SDP contenders—including possibly himself—had a reasonable chance in any leadership contest.
37. *Independent*, 3, 8 Dec. 1987.
38. *Independent*, 15, 21, 22 Dec. Grant was thoroughly fed up. In an article, 'Unworldly and unworthy Liberals', published in the *Independent* on 22 Dec. 1987, he referred to 'the continuing inability of the Liberals to jettison their futile role as a haven of protest in favour of a credible bid to achieve political power', and added: 'It is foolish for Mr Steel to pretend that a few Liberals may topple over the edge and all will be well. It is not some tiny lunatic fringe that is his problem. It is a substantial chunk of Liberal activist opinion. Those concerned are as deeply entrenched as Labour's Militant and will not go away.'
39. *Guardian*, 19 Dec. 1987.
40. *Guardian*, 17 Dec. 1987.
41. 22 Dec. 1987.
42. The figures were reported, in order, in *Observer*, 22 Nov. 1987; *Guardian*, 1 Dec. 1987; *Guardian* 30 Dec. 1987; and *Independent*, 11 Jan. 1988.
43. *Independent*, *Guardian*, 25 Sept. 1987. See also David Owen, *Sticking With It* (London: Social Democratic Publications, n.d.).
44. *Guardian*, 14 Oct. 1987. Andrew Rawnsley, in his *Guardian* account of a Campaign for Social Democracy rally in Finsbury Town Hall ('The Loneliness of the Long Distance Messiah', 15 Oct. 1987), noted that Owen was 'about to talk about the fifth force in British politics—himself' and that slips of paper on each seat in the hall invited support for the CSD—'the Campaign for Social Democracy to them, the Campaign to Save the Doctor to everybody else.' Photographs of Owen alternated around the hall and were then multiplied in gilt-edged mirrors, 'casting reflection upon reflection until there seem to be a hundred David Owens inside the hall'.
45. *Independent*, 23 Nov. 1987.
46. *Guardian*, 22 Sept. 1987. See also the National Committee Minutes, 21 Sept. 1987, and a fuller account that appeared in *Independent* on 22 Sept. Shirley Williams found herself in a difficult position. On the one hand, she was the party's president and, as such, expected to preside in a neutral way over National Committee meetings and meetings of the Council for Social Democracy. On the other hand, she was personally convinced that merger was the right thing to do and, once the August 1987 ballot results were known, had a duty to represent the views of the majority of party members. Trying to play both roles at once was not easy. Pro-mergerites claimed that the Owenites, instead of sympathizing with Williams' difficult position, exploited it and went out of their way to make difficulties for her. One described the 21 Sept. meeting as 'like something out of *Darkness at Noon*'. Another said the Owenites' behaviour resembled the kind of thing that used to go on in the American Teamsters' Union. For their part, the Owenites maintained that Williams was abusing her position as president to further the mergerites' aims rather than to keep the party of which she was president in being.
47. *Guardian*, 20 Oct. 1987.
48. *Independent*, 20 Oct. 1987.
49. *Independent*, 1 Dec. 1987.
50. Ibid.
51. The following account is based largely on interviews with most of the major participants in the episode but also on Robert Harris's excellent—and very well-informed—article in *Observer*, 17 Jan. 1988, 'The Day it All Ended in Tears'.
52. 17 Jan. 1988 (see n. 51).
53. See e.g. Michael Jones, 'The Misalliance', *Sunday Times*, 17 Jan. 1988. Jones wrote that Beith's

'final denunciation of the policy statement [was] described by the SDP leadership as "serpen-tine". The motive attributed by the SDP and senior Liberals alike is that Beith realised Steel could be so hurt by the SDP-inspired policy package that he would be pressured to resign and make way for . . . well, Beith, for example.'

54. Full summaries of *Voices and Choices* appeared in *Guardian* and *Independent*, 14 Jan. 1988.

55. John Carvel, 'Countdown to Chaos as Last-Minute Talks Falter', *Guardian*, 14 Jan. 1988. Another good account of the final negotiating session is Colin Hughes, 'Stormy Night that Ended in Disaster', *Independent*, 14 Jan. 1988. Hughes quotes a Liberal as saying that Maclen-nan 'seemed to go completely off the rails. He no longer seemed to be in control.'

56. A measure of how unexpected the ensuing developments were was that, quite late the follow-ing morning (Tuesday), Sir Russell Johnston did a pre-recorded BBC Radio Scotland interview in which he welcomed the document and praised it as though nothing were amiss (which, so far as Johnston knew, was true). The interview was actually broadcast.

57. *Guardian*, 13 Jan. 1988. The Liberal activist was Janice Lennon, leader of the minority group on Bedfordshire County Council and a member of the Liberals' national executive.

58. Some Liberals subsequently convinced themselves that the early circulation of *Voices and Choices* had been a deliberate leak in order to bounce the Liberals into accepting the SDP's position. There is no evidence to substantiate this view, and all the available accounts tell against it. As so often, the cock-up theory seems infinitely more plausible than the conspiracy theory.

59. Almost all those involved on the SDP side thought that Kennedy had devoted a great deal of time and emotional energy to sustaining Maclennan during the whole 'dead-parrot' episode. Some described Kennedy as Maclennan's 'shrink' and wondered whether Maclennan could have got through without him. Robert Harris provides a vivid description of the meeting between Maclennan, Kennedy and the Liberal MPs in 'The Day it All Ended in Tears', *Observer*, 17 Jan. 1988.

60. *Independent*, 14 Jan. 1988.

61. Not all the calls were critical of *Voices and Choices*. Some callers wanted to say how much they approved of its boldness and courage. They were impressed by Maclennan and his colleagues' willingness to think the unthinkable. A few who were opposed to merger even went so far as to say they would join the merged party—or, rather, would have joined it—if the document had been accepted.

62. *Independent*, 15 Jan. 1988.

63. *Guardian*, 19 Jan. 1988.

64. *The Times*, 15 Jan. 1988.

65. *Independent*, 19 Jan. 1988.

66. John Grant published a detailed account of the episode under the headline 'False Pretences', *Sunday Times*, 7 Feb. 1988. David Owen tells the story from his point of view in *Time to Declare*, 737–8. What Maclennan said to Grant in the course of three telephone conversations during the day is unknown, but Grant certainly got the impression that Maclennan had changed his mind.

67. No one will ever know what Maclennan would have done if Owen had done a volte-face and agreed to join him in mounting a combined 'no-to-merger' campaign. One can only imagine that by this time Maclennan would have been sorely tempted to wash his hands of the whole merger exercise and to see whether the SDP could not perhaps, after all, be kept together.

68. *Observer*, 24 Jan. 1988.

69. Of the Liberals' 101,084 members, only 52,867 (52.3%) voted. Of these 46,376 (87.9%) voted in favour of merger while 6,365 (12.1%) voted against. A small number, 126, indicated on their ballots that they were abstaining (*Independent*, 3 Mar. 1988). In all, only 45.9% of the Liberal party's members voted to support merger.

70. *Sunday Times*, 31 Jan. 1988.

71. *The Times*, 1 Feb. 1988.
72. Of the SDP's 52,086 members, only 28,908 (55.5%) voted. Of these, 18,722 (65.3%) voted in favour of merger while 9,929 (34.7%) voted against. A small number, 125, indicated that they were abstaining, while 132 spoiled their ballot papers. In the end, a total of only 35.9% voted for merger. Nearly twice as many, 64.1% either did not vote or voted against. Some of those who abstained probably did so because they were sure that merger was going to pass and did not mind. Even so, the membership's lack of positive enthusiasm for merger was evident. A postal survey of former members of the SDP, conducted several years later, found that former Labour and Liberal supporters among the SDP's rank and file were considerably more likely to have voted for merger than former Conservative supporters. See David Denver and Hugh Bochel, 'Merger or Bust: Whatever Happened to Members of the SDP?', *British Journal of Political Science*, 24 (1994), 409.

Chapter 23

1. There have been quite a few minor and breakaway parties in the twentieth century, most of them on the left. Sir Oswald Mosley's New party, formed in February 1931 by six Labour MPs, won considerable backing from press and intellectual circles but failed to take a single seat (it fought twenty-four) in the general election eight months later. In August 1931 the then Labour prime minister, Ramsay MacDonald, took a small group of colleagues into the Conservative-dominated National coalition. Thirteen of his National Labour candidates were elected at the 1931 general election and eight were elected in 1935, but all of them had Conservative backing. The Independent Labour party (ILP) disaffiliated from Labour in August 1932, won four seats (all in Glasgow) in 1935 and three in 1945 and rejoined the mainstream Labour party in 1947. A radical middle-class party of Liberal and Labour supporters, Common Wealth, was formed in July 1942. It won three Conservative seats at by-elections before the end of the war, but only because Labour withdrew its candidate under the terms of the wartime political truce. It fought no seats after the war. In 1975 two Scottish Labour MPs, Jim Sillars and John Robertson, resigned from the Labour party to form the Scottish Labour party; but both lost their seats at the 1979 general election and the party was wound up shortly afterwards. None of these tiny parties came anywhere near posing a threat, even briefly, to the existing two-party system. For a catalogue of minor British parties in the twentieth century, and brief notes on the more important of them, see David Butler and Gareth Butler, *British Political Facts 1900–1994*, 7th edn. (London: Macmillan, 1994), 157–67.
2. For detailed evidence see, in addition to ch. 16 above, Ivor Crewe, Bo Särlvik and James Alt, 'Partisan Dealignment in Britain 1964–1974', *British Journal of Political Science*, 7 (1977), 129–90, and Ivor Crewe, 'The Electorate: Partisan Dealignment Ten Years On', in Hugh Berrington (ed.), *Change in British Politics* (London: Frank Cass, 1984), 183–215.
3. See p. 285.
4. That said, the initial advances made by the centre parties from 1982 onwards undoubtedly contributed to the Liberal Democrats' much more substantial presence in local government in the 1990s. For example, see the impressive figures, which attest to the Liberal Democrats' advance, cited on p. 474.
5. See Patricia Lee Sykes, *Losing from the Inside: The Cost of Conflict in the British Social Democratic Party*, 2nd edn. (New Brunswick, NJ: Transaction, 1988). Sykes' thesis is implicit in her title and subtitle. The thesis is, however, not spelled out in any detail, and the author does not set her explanation against other possible explanations.
6. In this connection it is significant that, while support for the Liberals remained steady in the opinion polls in 1981–2, support for the SDP fluctuated. It seems that at that stage it

was the current popularity of the SDP that largely determined the current popularity of the Alliance.

7. This is a maximum estimate based on the generous assumption that all Alliance voters in 1983 would have voted Liberal had the SDP never been formed. Of the 14% of respondents to a BBC/Gallup survey who seriously considered voting for the Alliance, or who had actually voted for it at a local election or in a by-election, but decided against doing so at the general election, only 8%—that is, a mere 1.1% of all voters—said that they would have voted Liberal but for its link with the SDP. See Ivor Crewe, 'How to Win a Landslide without Really Trying: Why the Conservatives Won in 1983', in Austin Ranney (ed.), *Britain at the Polls, 1983: A Study of the General Election* (Durham, NC: Duke University Press/American Enterprise Institute, 1985), 194.

8. In 1987 27% of respondents told a BBC–Gallup election-day survey that they had seriously considered voting for the Alliance or had actually voted for it in the past but had decided not to do so at the general election. Of this 27%, 23%—that is, 6% of all voters—gave as their reason that 'it was unclear who leads the Alliance'. See Ivor Crewe, 'Why Mrs Thatcher was Returned with a Landslide', *Social Studies Review*, 3 (1987), 2–9.

9. See David Owen, *Time to Declare* (London: Michael Joseph, 1991), esp. 515–18.

10. See Crewe, 'How to Win a Landslide without Really Trying', 194.

11. For an example of a Conservative advocating this view, see Ronald Butt, 'The SDP's Problem', *Sunday Times*, 10 Oct. 1981.

12. In this connection the SDP suffered from a 'spiral of inertia', especially, but not only, after the initial efflux of Labour MPs to the new party in 1981 and early 1982. Friendly union leaders would only have come across and tried to take their unions across, and sympathetic council leaders would only have come across and tried to bring other councillors across, if many more MPs had defected; and large numbers of MPs were naturally not prepared to defect unless the trade-union leaders and councillors came over first. There is no reason whatever to think that many more senior figures in the labour movement would have joined the SDP in its first year or two simply because—and if—the Gang of Four had announced that what they were forming was meant to be a Mark II Labour party. What mattered in 1981–2 was not words but action—and sufficient action was not forthcoming. To have created a Mark II Labour party would have required a split in the existing Labour party on a much larger scale than actually took place—and it was simply not within the power of the Gang of Four or their followers to engineer a split on that kind of scale.

13. It is worth noting in this connection that, despite the well-publicized differences of emphasis between Owen and Steel, the Alliance's standing in the opinion polls remained serenely stable throughout the 1987 campaign. It averaged 21% between 31 May and 2 June, just before the muddle about coalition emerged on 3 June, and then 21.5% in the polls conducted after that. The proportion perceiving the Alliance as 'united' did drop suddenly on 21–2 May when Owen and Steel were appearing together on television (but well before their public differences on whom they would prefer to have as a coalition partner); but from 21–2 May onwards it, too, remained largely constant. See William Miller *et al.*, *How Voters Change: The 1987 British Election Campaign in Perspective* (Oxford: Clarendon Press, 1991), 157.

14. See Fig. 2.

15. One other possible exception is the National Progressive party in Canada, which at its first election in 1921 took 22.9% of the popular vote and sixty-four seats to become the second largest party in the Canadian parliament; but thereafter it steadily declined and by the early 1930s had disappeared altogether. In the United States, independent or third-party candidates for the presidency have occasionally secured more than 10% of the popular vote— notably Theodore Roosevelt in 1912 (27%), Robert La Follette in 1924 (17%), George Wallace in 1968 (14%) and Ross Perot in 1992 (19%)—but none of these four subsequently repeated their relative success and none succeeded in translating his personal popularity into seats

in Congress. Among centrist third parties, the most successful apart from the British Liberal party has been the New Zealand Social Credit party, which took 21% of the popular vote and two seats (in a parliament of ninety-five) in 1981. Canada's New Democratic party has frequently taken 15–20% of the vote since its formation in 1968, but it is, in most provinces at least, a left-wing social-democratic party rather than a true centre party.

16. On the rise of the Labour party and its displacement of the Liberals, see Henry Pelling, *A Short History of the Labour Party*, 8th edn. (London: Macmillan, 1985), chs. 2–3; Charles Loch Mowat, *Britain between the Wars 1918–1940* (London: Methuen, 1955), *passim*; Ross McKibbin, *The Evolution of the Labour Party, 1910–1924* (Oxford: Oxford University Press, 1974); Trevor Wilson, *The Downfall of the Liberal Party 1914–35* (London: Collins, 1966); Martin Pugh, *The Making of Modern British Politics 1867–1939* (Oxford: Blackwell, 1982), 64–86; Alan R. Ball, *British Political Parties: The Emergence of a Modern Party System* (London: Macmillan, 1981), 255–63; Duncan Tanner, 'Elections, Statistics and the Rise of the Labour Party, 1906–1931', *Historical Journal*, 34 (1991), 893–908; Duncan Tanner, 'The Parliamentary Electoral System, the "Fourth" Reform Act and the Rise of Labour in England and Wales', *Bulletin of the Institute of Historical Research*, 56 (1983–4), 205–19; H. C. G. Matthew, R. I. McKibbin and J. A. Kay, 'The Franchise Factor in the Rise of the Labour Party', *English Historical Review*, 91 (1976), 723–52; Chris Chamberlain, 'The Growth of Support for the Labour Party in Britain', *British Journal of Sociology*, 24 (1973), 474–89; Chris Cook, *The Age of Alignment: Electoral Politics in Britain 1922–1929* (London: Macmillan, 1975); and David Butler and Donald Stokes, *Political Change in Britain: The Evolution of Electoral Choice*, 2nd edn. (London: Macmillan, 1974), chs. 7–8.

17. See p. 115.

18. On the size of the total eligible electorate at the general elections from 1910 to 1929, see Butler and Butler, *British Political Facts*, 214–15.

19. The Liberals won 43.9% of the vote at the general election of December 1910, but by the time the divided party came together again in 1923 its share had fallen to 29.6%. In 1924 it fell to 17.6%, and in 1929 it recovered, but only partially, to 23.4%. The figures are contained in Butler and Butler, *British Political Facts*, 214–15.

20. Steel made the comment several times in the course of radio and television interviews.

21. According to a survey conducted several years later, 41% of those who had belonged to the SDP in 1987 declined to join the new party at the time of the merger and by the time of the 1992 general election an additional proportion, roughly 26%, had ceased to be members of any party. See David Denver and Hugh Bochel, 'Merger or Bust: Whatever Happened to Members of the SDP?', *British Journal of Political Science*, 24 (1994), 403–17. Further evidence of the political destinations (if any) of the former members of the SDP can be found in Wolfgang Rüdig, John Curtice and Lynn G. Berrie, 'Social Democrats, Liberals and Liberal Democrats: The Dynamics of Centre Party Membership', Report of Research Activities and Results to the Economic and Social Research Council (July 1994).

22. See Robert Shepherd, *Iain Macleod* (London: Hutchinson, 1994), esp. ch. 4, and C. A. R. Crosland, *The Future of Socialism* (London: Jonathan Cape, 1956).

23. Denis Healey, *The Time of my Life* (London: Michael Joseph, 1989), 480.

24. William Rodgers, 'What Happened to the SDP and What could Still Happen', *London Review of Books*, 7 Feb. 1991.

25. For details see the main document that emanated from the Labour policy review: *Meet the Challenge, Make the Change* (London: Labour Party, 1989).

26. On the sources of the post-1987 changes in Labour policy, see Colin Hughes and Patrick Wintour, *Labour Rebuilt: The New Model Party* (London: Fourth Estate, 1990). The authors refer to the SDP only occasionally and in passing.

27. Largely as a result of the merger row, the combined level of support for the Liberal and Social Democratic parties—no longer the Alliance—fell from 23.7% (in Great Britain) at the 1987

general election to 17.5% in the following month's polls and then to an average of only 15% during the rest of the year. In the June 1989 elections to the European Parliament, the new merged party, the Social and Liberal Democrats, secured only 6.4% of the vote in Britain and finished fourth behind the Greens.
28. The Liberal party on its own won 14.1% of the vote at the May 1979 general election. In 1979 its average support in the polls stood at 12% and in 1980 at 13%. In 1991 the average support for the new merged party in the Gallup Poll was 16%.

Figure Notes and Sources

Fig. 1. *Source*: *Gallup Political Index*.

Fig. 2. *Source*: *Gallup Political Index*.

Fig. 3. *Source*: authors' calculations.

Fig. 4. *Note*: The survey of Scottish SDP activists recorded an average self-placement of 4.1, i.e. to the left of Doring's SDP activists attending the 1982 council. See John Bochel and David Denver, 'The SDP and the Left–Right Dimension', *British Journal of Political Science*, 14 (1984), fig. 1, p. 388.

Sources: SDP members: David Goodman and David Hine, 'The SDP in Newcastle upon Tyne: A Survey-Based Analysis' (paper presented to the conference of the Political Studies Association, University of Kent, 1982), table 10, p. 18. Activists (all four parties): Terry Barton and Herbert Doring, 'Social Mobility and the Changing British Party System' (paper presented to the conference of the Political Studies Association, University of Southampton, 1984), table 8, p. 36.

Fig. 5. *Note*: The question was: 'In political matters people talk of "the left" and "the right". How would you place your views on this scale? And whereabouts on this scale would you place the —— party?' The scale read: 'Far left, substantially left, moderately left, slightly left, middle of the road [if volunteered by respondent], slightly right, moderately right, substantially right, far right', and for this table was scored 1, 2, 3, 4, 5, 6, 7, 8 and 9. Mean scores were calculated for each poll, and a mean of means for the three polls together. 'Don't knows', who typically amounted to about 15 per cent for self-placement, 20 per cent for the placement of the two major parties, 30 per cent for the placement of the Liberals and 35 per cent for the SDP, were excluded. The Gallup breakdowns did not distinguish between 'SDP' and 'Alliance' voters.

Source: Unpublished breakdowns, Gallup polls, 2–7 July 1986, 29 April–4 May 1987 and 18–22 June 1987.

Fig. 6. *Source*: *Gallup Political Index*.

Bibliography

• • • •

[Short articles in daily and weekly newspapers are excluded.]

ALLEN, WILLIAM S., *The Nazi Seizure of Power: The Experience of a Single German Town, 1930–35* (Chicago: Quadrangle Books, 1965).

AXFORD, BARRIE, and MADGWICK, PETER, 'Television News Monitoring Project, April–June 1986: Second Report' (unpublished paper, Oxford Polytechnic, 1986).

BAKER, BLAKE, *The Far Left: An Exposé of the Extreme Left in Britain* (London: Weidenfeld & Nicolson, 1981).

BALL, ALAN, *British Political Parties: The Emergence of a Modern Party System* (London: Macmillan, 1981).

BARTON, TERRY, and DORING, HERBERT, 'Social Mobility and the Changing British Party System' (paper presented to the conference of the Political Studies Association, University of Southampton, 1984).

—— —— 'The Social and Attitudinal Profile of Social Democratic Activists: Note on a Survey of the 1982 Council for Social Democracy', *Political Studies*, 34 (1986), 296–305.

BARTRAM, PETER, *David Steel: His Life and Politics* (London: W. H. Allen, 1981).

BBC/ITN Guide to the New Parliamentary Constituencies (Chichester: Parliamentary Research Services, 1983).

BBC TV, *Local Election Handbook* (London: BBC, 1983, 1984, 1985, 1986, 1987 and 1988).

BEER, SAMUEL, *Britain against Itself: The Political Contradictions of Collectivism* (London: Faber and Faber, 1982).

BENN, TONY, *Arguments for Democracy*, ed. Chris Mullin (London: Jonathan Cape, 1979).

—— *Arguments for Socialism* (London: Jonathan Cape, 1979).

—— *Out of the Wilderness: Diaries 1963–1967* (London: Hutchinson, 1987).

—— *Office without Power: Diaries 1968–1972* (London: Hutchinson, 1988).

—— *Against the Tide: Diaries 1973–1976* (London: Hutchinson, 1989).

—— *Conflicts of Interest: Diaries 1977–1980* (London: Hutchinson, 1990).

—— *The End of an Era: Diaries 1980–1990* (London: Hutchinson, 1990).

BERRINGTON, HUGH, 'The Labour Left in Parliament: Maintenance, Erosion and Renewal', in Kavanagh (ed.), *The Politics of the Labour Party* (1982), 69–94.

—— (ed.) *Change in British Politics* (London: Frank Cass, 1984).

BLUMLER, JAY, GUREVITCH, MICHAEL, and NOSSITER, T. J., 'Setting the Television News Agenda: Campaign Observation at the BBC' in Crewe and Harrop (eds.), *Political Communications* (1986), 104–24.

BOCHEL, JOHN, and DENVER, DAVID, 'The SDP and the Left–Right Dimension', *British Journal of Political Science*, 14 (1984), 386–92.

BOGDANOR, VERNON (ed.), *Liberal Party Politics* (Oxford: Oxford University Press, 1983).

BOYLE, ALLEN E., 'Political Broadcasting, Fairness and Administrative Law', *Public Law* (1986), 562–96.

BRADLEY, IAN, *Breaking the Mould? The Birth and Prospects of the Social Democratic Party* (London: Martin Robertson, 1981).

—— 'The SDP Mould', *New Society*, 27 Jan. 1983.

BULLOCK, ALAN, *The Life and Times of Ernest Bevin*, ii. *Minister of Labour, 1940–45* (London: Heinemann, 1967).

BUTLER, DAVID, and BUTLER, GARETH, *British Political Facts 1900–1985*, 6th edn. (London: Macmillan, 1986).

—— —— *British Political Facts 1900–1994*, 7th edn. (London: Macmillan, 1994).

BUTLER, DAVID, and JOWETT, PAUL, *Party Strategies in Britain: A Study of the 1984 European Elections* (London: Macmillan, 1985).

BUTLER, DAVID, and KAVANAGH, DENNIS, *The British General Election of February 1974* (London: Macmillan, 1974).

—— —— *The British General Election of 1979* (London: Macmillan, 1980).

—— —— *The British General Election of 1983* (London: Macmillan, 1984).

—— —— *The British General Election of 1987* (London: Macmillan, 1988).

—— and KING, ANTHONY, *The British General Election of 1964* (London: Macmillan, 1965).

—— and PINTO-DUSCHINSKY, MICHAEL, *The British General Election of 1970* (London: Macmillan, 1971).

—— and STOKES, DONALD, *Political Change in Britain: The Evolution of Electoral Choice*, 2nd edn. (London: Macmillan, 1974).

CACI Market Analysis Group, *ACORN: A New Approach to Market Analyses* (London: CACI Inc., n.d., *c.*1979).

CALLAGHAN, JAMES, *Time and Chance* (London: Collins, 1987).

CALLAGHAN, JOHN, *The Far Left in British Politics* (Oxford: Basil Blackwell, 1987).

CAMPBELL, JOHN, *Roy Jenkins: A Biography* (London: Weidenfeld & Nicolson, 1983).

—— *Edward Heath: A Biography* (London: Jonathan Cape, 1993).

CARROLL, ROGER, 'The Alliance's Non-Advertising Campaign', in Crewe and Harrop (eds.), *Political Communications* (1989), 87–92.

CATTERALL, PETER, *Contemporary Britain: An Annual Review 1990* (Oxford: Basil Blackwell for the Institute of Contemporary History, 1990).

CHAMBERLAIN, CHRIS, 'The Growth of Support for the Labour Party in Britain', *British Journal of Sociology*, 24 (1973), 474–89.

CLARKE, HAROLD, MISHLER, WILLIAM and WHITELEY, PAUL, 'Recapturing the Falklands: Models of Conservative Popularity, 1979–83', *British Journal of Political Science*, 20 (1990), 63–81.

CLARKE, PETER, *Liberals and Social Democrats* (Cambridge: Cambridge University Press, 1978).

CLEMENS, JOHN, 'The Telephone Poll Bogeyman: A Case Study in Election Paranoia', in Crewe and Harrop (eds.), *Political Communications* (1986), 254–64.

COATES, DAVID, *The Labour Party and the Struggle for Socialism* (Cambridge: Cambridge University Press, 1975).

—— *Labour in Power? A Study of the Labour Government, 1974–1979* (London: Longman, 1980).

COCKS, MICHAEL, *Labour and the Benn Factor* (London: Macdonald, 1989).

COOK, CHRIS, *The Age of Alignment: Electoral Politics in Britain, 1922–1929* (London: Macmillan, 1975).

COSGROVE, PATRICK, *Thatcher, The First Term* (London: Bodley Head, 1985).

CRAIG, F. W. S., *Conservative and Labour Party Conference Decisions, 1945–81* (Chichester: Parliamentary Research Services, 1982).

—— *Chronology of British Parliamentary By-elections 1933–1987* (Chichester, Sussex: Parliamentary Research Services, 1987).

—— *British Electoral Facts* (Aldershot: Parliamentary Research Services and Gower, 1989).

—— *British General Election Manifestos 1959–1987* (Aldershot: Parliamentary Research Services, 1990).

CREWE, IVOR, 'Why the Conservatives Won', in Penniman (ed.), *Britain at the Polls, 1979* (1981), 263–305.

—— 'Is Britain's Two-Party System Really about to Crumble?', *Electoral Studies*, 1 (1982), 275–313.

—— 'How to Win a Landslide without Really Trying: Why the Conservatives Won in 1983', in Ranney (ed.), *Britain at the Polls, 1983* (1985), 155–96.

—— 'The Electorate: Partisan Dealignment Ten Years On', in Berrington (ed.), *Change in British Politics* (1984), 183–215.

—— 'Great Britain', in Crewe and Denver (eds.), *Electoral Change in Western Democracies* (1985), 100–50.

—— 'Why Mrs Thatcher was Returned with a Landslide', *Social Studies Review*, 3 (1987), 2–9.

—— and DENVER, DAVID (eds.), *Electoral Change in Western Democracies* (London: Croom Helm, 1985).

—— and HARROP, MARTIN (eds.), *Political Communications: The General Election Campaign of 1983* (Cambridge: Cambridge University Press, 1986).

—— —— *Political Communications: The General Election Campaign of 1987* (Cambridge: Cambridge University Press, 1989).

CREWE, IVOR, DAY, NEIL, and FOX, ANTHONY, *The British Electorate, 1963–1987* (Cambridge: Cambridge University Press, 1991).

—— SÄRLVIK, BO, and ALT, JAMES, 'Partisan Dealignment in Britain, 1964–1974', *British Journal of Political Science*, 7 (1977), 129–90.

CRIDDLE, BYRON, 'Candidates', in Butler and Kavanagh, *The British General Election of 1983* (1984), 219–44.

—— 'Candidates', in Butler and Kavanagh, *The British General Election of 1987* (1988), 191–210.

CRITCHLEY, JULIAN, *A Bag of Boiled Sweets: An Autobiography* (London: Faber and Faber, 1994).

CROSLAND, C. A. R., *The Future of Socialism* (London: Jonathan Cape, 1956).

CROSLAND, SUSAN, *Tony Crosland* (London: Jonathan Cape, 1982).

CURTICE, JOHN, 'Liberal Voters and the Alliance: Realignment or Protest?', in Bogdanor (ed.), *Liberal Party Politics* (1983), 99–122.

—— 'Analysis', in Butler and Kavanagh, *The British General Election of 1983* (1984), 333–73.

—— 'Interim Report: Party Politics', in Roger Jowell, Sharon Witherspoon and Lindsay Brook (eds.), *British Social Attitudes: The 1987 Report* (Aldershot: Gower, 1987), 171–86.

—— and STEED, MICHAEL, 'Turning Dreams into Reality: The Division of Constituencies between the Liberals and the Social Democrats', *Parliamentary Affairs*, 36 (1983), 166–82.

—— 'Analysis', in Butler and Kavanagh, *The British General Election of 1987* (1988), 316–62.

—— PAYNE, CLIVE and WALLER, ROBERT, 'The Alliance's First Nationwide Test: Lessons of the 1982 English Local Elections', *Electoral Studies*, 2 (1983), 3–22.

DALYELL, TAM, *Devolution: The End of Britain* (London: Cape, 1977).

DE MONT, ALEX, *A Theory of the Social Market* (London: Tawney Society, 1984).

DENVER, DAVID, 'The SDP–Liberal Alliance: The End of the Two-Party System?', in Berrington (ed.), *Change in British Politics* (1984), 75–102.

—— *Elections and Voting Behaviour in Britain* (Hemel Hempstead: Philip Allan, 1989).

—— and BOCHEL, HUGH, 'Merger or Bust: Whatever Happened to Members of the SDP?', *British Journal of Political Science*, 24 (1994), 403–17.

DESAI, RADHIKA, *Intellectuals and Socialism: 'Social Democrats' and the Labour Party* (London: Lawrence & Wishart, 1994).

DORING, HERBERT, 'Who are the Social Democrats?', *New Society*, 8 Sept. 1983.

DRUCKER, H. M., *Doctrine and Ethos in the Labour Party* (London: Allen & Unwin, 1979).

—— 'All the King's Horses and All the King's Men: The SDP in Britain', in Paterson and Thomas (eds.), *The Future of Social Democracy* (1986), 108–26.

DUNLEAVY, PATRICK, and HUSBANDS, CHRISTOPHER, *British Democracy at the Crossroads* (London: George Allen & Unwin, 1985).

Edinburgh University Politics Group, 'Learning to Fight Multi-Party Elections: The Lessons of Hillhead', *Parliamentary Affairs*, 35 (1982), 252–66.

EVANS, HAROLD, *Good Times, Bad Times* (London: Weidenfeld & Nicolson, 1983).

FISHMAN, NINA and SHAW, ANDREW, 'TV87: The Campaign to Make Tactical Voting Make Votes Count', in Crewe and Harrop (eds.), *Political Communications* (1989), 289–303.

FLOWER, TONY, *Parties in the News* (London: Tawney Society, 1983).

FRANKLIN, BOB, 'Television and the House of Lords' (Leeds: University of Leeds Centre for Television Research, 1986).

GALLUP, GEORGE H., *The Gallup International Public Opinion Polls: Great Britain, 1937–1975* (New York: Random House, 1976).

GIDDENS, ANTHONY, and MACKENZIE, GAVIN (eds.), *Social Class and the Division of Labour: Essays in Honour of Ilya Neustadt* (Cambridge: Cambridge University Press, 1982).

GOLDTHORPE, JOHN, 'On the Service Class, its Formation and Future', in Giddens and Mackenzie (eds.), *Social Class and the Division of Labour* (1982), 162–85.

GOODMAN, DAVID, and HINE, DAVID, 'The SDP in Newcastle upon Tyne: A Survey-Based Analysis' (paper presented to the conference of the Political Studies Association, University of Kent, 1982).

GREAVES, ANTHONY, and PITCHFORD, RACHAEL, *Merger: The Inside Story* (Colne: Liberal Renewal, 1989).

GUNTER, BARRIE, SVENNEVIG, MICHAEL, and WOBER, MALLORY, *Television Coverage of the 1983 General Election* (Aldershot: Gower, 1986).

HALSEY, A. H. (ed.), *British Social Trends since 1900* (London: Macmillan, 1988).

HASELER, STEPHEN, *The Gaitskellites* (London: Macmillan, 1969).

HARRISON, MARTIN, 'Broadcasting', in Butler and Kavanagh, *The British General Election of February 1974* (1974), 147–74.

HARROP, MARTIN, 'Press', in Butler and Kavanagh, *The British General Election of 1983* (1984), 175–218.

HARROP, MARTIN, 'The Press and Post-war Elections', in Crewe and Harrop (eds.), *Political Communications* (1986), 137–49.

—— 'Press', in Butler and Kavanagh, *The British General Election of 1987* (1988), 163–90.

—— and MILLER, WILLIAM, *Elections and Voters: A Comparative Introduction* (London: Macmillan, 1987).

HATFIELD, MICHAEL, *The House the Left Built: Inside Labour Policymaking, 1970–75* (London: Victor Gollancz, 1978).

HATTERSLEY, ROY, *A Yorkshire Boyhood* (London: Chatto and Windus and The Hogarth Press, 1983).

HEALEY, DENIS, *The Time of my Life* (London: Michael Joseph, 1989).

HEATH, ANTHONY, JOWELL, ROGER, and CURTICE, JOHN, *How Britain Votes* (Oxford: Oxford University Press, 1985).

—— 'The Emerging Alliance Voter', *New Society*, 13 Sept. 1985.

HETHERINGTON, ALASTAIR, 'Miners and the Media', *Listener*, 17 Jan. 1985.

HODGSON, GEOFFREY, *Labour at the Crossroads: The Political and Economic Challenge to the Labour Party in the 1980s* (Oxford: Martin Robertson, 1981).

HOGGART, SIMON, *Back on the House* (London: Robson Books, 1982).

HUGHES, COLIN, and WINTOUR, PATRICK, *Labour Rebuilt: The New Model Party* (London: Fourth Estate, 1990).

HOWELL, DAVID, *British Social Democracy: A Study in Development and Decay* (London: Croom Helm, 1976).

HURD, DOUGLAS, *An End to Promises: Sketch of a Government, 1970–74* (London: Collins, 1979).

INGLE, S. J., *The Alliance: Piggy in the Middle or Radical Alternative?* (Hull Papers in Politics, No. 38; Hull: Department of Politics, University of Hull, 1985).

JENKINS, HUGH, *Rank and File* (London: Croom Helm, 1980).

JENKINS, PETER, *The Battle of Downing Street* (London: Charles Knight, 1970).

—— *Mrs Thatcher's Revolution: The Ending of the Socialist Era* (London: Jonathan Cape, 1987).

JENKINS, ROY, *Asquith* (London: Collins, 1964).

—— *What Matters Now* (London: Collins/Fontana, 1972).

—— *European Diary 1977–1981* (London: Collins, 1989).

—— *A Life at the Centre* (London: Macmillan, 1991).

JOHNSTON, R. J., 'A Further Look at British Political Finance', *Political Studies*, 34 (1986), 466–73.

—— PATTIE, C. J., and JOHNSTON, L. C. 'The Impact of Constituency Spending on the Result of the 1987 British General Election', *Electoral Studies*, 8 (1989), 143–55.

JOSEPHS, JEREMY, *Inside the Alliance* (London: John Martin, 1983).

KAVANAGH, DENNIS (ed.), *The Politics of the Labour Party* (London: Allen & Unwin, 1982).

—— (ed.), *Electoral Politics* (Oxford: Clarendon Press, 1992).

KELLNER, PETER, 'The Rabbit is in the Right-hand Pocket', *New Statesman*, 16 Nov. 1981.

—— 'An Everyday Story of Breaking the Mould', *New Statesman*, 8 Jan. 1982.

—— 'SDP Sunk in Private Gloom', *New Statesman*, 12 Nov. 1982.

—— 'With Enemies like These, Who Needs Friends?', *New Statesman*, 16 Nov. 1984.

KENNET, WAYLAND (ed.), *The Rebirth of Britain* (London: Weidenfeld & Nicolson, 1982).

KING, ANTHONY, 'The Election that Everyone Lost', in Penniman (ed.), *Britain at the Polls* (1975), 3–32.

—— (ed.), *Why is Britain Becoming Harder to Govern?* (London: BBC, 1976).

—— *Britain Says Yes: The 1975 Referendum on the Common Market* (Washington, DC: American Enterprise Institute, 1977).

—— 'Politics, Economics and the Trade Unions, 1974–1979', in Penniman (ed.), *Britain at the Polls, 1979* (1981), 30–94.

—— 'Margaret Thatcher's First Term', in Ranney (ed.), *Britain at the Polls, 1983* (1985), 1–38.

KOGAN, DAVID, and KOGAN, MAURICE, *The Battle for the Labour Party*, 2nd edn. (London: Kogan Page, 1983).

LABOUR PARTY, *Meet the Challenge, Make the Change* (London: Labour Party, 1989).

LEONARD, DICK, *Paying for Party Politics: The Case for Public Subsidies*, PEP Broadsheet No. 555 (London: Political and Economic Planning, 1975).

MACARTHUR, BRIAN, 'The National Press', in Crewe and Harrop (eds.), *Political Communications* (1989), 95–107.

MACLENNAN, ROBERT, 'Settling the Constitution', *The Social Democrat, the First Five Years* (London: SDP, 1985).

Market & Opinion Research International, *British Public Opinion, General Election 1983, Final Report* (London: Market & Opinion Research International, 1983).

MARQUAND, DAVID, *Ramsay MacDonald* (London: Jonathan Cape, 1977).

MATTHEW, H. C. G., McKIBBIN, R. I., and KAY, J. A., 'The Franchise Factor in the Rise of the Labour Party', *English Historical Review*, 91 (1976), 723–52.

MAYHEW, CHRISTOPHER, *Time to Explain: An Autobiography* (London: Hutchinson, 1987).

McCORMICK, PAUL, *Enemies of Democracy* (London: Temple Smith, 1979).

—— 'The Labour Party: Three Unnoticed Changes', *British Journal of Political Science*, 10 (1980), 381–7.

McGREGOR, ROBIN, SVENNEVIG, MICHAEL, and LEDGER, CHRIS, 'Television and the 1987 General Election Campaign', in Crewe and Harrop (eds.), *Political Communications* (1989), 175–85.

McKEE, VINCENT, 'Factionalism in the SDP, 1981–87', *Parliamentary Affairs*, 42 (1989), 165–79.

McKIBBIN, ROSS, *The Evolution of the Labour Party, 1910–1924* (Oxford: Oxford University Press, 1974).

MEADOWCROFT, MICHAEL, *Social Democracy—Barrier or Bridge?* (London: Liberator Publications, 1981).

MILLER, WILLIAM, CLARKE, HAROLD D., HARROP, MARTIN, LeDUC, LAWRENCE, and WHITELEY, PAUL, *How Voters Change: The 1987 British Election Campaign in Perspective* (Oxford: Clarendon Press, 1990).

MINKIN, LEWIS, *The Labour Party Conference: A Study in the Politics of Intra-Party Democracy* (London: Allen Lane, 1978).

—— *The Contentious Alliance: Trade Unions and the Labour Party* (Edinburgh: Edinburgh University Press, 1991).

MITCHELL, AUSTIN, *Four Years in the Death of the Labour Party* (London: Methuen, 1983).

MORAN, MICHAEL, *The Politics of Industrial Relations: The Origins, Life and Death of the 1971 Industrial Relations Act* (London: Macmillan, 1977).

MORGAN, KENNETH O., *The People's Peace: British History 1945–1989* (Oxford: Oxford University Press, 1990).

MOWAT, CHARLES LOCH, *Britain between the Wars 1918–1940* (London: Methuen, 1955).

MUNRO, COLIN, 'Legal Controls on Election Broadcasting', in Crewe and Harrop (eds.), *Political Communications* (1986), 294–305.

NORRIS, PIPPA, *British By-elections: The Volatile Electorate* (Oxford: Clarendon Press, 1990).

NORTON, PHILIP, *Dissension in the House of Commons, 1945–74* (London: Macmillan, 1975).

OAKESHOTT, MATTHEW, *The Road from Limehouse to Westminster: Prospects for a Radical Realignment at the General Election* (London: Radical Centre for Democratic Studies in Industry and Society, 1981).

OWEN, DAVID, *The Politics of Defence* (London: Jonathan Cape, 1972).

—— *Face the Future* (London: Jonathan Cape, 1981).

—— 'Agenda for Competitiveness with Compassion', *Economic Affairs*, 4 (1983), 26–33.

—— *A Future that will Work: Competitiveness and Compassion* (Harmondsworth: Penguin Books, 1984).

—— *A United Kingdom* (Harmondsworth: Penguin Books, 1986).

—— *Personally Speaking to Kenneth Harris* (London: Weidenfeld & Nicolson, 1987).

—— *Social Market and Social Justice*, Tawney Society 5th Annual Lecture (London: Tawney Society, 1987).

—— *Time to Declare* (London: Michael Joseph, 1991).

—— *Sticking With It* (London: Social Democratic Publications, n.d.).

—— and STEEL, DAVID, *The Time has Come: Partnership for Progress* (London: Weidenfeld & Nicolson, 1987).

PATERSON, WILLIAM E., and THOMAS, ALASTAIR (eds.), *The Future of Social Democracy* (Oxford: Clarendon Press, 1986).

PELLING, HENRY, *A Short History of the Labour Party*, 8th edn. (London: Macmillan, 1985).

PENNIMAN, HOWARD (ed.), *Britain at the Polls: The Parliamentary Elections of 1974* (Washington, DC: American Enterprise Institute, 1975).

—— *Britain at the Polls, 1979* (Washington, DC: American Enterprise Institute, 1981).

PIMLOTT, BEN, *Harold Wilson* (London: HarperCollins, 1992).

—— and COOK, CHRIS (eds.), *Trade Unions in British Politics: The First 250 Years*, 2nd edn. (London: Longmans, 1991).

PINTO-DUSCHINSKY, MICHAEL, *British Political Finance, 1830–1980* (Washington, DC: American Enterprise Institute, 1981).

—— 'Trends in British Political Funding', *Parliamentary Affairs*, 38 (1985), 328–47.

—— 'Financing the British General Election of 1983', in Crewe and Harrop (eds.), *Political Communications* (1986), 283–93.

—— 'Financing the British General Election of 1987', in Crewe and Harrop (eds.), *Political Communications* (1989), 15–28.

—— 'Trends in British Party Funding, 1983–1987', *Parliamentary Affairs*, 42 (1989), 197–212.

—— 'Political Parties', in Catterall (ed.), *Contemporary Britain* (1990), 29–45.

PONTING, CLIVE, *Breach of Promise: Labour in Power 1964–1970* (London: Hamish Hamilton, 1989).

PRIDHAM, GEOFFREY, and WHITELEY, PAUL, 'Anatomy of the SDP: Is the Party Structurally Top-Heavy?', *Government and Opposition*, 21 (1986), 205–17.

PUGH, MARTIN, *The Making of Modern British Politics 1867–1939* (Oxford: Blackwell, 1982).

RALLINGS, COLIN, and THRASHER, MICHAEL, 'Party Competition and Electoral Volatility: The Case of Local By-elections, 1983–87', *Local Government Studies*, 14, No. 6 (1988), 67–76.

RANNEY, AUSTIN, *Pathways to Parliament* (Madison: University of Wisconsin Press, 1965).

—— (ed.), *Britain at the Polls, 1983: A Study of the General Election* (Durham, NC: Duke University Press and the American Enterprise Institute, 1985).

RASMUSSEN, JORGEN, 'The Alliance Campaign, Watersheds and Landslides: Was 1983 a Fault-line in British Politics?', in Ranney (ed.), *Britain at the Polls, 1983* (1985), 81–107.

RODGERS, WILLIAM, *The Politics of Change* (London: Secker & Warburg, 1982).

—— 'The SDP and the Liberal Party in Alliance', *Political Quarterly*, 54 (1983), 354–62.

—— *My Party—Wet or Dry?* (London: Tawney Society, 1985).

—— 'What Happened to the SDP and What could Still Happen', *London Review of Books*, 7 Feb. 1991.

RÜDIG, WOLFGANG, CURTICE, JOHN and BERRIE, LYNN G., 'Social Democrats, Liberals and Liberal Democrats: The Dynamics of Centre Party Membership', Report of Research Activities and Results to the Economic and Social Research Council, July 1994.

SAMUEL, RAPHAEL, 'The SDP and the New Political Class', *New Society*, 22 Apr. 1982.

SANDERS, DAVID, WARD, HUGH and MARSH, DAVID (with Tony Fletcher), 'Government Popularity and the Falklands War: A Reassessment', *British Journal of Political Science*, 17 (1987), 281–313.

SÄRLVIK, BO, and CREWE, IVOR, *Decade of Dealignment* (Cambridge: Cambridge University Press, 1983).

SEMETKO, HOLLI, ' "Working Together"? Decision-Making, Coordination and Strategy in the Liberal–SDP Alliance Campaign' (paper presented to the Conference on Political Communications: The Media, the Parties and the Polls in the 1983 Elections, University of Essex, 1984).

—— 'The Impact of the Alliance in the Media: Television and the 1983 General Election Campaign' (paper presented to the annual conference of the Political Studies Association, University of Nottingham, 1986).

—— 'Political Communications and Party Development in Britain: The Social Democratic Party from its Origins to the General Election Campaign of 1983' (doctoral thesis, London School of Economics, 1987).

—— 'Images of Britain's Changing Party System: A Study of Television News Coverage of the 1983 and 1987 General Election Campaigns' (paper presented to the annual meeting of the American Political Science Association, Atlanta, 1989).

SEYD, PATRICK, *The Rise and Fall of the Labour Left* (London: Macmillan, 1987).

SEYMOUR-URE, COLIN, 'The SDP and the Media', *Political Quarterly*, 53 (1982), 433–42.

SHAW, ERIC, *Discipline and Discord in the Labour Party: The Politics of Managerial Control in the Labour Party, 1951–1987* (Manchester: Manchester University Press, 1988).

SHEPHERD, ROBERT, *Iain Macleod* (London: Hutchinson, 1994).

Social and Community Planning Research, *British Social Attitudes: Cumulative Sourcebook* (Aldershot: Gower, 1992).

STEED, MICHAEL, 'The Alliance: A Critical History', *New Outlook*, 22 (1983), 3–45.

STEEL, DAVID, *A House Divided: The Lib–Lab Pact and the Future of British Politics* (London: Weidenfeld & Nicolson, 1980).

—— *Against Goliath: David Steel's Story* (London: Weidenfeld & Nicolson, 1989).

STEPHEN, ANDREW, 'The Kicking, Squealing Birthpangs of the SDP', *Sunday Times Magazine*, 27 Sept. 1981.

STEPHENSON, HUGH, *Claret and Chips: The Rise of the SDP* (London: Michael Joseph, 1982).

SWADDLE, KEVIN, 'Ancient and Modern: Innovations in Electioneering at the Constituency Level', in Crewe and Harrop (eds.), *Political Communications* (1989), 29–40.

SYKES, PATRICIA LEE, *Losing from the Inside: The Cost of the Conflict in the British Social Democratic Party* (New Brunswick, NJ: Transaction Books, 1988).

TANNER, DUNCAN, 'The Parliamentary Electoral System, the "Fourth" Reform Act and the Rise of Labour in England and Wales', *Bulletin of the Institute of Historical Research*, 56 (1983–4), 205–19.

—— 'Elections, Statistics, and the Rise of the Labour Party, 1906–1931, *Historical Journal*, 34 (1991), 893–908.

TATCHELL, PETER, *The Battle for Bermondsey* (London: Heretic Books, 1983).

TAVERNE, DICK, *The Future of the Left: Lincoln and After* (London: Jonathan Cape, 1974).

TAYLOR, ROBERT, *The Fifth Estate: Britain's Unions in the Modern World* (rev. edn.) (London: Pan Books, 1980).

—— 'The Trade Union "Problem" in the Age of Consensus 1960–1979', in Pimlott and Cook (eds.), *Trade Unions in British Politics* (1991), 173–99.

Times Guide to the House of Commons: June 1983 (London: Times Books, 1983).

TOMLINSON, JOHN, *Left–Right: The March of Political Extremism in Britain* (London: John Calder, 1981).

WEBB, NORMAN L., and WYBROW, ROBERT J., *The Gallup Report* (London: Sphere Books, 1981).

—— *The Gallup Report: Your Opinions in 1981* (London: Sphere Books, 1982).

WHITELEY, PAUL, 'The Decline of Labour's Local Party Membership and Electoral Base, 1945–79', in Kavanagh (ed.), *The Politics of the Labour Party* (1982), 111–34.

—— *The Labour Party in Crisis* (London: Methuen, 1983).

WILLIAMS, PHILIP M., *Hugh Gaitskell: A Political Biography* (London: Jonathan Cape, 1979).

—— 'Changing Styles of Labour Leadership', in Kavanagh (ed.), *The Politics of the Labour Party* (1982), 50–68.

WILLIAMS, SHIRLEY, *Politics is for People* (Harmondsworth: Penguin, 1982).

WILSON, DES, *Battle for Power* (London: Sphere Books, 1987).

WILSON, HAROLD, *The Labour Government, 1964–1970: A Personal Record* (London: Weidenfeld & Nicolson and Michael Joseph, 1971).

—— *Final Term: The Labour Government 1974–1976* (London: Weidenfeld & Nicolson and Michael Joseph, 1979).

WILSON, TREVOR, *The Downfall of the Liberal Party, 1914–35* (London: Collins, 1966).

YOUNG, ALISON, *The Reselection of MPs* (London: Heinemann, 1983).

Newspapers and Journals

Alliance Magazine
Arcade
MORI, *British Public Opinion*
Campaign
Daily Mail
Daily Express
Daily Star
Daily Telegraph
The Economist
Evening Standard
Financial Times

Gallup Political Barometers
Gallup Political Index
Glasgow Herald
Guardian
Independent
Labour Weekly
Liberal News
The Mail on Sunday
New Democrat
New Outlook
New Statesman
Observer
Observer Magazine
Private Eye
Scotsman
Spectator
Sun
Sunday Telegraph
Sunday Times
Sunday Times Magazine
The Times
Times Educational Supplement
Times Higher Education Supplement
Today
Tribune
Western Mail

Reports

House of Commons Debates (Hansard)
Reports of the Annual Conference of the Labour Party
Report of the Committee on Financial Aid to Political Parties (Houghton Report) (London: HMSO, Cmnd. 6601, 1976)

Liberal–SDP Publications

A Fresh Start for Britain (London: Poland Street Publications, 1981)
Defence and Disarmament, report of the Joint SDP–Liberal Alliance Commission (Hebden Bridge: Hebden Royd Publications, 1986)
Britain United: The Time has Come
The SDP/Liberal Alliance Programme for Government (London: SDP, 1987)
SDP, The First Five Years (London: SDP, 1985)

Index

· · · · ·

Index

Index

Index

Index

Index

Grimond, Jo 11, 12, 140, 167, 288
Group of Twelve 48–9
Guardian:
  birth of SDP (1979–81) 60, 88, 94, 96,
    108, 114
  infancy of SDP (1981–3) 138, 161, 210
  anatomy of SDP 234, 245, 254, 260,
    261, 268, 272, 273, 280, 297
  maturity of SDP (1983–7) 263, 312,
    316, 350, 352, 357, 359
  decline of SDP (1987–8) 374, 415, 418,
    422, 432; disintegration 391, 393,
    398, 400–1, 403, 409

Hahn, Frank 95
Haines, Joe 261
Halmos, Tony 235
Hamilton, William 48, 109
Hancock, Mike 331, 379
Hardie, Kier 71
Harris, John, Lord Harris of Greenwich:
  birth of SDP (1979–81) 55, 57, 59
  infancy of SDP (1981–3) 154, 199, 213
  anatomy of SDP 258
  decline of SDP (1987–8) 369, 370, 372
Harris, Robert 400, 427
Harrogate Liberal Party Assembly (1983)
  339
Harrogate SDP Conference (1986) 349
Harrop, Martin 258
Harvey-Jones, Sir John 247, 248
Haseler, Stephen 162
Hattersley, Roy:
  birth of SDP (1979–81) 90, 107, 123;
    Labour Party and break from
    (1979–81) 37, 44–6, 78–9, 82, 84
  decline of SDP (1987–8) 399, 465
Hatton, Derek 424
Hayward, Ron 31, 98
Healey, Denis:
  birth of SDP (1979–81) 97, 105, 108,
    122–4; prehistory 13, 19, 22, 23, 26;
    Labour Party and break from
    (1979–81) 39, 44, 49, 72–6, 81–3
  infancy of SDP (1981–3) 131, 132, 148,
    200, 210
  decline of SDP (1987–8) 399, 462, 465,
    467–8
Heath, Anthony 295, 296
Heath, Edward 4–6, 10, 12–13, 53, 115,
  120, 167, 471
Heffer, Eric 37
Henderson, Arthur 71
Heseltine, Michael 330
Hicks, Robert 114
Hill, Anthony 143
Holland, Stuart 47

Holme, Richard:
  birth of SDP (1979–81) 63, 100
  infancy of SDP (1981–3) 174, 175, 199,
    202–3
  maturity of SDP (1983–7) 342, 351
  decline of SDP (1987–8) 432, 473
Holmes, Jack 440
Holmes, Sarah 434
Home Office 41, 52, 55, 56, 341
Home Thoughts from Abroad, *see* Dimbleby
  Lecture
Hoover Address, Strathclyde University
  332
Horam, John:
  birth of SDP (1979–81) 85, 93, 97, 107,
    120, 122; Labour Party and break from
    (1979–81) 36, 37, 48, 57–8, 65, 79,
    81
  infancy of SDP (1981–3) 150, 168, 213
  anatomy of SDP 221
  decline of SDP (1987–8) 473
House of Lords:
  abolition of 27, 29, 33, 49, 278
  television coverage 267
Howard, Anthony 180
Howard, Lord 268
Hoyle, Doug. 137–8
Hughes, Simon 192, 312, 351, 352, 359,
  434, 435
Huhne, Christopher 260

ICI 247, 248
Independent 364
  anatomy of SDP 259, 261, 268
  decline of SDP (1987–8) 378, 385–6,
    398, 400, 433
Industrial Policy Association 249
Industrial Relations Act 8
Industrial Reorganization Corporation (IRC)
  3–4, 5
Industry Act (1972) 5
Industry Act (1975) 13
Inner London Education Authority 359
In Place of Strife 8, 18
Institute of Economic Affairs 332, 333
International Monetary Fund 6
IRC, *see* Industrial Reorganization
  Corporation
Irish Home Rule 105
Isle of Ely by-election 284
ITN 102, 267, 270

Jenkins, Jennifer 57, 154, 206, 209
Jenkins, Peter 88–9, 106, 108, 260, 422
Jenkins, Roy:
  birth of SDP (1979–81) 85–9, 91–3, 96,
    97, 101–2, 118–20, 122–7; prehistory

Index

Index

Index

failure, reasons for 441–5
support for 442–7; mergerites, *see*
Jenkins; Rodgers; Steel; Williams
Midland Bank 135, 242, 244
Mikardo, Ian 16, 119
Militant Tendency (formerly Revolutionary
Communist League) 16, 27, 37, 44,
110, 119, 121, 424
miners' strikes 6, 7, 8, 326, 396
Ministry of Labour 41
Ministry of Technology 3
Mirror Group 261
missiles 40, 150, 296
see also Polaris; Trident
Mitchell, Bob 104, 105, 106, 113, 212
Mitchell, Parry 325
Mitterrand, François 349
Mole, Stuart 63, 199, 208
Moncrieff, Chris 436
Monster Raving Ego Party 393, 440
Monster Raving Loony Cavern Rock Party
440
Morgan, John 254
Morgan Grenfell 97, 239, 247
Morrell, Frances 39
Morris, Charles 109
Morris, Gouverneur 220
Mosley, Oswald 305, 455
Murdoch, Rupert 259, 261
Murphy, Sir Leslie 94, 96, 398

National Committee of SDP (formerly
Steering Committee) 162, 223, 225–9,
231, 236, 260
Jenkins as leader (1982–3) 152, 153
'partnership of principle' 170, 176, 183
anatomy of SDP 255; new institutions
218–20, 222–6, 235; machines,
members, and money 238–9, 245–6
Owen ascendancy (1983–7) 306–7,
316–18, 320–5, 336, 339, 345, 350,
356, 358
disintegration of SDP (1987–8) 386,
389–90, 393–6, 399, 400
merger with Liberals (1988) 411, 413,
423–4
blame for failure 448
National Economic Development Council
14
National Executive Committee of Labour
Party:
birth of SDP (1979–81) 137, 219, 222,
228; Gang of Three and 29–30, 32–3,
35–9, 42–5, 47–8; Jenkins and 56,
60, 65, 70; break from Labour 78–9,
81–2, 94
National Front 200

National Health Service 275
National Liberal Club 199, 200, 309–10,
372
National Plan (1965) 4, 13
National Union of Mineworkers (NUM) 18,
36
National Union of Public Employees (NUPE)
36
National Union of Railwaymen (NUR) 36
NATO 13, 278, 279, 341, 342, 343, 346,
348, 349, 353, 364, 419, 420, 421,
429, 431
Neuberger, Julia 234
new class 272–82, 561–3
new institutions 217–37, 550–5
Newby, Richard 244, 368, 369, 385, 387,
400, 416, 418, 434, 446, 473
New Labour Party 100
New Liberal and Social Democratic Party
419–20
New Outlook 140, 178
New Party 455
New Statesman 277, 364, 404, 405
Nixon, Richard 388
North Sea Oil 20
Northern Ireland 278, 287

Oakeshott, Matthew 56, 85, 92, 154
O'Brien, Ossie 192, 193
Observer:
birth of SDP (1979–81) 64, 90–1, 95
infancy of SDP (1981–3) 148, 155, 161,
181, 202
anatomy of SDP 254, 259
maturity of SDP (1983–7) 346
decline of SDP (1987–8) 374, 383–4,
400, 405, 427
Office of Public Service and Science 473
Ogden, Eric 48, 104, 106, 109, 141
O'Halloran, Michael 104, 107, 109, 141,
159
oil crisis (1972–3) 5
'one member, one vote' 86–7, 117, 118,
121, 151–2, 219, 220–21, 226, 321,
313, 392
Labour 33–4, 37, 48, 89, 92
SDP 153, 157
open letter 46–7
opinion polls:
birth of SDP (1979–81) 89, 95–6
infancy of SDP (1981–3) 132–3, 144,
146, 155, 161, 165, 170–1, 191;
general election (1983) 192–3, 200–3,
207, 210–11
anatomy of SDP 266; Alliance with
Liberals 283, 285, 286, 289, 297–8,
299

607

Index

Index

Index

Index